RETHINKING FRANCE

RETHINKING FRANCE

LES LIEUX DE MÉMOIRE

VOLUME 3

LEGACIES

Under the direction of

PIERRE NORA

Translation directed by

DAVID P. JORDAN

THE UNIVERSITY OF CHICAGO PRESS
CHICAGO AND LONDON

Pierre Nora is editorial director at Éditions Gallimard. Since 1977 he has been directeur d'études at the École des Hautes Études en Science Sociales. He is the founding editor of *Le Débat* and has directed the editorial work on *Les Lieux de mémoire* since 1984. In 2001 he was elected to the Académie Française. **David P. Jordan** is the LAS Distinguished Professor of French History at the University of Illinois at Chicago and the author of *Transforming Paris* and *The Revolutionary Career of Maximilien Robespierre*, both published by the University of Chicago Press.

The University of Chicago Press, Chicago 60637
The University of Chicago Press, Ltd., London
© 2009 by The University of Chicago
All rights reserved. Published 2009
Printed in the United States of America
18 17 16 15 14 13 12 11 10 09   1 2 3 4 5

ISBN-13: 978-0-226-59134-6 (cloth)
ISBN-10: 0-226-59134-4 (cloth)

Originally published as *Les Lieux de mémoire,* © Éditions Gallimard, 1984, 1986, and 1992.

The University of Chicago Press gratefully acknowledges a subvention from the government of France, through the French Ministry of Culture, Centre National du Livre, in support of the costs of translating this volume.

Library of Congress Cataloging-in-Publication Data

Lieux de mémoire. English
    Rethinking France = Lieux de mémoire / under the direction of Pierre Nora ;
translated by Mary Trouille ; translation directed by David P. Jordan
        p. cm.
    Includes index.
    Contents: v. 1. The State.
    ISBN 0-226-59132-8 (cloth, v. 1: alk. paper)
1. France—Civilization—Philosophy. 2. Memory. 3. Symbolism. 4. National characteristics,
French. 5. Nationalism—France. I. Nora, Pierre. II. Title.
DC33.L6513 2001
944—dc22
                                                            2001000375

♾ The paper used in this publication meets the minimum requirements of the American National Standard for Information Sciences—Permanence of Paper for Printed Library Materials, ANSI Z39.

CONTENTS

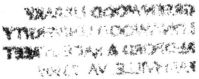

INTRODUCTION

PIERRE NORA

The English word "legacies" seems the best to characterize this collection of "lieux de mémoire," which in their diversity provide a unified and faithful image of a largely bygone France. "The Village Church," "Notre Dame of Paris," the "Sacré Coeur of Montmartre" illustrate well the Christian heritage of France. "Proverbs, Tales, and Songs" as well as "Vine and Wine" go right to the heart of popular and peasant culture, just as "The Industrial Arts" and "The Industrial Age" do for the traditions of French workers and artisans. "The Collège de France" explores a typical aspect of the culture of scholars: the independence and the liberty of academic institutions guaranteed by the state against the state itself. And what better expressions of the legendary "civility" of the French than "Gallantry," "The Café," and "Conversation"?

Here is the basic foundation of a certain idea of "Frenchness."

Of all these "lieux" in the nation's uniqueness, it is the *concept of patrimony* that deserves to be emphasized. It applies not just to the first essay in this volume, nor to the volume as a whole. In truth it might be said to encompass the entire series, since, from first to last, the essays aspire to be the scholarly and selective exploration, between memory and history, of our collective inheritance.

In France, as in most other countries, the last thirty years have seen a vast extension in the domain of "patrimony" that has stretched the definition to its limits. It is this imprecision, this sentiment of seemingly abundant confusion and uncertain interpretation, which the late André Chastel, that great historian of art and architecture, addressed in an article on the classical period: "A comprehensive idea," he said, "both vague and pervasive."

From a distance of nearly thirty years, this apparent confusion and disorder takes on an entirely different meaning, and it is precisely this shift in meaning that has inspired me and seemed to me to justify an altogether new understanding of a "lieu de mémoire." That is perhaps why clarifying the term here is not an unimportant exercise.

Traditionally, it is true that "patrimony," as commonly understood, designated the collective culture of the country: the châteaus, the cathedrals, the great monuments, the works of art in the museums—a complex meant to express the soul of the nation and the "genius" of France, for which the Service des monuments historiques has responsibility. The service was created at the beginning of the July Monarchy with Prosper Mérimée as its first inspector general.★ It is also true that this system, relatively undisturbed for so long, violently exploded just about the time the Year of the Patrimony was officially declared in 1980. That year can serve as a symbolic point of reference.

Patrimony and memory suddenly became almost synonymous.[1] By all at once expanding to include all traces of the past, the idea of patrimony underwent not a modest enrichment but in fact a true metamorphosis. It had customarily consisted of important artifacts, but then with peasant and ethnological patrimony, with the village washhouse and old kitchen recipes, it swept up, by contrast, the experiences of real life. Once it had consisted of objects no longer in use, a kind of scrap heap, but with the architecture of the second half of the twentieth century and with the purchase by museums of works by living artists, it no longer set itself apart from the contemporary anticipating the future. It was traditionally a phenomenon of culture; with laws protecting sites and the environment, it even appropriated nature. In short, by leaving its age of history to enter the age of memory, patrimony was not far from becoming the opposite of what it had been.

It was therefore perfectly legitimate to see in this silent metamorphosis, at the very moment it was taking place a quarter of a century ago, a disturbing yet straightforward expansion of the classical patrimony. It is therefore also legitimate to describe the stages of its development, as André Chastel has done better than anyone else, as a continuous and linear development to its final embodiment. Yet if one sees it as a true revolution of memory linked to a transformed awareness of the present and of the

---

★ Dramatist, archaeologist, short story writer as well as historian, Mérimée is perhaps best known for his story "Carmen," which Bizet used for his opera of the same name.

connection to the past, one would be rather tempted to interpret the history of the idea of patrimony as a series of successive mutations.

The first mutation, at the founding moment of the Revolution when the very idea appeared in the modern sense of the word (similar to "archives" and "museums"), could easily be defined as the *nationalization of the past*, since a vast number of assets, until then in the possession of powerful families and religious institutions, fell into the hands of the state. This idea of escheat for many years remained an inherent feature of the idea of patrimony. And from this nationalization of the past at least were born, and still remain, three of the major institutions of patrimony: the Archives nationales, the Bibliothèque nationale, and the largest of the national museums, the Louvre.

The second moment of patrimony might best be situated between 1820 and 1840, spanning the Restoration and the July Monarchy. In the years following the Revolution, the generation of Liberals and romantics understood that an absolute break in historical time had taken place and that the Revolution, by consigning all the past centuries to the register of the ancien régime, had distanced itself from the entire past, beyond any possible tie to the present. It was a time forever lost that historians could recover only through collections of authentic documents and could make speak by means largely borrowed from novelists like Sir Walter Scott. It was a poetics of the past expressed in a taste for ruins. Three great names illustrate this patrimonial moment: Hugo, by his plea for the "Gothic" (that is, the Middle Ages); Guizot, for the creation of those great institutions of memory, the Société de l'histoire de France and the Comité des travaux historiques; and Mérimée, to whom one owes the first classification of monuments. It was the *past experienced as the past*.

There is yet a third moment of patrimony. It occurs at the end of the nineteenth century, during the Third Republic, when *national history* completely subsumed the past, to the detriment, incidentally, of the physical legacy of the nation, which was abandoned to educated amateurs and artists, aristocrats, and connoisseurs. The beating heart of French patrimony of that era—and that would be true right up to the 1950s and 1960s—beat much less in the great edifices entrusted to subministry of fine arts in the Ministry for Public Instruction and the Fine Arts (Ministre à l'instruction publique et aux beaux-arts), so badly funded and so badly administered, than it did in those history books for young and old, degree and non-degree students, whose models were the *Le Tour de France par deux enfants* by Bruno and the *Histoire de France* by Lavisse in twenty-seven volumes. This shift in the idea of patrimony toward a fully developed, consecrated scientific and academic national history represented a vital movement of far-reaching significance. It helped give to the artistic past of France its "classicism" and was accompanied by a schism that gave birth, by contrast, to modern art, itself founded on the cult of the new.

★ ★ ★

It is within this new configuration that patrimony and memory relate directly to *identity*, from which the image of France derives its meaning. This is the image that emerges in the essays assembled here, of a France, let us note, that has entirely disappeared in the modernizing spirit of the 1950s to the 1970s. And these images are independent of each other, for we are not dealing with a systematic inventory nor a composite picture, but rather with illustrative samplings and deep plunges into a reality that is no more.

The years after the war indeed saw France experiencing a rapid transformation, all the more spectacular in a country that had remained, longer than others, sheltered from modernity. It was what one economist, Jean Fourastié, wanted to christen "the thirty glorious years of growth" and a sociologist, Henri Mendras, called, "the second French Revolution."[2] After a century of demographic stagnation and slow industrial growth, economic production quintupled in less than twenty-five years. The peasantry of old, the traditional bourgeoisie, and the classic working class disappeared in the face of the rising middle class. The great national institutions—the clergy and the army—lost their symbolic aura.

Several key dates mark this decisive and quiet revolution. In 1962, the end of the Algerian War constituted a turning point: France stopped projecting itself into the world and withdrew home to the "Hexagon." For the first time since 1939, France was not at war. With the end of the colonial adventure, one model of France and even one type of nation faded away—the statist, imperialist, and messianic nation that had been taught for a century to children in the primary schools in order to turn them into citizens and soldiers. In 1965, for the first time the president of the Republic was elected by universal suffrage, which radically transformed the functioning of republican institutions. Signs of this transformation as varied as they are vivid can be grouped around this date: the proliferation of large shopping areas that, by killing off family-owned shops, inaugurated the era of mass consumption; the conclusion of Vatican II, in which the reform of discipline and Catholic rites appeared to sanction the rapid decline of religious observance in the younger generation; the sudden appearance of nudity in magazines and movies, which indicated the emergence of an individualistic, hedonistic, and permissive society—many indices of a transformation of which the explosion of student protests in May 1968 appeared as the symbolic expression.

When juxtaposed to this new France many of these "lieux de mémoire" come into true relief. All of them have one point in common:

They presume the convergence of two points of view, the internal that entails a responsibility for a legacy and the external that objectifies this legacy and grounds it in tradition. They all refer to "lieux" that are actually or apparently integral to the French identity in its real and imagined depths: the antiquity of its religious, ideological, and social formations at the moment when no more than traces remain, like the "village church" or the "métier"; its popular cultures dating from time immemorial, such as its proverbs, its songs, its vineyards, and its wine when these cultures no longer exist except as folklore and an export. All of these illustrate the supposedly distinctive features of its civilization, like polite conversation or gallantry to the ladies, at the very moment when the rise in power of the world of business and the women's liberation movement has turned them into admittedly outdated practices and slightly "old France."

Do these "lieux" survive only by virtue of the charm that surrounds them or from the sentimental nostalgia that they inspire? I think not, for "mémoire" is not "souvenir." The merit of the essays you are about to read is that they highlight the distinction.

A "souvenir" in fact assures continuity, confirms permanence, and recalls a presence even as it fades away. A "mémoire" establishes an entirely different relationship with the past by producing a definitive separation and at the same time firmly reappropriating it. But it is a reappropriation of an order other than that of something living. It is of a symbolic and historical order. There is in most French villages the central presence of churches, today often closed; and there is the village church that, for example, has successfully served as the fundamental electoral image both for the "eternal France" of Marshal Pétain and for the "quiet force" of François Mitterrand. There is Notre Dame of Paris as one of the tourist monuments most visited in the capital, along with the Eiffel Tower; and there is what Victor Hugo's novel conveys from the medieval imagination and the nineteenth century of the romantics. There is the Sacré Coeur of Montmartre, an ideological construction that dates from the time after the Commune of Paris, signaling a desire for revenge by the royalist and Catholic majority and providing a sign of expiation; and there is the culminating point of the Montmartre quarter, the very name of which evokes, from Balzac's *Illusions perdues* to the Impressionist painters and the fin-de-siècle cabaret singers, certain great moments in art, literature, and poetry. One could say as much for any of these essays. They help define, each in their own way, what is a "tradition," that is to say, a "mémoire" that has become aware of itself.

One additional feature, finally, gives these traditions their homogeneity regardless of whether they arise from social models, long-standing traditions, distinctive features, or high places of worship. They all date from the nineteenth century or, if from much earlier, it is in the nineteenth century that they are rediscovered, recorded, and formulated. This is true even for the Collège de France, which, as an institution dedicated solely to knowledge ever since the sixteenth century, includes in that time, from Michelet to Claude Bernard, "the true leaders," in Renan's words, "of intellectual movement."

Certain British historians have succeeded in shedding light on the recent character of traditions considered ancient and venerable, including the Crown, for example.[3] What the present work illuminates, more particularly in the meticulous elucidation of depths and continuities, is a movement linked, on the whole, to the rupture of the Revolution in this country of history longer than memory. In the nature of the moment of patrimony and memory we continue to live by recovering the legacies of history and by fixing the points of anchorage. It is the nineteenth century in its entirety, even more than the others, that was the great century of French memory. It was the century that invented "la France," of which this series of essays is meant to be the memorial.

NOTES

1. I have discussed the emergence of this phenomenon elsewhere at length. See, in particular, the general introduction to *Rethinking France/Les Lieux de mémoire*, vol. 1 (Chicago: University of Chicago Press, 2001); the general introduction to *Realms of Memory: The Construction of the French Past*, vol. 1 (New York: Columbia University Press, 1996); and the general introduction to *Realms of Memory*, vol. 3 (New York: Columbia University Press, 1998).

2. A group of specialists at Harvard University in those years became the best observers of this transformation, in particular Stanley Hoffman, Charles P. Kindleberger, Laurence Wylie, and Jesse R. Pitts, together with Jean-Baptiste Duroselle and François Goguel, in their book *In Search of France* (Cambridge: Harvard University Press, 1963).

3. Eric Hobsbawm and Terence Ranger, *The Invention of Tradition* (Cambridge: Cambridge University Press, 1983).

THE NOTION OF PATRIMONY

❧

ANDRÉ CHASTEL

The word is an old one, the idea seems timeless. The Roman word *pat-rimonium* had to do with a familial legitimacy reinforced by inheritance. It made explicit a specific relationship between the legally defined group and certain entirely concrete material goods: a space, a treasure, or even less. By extension we speak of the *Patrimonium Sancti Petri* or the patrimony, the heritage, of the Institut de France, mindful of landed property that insures lasting resources as much as a kind of dignity. Problems start with what we must call the new dimension of the term. According to the meaning we give it today in standard usage, official definitions aside, this is a sweeping idea, vague yet pervasive, that came into existence barely two centuries ago. Its genesis, its chaotic development, and its final blunting will be the object of this study.[1]

As we are aware, there is a daily discussion these days of "cultural heritage" which embraces legends, memory, language itself. There is discussion of an "ecological" heritage as well, concerned with fascinating, sensitive, vital aspects of nature. Recent years have witnessed the appearance even of the startling metaphor of "genetic heritage." If we enlarge the discussion, the idea assumes a more pronounced emotional value to designate certain fundamental conditions of national, even human, existence. Perhaps this evolution of the term merely expresses the distress of a collective consciousness confronted by more or less specific and more or less obscure threats to its integrity. What we shall examine here is the domain of space, the products of art, the built environment—urban or

rural which, to no one's surprise, have justified the recent rather paradoxical creation of a cabinet-level "Direction of Heritage."

CHURCH AND MONARCHY AS CREATORS OF MEMORIES

The peculiarity of the contemporary world is, perhaps, that without really
realizing, and by fits and starts, it revives attitudes that are only discernible
when one looks at what historians are now calling the "long term" (*longue
durée*). There is an extralegal but symbolic source of the idea of heritage,
linked to the perpetuity of sacred objects essential to the community such
as the Palladium of Troy, the Black Virgin of Chartres, and the innumerable "treasures" that have played such an important role in the church. The
tangible network of sanctuaries, relics, and images has been consistently
perceived to be Christianity's treasury of heritage. Their double nature—
they are devotional as well as artistic—has guaranteed them the status of
marvelous objects (*objets merveilleux*) which deeply mark the sensibilities.[2]
When did we move from the *miracula*, which expressed a veneration of
the sacred, to the *mirabilia*, which merely admitted to aesthetic or intellectual admiration? This is what is nearly impossible to determine. Contrary to what is often thought, we constantly associate the two terms.[3] It
makes sense. By a shift that is characteristic of our times, the generalized
desacralization of social forms, except in a few cases, brings with it the desacralization of the religious apparatus, which tends to move the latter
into that category of heritage called "cultural." If we can use other terms
to more or less clearly explain to ourselves the reasons for so doing, we
have nevertheless preserved an instinctive attachment to forms and objects
of which we no longer directly perceive the "virtue," to use the name
that certain pockets of Provence once used to speak of relics. It has been
noted, for example, that the rehabilitation of "Gothic" necessitated and
included an appreciation of a high level of craftsmanship, leading, with
no irony intended, to the formulation of a "technological heritage."[4] A
certain vision of the Middle Ages, justified by France's prodigious artistic
creation, continues to be associated with the idea of a national heritage.
This intuition was so powerfully expressed by Michelet that it convinced
a fair part of the informed or vaguely cultivated public of the nineteenth
century, and probably the twentieth as well. How can we ever forget his
astonishing declaration: "The Middle Ages has left to us so poignant a
memory of itself that every joy, all the grandeur, of the modern age is not
enough to console us for its loss"?[5]

By comparison with the strong religious penetration that the calendar,
place names, and history subtly introduce in the collective consciousness or
half-consciousness, the spectacular demonstrations and "creations" of the

monarchic ancien régime carry perhaps less weight. They are, of course, impressive: France of the châteaus, large and small, is, theoretically, everyone's France. Versailles is the response to the Basilique of Saint-Denis, the Château of Chambord the answer to Mont-Saint-Michel, and so forth. But today's attachment is not like yesterday's, and the definition of "heritage" has been a long time coming. Aside from the exceptional sites such as Saint-Denis Basilica with its regalia of royal power, and Versailles, the Bourbons' only creation, historical analysis leads to the conclusion that the monarchy's numerous "houses" (maisons), impressive collections, and noble residences were not, in fact, as carefully tended and preserved as one might suppose. They were in no way treated like the wealth of a national heritage. What was important to the monarchy was above all else its "mythical" genealogy. For example: August 26, 1660, for the king's solemn entry into Paris, the houses on the Notre Dame bridge were decorated with medallions of the kings of France. First came the legendary ancestor, Pharamond, accompanied by the heraldic device which in one blow made the House of France larger and eternal: "Imperium sine fine dedit."[6] (It was no accident that Chateaubriand, monarchist, used the title "Founder" for Pharamond in his epic Martyrs.) These imposing memories were not tied to "relics." The liturgy of the king's consecration and funeral, passing celebrations, were more important than sacred objects and memorable visits.

This, then, is one of the points we should put in perspective. The sumptuous objects in the Saint-Denis treasure and in the ensemble we call the regalia "were the material expression of the enduring quality of the monarchy but they were no less a reserve of precious metal and stones liable to be pawned, cut up, sold, melted down,"[7] which did happen and more than once. As for the Crown's residences, which had been passionately cared for by certain kings and had greatly contributed to their prestige, they were so far from being considered inalienable and immutable that Chambord was given away, Fontainebleau transformed, Versailles renovated in the eighteenth century, and in 1787 a decree by Louis XVI suggested putting up for sale four châteaus that had become too costly to maintain: La Muette, near Saint-Germain-en-Laye (which was taken down several years later), the château in the Bois de Boulogne called the Château de Madrid (in ruins at the time and demolished in 1792), Vincennes (which remained a state prison), and Blois (which became a barracks). These were not "cultural sites" indispensable to the Crown, even less to the nation; they were subject to changes in taste and were not worth the sacrifice that the financial crisis had made exorbitant.[8]

This was obviously not true of the royal library (which had grown continuously since Saint Louis), nor of the archives, stored in a building attached to Sainte-Chapelle: *le Trésor des Chartes*. This collection of documents was too closely tied to the very history of the country and of its institutions to not merit special status. For the French mentality the idea of a heritage of political history finds its most eloquent form in its archives and documents. It is important, finally, to tie to the rise of erudition, which came later in France than in Italy or in England, the interesting expressions of a new state of mind during the ancien régime, stimulated by the press and sustained by great bureaucrats like Marigny and d'Angiviller. First, methodically, they opened to the public the "curiosities" of the royal warehouse and objects of the collections, arranging them in rooms that formed what was already being called the "museum." On the eve of the Revolution—we shall return to it a bit later—the problem was identified. One idea, timidly voiced at the start of the eighteenth century by R. de Gaignières (1703), was more often and more energetically expressed in the second half of the century. That idea was that it was wrong to demolish structures deserving of the name "monuments" without explicit permission. With the Enlightenment and the idea of a steady progress of societies, there was shaped a concrete attention to historical life which had as points of reference precisely those edifices, works of art, which one could no longer abandon to the caprice of those who happened to possess them.

What would become of the history of the arts if the "edifices wherein the genius of each century places itself, instead of acquiring with age the public veneration which should render them sacred, were condemned, no better than passing fads, to appear for a day then make way for tomorrow," read the February 1787 *Journal de Paris*. This letter from Quatremère de Quincy intervened in a press campaign to save the Fontaine des Innocents from the general destruction of the old Parisian cemetery.[9] Of course the term "heritage" was never used in these controversies. It seems that not even the idea appeared that such "vestiges" could interest the nation as a whole. One spoke of the "genius of each century." Most often they remained within the framework of monarchic history and religious history. The case of François Roger de Gaignières, that extraordinary scholar, who had the idea of a true archaeological, artistic, and sociological inventory of the country, is made all the more fascinating by the fact that his example was not understood. His vast documentation was scattered.[10] A scholar like Bernard de Montfaucon perhaps owed a more knowledgeable historical sensitivity to a certain familiarity with learned Italians, who were more evolved in this regard. But he finally concentrated his learning on the *Monuments de la monarchie française* (5 volumes, 1724–33), in which he obstinately confirmed the incorrect—and already controversial—interpretation of the column statues as royal portraits. The second work, not done, was to have been on the churches of France, *Églises de France*.[11]

MONUMENT D'HÉLOÏSE ET D'ABÉLARD.

Figure 1.1
Monument to Héloïse and Abélard, engraved by Réville and Lavallée from Vauzelle for the *Musée des Monuments français*, 1816.

In fact, in the minds of many scholars, such as the Abbé Lebeuf,[12] the idea of antiques had already evolved, and they had begun to approach their study with a new perspective which was, in a way, that of "culture." But the same author who in the Fontaine des Innocents so admired "the beautiful work which would have been the glory of Athens and Rome" had no objection to throwing down the "shameful traces of the Goths." In the Enlightenment perspective, the part to keep, the heritage of informed minds, was extraordinarily selective: it was limited to that which was of interest to and reinforced "neoclassical" dogma. The general upheaval of 1789–95 would be necessary for other ideas to take form in that great haste and for the insane, enraged, and deranged destruction of symbolic objects to provoke a birth by aftershock of new attachments.

THE AWAKENING: "HONORABLY PRESERVE THE MASTERPIECES OF THE ARTS"

The Year II* directive on "the manner of inventory and preservation . . . to the attention of administrators of the Republic" on the subject of buildings and works of art chose extremely strong language: "You are but the agents of property concerning which the great family is within right to demand an accounting."[13] At a time when the state, after the secularization of the clergy's property (from November 1789) and the confiscation of émigré property (especially of nobles who had fled revolutionary France), became responsible for an enormous share of the fortunes of the two great "traditional orders," the church and the nobility, new reflexes became necessary to the managers. They had to describe an area that was as intangible as it was explicit. It was unfortunate that these sound proposals had to come as a remedy to extreme disorder. One much earlier study has meticulously classified measures taken during the early years of the Revolution and meeting minutes for successive committees; under the pressure of events that swept away institutions, people, and property, it was necessary to define conservation procedures that became as precise as they were unenforced.[14] The idea of heritage took shape in France under the most dramatic and difficult conditions possible.

Defacements, profanations, statue toppling, the pulling down of buildings, all provoked at the urging of small groups of sans-culottes Parisian

---

* The revolutionary calendar, in which the months were named for their characteristics— e.g., Thermidor, the hot month, corresponded with the second half of July and the first half of August in the Christian calendar—and the Sabbath disappeared, to be replaced by the *décadi*, or every tenth day, which was designated as honoring the Revolution, and began the entire chronology anew. The year I began on September 22, 1792. This calendar remained in use until 1804, when Napoleon crowned himself emperor.—Ed.

workers, would become the subject of a long and lamentable narrative. The bronze from the bells, the lead of the roof cladding, the copper of the grillwork were collected everywhere. "Great saints into the crucible with ye / All fall down, that's the decree" (*Grands saints dans le creuset / Tombez, c'est le décret*) read Couthon's leaflet, the *Litany of Saints Turned to Coin* (*Litanie des saints convertis en monnaie*) distributed in the Puy-de-Dôme in 1793. The demolished bell towers and cloisters were a mine of bricks for builders. Examples are unlimited: Troyes, Agen, Cambrai, Le Mans . . . But very quickly there were too many bricks. In Clermont-Ferrand, in Chartres, the cathedrals were probably spared because their destruction would have created a long-lasting clutter in the center of town.[15]

Monuments and works of art have always shared, in times of trouble, the fate of the symbols they carried. It was, then, in difficult circumstances that here and there a sudden attachment to the works of the past was expressed, faintly at first but then more sharply. In some areas the motivation might have been resistance to de-Christianization and defeudalization that led to rescues by the population, as happened in many places in the West, for example. But those reactions could be discounted as sequels to "fanaticism." In other areas intellectuals, scholars, took it upon themselves to preserve, in the spirit of the legislators in the National Convention, those works made vulnerable to destruction by "vandals" by the dispossession of the clergy or the massive flight of the noble proprietors. The notion of heritage, that is to say fundamental, inalienable property, was extended for the first time in France to works of art, either because of the traditional values which they expressed and which explained them, or in the name of that new feeling of a common possession by the entire nation of a moral treasure.

Succeeding assemblies named commissions, unsure of how exactly to proceed, but able to talk a lot. To the Commission des monuments, already created by October 1790, was juxtaposed the 1793 Commission des arts, which absorbed the preceding by taking the title of Temporary Commission for the Arts (decree of December 18, 1793). This overlapping of commissions was not without conflicts and quarrels over exclusive jurisdiction. But it was thanks to these discussions that the key words of heritage (*patrimoine*) and vandalism (*vandalism*) were articulated with force. There were structures to preserve; there were vestiges to collect. A policy for museums was necessary. So said Jean-Baptiste Mathieu, president of the Commission des arts:

> Immense riches such as these [drawings] previously scattered among the émigrés [the fled aristocrats], after an appropriate selection, as is prescribed by the decrees, will be collected in the national museums

and will offer the most interesting possible collection for students who desire to instruct themselves in the arts for the good of the French people, which has become the single proprietor of these works of genius, of which it, the people, has always been the best judge. . . . The national palace, the formerly so-called [*ci-devant*] Bourbon Palace, the home of the émigré of Châtelet, the storehouse of the ci-devant Academy of Painting, has been inventoried as regards painting, sculpture, and architecture. . . . Monuments and antiques, those interesting remains spared and consecrated by time, which time seems to bestow upon us anew, because it did not destroy them, which history consults, which the arts study, which the philosopher observes, which our eyes do love to fix with that kind of interest inspired by the very age of things and by all that gives a sort of existence to the past, have been the numerous subjects of the inventories and research of the Commission des Arts.[16]

This remarkable text not only reveals the main concern of those responsible: to conduct an inventory, that is to say identify, recognize, and register for the benefit of the nation works which had, until then, never been the subject of any census. Why take on this task? It seemed no one had ever until then so eloquently articulated the power of those objects "which history consults, which the arts study, which the philosopher observes, which our eyes do love to fix" by reason of that very quality "which gives a sort of existence to the past." This time the barrier of prejudice was crossed: they did not merely define one original space, they identified a power of culture. The modern idea of heritage, *patrimoine*, began to appear through a care that was at once moral and educational.

THE "TROPHIES OF SUPERSTITION" AND THE TRIBULATIONS OF ABBÉ GRÉGOIRE

Unfortunately, the revolutionaries themselves had provoked the very attacks that the law sought to check. Had not Camille Desmoulins held out "as rich prey offered to the victors, the forty thousand palaces, mansions and châteaus of France"?

The most typical example is without doubt the matter of the royal emblems. Popular movements, as we saw in the attack on the Bastille, tended to immediately demolish buildings, gates, monuments that bore inscriptions proclaiming the names and the glory of the kings, that is, the evidence of oppression. Very quickly there arose a concern for what they referred to as excess. At the Châtelet de la Tournelle, at the south entry to Paris, how could one extract the royal reliefs worked into the whole structure without destroying everything? The Maison Rouge proposals were unable to prevent the destruction.[17] The spire of Sainte-Chapelle was destroyed with the sole purpose of annihilating the crown at its top. The devastation of the Gallery of Kings in Notre Dame Cathedral was an extraordinary illustration of the passion to destroy crowned heads, even those in the form of stone likenesses carved in the inaccessible heights of a façade which had been, among all of those so disfigured, considered venerable.[18]

As early as the summer of 1792, in the excitement provoked by the events of August 10 (the storming of the king's residence at the Tuileries Palace and the destruction of the monarchy), the Legislative Assembly had voted a decree with a first article which laid down that:

> All statues, bas-reliefs, inscriptions, and other monuments in bronze
> and in any other material raised in a public place, temples, gardens,
> parks and out-buildings, national residences, even in those which
> were merely reserved for the king's pleasure, will be removed by the
> diligence of the communes' representatives, who will oversee their
> provisional conservation.

The following article in that decree required they be converted to a kind of cannon (*bouche à feu*), unless request was made by the Commission des monuments to the legislative body to obtain dispensation for the "conservation of objects that might be of interest to the arts."[19]

That which is "artistic" should be preserved because it is worthy of entry into the national collection. But how was it possible to sort things out after the worst was done? The decree was so contradictory that, upon the entreaties of the committee, a new decree recommended an opposite procedure on September 16, 1792:

> Considering that while surrendering for destruction monuments suit-
> able for recalling the memories of despotism, it remains important
> to preserve and to honorably conserve the masterpieces of the arts,
> so worthy of filling the leisure and beautifying the territory of a free
> people . . .

The selection would, then, be made first, and then the transfers to holding areas, ever watchful in order to prevent disasters caused "by citizens of little instruction or ill-intentioned men." These terms were significant indications of the new idea that was taking shape.

Some years later the National Convention member the Abbé Grégoire recounted his torment and struggle during those difficult years:

Let us remind ourselves that those enraged people had proposed
burning the public libraries. Everywhere they seized books, pictures,
monuments that bore the trace of religion, of feudalism, of royalty;
it was incalculable, the loss of religious objects, of scientific and literary objects and documents. The first time I suggested putting a stop
to this devastation, they paid me the honor of branding me *fana-
tique*; they swore that on pretext of conserving the arts, I wanted to
save the *trophies of superstition*. Nevertheless, such were the excesses
to which some delivered themselves that at last it became possible to
make myself usefully understood and the Committee of Public Instruction consented to my delivering a report against vandalism to
the Convention. I created the word to kill that thing.[20]

Abbé Grégoire, whom David placed in the center of his *Oath of the
Tennis Court (Serment du Jeu de Paume)*, was the most ardent adversary of
the monarchy; September 21, 1792, he proposed its abolition to the Legislative Assembly. His hatred of the ancien régime was matched only by
his loyalty to the church (albeit a constitutional one after the Oath of the
Civil Constitution of the clergy made them loyal to the Republic and no
longer to the pope of Rome), and by an intellectual honesty that led him
to denounce with all his force and at no small risk the excesses and absur-
dities of revolutionary behavior.

The Committee of Public Instruction, which he joined in June 1793,
commissioned him to prepare a report "to unmask the counterrevolutionary measures by which the enemies of the Republic were trying
to dishonor the nation and to lead the people back into ignorance by
destroying the monuments of art." But the conclusions of this mission
could only be made public after Thermidor. On 12 Fructidor, Year II (August 24, 1794), the report on the destruction carried out by vandalism and
on the means of suppressing it was read to the committee, was accused of
being excessive by some, and was at last presented to the whole convention on August 31. On 19 Nivôse, Year II (January 8, 1793), Grégoire
had launched the term "vandalism" for the first time and denounced all
disorderly attacks on any work of art as "counterrevolutionary." But it was
the report—which came quite late—of the summer of 1794 that once and
for all classified the idea of vandalism as a criminal attack on heritage. At
that moment something changed, at least in the realms of judgment and
vocabulary.

These points of view, already difficult to convey effectively within the
commissions, no doubt had little effect on how people acted throughout
the country, where "iconoclasm" continued and was increasingly taken
over by demolition workers and speculators who knew very well what they

were doing. "All of it together cannot be considered a masterpiece of art which one should order saved," wrote quite simply the chief engineer of the Department of the Eure[21] on the subject of the Château of the Archbishops of Gaillon. Only its conversion into a prison saved the château. The list was extraordinary: edifices threatened by outright demolition in a moment of patriotic fever for a new beginning. In Blois, in Reims, in Fontainebleau . . . , the sale of national property, authorization promulgated April 4, 1793, to subdivide the great ecclesiastic, royal, or aristocratic domains, was able to give moral sanction to pure and simple dilapidation. The more or less honorable conversion and reuse that transformed churches, convents, or châteaus into warehouses or service centers seems to have been a necessary social humiliation. The insolent luxury of the churches deserved punishment. If they removed the sumptuous grills from the abbey choir in Pontigny, it was because "a sanctuary can exist without grills, but the Republic under attack cannot do without pikes."[22]

The idea of a heritage that was beyond the cares of history and worthy of escaping them could, then, be formulated only through arguments such as the "general" value of threatened works or the affirmation of their interest to education and history. An intellectual as well as cultural necessity was thus ripening. At the same time, pillaging and trafficking ("the shady gang," *la bande noire*) followed in the wake of passionate excess. This

Figure 1.2
La Petite Place in Arras: its condition in 1919.

Figure 1.3
The Tuileries fire, 1871: the Hall of Marshalls.

argument was periodically resumed in the course of the nineteenth and then the twentieth century. One could wonder if it really had convinced the French people. At any rate, by the end of the National Convention, strong initiatives had begun to depoliticize the problem.

THE PALACES OF HERITAGE

Royal palaces, convents, churches, châteaus, came to be turned to new uses. It had become necessary to store the innumerable vestiges, furnishings, statues that had been displaced, mutilated, or condemned. Two new approaches were developed to answer these circumstances: the inventory and the museum. The briefly descriptive lists give an idea of the extraordinary auction hall France became during these crucial years. But the very scale of the dispersal of objects, by its contrast, helps us appreciate the value of the adventure of the "Museum of French Monuments." For a quarter of a century, from 1793 to 1818, an original conservatory of stone vestiges was organized in the convent and gardens of the Grands Augustins. Enough has been said about the incredible liberties taken with history and archaeology by its director, Alexandre Lenoir. But this was the museum of a visionary, and it played a leading role, we know, by its stimulation of the "romantic" impulse, which lead to a definition of the medieval heritage that was theatrical as well as poetic. Thanks to the impulsive and generous character, somewhat prone to exaggeration, of its creator, the Museum of French Monuments attracted, enchanted, and struck the minds of its day. We can scarcely exaggerate the success of these historical "tombs," put together despite controversy, so that one went from surprise to surprise, roaming through that strange amusement park.[23] Alexandre Lenoir's romantic museography excited the feelings of the generation that had just rediscovered, with Chateaubriand's *The Spirit of Christianity* (*Le Génie du christianisme,* 1802), the notion of a past that was marvelous, chivalric, French.

This achievement played, then, a role that was the exact opposite of Napoleon's "Grand Louvre." Discussions that accompanied the development of the Museum of French Monuments introduced an element of thinking that would contribute more than a little to the ripening of problems. People were at last too well aware of the complications of makeshift warehouses not to advocate conservation in situ. Once again, members of the National Convention, overwhelmed by the problem, drafted ultimately ineffectual recommendations. Lenoir's great adversary, Quatremère de Quincy, had no trouble demonstrating the error of haphazard moving and reassembly of pieces. It was unfortunate that these observations came from a fine "neoclassical" mind for whom the Middle Ages quite simply did not exist and who would have rather seen Gothic buildings tumble down.[24]

The twelve editions of the Lenoir catalogue (1793–1816) well showed the groping toward knowledge and little by little revealed how one arrived at a level of scholarship.[25] Augustin Thierry found his vocation as he read Chateaubriand's *Génie.* Michelet discovered his in the melancholic garden of the Petits Augustins. To measure the impact of this change, we need only compare Séroux d'Agencourt's project (appeared in 1823), centered on Italy and the survival of classical beauty and typical of earlier scholarship, with the two important books by Alexandre de Laborde, *Les Monuments de la France, classés chronologiquement et considérés sous le rapport des faits historiques et de l'étude des arts* (*Monuments of France, classified chronologically and considered in relationship to historical events and the study of the arts*), which added to the classical foundation (1816) a careful contemplation of the Middle Ages (1836).[26]

Institutions took the problem into account. The Institut de France, organized by decree on 3 Brumaire, Year IV (October 24, 1795), took up where the Académie des Inscriptions left off. It included several specialists in national antiquities who were anxious to be heard: Aubin-Louis Millin, elected in 1804, Petit-Radel in 1806, Amaury-Duval in 1811. They took the measure of the immense gap in their knowledge and wanted to close it by conceiving what could have been a "General Inventory." Montalivet's well-known memorandum of May 10, 1810, ordered departmental prefects to collect all possible information about châteaus, abbeys, tombs, and so forth. Little by little the Middle Ages became essential to the national heritage. At last there was the desire to acknowledge the divers medieval elements that had survived in the geography and to make a kind of assessment.

Prefectural investigations were perhaps not the solution. In fact, the feeling was not unanimous, scholarship was dispersed and still too passionate, and the very idea of an inventory was uncertain. Results remained unconvincing. After the shock of 1814–15 (the defeat of Napoleon and the Bourbon Restoration with Louis XVIII), the question could have and should have been taken up again more forcefully. This time the reopened Académie des inscriptions intervened. Since the 1810 questionnaire was to be used again, the academy would be pleased to receive the results of the prefectures' research. It proposed clearer instructions: an April 8, 1819, memorandum drafted by Decazes took that into account. A kind of procedure was put in place. For 1819–26 the Academy of Registration archives had the responses filed by the minister of the interior. Between 1839 and 1862, documents were no longer classified by department but by year.[27]

Authorities were seriously pondering the "origins" of the French nation. As was usually the case, the oldest archaeological vestiges assumed vital importance in the discussion. But the authorities found themselves in an awkward position, trying to decide who their original ancestors were: the Celts, the Romans, or the Franks. The paper Lavallée wrote for the Académie celtique (1807) was particularly revealing: France needed the equivalent of what the Académie étrusque was to Florence, the Société scandinave to Stockholm and what the Society of Antiquarians, who since 1770 had published the *Archaeologia Britannica,* was to London. The need for historical depth can lead to mirages. By designating certain points of reference, monuments, sites, objects, which began to make up a revealing chain perceived as fundamental, a certain authority was conferred upon that young, searching scholarship. The publisher of the first treatise on national antiquities did not hesitate to affirm:

> Each new day reveals a fresh attraction to us, some new reason to
> be fond of those edifices raised for us by the hand of our forefathers,

joined to our sky and our lands as much as to our beliefs, our habits
and the most secret stirrings of our souls (1830).[28]

The sense of a national heritage was then less awakened by loyalty to
the work of the centuries than by a meditation, a funereal reverie on obsolescence. From that time on, the miserable condition of sanctuaries and
stately homes was emphatically described and decried by the new generation, who experienced a sort of remorse. When, in 1832, Victor Hugo
wrote his famous article, the still youthful violence of tone only seemed
excessive. It was a clear denunciation of the type of moral law which had
begun to take shape:

> Whatever property rights may be, the destruction of an edifice which
> is a historic monument must not be permitted to those ignoble spec-
> ulators who allow self-interest to blind their own honor. . . . There
> are two things present in an edifice: its use and its beauty. Its use
> belongs to the owner, its beauty to everyone; destroying it is, then,
> beyond his rights.[29]

The incubation of the feeling of heritage, like that of the national feeling, was long and dramatic, insofar as it inevitably concerned works shaped
by the institutions of religion, the monarchy, and the aristocracy. We can
set up a kind of symmetry between the impassioned reactions, of the people
or the scholars, between the will of scholarship and that of destruction. But
the sense of heritage, artistic and monumental inheritance in which one
recognizes oneself, was still far from definition in French society.

DEPLOYING THE MUSEUMS: THEIR FUTURE

The appearance of the museum as a viable institution only seems to con-
tradict the truth of this. The general establishment of those new conserva-
tories of interesting objects and works of art would occupy all of the nineteenth century and henceforth characterize national culture. But one must
more closely observe the birth and sudden growth of this phenomenon.

The notion of a coherent and accessible collection had appeared in the
eighteenth century, which, for that reason also, deserved its title of "the
age of Enlightenment" ("l'âge des Lumières").[30] The National Convention, which had created the museum of the Louvre, precipitated a general
movement. We all know this. But we must also remember that the first
establishment to call itself "museum," that of Elias Ashmole in Oxford,
with its bylaws, *Instituta*, presented in 1714, had above all, an educational
purpose. He had collected masterpieces, particularly those from classi-

cal art, with the object of forming or reforming the taste of his contemporaries. It was in this spirit of higher education that institutions would multiply in Great Britain and all over Europe. The monarchy at last had to answer the demand of pamphleteers like Lafont de Saint-Yenne that masterpieces "see the light of day" (*voient la lumière*) (1749). Most of all, Diderot, in the article "Louvre" of the *Encyclopédie*, laid out the complete plan for a scientific establishment, comprising at the same time a royal library, a natural history repository, royal collections, and those of the learned societies, in short, a "central museum of arts and sciences." Marigny, then d'Angiviller, took on the problem for which no one had been able to devise an administrative interpretation. The Grande Galerie of the Louvre, fitted out for displaying the collections, would see the light of day in 1788, when the Revolution interrupted that laborious enterprise to put something entirely different in its place.[31]

The concept of *museum*, a sanctuary for the human spirit and the place of initiation for the masses, haunted minds, occupied speeches, and would lead to hasty but fruitful developments. The encyclopedists' matrix museum (Museum central) burst into five or six establishments, among which were the Augustins museum for "monuments of stone" and the Jardin des Plantes. The Louvre became the National Museum of Art. To begin with, by September 1792, objects gathered in the royal residences were deposited there. At the end of several months of collecting, repairing, and discussing brought about by artists' demands that this "museum" was intended for them above all others (they were able to obtain the agreement that the museum was reserved for artists seven out of ten days in the new week of the new revolutionary calendar), the new national Louvre opened August 10, 1794, on the anniversary of the fall of the monarchy. But the necessary renovation was too vast and no doubt the confusion too great. The Grande Galerie was closed from 1796 to 1799 and the renovated Louvre reopened for more continuous activity July 14, 1800, in what had become a new world. France had, in fact, entered the expansionist era of the conquering Republic. Far from being considered a reliquary of French art and royal collections, a parallel, in other words, to Lenoir's French Monument Museum, the Gallery of the Louvre had become the gigantic conservatory for universal art.[32] The arrival of immense "treasure" caravans was celebrated by the festivals so fancied by that epoch: one famous engraving depicted the "triumphant entry of the monuments of art and science into France" at the Champ-de-Mars, 10 Thermidor, Year VI (1798).[33]

The story of the creation of the Louvre Gallery, through the energy of the astonishing Dominique Vivant Denon, has often been told.[34] In the city of liberty, Paris, the "Musée Napoléon" (1803–14) methodically

THE NOTION OF PATRIMONY

assembled distinguished works from all schools, all countries: all the Van
Eycks, all the Raphaels, all the Rubenses. By aligning the most famous
paintings in the world, they produced a concise statement of a "universal heritage" and offered a dazzled generation a show that must have ac-
counted for much in the renaissance of French painting. The "imaginary museum" really did exist during the Napoleonic empire. That was
a remarkable phenomenon but very different from the beginning of the
new consciousness that we are attempting to isolate here. When the collections of the Napoleonic Louvre were returned (with a few interesting
exceptions), in 1815, to the despoiled countries, the notion of the "ideal"
museum remained an aspiration equal in importance to the museum's
educational mission. And it influenced all future museum installations of
large European countries in the nineteenth and twentieth centuries.

The movement had reached the provinces, where the "depositories"
of confiscated property became the beginnings of museum collections.
It was in this way that the former convent of la Couture in Le Mans by
1799, the Augustins convent of Toulouse by 1793, and establishments in
ten other cities as well, piled up works which the social and economic
concerns of the times had either displaced or condemned. These foundations have lasted, with a generally less chaotic presentation. In the same
spirit, by the July Monarchy (of 1830), and then during the Second Empire
(of Napoleon III), mansions, convents, sanctuaries were transformed to
more or less organized settings for collections: the Hôtel Cujas in Bourges,
Unterlinden in Colmar, not forgetting the startling romantic bric-a-brac
that Alexandre Du Sommerard installed in the Hôtel de Cluny (opened
in 1844).

All these establishments accumulated poorly identified fragments,
vestiges of structures that had disappeared and were beginning to be
missed, and a hodge-podge of paintings. They gathered into these re-
positories the new category of "disused" edifices, the ones snatched from
destruction. They became increasingly fond of evocative decor. The scattering of Alexandre Lenoir's museum, after 1816, deprived amateurs of the
past of their most precious place of initiation. In the gardens of the Grands
Augustins, the ranked presentation of "monuments" had been composed
too arbitrarily and presented the advantage of miming historic development. The tomb of Heloïse and Abelard and the tomb of Diane de Poitiers became potent symbols of their corresponding periods of history and
art. Of course they were right to return to the Cathedral of Saint-Denis
monuments hastily disassembled during the Revolution (the Restoration
could do no less). But the idea of gardens where scattered fragments were
made available for meditation continued to please the "curious" and those

leading citizens who sensed more or less intuitively the necessity of somehow turning it to their own advantage. Local archaeology was born of this in nearly every province.

The concept of evocative "compositions" inherited from Lenoir produced a posterity which is nowhere near its end. Parks sewn with stone fragments, composed ruins, appeared everywhere. The temptation to be stylized was too strong. With the wreck of Lenoir's museum and with new medieval vestiges brought in by Haussmann's destruction of medieval Paris in his massive redrawing of that city during the Second Empire, Duban conceived the courtyard of the École des beaux-arts, which represented for numerous generations the model for an academic treatment of these kinds of objects.[35] The historic significance of such works as the Anet façade or the Gaillon portico was eliminated in favor of a theatrical presentation, a "synthesis" which no longer even claimed to arouse an awareness of the originality of those works. These were examples of decorative art, good for sketching and using in professional competitions.

Figure 1.4
Melun: café set up in former priory.

This didactic, pragmatic thinking resulted in a policy of systematic copying and casting to build up the "museum of comparative sculpture" and then the new "museum of French monuments" begun in 1882 at the Trocadero in Paris after a report by Viollet-le-Duc. The opposite of Lenoir's work, which assembled works, originals naturally, rescued from vandalism, the new museum gave an impression of resources of artistic heritage through plasters and renderings.[36] The educational rather than scientific intention was obvious. Moreover, the idea of faithful copies, easily arranged in a pedagogic order, was a dominant idea of the last century. The print, though it had become so important in the commerce of culture, obviously was not adequate for certain kinds of works. Photography had not yet been understood to be the extraordinary instrument of exploration and knowledge that it would later become. With castings and renderings, then, they endeavored to build up *duplicata*, which would lend themselves easily to commentary. At the beginning of the Third Republic, Thiers conceived a "musée des Copies" destined to rebuild, at great expense, the *musée "ideal."*[37] The least we can say is that the success of these initiatives has remained very limited. And it is peculiar—but, alas, revealing of a certain general lack of education—that the great museum of French architecture that France owed herself, easy enough to conceive from the often extraordinary maquettes in our depositories, has never been seriously contemplated by so many succeeding generations of authorities.[38]

BIRTH OF "HISTORIC MONUMENTS"

The expression "historic monument" appeared for the first time, it seems, in Aubin-Louis Millin's leaflet for his collection of national antiquities (1790): "We are primarily attached to historic monuments." "Monuments" here signifies edifices but also tombs, statues, stained glass, all that serve to fix, illustrate, to make more precise national history.[39] The term was kept: it adapted to France a notion formed a quarter of a century earlier by British archaeologists, but it failed to lead to the broad view of the ages of civilization, which had already been, for more than a century, common in Italy. In France one could scarcely imagine that idea except through Michelet, the translator of Vico. It was, then, with a remarkable delay, that the information so present in architecture and the arts was taken into consideration as facts of civilization. From there it was a quick step to the conception of an administrative apparatus and a state institution.

A half century had passed between the intuition of a monumental heritage essential to national consciousness and its translation to an official form. Provincial scholarship went into action with at least two remarkable centers, in Normandy, under Arcisse de Caumont and in the

Languedoc under Du Mège, whose passion and energy have often been commented upon.[40] Prefectural polls during the empire, continued during the Restoration, led to a stockpile of information which the Académie des Inscriptions, the transitory, logical administrator for this activity, was unable to put to use.

On October 21, 1830, Guizot (Louis-Philippe's minister of the interior after the Revolution of 1830) filed a report endorsing the creation of the post of "inspector general of historic monuments." It would be the full expression of the new desire to show "the admirable sequence of our national antiquities." You must know them to preserve them, was the slogan. His report added, rather naively, that the new inspector should prepare "in his first and general tour, an exact and exhaustive catalogue of the edifices or isolated monuments which deserve serious attention on the part of government." He added that catalogue documents would be kept by the Ministry of the Interior, "where they will be filed and consulted as needed." This seems to be the initial intention of the term "filed."

An administrative apparatus soon followed. The Comité historique des arts et des monuments in 1834 had as its mission the drafting of instructions to those reporting to the ministry. At the end of 1837, it gave way to the Commission des monuments historiques, with its instructions to compile the list of structures warranting protection and intervention. The work of this celebrated commission is by now well known. They were immediately thrown into all the kinds of problems that would develop more fully later.[41]

On the "scientific" level, the history of Guizot's committee was one of slow and discouraging discovery of the immensity of the French heritage. The historian, who was not an archaeologist, could conceive a magnificent inventory indispensable to any healthy preservation policy. But he would not have taken the true measure of the problem: he would have been ignoring the depth and complexity of real situations. He would not have grasped that heritage existed in space. The inspectors' missions always ended in a feeling of impotence. The provinces were inexhaustible and no one was prepared for the work required: "Each inspector should be able to draw up plans like an architect, to sketch fragments like an artist, to read old charters like an archivist, ride a horse or walk like a hunter and, what's more, for coherence, they should all share the same foundations in archaeology and the same system of analysis in the history of art" (Grille de Beugelin, December 1, 1835).[42]

Soon they were willing to accept a minimal "superficial but general recognition" (de Gasparin, 1838). They designed simplified questionnaires, supplied abbreviated definitions, decided to be satisfied with an informative map. For about twenty years the General Inventory revealed one after another of the concrete difficulties that would eventually bring the project to a standstill. But the problem had been stated: Philippe de Chennevières's exceptional energy intervened at the very moment the disaster of 1870 (the Franco-Prussian War and the massacre of Parisians by their own government) and the neo-Jacobinism of the commune were rousing minds, and the idea of "general statistics," amply conceived on a national scale, reappeared. This time it would be the kind of project in which German science had shown itself to excel. "Inventorization" had found its paradise in the Second Unified Reich, not in France.

Cultural development imperfectly and irregularly followed the administration's recommendations and demands. France had, for more than a century, lingered in error concerning the heritage that archaeologists were beginning to explore, that the public knew nothing about, that the bourgeoisie scarcely considered except for its economic aspect, and that the "modernists" had no qualms deprecating. The gap between official statements and the behavior of individuals or groups had never been so wide, so dangerous, as in a country where familiar reality, daily experience, the attachment to objects, to structures . . . were regularly obliterated by political eloquence. Depending on the direction it was given, that new social authority, the school, would only accentuate the indifference to "provincial" culture, exalting the nation but neglecting its immediate and visible symbols. This situation merits a detailed examination; short of being able to produce one, we can consider the particularly revealing experience of Mérimée.[43]

Mérimée responded to what was begun by Guizot and Vitet with a professionalism that was sometimes astonishing. He traveled throughout the provinces before the coming of railways, with a curiosity and stubbornness that were doubly revealing. Those edifices that became famous or at least familiar were nearly inaccessible. The monuments, rarely visited, were deteriorating into oblivion. But what is, after all, remarkable, is that it took a skeptic, a "libertine," a total agnostic, to rediscover Romanesque art, Gothic art, and medieval painting. There was no question of religious attachment or of some obscure loyalty to the ancien régime which, in any case, would only have drawn attention to structures that were already distinguished by tradition. No, here was the discovery of the country through its historical landscape, which no doubt assumes the need to explore a past sunk in rural monotony and compromised by ignorance and presumed truths. In this respect, Mérimée's experience showed a strong and, we should admit, modern intuition of heritage.

The trip diary and reports of the inspector general of 1832 have without doubt remained an excellent indication of this. If we examine the simple information on the state of mind of the population and local

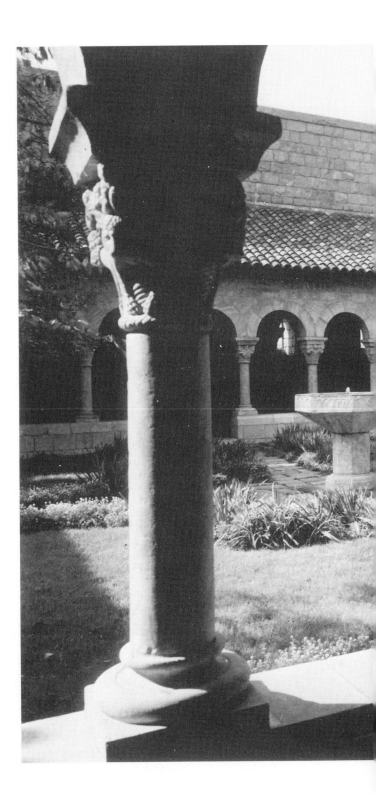

Figure 1.5
Restoration of the
cloister of Saint-
Michel-de-Cuxa at the
Cloisters in New York.

authorities, those who served the churches, those posted to military service, and so forth, we can only agree with Prosper Mérimée that there existed a distressing state of ignorance and apathy. Old edifices should be handled as most convenient or torn down without hesitation. The concern for knowing and interpreting existed in some leading citizens, some scholars, some ministerial agents. We learn their names. But they were constantly overwhelmed by the bad habits of owners and users, who cared little for archaeology and preservation. Most people were scarcely motivated; the civic-minded were indifferent or hostile. If this analysis, which Mérimée and the intellectuals of the last century have left us, is accurate, we can say that, for complex reasons that need a deeper understanding, the sense of the collective heritage that appeared during the Revolution, was defended by the romantics, and was celebrated in the language of officials, was, in actual fact, at its lowest ebb.

The problem was that they had to rescue all those scattered elements, all the minor aggregates. Rescue meant intervening on two levels, by protecting and by consolidating. A minority of people understood the vastness of the task. The majority of the population was unconvinced and never possessed the level of culture that would have changed their minds. The evidence of attachment to sanctuaries, relics, miraculous statues, to local mementos, did not extend to structures nor to the works taken by themselves. Conversely, the hatred of buildings that were symbols, so violent under the National Convention, lingered. We would see it in Paris, with the commune, which did not leave the city without first setting fire to the Cour des Comptes and the Tuileries. But that drama found its place of remembrance in Père Lachaise Cemetery. The Restoration had built the Chapel of Expiation. By the time of the Third Republic, there were thoughts of razing it, a symbol that had become too cumbersome.

Conservation problems assumed an overwhelming importance and finally consumed the service's time to such an extent that it was forced to give itself a structure. In fact, at the 1873 Exposition Universelle in Vienna, there was a sort of retrospective of the Service des monuments historiques français that was primarily an exact catalogue of important restorations, and its text, visibly dominated by the thinking of Viollet-le-Duc, spoke of nothing else but the new structuring.[44] Through inevitable developments, the idea of a vast inventory faded. Monumental statistics were ultimately confused with the ranking list for historic monuments, or with what would be called "the supplementary inventory," a list started gradually and as needed. The nearly random, occasional nature of work that consisted of a series of responses to appeals or political recommendations rather than the execution of a program had finally been accepted. In fact Viollet-le-Duc's overpowering personality set policy for the direction

of work and for a certain narrowness of view born in the old conviction
that the only veritable national architecture was that of the eighteenth
century.[45] For at least a century conceptualization and management of
the national heritage were guided by the dogma of the authenticity of the
eighteenth century, and during that same time, modern church architecture often received the same treatment.[46] The conviction, inherited from
romanticism, that medieval art represented par excellence the national
heritage, that it was the incarnation of "la France profonde," was used
to justify important interventions and lead archaeology to new research.
Inversely, this conviction made it difficult to admit that the works of the
seventeenth and eighteenth centuries deserved as much attention. Aside
from royal residences like Fontainebleau, which was put back into service,
innumerable Renaissance or seventeenth-century edifices were neglected.
Above all, they did not approach those edifices as automatically worthy
subjects, as was indicated by strange, scholarly, often very violent discussions at the end of the nineteenth century, to decide what was or was not
in keeping with the "French spirit" in the architecture of other times.
The very laudable reports of the Société française d'archéologie reveal
how long that hesitance lasted, leaving British historians the initiative in
treating French art of those periods.[47]

     Then too the restrictions of restoration brought with them a kind of
misunderstanding. They worked from a Viollet-le-Ducian idea of *proto-
type*. Restoration was to insure the prestige of heritage: it would by its
very nature be granted to remarkable works, the great examples. These
would be shown to their advantage as far as was possible. Rehabilitation
implied restructuring and additions. The analogy with the restoration of
paintings is worth examining. The nineteenth century was the age of
authoritarian and, it must be stressed, abusive, interventions: "A skillful
restorer should not confine himself to repainting damaged fragments; he
should paint everywhere so that the picture seems newly painted," this
from the treatise by Goupil and Desloges in 1867. It was the same doctrine,
the same ambition, the same error, which it has taken so long to be freed
of, for the presentation of paintings, doctored, run through the "juice"
of yellow varnish, as it was for the treatment of buildings, reassembled,
completed, without the smallest scruple. This intervention may well have
produced beautiful work quite satisfying to the restorer, but it struck at
the heart of the work of art, it released the unbearable doubt about the
work's authenticity, it broke the chain. If that seems intolerable, it is because it compromises the perception of "the work in time" which is the
key to the whole process.

     This general policy was attuned to the vast project of urban modern-
ization, as exemplified by Paris. A publication like the *Annales archéologiques*

by Didron l'Aîné shows the apprehensions caused by the double adaptation of some buildings. There began to appear acerbic criticism of the abstract definition of heritage, a definition which did not come out of an exploration of the neighborhood or site of the edifice but from a selection of worthwhile models. Elements deemed unnecessary were eliminated to call attention to those more in agreement with new courses. Guilhermy's protest in 1861 well conveys the extent and limits of Haussmann's "heritage policy":

> Instead of racking their brains to pull them [the old structures] down by the quickest possible means, they should have instructed men of taste to search for ways of keeping them. The experiment, made the first time with the Tour Saint-Jacques and repeated with no less success for the Hôtel de Cluny, could have succeeded equally well for the numerous monuments in the Latin Quarter, which have only left a few mysterious stones scattered in the gardens that surround the ruins of the Julian Baths. The transversal galleries of Saint-Jean-de-Latran could have made an elegant gallery on one side of the Rue des Écoles, across from the Collège de France. The dungeon of the Commanderie, less rich in ornamentation than the Tour Saint-Jacques but more interesting by the fact of the time it was built and by its intended use, might have lifted its crenellated roof above the rebuilt houses on the Rue Saint-Jacques. A little further, very near the last of the Philippe Auguste towers, at the entrance to the Place de la Sorbonne, an eighteenth-century building of the most elegant style which had been part of the Collège des Bénédictins de Cluny, could have opened its halls, decorated with columns and vaults, for a school or any other establishment of use to the public. As for the Chapelle du Collège de Beauvais, that would make a very useful extra chapel for the neighborhood. The Tour Saint-Jacques came close to disappearing. Today it is the monument most loved by Parisians.[48]

Thus would begin and grow in France a new conflict of doctrines on the theme of "historic monuments." Reactions to "vandalism" had given the country a certain lead in arousing a rather keen awareness of these problems, but then they settled into a long-lasting "ideological" conflict. It was, after all, a pity that the activity of an important administration be left indefinitely under the patronage on the one hand of a talented writer fascinated by the rich heritage of the country but perfectly incapable of organizing its methodical exploration, and on the other hand of a doctrinaire spirit that could conceive the complete restoration of buildings and was, unfortunately, only too able to accomplish it. Two great inspirations joined to two structural weaknesses heavy with consequence: in the exploration of works from the past, an impassioned approach that went from discoveries to omissions as the inexhaustible character of the "heritage" showed itself and, in the interventions of the architects, a legitimate concern for rehabilitation related to the disastrous idea of conformity to an ideal model.

The medieval portfolio had been subjected to an insistent and general remodeling for a hundred years. The example was set from above and justified by the policy for "great monuments." The observations, criticism, and reprimands from archaeologists who were forming their own idea of historic heritage were ineffective. The details were simplified to bring out the essence of a structure which one had sanitized, as it were. Paul Léon devoted one harsh chapter to those restorations that could affect the details (like the balustrades of Notre Dame of Paris or of Amiens), the furnishings, windows, chapels, sometimes the entire construction, as in Clermont-Ferrand or Moulins.[49] The complete hold of diocesan architects, supported by the commission's authority, is sufficient explanation of maneuvers that no scientific authority could have countenanced. The argument of usefulness was sometimes put forward, but more often that of competence, which reached arrogant proportion in Abadie's well-known comments: "The science of archaeology seems to have no other mission than that of blaming, accusing of ignorance, of barbarity and vandalism. . . . The archaeologist does nothing, produces nothing. He is satisfied to veto all innovative ideas."[50] In those discussions on method, on the limits to be placed on restoration, where architects as directors of the construction site and in the name of their obvious technical responsibilities always had the last word, one often wonders who the French building stock really belonged to. Abadie, the brutal restorer of Angoulême and of Saint-Front in Périgueux, was also the architect of that monument of national reparation after 1871 (financed by French conservatives through a national fund-raising campaign, as a peace offering after the commune massacre), the Sacré Coeur of Montmartre. Those two titles still guarantee his prestige.

THE PARADISE OF ANTIQUE DEALERS

Administrative practice, then, created development mechanisms, and their direction was immediately criticized. Montalembert, for example: "We must not create a vacuum around our cathedrals, thereby diluting the magnificent dimensions they were given by their authors. They weren't built for the desert like the pyramids of Egypt, but to float above the tightly clustered houses and narrow streets of our old cities."[51] This warning was perfectly inoperative under the advance of the Haussmann mandates, which were those of the engineers, the prefects, the municipalities. Historic vision has been transformed by it. In all of Europe, the French example was followed, if sometimes contested. In Austria, a country more attentive than the France of those times to the complete interpretation of the national heritage and to the imprudence of not always necessary modern solutions, they had a more subtle approach to the problem of the relation of the city to the works of earlier times.[52] In Central Europe, thinking focused more closely on the value and role of "monuments."

The German archaeologist G. Dehio had presented the *Denkmalkultus,* the worship of great monuments, as a sort of religious key to national assertion. It was applicable to more than Wilhelmian Germany. But is the national heritage more evident in the pathetic or picturesque ruin which conveys the shock of the passing of time or in the triumphantly restored monument? In the course of the nineteenth century both attitudes coexisted, the one nourished by a feeling of poetic nostalgia, the other responding to the exaltation of the present. In his *The Seven Lamps of Architecture* (1850), Ruskin, in the name of the "lamp of memory," denounced the French practice which for him amounted to "allowing edifices to deteriorate in order to restore them." If one followed the noninterventionist paradox to its conclusion, the ruin was preferable because more evocative, at least to the extent that it possessed the authenticity of a death.

One wonders finally if, at least in France, official action, conscientious though it was, did not unwittingly produce an unfortunate consequence. State intervention seemed to have accustomed collectivities and individuals to the idea that the authorities should take responsibility for the national heritage, for its definition and development. The lists for protection seemed to introduce into the French property stock a class of superior structures which it was proper to begin with: it was the category that in a way directed what we might call monumental history. Recourse to administration—so characteristic of French practice—has the obvious corollary of public indifference and the inertia of minor officials.

Political and social upheavals of the separation of church and state at the beginning of the twentieth century could not fail to revive old passions. The mediocrity of their debate was only too revealing of the inability of the clergy and faithful as well as opposing partisans of the laity to conceptualize church sanctuaries and other property as a shared heritage. The most refined and ultimately the freshest point of view was without doubt that of Barrès. His little book, *La Grande pitié des églises de France* (1912), continued Michelet's thinking on the rural and silent nation and Montalembert's protest against the triumph of mediocrity, the case the romantics made for "humble churches, without distinction perhaps, but

full of charm and touching memories which were part of the architectural character, the physical and moral face of the land of France."[53] In
fact, they always lost their statues or their cloister to the indifference of
city governments, just as some of the most sensational châteaus, Urfé's la
Bâtie or Biron, lost their decoration or tombs.

France is never simple, and its most annoying complexity concerns
the provinces. Regional archaeology took the lead at the beginning of
the nineteenth century and lost it around 1900. The Union of Departmental Art Societies was about to go out of existence.[54] "The provinces
are dead," Philippe de Chennevières had already predicted in 1847 at the
beginning of his *Recherches*. If each region no longer had the means or the
will to examine its own collection of monuments, the heritage would be
deprived of edifices deemed useless or old-fashioned. "Will we live forever in the midst of souvenirs of interest only to tourists?" France was one
of the countries where important development projects had been linked,
for more than a century, to the ideology of progress and a contempt for
national heritage. There had always been enough sites, châteaus, ruins,
useless ramparts. No longer a part of daily life, or barely so, the elements
of other times were abandoned to intellectuals, artists, scholars, who dog-
gedly persisted in making a history, in piecing one together. Villagers who
should have known everything about their area were surprised when an
archaeologist examined their local vestiges. No one complained when they
moved the second story of the marvelous cloister of Saint-Guilhem-le-
Désert or half of the cloister at Saint-Michel-de-Cuxa. One day, to our
great surprise, we learned they had become ornaments for the Cloisters
museum in New York. It was fair to say that France, every bit as much as
Italy, fully deserved to pass for the paradise of antique dealers.

Protected Areas and the General Inventory

For a variety of reasons having to do with the new phase of civilization
we now call "postindustrial," with its taste for complete occupation of
space and generational anxieties, the portfolio of national heritage has become, a little late, a serious, sometimes obsessive concern. Yet again it has
been confirmed that only disasters, crises, misfortunes attract attention,
as if we always turn, too late, to situations we are ill-prepared for. Perhaps
the value of these kinds of objects is apparent only in their absence.

Mauled by industrial expansion and by disorderly peacetime growth
and because of the tragic destiny of the West in the twentieth century, the
environment was subjected, twice over, to enormous upheavals and devastation. But the emotional shock of war brings symbols to life, and there
was an undeniable mass emotion on the subject of the cathedrals of Arras,

Noyon, and most of all, the Cathedral of Reims at the time of the 1916 bombardments and throughout its long and slow "rebuilding." A scholar like Émile Mâle even conducted an anti-German campaign by extending to the domain of erudition the pain and indignation of a damaged witness. How many cities discovered themselves in the ruins in 1940 and in 1944? The great uncertainty in peoples' minds at the time of postwar reconstruction was typical of a society placed abruptly before a problem which it lacked the appropriate culture, knowledge, and experience to master. The scale of works to be accomplished was equaled only by the absence of coherence and the improvised nature—sometimes bold, often mediocre—of the results.

And here we are at the heart of the problem. The advantages of the urban layout, the characteristics of its former configuration, the chain of old houses, suddenly assumed an importance so consuming that work could not stop until the urban "milieu" was made identical to its population. It was called the Warsaw phenomenon (1945)★ and it was often seen elsewhere. To the contrary, in Le Havre (1944) another city was rebuilt on another plan in another spirit. But the old church of Notre Dame, a vestige of the historic foundation, was preserved as a symbol. In the one case, they brought everything to the reverence of national heritage, in the other a single element. Nearly everywhere they were able to make compromises. Against an example like Orleans, where they were able to make a match, those of Lisieux or Beauvais, of Tours, Toulon, Saint-Malo are perplexing. Misfortune had made it necessary to find the intimate link between the city and its site, between the urban contour and the pulsing sites of the monuments, which meant searching for a valid point of connection with the past.[55]

The situation became serious and general when, toward the end of the 1950s, economic expansion and accelerated modernization brought an unprecedented amount of new construction and remodeling. That shock was so violent that it made obvious the authorities' lack of forethought. Plans for urban expansion had not been made or not approved, or, if they did exist, were not followed. And this was the origin, at the moment of greatest tension, of the important legislative innovation of August 4, 1962, which for the first time favored on a city-wide scale a scheme of constructed zones defined as zones of national heritage. There were some handsome results: both Sarlat and Uzès showed the benefit to be had from a measure that made possible intelligent handling of the building

★ The old center of Warsaw, damaged severely by the German bombing in World War II, was rebuilt as a facsimile of the original, often with the use of prewar photographs to get architectural details exact.—Ed.

Figure 1.6
Hôtel de Sully in Paris, photographed before its restoration.

Figure 1.7
Hôtel de Sully after restoration.

stock. Finally, they adopted the approach in use in Germany and Austria to distinguish between kinds of streets, to divert traffic from the city center, to rehabilitate neighborhoods and housing complexes. But we cannot forget the incredible conclusion, indicative of a deep confusion, that the first of these experiments led to in La Balance quarter in Avignon. With its split landscape—half in keeping with (if profoundly reshaped), half new (and without character)—Avignon is an enduring statement of malaise.[56]

If anyone still doubts the seriousness of these questions and of the new dimension of national heritage, it is enough to recall that the proportion of new, indifferent construction is far greater than that of old structures in French building stock. In less than a half century, the mass of French building has doubled. The treasure of stone and brick is surrounded, often swamped, always losing ground to concrete. The approaches to all the cities have changed. The same evolution has reached villages and changed the countryside. With the word "ecology" we at last discovered the reality of the natural milieu and it was finally obvious that this was a global phenomenon. In that context what constituted the national heritage became more prominent and its significance more distinct, just as some had predicted.[57]

The rediscovery of deserted human spaces formed over the course of the centuries; streets, old paths, trails[58] intervened here; and, just as much, the rediscovery, more difficult and laborious than one might think, of rural architecture.[59] That loose and oversimplified notion of "traditional form" comes in here as an alibi for the most questionable styles and dangerous, sudden fads. In reaction to the uniformity of modern construction, the unclad stone, the suddenly exposed wooden lintels, the roughed surfaces, became "pseudo-old-fashioned" elements, historical trompe l'oeil. These problems illustrate the dubious role of vague culture.

For romanticism, the treasure of the national heritage, defined by a historical landscape strewn with medieval silhouettes and ruins, was a priceless door to the national consciousness. A century and a half later, the more modest question arose of capturing the evolution of our societies through material reality, the regalia. That first definition of the heritage demanded greater historical density, by means of a constantly expanding selection of remarkable structures. The new, more modest definition requires an ethnological analysis which can leave nothing out—neither things nor customs. In the earlier case, a nation examined itself after a long and dramatic convulsion. In the current case, a society is amazed at its own complexity, one it was beginning to overlook. From this point of view, the investigation of the "arts and traditions of the people," open to daily life, how things were done, simple living, was unique. This work led to the regional museums, to specialized publications, to a new kind

of collection, and slowly enriched or changed the color of the consciousness of a shared store of national heritage.[60] The unused visible object took
on the value of an appealing sign, indicated a hard-working existence,
and revealed something of the human state. The farm, the workshop, the
shop of another time now became what the church, the picturesque site,
the château had been for earlier generations. To the great good fortune
of the antique dealers, all the utensils of the old structures thus entered
the category of curiosities. How, then, did they enter the national heritage? By their very typicality, which contradicted the uniqueness of the
work of art, answered the specialists. This is a definition which called for
a new approach, as yet incompletely elaborated. From the point of view
of the ethnologist, object and habitat are joined. Removed from their use
and function, they break apart. Recognition and preservation have neither
the same meaning nor consequences they once did.

Between the two wars and then again after 1950, preservation societies
attracted the attention of a certain intellectual audience to problems facing
the national heritage. These societies acted only in limited areas and were
probably hurt by their diversity, since they had been unable to federate in
the way pure political strategy dictated. Theirs was a role of intervention
with administrations and authorities in those cases where they saw the
national heritage thoughtlessly endangered. The chronicles of these lively
debates would draw attention, alas, as much to the cultural mediocrity
of the "authorities" as to the absence of documentation, which made it
impossible to present defensible dossiers. A few developments show the
historian the events upon which fate turned. One of these, which was a
sort of test, was the rehabilitation of Block 3, condemned as unfit for use,
in the center of Paris, across from the Place Maubert.

One of the most revealing quarrels, no doubt, remains the strange
and unfortunate ten-year battle for the central wholesale food market in
Paris, Les Halles. The departure of the market, announced years earlier,
exposed a stupefying lack of foresight: innovators indifferent to the city's
structure pushed against the handful of more or less well-informed people
attached to the neighborhood layout. The projects, entirely defined by
the old problem of underground and surface traffic, were based on flawed
analyses of the urban fabric. During the summer of 1970[61] the destruction of six Baltard pavilions was on the scale of the nineteenth-century
projects. It was executed by an authority which saw it as a condition for
raising a "monument" to the twentieth century on the Beaubourg plateau. That decision was in keeping with the Haussmann tradition, which
had practically never left the offices of the capital. Fifteen years after the
Pompidolian action, another point of view was necessary, and we clearly
saw three errors in one. In 1930 they razed the dilapidated zone separating

rue Beaubourg from rue Saint-Martin. That scandalous, gaping hole did
the spadework, so to speak, for Mr. Pompidou. At the Hôtel de Ville they
were far from thinking that one day someone would want to "save" the
Marais. What's more, it was revealing that, despite informed and timely
warnings, government authorities as well as those from the City of Paris
and the Paris public transportation system, the RATP, were in complete
agreement to take the easiest path, that is, to destroy the essential, univer-
sally recognized traces of "industrial architecture" which would, in the
following years, with the help of the popularity of the nineteenth century,
become a great, if late, political chestnut. Finally, what they had chosen,
went the formula dear to yesteryear's statesmen, was a monument forc-
ibly squeezed into the least suitable place. Parisians of 1986 agreed that
authoritarian destruction would no longer be possible. In short, in fifteen
years, the idea of national heritage had absorbed the recent past. Metal
architecture and service installations—train stations, covered markets—
were perceived in a new way. Those same Parisians had known that most
of the deteriorated, neglected, underexploited neighborhoods had, around
the fifties or sixties, nearly dropped from the respectable stock of the national heritage. Those who loved architecture and those who wrote its
history sufficiently lamented the fact. Fifteen years after the destruction
of Les Halles, those same neighborhoods, particularly the Marais, were
at the top of the list in the rehabilitation dossier.

The defining of the Marais★ district as the "Marais sector" was made
and a successful rehabilitation achieved thanks to the effort and intelligence
of far-sighted groups.[62] An urban ensemble was preserved and cared for.
Everyone agrees that the Marais is now a jewel among the French "urbanized preserves," with sensitive handling that has shown us the visible,
attractive face of the national heritage. At the same time, it seems that this
notion can no longer remain passive. It must be active: preserve means
develop, repopulate, revive . . . The experiment of the provincial "protected sectors" thus found its own remarkable confirmation and guarantee despite the difficulties that come with partial change of neighborhood
population. By a kind of mood swing peculiar to the French mentality,
one side had scarcely made the mistake of pulling down the Baltard pavilions to facilitate the open digs of the regional transport authority (RER)

★ The Marais ("swamp") is one of the oldest intact neighborhoods in Paris. On the right
bank, it is bordered, roughly, by the rue de Rivoli–St. Antoine, the place de la Bastille, the Beaubourg (Pompidou) Museum, and the place de la République. Originally a
wealthy *quartier* particularly favored by the legal profession, it contains some of the most
impressive town houses in Paris, as well as the place des Vosges, the first collective housing built in Europe. It fell into decline with the French Revolution and was not again
appreciated until the late twentieth century.—Ed.

when a version of remorse over the old industrial architecture appeared and the other side rather easily obtained both the acceptance of master historical monument ranking lists and the creation of a museum of the nineteenth century in the setting of Lalou's old Orsay railroad station. It all came to pass as if, after the "sacrifice" of the most beautiful example of nineteenth-century modernity, the rest would be admitted to the domain of the national heritage. There were even, as during the romantic period for Gothic art, impassioned pleas on behalf of everything produced during the last century, as if they were no longer subject to critical historical analysis. We went from rather generalized execration around 1950, when officials spoke casually about eliminating the Grand Palais, for example,[63] to a surprisingly fervent exaltation and found a new domain to include in the old French treasure. This movement culminated logically in an important rehabilitation of Viollet-le-Duc. This consecration of a great moment in the history of the national heritage was needed for us to glimpse the power and limits of that time and, finally, for us to understand the extent to which the example it gives us is ultimately tied to a time that is over.[64]

New Dimensions

Since 1960 we have seen the growth of a more attentive concern for the old courses of action, the tested itineraries, the plans. Despite the reminder of Camille Sitte, we had forgotten their value. The situation evolved in determined enough fashion, then, for a new factor of development and management to appear. This was an element of calmness, a sort of cultural thermostat, tending to slow, to channel, at any rate, to balance the general mandate for modernization by expressing a more complex insistence of the population. The same phenomenon appeared in all the countries of the West and New World, naturally coinciding with the end of the illusion of the technological era's unlimited good fortune. In the new age, christened postindustrial, growth conceived as indefinite expansion, production, consumption was accused of destroying the very base, exhausting the resources, compromising the natural stability of those societies that were growing. The unspoken demand of a more sensitive, more cautious approach more or less consciously referred to a system of achieved realities, one of inherited forms. We think this accounts rather well for the magnitude that the notion of heritage has attained in countries like France, where the idea has remained easily accessible. It explains as well the scale of the notion of ecology which has become superimposed on the concept of heritage or a substitute for it in other lands.

Thus we move to a plane that is somewhat technical, scientific. The extent of this development has taken the entire society by surprise for want of sufficient information. Now we must attempt to constitute a network of topographical and historic references that will function in a country where challenges have appeared nearly everywhere. This was what André Malraux's 1964 General Inventory addressed. Through the massive documentation he caused to be gathered, the computerized use of it he planned, and the regional exhibits he presented, his department exemplified the new strategy appropriate to a society with a complex and still imperfectly understood national heritage.[65]

The label "heritage" was applied to such diverse categories of objects that the difficulty of defining a reasonable use for each of them became evident. Destruction and ruin of that which is useless is a law of nature. Culture intervenes to annul or impede that law, in the name of a higher law. But what is to become, for example, of the immense "supply" of chapels and churches, gradually losing their natural support in the presence of the faithful? They must not disappear; they are essential to the landscape. We must find an alternative solution. An investigation recently published in Great Britain clearly showed the inevitable destruction and possible new uses, stressing throughout the awesome vastness of the heritage.[66] Merely to know this is to be encumbered by it. By an attachment to the national heritage we perhaps ourselves create extreme difficulties. This is perhaps the moment to recall that in every society that which is part of the national heritage can be recognized by the fact that its loss would constitute a sacrifice and its conservation implies sacrifice. That is the law of all that is sacred.

It is no accident that the events we are witnessing coincide with modern civilization's unprecedented flood of resources for our imagination and body of knowledge. Not only is there a fascinating accumulation of figurative documents, but whole new branches of learning are coming into being from aerial photography, from geology, from cartographic research, from parcel analysis of inhabited space, and from the interpretation of forms and materials of objects "made by the hand of man." There also we find a new, inescapable access to the heritage, with opportunities for deeper work that are one more proof of its importance.

A discipline like aerial photography, which obviously accompanies the exploration of the sky now familiar to all, has exposed the thesaurus of French ground: "The salvaging of a common archaeological and historic heritage, the very substance of which disappears every day because of mechanized, deep excavations, the reconfiguring of land, development of urbanized suburbs, the great public works . . . supposes an inventory backed by an exact cartography."[67] Revealing a submerged national heritage is not only an appealing job for young aviators and archaeological diggers, it is sometimes also the means to help properly resolve development problems in rural space and even in urban space.

A detour into scholarship seems then to have become indispensable to all successful operations. The only means of resisting the eradication of the national heritage by the deployment of industrial civilization is to use that civilization's own extraordinary equipment in every area where it ruins the "development." In this way we can explain the paradox that exists when one assembles information of this kind in a computer.[68] Moreover, the scientific apparatus can rouse the attention that was missing by stimulating curiosity for detail and the discovery of subtle groupings. We have never seen so many exhibits in the provinces, in Paris even, where structures, villages, and sites are shown in relationship to each other. Their relationships become the basis of collective memory for a given society because they are a statement of the social setting: the intersection of nature shaping the ground and the culture giving it meaning. To the taste for physical experience people would be forced to add the dominance of that which was known. All else depended upon that taking place.

TREASURES, INHERITANCE, AND HERITAGE: THE NATIONAL FABRIC AND UNIVERSALISM

"There is not a bit of doubt that Napoleon invented individualism," André Malraux declared, thus reminding us that Stendhal, by his own admission, respected a single man: Napoleon. Indeed, "Napoleon erased birth. That represented something extraordinarily profound: humanity lived by the position guaranteed by birth. In place of that he set the conquest guaranteed by civil equality."[69] Let us accept this great simplification to understand how the sudden appearance of the shared feeling of "national" heritage, which we are attempting to define, could have been contemporary with individualist "liberation." Treasures, inheritance, heritage no longer coincide. If we so willingly gather the bequest of history and the gifts of the earth, literature and landscapes, space and tradition into the same reassuring basket, and so inhale the promising warmth of the "long term," it is because we are increasingly pressed to rely on that shared heritage.

The national group thus describes its inheritance to itself by calling upon, by expanding upon the notion of heritage. Just as there has been a slow deterioration of private riches, land, collections, in favor of public property, parks, museums, in the same way and by the same evolution, family and personal inheritance came to appear less worthy of attention than the "national" collection. In that sense, the consciousness that developed in 1789–95 has now reached its conclusion. The individual, "freed"

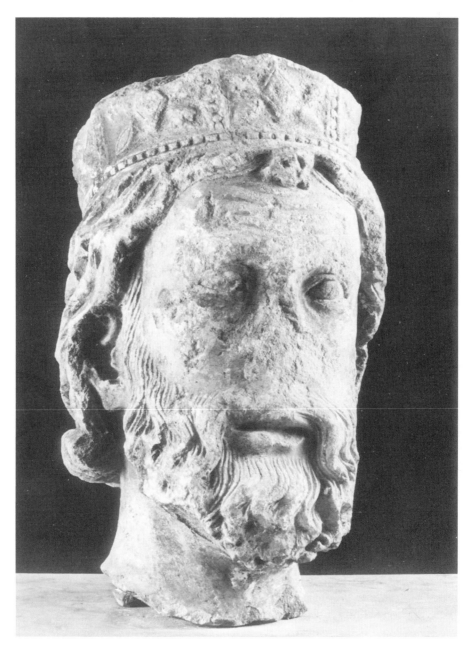

Figure 1.8
King of Juda. Stone head found at the time of the Notre-Dame de Paris archaeological digs, from the Gallery
of Kings, ca. 1220.

from the privilege and obligations of birth, had not succeeded, could not succeed in becoming self-sufficient. One of the characteristics of those times was no doubt the reduction of "privatization," the "private" domain being both the possibility of solitude and that of quiet possession. In any case, the slow and regular decline in the public domain of private collections,[70] the progressive opening of historic residences to crowds of visitors—exemplified by the British experience with its National Trust— are typical phenomena. There is a question here of the evolution of aristocratic land and wealth, whose problems are far from being over. For a long time the notion of heritage signified privatization. For certain social categories, the petite bourgeoisie, artisans, the peasantry, it had very little meaning at all. In the course of the last century, culture was given an official form and its direction taken by the state. That, in combination with the degenerating regionalism that spread through the French community, only accentuated the feeling in working-class milieus of being outside the circuit of properties acknowledged to be appealing and worthy of conservation. It was as if those riches belonged to the anonymous and distinguished world of fine arts or to the happy few of this world.

We are right to wonder if the expansion of the idea of heritage is not about to lead to the sudden discovery of those values by the people who might have believed themselves excluded. What are the reactions of provincial people, rural people, of craftsmen today to the economic devices being built for them, the *écomusées* (collections of material objects signifying how our ancestors earned a living, practiced a trade). What are their reactions to the tourist itineraries that bring foreigners and tourists face to face with their churches and their châteaus, edifices they themselves have only ever seen from afar? Or to exhibits by the local office of tourism or the General Inventory? When grandfather's tools, once useless and stored, are collected by the ATP curator or a passing antiques dealer, when barn or chapel are photographed by agents of the General Inventory, are they still grandfather's tools, still the dwelling or structure of another time? What hidden transformation have they been subjected to, when, after their elevation, they are once again contemplated en famille? Now an element of the national heritage, the object's nature and function change. It is used for something else.

And what else, if not illustration of the heritage? This is a vast area where the inevitable insatiability of commerce insinuates itself into the attention of sensitive minds and the attachment of the local people. Can we accept the new value of objects and properties formerly doomed to wear out and disappear? In the face of these new cities of the dead—useless objects, lifeless mannequins, and memories—one needs much culture and conviction to feel anything other than a sometimes tender, amused sense of the picturesque and of being very far away from something. The national heritage will be defined, they tell us, on the basis of well-documented and duly clarified items. But is that enough? Deep memory is less linked to possession than to pleasure. That is the crux of it.

History appears to be cyclic. At least it seems so on the planetary level. The great sanctuaries were for Christianity the tangible and necessary proof of its existence. The great pilgrimages attracted the faithful from all countries. Thus there existed for Western consciousness a valued resource, its religious heritage. One may think that the sacred places of tourism have taken this over in the twentieth century's civilization of the masses. The *Denkmalkultus* is followed by the national and international tourist attraction which, unfortunately, might in turn destroy what it seeks to value.

The concept of "universal masterpieces of art" fostered by UNESCO and acted upon by the ICOMOS, signals a return to the prestige-laden tallying of "wonders of the world" invented by the universalism of antiquity. In 1972 UNESCO adopted a "Convention for the protection of world cultural and natural treasures." That agreement intended to define a policy for intervention which was spectacularly demonstrated in Philae in Egypt and in Venice (1973), in Borobudur and in Mohenjo Daro (1974). The idea of a universal cultural heritage took shape; a catalogue of edifices to be listed in priority was created. That list of new "wonders of the world" was published after a meeting of the Committee for World Heritage held in Luxor in October 1979.[71] The practice has continued under the supervision of experts.

This initiative, which will create a new reference plan, requires several observations. The notion of a cultural property is not or should not be confused with that of property of national heritage. Collection pieces, ethnological testimony, are or can be cultural riches worthy of attention. It seems that does not make them, except, perhaps, metaphorically, elements of the heritage. Many Third World countries have come to so designate monuments, groupings, sites that could, because of their local interest, constitute a "heritage." But the apparatus of customs and traditions, a real framework for these societies, did not imply for them a system of monumental symbols comparable to that of countries in the West. They had to make one up. It was a question of dignity. The device is painfully obvious.

We can easily see how deceptive this alignment of the two distinct heritages really is when we consider the case of the country which is justifiably taken for the one most faithful to its own identity: Japan. Certain behavior with regard to the national heritage can only disconcert Westerners. For example, whether they are damaged or not, the great sanctuaries are periodically and totally rebuilt, with materials that are identical but new. Sometimes, as was the case at Ise, the site planned for the new edifice was duly prepared while the old structure still stood.[72] This practice assumes faithfulness to the techniques of construction and craftsmanship, to decoration, to the kinds of decisions made and followed, to the customary uses of the original structure, which perfectly demonstrates the care the Japanese have for the dignity of the edifice. To this sense of the existence of an ideal continuity we can oppose the Western attitude, haunted by the awareness of decline, of the impossibility of replacing that which went before, and of the twin deaths of objects that decay and feelings that change. The modern idea of heritage, come to us from so many layers of ideology and emotion, seems to be undergoing a development lately which will, perhaps, become one of the important characteristics of our mentality. If the extreme "formalism" of the Japanese civilization has made a "land with a wealth of signifiers (*signifiants*), possessed of the charm of having no signifieds (*signifiés*)" (Roland Barthes), we should no doubt state that France, the Extreme Occident, seems to be, on the contrary, a domain so loaded with signifieds (that is the concepts themselves not the signs or sounds-signifiants that represent them) that one forgets their signifiers, and so neglects their implied originality and complexities.

It is rather by a respectful and faithful description of behavior that we are able to grasp and preserve what is important and original in each society. By posing the problem in this way, we are not ignoring devastation and emergencies. UNESCO's suggestions, moreover, were formulated in a style striking in its pessimism. The preamble of the convention is solemn and explicit: "The cultural patrimony and natural patrimony are increasingly threatened with destruction, not only from traditional causes of deterioration but also by the evolution of social and economic life which aggravates these by even more fearsome sources of alteration or destruction." Even if one might wonder how the "traditional" causes differ from the new ones, in the undermining of the ill-defined "treasures" of national heritage, this declaration is important. It is evidence, at last, of serious attention to the concrete inconveniences of "universal progress." By disturbing and distorting the old configurations everywhere, the world's business and industrial civilization is causing their qualities to be discovered, which are then immediately arranged, rightly or wrongly, in the system of the heritage.

We do, after all, live in time. All that is human is made of duration. "Use is a sort of slow vandalism, unfelt, unperceived, which ruins and deteriorates nearly as much as a brutal devastation," wrote Vitet in a study of English medieval art (1867). "Nearly as much"? Perhaps not. But the permanent and effective cause of deterioration really is use, that is, life going on, the wear of time, the very risk of existence. Attention to the store of the country's heritage is unquestionably connected to the poignant sense of growing old, of fatigue. The things that surround us, that we are attached to, express this feeling to us by their mutability, their misfortunes, and the more or less artificial and cosmetic appearance of an enduring existence. In fact, no element of national heritage makes sense outside the attachment of the societies in question, outside, why not say the word, the love that shows itself in instinctive ways in the consciousness of the various regions and in enlightened fashion in the ways scholarship approaches those elements of patrimony. Modernism's "disenchantment" inevitably feeds on the nostalgias and loyalties that are proper in an old country. But if we were right to extend the idea of national heritage to the unique features of space and architecture, we should find in it a store of experience to confer with and see ourselves to be less disarmed as we face a future where nothing will ever be simple again.

NOTES

1. This study takes advantage of a certain number of previous articles: "Le Problème de l'inventaire monumental," *Bulletin de la Société de l'histoire de l'art français* (henceforth referred to as *BSHAF*) (1964): 137f.; "Les Nouvelles dimensions du patrimoine," *Cahiers de l'Académie d'architecture* (1980): 6–12; "Patrimoine," *Encyclopaedia universalis,* Supplément, Paris (1980): 41–49; "La Notion de patrimoine" (in collaboration with Jean-Pierre Babelon), *Revue de l'art* (henceforth referred to as *RA*) 49 (1980): 5–32.

2. On the subject of relics: Marie-Madeleine Gauthier, *Les Routes de la foi* (Fribourg, 1983).

3. Valuable information from Meyer Schapiro, "On the Aesthetic Attitude in Medieval Art" (1947), *Selected Papers,* vol. 1, *Romanesque Art* (London, 1977), 1–27.

4. Louis Grodecki, in the catalogue for the exhibit "Le 'Gothique' retrouvé avant Viollet-le-Duc," Paris, Hôtel de Sully, 1979–1980.

5. Jules Michelet, *Histoire de France* (Paris, 1895), 7:193.

6. Victor L. Tapié, *Baroque et classicisme,* last edition (Paris, 1980), 204f.

7. Jean-Pierre Babelon, *RA* 49: 9.

8. F. Vauthier, "Quatre châteaux royaux à vendre en 1787," *BSHAF* (1913): 164–73.

9. Complete text in *RA* 49: 15.

10. On this inexplicably neglected scholar: G. Duplessis, "Roger de Gaignières et ses collections iconographiques," *Gazette des beaux-arts* 1 (1870): 468–88; Alain Erlande-Brandenburg, "Une initiative mal récompensée: Roger de Gaignières (1642–1715)," *RA* 49: 33–34.

11. On Bernard de Montfaucon: André Rostand, "La Documentation iconographique des monuments de la monarchie française," *BSHAF* (1932–1933):

104–49. Alain Erlande-Brandenburg, "L'Érudition livresque: Bernard de Montfaucon," *RA* 49: 34–35. Jacques Vanuxem, "The Theories of Mabillon and Montfaucon on French sculpture of the twelfth century," *JWCI* 20 (1957): 45–58.

12. On the Abbé Lebeuf: Jacques Vanuxem, *L'Abbé Lebeuf et l'étude méthodique des monuments du Moyen Âge* (Auxerre: Cahiers d'archéologie et d'histoire, 1963).

13. Frédéric Rücker, *Les Origines de la conservation des monuments historiques en France (1790–1830)* (Paris, 1913), 95. On the Revolution, aside from this work, see Louis Hautecoeur, *Histoire de l'architecture classique en France,* vol. 5 (Paris, 1953), 103f. and 109f. on chaotic legislative policies ("la politique confuse des assemblées"); see also G. Brière, "Les monuments de France pendant la Révolution, de 1789 à 1795," *BSHAF* (1952–1954): 58–63.

14. Rücker, 23. Louis Réau, *Les Monuments détruits de l'art français,* vol. 2, pt. 2, "Tableau d'ensemble des saccages divers."

15. Paul Léon, *La Vie des monuments français,* 2nd ed. (Paris, 1951): 255f.

16. Quoted by Rücker, 93.

17. André Chastel, "Le problème de l'inventaire monumental," *Bulletin de la Société de l'histoire de l'art français* (1964): 137.

18. Alain Erlande-Brandenburg, Michel Fleury, François Giscard d'Estaing, *Les Rois retrouvés* (Paris, 1977).

19. Rücker, 23.

20. On the Abbé Grégoire: James Guillaume, "Grégoire et le vandalisme," *Révolution française* (1901): 155–80 and 242–69; Pierre Marot, "L'Abbé Grégoire et le vandalisme révolutionnaire," *RA* 49: 36–39. See also *Mémoires de Grégoire, ancien évêque de Blois, précédés d'une notice historique sur l'auteur par M. Carnot* (Paris, 1837). Eugène Despois: *Le Vandalisme révolutionnaire* (Paris, 1868), is more a retrospective apology for the revolutionary activity in this area.

21. Quoted by Hautecoeur, 103.

22. A. Vialay, *La Vente des biens nationaux pendant la Révolution* (Paris, 1908).

23. Lastly, on this important matter see Alain Erlande-Brandenburg, chap. 5 (with bibliography), in *Le "Gothique" retrouvé. . .* ; and Louis Courajod's publication, *Alexandre Lenoir, son journal et le musée des Monuments français,* 3 vols. (Paris, 1878–87).

24. *Considerations morales sur la destination des ouvrages de l'art* (1816). See A. Erlande-Brandenburg, *Le "Gothique" retrouvé. . .* , 78.

25. Jacques Vanuxem, *La Sculpture religieuse au musée des Monuments français, Positions des thèses des élèves de l'École du Louvre (1911–1944)* (Paris, 1956): 200–203.

26. Ferdinand Boyer, "Les Collections et les ventes de Jean-Joseph de Laborde," *BSHAF* (1961): 137–52. On Séroux d'Agincourt: Henri Loyrette, "Séroux d'Agincourt et les origines de l'histoire de l'art," *RA* 48 (1980): 40–56.

27. Pierre Marot, "L'Essor de l'étude des antiquités nationales à l'Institut, du Directoire à la monarchie de Juillet," *Académie des inscriptions et belles-lettres,* read at the annual public meeting of November 22, 1963.

28. These are the terms of L. Prevost's brochure for the publication of Arcisse de Caumont's *Histoire de l'art dans l'Ouest de la France depuis les temps les plus reculés jusqu'au XVIIe siècle,* vol. 7(Paris: 1830).

29. Victor Hugo, "Halte aux démolitions!" *Litterature philosophie mêlées* (Paris, 1884).

30. Germain Bazin, *Le Temps des musées* (Brussels, n.d.), chaps. 8 and 9.

31. Louis Hautecoeur, *Histoire du Louvre des origines à nos jours: 1200–1928* (Paris, 1928), chap. 7, "Le Louvre musée."

32. Cecil Gould, *Trophy of Conquest: The Musée Napoleon and the Creation of the Louvre* (London, 1965).

33. *Les Fêtes de la Révolution* (Clermont-Ferrand, Musée Bargoin, 1974), no. 63.

34. Jean Chatelain, *Dominique Vivant Denon et le Louvre de Napoleon* (Paris, 1973).

35. See Catherine Marmoz, "Duban et l'arc de Gaillon à l'École des beaux-arts," *BSHAF* (1977): 217–23; Philippe Canac, C. Marmoz, and Bruno Foucart, "L'École nationale des beaux-arts," *Les Monuments historiques* 102 (1979): 17–37.

36. On the Musée des Monuments français at the Palais de Chaillot: Philippe Chapu, "Le Musée national des Monuments français," *RA* 49: 40–41.

37. Albert Boime, "Le Musée des Copies," *Gazette des beaux-arts* (1964): 237–47; editorial, "Copies, répliques, faux: Les Modèles élusifs et le 'musée des copies,'" *RA* 21 (1973): 23–29.

38. Editorial, "Les Musées d'architecture," *RA* 52 (1981): 5–8.

39. See Rücker, 180, no. l; Jean-Pierre Bady, *Les Monuments historiques en France* (Paris: PUF, Collection Que sais-je? 1985).

40. See Marcel Durliat, "Alexandre Dumège et les mythes archéologiques à Toulouse dans le premier tiers du XIXe siècle," *RA* 23 (1974): 30–41; and *Le "Gothique" retrouvé,* chap. 6.

41. Françoise Bercé, *Les Premiers travaux de la Commission des monuments historiques (1837–1848)* (Paris, 1979).

42. See Léon, 121.

43. Besides the article by André Fermigier, "Mérimée et l'inspection des monuments historiques," *Les Lieux de mémoire*, vol. 2, *La Nation: Le Territoire, l'état, le patrimoine* (Paris: Gallimard, 1986), see the catalogue for the 1963 exhibit at Hôtel de Sully and the important *Notes de voyage* presented by Pierre-Marie Auzas.

44. A. du Sommerard, *Les Monuments historiques de la France à l'Exposition historique de Vienne* (Paris, 1876).

45. Viollet-le-Duc in *Annales archéologiques* 4 (1846): 333.

46. Pierre Lavedan, "Églises néo-gothiques," *Archives de l'art français* 26 (1978): 351f.

47. For example the treatises of William Henry Ward, *French Chateaux and Gardens in the XVIth Century* (London, 1909); and Sir Reginald Blomfield: *A History of French Architecture from the Death of Mazarin to the Death of Louis XV (1661–1774)* (London, 1921).

48. F. de Guilhermy, "Trente ans d'archéologie," *Annales archéologiques* 21 (1861): 254.

49. Léon.

50. See catalogue for the Paul Abadie exhibit (Angoulême, 1984).

51. Montalembert, speech, July 11, 1845, Chamber of Peers, quoted by Léon, 349.

52. C. Sitte, *Der Städtebau nach seinen künstlerischen Gründsätzen* (Vienne, 1889), French translation: *L'Urbanisme et ses fondements artistiques* (Paris, 1979); and, most of

all, A. Riegl. On all of these points see André Chastel, "Patrimoine," *Encyclopaedia universalis.*

53. Maurice Barrès, *La Grande pitié des églises de France* (Paris, 1912); *Tableaux des églises rurales qui s'écroulent* (Paris, 1913). There is much to say on the subject of the impotence of "sentimental" archaeology. See Léon, 141f.

54. See the editorial, "L'érudition locale en France," *RA* 4 (1969).

55. See *The Future of the Past: Attitudes to Conservation, 1174–1974,* ed. J. Fawcett (London, 1976).

56. The proliferation of reactions, exhibits, commentary, and discussion of these experiments has not noticeably influenced the public's attitude. See catalogue for the exhibit "Construire en quartiers anciens" (Paris: Grand-Palais, 1980); *Centres et quartiers anciens, Les Monuments historiques de la France* (Paris, 1976), no. 6.

57. Henri de Varine, *La France et les Français devant leur patrimoine monumental,* Report of the Fondation pour le developpement culturel, February 1975.

58. See Françoise Choay, "Haussmann and the system of Parisian green space," *RA* 29 (1975): 83f.

59. Among the numerous analyses "at ground level" of French country places, we can cite, in addition to the important investigation of *L'Aubrac, étude ethnographique, linguistique, agronomique et économique d'un établissement humain,* 6 vols. (CNRS, 1970–1976), more modest works such as one by Paul Dufournet, *Pour une archéologie du pays* (Paris, 1978) (about a small area in the Mâconnais), and the work of Dr. Cayla. The diversity, age, and originality of rural dwellings are resituated in the context of their long evolution by the lofty text of *l'Histoire de la France rurale,* 4 vols. (Paris, 1975). A collection in progress, "L'Architecture rurale française" (Paris, 1977f.), approaches this production of housing stock province by province.

60. On this creation of Georges-Henri Rivière and its multiple extensions, numerous studies have appeared in reviews: *Museum* (UNESCO) and *Arts et traditions populaires* (1957–1970), which became *Éthnologie française* (1971f.).

61. A. Chastel, "La fin des Halles ou le miracle inutile," *Le Monde,* December 11 and 23, 1970.

62. *Monuments historiques de la France,* special issue, 1977: "Les restaurations françaises et la charte de Venise."

63. Editorial from the *Revue de l'art* 15 (1972). J.-L. Bady, *Les Monuments historiques* (Paris: Collection Que sais-je? 1984).

64. *Viollet-le-Duc,* under the direction of Bruno Foucart (Paris: Grand-Palais, 1980). The phenomenon is better explained in a special issue of *Monuments historiques de la France* (1977) than in the proceedings of the Viollet-le-Duc colloquium.

65. On the General Inventory, *RA* 65 (1984).

66. M. Binney and P. Burman, *Change and Decay: The Future of Our Churches* (London, 1977).

67. Raymond Chevallier, *L'Avion à la découverte du passé* (Paris, 1964). See also Pierre Gascar, Alain Perceval, Raymond Chevallier, and François Cali, *La France: Cent cinquante photographies aériennes* (Paris, 1971).

68. On this subject, see computer organization in General Inventory, *RA* 65 (1984).

69. Roger Stéphane, *André Malraux: Entretiens et précisions* (Paris, 1984), 144.

70. The institution of the dation, for guardianship applied to "works of art" but not to edifices; see editorial, "La fiscalité des successions au secours du patrimoine artistique et historique national," *RA* 23 (1974); and catalogue for the exhibit "Défense du patrimoine national, 1972–1977" (Paris: Musée du Louvre, 1978).

71. "Patrimoine culturel de l'humanité," *Bulletin de l'Unesco* 15 (April 1980). Also see G. Fradier's article in *Monumentum,* special issue, 1984, "The World Heritage Convention."

72. See Shikinen-Sengu of Jingu, *Renewal of the Grand Shrines of Ise at Fixed Intervals of Twenty Years* (The Grand Shrine Office, 1973). I owe this reference to the kindness of my friend and colleague, Bernard Frank.

The Village Church

✠

PHILIPPE BOUTRY

I

The Ars church has two steeples: one is brick, rebuilt in 1820 after it was toppled in Year II of the French Revolution. The other is stone, capping the dome of the new basilica that was begun in 1862.[1] What happened in the interval was that Jean-Marie-Baptiste Vianney, the priest who served that church for forty-one years (1818–59), became the "holy curé" or parish priest, beatified by Pius X in 1905, then canonized by Pius XI in 1925 and in 1929 promoted by him to patron saint of all the curés in the universe. By the same stroke Pius XI made the curé's poor parish of Dombes (268 souls when he arrived) the object of one of the most fervent pilgrimages in France. As it now exists, the Ars basilica is a heterogeneous ensemble of two churches built side by side. The first, a shingle and brick Romanesque structure, was made heavier by the nineteenth century addition of chapels and is powerfully marked by the presence and spirituality of the village's saintly priest and confessor. The second, a little known work of Fourvière architect Pierre Bossan, was built on the site of the former chancel. Until the early 1960s its octagonal plan, sumptuous and mystical, was the setting for the reliquaries of Saint Philomena and the Curé of Ars, whose body reposes there as the object of devotion for the faithful. From its low hill overlooking the village roofs, this church is not only one of the great shrines of French Catholicism, it is as well a concentrate of the tradition of that place and the memory of the centuries: a sign, a witness, and a symbol all at the same time.

Figure 2.1
Colombey-les-Deux-Églises, November 12, 1970.

This is where Pope John Paul II arrived by helicopter Monday, October 6, 1986, during his third trip through France. From Lyons he had proceeded to Dardilly, the saint's birthplace on the eve of the Revolution two hundred years earlier. To greet him were the seven hundred and twenty inhabitants of the commune of Ars, several thousand faithful from the diocese of Belley, but particularly one hundred and fifty bishops, nearly three thousand priests, one thousand three hundred seminarians, two hundred monks and nuns, and one hundred deacons, all privileged guests of a short retreat consecrated to a meditation on the meaning and direction of the priestly ministry.[2] It was a meeting prepared by Rome with a "Letter to Priests on the Subject of Holy Thursday" (March 16, 1986),[3] entirely consecrated to Jean-Marie-Baptiste Vianney, Curé of Ars, "a witness for our times," "the extraordinary model of priestly life and service."

The short, dense text, appearing nearly thirty years after John XXIII (who dedicated one of his most personal encyclicals to the Curé of Ars in 1959 on the occasion of the first centenary of the curé's death)[4] provided, for the post-Council Pope John Paul II, the opportunity to remind French clergyman of the nature and foundation of a "specific ministry," since they were far removed in their concerns and activities from the sacerdotal models of the nineteenth century and might be tempted by "certain challenges to the priest's role." "The priest," wrote the Polish pope, "always and by an immutable process, finds the source of his own identity in Christ the Priest. It is not for the world to fix his status according to its needs or its conception of social roles." This is a discourse of "re-centering"—no one would called it "restoration"—in which, beyond the search for a "more balanced position" (for example "the priest is on the side of the laity: he instructs and supports them in that common priesthood of the baptized"), the historian is able to discern the terms of a spiritual affiliation with the more "sacrificial," more "hierarchic" concepts of the church represented by the Council of Trent, which were those of the Curé of Ars himself. "Attempts to create the lay priest harm the church," wrote the pope. "The priest is the witness to and the dispenser of life beyond earthly life. It is essential to the church that the priest's identity, with its vertical dimension, be protected." "In order for priests to play this role, which is prophetic, priestly, and royal," the pope told the assembled clergy at Ars, "the baptized need the priestly ministry by which they learn in tangible and privileged ways of the gift of divine life that comes from Christ. . . . Precisely for this reason, priests . . . must not forget that they are the dispensers of life beyond earthly life and that theirs is not to model themselves on the present world but to confront it in the name of the Gospel."

Figure 2.2
Jean-Marie Vianney arrives at Ars, February 9, 1818; stained glass from the gallery of the old church, by Émile Ader and Georges Decôte, beginning of the twentieth century.

Figure 2.3
View of the Ars church with its two steeples.

Beneath the steeples of Ars, then, is regenerated a discourse on church and priesthood which implies reassertion of belief and Christian identity in time and in space, here and now. And it was exactly in these terms that the pope evoked the Curé of Ars in his homily: "Jesus traveled through all the cities and all the towns (Matthew, IX, 35). . . . Sometimes that presence—that redeeming presence of Christ—is felt in a special way. At that moment, on the great world map of evangelism, a city or a town takes on a particular kind of glow. . . . Jean-Marie Vianney came to Ars to perform the sacred priesthood. . . . And behold, that to those people of Ars . . . he feared not to proclaim, by his word and by his life, that message from Peter which resounded so powerfully in the teaching of the Vatican II Council: You are the chosen people, the royal priesthood, the holy nation, the people which belongs to God. . . . Christ stopped here."

2

Thus, the pontiff's speech and the choice of a pilgrimage to Ars have contributed to restore, at the end of the twentieth century, a universe that is at once near and far, tucked away but not erased from shared memory and mentalities, and yet, has become foreign to the behavior of a great number of French: the parish as the limited, measured, mastered, sensitive, and nearly carnal space for religious life; the priest as pastor of souls and Christ's representative in the human flock; nave and steeple as the point of geometric intersection of the horizontality of the earth of mankind and the verticality of the aspiration to seek God. This is the "vertical dimension" that the pontiff makes part of the priest's identity and that the steeple revives from village to village across the landscape of rural France.

The bell tower, here envisaged as the architectural sign par excellence of the memory of nearly two millennia of Christian life rooted in territory, rooted also in the sense of belonging to a community, in a church and in a daily relationship to the sacred, is thus the bearer, as are all places of the collective memory, of contradictory information. It conveys a feeling of familiarity and a bond of emotional attachment. It is not at all anecdotal to recall here that no less astute a politician than François Mitterrand placed the reassuring silhouette of the village steeple behind his own picture on his 1981 electoral campaign poster. But it also communicates the mythic qualities of a rhythm of country life that no longer really exists and of a church rarely attended, and a belief now in part deserted. Ars is a model of rural and parish life that is of the past but was never banished and so has taken root and become virtually sacred and now holds a fundamental place in the collective memory. Accompanying Ars into the space of public memory is the souvenir of a long

Figure 2.4
Claude Laydu in *Le Journal d'un curé de campagne* (*Diary of a Country Priest*) by Robert Bresson, 1951.

nineteenth century (circa 1800–1940) where those values of rural and parish life seemed, rightly or wrongly, to have reached their peak and participated in that most intangible of realities, nostalgia.

For memory has basis outside of history and ways that do not rely on truth. In a publication that appeared in 1925, the year Jean-Marie Vianney was canonized, Marcel Halbwachs wrote: "All remembrance, no matter how personnel . . . is in direct rapport with series of notions that we are not the only ones to hold, with people, groups, places, dates, words, and forms of language, with ways of reasoning, too, and ideas, that is, with all material and philosophical life of all the societies we belong to or have ever belonged to."[5] And in the favorable and critical account he gave to Halbwachs's work the very year it appeared, Marc Bloch—who, in one of those coincidences through which the blind logic of terror comes to foul the tradition of place, would die in a ditch, near a cornfield, June 16, 1944, just four kilometers from the church at Ars—enthusiastically developed the concept that closely linked memory, tradition, history, and the writing of history: "The collective memory," he wrote, "like the individual memory, does not exactly preserve the past: it endlessly rediscovers it or rebuilds it, with the present as point of departure"; memory works a " 'reconciliation,' if we can call it that, of tradition with the present." . . ."All memory is an effort of will."[6]

It is, then, from that long nineteenth century that one must begin, if one is to capture in all its vitality, its emotional power, and even its ambiguity and illusions, that place of memory which is the steeple. In 1925, in a Strasbourg just restored to France, Marc Bloch was already urging his colleague, Gabriel Le Bras, to undertake this project, "to write for [the collection] *Le Paysan et la terre* [peasants and land] a volume that was to have launched the collection under the title *L'Église et le village* [church and village]."[7] That was the year of Abbé Trochu's important biography of the Curé of Ars,[8] followed in 1926 by the Georges Bernanos novel, *Sous le soleil de Satan* (*Under the Devil's Sun*) with its hero, the Curé of Lumbres, directly inspired by the Curé of Ars.[9] Marc Bloch encouraged Gabriel Le Bras, and much later the founder of French religious sociology recalled that "his wish was that we determine the role of the actual church building in the town, the part the clergy plays in country civilization, the relationship of the small community to the world. . . . In short, it was a question of situating the church and in a more general sense, the sacred, in rural history."[10]

Truly a vast design, which we are pleased to recall here because it situates in the personal itineraries of two great historians this project—shared but very differently executed—of reintroducing the church, the parish, the steeple, the sacred, into rural history and into the memory of them held by the present. In these pages we shall limit ourselves to a more modest plan: to restore to the parish structure, as it was refashioned after the Revolution, its meaning and limits. Using an approach of territorial, collective, and religious realities we shall attempt to rediscover the historical and emotional content of memory of the steeple from the more distant past of centuries of tradition. We hope, thus, to perceive what has, since the Revolution and in these same domains, kept this *lieu de mémoire*—fragile, uncertain, illusory—still alive.

3

The parish map of France of the ancien régime offers the first view of this tradition of place, this minimal geography of human space, which is more complex in its detail than that which the nineteenth century will leave us, but which shows in the long term the shape of a thousand years of history in the making of a nation.[11] First, it reflects the uneven concentration of the rural life: a France inhabited in clusters in the north, to the east, in the Parisian Basin; a sparsely inhabited France in the Brittany farmlands of hedgerows and the inland West, the Boulogne region (the Boulonnais), and that of Bresse; a France of small market towns, "bourgs," in Provence or in the Languedoc; a France of "villages," dependencies, and hamlets in the mountains of the Massif Central, the Alps, or the Pyrenees. The "communities of inhabitants" thus fit into a latticework of uneven density made up of vast collective territories in the Midi as well as criss-crossed farmlands and high mountain villages and the "swarming" of human microentities whose fine mesh covers not only the "countrysides" of the Northwest, of the North, and of the East, but also the densely populated valleys of the Loire, the Rhone, and the Garonne.

The form of the habitat and the strength of the collective traditions determine the regional characteristics of the parishes: the small, clearly delimited parishes in a village in the Franche-Comté, Normandy, or Aquitaine; the vast parishes, part rural and part urban, of inland Provence; mountain parishes in the Dauphiné or the Rouergue, pulled roughly between three or four distinct if not rival "villages," which are joined by their very weakness but never submerged in the whole; or yet again immense Breton parishes like a "cloud atomized into innumerable hamlets, dependencies and isolated farms,"[12] in the image of that "mother parish" of Iffendic (Ille-et-Vilaine), still strong in 1826 with its 4,500 souls scattered over 249 inhabited places. In 1789 the parish matched the peculiarities of its region in its configuration, practices, and geographic and human coherence. The parish is worthy of a shared history and a memory of a people gathered around the same steeple.

4

It was this inheritance of more than a thousand years of local tradition that the Constituent Assembly undertook to rethink and remodel. The parish, as it would mark both the landscape and contemporary memory with its idealized and competing trilogy of church, town hall, and school, was simultaneously the fruit of that break—the Revolution—and of the attempted restoration that followed, the tremendous religious surge of the nineteenth century.

In 1790 the Revolution fundamentally modified the organization of "communities of inhabitants" in France of the ancien régime. It created the "commune," the "free town," as the civil entity and legal framework for local political and administrative life. From that time on the parish would have only a peripheral relation to the state. It was to be secondary, subordinated; its legitimacy of several centuries disappeared. In place of that time-honored status was an institutional mutation which represented both a usurpation of inheritance and the conclusion of a very long process of secularizing society and power.

But by redefining the civil and religious spatial framework of France the Revolution had once again—even before the upheavals and antireligious persecutions of Year II—deeply disturbed the church's membership bond. As drafted in the Civil Constitution of the Clergy (July 12, 1790), the overlap of the old dioceses with the eighty-three new departmental districts led to the suppression of more than fifty bishoprics, some of them over a thousand years old, and to a nearly total transformation of the ecclesiastic geography of France, particularly in the small Gallo-Roman or medieval episcopal towns of the Midi. The Civil Constitution also stipulated a drastic reduction in the number of urban parishes (only one parish for cities of less than six thousand inhabitants) and authorized "administrative assemblies" to designate, "in concert with the diocesan bishop," the "annex or branch parishes of towns or countryside it shall be appropriate to preserve or extend, establish or suppress . . . according to the needs of the people, the dignity of worship, and local differences."[13]

Napoleon's Concordat of 1801, which ended a decade of revolutionary religious history, nonetheless produced further upheavals within the spatial framework of religious life. At the request of the First Consul, Pope Pius VII ratified the new diocesan district, which was even smaller than the one described in the Civil Constitution; bishops were given the right to make "new parish districts in their dioceses, which would take effect only after government consent."[14] Under pressure from civil authorities, the application decrees for the Concordat tended to reduce the number of parishes. In 1803, when the state took responsibility only for salaries of bishops and parish priests in the towns (*cantons*), an early constituency of "branches" was confided jointly to the prefect, who made the actual decisions, and to the bishop, who usually confirmed those decisions. These "branches," or *succursales*, were isolated parishes whose vicars or "service providers" (*desservants*) had been abandoned to the financial goodwill or whim of the local community. The full range of difficulties resulting from this first reorganization forced the state to assume direct responsibility for the branches and to fix their number. This operation was accomplished in part by 1804 and was totally achieved in 1807, confirmed by the decrees of September 30, 1807, and August 28, 1808, which drew up the plan of dioceses, vicarages, and parish branches for the empire.

In numbers, that assessment showed a considerable transformation in the parish fabric of France. In 1789, ancien régime France (including Avignon and Comtat Venaissin) counted 141 dioceses with seats within royal territory, 36,000 parishes, and 5,500 annexes. France in 1814 showed 60 dioceses and 29,000 parishes. The parish fabric of urban and rural France had shrunk in proportions that varied according to place from a fifth to a third of its previous size. Priestly presence in towns and cities collapsed everywhere: the 60,000 secular priests in France of 1789 had dwindled to 36,000 at the dawn of the Restoration (1814–15).

Then came the time of "pruning" and of "unification" for the free towns as well as for the parishes:[15] a simplified administrative geography removed thousands of "hamlets," "dependencies," or "villages" of ancien régime France from the people's memory and condemned them to the mere status of "locality." The shrinking of the collective fabric after the Revolution seemed considerable. Less affected, the departments with large towns were nonetheless not spared; the Department of the Herault, which counted 359 parishes in 1790, had no more than 311 in 1803 and 291 in 1808.[16] The diocese of Rennes, for those same dates, saw the number of its parishes go from 380 to 342, then to 314.[17] But it was in the departments with densely populated towns that the authoritarian reduction of the parish framework assumed the most dramatic proportions. The mountain diocese of Grenoble went from 640 places of worship in 1789 to 503 in 1803 (of which only 459 were provided for), then to 397 parishes in 1808, or a 38 percent drop.[18] The diocese of Évreux, which numbered 882 parishes in 1790, saw that number reduced to 503 in 1803—a 43 percent drop—then rise to 573 in 1808 in response to widespread protest among the inhabitants.[19]

"And so, in two days," wrote the unfortunate Bishop of Évreux to the minister of worship, Portalis, in Vendémiaire, Year XII (October 1803): "I decreed nearly three hundred of these unions, one alone of which, in an earlier day . . . could have occupied by its rigorous formalities the Officialities and the Sovereign Tribunals for two or three years." Beyond the statistics and clashes of Year II the Revolution was also the destabilizing of old law, an irruption of civic power into the order of the sacred space of the parish, and a violent rupture of the group's habits as well as its spatial definition.

5

After the Revolution parish restoration of the nineteenth century was the reaction of a threatened communal sensitivity and an identity perceived to be amputated or denied, in which was elaborated for modern times a new perception of the local now rooted in the contemporary nostalgia of the church steeple. It was a tremendous surge in a few decades:[20] in raw figures, the number of parishes went from 29,000 in 1814 to 32,000 in 1848 and 35,000 in 1875; the number of places of worship truly serviced went from 36,600 in 1830, to 39,000 in 1848, to 42,000 in 1870; and the ranks of the lay clergy swelled to 40,600 in 1830, to 47,000 in 1848, and to 56,400 (including 44,000 curés and vicars) in 1870: or one priest per 913 inhabitants in 1810, one per 639 in 1870. At the decline of the Second Empire, as far as parish order was concerned, the Revolution seemed overcome, erased.

By the Second Empire, in the Christendoms of Western France of vast, old parishes and the dioceses of Rennes[21] or Nantes,[22] there were more parishes than communes and the number of places of worship, chapels, and public or private oratories had very visibly increased. But in raw figures and sometimes even in percentages, the multiplication of new parishes was even more apparent in those departments with a dense communal network. In Albi,[23] Belley,[24] Arras,[25] and Montpellier,[26] the organization of hundreds of new parishes made possible the reduction of the number of communes in need of a priest without completely eliminating, however, that indispensable base of rural microcommunities with populations under two or three hundred. At the same time the new organization roused the spiritual autonomy of a few militant "sections."

In the Orléans diocese Monsignor Dupanloup tried, with relative but ephemeral success, to combat the practice of "binage," that is, the celebration of two consecutive masses, usually by the same priest but in two separate churches. This ecclesiastical term was a metaphor drawn from agriculture, when farmland was plowed twice, first for planting, then again to break up the soil, aerate it, and get rid of weeds. "Most of the parishes that no longer observe Easter, where religion and the faith are extinguished," he noted, "are parishes that have long practiced 'binage' . . . 'Binages' must cease in a number of churches. [They] ruin the piety and the health of priests and have been the ruin of religion in many villages for the past fifty years."[27]

It was not a whim when Zola, in *La Terre* (*The Earth*, 1887) wrote of a church undermined by binage in the backward commune of Rognes. By twenty years (1849–69) of hard work, however, Dupanloup appealed to "itinerant" priests to reduce the number of communes served by binage from sixty-five to eighteen. The figures speak for themselves: in a few decades the parish fabric everywhere had undergone an intense period of increasing density, with the area of commune and parish becoming one.

Against these suppressions, "meetings," and binages, parish agitation of rural communities insistently colored the flow of events of the first third of the nineteenth century. Jean Godel wrote of the Dauphiné, "It was asking too much of these farm people, still attached to their church, despite its being in ruins, attached to their cemetery, though it was choked with weeds, asking too much of them to go to the neighboring village to be married or buried. For people rooted in their land it meant the loss of their soul."[28] A resident priest paid by the government; mass and catechism close at hand; sacraments in their own church; their dead within the enclosure of a familiar cemetery; and the silhouette of their own steeple—the triumph of neo-Gothic architecture made it possible, precisely during those years, to rebuild the most beautiful, and above all the highest[29]—boldly soaring to heaven: that was the unanimous demand of the faithful, and the reality of the church in 1870, highpoint of parish and priest in nineteenth-century rural France.

How can we understand this irrepressible momentum toward spiritual autonomy? First one must take into account the immense and universal local emancipation movement that covered the French countryside in the course of the nineteenth century and was, with the ascent of the republican democracy, confirmed by the Municipal Law of April 5, 1884. All the rural communities aspired to self-management, self-government, self-sufficiency. It was a unanimous demand that arrived with the same momentum at the earthly and the spiritual and was a bit hastily denigrated by the label "steeple mentality" (*esprit de clocher*). Every rural community held that a real or supposed communal uniqueness was the basis of an indomitable civic and religious "personality" and demanded "liberty" for the community and for all its components: mayor, curé, and soon, that newcomer, the elementary school teacher. After the Revolution, the desired identification of commune with parish was the first article of village faith from East to West and from North to the Midi.

There were no worthy prayers outside the shadow of one's church spire, nor beautiful ceremonies outside one's own little church, and no eternal peace except within one's own burying ground: the faith of the countryside expressed itself above all within the narrow, consecrated confines of its land. At the end of the Revolution there is ample testimony to this in the piles of archives that exalt "immemorial" local traditions, where thin-skinned sensitivities of neighboring or even rival villages quickly and sometimes violently set dependency parishes and "incorporated" parishes against one another. Among so many others we have the grievances of the annexed or "subjugated" communes of the Ain: "The commune of Lochieu, former parish seat, was unthinkingly annexed to Brénaz parish by the Concordat of Year X," wrote the indignant mayor of the tiny locality of Bugey (population 340), who had been made the assistant of his rival in Brénaz (population 393). "We have become a mere branch. . . . After having enjoyed for centuries the advantage of being the home Church, my constituents [must] now go to an outside parish to hear the divine office. Their repugnance is such that they prefer to go to other churches."

"Monsignor," moaned in 1853 the inhabitants of Champteins, the former parish and community of Dombes abolished by the Revolution, "why doesn't he [our curé] want to come to bury us? What we all ask, and inasmuch as we are the inhabitants of our commune, is to be buried in our cemetery when we die."

That same year of 1853, the people of the hamlets of Gévrieux and Mas-Durand in the Valley of the Ain, threatened with incorporation into the new parish of Bublanne, protested, "In the name of the Author of Justice whom we adore and who will one day judge us, we beseech you, Monsignor, to prevent all the misfortunes that threaten us by leaving us in the parish we have always known, in order that we might continue to fulfill our duties in peace and have the hope of one day sleeping next to our fathers' bones, without the fear of being carried off somewhere else."

Changing cemeteries was perhaps worse than changing parishes: it meant giving up all hope of awaiting the hour of resurrection among loved ones under home ground. It would be a long and repetitious job indeed to conjure up the lament that went up all over France from those orphaned communities that missed having their own parish, church, or curé. Their structure is of greater interest to us. Group petitions and intercessions by prominent citizens remained discrete about what could be properly called the religious content of their requests—almost as if their intentions went without saying. There were no acts of faith, but

Figure 2.5
The Village Awards Ceremony (*La Distribution des prix au village*) by Aimé Perret, 1890. On the rostrum, the mayor, the elementary school teacher, and the priest.

their needs were clearly expressed: "instruction for the young," "consolation of the old," "holy mass," the sacraments, especially the last sacraments, when death's urgency—one could know neither the day nor the
hour—that crucial and necessary moment for reconciliation with God
and the family of man ("from sudden death deliver us, oh Lord"), turns
the absence of a resident priest into tragedy. Mute on explicit religious
feelings, the village texts become verbose with detailed reflections on
the "great separation" of their village, the "exceedingly great distance"
that prevented their "people" from frequenting the neighboring church.
A historian like Eugen Weber would easily find there the elements of a
(somewhat forced) demonstration of the insuperable impacting of rural
France in the first part of the nineteenth century.[30] Wherever one turned

one found only "paths on the edge of frightening precipices," "snow and ice" (Montpellier), "impenetrable trails," "precipices, gorges, eight months of winter," "terrifying torrents," "flooding waters" (Belley), as if a suddenly more savage nature had forbidden the faithful to go beyond their steeple to hear mass.

And that was because the surest basis of the petition for spiritual autonomy rested beyond doubt in the hatred of the neighboring community. "Invincible and reciprocal repugnance" and "ageless hatred" more surely separated many villages than the violence of the streams or blocked roads. The nineteenth-century parish was that measured, limited, compartmentalized space, understood and cherished—*Heimat* rather than *Vaterland*—from which none could agree to withdraw without suffering a violence, whether it was being drafted into military service or seasonal or temporary emigration. And the community defined itself as much by a collective feeling of belonging to a group of houses, families, and traditions as by the excitement caused by a difference fed by hostility toward the other—neighbor, itinerant worker, the outsider (*horsain*, a regional, Norman word), the stranger. Through the demand for a parish, the steeple mentality sanctified the land, the better to consecrate its own borders. Spiritual autonomy's demand for unity—a single flock, a single church, one pastor—made sacred the very fact of being different and located that sacred separateness in a physical space.

                                    6

There are dubious victories, though, the preludes of a difficult future. Just when the Catholic Church, 35,000 parishes strong, had restored the custom of the village priest nearly everywhere, there suddenly appeared the first anxieties about priest recruitment in the wake of a powerful and diverse movement that challenged clerical authority and the church's ascendancy.

Very quickly the significance of the nineteenth-century pastoral restoration was questioned. As early as the 1840s there was evidence that bishops and priests were concerned about the long-term consequences of a too rapid increase in the number of rural parishes brought about by easy, abundant recruitment. "If the clergy ages or the population moves around," wrote Gérard Cholvy, "problems are going to multiply. . . . The inflexibility of the parish network, obedience to sclerotic traditions of the ecclesiastic program, complicity between the public and public authorities who are most concerned with containing costs, all these will help make the distribution of parish clergy less and less adapted to changes in the ways people live."[31] Yves-Marie Hilaire has also noted, "The Second

Empire passed on to the first half of the twentieth century a fairly large number of parishes that were too small and served by underused priests. The migration from the countryside to the cities and the shrinking of ecclesiastic recruitment would later make it clear that between 1850 and 1880 they had built up an unnecessarily dense network of parishes in the rural world."[32]

Doomed by the narrowly spatial conception of the sixteenth-century Tridentine model of their ministry, priests already rebelled against spending their lives in the heart of a tiny locality, in the shadow of their steeple and shelter of their rectory walls. In 1876, in an admirable and premonitory plea, *Le Grand péril de l'église de France au XIXe siècle* (*The Grave Danger of the French Church in the Nineteenth Century*), the Abbé Bougaud, vicar general of Dupanloup in Orléans, quotes a young priest in the Loiret (considered a "detached" area, and not a hotbed of Catholicism): "During the week it's not so bad, but Sunday it is horrible! I arrive at mass, I find thirty or so women, two or three men: what can I tell them? I would rather weep than speak. At Vespers, no one. I lock myself in the rectory all day."[33] And Fernand Boulard attributed this unusually bitter and violent comment to Cardinal Suhard, during his visit to Vézelay in the Yonne: "We are never going to have priestly vocations in those regions, with the spectacle of those priests' lives of misery and isolation. It is said that people want to have their curé close by: yes, but when they have him what do they do with him? He's a piece of furniture!"[34]

The collective religious significance of restoration is no less ambiguous. Church restoration in the nineteenth century did not strictly speaking reproduce the eighteenth-century ecclesiastic map. By rebuilding churches and enlarging or moving cemeteries, it did, in part, rearrange the epicenters of community life, favoring even the smallest market town over hamlets and out-of-the-way places. In Bresse or in Brittany it created new centers in the hedgerow region, gave the advantage to the new towns along the main roads or on the plain to the detriment of the old villages. Most of all it accentuated the opposition between the Christian lands of the West, the highlands of the Massif Central, the Boulonnais, Flanders, Alsace and the Haut-Doubs, Bresse and Savoie and the Basque Country to the lands of indifference or abandonment of Christian practices. "There are extreme cases," noted Claude Langlois, "like the diocese of Rodez, which can have more than two parishes for a single rural commune, or that of Tarbes, which only has six parishes for ten communes."[35] In this way parish geography, as it became differentiated in the nineteenth century, became one of the means, still not fully explored, of analyzing the religious detachment of the rural population.

Figure 2.7
Sunday blessing in an illustrated catechism published by *La Croix* at the end of the nineteenth century.

7

In the final analysis was it, then, an illusion, that dream—unanimously fostered for most of the nineteenth century by church, state, the clergy, and their flock—of a Christianizing influence close to home, a religious life in the shadow of the parish steeple? Generations of priests and faithful lived with this narrow and uncompromising concept from the Restoration until and beyond the rise, between the two wars, of the Catholic Action movements. And nostalgia for an earthly and spiritual community, a closed group of faithful on their land, a place of sanctuary from the hostile world or an indifferent century, a sacred fortress, a steeple-stronghold, still haunted memory and gave the Ars model part of its imaginative force.

"I desire a little parish the better to watch over it, where I shall be better able to achieve sanctity," thus confided Monsieur Vianney to his aunt in 1818 on the eve of his being named to Ars.[36] "He would often tell us," said the château farmer, Guillaume Villier, "Oh, my brothers! Let us all seek paradise; it is there we shall see God; there we shall be happy! We shall all go together in a procession, if the parish is good, and your curé will lead you."[37] And it was in a procession to Notre-Dame de Fourvière, August 6, 1823, covering on foot then by boat on the Saône the ten leagues that separated them from Lyons, that the young Curé of Ars soon took his converted parish five years after his arrival. "We left before midnight," recalled Guillaume Villier. "I think two-thirds of the parish were on the pilgrimage. We went in procession until Trévoux, preceded by three beautiful banners, singing hymns, reciting the rosary. . . . People crowded around us as we passed and showed they were astonished."[38] Defense and illustration of unanimity found, at the foot of a restored steeple, a church once more cared for, a priest restored and acknowledged in his pastoral duties for a "flock" reunited under its banners. The Revolution seemed to have disappeared in that 1823 of missions and processions. The steeple once again rose in the center of a community's existence, and the priest had once more found his place at the heart of a group's microhistory of salvation.

Monsieur Vianney belonged to the school of the unanimous parish, "an island of Christianity," a protected land of consolation. He used the concept of sacrifice and "priesthood" in the full, Christ-like sense of the term that Pope John Paul II would further develop two centuries later: "What is a priest? A man who stands in for God. A man who is invested with all the powers of God. . . . If I encountered a priest and an angel, I would greet the priest before greeting the angel."[39]

He had rediscovered, perhaps unknowingly, an old image that was an architectural reality of the "bad old days" of the history of the Christian people. In this image the parish was both holy and walled; and safe within what were perceived as protective walls was the fortified church and the steeple that was rampart, wall, tower, or keep.[40] This was a religious, defensive, and community tradition that, in the name of a long history of memory, no doubt deserves more attention that it has received. For the military-ecclesiastic architecture of rural France was not only a matter of archaeology or the picturesque, but of a shared feeling and hope, in the manner of the protective saint,[41] the roadside cross,[42] the bell,[43] or the parish or confraternity banner.

Fortified churches appeared as France was Christianized, first in the episcopal cities—"in the cities, most of the time, the cathedral met the ramparts," noted Raymond Rey.[44] Then, quickly, it was done in the countryside as well: *ecclesiam incastellare* or *ecclesiam incastrare,* "to enclose the church in the castle," read the Latin documents of the feudal period.[45] Already in 1087 the people of Mantes, who had taken refuge in its churches, were exterminated by William the Conqueror's soldiers. In 1105 in Bayeux, Robert Fitz-Haimon tried to escape the Duke of Normandy by fortifying the abbey's bell tower: Alas! The besiegers set fire to it and he had to surrender.[46] And canon law XV from the first Lateran Council (1123) forbade, in vain, the laity to both "fortify churches and capture them," and "to use the church like a castle taken in subjection" wrote Gabriel Fournier.[47] Nonetheless, fortified churches spread through the Midi in the twelfth and thirteenth centuries, with the French conquest and the Albigensian crusade,[48] and through all of France in the fourteenth and fifteenth centuries with the Hundred Years' War and its parade of battles and looting.[49] And then in the sixteenth and seventeenth centuries, in the border provinces devastated by roaming armies—Thiérache,[50] Bourgogne,[51] Lorraine,[52] Alsace[53]—the fortified village churches became the ultimate protection of populations exposed to all the horrors of war. And "it was only in the seventeenth century, with the disappearance of private wars and with advances in artillery, that the military role of religious buildings vanished."[54]

Entire parishes, men and beasts alike, lived inside those church fortresses at the top of the steeple-keeps, placing themselves under the protection of the altar, watchful, fearful, prayerful; hours or days of waiting or fighting, abandoning their houses and fields to marauding soldiers and seeking refuge within the sheltering walls of the shared sanctuary. "The Lord is my keeper, I shall scorn my enemies. . . . All nations have besieged me. . . . They have swarmed over me like the bees and they have burst into flame like a fire in thorns; but it is in the name of the Lord that I have avenged myself. . . . The Lord is my force and my glory and he has become my salvation."[55]

Figure 2.8
Fortified churches in the Thiérache: Plomion.

Figure 2.9
The church at Oradour-sur-Glane, in November 1944.

In the Parisian countryside ravaged by armed bands in those gloomy years of 1356 and 1357, "the country people fortified their churches and steeples and, when necessary, hid their valuables in them for safe-keeping. They posted children to stand watch at the top of the steeples and signal the approach of robber bands or enemy hordes. As soon as they saw them, those sentinels sounded the horn or rang the bells and everyone ran to the church."[56] Again, in 1636 in the Burgundy valley of the Vingeanne, the male inhabitants of Poinson-lès-Fayl "were constrained to withdraw into the village church, which is the only place remaining whole, and in the aforesaid church they, their wives, and their children slept, as well as the few beasts that were left to them. In which place, they defended themselves several times from the top of the bell tower against the enemies who came to force them."[57]

Architectural traces of that last resort of the shelter of the steeple are numerous, and the rudimentary nature of their defense mechanisms cannot fail to move us. The church of Saint Radegonde in the Aveyron, a modest thirteenth-century structure, has preserved the modifications it made in the fourteenth century at the time of the English invasion of Rouergue. "In the first bay of the nave a well, two fireplaces, and forty or so rooms built into the upper parts of the building, the steeple, the attic attest to the inhabitants' intention to arrange a refuge for a possibly extended stay inside the church. Family property and rooms, kept conveniently close to each other over five or six stories and connected by corridors, were kept available. Their revenue was the bishop's. The inhabitants refused outsiders the use of these rooms. They were responsible for the repair and guarding as well as the defense, which was assigned to a captain appointed with the bishop's approval. On the outside, cantilevered machicolations on the corbels originally surrounded the structure. The steeple, a true castle tower dungeon, is fitted with a watch tower on every side."[58] And even today the dense network of fortified country churches in the Thiérache attests, in all of its poignant roughness, to that shared quest for safety in the shelter of the steeple.

It was, however, a precarious protection. The sanctity of the altar and the right of sanctuary were slight indeed in the face of the cruelty and rapacity of warriors.[59] More often than not chronicles and archives have left us accounts of attacks and fires, of carnage and massacres. In the fortress church of Orly, defended by nearly two hundred inhabitants, the English, after having attacked on Holy Friday, April 3, 1360, massacred nearly one hundred people. Nearby in Châtres, the peasants, abandoned by the French captain, resisted all the English attacks for a week in their church. The English set fire to the building and nearly nine hundred perished inside.[60] On November 9, 1636, in Dampierre-sur-Vingeanne in the Côte-d'Or, "the said inhabitants withdrawn into their said church, the said enemies, having forced their barricades, attacked them in furious manner in their said church, setting fire at the top and bottom of the nave, reached the tower, killed and burned in the aforesaid church more than two hundred persons as much from said Dampierre as from the neighboring places; burned entirely said church, chests, furnishings and grains that said inhabitants had withdrawn into that place."[61] And we know that on June 10, 1944, in Oradour-sur-Glane in the Haute-Vienne, 643 people, nearly 500 of them women and children, were burned alive and massacred in their church, where they had sought safety, by German troops in the Das Reich division.

8

Is the steeple then powerless to protect the community from the fury of the times? The violent paroxysm of the attack on a fortified church that runs through a thousand-year history of French village life is inseparable from one other strong moment in memory: the brief period of the revolutionary destruction of the church steeples. After Abbé Grégoire invented the word during the Revolution, both sides chose to keep it: "vandalism."[62] But this expression is too vague and does not begin to convey the diversity of forms and the significance of all the destruction, scattering, or transfers of title of religious and civil buildings, collections, libraries, and furnishings enacted during the Revolution and in the no doubt even more "vandalistic" half-century that followed.[63] If the steeple was part of the balance sheet of "revolutionary vandalism," it was a direct effect of the willful, violent, radical de-Christianizing of Year II.[64] The policy of systematic eradication of the steeples carried out by the revolutionary conventionnel Antoine-Louis Albitte[65] is of even more importance to us than the inexorable and slow dismantling of the abbey at Cluny or the threats made against Strasbourg Cathedral's tower. It was Albitte who, in the winter of 1794, ordered the revolutionary destruction of the steeple on the church at Ars:[66]

Citizens," he exclaimed in a decree published in "Regenerated" Bourg, 21 pluviôse, Year II, and read at the National Convention (which ordered its printing),

> I call that government revolutionary which destroys fanaticism to its
> last atom, which annihilates all the despicable remains of royalty and
> feudalism and which rips from the *ci-devants* any means of causing
> further harm, which crushes counterrevolutionaries, federalists,
> and rascals, which revives patriots, honors the sans-culottes, and

dispels indigence. . . . From the attached list of former priests who
have abdicated you will see, colleagues, that believing that the people
are disposed for one minute to support fanaticism is to insult them.
You will see, colleagues, that the best way to establish freedom of
worship is to prevent imposters from enjoying any advantage whatsoever. You will be convinced of this truth when you see the more
than 400 silver marcs I am sending you which came from those former churches and the melting of more than 300 church bells from the
department of the Ain.[67]

And, in the name of this singular conception of freedom of worship nearly
two hundred priests were forced to sign the following abdication text:

> I, the undersigned . . . having exercised the profession of priest
> since . . . under the title of . . . convinced of errors too long pro-
> fessed by me, declare in the presence of the municipality of . . . to
> renounce them forever, declare as well to renounce, abdicate and
> repudiate as a lie, illusion, and imposture all of the so-called charac-
> ter and function of the priesthood, of which I testify that I surren-
> der on the desk of the aforementioned assembled representatives all
> certificates, diplomas, and letters of authority: consequently, I swear
> before the People's Magistrates, whom I acknowledge to be all pow-
> erful and wise, to never again take advantage of the abuses of priest-
> trade, which I renounce; to uphold Liberty and Equality with all my
> strength; to live and to die for the affirmation of the Republic, one,
> indivisible, and democratic, under pain of being declared vile per-
> jurer and enemy of the people and treated as such.

It was by virtue of principles such as these that the majority of the
steeples in the region of the Ain perished under the pickax within a few
months by authority of "commissioners appointed to supervise the demolition of steeples and of the former châteaus and to see to the preservation of the furnishings and personal effects found in them." Among those
Ain steeples were the admirable Romanesque stone towers of Arbigny,
Boissey, Chevroux, and Sainte-Bénigne, built on the Abbey of Cluny
model, of which the Saint-André-de-Bâgé steeple in western Bresse is
the last remaining example. Commissioner Juvanon reported that in the
month of Ventôse, in Marboz, a sprawling, unrepentant commune, "the
steeple was torn out all the way to the choir vault but the vault was pretty
well damaged and repairs would be costly. It will also be demolished. Stuck
to the body of the church are chapels which do no more than represent
emblems of superstition. It is advisable to demolish them, in order to en-

tirely divest the church of superstitious emblems and make the church the body of a square building intended for the people's assemblies. As for the demolition of the chapels, only one will be excluded: the one that exists in the middle of the body of the former church; that one will be used for sessions of the people's society after we have cleared out everything that gave it the character of a chapel."[68]

A de-Christianizing *furia*?[69] No doubt. (In all of France, only the Lozère, under the authority of Châteauneuf-Randon, would be subjected to such a deliberately destructive policy.) But above all it was an attempt to substitute in space and in the architecture itself the sacredness of law for that of God. It intended to make the nave the temple, make the vault the roof, the altar the rostrum, to replace the roundness of Romanesque with classical geometry, and put the bare space of a citizen's meeting in place of the devotional proliferation of apse and chapels. It would oppose the horizontality of the public place to the verticality of steeple, the sovereign people to the gathering of faithful; and at the heart of the public mechanism it would set the political society where the confraternity had been.

Thus the people's, especially the women's, resistance to destruction of their steeples—and it was far from being a universal expression of explicit opposition to the revolutionary Mountain's politics—was carried out in the name of a new religion that was collective, civic, and inclined to hold festivals. The directory of the Trévoux district wrote on 30 Pluviôse, Year II, "Several municipalities are using different pretexts to delay the destruction of their steeples: some claim that a tower is necessary for various gatherings of the commune inhabitants; others ask us who will pay the demolition expenses. We must begin by the representative's point-by-point execution of the decree. revolutionary measures can suffer no delay. The republican ear must no longer be struck by the sound of the bells; they were invented by priests to dizzy the people and incline them to slavery. Military instruments lift the soul and strengthen it; let each commune supply itself with a drum and fife. They will be useful for more than one use; in case of alarm, they will be heard every bit as far as the bell. Republicans are all soldiers; they cannot do without a drum, and every tenth day of the week [*décadis* of the revolutionary calendar] the fife and drum will be used to animate country dances. . . . Rush, then, brave republicans, to overturn your steeples, which still offer a rallying place to superstition; and finally, a wise representative has not commanded this in vain; you must obey."[70]

In 1934 Eugène Dubois, the lay radical historian of the Revolution in the Ain region, wrote, "The truth is that peasants in the rural communes were as attached to their steeples as they were to family possessions. For

Figure 2.10
Atavism at Dusk (Obsessive Phenomenon)
(Les Atavismes du crépuscule [phénomène obsessif]), by Salvador Dali, 1933–34.

Figure 2.11
L'Angélus, by Jean-Francois Millet, 1859.

fifteen centuries the steeple had been the soul of their countryside. Its bronze voices had announced all the joys and all the sorrows, the coming into life of the small infant and the union of lovers. Those voices of the bells were the foundation of the family, just as they presided over the laying in the ground of ancestors and loved ones. The peasant watched with pleasure as the menacing, arrogant tower of the feudal castle disap-

Figure 2.12
1789: L'Angélus by
Millet, appropriated by
Yves Yacoël, 1981.

peared. . . . But he could not bear to see his steeple, the pride of his parish, his own rallying point, vanish."[71]

9

"Rallying point": the expression, common to both the sans-culottes of Trévoux and their historian (but used with opposite intentions), is a clear indication of what was at stake in this destruction. Could the steeple ever again be the center of group life, the heart of community life? In Lagnieu, a large market town in the low plain of the Ain, "in December of 1793, the church was handed over to the commune's society and the curé came to receive, in exchange for his titles of priesthood, the President's embrace. On January 21, 1794, to celebrate the memory of we know which event [the execution of Louis XVI], a bonfire was lit in the surrounding hills, then the town was lit up, then the people ended the day with a big, noisy banquet inside the church. However, two months later, April 20, Easter Day, before dawn, the priest, dressed in those bizarre disguises of another time, gave three children their First Communion in a small room that was low, dark, bare, and that I can still see. When I was ten years old I was led there myself by one of those communicants of the first of Floréal, Year II. The piece of furniture, oak, worm-eaten, was still there, as were the crucifix of irregular ivory and the once gilded copper torches used in the service and, near the door, the cheap holy water font."

"If I ever did feel an emotion," concluded Charles Jarrin, the great nineteenth-century republican (and anticlerical) historian of the Ain region, "it was as I knelt with my mother before that humble altar."[72] The childhood memory recreates the double event of the moment of rupture: that of a collective and public ceremony in honor of the Republic and that of a sacrament administered privately, to which the inexpressible experience of persecution and loyalty restore value, meaning, and fervor. That split—beyond the extraordinary aura of clandestinity that the Terror had conferred on the Christian community[73]—gradually sanctioned the two trends of the nineteenth and twentieth centuries: the increasingly lay quality of daily life and the individuation of religious convictions and behavior. By the terms of Napoleon's 1801 Concordat, "The apostolic Roman Catholic religion was nothing more than the religion of the great majority of French citizens." The parish became the communal framework for individual beliefs. The history of nineteenth-century parish restructuring as we have briefly sketched it is then seen in a new light. The image of a territorial and human unanimity is diffracted. The steeple, symbol of a communal Christianity and of a sanctified space, gives way to a fragmented story of beliefs and practices, loyalties, separations, and desertions: in short, to a modernism of autonomous moral behavior and personal spiritual orientations.

Repositioning this evolution at the heart of more than one thousand years of French Christian parish history would without doubt exceed the scope of this brief sketch.[74] And anyway, the aim is rather to stress the dynamic aspect and the ambiguity of the reinvention of the parish in the nineteenth century, which the birth of the expression "steeple mentality," midcentury, is enough to indicate. The convergence, around 1925, of historic interest in priest and parish that we have noted, from Marc Bloc to Gabriel Le Bras and Georges Bernanos, which coincided with the canonization of the Curé of Ars, revealed, in its way, an observation: that a model of spatial, human, and ecclesiastic organization created by the "feudal revolution" and the mantle of the churches of the year 1000, consolidated by the Catholic Reformation, shaken by the Revolution, restored with great difficulty and not without ambiguity by the nineteenth century, was tending, around 1925, under the impact of the Action Catholique movement, to become weakened. That model of organization deeply marked the religious and social memory of rural France. At a time when we seem—by lack of priests as much as by the dwindling of the faithful—to be watching the accelerated dissolution of this model, it would be a strange but instructive experience to compare the very contemporary map of parish service in the France of 1990 with France of the fourth or fifth centuries, a world filled top to bottom with churches and village steeples. We would no doubt recognize everywhere the common existence of vast ecclesiastic districts, of a sparse clergy in direct contact with its bishop, of weak but fervent clusters of faithful, of the fervor and uncertainty that are common to minorities and of the rivalry of sects and beliefs.

Cyclic history? That would be, if we are considering memory, a lazy hypothesis, for memory sustains itself also by its own history and feeds on its own tradition. The figure of a priest in Pope John Paul II's 1986 speech in Ars stems from a desire to reaffirm and restore the priestly identity. More than any earlier period, the first part of the nineteenth century lived a similar quest for restoration. Wasn't rebuilding the steeple, as Monsieur Vianney would do, a strong attempt to return order to Christianity, to return its rhythm to the space of worship, to return its vital center and its memory to the society of men? "Leave a parish without a priest for twenty years," he said (and the church at Ars was without priest from 1794 to 1803), "they'll worship beasts at the end. . . . When they want to destroy religion they start by attacking the priest, because when there is no more priest, there is no more holy sacrifice and when there is no sacrifice, there is no longer religion."[75] But in 1830 already his priestly project was imperceptibly changed by the double shock of a new, strongly lay state and, within the church, the increasing popularity of the mission and the pilgrimage.[76] Immense and motley crowds—from 60,000 to 80,000 in the 1850s—pressed into the Ars confessional. They were joined by a common belief or hope rather than any similarities of where they came from or even their lives. The sacrificial character of the priest would not go away.

Figure 2.13
The Lavaur (Tarn) bell and its *jacquemart* (armed metallic figure) bell-ringer.

On the contrary. But it too was distorted by the very spatial and human transcendence of the pilgrimage.

The two steeples of the church at Ars are the two periods of this history, less unequivocal than they might seem: the brick steeple, rebuilt in 1820 after having been pulled down in Year II by a young parish priest who pulled down his own share of heritage with it; the other, stone, capping the dome of the new basilica begun in 1862 and financed by a lottery that honored devotion to the "holy Curé."[77] We have no doubt that both steeples are *lieux de mémoire* and the signs of a rallying in the still unfinished work of a tradition.

NOTES

1. Cf. the remarkable iconographic analysis done by the regional department of the Inventaire général des monuments et des richesses artistiques de la France, *Le Curé d'Ars et son église,* text by Marie-Reine Jazé-Charvolin and Geneviève Jourdan, photographs by Eric Dessert and Jean-Marie Reffle (Lyons: Inventaire Général, 1990).

2. Detailed account in *La Croix: L'Événement* of Tuesday, October 7, 1986. Cf. also *La Route de Jean-Paul II,* a special issue edited by *La Croix: L'Événement,* September 1986.

3. *Le Témoignage du curé d'Ars: Un Appel pour notre temps; Lettre du pape aux prêtres pour le Jeudi saint,* supplement to *la Documentation catholique* 1915 (April 6, 1986). All references to the spoken words and texts of the Curé of Ars are excerpted from *Jean-Marie Vianney, curé d'Ars: Sa Pensée, son coeur,* presented by Bernard Nodet (Le Puy: Mappus, 1958). The Abbé Nodet (1911–89), who, as priest and historian at Ars for several decades, was the "face of the Curé of Ars," had the joy of welcoming the pope in the church at Ars; these pages are dedicated to him.

4. *Nostri sacerdotii primitias,* July 31, 1959, at the occasion of the first centennial of the death of the Curé of Ars. French translation, *Encyclique de sa sainteté le pape Jean XXIII sur le curé d'Ars* (Belley: Imprimerie du Bugey, 1964), according to *La Croix de Paris,* August 1, 1959. "The simple joys that came in the springtime of our priesthood are forever joined, in Our memory, to the deep emotion that We felt January 8, 1905, in the Vatican Basilica, during the glorious benediction of this humble French priest who was Jean-Marie-Baptiste Vianney." Angelo Roncalli, twenty-four at the time, went to Ars that same year of 1905 with Monsignor Radini Tedeschi.

5. Maurice Halbwachs, *Les Cadres sociaux de la mémoire* (Paris: Alcan, 1925), 51–52.

6. Marc Bloch, "Mémoire collective, tradition et coutume: À propos d'un livre récent," *Revue de synthèse historique,* 39 (1925): 77.

7. Gabriel Le Bras, "Un Programme: La Géographie religieuse," *Annales d'histoire sociale: Hommage à Marc Bloch* 1 (1945): 89.

8. Francis Trochu, *Le Curé d'Ars, saint Jean-Marie-Baptiste Vianney (1786–1859)* (Lyons: Vitte, 1925), the first important scholarly biography based on the testimony

of the canonization trial and the ensemble of historic sources. A first biography had preceded it, the work of an eyewitness of the last years of the pilgrimage: Alfred Monnin, *Le Curé d'Ars tel qu'il fut: L'Homme et son entourage* (Paris: Fayard, 1971).

9. *Sign of the Times?*, the admirable film that Maurice Pialat made from this, received the 1987 Cannes Festival Palme d'Or.

10. The book commissioned in 1925 would not be published until 1976, six years after Gabriel Le Bras's death: *L'Église et le village* (Paris: Flammarion, coll. "Nouvelle bibliothèque scientifique,"1976), preface, 16. It remained dedicated "to the memory of Marc Bloch."

11. Of which an echo, albeit imperfect and quite late, comes to us through the admirable map of communal borders in the France of 1958, drawn up by Jacques Bertin and the Laboratoire de graphique of the EHESS, in "La Carte, instrument de recherche: Les Communes de France," *Annales ESC* 13, no. 3 (1958): 447–87, with commentaries by André Meynier, André Perpillou, Etienne Juillard, Henri Enjalbert, Georges Duby, and André Piatier.

12. Michel Lagrée, *Mentalité, religion et histoire en Haute-Bretagne: Le Diocèse de Rennes, 1815–1848* (Paris: Klincksieck, 1977), 262.

13. *Constitution civile du clergé, titre I ("Des Offices ecclésiastiques")*, articles 1, 15, 17.

14. The Concordat of 1801, articles 2 and 9.

15. The Department of the Seine-Inférieure, which numbered no fewer than 1,003 municipalities in 1790, had no more than 757 in 1801. In the Department of the Ain there were 682 communities on the eve of the Revolution, but only 468 by 1790, and by 1815, 439.

16. Gerard Cholvy, *Religion et société au XIXe siècle: Le Diocèse de Montpellier* (Lille: SRT, 1973), 1:33, 357.

17. Lagrée, 259.

18. Jean Godel, *La Reconstruction concordataire dans le diocèse de Grenoble après la Révolution (1802–1809)* (Grenoble: Eymond, 1968): 129–31.

19. Marcel Baudot, "La Répartition des paroisses dans le diocèse d'Évreux," 101e Congrès national des sociétés savantes (Lille, 1976) (Paris: Imprimerie nationale, 1978), vol. 2, "Histoire moderne," 365–75.

20. Overall assessment in Claude Langlois, "Le Prêtre et la paroisse," in *Histoire des catholiques en France,* under the direction of François Lebrun (Toulouse: Privat, 1980): 298–302. On the growth of total French clergy, see Fernand Boulard, *Essor ou déclin du clergé français?* (Paris: Éd. du Cerf, 1950); Dominique Julia, "La Crise des vocations: Essai d'analyse historique," *Études* (February 1967): 238–51, and (March 1967): 378–96; and, more specifically on the first part of the nineteenth century, Charles-Hippolyte Pouthas, "Le Clergé sous la Monarchie constitutionnelle," *Revue d'histoire de l'église de France,* 29 (1943): 19–53. On the ensemble of these questions, see also volume 1 of this work, Claude Langois, "Catholiques et laics."

21. The diocese of Rennes (314 parishes in 1814) obtained, from 1815 to 1848, 62 new creations (+19%). Cf. M. Lagrée, 260.

22. The diocese of Nantes, already well endowed (200 parishes for 209 communes in 1814), obtained, from 1815 to 1870, 58 new creations: in other words, in 1869, for 214 communes, 258 parishes (+29%) and 264 vicarages. Cf. Marius Faugeras, *Le Diocèse de Nantes sous la monarchie censitaire (1813–1822–1849)* (Fontenay-le-

Comte: Lussaud, 1964), 2 vols.1:55–58 and 2:215–22; Marcel Launay, *Le Diocèse de Nantes sous le second empire: Msgr. Jacquemet, 1849–1869* (Nantes: CID, 1982), 2 vols.1: 8–45 and 2:483–89.

23. The diocese of Albi counted 392 parishes in 1807, 458 in 1848, 500 in 1900. Cf. Jean Faury, *Cléricalisme et anticléricalisme dans le Tarn (1848–1900)* (Toulouse: Service des publications de l'Université de Toulouse-Le Mirail, 1981), 287.

24. The Department of the Ain counted 329 parishes for 439 communes in 1814: the erection of 112 new parishes (+34%) made it possible to reduce the number of communes in need of a resident priest from 110 to 30 in 1880 (30 being the irreducible minimum of rural microentities) by granting spiritual autonomy to a few militant "sections"; Philippe Boutry, "L'Esprit de clocher," in *Prêtres et paroisses au pays du curé d'Ars* (Paris: Éd. du Cerf., 1986), 17–62.

25. The diocese of Arras already had 566 parishes in 1814: from 1815 to 1881 it obtained 129 branches (+22%) and 86 supplementary vicarages. Cf. Yves-Marie Hilaire, *La Vie religieuse des populations du diocèse d'Arras, 1840–1914* (Lille: SRT, 1976), 2 vols.1:750–55.

26. From 1814 to 1890, the number of parishes in the diocese of Montpellier went from 291 to 350. Cf. G. Cholvy, 1:343–59.

27. Christianne Marcilhagy, *Le Diocèse d'Orléans sous l'épiscopat de Mgr. Dupanloup (1849–1878): Sociologie religieuse et mentalités collectives* (Paris: Plon, 1962): 74, 100.

28. Godel, 133.

29. Cf. on this point, Jean-Michel Leniaud, "Les Constructions d'églises sous le Second Empire: Architecture et prix de revient," *Revue d'histoire de l'église de France* 65 (1979): 267–78; as well as Philippe Boutry, "Les Mutations du paysage paroissial: Reconstructions d'églises et translations de cimetières dans les campagnes de l'Ain au XIXe siècle," *Éthnologie française* 15, no. 1 (1985): 7–34.

30. Eugen Weber, *La Fin des terroirs: La modernisation de la France rurale, 1870–1914* (Paris: Fayard, 1983) (translated from *Peasants into Frenchmen: 1870–1914* [Stanford University Press, 1976]).

31. G. Cholvy, 2:109.

32. Y.-M. Hilaire, 1:755.

33. Émile Bougaud, *Le Grand péril de l'église de France au XIXe siècle* (Paris: Poussielgue, 1878), 29.

34. F. Boulard, 366. On the Christian parts of the Yonne in the nineteenth and twentieth centuries, see the beautiful and sensitive study by the Abbé Alype-Jean Noirot, *Le Département de l'Yonne comme diocèse,* vol. 1, *Un Feu pour illuminer la nuit*; vol. 2, *Quand refleurissent les déserts*; vol. 3, *La Belle Époque*; and vol. 4, *Ils danseront les os broyés* (Aillant-sur-Tholon: By the author, 1979–81).

35. Cl. Langlois, 302.

36. Parish archives of Ars, *Procès de l'ordinaire,* Marguerite Humbert, 1324.

37. Ibid., Guillaume Villier, 628.

38. Ibid., 645–46.

39. Ibid.

40. On fortified churches and steeples in medieval and modern France, there are few or no general studies with the exception of some older and still fundamental works: René Fage, "Les clochers-murs de la France," *Bulletin monumental* 80 (1921):

159–85, and 81 (1922): 28–71 and 310–39; and Raymond Rey, *Les Vielles églises fortifiées du Midi de la France* (Paris: Laurens, 1925). A brief synthesis by G. Le Bras,
L'Église et le village, 48–49; and another by Gabriel Fournier, "Les Églises fortifiées,"
in *Le Château dans la France médiévale: Essai de sociologie monumentale* (Paris: Aubier,
1978): 201–9. I heartily thank François Bougard for this highly useful information.

41. See on this point the remarkable investigation (but astonishingly lacking
in all religious perspective) by Emmanuel Le Roy Ladurie and André Zysberg,
"Géographie des hagiotoponymes en France," *Annales ESC* 38 (1983): 1304–35.

42. About this fundamental element in the Christianization of the rural landscape, see Gabriel Le Bras, "Sur l'histoire des croix rurales," in *Miscellanea historica
Alberti de Meyer* (Louvain, 1946), 319–36, reprinted in *Études de sociologie religieuse*
(Paris: PUF, 1955–56),2 vols. 1:85–99; and Hervé Martin and Louis Martin, "Croix
rurales et sacralisation de l'espace: Le Cas de la Bretagne au Moyen Âge," *Archives
de sciences sociales des religions* 43, no. 1 (1977): 23–38. On the Christianization of the
rural landscape in the nineteenth-century, see Yves-Marie Hilaire, "La Christianisation de l'espace," in *Une chrétienté au XIXe siècle? La vie religieuse des populations du
diocèse d'Arras (1840–1914)* (Lille: Publications de l'Université de Lille-III, 1977), 2
vols.1:374–83, as well as, on the urban landscape, Regis Bertrand, "De la toponymie
à la statuaire: Les Formes de christianisation du paysage marseillais depuis le XVIIIe
siècle," *Annales du Midi* 148, no. 173 (1986): 95–120.

43. *A fulgure et tempestate, libera nos domine* ("from lightning and storm, deliver
us Oh Lord"), would be engraved on the bells of Saint-Pierre d'Ivry (sur-Seine), by
a contract signed in 1556 by the priest, three churchwardens, and fourteen parishioners with Laurent Le Roy, master bellcaster, residing in Meaux. Cited by Yvonne
Bézard, *La Vie rurale dans le Sud de la région parisienne de 1450 a 1560* (Paris: Firmin-
Didot, 1929), 277.

44. Rey, 12. And note the examples of Dijon, Tours, Le Mans, Angers,
Nantes, Paris, Soissons, Noyon, Senlis, Cologne, Bourges, Bordeaux, Cahors,
Rodez, Toulouse . . .

45. According to *Le Glossaire* by Du Cange, in the article "Incastellare." Notes
Rey, "Military concerns appeared in church architecture as early as the eleventh century. Means of defense, minimal at first, were only as good as the topographical position or importance of the building" (29).

46. "Robert s'embati el mostier / Sus en la tor très h'ol clochier / Mais il n'i
pout gaire attendre / Volsit n non l'estut descendre / Kar li feu i fu aportez / Dunc
li mostier fu alumez" (Robert was embattled in the monastery / From the tower of
the steeple / But he could scarcely hold it; Soon he was forced to come down / For
a fire was set to it / And thus the monastery was burned down), *Le Roman de Rou*
5.16.194f., cited by Rey, 23.

47. Rey, 205.

48. Fernand Benoît, "Église des Saintes-Maries-de-la-Mer," *Bulletin Monumental* 95 (1936): 145–80; Xavier Barral y Altet, "L'Église fortifiée des Saintes-Maries-
de-la-Mer," in *Congrès archéologique de France, 134e session, 1976, Pays d'Arles* (Paris:
Société archéologique de France, 1979), 240–66; Jean-Louis Biget, "La Cathédrale
Sainte-Cécile d'Albi, l'architecture," in *Congrès archéologique de France, 140e session,
1982, Albigeois* (Paris: Société archéologique de France, 1985), 20–62. H. Sigros,
"L'Église de Saint-Andéol," in *Congrès archéologique de France, 120e session, 1963, Avignon et Comtat Venaissin* (Paris: Société archéologique de France, 1966), 433–41.

49. Abbé Mandon, "L'Église fortifiée de Saint-Angel," *Bulletin de la Société scientifique, historique et archéologique de la Corrèze* (1931): 125–36; Bernard de Galejac, "Sainte-Radegonde," in *Congrès archéologique de France, 100e session tenue à Figeac, Cahors et Rodez en 1937* (Paris: Picard, 1938), 401–7; René Cuzacq, "Une église fortifiée landaise: Lesgor," *Bulletin trimestriel de la Société de Borda* 83 (1959): 9–26, 135–50; Jean Martin, "Églises fortifiées en Bigorre," in *Tarbes et la Bigorre, 33e Congrès de la Fédération des sociétés savantes de Languedoc-Pyrénées-Gascogne (Tarbes, 1978)* (1979): 73–78; Roger Piotet, *Saint-Dier d'Auvergne, église romane fortifiée, XIIe siècle* (Saint-Dier d'Auvergne: Association paroissiale d'éducation populaire, 1978); Daniel Gibert, "L'Église fortifiée de Feigneux (Oise)," *Revue archéologique de l'Oise* 25 (1981): 17–25; Jacques Miquel, "L'Église fortifiée d'Inières dans le Rouergue, 1442–1445," *Donjons et forteresses* 2 (1982): 11–20.

50. Roger Rodière, "Notes archéologiques sur les églises fortifiées de la Thiérache," *Bulletin de la Société des antiquaires de Picardie* (1952): 194–201; (1953): 54–65, 97–111; (1954): 199–203, 280–85; Mathilde Renaudin, "Militarisation des campagnes et rôle des fortifications secondaires dans le contexte guerrier des XVIe et XVIIe siècles dans les Ardennes," *Revue historique ardennaise* 22 (1987): 1–5.

51. Albert Colombet, "Les Églises fortifiées de Bourgogne: À propos d'une étude récente," *Annales de Bourgogne* 31 (1959): 250–58; and "Une église fortifiée de Bourgogne, l'église de Maulay," *Mémoire de l'Academie des sciences, arts et belles-lettres de Dijon* 115 (1965): 129–37.

52. René Truttmann, "Les Églises fortifiées de l'est de la France," *Le Pays lorrain* 7 (1959); Albert Haeffeli, *Les Clochers fortifiés du pays messin* (Montigny-les-Metz: by the author, 1976–81), vol. 1, *Rive droite de la Moselle,* 1976; vol. 2, *Le Mont Saint-Quentin,* 1979; vol. 3, *Le Val de Metz,* 1981.

53. "Le Problème des églises et cimitières fortifiés d'Alsace à la lumière de l'architecture militaire du Moyen Âge en France," *Les Vosges* 34 (1954): 1–8; Bernard Metz, "Le Clocher fortifié d'Allenwiller (Bas-Rhin)," *Société d'histoire et d'archéologie de Saverne et environs,* Cahier hors-série 124 bis (1983): 93–108.

54. Rey, 59. "Until 1676 in some regions, the fortification of churches was continued," M. Raudin noted about the Ardennes in "Militarisation des campagnes," (article cited). "On the other hand, in other regions, between 1663 and 1679, after the war with Holland, the fortifications of certain churches were deemed no longer useful and were pulled down. An example was the Church of Saint-Nicolas de Givron, for which the demolition of three sentry boxes built during the wars in 1673 was ordered."

55. Psalm 117 (translation Lemaitre de Sacy).

56. Henri Denifle, *La Guerre de cent ans et la désolation des églises, monastères et hôpitaux en France* (Paris: Picard, 1899) 1:181, according to Froissart.

57. Quoted by Gaston Roupnel, *La Ville et la campagne au XVIIe siècle: Étude sur les populations du Pays dijonnais* (Paris: SEVPEN, 1955), p. 15, no. 28.

58. Gaulejac; other examples in Nicole Lemaître, *Le Rouergue flamboyant: Le Clergé et les fidèles du diocèse de Rodez, 1417–1563* (Paris: Éd. du Cerf, 1988), 127.

59. On this point see Pierre Timbal's fundamental synthesis, *Le Droit d'asile,* preface by Gabriel Le Bras (Paris: Sirey, 1939).

60. Denifle, 1:352.

61. Quoted by Roupnel, 254.

62. Henri Grégoire, *Convention nationale: Instruction publique; Rapport sur les destructions opérées par le vandalisme et sur les moyens de le reprimer,* session of 14 fructidor an II; *Second rapport sur le vandalisme,* session of 8 brumaire an III; *Troisième rapport sur le vandalisme,* session of 24 frimaire an III (Paris: Imprimerie Nationale); as well as James Guillaume's fundamental study, "Grégoire et le vandalisme," *La Révolution française* 41 (1901): 155–80 and 242–69; and the thoughts of Stanley J. Idzerda, "Iconoclasm during the French Revolution," *American Historical Review* 60 (1954): 13–26; Daniel Hermant, "Destruction et vandalisme durant la Révolution française," *Annales ESC* 33, no. 4, 1978): 703–19; Gabriele Sprigath, "Sur le vandalisme révolutionnaire," *Annales historiques de la Révolution française* 52 (1980): 510–35; and Claude Langlois, "Le vandalisme révolutionnaire," *L'Histoire* 99 (April 1987): 8–14.

63. For an assessment of "revolutionary vandalism," see the balanced summation of Louis Réau, *Histoire du vandalisme: Les Monuments détruits de l'art français* (Paris: Hachette, 1959)2 vols.; as well as Michel Heurdeley's indictment, *La France à l'encan, 1789–1799* (Paris: Tallandier, 1981).

64. A recent synthesis in Michel Vovelle's *La Révolution contre l'église: De la raison à l'être suprême* (Brussels: Complexe, 1988) ("La Table rase," 67–100), in addition to the preceding investigation by the same author on the larger Southeast region: *Religion et révolution: La Dechristianisation de l'an II* (Paris: Hachette, 1976). Interpretive presentation by Serge Bianchi, *La Révolution culturelle de l'an II: Élites et peuple (1789–1799)* (Paris: Aubier, 1982) ("La Révolution culturelle: Table rase et régénération," 153–93).

65. On Antoine-Louis Albitte the elder (1761–1812), from Dieppe, deputy of the Seine-Inférieure at the Legislative Assembly (l'Assemblée législative) and the Convention, influential member of the Club des Jacobins in Paris, representative on mission in the Departments of the Ain and Mont-Blanc from January to April 1794, see A. Boudier, *Albitte* (Rouen: Wolff, 1931); Louis Meunier, "Albitte, conventionnel en mission (plus spécialement dans l'Ain et le Mont-Blanc)," *Annales historiques de la Révolution française* 18 (1946): 49–66 and 238–77; Richard Cobb, "Les Débuts de la déchristianisation à Dieppe," *Annales historiques de la Révolution française* 28 (1956): 191–209.

66. On the subject of Albitte's "hundred days" in the Department of the Ain (January 22–April 30, 1794), see Charles Jarrin, *Bourg et Belley pendant la Révolution* (Bourg: Authier et Barbier, 1881): 119–81; and Eugène Dubois, *Histoire de la Révolution dans l'Ain*, Bourg: Brochot, 1931–35) vol. 4, *L'An deux de la République Française, 1793–1794,* 141f.

67. *Archives parlementaires* 85, séance du 29 pluviôse an II, 157–61.

68. Quoted by E. Dubois, 4:435.

69. The statement comes from M. Vovelle, 81–82.

70. Quoted by E. Dubois, 4:432.

71. Ibid., 431.

72. Jarrin, 214–15. Charles Jarrin, a republican in 1848 and 1870 and correspondant of Quinet, is the author of an extraordinary roman à clef on society in Bourg and Belley, *Grandeur et décadence de la bourgeoisie de Montbeney* (Bourg: Authier et Barbier, 1884–93), 2 vols.

73. "Taking the sacraments to the faithful" during the revolutionary period constitutes one of the richest areas of recent religious historiography of the Revo-

lution; cf. in this domain, in *Pratiques religieuses dans l'Europe révolutionnaire (1770–1820): Actes du colloque de Chantilly (November 27–29, 1986),* collected by Paule Lerou and Raymond Dartevelle under the direction of Bernard Plongeron (Turnhout: Brepols, 1988), the contributions of Bernard Cousin, "Prêtres et laïcs: Les Sacrements dans la clandestinité (Avignon, 1793–1801)," 191–200; Patricia Lusson-Houdemon, "La Vie sacramentelle des fidèles de l'Ouest à travers les registres clandestins," 216–24; Dominique Varry, "La Paroisse de Phaffans d'après le registre du curé constitutionnel Berdolet (1789–1805)," 236–45; Marie-Paule Biron, "La Résistance des laïcs à travers les messes blanches [*sic*] et le culte laïcal," 293–99. See also the first synthesis of Bernard Cousin, Monique Cubells, and Rene Moulinas, "La Vie religieuse des catholiques," in *La Pique et la croix: Histoire religieuse de la Révolution française* (Paris: Le Centurion, 1989), 223–55.

74. For a long-term parish history, see the classic and still fundamental synthesis by Pierre Imbart de la Tour, *Les Origines religieuses de la France: Les Paroisses rurales du IVe au XIe siècle* (Paris: Picard, 1900), as well as the program articles of Joseph Guillaume, "Comment concevoir une monographie paroissiale," *Revue d'histoire de l'église de France* 14 (1923): 369–88 and 493–523, reprinted in Victor Carrière, *Introduction aux études d'histoire ecclésiastique,* vol. 2, *L'Histoire locale à travers les âges* (Paris: Letouzey et Ane, 1934): 303–45; and of Gabriel Le Bras, "Pour l'étude de la paroisse rurale," *Revue d'histoire de l'église de France* 28 (1937): 486–502. Recent perspectives in René Metz, "La Paroisse en France à l'époque moderne et contemporaine," *Revue d'histoire de l'église de France* 60, no. 165 (1974): 269–96, and 61, no. 166 (1975): 5–24; Michel Aubrun, *La Paroisse en France des origines au XVe siècle* (Paris: Picard, 1986); Francis Rapp, "Le rôle des paroisses dans l'encadrement religieux des fidèles (XIIIe–XVIe siècles)," in *Idéologie et propagande en France,* under the direction of Myriam Yardeni (Paris: Picard, 1987), 75–86; Joseph Avril, "La Paroisse médiévale: Bilan et perspective d'après quelques travaux récents," *Revue d'histoire de l'église de France* 74, no. 192 (1988): 90–113.

75. *Catéchismes de la Providence,* quoted by Monnin, 1:277–79.

76. On this point we wish to refer to Philippe Boutry and Michel Cinquin, *Deux Pèlerinages au XIXe siècle: Ars et Paray-le Monial* (Paris: Beauchesne, 1980): 11–169.

77. Philippe Boutry, "Un sanctuaire et son saint au XIXe siècle: Jean-Marie-Baptiste Vianney, curé d'Ars," *Annales ESC* 35, no. 2 (1980): 375.

Figure 3.1
A painter on the Eiffel Tower.

CHAPTER 3

THE INDUSTRIAL ARTS

❧

YVES LEQUIN

O n February 15, 1848, the people of Paris gathered at the Hôtel de
Ville before setting out on a march to celebrate the return of liberty.
One group after another—the cabinetmakers, the joiners (woodworkers),
the tailors, the mechanics—in short, there were all the countless trades of
the capital in procession. A surprising cortege, an explicit reference to the
Revolution of 1789. Although on so many occasions it gave evidence of
its strength and sovereignty, it had nothing in common with the undifferentiated mob of *sans culottes* distinguished by its adherence to a common
political purpose. From this time forward, these working people were
to be found every spring pounding the pavements of the city, notably on
March 16, when they were 100,000 or perhaps 200,000 strong. And from
that time forward, they fell into place as a single profession: trades established the elementary cells of the social body, the little republics of labor,
to use the language of the time, the prominence of which the Luxembourg Commission had just sanctioned by aligning them with the electoral colleges. The new social republic was supposed to emerge from their
association, and it was logically within each group that they began to debate and let the democratic effervescence spread, at least as much as in the
clubs, through discussions, organizational projects, and general meetings—
twelve for the tinsmiths alone between March and June.[1]

A unique moment where the political did not diverge from the social, where the discovery of universal suffrage and the workers' question
occurred simultaneously. It mattered little that the dream soon collapsed

and that it never afterward took on the same colors. And that history would stammer when it met up again, between 1940 and 1944, with the nostalgia for the lost trades, when the Vichy Regime would revive in its own name the words of an obsolete discourse, that of the "ancient artisan traditions," when one René Belin would dream anew of a society where those corporations came into association by, in a perversion of words, linking to the snares of memory.[2]

It is true that a society of corporations and artisan traditions, modernity and archaism, are not completely absent in the language of 1848. People speak not just of trades but also of a "corps," the "state," or indeed a corporation, a whole vocabulary echoing, in fact, the society of the ancien régime that the Revolution had supposedly eradicated, and successfully, at least at the legal level. In 1790, to tell the truth, the Typographical Society of Paris avoided such language lest it be suspected of nostalgia. There was, as William Sewell notes, a "comfortable shorthand" in the use of ordinary everyday words even if they did go back to the past. We see the old rupture in mental machinery, so often not in step with reality.[3] In 1848, in fact, the printing trade was already a *lieu de mémoire* for the workers. More astonishing is the fact that even today it has not stopped being so, although most historians—and, more recently, sociologists—chart the chronology of its disappearance in industrial development.

The explosion in the spring of 1848 expressed the uneasiness of the workers, their feeling that a world was slipping away.* Since the beginning of the century, the direction of wages had been down and, for the short term, they were increasingly unstable: even a skill no longer guaranteed the means of existence, which increasingly depended on credit. Unemployment occurred periodically without anyone's being able to anticipate it, and it could affect even the most capable. Work itself stopped being steady. Machines were brought onto the factory floor to replace work done by the hand of the workingman, like the mechanical saw in the faubourg Saint-Antoine, the printing press in the publishing houses. The wool workers of Vienne, in the Isère, put up a fight to remove the mechanical shears.

---

* The "explosion" is the Revolution of 1848, often considered the first violent confrontation between the dominant bourgeoisie and the workers. The Revolution had two distinct phases. In February 1848 the workers united with the bourgeoisie to bring down the July Monarchy and King Louis-Philippe. A new provisional republican government was established. In June the workers of Paris, still without work and significant economic and social change, set up barricades in the capital. The urban insurrection was savagely repressed by the army.—Ed.

With this machinery or even without it the division of work, or, by contrast, the interchangeability of tasks, was expanded.[4] And in a world that exalted property and property alone, work was devalued, subject to the pitiless law of the market, the extent of which was distant, thus mysterious. For the statutes, revenues, and conditions of work to be threatened, no drastic change was necessary, and the artisan workers of Toulouse had no illusions about this.[5] Henceforth, no trade was sufficient to protect one from accidents, illness, off-season unemployment, or even boredom, to use the words of one Ledreuil, who spoke of the "inner drought" of Georges Navel. The good workers were no more protected than any other from the "inquisitorial demands" of work,[6] and one's own community split apart because of growing conflicts, heretofore unthinkable, with the masters: the chair maker Bené never got adjusted to a society given over to individual selfishness.[7] Outside the workplace there was the degradation of the manufacturing cities, with their hideous living quarters where poverty oozed out from everywhere and where the proletariat, in Villermé's words, lived like a "half animal."[8] This horror was in a world that had developed a morality of work, and to the sensation of professional spoliation was added the denial of this misery in which the philanthropists of the 1840s had confined the working class. Defying this definition, the workers organized a movement that arose by poverty alone. That poverty would remain an obsession.[9]

The industrialization of France in the first half of the nineteenth century was thus novel enough to transform the reality of the workers' condition. It was not cataclysmic enough to cause associations to disappear, especially in the trades.[10] Outside the mining and metalworking industries, all the more visible as they were rare, the cities were essentially where the dynamism of industry flourished; the French world of trade remained that of the urban trades, particularly in furniture, building construction, and clothing, swept along by expanding demand and consumption, as well as that of the textile trades, whose world was closer to modern large industry. In the silk industry in Lyons and the cotton and wool industry of Lille, expansion did not transform the organization of production as a whole. All it did was add new workshops to those already in existence. As late as 1876, artisan workers were twice as numerous as factory workers in France, and by the end of the nineteenth century, Paris was one of the largest workshops in the world.[11] In sum, French workers of the nineteenth century already had a certain collective awareness, and 1848 proves it, that foreshadowed the contemporary proletariat. They did not retain any less the capacity to exercise their tasks freely, tasks that linked them to the artisans of the ancien régime, which called them *gens de métier* (tradespeople) as distinguished from the simple *gens de bras* (manual laborers), through their know-how, the fruit of a long apprenticeship and long experience that did not separate physical effort from intelligence or the capacity for execution from the power of creation. The worker poets of the July Monarchy spoke of this in their way, as did Charles Poncy, a mason from Toulon with his "ringing hammers" that gave "life to the rebellious metals" and to his fellow stonecutters, who "breathed soul into the coarse block."[12]

The law might try to proscribe that set of conventions, customs, rites, and ways of speaking that very much tied workers in the same trade in the France of the Restoration to those in the France of the July Monarchy, which were expressed in proper corporate language that bore specific values and had the immense advantage of being understood by the masters, thereby illuminating any possible negotiations.[13] If the words "society" and "association" came to be substituted over time for *jurande* (those members of the trade corporation responsible for defending its interests and upholding standards), "community," and "corps," it was because the state recognized only individuals and citizens, and it was better to translate what joined them together through professional qualifications, which signified a discipline as well as a certain personal commitment. Here then was the *corps d'état* or the *corps de métier,* and later it is the name of the trade itself that occurred more frequently. Much later, "metalworker" would be the term used by the economist. As for the workers, they would become mechanics, puddlers, blacksmiths, or fitters in contrast to those people *sans état,* those day laborers and unskilled workers doomed to anonymous jobs, undifferentiated and interchangeable. They were the ones picked to do everything because they had no skills in anything. Buchez understood this very well and had hopes for the urban trades precisely because of their professional qualifications.*[14]

That the first workers' movement may have grown out of the workers' own efforts cannot be denied.[15] The second youth of the workers' associations, during the Restoration, did indeed lead to different duties linked to several *corps d'état.* But it was within the community of a single trade where current issues were resolved and rules of hierarchy and mobility were defined. The "mold" was true for only one of them. The hatters were at least as preoccupied by technical examinations validating competence as they were by observation of the rituals.

As for the mutual aid societies, which the Restoration encouraged,

---

* Philippe-Joseph Buchez, a socialist theorist, historian, lecturer, and former Saint-Simonian, developed schemes for workers' cooperatives in the 1830s in which everyone would be equal, be their own masters, and draw equal pay. He argued for a "common social capital," formed by the dues of the associated workers, which was to be "inalienable and indissoluble."—Trans.

though with some ambivalence, there was variety, some not even managing to encompass an entire profession. But beginning with Napoleon, the oldest—the glovemakers of Grenoble are a good example—organized around a trade and took over, under the auspices of a patron saint, the moral traditions and practices of the community. In 1823, of 160 mutual aid societies in Paris, 32 of them were identical to a *corps d'état*. Ten years later, the Society of the Rights of Man, the activities of which showed up in an entirely different arena, modeled its sections on the professions— the tailors, cabinetmakers, shoemakers, glovemakers, typesetters—and found itself, without always meaning to, drawn into the big strikes that the various groups would call in autumn. Failures led a number of them to create—in the clothing, furniture, and packaging businesses—cooperative workshops, forebears of the great movement of producers' associations that burst forth in 1848 and again during the Second Empire. There were 300 in Paris and more than 800 in the provinces. Is it surprising that the Commune of Paris and the Third Republic in its beginnings wrote financial assistance into their program because that seemed so strongly to convey the will of the workers?[16] Certain forms would last even if some French historians more inclined to attach themselves to the so-called avant-garde ignored them. Those forms would come to be discovered and with that the contamination that would end up affecting large industry, glass-making, printing as well as the construction business, and even those miners who until 1914 dreamed of "mines for the miners."

More generally, to have a trade meant having a specialized skill ("I have a skill, I can go anywhere, I don't need anyone," wrote Proudhon, "an immense pleasure"),[17] good pay, and also to be in the prime of life, in short everything that brings one recognition. And perhaps also a certain access, in a way, to the culture of the elite. We need only recall the well-deserved reputation of the shoemakers during the July Monarchy. They were agitators, but because they were also thinkers, they played a central role in labor agitation. There is no doubt that they were also a secret organization with ties across the nation.[18] In 1830, again in 1848, and yet again in 1871, the building, furniture, clothing, and mechanical trades furnished manpower for the uprising disproportionate to their numbers in the population of Paris. The First International in 1869 took root among the mechanics, bronze workers, plumbers, and men working with chisels. All these, like the carpenters and woodworkers, painters, and masons, and even the journeymen bakers, were there at the beginning when unions burst on the scene in 1875–76 at the culmination of the first phase of the industrialization of France before we find them again at the birth of the workers' political party several years later.[19]

To be sure, in 1884, *Le Cri du peuple* did denounce the treachery of

Figure 3.2
Cards and labels of different trade associations, 1848.

the typographers and the carpenters, among others, that false avant-garde tangle of ceremony and obsolete rituals. In those times of the "youth on strike," they did indeed seem to fade away. And the shoemakers too disappeared from center stage to the margins of anarchism. Those who saw the new society emerging from their cooperative and mutual aid society dreams were discouraged—for what had they sacrificed so much? They were more ready now to negotiate, and thus to accept, than to struggle. They were in fact paralyzed by a certain bourgeois fascination with ability, which gave the advantage to experience and rejected those who did not have it, namely, the young, the female, the clumsy, and, soon, foreigners. In 1882, it was an event when the "railway men," and they were the ones pushing the trades, joined a strike by the weavers in Roanne. But then in Angers and Le Mans, the "shoe cutters" refused to join the strike by the "shoe finishers." More generally, in the hat business, it was the *approprieurs*, "men who shaped the hats for the *chapelliers*," who insisted on distancing themselves from the "fullers." The cutters, the "clothing jobbers," and the "piecework men" rarely made common cause in the clothing industry. They were skittish specialists, as were the glass workers; in the Lyons region, they were the "big boys" or "blowers," who wanted nothing to do with the unskilled workers with whom they nevertheless had close daily contact and without whom they could not do their work. Then there was the textile industry in the North, where up until the end of the century the "sorters," "washers," and "combers" led their own individual actions that made them suspicious of collective distractions.[20] And again in 1903, the union of copper workers in Paris admitted to its numbers only "foundry men" and "casters" and rejected the "trimmers" and other helpers.[21]

And yet, the spreading number of strikes tended to mask the role the trades continued to play as if their apparent fading away were only the effect of experience. If they stopped work less frequently than others, they still did so with obvious effectiveness, at least in part—three out of five times during a period when the rate of success for the unskilled did not exceed 40 percent. In the new metallurgy industry, puddlers, ingot rollers, and casters would exploit their strategic position in the production process when declaring the thrombotic strikes of the next century. It is true that two out of five times the struggle was propped up by the strength, cohesion, and ability of a union organization.[22] In the years 1871–90, unions pushed easily into the compost of mutual aid and cooperative societies from which had sprung over time those organizations dedicated to resistance which the law of 1884 had legalized, although in equivocal terms, since what the law authorized was the free association of "persons exercising the same professions, similar trades, or related professions."[23]

The workingman's association might disappear—it had no more than 25,000 members in all of France during the Belle Époque, compared with 100,000 in the middle of the nineteenth century—yet its traces remained, strong and effective. Putting an organization on the index or using the boycott remained ways to rally the small business owner, but those tactics evoked a distant memory of damnation. And we can still see the origins of the association in the complicity of slang, in the workers' fraternity, in the pride of the trade, in the obvious taste for physical confrontation, and in their heroic legends. We must not forget certain forms of sociability, which, for example, were still bringing the tanners together in the 1880s at their collective "kitchen" on rue Lafayette.[24]

In sum, there was no fracture between the cooperatist tradition and revolutionary socialism at the end of the century. Behind the apparent metamorphosis in the workers' organizations, be they union or political, the effect of the structure did not play a role. It was the change in the context, the founding of a republic based on representative democracy. The Marxist intellectuals of the 1920s were not in error when in *La Vie ouvrière*, the newspaper of the CGT (Confédération générale du travail), which was the major association of French trade unions and was affiliated with the Communist Party, they denounced, as did René Garmy in 1933, those "worker aristocrats" as the last guard dogs of capitalism. Nor did it matter that they got the meaning of the expression wrong.

The direct action of the 1900s no doubt brought the unionism of the trades to its peak, and the organizational reality, the stock exchange of work, was nothing but the consolidation at the local level of cooperative organizations. It was not by chance that the men in the various construction, leather, and clothing industries were present in force.[25] But, then, what about the metalworkers, who embodied modernity? And where was the federation born that laid claim in 1883, too soon as it turned out, to all of industry? Its entire subsequent history is precisely that of a series of splits and belated revivals in the trade federations—the copper workers, casters—still called the "republic of casters"—the automobile workers, and so forth. A new attempt at unification failed in 1899. The casters joined in 1909 but the mechanics declined.[26] The automobile of the Belle Époque had three coexisting unions, at least one of which, the mechanics, maintained a strong loyalty to the trade just like the woodworkers, accessory fasteners, and carriage painters.[27] As for the railway workers, united since 1884 in their own association, the Syndicat Guimbert, they avoided a decision between 1889 and 1891, when a more all-encompassing organization, the Syndicat Guérard, was formed that allowed them to practice dual membership.[28] The difficulties of the CGT at the beginning of the century are well known, when it wanted to replace the trade federations with industry federations, and it did just that, taking the long view, when they yielded for a time to the casters and their organization.[29]

The strength of those large consolidations in the professions during the years 1880 to 1890 could not be opposed. Those consolidations are forgotten today because they correspond so little to the self-styled image of trade unionism, in the French version, among the glassworkers, leather workers, hatmakers, textile workers, and we must not omit the printers. They drew their strength from the geographical tension of the places of production between which the workers and the militants moved about. For a time at least they imposed control over the terms of apprenticeship, the setting of norms of production, and even the union monopoly over hiring, and one suspects that they did not accept skilled workers.

There were also, in one inverted image but in the same sense, large protest movements at the local level, which though occurring at the same time had no knowledge of each other. This situation drove to despair those who dreamed of a general strike even when they could not get the interprofessional groups to join forces. In 1901, the gold and metal trimmers and the miners marched in the streets by the thousands, and their processions crossed each other without any notice of the other being taken. Several years later, it was in the Lorraine of iron and steel where the miners and the steelworkers avoided each other when they were not battling each other. It was, as Jacques Julliard has noted, the dream of the workers not to take control of society. Their revolution was the moment when they appropriated the instruments for the exercise of their trade. In the CGT one imagined a future world still as a collection of professional federations of which the little islands of worker autonomy with the capitalist world were so many "toothing stones," those stones left at the end of a wall to allow the wall's continuation.[30]

One might also note that at the beginning of the twentieth century only the trade unions managed to gain headway on the mass of workers in an industry. The reason: they spoke the language of concrete matters, salary, working conditions, overtime. They were the one visible organization that was not limited to a particular business, the single closest point of reference in the unknowns of the market. As such, they constituted well and truly the most elementary line of sociability for these men at work, the visible expression and concrete symbol of solidarities, community, condition, and interests, using Georges Friedmann's words for that derangement of men and things that is industrialization. It was obvious that it was the union, like the strike, that assumed the shape of the trades. It had a vitality that was not necessarily at odds with a collective conscience that went beyond it. Still, proletarian associations did not signify confusion. And if the French working class at the end of the nineteenth and the beginning of the twentieth century displayed what could be called class awareness, it was always through the mosaic of its trades, which affirmed their first identity in the trilogy of skill, effort, and, at the end of the chain, work well done. Furthermore, it truly came as a surprise to the business owners when the demands of their workers were presented by the one person, of all of them, who was their best and most skillful worker. This was the first face, therefore, of union action, the face of the "proud conscience," if the sociologists are to be believed, but destined to fade away with modernity.[31] Time would be needed for discourse and reality to mirror each other.

Blue overalls for the locksmith, white dungarees for the mason, overcoats for the painters, who inhabit Zola's world: the habit does not the monk make, but it does make the trade visible. In the Belle Époque, the long smocks, the high leather apron, the wooden shoes, and the hats with wide brims made the blacksmiths of Lorraine recognizable before Georges Navel, some years later, went into ecstasies over the trousers of the tough women in the beautiful velvet, red, and blue belt of the building laborers who harmonized so well together in the beauty of their voices and in solidarity with the "good guys . . . so proud of [their] trade to be wearing its garb."[32] From the description of their clothing to the literary imagination, but one step was needed to fix the emblematic silhouette of the trade worker: Arthur, Alphonse Daudet's mechanic; Goujet, that blacksmith whose wisdom stood in contrast to the turpitudes of L'Assommoir. We have to wait for the more ideal types in their operations, drawn by the engaged writers of the twentieth century—, Le Mot "mineur," camarade[33] and the foundry workers of André Stil: "The fire is in them and flares up in the agitation of their dreams."[34] All were virile figures who also evince the symbolic iconography of work, and not only in France.[35] All were great meat eaters in a population that remained deprived. In the 1880s, that iconography was still a familiar site where the glassmakers of Douai and Baccarat or the miners of Liévin and Alès or the mechanics and blacksmiths of Pont-à-Mousson and Montataire took their meals. And they were all great drinkers of wine, for whom there was a symbolic meaning: the drinking of wine was the sign of the glassmakers and coal miners. Did not Denis Poulot model the scale of skills and unique behaviors on the hierarchy of drinking in the Paris of the Second Empire?[36] When the laundresses of Saint-Étienne in the 1920s wanted to get themselves recognized in the working community, they stuffed themselves with sausage and red wine.[37]

But in the abuse of strong drink that on occasion underscores the loudmouthed arrogance of certain trades was there not also an unconscious desire to stave off death? Danger was everywhere, and industrial death had just been added to the traditional threats that weighed on the condition of the people. In the 1840s, physicians could spot the often insidious signs—dust in the workplace, not to mention intoxication from burning hot air and gases—and by the end of the nineteenth century, they could tell some by their hacked-off fingers and others by their maimed limbs. If the image of the glass workers is youthful, it is only because they hardly lived beyond forty. The mill worker risked at every moment being pierced by rods in motion. The foundry man might fall into the mouth of a blast furnace if he slipped. Then there were the miners, who, apart from the explosions from firedamp, confronted the violence and hostility of the entrails of the earth. How can we not be astonished by the fantasies of physical anthropology and those of its "race of miners"? The material resists the Promethean enterprise, and physical force may be, right at the outset, a question of survival.

Muscular effort and constant alertness is what prematurely wore out the miners, glassmakers, and locomotive firemen. Specific pathologies were soon spotted. But it is precisely the enforced brevity of their intense careers that gave them grandeur. The sweat of their faces, as well as their darkness, revealed the essence of the blacksmiths in the steel industry: tall, solid, and a little bent over. Georges Navel spoke his admiration before the efficient and muscular body of his brother Lucien, a foundry man, and, for him, no greater praise could be made of the mechanics than to find them "as brawny as the masons."[38]

The practice of a trade meant first of all the perfect mastery of the body, fit and trained, that allied work to athleticism, said Simone Weil. That practice, which had no tinge of complacency, was not any less sensitive to the economy of motion, the alternating use of each arm and each leg that ensured the efficacy of the productive act and at the same time the minimum of fatigue.[39] And the welder in the Batignolles railway engine and repair plant in Nantes, in a time not too long ago, was above all an acrobat on the ground.[40] Well before Navel, the carpenters of the nineteenth century could be identified by their large chests and their high waists.[41] The miners who hewed the coal face were always solid, strapping fellows in the mining communities who, quite logically, soon came to discover the sports involving force: football and, later, boxing.[42] André Stil became lyrical about the steelworkers, who, even in their sleep, "marched," "ran," "struggled," "the body ever alert," but who also "stroked."[43] Precision is what the fitter or the tracer demonstrates; agility, the fitter and the ingot rollers, whose jump to the side avoids the murderous rod. For others it is a matter of the eye: the glassmaker or the foundry man opens the furnace, and melted glass might fly up. For still others it is a matter of the ear, staying attuned to the noises of the machine or the workshop, or the nose or

Figure 3.3
Workers, great eaters of meat and drinkers of wine. Raffaelli, *Les Forgerons* (The blacksmiths), Museum of Douai.

the skin, getting away from the mouth of the blast furnace. The interior meanings of the rhythm and profound ambiance of the material, Michel Verret notes, are at least as important as muscular touch.[44] This mastery of the body is what perhaps gives birth to the happiness of work, "this cadence" where it "finds its bliss," when the earth "sings on the shovel of the building laborer." "There is at least one hour in the day when the body is happy."[45] Simone Weil herself confesses, even in the evening after a day's work on the assembly-line, beyond exhaustion, to a "certain joy in the muscular effort."[46]

In this gymnastics of work there was for a long time what the anthropologists have identified as the extension of the gesture by the tool.[47] This in turn points to another emblem of the trades, alongside the abilities and misfortunes of the body. There is a lithograph from 1848 that shows the trades of the Luxembourg Commission: the tailors are naturally recognized by their scissors, the printers by the press, and the masons by their mortarboard and trowel.[48] And in the photographs at the end of the century, the men shatter the anonymity of the image by shouldering their hammers, holding the tongs in their hands, and clutching the blowpipes with their legs. The cabinetmakers of faubourg Saint-Antoine never stopped making their own tools, and with Jean Baptiste Dumay and Georges Navel, one recognizes the fitter or the mechanic by his file and, in the 1920s, spots the diggers by the folding rule that sticks out of their pockets and the little spoon they used to scratch. Ownership of one's tools was a traditional point of pride in the building trades.[49] It required a new regulation, in 1906, stating that "the company had to furnish all the tools necessary for the worker to perform his job" so that the Renault workers could stop bringing their own tools to the factory and risk seeing them confiscated.[50]

Having one's own tools, and those tools were often simple and multipurpose—the poker remained essential to steelmaking right up to the middle of the twentieth century—was both a sign of technical skill and a surety of liberty. Georges Navel again, going from one factory to another, carefully hung on to his caliper rule, his awl, his toolmaker's hammer, and his "set squares fashioned with patience."[51] A stone quarrier of today, with a longing for his stonemason's hammer, expresses nostalgia for a time when it was not the tool (or the machine) that made the rules.[52]

What is more, who but another tradesman could know what a "rabbler" or a "turning chisel" or a "routing plane" meant?[53] How can one not be fascinated, when one is not part of it, by the three types of hammer (sledgehammer, riveting hammer, ball-peen hammer) and the six kinds of drills (bow drill, drill bow, center bit, etc.) that were used in the early days of the airplane industry and the uses of which—with the punch, the

Figure 3.4
The quality of the casting depends on the worker. *La Coulée* (The casting), stained glass made at the Majorelle workshops in Nancy for the headquarters of the Steelworks of Longwy (Usinor) Hotel in Mont-Saint-Martin.

Figure 3.5
An athletic body, an economy of motion. Caillebotte, *Les Raboteurs de parquets* (The floor planers), 1875.

bevel, and the chipping chisel—the apprentice had to learn to recite by heart?[54] "Workers could not preserve their trades if they did not use words manufactured by them and unknown to us," wrote Joachim de Bellay. The trade was in fact also a shared language that varied infinitely according to the workplace and the factory. The old trade jargon, which for the miners of the nineteenth century penetrated the entire community beyond the pit and the shaft, was understood by one's fellow workers in the same trade. It designated not only objects, but also practices, in the variety of their nuances and circumstances. These so-called ergolects, or words of work, are turned to good use by the anthropologists of industrial society and are recognizable in that they reflect the (so-called?) specificity of knowledge all the more esoteric when you do not want to share it or fear someone will dispossess you of it.[55] In the mystery of the words are displayed those famous professional "secrets," those "tricks of the trade" about which no one had any suspicion for a long time.

"The worker alone has the instinct and secret of what he does," said Louis Reybaud in 1874, when pointing out the "more or less instantaneous glance" and the "hardly appreciated details" guiding the arm of the puddler. Even on the eve of war in 1914, it was the Comité des forges that still determined that the quality of the casting depended on the technique—there were several—used by the foundry men to pressurize the nozzles to the blast furnace. There was nothing to replace the empirical intelligence of the first foundry men for appreciating the "cracks" in the steel samples they took.[56] There is no need to evoke the "strange and grand calls" of the smiths or the atavistic knowledge of these families alone capable in the middle of the nineteenth century of giving form and measure to the new blast furnace, since in an activity as emblematic of the industrial revolution as the steel industry, empiricism long reigned as master by leaving intact the role of the trades, hidden behind the "veil of professional secrets," to use Marx's words.[57] Navel marveled at the thousand possible uses of the hammer according to whether the rod in the forge was "cherry red," "straw yellow," or "dove colored" when, during the 1920s, the work was done in the old manner.[58] Well into the twentieth century the toolmakers of La Fure in Dauphiné started with the color of the material, the odors from the hearth, and the resonance of the piece.[59] One spoke of "the art and mystery of printing" for the English typographers.[60] And by the end of the nineteenth century, the engineers in the glassworks were the ones becoming annoyed when unable to penetrate the mysteries; doubtless the coal miner at the coal face alone had the capacity to deal with every situation, like the spinner who gauged the temperature and humidity of the wool or cotton fiber, the tailor the resistance of the fabric, the glovemaker and shoe smith the elasticity of the leather. Right up until today, the recurrence of terms of speech refers to skills not formalized, those bodies and hands in motion that fashion the trade in every sense of the term, another way of saying job experience.[61] The Encyclopédistes did not really give up on describing their practices when they chose to depict them in the book-plates, in which, however, the essential was lacking, namely life.[62]

"I spent a lot of time at the forge working the ventilation. Whenever it was necessary, I would hammer the material. I would observe the movements of the journeyman who was training me." No one could express the progressive knowledge of motions and gestures that rightly signified apprenticeship better than Navel and the uses the journeyman put them to in the factory and the workshop. His brothers had learned to be a boil-ermaker and a caster by this pedagogy of example and imitation, and he himself, at Berliet's side, "a good *compagnon* ready to help when needed."[63] We might ask what exactly was the "trade" of the coal-pick man. It was something that dealt with physical force, simple tools, and an effective-ness that assured recognition from one's peers and an indisputable author-ity over others. And it drew on years of experience where one learned, on the job, how to recognize the hardness of the vein, how to interpret the cracks in the timbering and the putrefaction in the air.[64] The first caster at the blast furnace at the end of the nineteenth century was hardly more qualified in the strict sense of the word, but he knew how to sniff the noxious gases at the throat of the blast furnace that made novices faint.[65] And in a less dramatic manner, let us note the earthwork labor-ers of Paris in the interwar period with the intelligence of their well-measured gestures, their way of tossing the earth with their shovels, that productive rhythm that is born from repetition, from their experience with the timbering of the trenches and the protective arrangement of the planks and pillars.[66] It matters little, in the last analysis, that all through the nineteenth century complaints were heard about a crisis in appren-ticeship. At issue were the forms and contractual practices of the ancien régime, not the reality of that physical and personalized mimesis of which Gerard Noriel speaks, but the tricks of the trade that were transmitted by observing the motions of others, the pedagogical relationships between the master with the skill and the apprentice who was learning it. It was a relationship of action more than words. Autobiographies by workers who did not omit their masters described them as both affectionate and severe.[67] In the foundries of Paris in the 1900s, for example, it was under-stood that a journeyman helped the one who did not understand or who understood poorly.[68] One pedagogical example may serve as an example, in almost the same period of time, for a toolmaker from Dauphiné: One entered an apprenticeship at age sixteen, and became a stoker who put the pieces into the oven. Later, he was entrusted with the finishing tasks, the planing and straightening, through which he came to observe the work of the smiths. Then it was up to the apprentice to practice outside regular hours if he wished to become a planer and master a complicated technique through which a single plate of steel could be turned into a particular tool. All in all, it took him ten years.[69] Similar training could be found in the mining, glassmaking, steelmaking, and other industries.

Lumbermen, puddlers, casters, foundry men . . . the recurrent discourse of the trade is quite far, it would seem, from the world of the workshops where the workers' movement was shaped. That world did not disappear after 1850: in an industrial milieu that remained for the most part urban, tailors and shoemakers, carpenters and cabinetmakers, and especially masons, plasterers, and painters held a considerable place and still played the premier role in the great waves of demands. Even more, the increasing variety of manufacturers and specialties expanded the checkerboard of that large mosaic of trades that was the French working class. Thus it was with Parisian furniture, beginning in the Second Empire, about which, from an outside perspective, one spoke of the cabinetmaker, or "carpenter in veneer," but in addition there were the pit sawyer, the worker in marquetry, the sculptor in wood, the tapestry maker, the chair stuffer and caner, the worker in bronze or gold. Those who make "chairs" must not be confused with those who make "armoires" or "chests." Buildings likewise saw the emergence at the end of the century of the stucco worker and the heating engineer.[70]

As for large industry, the change was not such, even after 1850, that it eliminated the old trades. Labor was sufficient for a long time so that the employers' project for mechanizing had radical effects and reduced the factory to a one-on-one between a machine and its auxiliary equipment. The factory remained largely an aggregate of specialized or similar workshops, hence one of skilled trades. What helped bring this about was the survival of certain skills like haggling, jobbing, custom building work, woodworking, and coach-making industries in the first half of the nineteenth century, later extending to mining, steelmaking, glassmaking, and even to the large metalworking industry, locomotive manufacture, for instance. Indeed the system delivered the employers from direct management and accounts for the long survival of piecework. Take the team of the coal-pick man, with twelve to fifteen complementary categories, connected or ancillary but clearly specified; or another team, also diversified and hierarchically organized, that of the caster assistants, the weighers, loaders, rollers, lifters, and stackers, who are not to be confused with the underlings of unskilled workers and who, fortified by experience and high recognition, served as the "first worker of the foundry" of a blast furnace in Lorraine. During the Belle Époque a tooling platemaker in Dauphiné

Figure 3.6
Artist or artisan? The same motion, the same tool for the locksmith at his forge, under the watchful eye of the apprentice, and for the solitary sculptor in his workshop. A locksmith at his forge in the 1950s.

trained his own stokers and paid them out of his own salary. In the textile mills of Lille, the "spinner" directed, in his "domain," the same ordered world of slipshod workers, textile finishers, and machine operators.[71]

New products, new processes of work, new technologies: industrial modernization, before the "new factory," created new trades to be named and extended the list of terms for the professions by the end of the century. Mechanization itself played an essential role: First came the "new craft industry," identified by Jean Fourastié, with machine builders but also their regulators, their toolmakers, and their repairmen who found new employment using their technical skills.[72] The mines became populated with machinists, engineers for the mine locomotives, and haulers at the bottom—10 percent of the total workforce in Hussigny in Lorraine around 1910—and on the surface the fitters, electricians, and blacksmiths. In the steelmaking industry, though the "loader" faded away after 1905, the entry of electricians, machinists, and especially the newcomers like the coil winders, the casters, and the machine operators pushed unskilled

Figure 3.7
The sculptor Yves Loyer in his workshop in the 1980s.

workers into a collection of jobs. True, there were still blast furnace workers and mold pourers, but they had to make room for the mill hands who rolled the ingots and others who cored the mold. In 1939, they still needed "second metalworkers" to handle with their tongs the casting from the mold that an engineer would check. In the foundries of Paris in the first years of the twentieth century, the molding process was completely mechanized, but it could not be done without the manual assistance of those who knew how to prepare the sand, fill the mold box, tighten the molds, and get the tubes to flow. In 1914, it was still the trades who qualified two automobile workers out of three. Finally, the second industrialization with its wide array of experiences did not mark a true rupture. In the electrical plants of La Praz, in the Alps in 1906, a new trade emerged, the "fermenter," originally from the countryside. The fermenter had to learn how to mix the baths, fill the vats, and position himself in such a way as to gauge when to intervene and evaluate the risks that might arise. The aeronautical industry too, in its beginnings from 1920 to 1930, was a collection of trades—fitters, turners, milling machine operators, model makers, electrotypers, decorative painters, woodworkers, cabinetmakers, and the men who applied glue to the wing surface. All of them functioned in a system of incessant intermingling of qualified workers. And well after World War II, this industry would see its sand men, its carpenters, and its metalworkers disappear, its riveters and welders blur into the background as electricians and the specialists among them, the wiring specialists, suddenly appeared, followed by the electronics engineers.[73]

Besides manufacture itself, the factory generated the world of the maintenance workers that the incertitudes of the functioning of machines necessitated and those in manufacturing for the small runs and prototypes where their polymorphic skill was more necessary than ever. They amounted to a third of the workers at the Micheville steelworks in 1929![74] It was "varied" work in which one was "sensitive to the quality of one's work" and where the adjusters and the toolmakers let themselves be seduced by the "changing interest of their task." James Laux has called attention to the exemplary destiny of the smelter steelworkers of Nouvion, in the Aisne, and the reputation of their skills. Around 1900, their number grew and their salaries rose because these were the workers to whom the automobile industry turned for the manufacture of complex molded pieces that were always changing with new models, cylinders, and engine blocs.[75]

And very soon there came, in addition to salaried work, the time of the car mechanics and the engineers for agricultural machinery, followed by the radio and television repairmen. Was this the opportunity to recover the independence of the artisans of long ago, another history? Not really. The arrival of women in the workforce during the interwar period assuredly would lend support for that by facilitating the return of men to the manly trades of skill. Before, in the textile trade of Lille during the Belle Époque, there had been massive hiring of a female workforce that had enabled men to requalify themselves as wool sorters, washers, combers, and transporters by affirming, notwithstanding general opinion, that "to be a wool spinner was to have a trade."[76] World War I was a turning point: the iconography indeed shows it, with women feeding the flow of pig iron or working the lathes. If they were the ones turning the shells, it was the men who adjusted the machines, and if women were the ones who fed the men, got them going, and served them, they never interfered with the machines. The massive arrival of women in the factory—like that of immigrant unskilled workers—might seem to threaten for an instant the manly trades, but it only shifted them, not allowing them to escape back into the autonomy of the artisan. Elsewhere it restored to the image of those screw cutters of the Saint-Etienne cycle "intact masculine sites" when the number of "female screw cutters" was increasing.[77]

New trades, with the same manly references, to be sure, but were they the same men? Most certainly, even from one generation to the next. In the nineteenth century the plasticity of employment was already evident in the recruitment of mechanics from the reservoir of steelworkers and automobile workers in the former sites of metalworking. This reappropriation of traditional skills for new uses was sketched out very early by imperceptible shifts. The turners of steel in the nineteenth century worked first in wood, and there were a number of mechanics in the 1920s who were first forgers, cartwrights, locksmiths, or cabinetmakers. The change took multiple paths: It went through the permanence of the tool, like the poker, inherited by the foundry worker-puddler and now useless. Through the object that was born in the same work but applied to different fabrications: from the Saint-Etienne gunsmith to the cyclic worker, the form follows the same spiral from the machine-gun loader to the gearwheel in the gearbox. Through the excellence and the efficiency of the motion especially, as if these were inscribed in some kind of atavistic skill set, it was the visual sensitivity that qualified the ancient boilermakers when composite fibers revolutionized the aeronautical industry and, in the Saint-Junien (Limousin) of today, it was the sense of precision acquired by the "tawers" and the tanners in the preparation and smoothing

Figure 3.8
The Revolution "took care of its art" and "left its deputies alone."

Figure 3.9
A shoemaking work-
shop for the blind in
Dijon at the beginning
of the century. The intelligence of the hands
made up for visual
deficiencies.

Figure 3.10
A boot maker in
Ménilmontant.

of pelts that turned them into servants of precision machinery in which
one slices metal by the micron.[78]

And yet, to be current in the terminology that exalted the trades, the
congress of workers of 1871 felt in addition that it was finished for the
"artisan"—a word that, in English, has first of all meant skill—and that
they had gotten rid of the artisan's liberty in the "industrial prisons" of
factory discipline and, even before that, in the trend toward rationaliza-
tion. Was not the vocabulary itself a deception? In the faubourg Saint-
Antoine one was, to be sure, a "cabinetmaker," but work was no longer
the same and had not been so for some time. Workers were just repeating
models developed earlier or elsewhere, and the power of creation had fled
in favor of artists, schools, or the state. If one spoke in 1914 of the "makers
of ballet shoes" of Fougères, one was referring to no less than three very
different categories of workers, of which one at least had been reduced

to serve precision manufacturing. Likewise in the interwar period, there were still "foundry workers" in the blast furnaces of Lorraine, but where was their autonomy with respect to the "instrument panel"? And for the mill hand, there remained only the husk of a word.[79]

Contemporary sociologists have laid great stress on the personal tragedy caused by this drop in status. It marks irremediably the memory of the demoted worker in the 1960s after the absorption of his company who had no taste for unskilled work; the mason who builds chimneys now at the age of forty-two, a "feeder" at La Sollac—"so there I was again an unskilled laborer"—the woman whose diploma in sewing and home economics is of no use, who is "one day here, another day there," who says she no longer knows who she is.[80] The task of pinpointing the drop in social status is infinitely more delicate, except when that drop is the subject of conversation by business leaders or is discussed in general terms like that seen in the *Bulletins des usines Renault* of August 1, 1918, which blames the French worker for wanting to be "too universal" and "who knows a little of everything, but nothing in depth," a reference to that apologetic anthem of the unskilled worker and, curiously, an echo of Merrheim denouncing the vanity of the professionals.[81] Dispossession occurs imperceptibly and, especially at the right conjuncture, in a particularly insidious manner. One realizes it when the trade is lost and the words triggered evoke the memory of mourning—always the beauty of death. If the figure of the shoemaker took up the first rank of the trades between 1770 and 1880, it was even then an indication that there were fewer of them. The market was eliminating their traditional role. Changes were occurring that would chase the shoemaker from manufacture to the simple role of maintenance. Like the "songs of the workplace" arising in the nineteenth century, the words of the cabinetmaker Chausse, the clog maker Malinvaud, and the watchmaker Vincent Prost at the first Workers Congress in 1876 had the flavor of a paradise lost and the tint of Rousseauism. *La Fonderie*, the journal of the mold pourers of Paris, dedicated a quarter of its pages, at the beginning of the twentieth century, to technical advice and regularly called attention to innovations in work. At the same time, a machine mold had been developed that would eliminate the delicate work of securing the coupling, the essential part of the skill; the impression runs through these articles that everything was "degenerating" and that everything "was in jeopardy." A final touch, the *clapeuses* of Saint-Etienne, those women who sorted coal, disappeared after 1920. They then intoned the hymns of this "true craft" resting on legends, promoting a memory of exaltation inversely proportional to the scorn of which they were the object, which held them to be coarse, dirty, and libertine, not to mention incapable.[82]

The tone and its ambiguities matter little in the long run. There was a Taylorian turning point in French industry that was seen in outline in the 1880s, was more fully developed in the First World War, and was made prominent in the years afterward, and which depended on the workers' explicit desire to appropriate knowledge in order to "replace them by new men lacking in experience," so wrote C. A. Costaz as early as 1917. To impose new norms of work "against [their] will" was spoken by someone a century before.[83] Rather than turn to Marx and to his commentators, one can simply refer to Adam Smith and his prophetic text, *Wealth of Nations*, which announced that, with the division of work, the "man whose entire life passes in accomplishing a small number of simple operations, the effects of which are perhaps always the same or pretty much the same, [who] never has the opportunity of exercising his intelligence or his faculty for invention to find a way to remove the difficulties that are ever confronting him" ends up "as stupid and as ignorant as is possible."[84] Nor is it a question of resuming the long accusation concerning the effects of his subdivided work and his motivations, from the *rabcors*★ of the 1920s to Marglin or Gorz, after the shock Georges Navel had on entering the Citroën factories in the 1920s or the shock Robert Linhard had fifty years later when faced with "merging into the assembly line, with the repetition of identical gestures, the job never done," "that gray slippage of the line," "the factory's war of death against life, of life against death."[85] It is fallacious to hope to identify in certain appearances recurrences of creativity, intelligence, responsibility in the curse that spares no sector, not even that of the office with its machines, where the new, generic employee is limited to "simple manipulations of paper."[86]

To be sure, there were more intellectuals, before they were identified as such, who denounced the crime of subdivided work than there were workers. Simone Weil was astonished to see some "who did not do that" and who did not have that "concentrated rage that had invaded the heart." To the contrary, the image of the trades was constructed by the turncoats of that world, like Anthème Corbon, eminent defender of the dignity of the work he had left to become deputy and senator. They were the ones who had lost their status and now dreamed of "the proud professionals in immaculate overalls."[87] It was rare that one spoke of work now that the factory and assembly line had become permanent.

The denunciation of the origin of work speaks more to the periphery

★ "Rabcors were workers in hundreds of business enterprises who sent reports on working conditions, strikes, and so on to *L'Humanité* [the communist newspaper in France]." Leopold Trepper, *The Great Game: Memoirs of a Spy Hitler Couldn't Silence* (New York: McGraw Hill, English translation, 1977), 81.—Trans.

1. - CARON Juliette, née le 6 Mai 1882, à Senlis (Oise)
La seule femme en France exerçant le métier de charpentier
Travaillant actuellement aux casernes de Montluçon

of the factory and assembly line. The perversion is elsewhere when routine mediocrity finds itself better paid than skill and autonomy. Already in 1840, in Paris as in Marseille, there was outrage that the unskilled workers were earning more than the workers in the trades. In 1891, a major survey, *Salaire et durée du travail dans l'industrie française* (Salary and time at work in french industry) noted that the salary of the man at the tool machine was higher than that of the fitter, the latter having gone through the discipline and fate of a long apprenticeship. On the eve of 1914, in the spite shown by automobile mechanics for the "makers of boilers," there was also jealousy between the less well paid.[88] It was that raw egoism, seen at the Anzin mines, being rationalized in the 1930s and already anticipated by Merrheim, that pointed to the end of solidarity when the best miners were chosen to standardize the cadences and end reliance on force and dexterity. When the trade vanished, "everyone worked for himself." "All that remained were the low appetites that one satisfied at any price" (Merrheim again). And the workers reacted with hatred for the tool, the machine, the workshop, the family, and one's comrades, in brief with hatred for work itself. Freedom, skill, conviviality, and time took refuge in that form of work known as *bricolage*, handiwork, do-it-yourself. "I know how to do everything," says the worker of today. We will see him again, but in another context.[89] That is quite far from that creative pleasure of which the mechanic Cail dreamed in 1881, and the paradox is that this new *homo faber* finds fulfillment everywhere, except at the core of his manufacturing work.[90] The worker of affluence no longer has a trade, but a job. And it matters little that he does not think of leaving it. He has invested himself elsewhere, in material ease, in family or personal projects that are in line with his accession to mass consumption. Logically, the union is no longer a form of identity, but rather a simple instrument for the defense of one's standard of living.[91]

If we come back to the factory, though, the tableau will require some retouching. What about subjugation by the machine, creator of that "clumsy man" of whom Michel Verret speaks? The one who is all too human, who ends up stealing the gestures of work after having imitated them? The machine itself does not coincide with the "new factory," and the workshops of the nineteenth century are already filled with sewing machines beginning in the 1860s, as well as lathes, drills, and planing machines from the beginning of the Third Republic. Hundreds of minor incidents mark the machine's presence for most of the century in the urban industries—printing, clothes making, woodworking, wallpaper.[92] Yet it is in the machine that the cabinetmakers of Paris in 1890 put part of their experience, since it would relieve them of the most difficult tasks and thus reinforce their creative capacities and thus purge the artist of the gangue, the unwanted components, of manual work, defined and driven by his intelligence alone. It is so familiar, the simple improvement through the tool that extends the hand. In 1874, Louis Reybaud noted that a forge hammer is never a motorized animal, and just because it is more powerful does not mean it is less docile to its creatures. The mechanics of the Second Empire were proud to make their own machines, which remained in their hands, in all senses of the term. One looked for machines on a small scale, like the *jeannettes*, the sleeve boards for ironing, precisely because one could harness them and, as the *Echo de la fabrique* asserted, avoid many troubles, thanks to them.

An entire technical pedagogy had for a long time helped tame machines through innumerable tracts on manufacture and popular periodicals like *Le Journal des connaissances utiles*, started in 1832, or *Les Merveilles de l'industrie*. Then came the grand book of the expositions at the end of the century, with their galleries of machines. After 1871, the workers' congresses were influenced at least as strongly by laments to lost trades through the most vibrant homages to these "instruments of progress." These "instruments" were easy to see and to understand because the secret of artisan skills had until then impeded the necessary diffusion of technical capacity. In the admiration of a Denis Poulot as well, there is, in Michelle Perrot's view, the trace of a certain worker Saint Simonism, all the more reassuring as the machines themselves are the creation of the workers.[93]

●For a long time, the connivance was deep, and that led to all sorts of carelessness: the refusal to stop the machine or to leave its settings to others, leading to a rise in the number of accidents that took away a hand, an arm, or a life in their toils. One might doubt that the thread was ever broken. In 1918, Georges Navel found machines to be quite mysterious, and he admitted little taste for machinery. The mechanics, however, fascinated him because they shared, in their attention to innovation, in the creative universe of the engineers and the inventors. As strange as they might be, machines had something human about them. Man was in them and one saw how they increased the number of trades in their turn by relocating the experience of skills to the requirements of their functioning. One spoke of them in feminine terms at home, in the evening, with one's companions. One dreamed of making them more efficient and, in the twentieth century, one turned to filling up the "suggestion box." The heart breaks to see the men put on the scrap heap; and in a factory like that for cars in the 1960s, the seniority of the journeyman and his capacity to make himself known were marked by the indefinite appointment to one of those machines. From the machines' hierarchy too, depending how difficult or how dirty they were, came the hierarchy of the workers, as if *in fine* the machines remained the sole means of holding onto control

Figure 3.13
The skill outside the factory in do-it-yourself creations, or the dream realized. Raymond Isidore at the window of his home in Chartres, which was entirely decorated with his own hands.

over work over which they had lost mastery, at the heart of a "reignit-
ing" of productive experience by way of dead or crystalized social work,
as Michel Verret, for one, noted.[94]

Then there were the porosities in space and time in the new factory:
the night shift in less of a hurry than the day shift, when an apparatus was
not free, or stopped, that allowed a gain here that one lost elsewhere. During the period 1880 to 1920, there were numerous worker categories that
mitigated the pernicious effects of the intensity of the work, right up to
limiting production. The workers in leathers and hides were, before 1890,
the unskilled worker before being so labeled, little qualified, ill-paid, and
scorned. They were dirty and smelled bad. Nevertheless, they knew how
to play the hot days, which could spoil the hides if they were neglected,
to put forward their demands. And the list is long of the thousand forms
of resistance by workers who had no other assets than their arms. That
resistance got them around the letter or the spirit of the regulations and
enabled them to appropriate for themselves a piece of the space—placards,
the area around the machines with its secret hiding places; and of the technology—through the settings, the changes in the tools used, all difficult
to formalize, and to deflect the constraints of management, doing one's
own work on company time and causing slowdowns, and so forth. They
"stuffed" the machines at the beginning of the day so that they could slack
off at the end without violating standards. At the Berliet factory, it was
the clandestine cigarette, conversation, or the reading of a newspaper in
the bathroom. Elsewhere it was absenteeism or the self-inflicted wound,
and all the time slots made up for by gossip in the yet "very dirty place"
of Simone Weil.[95] In sum, all were signs of the autonomy that marked the
traditional trades, and that the assembly line could never totally shatter,
the autonomy which, with the unskilled worker as well, was not the first
phase of the worker's awareness but, in a productive universe that was so
different, was an immediate and permanent given.[96]

Even that certain joy of work did not entirely disappear, very surprising if one believes the theorists. The most tedious and the most monoto-
nous of tasks, in appearance, may well have been experienced differently
by the person who spent his life at them, and work was rarely hated in
the memory of the workers of today.[97] "It's necessary to do it fast," wrote
Georges Navel about assembling the bearings, "but it is also a game . . .
work well paced, intelligence well used." At the same time, he exploited
the dexterity of his fingers and "the precision and suppleness of each gesture." "When that changes, you have to think about the job it does," said
some metal trimmers from Lyons in 1949, who expressed the desire to
remain as long as possible on one piece, since "it is the hand that does
it." The juxtaposition of languages is astonishing. "To finish the things

is to finish the work," in the words of a sheet-metal welder in 1970, who sings all the more loudly as the machine devours him, in Jacques Frémontier's analysis. "The weld, it's really beautiful . . ." Because one loves one's (new) trade, does that deny the fact that one has been downgraded? With the unskilled worker there is the confirmed reference to an artisan's trade with its variety, its quality, and its independence because when one cannot suppress reality, one takes refuge in the dream, as Michelle Perrot once noted.[98]

Not just that. To be sure, the vitality of the old nomenclature remains, and in the automobile factories of the twentieth century a person is still called *compagnon*. Is it not, however, blindness to look for the skills of the tradesmen of years gone by only in the quality of the individuals alone? "The more the pieceworker is incomplete and even imperfect, the more he is perfect as part of the collective worker,"[99] to quote Marx, but his remark has another meaning and, by putting the accent on the collectivity, it goes to the heart of the analysis. The zones of autonomy of the unskilled worker are not personal; they are shared with people like himself, through codes and languages, like the hatmakers, woodworkers or cabinetmakers in the workshops of the nineteenth century. These were the ones who, as individuals fragmented by the individuality of the tasks that formed the basis of employer management, reconstituted the communities that were also, and perhaps at first, the traditional trades. They did not need to remember, since, as was seen, the workers in the trades, who were now labeled unskilled workers, were always there, within the factory, and even more numerous and varied. They had only to imitate them, those men who existed especially through a certain control over the technical management that seniority and their working-class origins conferred on them. These then were the unskilled workers who, in their turn, stopped work when the equipment was obsolete or badly maintained, because the pieces were defective or because the "line" was poorly organized. What followed was the wildcat strike, specific to one team or one workshop, without warning or union support, right at the heart of the production process, to show that without you—that shared, collective professional cadre with an efficiency that was at least as tough as that of the professional secrets of old, and the contours of which adhered to the community whose identity they expressed—production stopped.[100]

What made the unskilled workers of De Dion in Languedoc and elsewhere, at the end of the nineteenth century, as much as the work itself did, was their peasant origins. Those working in Brasier automobiles at Rennes had been fishermen or vine growers. Men from Limoges were recruited by the Compagnie de l'Est in Paris after a nonpaid probation of several weeks. None of these were without the tradition or memory enabling them to master in a moment the ways and rhythms of industrial work.[101] A trade then was not only a skill, it was a community and its memory, which for a long time were just part of the geography. They were squeezed into the specialized quarters of the large cities: the jewelers flocked to the rue de la Temple in Paris, the bookbinders to the faubourg Saint-Germain, the mechanics to Popincourt. Faubourg Saint-Antoine especially did not quite form a single factory in the nineteenth century, since it was torn between the perpetual movement of the cabinetmakers between the first factories and the artisan shops and domestic workplaces. Even at the end of the century, the topography of Lyons was a shared arrangement of trades, between the Croix Rousse of the silk workers and the La Guillotière* of the glassworkers and the metalworkers. In Saint-Etienne, each to his own hill—the miners here, the gunsmiths there, and over there the *passementiers*, the makers of the decorative gold or lace for chairs. Just about everywhere along the water's edge one perceives the density of the "people of the river," the boatmen, as well as the tanners of hides and the dyers. And if the mining and steel towns with their *corons,* or houses, had other purposes, they did gather into one limited space those whom the same work joined together.[102]

But there was another faubourg, on the scale of France, which was shaped by the journeys of the *compagnons* in the nineteenth century, where skill was synonymous with mobility, thanks to varying circumstances and distant opportunities. The geography of the tours of the *compagnons* certainly did not draw its inspiration from chance encounters, with its network of compulsory urban stopping places. When those faded, the mobility of the trade workers became part of the same reticulated logic of the route marked out by the similarity of manufactures. Great travelers like the mechanics and fitters saw the geography of their journey change simply with the renewal and increase of sites in a sector of permanent change. The men from Le Creusot in Burgundy came and went between the Schneider armaments factory and its machine shops in the countryside and area around Lyons, before heading to the first automobile factories in the suburbs of Paris. It was the same in Genoa. It applied to the tawers, always on the road between Millau in the southwest and Annonay south of Lyons, or Grenoble and Chaumont to the east, as well as to the glassmakers wandering like nomads from one glassworks to another, starting in Carmaux, apprenticed at Sin-le-Noble, "big boys" at Rive-de-Gier, glassblowers at Choisy-le-Roy, in a life's trajectory that lasted into the 1920s. At the same time, did not Georges Navel see in the restlessness of

* These are regions of Lyon.

the building laborers, which meant everyone involved, "one day here, eight days there," the sure sign of their proletarian essence?[103]

In that perpetual wandering, the sharing of the trade belonged to family members, distant relations, and the fraternities back home. With the miners, up to 1914, the circle of the family was nourished by "tales from the mine" in those patriarchal households where the father was the model one dreamt of imitating. Therein lay the secret of the heredity of this "race," founded on a true tribal memory, and in the middle of the nineteenth century, the nomenclatures of the first professional censuses made reference to this patrilineal transmission of the trades well before Le Play and his school turned it into the chief prescription for their utopia by putting the pairs master–journeyman and father–son in parallel.*[104] The new teams in the large factories had no other foundation. The team for the blast furnace was not a simple addition of individual skills; it drew support from a practical collective as well. And in the car-manufacturing concern of Panhard-Levassor, previously a woodworking business, which employed 1,200 workers in 1905, the woodworking machines were operated by small teams who recruited their own members. Right here we find links to family background and distant cousins. The same was true in the glassworks industry and in some machine shops. Yet just as the authority of the mining engineer stopped at the coal face—a small workshop with two to twenty members, bound together by common work but who also saw each other in town—coercion and surveillance were exercised only at the peripheries of the [metallurgy] industry, [confined to] materials handling, for example. In this instance, the team became united not just through traditional personal ties but also through the complementarity of the trades.[105] Friendly relationships established the unity of the factory or its branches, along with a certain tempo, created from the noise and the smells, that grand rhythm of the machines sung by Mayakovsky and close friends, not to mention the contribution of connivance and complicity. Your companion was the person who shared the same motions, with whom you shared bread and wine, for whom you substituted in case of absence, whom you helped out when necessary because he had slowed down or was getting on in years. This was camaraderie, that *Kameradschaft* of the German miners, that was reinforced by the solidarity of the struggles and that, practically everyday, lived on sparring, roughhousing, jokes, and rituals. There were other means, just as important and within the mutual recognition by those communities "with active hands and a quick and alert tongue," revealing a mixture

* Pierre Guillaume Frédéric Le Play (1806–82), engineer, sociologist, and economist, who collected and analyzed material on the working classes of Europe.—Trans.

of moral density and rituals.[106] Who did not recognize in that the supposed fraternity of the workshops of the nineteenth century, even if that included a touch of deceptive nostalgia?

In the last analysis, the trade, or whatever served for that, remained the accepted framework through which the entire ascent of a life progressed without ever leaving the conditions of working-class life. That is indeed the reason why, if women work, they rarely have trades, notes Michelle Perrot. It was long thought a matter of a technological frame of mind that was also dexterous, meticulous, and supple, with a supple body and agile fingers, according to Paul Leroy-Beaulieu and Jules Simon. From weaving and the clothing of yesterday to the assembly of microprocessors, have the words and realities changed? Alas, only with the "copyists of the first order." So, there we are, it seems, and all the apprenticeships in the world can do nothing about it. Still the reason lies elsewhere: for women, work and its types of trade constitute only one moment of existence, and the communities of apprenticeship in the family, or the sewing circle, are ephemeral. Clothing, sewing, fabrics—do they not come before office jobs? The nature of work and the acquired capacities can well transcend places and generations, but they do not create an identity or a permanent community, since they constitute a single moment of life, before marriage or the first child, unless it is work after the last child or as a widow. The laundresses of Saint-Étienne, though proud of their washhouse and their rough, gossipy language and the hint of a career, admitted their inexistence by dressing in blue work overalls during Lent just to ape the men.[107] "It is not a career just sewing breeches, underpants, and stuff like that," says a worker of today.[108] Conversely, if the hierarchy of a mining team is so completely internalized, it is not just that it marks the barriers and the levels as well as the way to advance: work on the timber frame at fourteen, cart pusher—he pushes the tubs—at fifteen, miner's assistant at twenty, and foreman at twenty-five. Similarly in the glassmaking and steel industries—there were eighteen levels and fourteen qualifications in working steel at Forges et Aciéries de l'Est in Valenciennes around 1920 for the top ranks. There were forty and thirty-six for the medium-qualified, and seven at the lowest level. In the logging industry, for one starting out, progressive qualifications followed the progressive mastery of the trade, and the trade did not abandon one when one's strength declined: from repairman one became an official for surveillance at forty-five and for the timber work at fifty-five. The trade provided security with the onset of old age. Even today, the entry into metalworking, when one begins one's life at work, brings with it the memory of an extraordinary ascent.

The first *Dictionnaire des professions*, published in 1842 by E. Charton, member of the Institut de France, did not define in terms of career. Its intention was rather to propose a guide indicating for each entry "the methods of establishment, the chances of advancement and of success, the duties" even though the author was not really taking into consideration the "mechanical arts."[109] We are thus once again at the recurrence of a society of orders founded on competencies, guaranteed henceforth by "jurors" of another sort by which, on entering the trade, one was assured of a position—an estate—in life and in society. The factory at its most basic reproduced in its way the clarity of a tripartite hierarchy—the master, the journeyman, and the apprentice—and clarified the rules, the fluidity of their limits, and the final distinctions, signifying that there was competence to be acquired and accessibility to all. The censuses of the nineteenth century for a long time had difficulty in distinguishing the masters from the journeymen, which no doubt reflected the reality of French industry, which was not moving forward; the true point of division was with the unskilled manual laborers, who had neither specialized knowledge nor any future.[110]

Even today is it not said that "between the professionals and the unskilled workers there is no agreement"?[111] For the price of greatness and luck in the trades is the scorn of others, and the system of marriage alliances serves to demonstrate, if it were required, the repugnance people have, even outside of work, to mix with each other in that "petit-bourgeois illusion of difference" so strong among the metalworkers of the nineteenth century.[112] From the time of the Second Empire, that illusion was spreading among the railroad mechanics of the Compagnie du Nord, who were troublemakers for their bosses and were scornful of the simple railway worker all the more because they were part of them. As for the aristocracy of the metalworkers in the first automobile industry—the mill workers, the fitters, and the wood turners who wore a blue outfit and a cap—it was an aristocracy that took pains not to be confused with the men who did the body work and merely assembled the car and wore blouses and clogs. Condescension simply changed direction in Les Batignolles factory in Nantes when, in the twentieth century, the work of the boilermaker was stripped down and that of the welder became professional.★[113] Inside the same sector there was hardly any tenderness. The core group had nothing in common with any egalitarian community. The bully could behave like a tyrant. He pretended to ignore the weaker men; he shoved the young around and bombarded them with scatological insults as well as blows. In the steel plant at Longwy, around 1920, the maintenance workers refused to repair the tools of those "whom they did not like the looks of" or

★ In 1917, the Société de construction des batignolles (avenue de Clichy à Paris) built a factory in Nantes for the manufacture and repair of locomotives.—Trans.

made them wait around for a few days.[114] As for the apprenticeship, it was often based on crushing the inexperienced. The bullies laughed when the hammer hurt the inexpert hand, and during the July Monarchy, violent death or suicide sometimes occurred. Norbert Truquin never forgot in later years the lashes by rope he took. Jean Baptiste Dumay suffered kicks, Eugène Saulnier the hostility of "drunken louts"; it was advisable to get out of their way. The worker's memory of today more often becomes the echo of bullying than of good times.[115]

Apprenticeship in fact had the harshness of a rite of passage. Some clearly could not restrict themselves to merely conveying a skill even if it were totally visible. Trying to control this was a constant effort by the union at the end of the nineteenth century. Talk was not supposed to deceive, it was supposed to evoke competence. The real issue was the removal of the outsider, since the dream to pass the trade on to one's heirs had never completely disappeared. The feeling of belonging was a reference as well to the seniority of condition, marking the line from the father in every case. The boilermakers of Les Batignolles said that explicitly, confronting the neoworkers that the welders had been for so long, whose work was limited to earning one's livelihood.[116] When Navel began his apprenticeship in 1918, he was taught to cut straight, but he was also told to sweep out the workshop, do the shopping, and perform other services. Those were the conditions, finally, for being admitted.[117] The community was itself sufficiently polymorphous that there were a thousand ways of learning and joining. What remains today of the trades as a "powerful contribution," as Denis Segrestin has said, is there to illuminate the past. Those typographers, longshoremen, maritime students who behind the appearance of resistance limited to modernity have been able to successfully negotiate the technological changes of the last two decades have emerged from a vigorous apprenticeship in good form. And what would they have done with motions that had become obsolete? The only reason those motions remained was that they had acquired resistance through tradition reinforced by the incertitudes of the market in sectors marked at all times by high instability. It is clear: the "worker's custom" is quite something else besides the preservation of technical skills. This brings us back again to the Vichy myth in which the Charter of Work claimed to recreate in 1943 the community of trades, starting with essential forms. Vanity aside, dismantling the industrial economy was impossible, as it also meant forgetting that the journeymen of the nineteenth century were the vanguard of worker protest, if not revolutionary planning. And for cause![118]

And what if the golden legend of trades were nothing but illusory talk? Jacques Rancière has denounced the centrality of this "worker myth," imagining those artisans of long ago as the defenders of the "good work" and of a culture where the hand was in accord with intelligence. Likewise, the doubtful legend of the shoemakers and their reputation as thinkers was rather an openness to the world and a knowledge, spanning the towns and villages and based on practical experience, where it was illicit to link professional practice and an aptitude for thinking and writing. Does not qualification, according to Jacques Rancière, mean something more than a lottery ticket? Under the July Monarchy, any mason who knew how to read a plan was still not far from being a domestic in the eyes of society, and if the tailor and the typographer seemed to be at the top, that was due less to their knowledge than to their proximity to the elite whose sumptuary and intellectual needs they satisfied. More generally, promotion in the evolving career of the trade was an effect of a manager's decision, dictated by the conjunction of circumstances and production needs rather than the recompense of an apprenticeship. As to the family background of the miners, and certain metalworkers, the effect of the attractive image of the father is visible. How could it be otherwise in cities where large industry was the only horizon and where elementary school prepared one for nothing else?[119]

Today it is doubtful that the radicalism of the shoemakers can be explained by imagined interior monologues to which the solitary exercise of making shoes supposedly disposed them. Sociologists find no evidence of similarity between the exercise of a trade and the collective behavior of the practitioners of that trade. Union traditionalism is not the necessary consequence of such a work situation. Conversely, the vitality of the trade does not stand in contradiction to a strong class sentiment or solidarity that, as the poet-worker Poncy in the nineteenth century wrote, "exists among us . . . an admirable thing and a dream held in common from which no link could be detached without it all shattering to pieces."[120] And the same words and the same apparent references, it must not be forgotten, may have produced, up to the Second World War in any case, nostalgia and plans that had nothing in common with proletarian eschatologies but yet were powerful enough, during the Vichy times, to bring back certain leaders of the CGT from before 1939. Meanings became confused with the polysemy of the words, and we are entitled to ask the reason for these contradictory recurrences right at the heart of the world of work that for some time was no longer the workshop of the artisan. In the companies of the 1970s, were not the "unhappy ones" those, it was said, who did not have a trade?[121]

The history of socioprofessional classifications sheds some illumination. Without doubt, recognition starts with the seminal cleavage, at the end of the nineteenth century, brought by the connection to the wage earner. And the collective conventions of 1936, continued in the job classification Parodi grids of 1946, seem to get locked into the trilogy of the highly skilled worker in a trade, the unskilled worker, and the unskilled manual worker, but they do this using a complex combination of criteria that takes into account the task to be accomplished, the degree of responsibility, and prior training, meaning apprenticeship, even if that had theoretically occurred outside the factory and was known to be part of a universe much larger than simple technical pedagogy. Beyond the figures imposed by the state and its analytical instruments—the INSEE, the INED, the Planning Administration, and so forth,* this combination of criteria absolutely rejects the ideal type of trade worker, notwithstanding the declarations of those concerned who have difficulty in slipping into the rationality of taxonomies. The *Dictionnaire des professions* of the INSEE of 1955 has to recognize more than 12,000 different terms for people in trades and 1,129 trades in which the *aconniers* (bargemen), and the eight kinds of *abatteurs* (the men who fell trees, slaughter animals, blast the coal faces, etc.), are included with the *ramoneurs* (the go-devils, the men who clean out the oil pipelines, the earlier term for chimney sweep) and the *radaristes* (radar operators). When in the 1970s the new PSP (*professions et catégories socioprofessionelles*) were introduced to replace "trade" with "job" through a standardized division in the chain of production, Force ouvrière, one of the five major union federations in France, protested and proposed a grid built on multifunctional trades adaptable in themselves to all the professional branches and industrial sectors.[122]

The Popular Front, it is true, by creating here and there workshop delegates, matched up the electoral colleges with the organization of the trade. In the book trade could one even conceive of a book trimmer speaking for a linotypist? The case of the glass industry is even more striking: the trade disappeared a good fifty years ago, and making flat glass has for a long time had nothing in common with the manufacture of hollowed-out glass. Nevertheless the Fédération de la CGT changed neither the term nor the identification code, and even though it had disappeared as a form of work, the trade of the glassworker survives through an organization that constantly tries to get conventional texts passed with management and recognized by public authorities. It is the same for the men in the book trade and the longshoremen whose registered members over

---

* The INSEE (Institut national de la statistique et des études économiques), created in 1946, is the government agency that collects and publishes information about the French economy and society. It also carries out the national census. The INED (Institut national d'études démographiques), created in 1945, is a government agency that works and publishes reports on demographic issues, studying material and moral means that might contribute to the population's quantitative augmentation and qualitative amelioration.—Trans.

the last decades seek to fix in the textbooks that which has been erased from reality.

A persistent sign of archaism? The obstinate attachment to the past and refusal to abandon an inevitably condemned preindustrial model of organization? The longing for an immutable order of qualifications and worker jobs? Is it a fight doomed to failure? Denis Segrestin has shown the real and successful handling of the inevitable technological changes. Over time, the meaning of the trade is something else: a social logic, as opposed to an economic logic, is henceforth part of the enterprise, as is the rejection of a trade unionism by industry that would be, according to the CGT, the "negation of true professional trade unionism." We are far from the "new working class" of the prophets of the 1960s, who were perhaps a little too anxious. True trade unionism is less and less the sharing of a skill. Rather it relies on a community of culture, history, and collective memory, everything that was formerly called the "working custom."[123] The spokesmen for their demands, chosen as in the years 1871–90 among the workers of the factory, had that in them as least as much as the level of their professional qualifications.[124]

We are then at that "birth of the trades," paradoxically announced in contemporary France by Geneviève Latreille, and, with the service sector, the trades of nurses and social workers who are constrained to "invent tradition." That "birth" passes through a kind of "groupism" or "sets" made up of sociabilities and discussions that occur outside work, the gestures of which would be difficult to pinpoint. These motions bring about in their turn a collective identity that transcends the job and defines a role that goes beyond a common way of being labeled.[125] The definition turned out to be simplistic when Halbwachs, in 1912, made a trade interdependent with a technique, a level of salary, and structure of work. Women were not mistaken when they grumbled at being dismissed after the war in 1918–19. They lost some material advantages, but what they mainly lost was membership in a community and all its cultural trappings, all the more precious because the trades termed feminine forbade them access to things like tradition.

"There will always be furniture makers, there will always be mechanics." The dream of the trade is expressed in any way possible unless it is through what one manufactures. For once Navel was absolutely right when he justified work by the immediate social utility of the object: "You always looked at the boats," he said in Nantes at the shipyards.[126] The shoemakers had taught "the knowledge of their misfortune," as Merrheim would later say, less in the gestures and the skills of their shop than in an early access to writing—there were poets, journalists, songwriters, and preachers—which permitted them, sooner than it did others, to feel,

Figure 3.14
Jean Gabin in Jean Renoir's *La Bête humaine*, 1938.

Figure 3.15
A locomotive, symbol of France, in the parade of Jean-Paul Goude on the Champs Élysées on the occasion of the bicentenary of the French Revolution, 1989.

to say, and to write the forms of a collective identity. For "being of the trade" even today is, beyond the transformations in the economy and in society, to be inscribed in a line and a polymorphic memory—even if one has to establish or invent them—that transcend life. And therein without doubt resides the ambiguity of technical teaching, which in the aftermath of the Astier Law of 1919 was limited to an apprenticeship of techniques even if it ignored the intellectual training without which, in the time of the trades, the skill would have been limited to a repetition of motions without the necessary creativity. In so doing, it set aside the social and indeed the political aspects at a time when it was only in the market and in the shared experience of work that a collection of competencies could become a trade, that collective entity made by history and thus by memory.[127]

Once again, is this not speaking in the place of others? That shadow a trade makes, is it not the deceptive reflection of French historiography that for a long time did not tackle the history of work except through that of the workers' movement using deduction and reasoning rather than empirical analysis? This historiography would not have found the trade when it continued to trace the form of demands and collective actions, which elsewhere in England, the United States, and Germany took such a different path. The fact remains that those young workers certified by a mediocre CAP in the period right after the war dreamt no less of an (imaginary?) autonomy of a trade. And there are families today, who,

Figure 3.16
Equipment for the amateur. Catalogue, *Manufacture d'armes et cycles*, at Saint-Étienne, tools for making arms and bicycles.

when asked, express their hope that their children will have "in their hands"—what a trap these words are!—"a good trade."[128]

NOTES

The interested reader may wish to refer to the essays by Michelle Perrot, "Les vies ouvrières," and by Louis Bergeron, "L'Âge industriel," in volume 3 of *Les Lieux de mémoire*.

1. William Sewell, *Gens de métier et révolutions: Le Langage du travail de l'ancien régime à 1848* (Paris: Aubier-Montaigne, 1983), 338–52. (Trans. of author's *Work and Revolution in France: The Language of Labor from the Old Regime to 1848* [New York: Cambridge University Press, 1980].)

2. Robert Paxton, *La France de Vichy, 1940–1944* (Paris: Éd. du Seuil, 1973), 207–8. (Trans. of author's *Vichy France: Old Guard and New Order, 1940–1944* (New York: Random House, 1972].) Christian Faure, *Le Project culturel de Vichy* (Lyons: Presses universitaires de Lyon, 1987), 115ff.

3. Sewell, 17ff.

4. Ibid., 219ff.

5. Ronald Aminzade, *Class, Politics, and Early Industrial Capitalism: A Study of Mid-Nineteenth Century Toulouse, France* (Albany: State University of New York Press, 1981).

6. Jacques Rancière, *La Nuit des prolétaires: Archives du rêve ouvrier* (Paris: Fayard, 1981), 19, 20, 223.

7. *Un ouvrier en 1820: Manuscrit inédit de Jacques Étienne Bené*, introduction and notes by Rémy Gossez (Paris: PUF, 1984).

8. Sewell, 308–11.

9. Alain Touraine, Michel Wieviorka, and François Dubet, *Le Mouvement ouvrier* (Paris: Fayard, 1984), 28.

10. Bernard H. Moss, *Aux origines du mouvement ouvrier français: Le Socialisme des ouvriers de métier, 1830–1914* (Paris: Les Belles Lettres, 1985), 29. (Trans. of author's *The Origins of the French Labor Movement, 1830–1914: The Socialism of the Skilled Workers* [Berkeley: University of California Press, 1976].)

11. Ibid., 21; Sewell, 214ff., 318.

12. Sewell, 17, 18, 40; Moss, 32.

13. Sewell, 249, 250.

14. Sewell, 256, 265, 266, 277, and passim.

15. Note, however, the reservations of Rancière and the debate that they have fueled; *International Labor and Working Class History* 24 (1983): 1–26.

16. Sewell, 83, 225–28, 237, 284; Moss, 20, 21, 41.

17. Quoted by Rancière, *International Labor and Working-Class History*, 24 (1983): 48.

18. Eric Hobsbawm and Joan W. Scott, "Political Shoemakers," *Past and Present* 89 (1980): 86–88.

19. Moss, 25, 26, 33,34; J. Rougerie, *Procès des communards* (Paris: Julliard, 1964), 128–32.

20. Michelle Perrot, *Les Ouvriers en grève, France, 1871–1890* (Paris: La Haye, Mouton, 1974), 1:341, 361, 362; 2:508, 509.

21. Christian Gras, "L'Ouvrier mouleur à travers le journal de sa fédération, *La Fonderie, 1900–1909," Le Mouvement social* 53 (1965): 57.

22. Perrot, 1:344, 345, 386.

23. Quoted by Jacques Julliard, *Autonomie ouvrière: Études sur le syndicalisme d'action directe* (Paris: Gallimard-Éditions du Seuil, 1988), 118.

24. Michel Verret, *Le Travail ouvrier* (Paris: Armand Colin, 1982), 140; Perrot, 1:392, 393; 2:429, 430, 487.

25. Moss, 33, 34; Julliard, 11.

26. Gras, 52.

27. Patrick Fridenson, "Les Premiers ouvriers français de l'automobile, 1890–1914, " *Sociologie du travail* 3 (1979): 302; James Laux, "Travail et travailleurs dans l'industrie automobile jusqu'en 1914," *Le Mouvement social* 81 (1972): 20.

28. François Caron, "Essai historique d'une pyschologie du travail: Les Mécaniciens et chauffeurs de locomotive du réseau du Nord de 1850 à 1910," *Le Mouvement social* 50 (1965): 26, 27.

29. According to an agreement reached by the Fédération de la métallurgie in 1906, "the federation of mold pourers justifies an exception in any case because it embraces a well defined trade which, by its special professional nature, encounters no difficulty in setting limits to its recruitment." See also Gras, 68.

30. Perrot, 1:342; Yves Lequin, *Les Ouvriers de la région lyonnaise dans la seconde moitié du XIXe siècle, 1848–1914* (Lyons: Presses universitaires de Lyon, 1977), 1:298ff.; Patrick Fridenson, "France–États-Unis: Genèse de l'usine nouvelle," *Recherches* 32–33 (1978): 379, 380; Jean Lorcin, "Un essai de stratigraphie sociale: Chefs d'ateliers et compagnons dans la grève des passementiers de Saint-Étienne en 1900," *Cahiers d'histoire* 13 (1968): 191, 192; Serge Bonnet, *La Ligne rouge des hauts fourneaux* (Nancy: Édition Serpenoise, 1981), 281ff.; Julliard, 370ff.

31. Georges Friedmann, *Le Travail en miettes* (Paris: Gallimard, 1964), 150, 151 (English trans. by Wyatt Rawson, *Labor, Leisure, and the Implications of Automation* [New York: Free Press of Glencoe, 1962]); Claude Durand, "Conditions, objectives et orientations de l'action syndicale," *Le Mouvement social* 61 (1967): 76–80.

32. Perrot, 1:227, 228; Georges Navel, *Travaux* (Paris: Stock, 1945), 186; Gérard Noiriel, *Longwy, Immigrés et prolétaires, 1880–1990* (Paris: PUF, 1984), 31, 32.

33. Perrot, 1:384; Marc Lazar, "L'Ouvrier imaginaire du Parti communiste français," *Annales ESC* 5 (1990): 1071–96.

34. Quoted by Odette Hardy, *Industrie, patronat et ouvriers du Valenciennois pendant le premier vingtième siècle* (Thesis, Université de Lille, n.d.), 1, 2.

35. Eric Hobsbawn, "Man and Woman in Socialist Iconography," *History Workshop* 6 (1978): 121–38.

36. Perrot, 1:232ff.

37. Jean-Paul Burdy, Mathilde Dubesset, and Michelle Zancarini, "Rôles, travaux et métiers de femmes dans une ville industrielle, Saint-Étienne 1900–1950, " *Le Mouvement social* 140 (1987): 27, 34–36.

38. Georges Navel, *Passages* (Paris: Le Sycomore, 1982), 238; Noiriel, 32, 52; Caron, 5; Joël Michel, *Le Mouvement ouvrier chez les mineurs d'Europe occidentale (Grande-Bretagne, Belgique, France, Allemagne): Étude comparative des années 1880 à 1914* (Thesis, Université Lyon II, 1987), 118–26.

39. Simone Weil, *La Condition ouvrière* (Paris: Gallimard, 1951), 52, 53.

40. Joëlle Deniot, "Métiers ouvriers," *Sociologie du travail* 3 (1983): 359.

41. *Le Cri du peuple*, April 22, 1884, cited by Perrot, 1:340.

42. Michel, 142, 178.

43. Hardy, 1.

44. Michel Verret, *La Culture ouvrière* (Saint-Sébastien: ADL-CROCUS, 1988), 23ff.

45. Navel, *Travaux*, 187, 188.

46. Weil, 52.

47. Georges Friedmann, *Où va le travail humain?* 3rd ed. (Paris: Gallimard, 1963), 37–39.

48. Sewell, 357.

49. Navel, *Travaux*, 183–86.

50. Fridenson, "Les Premiers ouvriers," 316.

51. Navel, *Travaux*, 231.

52. Jacques Frémontier, *La Vie en bleu: Voyage en culture ouvrière* (Paris: Fayard, 1980), 79.

53. Friedmann, *Où va le travail*, 351, 363.

54. Yvette Lucas, "L'Aéronautique, une industrie productrice de savoir-faire," *Le Mouvement social* 145 (1988): 45.

55. Verret, *La Culture ouvrière*, 25ff.; Michel, 178ff.

56. Louis Reybaud, *Le Fer et la houille* (Paris: M. Lévy, 1874), 44–47; Noiriel, 31, 32.

57. Noiriel, 45, 46.

58. Navel, *Travaux*, 72.

59. *Cultures du travail: Identités et savoirs industriels dans la France contemporaine* (Paris: Édition de la Maison des sciences de l'homme, 1989), 4, 5.

60. Sian Reynolds, "Allemagne avant l'allemanisme: Jeunesse d'un militant, 1843–1880," *Le Mouvement social* 126 (1984): 9.

61. Michel, 164, 167; Friedmann, *Où va le travail*, 360ff.

62. Cynthia J. Koepp, "The Alphabetical Order: Work in Diderot's *Encyclopédie*," in *Work in France: Representations, Meaning, Organization, and Practice*, ed. Steven L. Kaplan and Cynthia J. Koepp (Ithaca: Cornell University Press, 1986), 247ff.

63. Navel, *Travaux*, 72, 87.

64. Michel, 161ff.

65. Noiriel, 46, 47.

66. Navel, *Travaux*, 183–88.

67. Noiriel, 51; Yves Lequin, "L'Apprentissage en France au XIXe siècle: Rupture ou continuité?" *Formation-Emploi* 27–28 (1989): 98, 99.

68. Gras, 56.

69. *Cultures du travail*, 20, 21

70. Moss, 29; Michell Perrot, "Les Ouvriers et les machines en France dans la première moitié du XIXe siècle," *Recherches* 32–33 (1978), 349; Leora Auslander, *The Creation of Value and the Production of Good Taste: The Social Life of Furniture in Paris, 1860–1914* (Ph.D. thesis, Brown University, 1988).

71. Moss, 31; Noiriel, 46, 47; Touraine, Wieviorka, Dubet, 133; Michel, 134–48; Laurent Marty, *Chanter pour survivre: Culture ouvrière, travail et techniques dans le textile; Roubaix, 1850–1914* (Lille: Fédération Léo-Lagrange, 1982), 48ff.; Bernard Charlot and Madeleine Figeat, *Histoire de la formation des ouvriers, 1789–1984* (Paris: Minerve, 1985), 41.

72. Friedmann, *Où va le travail*, 354ff.

73. Noiriel, 129, 143, 147ff.; Gras, 57; Laux, 10, 11; Lucas, 98, 107; Nicolas Bourginat, *Conception et exercice d'une politique sociale d'entreprise: Péchinery dans la vallée de l'Arc de 1896 à 1921* (Thesis, Université Paris-IV, n.d.), 111ff.

74. Verret, *Le travail*, 41ff.; Noiriel, 143.

75. Laux, 12; Navel, *Travaux*, 84–91.

76. Marty, 48ff.; Fridenson, "France–États-Unis," 78; Sylvie Zerner, "De la couture aux presses: L'Emploi féminin entre les deux guerres," *Le Mouvement social* 140 (1987): 21; Perrot, *Les Ouvriers en grève,* 1:361, 362.

77. Michelle Perrot, "Qu-est-ce qu'un métier de femme," *Le Mouvement social* 140 (1987): 5–8; Madeleine Guilbert, "Les Problèmes du travail industriel des femmes et de l'évolution des techniques," *Le Mouvement social* 61 (1967): 34, 35; Zerner, 22.

78. *Cultures du travail*, 35, 124ff., 166; Navel, *Passages*, 238, 239; Perrot, "Les Ouvriers et les machines," 370; Noiriel, 147, 148.

79. Perrot, *Les Ouvriers en grève*, 2:518; Noiriel, 145; Bernard Legendre, "La Vie d'un proletariat: Les Ouvriers de Fougères au début du XXe siècle," *Le Mouvement social* 98 (1977): 10.

80. Frémontier, 76–79; Serge Mallet, *La Nouvelle classe ouvrière* (Paris: Éd. du Seuil, 1963), 121, 122; Patrice Augereau, *Les Événements dans la mémoire des ouvriers* (Thesis, Université de Nantes, 1981), 83–88.

81. Fridenson, "Les Premiers ouvriers," 318.

82. Hobsbawm and Scott, 105, 108, 115; Perrot, *Les Ouvriers en grève*, 1:296, 382, 383; Gras, 57; Burdy, Dubesset, and Zancarini, 46.

83. Perrot, "Les Ouvriers et les machines," 352; Fridenson, "France–États-Unis," 375, 386, 387; Aimée Moutet, "Patrons de progrès ou patrons de combat: La Politique de rationalisation de l'industrie française au lendemain de la Première Guerre mondiale," *Recherches* 32–33 (1978): 455.

84. Quoted by Friedmann, *Où va le travail*, 350.

85. Robert Linhardt, *L'Établi* (Paris: Éd. de Minuit, 1978), 13; Navel, *Travaux*, 110; André Gorz, ed., *Critique de la division du travail* (Paris: Éd. du Seuil, 1973), 47, 96, 101; Sylvie Schweitzer, *Des engrenages à la chaine: Les Usines Citroën, 1915–1935* (Lyons: Presses universitaires de Lyon, 1982), 117ff.

86. M. Ponthière, *Le Bureau-moteur, fonction et organisation des bureaux* (Paris: Delmas, 1935), 262, quoted by Zerner, 23, 24.

87. Frémontier, 282; see also Weil, 40; and Rancière, 11, 12, 49, 69.

88. Perrot, *Les Ouvriers en grève*, 1:337; Hobsbawm and Scott, 337; Laux, 10, 11.

89. Frémontier, 93; Fridenson, "Les Premiers ouvriers . . . de l'automobile," 320, 321; Verret, *Le Travail*, 37; Odette Hardy, "Rationalisation technique et rationalisation du travail à la Mine d'Anzin, 1927–1938," *Le Mouvement social* 72 (1970): 37.

90. Perrot, *Les Ouvriers en grève*, 1:290; Friedmann, *Où va le travail*, 405.

91. J. H. Goldthorpe, D. Lockwood, F. Bechhofer, and J. Platt, *L'Ouvrier de l'abondance* (Paris: Éd. du Seuil, 1972), 14–16 (translation of *The Affluent Worker: Industrial Attitudes and Behavior* [London: Cambridge University Press, 1968]); Friedmann, *Où va le travail*, 121.

92. Moss, 28–31; Perrot, "Les Ouvriers et les machines," 1:355; Verret, *La Culture*, 26.

93. Perrot, "Les Ouvriers et les machines," 1:335; David Landes, *L'Europe technicienne*, trans. Louis Évrard (Paris: Gallimard, 1974), 211, 212 (trans. of *The Unbound Prometheus: Technological Change and Industrial Development in Western Europe from 1750 to the Present* [London: Cambridge University Press, 1969]).

94. Verret, *La Culture*, 26, 27; Navel, *Travaux*, 84; Perrot, *Les Ouvriers en grève*, 1:238, 239; Fridenson, "France–États-Unis," 375; Philippe Bernoux, *Un travail à soi* (Toulouse: Privat, 1981), 26ff.; Bernoux, "La Résistance ouvrière à la rationalisation: La Réappropriation du travail," *Sociologie du travail* 1 (1979): 411.

95. Navel, *Travaux*, 86, 110; Perrot, *Les Ouvriers en grève*, 2:389, 390; Fridenson, "France–États-Unis," 378, 379; Bernoux, "La Résistance ouvrière," 423.

96. Julliard, 13.

97. Augereau, 75, 76, 94.

98. Navel, *Travaux*, 110, 238; Friedmann, *Le Travail*, 53; Frémontier, 82, 87.

99. Quoted by Gorz, 25.

100. See Bernoux, 25, 147; Maurice de Montmolin, *Le Taylorisme à visage humain* (Paris: PUF, 1981), 80ff.

101. Fridenson, "France–États-Unis," 384.

102. Moss, 30; Lequin, *Les Ouvriers*, 1:173–81.

103. Perrot, *Les Ouvriers en grève*, 1:466; Lequin, *Les Ouvriers*, 1:253ff.; Navel, *Travaux*, 183, 184.

104. Michel, 118, 175; Alain Derosières and Laurent Thévenot, *Les Catégories socio-professionelles* (Paris: La Découverte, 1988), 11.

105. Perrot, *Les Ouvriers en grève*, 1:355, 356; Noiriel, 41, 42, 46, 47; Michel, 142; Michèle Flageolet-Lardenois, "Une firme pionière: Panhard-Levassor jusqu'en 1918," *Le Mouvement social* 81 (1972): 36.

106. Navel, *Travaux*, 185; Goldthorpe et al., 12; Michel, 133, 134; Verret, *La Culture*, 28–31.

107. Perrot, "Qu'est-ce qu'un métier de femme?" 3–5; Burdy, Dubesset, and Zancarini, 34–36; Yvonne Verdier, *Façons de dire, façons de faire* (Paris: Gallimard, 1979), 197ff.

108. Augereau, 211, 212.

109. Michel, 137–40; O. Hardy, "Industrie, patronat et ouvriers de Valenciennois pendant le premier vingtième siècle" (Thesis, Université de Lille, 1985), 899; G. Latreille, *La Naissance des métiers en France, 1950–1975* (Lyons: Presses universitaires de Lyon, 1980), 31.

110. Sewell, 53, 69.

111. Frémontier, 76.

112. Perrot, *Les Ouvriers en grève*, 1:335, 385, 386.

113. Caron, 11–13; Flageolet-Lardenois, 36; Laux, 10, 11; Deniot, 359ff.

114. Michel, 169ff.; Noiriel, 156.

115. Rancière, 64, 65; Lequin, "L'Apprentissage," 43, 44; Augereau, 76ff.

116. Gras, 56, 57; Deniot, 357.

117. Navel, *Travaux*, 64, 72.

118. Paxton, 207, 208; Faure, 115ff.; Denis Segrestin, "Du syndicalisme de métiers au syndicalisme de class: Pour une sociologie de la CGT," *Sociologie du travail* 2 (1975): 162, 163.

119. Rancière, 48–50; Hobsbawm and Scott, 94; Michel, 175.

120. Quoted by Sewell, 323; see also Segrestin, 75, 155, 156, 173.

121. Renaud Sainsaulieu, *L'Identité au travail* (Paris: Presses de la Fondation nationale de science politique, 1977).

122. Desrosières and Thévenot, 10–16, 186; Latreille, 15–23.

123. Segrestin, 164–69.

124. Verret, *Le Travail*, 33ff., 44, 45.

125. Latreille, 310.

126. Navel, *Travaux*, 94; Frémontier, 155; Deniot, 355–62; Hobsbawm and Scott, 88, 89; Verret, *Le Travail*, 33.

127. Luce Tanguy, "Les Savoirs enseignés aux futurs ouvriers," *Sociologie du travail* (1983): 336–54.

128. Frémontier, 155; Latreille, 355.

CHAPTER 4

THE INDUSTRIAL AGE

❧

LOUIS BERGERON

D oes it take the brutal threat of loss to become attached to things? The full implications of that question become apparent in the salutary reactions, over the last twenty years, that have revealed the accelerated erosion and even the massive destruction of the vestiges of the different phases of industrialization in France. From the 1960s to the 1980s, France has moved from a phase of rapid growth to both a structural and cyclical crisis, from an infernal rhythm of modernization to obsolescence, from destruction to the relocation and redefinition of activities, and it is now finally emerging from the crisis. Large factories have halted, the roar of their motors and the smoke from the chimneys and furnaces have stopped. Thousands of tons of material have been turned into scrap metal or junk. Within a few days in some cases, a few months, or a few years, entire urban areas, microregions, and localities have assumed, in silence and in the re-covered purity of the air, the impressive look of the decor of an empty theater inexorably turning into a landscape of ruins.

Certain perceptive minds have felt that a memory, until then ne-glected, was about to be swallowed up—the memory of industry. The first ecomuseums (Le Creusot, in 1973), inspired by Georges-Henri Rivière, encountered this prospect in the intellectual probings and inquiries about the land.[1] Historians of technology and industry (quite few in number) and museum specialists (even fewer in number) seeking guidance in the practice of "industrial archaeology" developed here in the 1950s looked to England, the oldest industrial power and the first hit by the decline in

Figure 4.1
Cartier-Bresson, the industrial landscape between Lille and Roubaix (Nord): brick, smokestack, wall.

those sectors and areas. They also looked to the German and Scandinavian countries where the long-standing practice of open-air museology was now being applied to fossilized industrial sites. Architects, architectural historians, and photographers curious about the evidence of work or local identities suddenly seemed to see what the man of taste had up to then turned away from in horror and condemnation, that is, the power and functionality of the structures, the quality of the materials, the boldness of certain technical solutions, the aesthetic value of certain stylistic and ornamental exterior features that strove to link the industrial building to other categories of civil, religious, or military architecture. And then, there are the mass effects, produced by the modular repetitiveness of the industrial buildings themselves or the individual workers' homes, creators of an urban morphology and social landscapes.[2]

Then again, some professional historians had an insight around 1980 that all the physical vestiges—walls and furnishings, the extremely modest archives of the businesses, the memory of the unemployed, the retired and the trade unionist, men and women—could reframe the problems, methods, and interpretations of industrial history. For reactions to this insight it is easy to list names: Marcel Évrard, Dominique Ferriot, André Desvallées, Maurice Daumas and his disciples, Philippe Robert, Maurice Culot, Yves Lequin, Serge Chassagne, Denis Woronoff, Bernard Rignault, Yvon Lamy, and a handful of others, from all disciplines and all viewpoints, including political (elected officials from the departments of Nord and Pas de Calais, for example). Not to be omitted are the hundreds of volunteers who, at the level of even the smallest commune, gradually mobilized themselves in a spirit of respect for all aspects of the local patrimony. Lastly, the public at large showed awareness of the industrial patrimony on the occasion of major public debates concerning monuments, which, in actual fact, were more evidence of the classical age of industry (the nineteenth century) and its new materials (iron) than were the industrial monuments in the proper sense of the term.[3] We can measure the distance covered, the evolution of attitudes, from the conflict over Les Halles in Paris (only one wing survives, the market itself relegated now to the eastern suburbs of Paris) to the sumptuous rehabilitation and redefinition of the great hall (Halle aux boeufs) at La Villette,[4] and the Orsay train station.

Still we must not forget that a few fortified posts do not suffice for holding new territory. Compared to the elements long since recognized and appreciated as the most noble of the national cultural patrimony, the patrimony of industry (at once both the foundation of a memory of industry and the protective efforts that call forth that memory) remains the poor relation of our general culture. Its history at the evolutionary core of the very idea of culture and patrimony, reproduces, with a lag of several

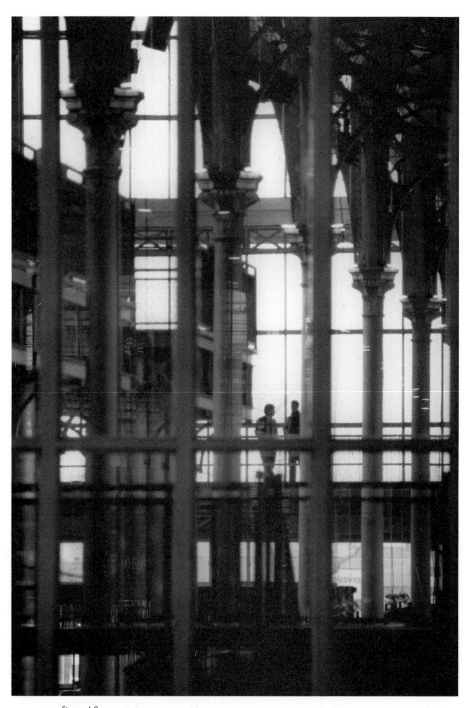

Figure 4.2
The former Halle aux boeufs at La Villette in Paris. Cast iron and steel: an architecture of great technical and stylistic boldness serving the vast halls for many uses.

years, that of the patrimony of rural societies. But up to now it does not seem destined to much popularity or a sympathetic reception of spontaneous sympathy—no doubt because, in comparison to the "popular arts and traditions" it arouses more socially circumscribed echoes.[5] Its access is less inviting, and less immediately comprehensible. It lacks without exception the nobility that antiquity confers. Its image has the defect of not hearkening back to a golden age. The awareness of the existence and interest in an "industrial patrimony" is strong in some parts of the country and certain circles of opinion, but it is far from widespread. Still it is desirable that we in our society grasp that it is against our interest to let ourselves be cut off from our industrial past, recent or remote, at the moment when we are entering another phase of economic growth that will doubtless be characterized by radically different industrial structures. As a matter of urgency, let us take the means necessary to conserve this particularly volatile memory and this patrimony with its unusual contours.

I. The Organization and the Construction of the Memory of Industry

1. Museums of Varying Types

Can the patrimony of industry be a subject—or perhaps the only subject—of procedures that the state of France has devised for safeguarding other forms of the memory of our national culture, artistic in particular, even if those procedures are essentially administrative and technical in character? Indeed the 1980s were marked by an agreement and a commitment to a significant expansion of the concept of patrimony.[6] The preservation of a memory of industry was among the first beneficiaries. From that moment on, the industrial past of our country with the vestiges of its buildings and furnishing was in turn inventoried, registered, classified, and, when possible, restored.[7] As for the archives, included in a vast collection baptized "archives of the world of work," in principle they ought to be deposited, conserved, and classified in specialized establishments. One part of this initiative, in fact, comes within the scope of regional administrators.[8]

But behind the screen of the institutional analogy there was a not so well hidden distortion introduced when the industrial patrimony was taken into consideration. It was perhaps already perceptible with regard to the classical architectural patrimony, for example, when it was a question of providing protection for entire quarters of unusual and harmonious character and when it was desirable, from that point on, to protect the totality against urban expansion or land and real estate speculation. Our industrial heritage is often very cluttered or of a modest and repetitive appearance. Criteria for evaluation remain more uncertain than those that apply to the fine arts; and investigations as to the reallocation of funds, for the means to make durable what one would like to save, have only just begun. To survive, the industrial patrimony needs to be supported at the outset by public intervention and carried by social action on which this intervention can confidently be based.

To facilitate the establishment and reappropriation of a memory of industry at the ground level is the objective ecomuseums have set for themselves for nearly twenty years. Their rule is not just aligned with safeguarding this memory alone, since their basic purpose is to seek to be the conservators of all the cultural ties that can join a population to a given territory: the ecomuseum, therefore, intersects with and in passing takes into account the memory of industry. Nevertheless, several among them have an explicitly industrial purpose: that is the case with the ecomuseums of Le Creusot, Fourmies-Trélon, Beauvaisis,[9] and Roannais, among others. Their task is not easy, for their funding depends largely on elected politicians, which means running the risk of doing something completely deplorable, politicizing a cultural issue. But they have to deal with the moods of the local employers, some of whom have refused cooperation (Le Creusot), whereas others have extended cooperation and offered great encouragement (Mulhouse).[10]

Figure 4.3
A factory at Fourmies (Nord) was transformed into the principal location of the ecomuseum for the Fourmies-Trélon region.

In Le Creusot are the "classical" forms of industrial memory that were promoted in the heart of a microregion where factory owners-entrepreneurs knew the king of France himself at the very end of the ancien régime and later the great, almost feudal dynasties of the Chagots and especially the Schneiders.[11] These were the places where the coal mine, new metallurgy, and other fire-based industries came to symbolize the entry of France into a new technological era, where the chateau of the Schneiders—once the home of a secret, aristocratic life, today the seat of an ecomuseum—tried to set the institutions and mechanisms of a very elaborate paternalism in opposition to the virulent labor struggles recalled in the celebrated autobiography of the worker Jean Baptiste Dumay,[12] a masterpiece of the written memory of work. In Fourmies, just the opposite: the ecomuseum had the luck to find its shell in a small but typical factory to which the architecture of a very well maintained smokestack confers a particular charm. The place is situated in a region that forms an isolated link in the chain of industrial sites that run along the northern and eastern frontiers of France. Fourmies is located between the regions of Valenciennes-Maubeuge and the Meuse Ardennes; it was a small town filled with spinning, combing, and weaving mills; and it became engraved in memory less by its industrial output than by the bloody event of May 1, 1891.* Today one of the most beautiful French collections of textile machines is found there, but the real ecomuseum there takes the form of an "exploded" museum—its branches, all in a close radius, are attached to safeguard the traces of all local activities, notably that of the glassworks at Trélon. That is also the pattern for the ecomuseum of the Beauvaisis, which found its current setting in the Pays de Bray, which is both Norman and Picard and perfectly representative of a long cohabitation that interlocked agricultural and industrial life along the valleys and on the plateaus, in the villages and large towns that could rely on the availability of hydropower and the richness of earth ideal for pottery and ceramics, and on a rural society that gave rise to the proliferation of mechanized agriculture. At Roanne, by contrast, another form of the French version of industrialization found an echo in a city heavily industrialized in weaving and processing cotton, and it acted as a pole for the whole backcountry mountain area on the western slope of the Beaujolais. Memory here takes into account an entire protoindustrial heritage.[13]

Every national culture generates the modalities appropriate to its museography. The institution highly prized elsewhere in (northern) Europe

* In 1891, Fourmies was a town of 16,000 with a working population of over 75%. On May 1, workers demonstrated, demanding an eight-hour workday. Soldiers who were called in because of the demonstration fired on the workers, killing nine and wounding thirty.—Trans.

Figure 4.4
The Buffon forge (Côte d'Or). The hall for casting and the blast furnace, seen from the grand staircase.

and North America has up to now in France hardly been attempted, namely the open-air museum. The ecomuseum in Alsace at Ungersheim stands in brilliant contrast to this inaction. It opens out onto an abandoned industrial site, formerly a potash mine, with the goal of coordinating and inspiring the development of all the museums in the greater Mulhouse area.

The recent tradition of the ecomuseum, though, is not the only tradition supporting the cult of industrial memory. Industrial and technical museums specializing in local or regional history preserve this memory with a focus on an activity or a branch that had a particular success in a specific area. Mines lend themselves in a spectacular way to the conservation of memory in situ when a whole group of extractive installations manage to escape destruction, like the salt mine at Salins[14] or the coal mine at Lewarde. But then too the old metal and textile industries can enjoy analogous opportunities, for instance, the old metal works at the forges of the Marquis de Buffon at the chateau and village of the same name,[15] or the textile mill of the Vallois rope factory at Notre-Dame de Bondeville. Soon there will be hundreds of places we can count on for museums of this type, gradually created in the territorial fabric by those inhabitants keen to know the skills, the methods of production, and the people of their place and their past. They readily see in those museums a guarantee of creative capacity for the near future. These technical and industrial museums are, in the best cases, remarkable places for reflecting and experimenting on the difficult problems of transmitting to the public of today the cultural content they mean to preserve. From a possible archaeological dig to site restoration or repair of restored tools, to education and the sheer pleasure of the eyes or the mind, there is a more arduous course yet to be taken than that which leads to making a Roman ruin or medieval stained glass accessible. Indeed, we belong to a country in which the history of technology is practically not taught at any level within the educational system and where (except for the new school dedicated to the patrimony, the Institut national du patrimoine) no one learns in any systematic fashion the way to tackle and present the technical and industrial aspects of a national culture. We see how the history of the patrimony returns to the fundamental structures.

Are there not in the end some other ways, less sophisticated and more prosaic, of making a place in our civilization for the memory of industry? Our cities and contemporaries have thoroughly incorporated the idea that an urban setting worthy of the name must be the synthesis of all the stages marking the architectural, functional, and physical development of the city. It is a recent idea to be sure, since in the interwar period certain individuals dreaming of doing Haussmann* one better even suggested eviscerating a good part of the twenty arrondissements of Paris for the sake of a new traffic system. It was not too long ago when a proposal to dismantle the Eiffel Tower was rejected. The Halles of Baltard† would no doubt not have been demolished were the question posed in 1990. The architecture of the nineteenth century, as well as that of the Belle Époque, became in its turn part of the patrimony like a townhouse in the historic Marais district or the foundations of the Louvre of Philip Augustus (which was demolished to make room for the present structure begun in the sixteenth century).[16] Only the industrial patrimony, at least in Paris, was pursued with a devastating hatred directed indiscrimi-

---

* Georges-Eugène Haussmann (1809–91) was appointed préfet of the Seine, the most important administrative job in the authoritarian state of Louis Napoleon Bonaparte (1853) and charged with the transformation of Paris. He accomplished his task and made modern Paris a city of boulevards, monuments, parks, and a remarkable sewer and water system. He was accused at the time (and since) of being excessively brutal. *Haussmanization*, a contemporary coinage, meant urban renewal by destruction.—Ed.

† Victor Baltard (1805–74) was the architect of the glass and iron structures of Les Halles, the central markets in Paris, which were one of the key projects in the city's transformation. These sheds, now destroyed, were considered a model of modern industrial architecture.—Ed.

nately at the traces of the glorious craft industry in the Paris of the old faubourgs or at the remains of the powerful industries in the periphery of Paris born at the dawn of the twentieth century and dead well before the century's twilight. If a citizen is a person whose awareness has deepened over the course of his life by frequenting all the articulations and landmarks of his city, then it will have to be admitted that a part of his heritage, without justification, has been amputated from his consciousness. Working on the hypothesis of a sustained process of enriching and adding to the national memory, we will surely have to obtain some developers, project managers, and political decision makers who can apply the indispensable intelligence and imagination for integrating, within the ever evolving city, those elements and lines of the industrial trajectory of urban development. Even in the United States, where cities traditionally erase urban quarters and start again from zero, the concept of "historic district" has contributed to protecting certain urban museums like Soho.[17]

Finally, there are the architects who were among the first to draw attention to the patrimony built from industry by keeping steadfast in their approach, a formal and aesthetic bias that has earned them much hostility. They remain today, in more than one case, the most reliable artisans for reviving and stabilizing the memory of industry each time they decide to take over a site and a monument to give them a new purpose, to extract them from the temporarily tolerated ruin, and to reintegrate them into a new cycle of urban development. They allow them, so to speak, to "earn their living." As the technicians and practitioners that they are, the architects know the particular qualities of the industrial building site: the spaces, the materials, the pastiches, or the provocations of style. They run the risk, however, of splitting into two camps. Originality at any price. The architect takes over the legacy that he has found abandoned with the idea of seeing in it only a pretext for some personal acrobatics. Then he devours what one could expect him to save. The other camp is the historian of his subject, seeking to understand its meaning and then trying to preserve its historic and technical intelligibility all while conferring new qualities on it that its reuse will require. Was there ever a more reprehensible manipulation than that of the relentless restorers of Gothic art in the last century? Certainly not. All those who campaign for the fusion of the aspects of the patrimony into a single common benefit have to give equal attention to the archaeology of industry and to the rehabilitation of the vestiges every time that it can be undertaken. Beyond that, it is up to them to elaborate the scientific instruments thanks to which the memory of industry will come to enrich the understanding of the beginnings of contemporary society.

2. The Testimony of the Actors

The sensitivity to one's own culture of industry and the desire to safeguard the traces of it have been sharpened within the context of crisis and of a redistribution of roles and locations that lead to accelerated loss. One of the initial steps for expanding the collective memory of industry seemed to consist in appealing to individuals or groups, inviting them to go back deep into the memories of their professional life. Three broad categories of memory may be drawn upon: the salaried personnel involved in production, the managers and directors, and the professional staff, in particular, the engineers. The recourse to oral history in this field is unavoidable given the penury of direct written sources. Of the trade union newspapers and professional and technical presses which existed for a long time, from the two sides of the capitalism barrier, nothing remains now but the actors from the world of production and business, who have expressed themselves very rarely in private correspondence or printed publications on their work, their ideas, their passions. Over the last twenty years, French publishing has managed to produce only a handful of memoirs through which the skilled worker spoke. Letters or autobiographies are just as rare, but are guaranteed best sellers. The engineer keeps to himself even more when he is in retirement, if that is possible. Unfortunately, oral history is seldom a satisfactory substitute, not just because the information it provides is limited to a given slice of time, but also because it constitutes a source difficult to analyze and, outside the total collection of such testimony, to exploit and present.

Oral testimony from the head of a company, whatever his status, is often the most difficult to get. That person becomes evasive at times, fearing like someone in the dock that anything he says may come back to haunt him. Then again his testimony might be overly apologetic, dynastic, and family-centered. More benefit is to be gained from the history of the business or from that of its managerial divisions than from that of an industry as a social microcosm. However, those who come from technology enterprises or who are high-level employees, and increasingly these individuals are the heads of modern businesses, have more to say and say it freely because they can stand back from their own business. They have distance and almost an independent view of it.

The testimony of the worker has going for it spontaneity, audacity, the smell of real life, and the sense of the practical. This testimony does not come to light without difficulties of another kind, and the practitioners of oral inquiry in the workers' milieu know the bareness and stereotypes into which one must dive for precious pearls. As Danièle Miguet so nicely put it, "For memories, as for life, there are the poor and the well-off. In the worker's milieu the supports are missing for putting together and transmitting a family memory over one or more generations: In bourgeois families, silverware, jewels, family portraits, and sometimes letters are handed down with devotion. Such things stimulate the imagination and allow a way of life to be put into thought. For the other, nothing."[18] If the managers have their prejudices, their preconceived notions, their sanctimonious jargon, so too do workers with their ready-made formulas, which are not always their own. Chronological precision is often lacking. Time in the past is organized around episodes in one's personal life, like the date of hiring; violent events in particular have a decisive impact. Many of these episodes are drawn from the depths of memories that are dreadful—destitution, illness, unemployment, injury.[19] On many points simplification or confusion fixes and biases the memory. For the factory, that often occurs where the testimony is fragmentary and uncertain. Years ago, progress in the organization of work and discipline, at least in businesses of some sizes, partitioned the work space to the point where the worker saw only the immediate surroundings visible from his work station. The worker was unable to place his work station within the total production unit. Still the testimony of the worker remains indispensable for reconstructing the conditions of work, illuminating the relationships with other wage earners and with the employer, understanding the forms of sociability proper to one division or to a region, comprehending the skills and their transmission, and certainly learning what the standard of living was. Everything in the memory of industry concerns the social anthropologist and necessarily passes through the analysis of these responses from evocative questionnaires or, in the best cases, from life histories.

The memory of the engineer, lastly, is perhaps the one most sought after. If, by virtue of his position in the business enterprise, he cannot escape his condition as an employee with a share of authority, he is nevertheless, by virtue of his training and competence, a kind of intellectual often capable of the acute, critical, and best-formulated observation of the life of the places where his career unfolded. On the other hand, he is the living technical memory of businesses, especially at a time when many of them are neglecting to preserve that memory and instead are destroying their old technical archives, eliminating or selling off outdated materials on the cheap—obsolescence, the never-ending dread of a business between a future that it seeks to master and a history it does not try to keep. The engineer is the one who remembers all that. He is, notably, the intermediary who knows all about the "living" machine, not just from the catalogs and instructions, but also what is needed to set up, maintain, and adapt to the space and the users, in short, to "acculturate."

In any event, the vigor of the memory of industry varies according to the branch and the specialty. It has particular originality and vitality in the masculine trades that bask in the glow of a precise technical competence and necessitate particular physical strength or confrontation with constant danger. It has become common, and with good reason, for historians or anthropologists/ethnologists to speak of the "man of iron" at the forges in the Périgord or in the mines and steel mills of Lorraine.[20] The workers at the bottom of a coal mine, the *gueules noires*, the black maws, had a strong cultural identity too in the world of work, as did the weaver, the silk worker of Lyons, the ribbon maker from Saint-Étienne or the protoindustrial helpers in the huge cotton industry—before, one did not talk about the "thread man," because strength and competence still were indispensable when it came to moving the lever or following a pattern. As for the *métallos*, the metalworkers in the big cities, a whole range of mechanical engineering proliferated that assumed legendary proportions even during their lifetime. By contrast, memory was surely deleted; indeed, it was nonexistent for millions of women whose work coexisted with the men in big industry. At best it was diluted in an infernal combination of domestic tasks and ill-paid jobs in the service of companies exploiting the inexhaustible store of home-bound labor for certain steps in the manufacturing process.[21] In the first case, deletion came about from the sexual division of work that always forced women into tasks requiring little or no competence. In the second case, there was the prevalent image of a kind of "antiprofessionalism," if it were even one of social scum (recall the judgments made about the morality of female textile workers or dressmakers working at home). The nobility of work takes refuge here in the legacy, more artisan than industrial, of trades like lace making or embroidery, reflected in the prestige of the luxury article. An entire piece of the culture of work, in short, is done a disservice as much by the quantitative sources as by qualitative assessment.

3. Vestiges by Category

Like the other forms of collective memory, that of industry is, in addition, largely dependent on the monuments built by this particular form of civilization. In its demand for recognition and analysis the industrial structure poses all sorts of problems; one could say that by turn it is taken for what it is not before it compels one to look at it as disputed architecture and then evaporates into anonymity or meaninglessness. Consequently, its maintenance, its conservation, and its reuse often remain an object of controversy. Despite its bold appearance in the landscape and its fact as a landmark, an industrial building constitutes a particularly fragile element of the national patrimony.

Figure 4.5
The Dijonval factory at Sedan (Ardennes). The architecture is much more adapted to the dignity of an entrepreneur favored by the king than to the kind of work done.

Figure 4.6
The Congo or Vaissier chateau near Tourcoing (Nord). In contrast to the purely functional and repetitive architectures of the workers' quarters, the business owner freely indulged in luxury and fantasy for his living quarters. Ostentation and eclectic taste.

There is little doubt that now in France, as in other countries, attention is increasingly being paid and consideration given to the architecture of industry, insofar as it does not reveal the material circumstances of the actual operations of what is going on behind the walls and approximates in some old fashion the standard look of "noble" architecture, meaning a palace, a town house, and sometimes a church.[22] Among the first industrial buildings to have been restored, studied, and made much of even if no restoration followed, one can cite the rope-making factory at Rochefort, today completely restored and in use, the Van Robais factory of Les Rames at Abbeville, the factory of Le Dijonval at Sedan,[23] or the factory of Fontaine-Guérard—four examples from the seventeenth to the nineteenth centuries. The first, an immense, low, one-story building, evokes the outlying buildings of a royal residence, even though for the specialist it expresses its function well through its size. The technology of the time required stretching the rope to full length as part of the manufacturing process. The second and third take as their model the town house or the chateau, each with a large inner courtyard, executed by the best architects of the region. The fourth was a cotton mill that the owner had situated in a building the ruins of which could pass today for a Gothic abbey church, other parts recalling a fort. The choice of such "envelopes" can be explained at two levels: whether it is a matter of equipment for the navy (Rochefort) or fine fabrics (Abbeville, Sedan), its meaning is more social and political than industrial. The state with its needs and the privileges it accorded to the factories producing luxury goods, the exalted relationships among the owner-entrepreneurs at the top of the trading caste and the office holders—everything meant that the places where work was carried out manifested on the outside a majesty that reflected the power, the prestige, and also the nobility of the manufactured product.

On the other hand, nothing in industrial work imposes a specific, functional architecture. One does need space to be sure to hold the initial concentrations of workers bought about by the necessity to oversee the quality and regularity of the work (and not to fulfill some technical imperative). Vast proportions and several floors are therefore sufficient. Even at the time of the Revolution of 1789, what aroused the interest of the manufacturers was the chance to acquire ecclesiastical buildings and seigniorial residences. Is it necessary to speak of an "industrial" architectural patrimony? In some ways, yes. For if one looks closely at the attached buildings, the interior plan, or if one has the luck of coming across some inventory, one will notice the presence of an internal logic responding to the needs of the different operations, like work flow and oversight. Some details, like the added number of high and narrow windows, show that the Le Dijonval plant was designed to dispense the maximum amount of light into the rooms. The place is no longer a chateau to be saved: it is precious evidence of work done in the time of the "protofactories."

As for the extravagance of Fontaine-Guérard, it comes under the heading of "industrial castles," a notion disseminated by architectural historians in the late 1970s. The occasion was a well-publicized photographic exposition and a book dedicated to the large factories around Lille. These factories, for the most part, were textile companies with a large physical plant that dated from the second half of the nineteenth century or the beginning of the twentieth. The reality of the proportions was an exercise in virtuosity realized in an architecture of bricks that covered the buildings. The structure was set strictly according to the requirements of the material, energy, and organization of the work. The decorative trappings were borrowed from the traditions of the region or hearkened back to all the fantasies of eclecticism. How can we explain these stunning events except by the complicity (of which we know next to nothing) between an architect or an engineer, on the one hand, and an owner of a company, on the other, who all agree on a program that could only be costly? In any case, the result is the glorification of the industrial economy, the display of success, the reputation of a brand all coming to the forefront. As time went on, quite late in the nineteenth century the custom took hold among the factory owners to loosen and separate the place of work from one's residence. Architectural ostentation was transferred to the villas, now with a park, in the urban or suburban areas of Roubaix or Tourcoing, for example,[24] of which the most amazing have unfortunately disappeared after a century or less of existence thanks to the pressure of urban real estate. This behavior must not be generalized. In many cases, a more reasonable policy and more restricted resources have brought back the luxurious part of the architectural ornamentation of industrial buildings, the main gate, or provided care for the business administrative quarters. Conversely, in the north, the style of the factory-chateau extends and imposes itself on all urban public architecture.

If we were to limit ourselves to an inventory and typology of complacency for such vestiges, we would surely get no further than the exterior of this patrimony of industry. The truth of this patrimony is, in reality, found in the constantly renewed creation of constructed forms being adapted to the diversity of techniques, from branch to branch, and to their transformation and their substitution more or less rapidly, depending on the times. The memory of industry is tied to the genealogy of buildings, thus something to be reconstructed, even if only from the bits and pieces on the ground and old iconographic icons. Attention has to shift from the formal characteristics to the intrinsic rationality of the installations. This rationality, if it rests on the use of appropriate and worthwhile materials,

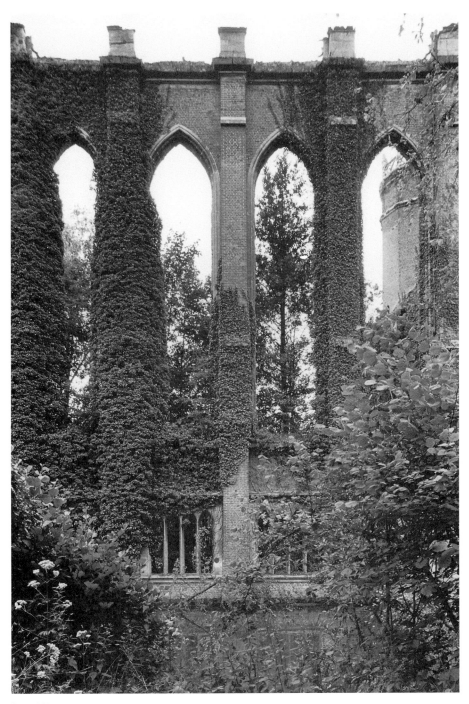

Figure 4.7
The ruins of the factory of Fontaine-Guérard (Seine-Maritime), an example from the age of ornate decoration in industrial architecture that stands in contrast to the functionality of the rope-making factory of Rochefort.

can only lead a different aesthetic, which it is our task to decipher once we have overcome the feelings of unfamiliarity regarding the traditional objects of our admiration. The water-powered mills, the structures inside of which one utilizes energy transmitted from falling water to a rotating wheel, have for nearly a millennium and at thousands of sites formed the matrix of industrialization in the long term, everywhere that grain and olives or other raw materials were ground or that fulling rollers, mallets, and hammers were set into motion. Starting in the eighteenth century, the flour mill was organized from the top down with the view of ratio-nalizing the grinding function. By changing the dimensions and internal arrangements, the mills evolved into primitive textile plants, powered by water. Even when they began running on steam power and were housed in a separate building, the first factories kept the high, elongated appearance of those buildings, at the dimensions required by the machines of the time. Within these buildings of no great originality, there arose a new kind of construction engineering to meet the growing requirements for free space between the supports with resistance to load, vibration, combustibility in case of fire, and so forth. Wood, brick, plaster, iron, and cast iron to this purpose were worked into complicated combinations in the floors and ceilings. The memory of industry for twenty years has exploited the ar-chitecture of metal, the preferred example of industrial architecture. We know now all about its progressive triumph, despite the grumpy doubt-ers, in works of art, halls of all kinds, public and private buildings, Pari-sian passageways, and, of course, railroad stations and symbolic buildings serving no practical purpose (the Eiffel Tower).[25] But architecture for use by industry, more modestly, despite the attention that a specialized and at times popularizing press has brought to it, has not contributed less to testing and setting rules for a new way of building.

Another genealogy could be pursued in the steel and metallurgical industry, from the introduction into France of the first blast furnaces in the fifteenth century up to the revolution in technology in the second quarter of the nineteenth century, which saw the birth of the blast furnace, the *forge à l'anglaise*. The forge of the Marquis de Buffon in his Burgundy chateau is currently undergoing repairs to restore authenticity to all its parts. It is one example among hundreds of others of these "large forges," characteristic of secular and ecclesiastical domains that reached their apogee at the end of the eighteenth century and often continued well into the following cen-tury.[26] The center of the installation is a flat-top pyramid which goes from six to eight meters to twelve to fifteen, from top to bottom. Here was the blast furnace, the heart of the operation, which, with an almost magical quality, through the indirect manufacturing process, gave rise to cast iron. The transport of minerals, charcoal, and other ingredients converged at the upper opening by means of a ramp. Loads and temperatures required the careful construction of beautiful hewn stone into well-calculated geometric forms, at certain points set off by reinforced arches. Apart from the blast furnace, the only piece of architecture was the steward's house. The other buildings were copies of rural architecture: huge sheds with massive roofs covering supplies and product stock awaiting shipment, workshops in the countryside for refining cast iron, smelting or rolling iron, though they were not always found in the same spot. The whole affair existed in happy disorder. To this were added the houses for the salaried workers in the "forge" (the term designated the whole complex). It was a worker's village in the rough under the eye of the master of the forge, and, as such, it did indeed exert an influence on the utopias of the same period (late eighteenth century, early nineteenth century) or at least on similar establishments modeled in the image of others like the royal saltworks at Arc et Senans or the workshops of the Grand Hornu.[27] Yet even greater rigor was introduced when it came to imitating the English technique of utilizing coal at every stage, from converting the ore to working the iron. At that point in time, apart from the blast furnace, which simply grew in size, there appeared vast, carefully constructed workshops where the hewn stone and the brick were judiciously combined with openings at the top to let out the smoke and with carefully laid-out work stations inside. Today, alas, Le Creusot is no longer in Le Creusot, and Schneider still remains the owner's castle. But perhaps some day, when the Guérigny forges are restored, the landscape of the steel industry of the first industrial revolution will be returned to us.

Since the second industrial revolution, genealogies have scarcely had time to be established. So, for example, the coal gas industry, which used to illuminate and heat municipalities, has practically been wiped off the map after having produced in the interwar period strange technical architecture going well beyond the simplicity of the gas meter. No less strange was the destiny of the automobile industry, with its long assembly lines in the post–World War I years; from that time these have become obsolete, and in Paris, the automotive capital, are completely blotted from the city dweller's view and thus from his memory. There is a recent author, by contrast, who speaks to us of the "electric cathedrals": from the manmade waterfalls to the nuclear power industry, the Alpine mountains retain a rich variety of industrial monuments in which the evolution in its entirety from the decorative to the functional may be found.[28]

Does not the recent evolution of the architecture of industry call this very architecture into question as an element of the patrimony? The generalized use of "mechanized tents," easy to adjust and disassemble, renders obsolete any idea of the permanence, safeguarding, and even the identity

of the industrial building. The memory of industry will no longer be attached to those prefabricated walls that push into the anonymous and undifferentiated industrial zones surrounding the cities. In point of fact, the memory of industry has always been, to some extent, somewhere else.

A second category of vestiges has actually been formed by the tools and technology of a given industry within a defined time frame. Let us include in this category all the objects that industry has produced. Unfortunately we enter into a domain where vestiges assume the character of archaeological fragments, traces, or indirect evidence. Fragility and rarity characterize them even more than do the vestiges of the buildings. If one proceeds in a regressive fashion, one first notes that every business stands opposed to any concerns about preserving its equipment at the time it is replaced. At that moment it can be sold to a business with fewer technological demands or better provided with cheap labor. It can also be sold as scrap metal or sometimes left out in the open to rust. A machine that is taken out of service is good only for a museum. To be sure, there is the school of science and technology in Paris, the Conservatoire national des arts et métiers, created in 1794 to be the depository "of the originals of the instruments and machines invented and perfected," as well as the place where people would be taught how make and use them. But for some time now, it has been unable to receive the proliferation of tools arising from the speed of technical progress and the amorphous diversification of industry. What is needed, therefore, is the specialized museum, though certain equipment (a paper-making machine, a rolling mill, an assembly line) will require enormous space and area. Maintenance and utilization pose many problems not yet resolved. The "lines" or the assemblage of the technologies are as a consequence, even with printed documentation, difficult to reconstruct on a full scale. As for the products, the situation is even more variable. How many textile manufacturing and processing plants have burned countless cartons containing their samples and their archives![29] And when the desire comes to reconstruct the memory of the civilization of domestic consumption, despite high levels of mass manufacturing, will it not be necessary to have recourse to store catalogs to compensate for the losses? That notwithstanding, in the first half of the nineteenth century, the calico mill in Mulhouse took pains to keep a sample of all its fabrics, thereby preparing from early on the accumulation of wealth for the museum of textile printing, the Musée de l'impression sur étoffes. The museum of wallpaper, Musée du papier peint, in Rixheim near Mulhouse, likewise today preserves the entire creativity of the company, founded at the end of the eighteenth century by Jean Zuber.[30] The frenzy of the automobile collectors, on the other hand, is well known. Here at least there is little likelihood that any model by any manufacturer will be lost, a phenomenon without doubt unique for its kind but that only contrasts harshly with the general disdain for the preservation of the memory of work in the automobile industry. Let this be a caution: a machine tool will never be put together in the manner of a skeleton assembled from a few remains. It is not for us to laugh at the explorers of ancient granaries, and we must accord the same consideration to the technical manual as to an old book. If we fail to do that, we will know less about certain stages of industrialization than we do about Mesopotamian civilizations.

II. THE HANDICAPS OF INDUSTRIAL MEMORY

Between the riches of the traditional patrimony and the materials with which the memory of industry is constructed there exists a major difference. If we look into the archaeology of the most ancient periods (the Middle Ages, antiquity, prehistory), we will note today a progression in the volume of knowledge due either to the attentive conservation of remains in the open air or, paradoxically, to the burial of civilizations by the accidents of history or simply by its evolution. This comes about thanks to the refinements of techniques of location and excavation, combined with strict regulations for excavations and public construction. In that way, the archaeology of the Parisian subway has yielded some good surprises, as has work done on the underground parking lot at Notre Dame and the restoration work at the Louvre and the Tuileries. In contrast, the materials from industrial archaeology, from the entrance to the sites and installations, have started down the slope of irremediable impoverishment because of the organized "breakage" to which valuable objects are subject in recovering the soil, or through the wish to erase and forget. Just the same, the oldest and least exposed of the industrial patrimony has more difficulty than other monuments in mobilizing the social environment and government protection. As a consequence, the historian of industrial patrimony sees himself obliged to leave without delay the world of inventories and research for that of public action: sensitizing, informing, defending, promoting. He cannot stop being the one who collects and gathers the fragments before he is even able to orchestrate them at the risk of never getting to that stage.

Let us take a closer look at the handicaps peculiar to industrial memory.

1. Fragility of the Industrial Patrimony

The industrial landscapes, such as those formed over the course of the years from 1820 to 1970, are characterized by significant control over land and continually growing units of production as well as by urban concentrations or microregions of businesses announcing their presence in a quantitative and architectural manner simultaneously. These landscapes have created, through the intermediary of literary description, social criticism, or aesthetic rejection, the image and, in the end, a snapshot of the deleterious influence and irreversible deterioration of a preindustrial landscape seen by contrast as bucolic or monumental, depending on whether it is rural or urban. The idea has gained currency that a previous equilibrium was destroyed by the sudden emergence and expansion of industry and replaced by "skylines" and dark shapes that produced quantities of pollution and visions of horror. In an atmosphere that is ruralist, anti-industrialist, hostile to capitalist concentrations, or particularly sensitive to social clashes arising from industrialization-urbanization, many French people have formed a negative picture of the physical presence of industry as that necessary evil.

Nevertheless, we find ourselves in the last quarter of the twentieth century observing that industry's dominance over the landscape can be washed away. With certain exceptions, to be sure. The slag heaps are stable and planted, and they will leave for the future lines of artificial hills rising above the flat plains. The extractive industries with their unrelenting consumption of sand and stone tend by contrast to make the horizons retreat by removing the hilltops. The formidable techniques of land management in the hydroelectric industry have reconfigured entire valleys according to totally artificial mathematical profiles. Underground mining leaves surfaces unstable and unfit for building. The sand quarries create landscapes with lakes along the valleys of the Seine and Marne just as the forest policies did ex nihilo for the department of the Landes in the nineteenth century. The slate quarries fashion at the gates of Angers, a calm and sumptuous provincial capital, a landscape of disquieting shapes, a burlesque note in the landscape of great culture. All that means really very little compared to the vegetal covering inscribing the soil, the different types of habitats and networks capturing all the territory—phenomena of great expansion and long duration.

In the kinds of work that are technically and geographically concentrated, industry settled in places where resources are distributed in an unpredictable way. More often, it joined with preexisting urban bodies that were much older and more complex, ingratiating themselves into the fabric of the community before setting out to build industrial extensions outside the city limits. When on its own it instigated the creation of new towns, the latter were always of modest size unless they diminished or disappeared as a result of shortages, economic circumstances, or worldwide competition in the workforce. The modern forms of industry have coexisted with only a few generations of mankind, not very long in comparison to an economic and historical memory whose beginnings go back to Neolithic times. There exists a striking contradiction between the values of the majority, produced by industrial activities in the developed countries, and the subordinate place these activities physically occupy within urban bodies the legacies of which in the end are restrictive and dynamically varied.

Subject to technological renewal, changes in the market, and utilitarian calculations, industry does not possess in itself the resources of other forms of culture rooted in a long history. Once an activity or a site falls into obsolescence or is hit by a halt in production, the fragility of all the elements entering into the patrimony of industry is revealed with frightening speed. Often of mediocre quality, buildings already inadequately maintained in the phase of economic decline age in very few years. The glass walls of the great manufacturing plants do not have the resistance of Roman vaults. Archives are burnt with wood chopped from the building or with old furniture in the factory courtyard. The no longer guarded walls are easily penetrated by looters or scrap dealers. The places also serve as illegal dump sites. Tools are sold again or turned into scrap metal. Except in economically depressed zones, the land, the capital asset, very quickly comes under enormous pressure. In the end, there is not the least risk; the actors of the industrial past have departed, proprietors and managers along with the workers. The retirees remain; the working population and the young leave. The memory of skills and the histories of life there become as nothing right from the moment when there is no longer anyone to transmit them, either through one generation to the next or through circles of social and work contacts. Extinction follows its own logic, and there is no going back. Elements of the industrial landscape with the most potent symbolism are impossible to preserve. Whether it is a matter of the high brick chimneys or the pithead mine frames about to rust, no budget by itself would suffice.[31] At a time when an administration, archaeologists, or historians are planning preservation work on the great abbeys of the Middle Ages or of more recent times by engaging masons, stonecutters, and earthwork men (note, for example, the site at Villers la Ville in the Brabant), one can imagine the dizzying effect that would overcome such a group if charged to maintain in good condition the many hectares of a steel factory or an oil refinery.

So then, a century after its start-up, the ordinary man just looking with his eyes might wonder if that coal basin or steel mill in the department of Nord or in Lorraine ever existed. Less than a century after the birth of the automobile industry there is nothing left of it in the fifteenth arrondissement of Paris that could suggest to a resident or a passerby that

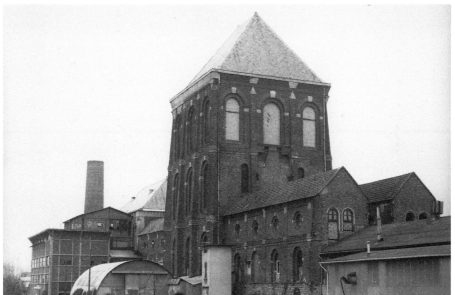

Figure 4.10
The Sabatier shaft at Raismes (Nord); the metal pithead built in 1920. Operations ceased in 1980.

Figure 4.11
The pithead frame for the Sainte-Fontaine shaft in Freyming-Merlebach (Moselle). Built in 1955; operations ceased in 1986.

Figure 4.12
The Hottinguer shaft at Épinac (Saône-et-Loire), pithead frame with masonry construction. Built in 1870; operations ceased in 1936.

in the angle formed by the Seine and those boulevards named after the generals the Citroën factories had once been set up. The space in that outer arrondissement has been filled up, thanks to urbanization. The powerful metropolis has digested all in the urban trajectory on which it has embarked.

The fragility is around elsewhere still. "Industry before industrialization" has over the centuries cohabited with rural society, interwoven with the agricultural economy, as with the urban society so hospitable to the trades.[32] And this cohabitation in no way disappeared with industrialization. It survives today. Yet the signs and markers are almost all missing. One needs the eye of the specialist to discern in the structure of a rural habitat of Le Choletais in western France near Nantes or La Pévèle, in northern France, an area near Lille, the bygone combination of domestic textile work and private life, the half-buried room in the basement or the room reserved for the weaver on the other side of a corridor. It becomes just as difficult to reconstruct through one's imagination what the industrial glory of Paris accomplished from the nineteenth century to World War II, when the work done by the mechanical and artistic trades and the small metalworkers was embedded in the hundreds of little islands to the east and the south of Paris, pierced with the branches of dead-end streets, fringed by tiny workshops or leading to factory enclosures, and closely interwoven with working-class or lower-middle-class housing. Every day here the memory of industry is smoothed away by modifications done by the locals with their changing affections, the demolition completed in a surgical way through real estate operations. In brief, industry, in contrast to religion or the powers of the state, does not by itself have those prestigious edifices or consecrated places that the centuries and the regimes are all willing to hand down as emblems and markers that guide the steps and thoughts of the subjects and the faithful from age to age.

2. Unpopularity of the Industrial Patrimony

Worse, we in France in the last years of the twentieth century, with a profound disaffection, have often been pursuing the instrument that enriched us. The vestiges of the recent industrial past have attracted the disapproval, implicit or active, of economic authorities and the heads of business themselves: by definition oriented resolutely toward the future, they are brought to consider as out of date and lacking in interest that which no longer corresponds to the contemporary necessities of production. But if indeed the past did close on a defeat, the obsession becomes the failure to efface the memories of that failure. All traces have to disappear.[33] Curiosity would be unhealthy. The workers and the union leaders in addition may find themselves having the same negative attitude as their managers: rejection of bad memories and hard years, scandal of a badly understood "recovery" of those memories by "aesthetes" who would make it their business.

To an even greater extent, the amateurs and the specialists of the grand classic categories of the architectural patrimony that for a long time excluded the nineteenth century and twentieth century have welcomed with more reticence still the building vestiges of the industrial patrimony. This last runs great risks in being valued only according to criteria used for the analysis, maintenance, and conservation of artistic works. The absence of aesthetic value and the banality of one element of industrial patrimony are not cause for justifying its neglect or its loss. This patrimony, in certain cases, may appear repellent because we are not educated or used to deciphering it.

It is at this point that one touches, without doubt, on the most basic reasons why the incorporation of the industrial patrimony into the cultural patrimony of the nation in its entirety is so complicated and so slow. It is true that the matter has been talked about for less than twenty years. Every cultural memory is a voluntary act, and so many are averse to even considering the industrial patrimony as anything but an eccentric subset of the cultural patrimony, of marginal curiosity. There is no doubt about that because those same individuals do not want to admit that the technical culture and the culture of work make up part of the general culture of respectable people. So it is that a part of contemporary society turns its back on the world of production, the fruits of which nevertheless de-

Figure 4.13
The industrial wasteland of Cornillon, in the Saint-Denis plain north of Paris: gasworks no longer in use. A harmonious industrial architecture of the interwar years for an "ungrateful" industry and at a very contested site.

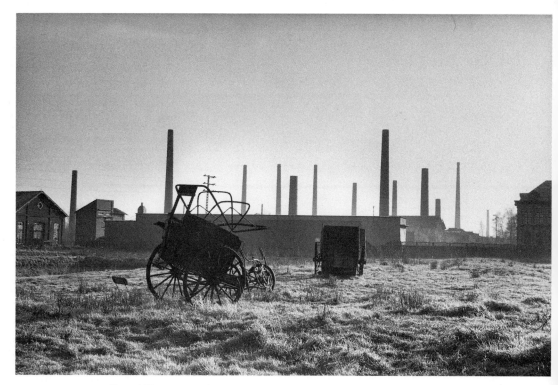

Figure 4.14
Between Port sur-l'Escaut and Saint-Amand (Nord) in 1976. Cartier-Bresson's interpretation.

termine at each instant the kind of life society leads. Condemning the tyranny of technology, the master might just as reasonably complain of letting himself be subjugated by his slave. Great courage is therefore necessary to "tame" the industrial patrimony because that act presupposes changing minds, the heirs of twenty centuries of classics periodically rejuvenated and dressed up, deformed by those social habits that so sharply reorganize the different types of culture among them, believing they can leave technology to the technicians. Technology is everywhere, and it does a great injustice to those men to believe that the mind that perfected the blades of waterwheels is inferior to that which conceived the cupola of Santa Maria del Fiore in Florence. Industrial patrimony and technical culture therefore will save each other.

3. Potentiality, Unity, and Necessity

To keep, awaken, or quite simply construct the memory of industry does not fit with an attitude of acquiescence or devotion to the past. On the other hand, memory is not the automatic guarantee of innovation. It is not a recipe book. Instead, it forms, or at least can form, a link in the identity in the territorial framework and contribute to maintaining a culture the technical dimension of which facilitates the evolution or the reorientation of economic activity. The memory of industry is cultural wealth, but it can also constitute an economic potential beyond what might promote new forms of specialized tourism. Industry creates patrimony in every sense of the word. To neglect the transmission of it is an error and a risk that can lead to impoverishment and dependence. In accord with its different aspects, it must be preserved, given media attention, and taught in the same way literary and artistic patrimony are. In a country like France, the acceptance of such ideas still constitutes the object of a cultural revolution hardly begun. These ideas will upset many individual or group prejudices as well as land management and restructuring policies, of which one of the dogmas remains the eradication of all traces and images even of industries that have collapsed. Respect for the memory of industry is at the heart of development even if that memory is not sufficient to guarantee it. From a narrowly academic point of view, it is necessary to add that historians whose task is to elaborate the image of society have by the same token an interest in what the archaeology of industry, an essential source of information, makes impossible for them by imprudent barbarisms.

There is no patrimony that has as its purpose to be preserved. Nor is there a patrimony whose purpose is to vanish. Might we have lost the enthusiasm that animated in the last century the organizers and visitors to

Figure 4.15
The Vernes power station, built in 1918 on the Romanche River (Isère). The hydroelectric power stations in Dauphiné made pioneering efforts to harmonize with the architectural patrimony of the region.

the universal industrial expositions? It is true that France has hosted only two expositions over the course of the twentieth century (1900, 1937) and that the grand expositions of the nineteenth century have today become objects of the historian's curiosity, indeed an object of celebration (1989, the centenary of 1889, was also celebrated!). One political test is cultural and it is about to unfold. Who can say if attitudes will change: the renovation of the museum of engineering, the Musée national des techniques, has been announced. That museum had been deteriorating while the site of La Villette was the object of much attention. If it is done right, it will be indifference that will be in retreat and the memory of machines will have found in us the right to be put on display.

NOTES

For further discussion of the subject, the reader will wish to consult François Caron, "L'Entreprise," and Daniel Fabre, "Le *Manuel de folklore français* d'Arnold van Gennep," in *Les Lieux de mémoire*, vol. 3, *Les France: Traditions* (Paris: Gallimard, 1993); and Michelle Perrot, "Les Vies ouvrières," *Les Lieux de mémoire*, vol. 3, *Les France: De l'archive à l'emblème* (Paris: Gallimard, 1993).

1. Georges-Henri Rivière (1887–1985) had been the one, along with Paul Rivet (1928) to modernize the Musée d'éthnographie du Trocadéro before creating (1938) and directing until his retirement the Musée national des arts et traditions populaires (established in the well-known modern building at the edge of the Bois de Boulogne). The launching of ecomuseums by Rivière belongs to the last phase of his life, when he was already retired, and constitutes the culmination of his interest in protecting environments, especially the natural parks that opened up the field of museology.

2. Cf., in very different genres: Lise Grenier and Hans Wieser-Benedetti, *Les Châteaux de l'industrie: Recherches sur l'architecture de la région lilloise de 1839 à 1930* (Paris-Brussels: Archives de l'architecture moderne, 1979), vol. 2; and *La Mine dans le paysage stéphanois* (Saint Étienne: Maison de la Culture, 1979).

3. Bernard Marrey, *Les Grands Magasins* (Paris: Picard, 1979); idem, *Architectures à Paris, 1848–1914*, with Paul Chemetov (Paris: Dunod, 1980); idem, *Gustave Eiffel: Une entreprise exemplaire*, 2nd ed. (Paris: Institut, 1989); idem, *Le Fer à Paris: Architectures* (Paris: Picard, 1989).

4. Through the efforts of the architectural firm of Philippe Robert and Bernard Reichen. Among his other realizations: the factory of Le Blan in Lille, the factory of Blin at Elbeuf, and the pavilion of the Arsenal in Paris.

5. And yet where is the limit exactly to be situated, in the "popular arts and traditions," between the culture of the peasant and that of the worker? France is without a doubt one of the countries in which the familial and territorial overlapping of the agricultural and the industrial spheres was maintained the longest. Among many possible examples, see Claude-Isabelle Brelot and Jean-Luc Mayaud,

L'Industrie en sabots: La taillanderie de Nans sous Saint Anne (Doubs); Les conquêtes d'une ferme-atelier aux XIXe et XXe siècles (Paris: J.-J. Pauvert-Garnier, 1982).

6. In 1979, Georges-Henri Rivière received the Grand prix national du patrimoine. In 1980, the demonstrations of Year of the Patrimony awarded an "official seat," a *strapontin* or foldout chair, to the major figures of the industrial and technical patrimony.

7. Since 1983 and thereafter, through the creation of a "Unit of the Industrial Patrimony" as part of the Inventaire général des monuments et richesses artistiques de la France, then through the reorganization of the Commission supérieure des monuments historiques, which took into consideration in one particular section the industrial and technical patrimony.

8. Of the five centers named in principle to receive specifically the deposit of the archives of businesses, only one is in the process of realization, the one for the region of Nord–Pas de Calais. It is being established in the Roubaix in the former factory, Motte Bossut, an essential architectural landmark of the city.

9. See the fourteen issues of *Cahiers de l'écomusée* (1980 to 1987).

10. In Mulhouse, now also reputed for the number and quality of its museums, the Centre de culture scientifique, technique et industrielle, formed in 1982, benefited thus from the patronage of Jacques-Henri Gros, a descendant of one of the founding families of the Wesserling industrial center, president of honor as well of the venerable Société industrielle of Mulhouse.

11. Marcel Sutet, *Montceau-les-Mines: Essor d'une mine, naissance d'une ville* (Roanne: Horvath, 1981); Marcel Sutet and Jean-Pierre Brésillon, *Le Creusot Montceau-les-Mines autrefois: Du terroir à l'usine* (Roanne: Horvath, 1983). The Schneiders are still waiting for their biographer; the American historian, Jean Joughin, does not appear to have published the results of her extensive research on the Chagots.

12. Jean-Baptiste Dumay, *Mémoires d'un militant ouvrier du Creusot (1841–1905)*, introduction and notes by Pierre Ponsot; preface by Ernest Labrousse (Grenoble: Presses universitaires, 1976).

13. Jean-Pierre Houssel, *Le Roannais: Une région textile* (Roanne: Les Cahiers de fabrique, 1986); Danièle Miguet, *Hortense et Jean-Marie: Ouvriers tisseurs* (Roanne: Les Cahiers de la fabrique, 1986).

14. Claude-Isabelle Brelot and René Locatelli, *Les Salines de Salins: Un millénaire d'exploitation du sel en Franche-Comté* (Besançon: CNDP, CRDP de Besançon, 1981); Claude-Isabelle Brelot, *La Saline comtale de Salins (Jura)* (Besançon: CNDP, CRDP de Besançon), 1985.

15. Serge Benoît, *La Grande forge de Buffon*: *Monument historique; Historique et guide de visite Musée de la sidérurgie en Bourgogne du Nord* (Buffon: Association pour la sauvegarde et l'animation des forges de Buffon, 1990).

16. Special protection has been in place in Paris for the Marais since 1970 (plan for protection of 126 hectares). In a limited intervention on 3.5 hectares a spectacular renovation was achieved in the Thorigny sector (Hôtel Salé).

17. Manhattan has preserved in the Soho district (south of Houston Street) a large number of buildings, including almost entire streets, with their façades of cast-iron architecture. On this subject see Kaisa Broner, *New York face à son patrimoine* (Brussels: Mardaga, 1986).

18. Danièle Miguet, *Hortense et Jean-Marie ouvriers tisseurs* 15 (collection "Les Cahiers de Fabrique," Écomusée du Roannais, 1986).

19. For example, Serge Grafteaux, *Mémé Santerre: Une vie* (Paris: Marabout, 1975). This work has been translated by Louise A. Tilly and Kathryn I. Tilly, *Mémé Santerre: A French Woman of the People* (New York: Schocken Books, 1985).

20. Serge Bonnet, in collaboration with Étienne Kagan and Michel Maigret, *L'Homme du fer: Mineurs de fer et ouvriers sidérgistes lorrains: 1889–1930* (Nancy: Centre lorrain d'études sociologiques, 1976), vol. 1; Yvon Lamy, *Hommes de fer en Périgord au XIXe siècle* (Lyons: La Manufacture, 1987).

21. See, for example, Helen Harden-Chenut, *Formation d'une culture ouvrière féminine: Les Bonnetières troyennes, 1880–1939* (Thesis, University of Paris IV, n.d.).

22. See in particular the journal *Monuments historiques* 3 (1977): "L'Architecture industrielle"; 128 (August–September 1983): "Colbert et les manufactures"; and 150–51 (April–June 1987): "Ouvrages d'art,"150–51.

23. See *La Manufacture du Dijonval et la Draperie sedanaise, 1650–1850, Cahiers de l'inventaire* 2 (1984).

24. *Tourcoing 1711 –1984: Architecture du centre-ville* (Lille: Inventaire général, 1984), 2 vols.

25. See Henri Loyrette, "La Tour Eiffel," *Les Lieux de mémoire*, vol. 3, *Les France: De l'archive à l'emblème* (Paris: Éditions Gallimard, 1992), and more generally, Yves Lequin, "The Industrial Arts," in the present volume.

26. "Les Forges du pays de Châteaubriant," *Cahiers de l'inventaire* 3 (1984); "La Métallurgie du fer dans les Ardennes (XVIe–XIXe)," *Cahiers de l'inventaire* 11 (1988).

27. Hubert Watelet, *Le Grand-Hornu: Joyau de la révolution industrielle et du Borinage* (Brussels: Grand-Hornu Images, 1989).

28. Jean-François Lyon-Caen and Jean-Claude Ménégoz, *Cathédrales électriques: Architecture des centrales électriques du Dauphiné* (Grenoble: Cent-Pages, 1989).

29. Author's note: Truly said, one must acknowledge the efforts made by quite a number of big businesses in order to "rediscover" and valorize their collections of black-and-white photographs, sometimes coming in tens of thousands. See, for instance, the collection kept by the Académie François Bourdon in Le Creusot, a treasure for the physical, technical, or human history of the Schneider enterprise. Not to mention, somewhat later, of the "businesses filmography."

30. "Musée du papier peint," *Bulletin de la Société industrielle de Mulhouse* 793 (1984).

31. Pierre-Christian Guiollard, *Les Chevalements des houillères françaises de 1830 à 1939* (N.p.: printed by author, 1989).

32. On what still remained of this cohabitation at the turn of the nineteenth century, consult the volumes in *Voyage en France* by Victor-Eugène Ardouin-Dumazet (Paris: Berger Levrault, 1893–1917). Ardouin-Dumazet, the son of a calico textile worker in Vizille, was a journalist for *Le Temps* and later *Le Figaro*, specializing in economic news.

33. DATAR (Délégation à l'aménagement du territoire et à l'action régionale), *Les Grandes Friches industrielles*, report produced in 1985 under the direction of J.-P. Lacaze by the Groupe de travail interministériel, Ministère de l'équipement, du logement de l'aménagement du territoire et des transports (Paris, 1985) and published (Paris: Documentation française, 1986).

CHAPTER 5

PROVERBS, TALES, AND SONGS

❧

DANIEL FABRE

Si l'esprit français, strictement
Imaginatif et abstrait, donc poétique, jette un
éclat, ce ne sera pas ainsi: il répugne, en cela
d'accord avec l'Art dans son intégrité, qui est
inventeur, à la Légende.

Stéphane Mallarmé, *Richard Wagner*, 1886.[1]

If the French mind—strictly imaginative
and abstract, and therefore poetic—is to
radiate brilliance, it will not do so in this way:
it is put off—and in this it concurs with the
whole integrity of Art, which is inventive—by Legend.

"Clustered images," an "irregular pace," "frequent repetitions," "large objects of nature" beside "familiar objects of life," such are the characteristics that Jacques Turgot underlined when he presented to the *Journal étranger*, in September 1760, his first translations of the Ossian poems.[2] This extraordinary literature is not the fruit of an extreme climate or a particular political system; the work of bards from the Scottish highlands is not too far removed, stylistically, from the more familiar work of Asian poets. But then where does its charm come from? According to Turgot, "The poverty of their language, together with the simplicity of their mores,

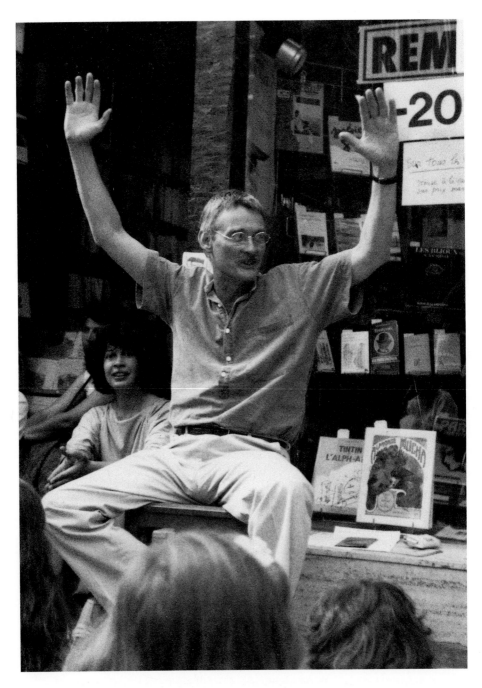

Figure 5.1
Jean Baudin with storyteller Susana Azquinzer in the background.

offers a very natural [explanation]. It is quite certain that the fewer terms a people has for expressing abstract ideas, the more it is obliged in making itself understood to borrow help at every moment from images and metaphors, and at the same time the more its ideas are necessarily enclosed within the field of concrete objects." Turgot thus sketches the outlines of a new world, that of the poetic word. But he situates it apart from the great cultures of Europe, far from "civilized peoples," from "cultivated nations" whose idioms—richer in objects and in turns of phrase, more abstract as well—have lost their expressive vividness. In the West, therefore, it is outside cities and away from educated citizens that one must search for the words and the works that Turgot calls "untamed language."

Half a century later, when the official art of the empire was making faint references to the tales of Ossian, the Celtic Academy (1805) undertook to realize the aspiration that was very briefly shared, in 1760, by Turgot and Diderot. In the same way that it dealt with the most imposing stone relics, it named oral works of art "monuments."[3] Later still, from 1840 to 1900, by combining their study of living speakers with their inventory of traces deposited little by little over the centuries, a few scholars drew French oral literature out of the shadows and struggled to organize it. They wanted to find within it a body of wisdom (proverbs), a mythology (tales), a poetry (songs). Although those three genres, in that order, had surfaced in the course of history under conditions whose specific features and inflections we are going to consider, they now came to rub against one another as shared property, as common knowledge transmitted at once by peers, families, and schools. A modest treasure, no doubt— one that does not claim to establish a French national identity, but one that circulates intensely like small change, a discreet sign of recognition, an ordinary childhood memory capable of reactivating itself from time to time, so as to transform these venerable "frozen words" into emblems of difference.

WORDS FOR THE RECORD

In positing the relation between native language, social world, and poetic forms, Turgot doubtless risked a somewhat hasty shortcut, but he put his finger on the first perceived source of oral tradition, that is, on the idiom itself. A locution, a turn of phrase, an expression thought to be untranslatable: are these not the mark—a bit enigmatic if one lingers over it—of membership in a group? In the dictum and the proverb, this mark of singularity is enriched on two levels. First on the level of form: antitheses, anaphoras, syntactical parallelisms, assonance, and internal rhyme always abound in them. Second, on the level of utterance, they aim to produce a very particular effect: to utter a proverb is to illuminate conversation with a spark of timelessness, an indisputable maxim bolstered by the archaism of its appearance and the metaphorical openness of its meaning.[4]

It is not surprising, therefore, that all self-aware speech turns toward the proverb in search of the source and the irrefutable proof of its identity. This was the case in France as early as the twelfth century, when, in addition to literary works in the nascent form of romance (*roman*), people gathered and recopied collections containing dozens, sometimes hundreds of *respits*, as proverbs were called in French before the word *proverbe* appeared at the end of the century. This latter word, a scholarly Latinism applied to a kind of language whose "common" coarseness people were occasionally fond of emphasizing, signals the variegation of the manuscripts in which proverbial turns of speech were transcribed between the thirteenth and the fifteenth centuries.[5] All these collections stage an encounter with what they take as a novelty to tame, a language to capture: the "vulgar tongue" spoken *in gallica* (thirteenth century), to which the "silly jokes [*bourdes*], idle sayings [*folies*], and proverbs of France" (late fourteenth century) bear such abundant witness. But Latin was never far away; Latin translations or equivalents accompany most of the anthologies, and such adaptations are mostly in verse. They are signed "Serlon" in one of the most prolific manuscript traditions of the Middle Ages. Several decades later, this Latin coating gave way to the assonanced, six-line stanzas in French that would henceforth clothe the famous "common proverbs." This formal transposition acknowledged the oral proverb to be a deliberate discourse, but one that was still unsure of itself and that only writing could endow with the dignity of a memorable text. Such dignity went together with the recognition accorded to illustrious authors about whom little was known, authors all the more revered for remaining haloed in legend. The most authentic collections of precepts were attributed to Seneca, who was nothing but a name; to Cato, who apparently had nothing to do with either "the ancient one" or the citizen of Utica; and especially to Solomon, in whom the twelfth century saw a magician-king, master of animals and elements, inventor of Syrian and Arabic letters, keeper of all the natural wisdom revealed to him by "the queen of ants [who] halted one day in his hand." Above and beyond the formulaic *Wisdom* with which the Old Testament credits him, Solomon was the most sacred originator of proverbial sayings.[6] He was associated, in a dialogue that enjoyed great popularity up to the sixteenth century, with the peasant Marcoul (or Marcolf), a lout who spoke his mind with the unvarnished idiom of the people and demonstrated that an acquaintance with maxims and their proper uses permitted its possessor to converse with the most renowned kings.

The proverb thus remained in circulation—between languages, between anonymity and authority, between linguistic forms. Its usage was universal. Even if some recalled how diverse were its roots, the proverb was an instrument everyone could use, and every social condition was defined by its own panoply of proverbs. As evidence, consider the notebook of a schoolboy from Arbois in the 1320s: he copied out sixty-five proverbs in dialectal French and, as a matter of course, translated them into Latin. At first sight, his choice reflects that of a habitual practitioner of scholastic adages such as the "golden words" of Cato. The most general precepts—"Better to die in joy than to live in shame" (*Mieux vaut mourir en joie que vivre en honte*), "Wisdom is worth more than wealth" (*Sagesse vaut mieux que richesse*)—are often converted in terms of practical morality: "Don't forget that less can be more" (*On ne doit pas perdre le peu pour le prou*). But once in a while one glimpses the pride of the little scholar ("If you anoint the peasant, he'll shit in your hand" [*Oignez le vilain, il vous chiera dans la main*]) and the boisterous jollity of the schoolboy ("God thinks on those who drink" [*Qui bien boit, Dieu voit*]). An entire station in society is exposed in these quintessential phrases, which the schoolboy adopted and no doubt carried around with him.[7] Preachers used other maxims, recopied or noted in passing, to enliven their sermons; one thirteenth-century cleric even composed a little treatise on this aspect of pastoral rhetoric. Jurists practicing either canon or civil law made personal collections of proverbs mixed in with quotations from the Decretals or the Digest. Physicians similarly noted their principles of diagnosis and therapy, their rules for diet and hygiene; their adages can still be found in the oral proverbs of modern times. The ultimate proof—if it were needed—of the quasi professional use made of these collections lies in their written form: writing came to shore up verbal memory because it permitted rapid access to the treasure trove of maxims by means of alphabetical lists, which appeared in this context at the end of the thirteenth century.

The Renaissance did not instantly efface these practices. When printing presses set the *Cathon en français*, the *Dits de Salomon*, or the *Proverbes communs*, it only added finishing touches to a manuscript tradition three centuries long. Yet even before printing emerged, and thereafter throughout the sixteenth century, people developed what one might call a modern proverbial consciousness, that is, a fairly broad range of critical and theoretical attitudes that took this type of expression as an object for reflection. There thus arose in France a new and at first very distinct ensemble of approaches to oral tradition.

A Light-Hearted Science

A first approach originated far from Paris, in the capital of Languedoc. It repeated the separation by which the literature of proverbs—whose various faces we have just sketched out—established itself in the eleventh and twelfth centuries, but this time it was normative French that found itself at least implicitly in question. Here we are, then, in Toulouse in 1323. Seven of its bourgeois have founded the "Very Joyous Company of the VII Troubadours of Toulouse" (*Sobregaya companhia des VII trobadors de Tolosa*), which hoped to restore the fortunes of literature by giving prizes every year to the best poems. This institution would later codify its rules for writing: Guilhem Molinier drafted them in 1341, and they were promulgated in 1356. *The Laws of Love* (*Las Leys d'amor*): such is the handsome title of a treatise on grammar and rhetoric that parades through figures of language and forms of poetry. Among the latter, the proverb holds a prominent place. Guilhem Molinier distinguishes two kinds: proverbs whose source is cited—Solomon, Cato, Seneca—and proverbs that people habitually use without knowing the author, or "common proverbs" that in the south of France are sometimes called *reproverbis*. This grammarian from Toulouse imposes no explicit hierarchy; since he needs to restore the dignity of the (Provençal) language, he makes a virtue of necessity by using whatever comes to hand. Besides, the greatest troubadours of the twelfth and thirteenth centuries did not hesitate to stud their verses with proverbial locutions of either enigmatic or transparent import. However, the examples given by Molinier—except for a few meteorological adages that are still alive today, such as "From lots of wind comes little rain" (*De gran vent pauca plueja*)—derive mostly from moralizing distiches whose regular, swaying rhythm he cherishes. There existed in Languedoc no anthologies of "ordinary proverbs" or "common proverbs," and the rhetorician, concerned to reestablish a language that seemed likely to disappear in written form, hesitated to give proverbs the same place they occupied in everyday speech, even if he was the first to treat the proverb as an islet that still broke the surface and witnessed to a submerged world, according to an image that would later come into vogue.[8]

This was not the concern that, in the sixteenth century, attracted writers fond of proverbs. Despite the nuances among their attitudes, they were united on at least one point: a certain idea of the "popular." Montaigne pursued his meditation on this subject the farthest, and he therefore embodies for us this second approach. One may remember that "on the day of the calends of March 1571," on the eve of his thirty-eighth birthday, having relinquished all his public offices, he withdrew into his library, ordered the painting of a Latin phrase that announced his choice of lifestyle, and would soon spangle the woodwork with fifty-seven adages, twenty-five in Greek and thirty-two in Latin.* A formulaic style of writing would be one of the constants of his *Essais*, which reveal his knowledge and his habitual manipulation of proverbs.[9] These expressions appear by the dozen beneath Montaigne's pen. He draws some of them from his reading of ancient authors or from contemporary manuals such as *La civila conversazione* by Stefano Guazzo (Venice, 1581), but it is from within himself—his memory, his way of speaking, his encounters—that he draws most of them: "I am the form of speech that is born with me, as simple and naive as possible." However, within the flow of each "Essay," the proverb makes audible a still more fundamental "simplicity," a more radical "naiveté." It refers us back, as it were, to the real, the concrete, and the perceptible—"So says a peasant, so says a woman. He [Socrates] never opens his mouth but to talk of coachmen, carpenters, cobblers, or masons. He draws inductions and comparisons from the most common and familiar actions of men; everyone understands him." The proverb gives resonance to the harmony of language, a kind of beauty that is "delicate and hidden; one needs very sharp and well purified vision to discover this secret light." It speaks the truth: "The talk of peasants, I commonly find, is better formulated according to the prescriptions of true philosophy than that of our philosophers." This proverbial knowledge—concerning both what to say and what to do—cannot be learned at "schools for speechifying" but only in the fields, the streets, the markets, and the taverns. It passes from one nation to another; it travels across history; it constitutes not a fixed collection of tried-and-true moral sayings but rather a critical tool to be used on the illusions and vanities of the great theater that is the world. At the foundation of the proverb, beneath the impersonal saying that one ought to make one's own in order to progress toward self-knowledge, the essentials of the human condition are thus to be discovered.

Its language (for the new "troubadours" of Toulouse) or its naked truth (for Montaigne) made the proverb valuable for reviving the splendor of a forgotten literature or for concluding an argument with what is called the *definitive word* (*fin mot*). None of its connoisseurs claimed to study the proverbial expression solely for its own sake: that would be the aim of a third approach, the one inaugurated by Erasmus in 1500, when he defined the proverb in the introduction to his *Adages* as "a window opening onto the ancient world." It indeed hands down to us not only the advice of old sages, but also the customs that have disappeared. The proverb is a

---

* All translations from Montaigne are my own, but in making them I have on occasion consulted Donald Frame's translation of *The Complete Works of Montaigne* (Stanford, CA: Stanford University Press, 1957).—Trans.

document, a source, and the founders of a national history would apply themselves to demonstrating this. In their work, the archaeology of the spoken word served to support their convictions about the autonomy and the continuity of the *lingua gallica*, convictions that were affirmed as early as 1531 by Jacques Dubois, nuanced two years later by Charles de Bovelles, a great collector of proverbs, then taken up again and amply orchestrated by one of the scholars of the era, Étienne Pasquier.[10] Does he not, after all, devote several passages from his *Recherches de la France*, composed between 1560 and 1607, to describing a nation of Gallic origins, whose ancient mores are revealed by certain proverbs to those who know how to decode them? With subtlety and erudition, Pasquier glosses locutions that refer to symbolic punishments ("To cut the beard short" [*Faire bien la barbe*], cautionary edicts ("A good name is worth more than a gold belt" [*Bonne renommée vaut mieux que ceinture dorée*]), and the immemorial antagonism between peasants and wolves. Pasquier thus comes close to treating the proverb as witness to a culture that survives *without knowing it* because its originary institutions and customs have been forgotten, because the "popular corruption" of language has made the allusions preserved in its ways of speaking unrecognizable.

On the brink of the seventeenth century, and in a way that was to last, the study of proverbs had thus put some very firm perspectives into place. Even if the most extreme advocates of classical "good usage," speaking through Vaugelas, would later shelve the "common adages" that Father Bouhours compared to "those old clothes that people keep in their wardrobes and use, at the most, only for masquerades," the proverb would always remain present in literary taste, in reflections, in writing.[11] For some, it harbored all the pith of a language saved from obsolescence: in 1607, Larade and Voltoire brought out the first collections in Gascon—which was at the time, admittedly, the king's own language; in 1657, Oihenart recorded Poitevin adages.[12] For others, the truth of natural reason was expressed in these splinters of discourse: natural reason was not assigned the same role that it played for Montaigne, but it grew in scope to embody the "wisdom of nations" in more and more cosmopolitan compilations of proverbs. As for the erudite vein initiated by Pasquier, it was never interrupted among scholars: in 1656, the Flemish Fleury de Bellingen published an *Étymologie ou explication des Proverbes français* that assured its future.[13]

Too Common a Discourse?

A long history, an extensive range of geographical areas, repeated validation by writings that confirmed its widespread circulation even in a very hierarchical society, a close tie to the identity of the languages of the state and the countryside—everything seemed to conspire to make proverbial wisdom the first object of ethnological study in France, the most evident sign of self-recognition at the moment when the nation began cataloguing the diversity of its manners and promoting a meticulous science of local mores. It is true that in 1789 a learned canon of Sens, the abbot Tuet, published his *Matinées sénonaises, ou Proverbes français*—the version reprinted in the year III would retain only the subtitle—in which he used rich colors to paint the study of proverbs in France while deploring the rupture between men of letters and ordinary people. He felt that only the latter—especially its feminine contingent—had preserved proverbial turns of speech and thought. The inquiry conducted by the abbot Grégoire (1790) dealt with proverbs, as did the questionnaire of the Celtic Academy (1807). The statistics compiled by prefects often inventoried proverbs, which were also published in departmental yearbooks. However, and here lies the paradox, no research, no large-scale analysis would prolong this new curiosity. Although the proverb had been recognized for centuries as the indestructible heart of authentic speech, the rise of romantic ethnography neglected it, or rather abandoned it to a kind of learning that had already insidiously taken it over, that of lexicographers. Indeed, as of the 1606 publication of Nicot's *Trésor de la langue française*, and in addition to the contrasting approaches that we have just depicted, the proverbial locution entered the domain of the illustration for other dictionary entries, sometimes in alphabetical collections of proverbial expressions. The rigidity and monotony of this presentation triumphed, giving birth during the first half of the nineteenth century to a series of "proverb dictionaries" by authors of all kinds.[14] These would contribute, by way of example, to the great works of Larousse and Littré. Such lists dissolved the originality of proverbial forms, their semantic subtlety, the rhetoric of their appropriate usage, and the coherence of their grouping by locality. Even in the work of folklorists and ethnographers, nothing remained except these forbidding lists, which gave the impression that proverbs were uttered anonymously and with transparent signification. Fashion turned instead to the song and the tale, which were more obviously endowed with meaning, closer to real works of art, easier to associate with the person of their interpreter, with the society of their listeners, and with the region of their transmission. For proverbs, there lingered only some solid compilations of past collections (Leroux de Lincy, 1845 and 1859) and some regional monographs organized around tightly limited topics, such as Canel's study of taunts used between villages in Normandy (1840 and 1859) or Daugé's work on expressions concerning marriage and the family in Gascony (1916–30).

Thus, in contrast to the proliferation of curious proverbs under the

ancien régime, the study of proverbs never acquired the dignity of a recognized field of knowledge. To collect them seemed futile, and their
interpretation remained a rare and marginal pursuit. In France, neither
history nor ethnology nor linguistics took the proverb as a serious and
autonomous object of inquiry. This lasting neglect, this divorce between
practice and knowledge, left the field free for other uses and other approaches. Since no intimidating science got in the way, and since proverbial
discourse appeared only in a passive form, dispersed throughout a string of
dictionaries and anthologies, anyone could revive it in his own fashion. As
of 1830, the mass media—almanacs, daily newspapers, and magazines—
were stuffed with it; even today, radio and television are unable to talk
about gardening or the weather without citing some "old proverb." Furthermore, literature unceasingly parodied proverbial forms or meditated
on their poetics, while the novel tried for a long time to reconstitute the
unique life of proverbs in everyday speech.[15] It is in the novel that habits of
speech reveal themselves down to the finest grain and that one perceives
the truth—all the more noticeable for having been transfigured—of proverbial discourse in action.

One ought to follow step by step the treatment that Balzac and Flaubert impose on this "wisdom of nations," but only Proust will occupy us
for the moment, because he spotlights the imagery of oral expressions in a
way that is more deliberate, more complete, and more conscious of social
distinctions. In any case, whereas Bergotte, the ideal writer, struggles to
transpose life's most banal situations into a noble style, the narrator of the
Recherche, on the contrary, avidly composes duets or fugues from the flow
of overheard conversation. Françoise, Aunt Léonie's cook, is the incarnation of a very powerful manner of speaking. In diametrical opposition to
the presumed spontaneity of popular speech, her words, like her actions,
are "governed by an imperious, extensive, subtle, and intransigent code,"
on the basis of which she restores the vivacity of a decisive act to "the
old ways of speaking in which we see a dead metaphor." It is thus that
she gets at the truth when embroidering on the chronicle of Combray
life as it passes under Aunt Léonie's windows or when finishing off the
kitchen maid, who is ill after giving birth, with the final thrust of her
loudly declaimed monologue: "All she had to do was *not* do what it took
for this! But she enjoyed it! So she had better not put on airs now. Any
boy must surely have been lost to God before he'd take up with the likes
of *that*. Oh, it's just like they said in my poof mother's patois: 'If you're
besotted with it, then to your nose / A dog's hind end smells like a rose.'"
Here, as is often the case, the maxim is shored up with a reference to
the tradition and the heritage by which Françoise—"a medieval peasant

(surviving into the nineteenth century)"—comes to take her place in the long procession of faces and speech patterns evoked for the narrator by the sculptures in the porch of Saint-André-des-Champs.[16] But this singular resurrection of the immemorial is no longer the sole way in which locutions, adages, and ready-made comparisons reappear. In the world of cities and bourgeois citizens, they continue to nourish memory, but they do so according to wholly different principles, which Charlus explains very well in regard to the superficial M. de Norpois, so susceptible to the latest linguistic crazes:

> have you noticed this proliferation of new expressions that, when they have at last worn out from daily use . . . are immediately supplanted by other commonplaces? In the past, I recall, you amused yourself by noting linguistic fashions that appeared, remained for a while, and then disappeared: "he who sows the wind harvests the storm," "the dogs bark, the caravan passes," "give me good policies and I'll give you good finances, said Baron Louis," . . . "Work for the King of Prussia" (that one, moreover, has come back to life, as was inevitable). Oh well, since then—alas—I have seen a lot of them die![17]

TALES TO TELL, TALES TO READ

Just like the proverbial expression, the tale seems to belong to a past without limits. However, if the Middle Ages clearly identified the former, they let the latter go unnoticed, or rather they failed to define its character because every narrative could at that time be called a "tale." Of course, there are many allusions to oral tradition—that of the Bretons in Marie de France, that of peasants in preachers' sermons—but it does not fit the mold of any one genre, it has no specific content, and it implies no rite of transmission. It is therefore from our present perspective, enriched by a history that discovered *the* tale, with the whole range of its recurrent plots, that we are able to flush it out from the cover of sermon exempla, saints' lives, and romances.[18] In fact, one must wait until the Renaissance to begin glimpsing what we call tales, and even then one sees them indirectly, through the situations in which they are uttered and exchanged. Boccaccio superbly constructed an exceptional occasion for storytelling: Florence in 1348, the black death, the seven young women in mourning in the church of Santa Maria Novella, the three handsome young men, the palace preserved on a hill, the election of a queen for the day, the order she gives to tell tales.[19] In France, tales were evoked by a setting altogether different from the aristocratic oasis; the very source of oral tradition was located elsewhere.

The Distaff Gospels (Les Évangiles des quenouilles), written in Flanders around 1460, were dictated, according to their amusing author, by a circle of neighbors who gathered "after supper for the sake of jollity and pastimes, in the long nights between Christmas and Candlemas." They talked of love, evil, and magic during these evenings, about which the scribe specifies, "In France they are called série (serée), in Artois siète, and in Hainaut escriène." The organization of the latter is reported in detail by a Burgundian lawyer, Étienne Tabourot, in his "Dijon Evenings" (Escraignes disjonnaises) (1592). It takes place in a hut made for the occasion out of branches that appear, when seen from the outside, to form "a swallow's nest." Inside, girls and women spin, receive timid homage from their lovers, and above all unwind "an infinite string of witticisms and graceful tales." These are doubtless similar to the ones that Noël du Fail heard during Breton evenings (veillois): "And thus occupied with diverse tasks, the good gentleman Robin (having imposed silence) began a beautiful tale of the time when animals could talk . . . : how the fox sneaked the fish away from the fisherman, how he had the wolf beaten by washerwomen when teaching him to fish . . . , about Mélusine, the werewolf, Cuir d'Anette, fairies. . . ." A winter evening, with all the neighborhood assembled around the hearth, the women spinning, the men carding hemp or repairing wooden tools: such is the scene in which "beautiful" and "graceful" tales arise out of the silence. One can sense that they are very different from particular local anecdotes; even if they are barely sketched out, their subjects portray situations and call forth figures—the wolf, the fox, the young girl, the fairy—that are elevated to the scope of the universal. But about the details of such narratives, the era teaches us very little.[20] The only collection that circulated in France with a certain amount of success—twelve editions between 1560 and 1614—was adapted from Straparole, a Venetian author who tried to disguise oral fables (fiabe) as historical novellas (novelle) in his Facétieuses nuits.[21] One had to wait for their rediscovery in order to know what the tales recounted and to revitalize the nearly defunct drama of the storytelling evening.

In fact, it was another setting that brought such evenings back to life, a very different social world that showed interest in the tale as of the 1650s, much earlier than is generally believed. Allusions to it flow increasingly from the pens of writers at the time: Scarron, Molière, La Fontaine, and so on. Furthermore, we learn that the art of storytelling was alive and well in the best society. La Porte, a valet to Louis XIV, regrets that the young king, "removed from the care of women" at age seven, was deprived "at bedtime of tales like 'Donkey Skin'" and missed them sorely.

In October 1656, Madame de Sévigné recounts for the Grande Mademoiselle★ a narrative she doubtless heard from the people of Montfort-sur-Meu, not far from her property at Rochers, in Brittany: "It is not a tale of Mother Goose, but rather of the Montfort duck, which, upon my word, resembles her closely." In August 1671, Madame de Sévigné writes to Madame de Grignan about "the tales with which one amuses the ladies at Versailles: we call that *simmering them*." And she herself goes on to *simmer* her daughter with the story of a "princess more beautiful than the day" on whom "the fairies breathed . . . at every moment," although she gives an abridged version because "the tale lasts a good hour." Just as ballets and operas, with their special effects, put the marvelous and its metamorphoses on stage, so the witty minds of the age were ready to welcome what was the ultimate infatuation of the "great century": the fashion for fairy tales.[22]

PERRAULT, THE INVENTOR

Published in 1697 under the name of Pierre Darmancour (the young son of Charles Perrault), *Histoires, ou Contes du temps passé* did not inaugurate this vogue. The way had been opened by Mademoiselle Lhéritier, Perrault's poor and virtuous niece, and also by the very scandalous Madame d'Aulnoy, the first writer who, in 1690, slipped into her *Histoire d'Hypolite, comte de Duglas* an "Island of Felicity" whose source is certainly oral. But a marked difference sets Perrault—father and son together if one posits, with Marc Soriano, their intimate collaboration—in opposition to the other twenty or so authors who brought fame to this genre.[23] Madame d'Aulnoy, descended from good Norman nobility, undoubtedly possessed a more extensive knowledge of oral material. She reworked sixteen tales drawn from oral tradition, decorating them with turns of phrase that carried the scent of their native soil. But like her contemporaries and her followers, she deployed and dissolved their plots in fabulous novelistic abundance; she multiplied their magical elements at will; she turned the initial narrative into a perpetual wellspring of surprises and enchantments. Conversely, as soon as Perrault gave up the precious style of versification that he practiced at first—in "The Patience of Grisélidis," "Donkey Skin," and "The Ridiculous Wishes" that he collected into a volume in 1695—he quickly achieved a sort of distilled perfection in which one recognizes not the

★ Anne Marie Louise d'Orléans, duchesse de Montpensier (1627–93), was the daughter of Gaston d'Orléans (brother of Louis XIII) and thus a first cousin to Louis XIV. She was known as La Grande Mademoiselle. One of the richest heiresses in Europe, she wrote controversial memoirs that were suppressed by Louis XIV.—Ed.

faithful notation of a storyteller's words, but the refined art that makes the illusion of oral storytelling seem truer than the reality.

Let us simply note a few features of Perrault's stylistic originality. It implies that he was profoundly conscious of the poetics of the tale, which requires him to renounce—largely but never quite completely—the common ways of fashioning a novel or a novella. Picturesque description on one hand and psychological justification on the other give way to a simple chain of actions whose necessity seems self-evident because it derives from the tacit ordering principles of the genre. It also derives from a nexus of fundamental relationships that Perrault may have accentuated by turning the disinherited younger child, violently rejected by his parents, into the hero—or, more often, the heroine—par excellence. But on the level of detail, Perrault takes a number of liberties with the oral heritage he claims to follow. It is well known, for example, that the art of storytelling very often relies on the reiteration of episodes, as when the misadventures of two heroes precede the success—glorified by contrast—of a third. Perrault uses this formula, but without becoming enslaved by it. He forgets about it midway through "Puss in Boots," and he cleverly distorts it in "Cinderella," where the third ball is replaced, as it were, by the redoubled description of the second, from the viewpoint of the heroine and then also her evil stepsisters. Only writing can authorize such a displacement of the ternary rhythm. Similarly, Perrault manipulates as he sees fit the repetition of stock phrases, knowing as he does the fascinating power and the mnemonic force of such refrains. Treated as sources of humor in "Little Red Riding Hood," which is permeated with imitations of baby talk, repeated formulas become the focal points of dramatic suspense by the end of "Bluebeard." There is nothing, not even the position of the narrator, that Perrault does not toy with: he varies from immediate participation in the terrifying movement of the narrative in "Tom Thumb" to ironic or comic distance in "Riquet with the Tuft" and "Puss in Boots." Is this the sovereign liberty of the writer or a desire to show the range of viewpoints that every storyteller may occupy?

To these choices, barely touched on here, Perrault adds his own, personal conception of the tale. In the first place, he ennobles it in the name not of a distant origin—such as the Middle Ages of the troubadours so dear to Mademoiselle Lhéritier—but rather of a mode of transmission: "Connoisseurs claim . . . that one must regard [tales] as being authored by an infinite number of fathers, mothers, grandmothers, governesses, and nurses, who for perhaps a thousand years have added to them, each teller detailing more agreeable circumstances that have remained part of the tales, while everything that was badly conceived has been forgotten." "Original tales" are thus, for Perrault, "tales of an old rock" that have undergone the slow erosion of time, that stay in tune with memory, and that offer "a clear moral."[24] They are less the fruits of remote history than the slowly polished products of *tradition*, which Perrault imagines and places at the opening of his book under the engraved features of a storytelling maidservant—the old lady, the nurse, Mother Goose, the governess—who gathers children of all ages in a circle around the bourgeois hearth. She tells stories while thread turns in her fingers.

The storytelling evening in Brittany, an affair of grown-up country folk as Noël du Fail portrayed it, henceforth took on this new ambiance, underwent a change of setting and meaning. Since tales represent the art of storytelling in its childhood, children naturally enjoy them, and Perrault wished with all his might that writing might prolong, disseminate, and refine their pleasure by spelling out the moral of the stories. Himself a widower, he raised three sons and a daughter. He wanted to take his place in the pedagogical debate that Madame de Maintenon and Fénelon were then bringing into prominence. After the publication of his tales, he translated the *Fables* of Faërne (1699) for young readers. By establishing the equivalence of the traditional, the popular, and the childlike, he opened a decisive gap between salon entertainment, in which he had played his part, and his *Histoires, ou Contes du temps passé*.

THE TWO TRADITIONS

Perrault nonetheless benefited from the fever that swept through Paris and also the provinces, seizing on the little world—largely feminine—of those who wrote and appreciated fairy tales. He did not challenge this term, which now sounds hackneyed but at that time signaled a literary novelty. The fairy godmother, a sort of Fate in reverse, is present in "Cinderella" and "Riquet with the Tuft"; oddly multiplied (since there is only a single fairy in this tale), she even figures in one title, "The Fairies." If Perrault did not make the omnipresence of fairies into a principle of construction for his tales, he did consent to their predominance and certainly also to their recent metamorphosis, the one announced by Madame de Murat in the "Dedication to Modern Fairies" that opens her *Histoires sublimes et allégoriques* (1699):

> The former Fairies, your predecessors, no longer pass for anything
> but frivolous pranksters in comparison to you. Their occupations
> were lowly and childish . . . ; their amusements were to dance in the
> moonlight or to transform themselves into old ladies, cats, monkeys,
> and surly monks so as to frighten children and the feebleminded. . . .
> But you, my ladies, you have taken another path; you occupy your-

selves only with important matters, the least of which are to give wit to those who have none, beauty to the ugly, eloquence to the ignorant, wealth to the poor, and brilliance to even the most obscure things.

In Perrault's works, as elsewhere, fairies left forests and caves, stables and kitchens, so as to weave destinies in broad daylight throughout their realm. Moreover, the editions of Perrault's *Histoires* were carried along by successive waves of educated taste for these modern divinities: the edition of 1697 coincided with its highest tide; the new Paris edition of 1742 came in the midst of a strong resurgence; the reprinting of Perrault's work in the "Bibliothèque universelle des romans" (1776) and at the head of the grand edition of the "Cabinet des fées" (1785) confirmed his preeminence.

But, remarkably, there was also a parallel development that might seem to be a just reversal of the situation. The learned Perrault did not disdain "blue paper books"; he faithfully borrowed from them the plot for "The Patience of Grisélidis." His writing very quickly ended up, however, in book peddlers' packs, something that was not his prime ambition. From 1723 on, print shops in Troyes obtained permission to print his tales. Their editions appeared one after another beginning in 1737. Between 1760 and 1820, Perrault's writing made the round of all the chapbook printers: Rouen, Orléans, Metz, Toulouse, and so forth, especially since printers fell during this time into the habit of publishing each tale separately in small, illustrated booklets. Their success did not fade in the nineteenth century, and Charles Nisard, in his 1853 report to the minister of the interior on the chapbook trade, could only underline and celebrate their unanimously favorable reception. As the narratives in these chapbooks were increasingly simplified and spaced out on the page in such a way as to encourage inept readers, visual images came to prop them up. The images served less as illustrations than as separate commentary, more and more independent of the text. Before the Revolution, the first copper engravings had appeared, with the accompanying stories reduced to brief captions. These were followed, after 1830, by large images divided into frames, engraved and colored in Épinal.[25]

Such widespread circulation produced a double effect. First, Perrault was gradually erased from memory, or rather he was elevated to the level of allegory. As early as 1716, stories he had not written were attributed to him; he became the generic author, the "master of tales." He acted as scribe for a tradition that made itself so visible, so readable, that it finally took its proverbial place in everyday language: "We have ended up using some of his proper names as if they were common nouns: we talk in this way about a Cinderella, a Bluebeard, a Little Red Riding Hood, or a Prince Charming; and we also commonly use certain expressions to characterize a given situation or sometimes merely as a game: 'You certainly made us wait for you,' or 'Anne, my sister Anne, don't you see anything coming?' or 'Pull out the peg and the latch will fall.'"[26] This dilution of the author into the commonplace goes together with a deeper and more complex movement: in the eighteenth and nineteenth centuries, there arose between the oral and the written tale a zone of interference, a hybrid domain. On one hand, the tales of Perrault and a few other writers—Madame d'Aulnoy ("The Bluebird," "Beauty with the Golden Hair," "The White Cat") or Madame Leprince de Beaumont ("Beauty and the Beast")—called forth echoes, because they were drawn from oral tradition. Writers and illustrators explored their memory and questioned those around them. Printing houses thus brought to light fragments of oral culture from various localities, including whole tales that followed in the wake of canonical narratives. "Tom Thumb" called to mind "Thumblet" (*Pouçot*), the story of a minuscule boy swallowed by a cow, whereas "John the Strong," "The Man without Fear," or "John the Bear," which were also told with pictures by the middle of the nineteenth century, could do without literary mediation. On the other hand, especially among literate Francophiles in the northwestern corner of the country, oral tradition moved in the opposite direction by feeding on the printed word. It adopted the previously unknown "Sleeping Beauty," it reworked "Little Red Riding Hood," and it sprinkled oral narratives with water sprites (*fées "Truitonne*) and "birds the colors of weather." The unusual conjunction of these movements insured that a dozen or so tales became ubiquitous well before primary schools deigned to adopt them around 1885.

This underground propagation corresponded to a long period in which Perrault faded from view together with the whole question of tales as he had formulated it. In eighteenth-century intellectual circles, fairies retained a bit of their former dignity only by appearing as mythical creatures whose lineaments and adventures were to be compiled for the use of poems and artists. But the tales themselves reemerged from the shadows—that is, from the haze of banality maintained by their constant circulation—only with the beginnings of romanticism. Nodier positively worshipped Perrault; Leroux de Lincy published his works with care, as befitted an ancient author; and Baron Walkenaer, in his *Lettres sur les contes de fées attribués à Perrault et sur l'origine des fées* (1826), tore off the veil as follows: "A belief in fairies was the mythology of our ancestors and was produced by the soil of our fatherland; it came to us from neither the Greeks nor the Romans, as several scholars have claimed: it was born in our own France, it is native here, it belongs to us." To each his own paganism. Many of the great collections of tales made during the Second

Empire in remote regions of France—Brittany, Gascony, Velay, and so
on—were assembled in light of this interpretation; one can even say that
it was what rendered them conceivable and possible. Of course, these collections largely obscured the give-and-take between the oral and the written that produced the tales stored in French memory. They rediscovered
modes of circulation that had been forgotten—storytelling evenings for
grown-ups, such as sailors, soldiers, woodcutters, and pilgrims—but Perrault remained the paragon for everyone in quest of the tradition. Such
collectors as Smith, Sébillot, Arnaudin, or Pourrat, who went in search
of people like the "old women" and the "governesses" of their childhood,
were able to relive their originary experience of storytelling, an experience that Bladé, the discoverer of Gascony's oral tradition, recorded in an
exemplary narrative:

> Summer had come. The sun was going down. In our garden in Lec-
> toure, the fledgling birds were singing among the high branches of
> the cypress trees. In the shade, with her servants, my grandmother
> was spinning wool or flax, like a Roman matron. Sitting at her feet, I
> waited quietly. "My servants," she said, "let's entertain the little one."
> And they stayed at it until nightfall. In our local idiom, the beauti-
> ful tales unfolded, recited by slow, rhythmic voices. They unfolded
> in their invariable, ritualistic formulas, often broken by silent pauses
> in which the spinners, with the broad gestures of the Fates, reknotted
> their broken thread and their distant memories.[27]

The Unanimous Song

In 1773, in an *Extract from a Correspondence about Ossian and the Songs of
Ancient Peoples* (*Auszug aus einem Briefwechsel über Ossian und die Lieder alter
Völker*), Herder reproached his compatriots for not yet having undertaken
to collect songs heard "in the streets, alleys, and marketplaces," as well
as those that accompanied "the naive found dances of the peasants"; "they
often cannot be scanned and their rhyme is incorrect," but they were the
very voice of the people. This German apathy was all the more scandalous for the bard of *Sturm und Drang* because the English, with Macpherson
and Percy, had put together vast collections of "the relics of old poetry"
and because the French, for their part, were also active in this domain.[28]
This second reference never fails to sound surprising, but Herder can
be trusted. He knew that a link so durable as to be nearly proverbial in
Europe attached the French to dancing and song. He had certainly read
passages by the great writers who celebrated the simplicity of rustic song:

Rabelais, Montaigne, Malherbe, Molière, and most recently Rousseau, who described in *La Nouvelle Héloïse* (fifth part, seventh letter) the evening of stories told by the hemp carders of Clarens. During that evening are heard "some old love songs [*romances*] whose tunes are not engaging; but they have something sweet and antique about them that is touching in the end. The words are simple, naive, often sad; nonetheless, they are pleasing."

This relative consecration of the song does not in itself imply a secure and stable place for it (in cultivated circles) during that era. Song texts and, above all, song tunes circulated intensely. As inventors of songs and professional performers, the Pont-Neuf chansonniers were, by virtue of both their vocation and their position, universal mediators. Their compositions were heard at fairs and courts, in castles and taverns, in workshops and barracks. Until the end of the eighteenth century, the urban setting that often gave rise to such compositions formed a world buzzing with song lyrics. A song could blossom, circulate, polish itself in the course of its oral transmission, proliferate in multiple variants. Yet, the very notion of "popular song" emerged with the consciousness of a real distance separating what was sung by educated people—the nobility and the bourgeoisie—from what was sung by everyone else. All the more so since the song was a very particular kind of oral art. The proverb came to life in the mouth of anyone who uttered it; the tale was told by a few storytellers to a small audience; the song aspired to be taken up in chorus, tended toward a fulfillment that was immediately collective. A given community tested its strength and put itself on display in the act of singing together. It is not surprising, therefore, that the "people" and the "popular" acquired, in and by the song, a cultural definition that made their separation audible. It was on this basis that the existence of a different poetics became recognizable, thriving in a social world that was enigmatically creative.[29]

A DIFFERENT POETRY

The taste that Malherbe evinced, according to his biographers, for the Pont-Neuf tunes was doubtless just another way of disparaging Ronsard. The praise for "the old song" that Molière put into Alceste's mouth was first of all a critique of the "bad taste of the century" that tended toward "pure affectation." Only Montaigne gave substance to this literature whose character he was the first to point out: "Popular, purely natural poetry shows certain kinds of naiveté and grace by which it can be compared to the principal beauty of poetry perfected according to art; as can be seen from the villanelles of Gascony and from the songs that are brought back to us from nations that have no knowledge of any science, not even of writing" (*Essais* 1.54). We never learn anything more about those Occitan "villanelles" that charmed him; on the other hand, elsewhere in the *Essais* (1.31) he quotes battle chants and a love song from the Amerindian "cannibals" so dear to him. "Popular poetry, "natural" poetry, an untamed courtliness in which one seemed to recognize the lyrical imagery of the Greeks: none of these captured the attention of contemporary humanists and baroque writers, but Montaigne's remarks would be remembered two centuries later. It was under his aegis that the discoverers of the eighteenth century and of romanticism would place themselves, having first launched their quest for a universal poetic style whose "nature" they attempted to recognize, to delimit, and to imitate. But how were they to define this "nature," and how were they to make room for it in the world of poems? An initial way opened up before them. It consisted in an effort to retrieve some genres from oblivion or from confinement in their region or origin—to *invent* them in an archaeological sense. In opposition to the ode, the sonnet, the idyll, or the fable, they set the *romance*, the ballad, or the historical song.

Let us not mistake the meaning of the first term. When Brantôme began using it as of 1599, *romance* was the precise designation for a song heard in Spain, divided into stanzas and devoted to some exalted deed; this was just before the *Romancero del Cid* was first published.[30] Moncrif widened this definition somewhat with his 1751 publication of the *Infortunes de la Comtesse de Saulx*, which enjoyed lasting success. He composed it from the lament of an unhappily married wife that he drew from oral tradition and whose text he also printed. Here is his brief recipe for the new genre: "The action must be touching and the style must be naive." Dozens of such songs published at the end of the old regime allow us to refine this definition: a brief but complete narrative ("an often tragic love story," specifies Rousseau in his *Dictionnaire de musique*) and a series of stanzas strongly marked by a recurrent melody are enough to make the *romance* into an air "in the old manner" that recognizably combined the "popular" and "troubadour" styles, which were not at that time distinguished from each other. But did not the *romance* also evoke a poetic countryside? Do not the three heroes—Languedocian, Spanish, and Moorish—who compete in a singing contest in Chateaubriand's *Les Aventures du dernier Abencérage* sound forth the rival yet concordant harmonics of the same South?[31]

This infatuation with *romances* provided the initial impetus and justified future inquiries into memory as preserved in song. The *Essai sur la musique ancienne et moderne* by J. B. de La Borde (1780) contained several Occitan songs—the *pastourelle* and the *maumariée*—introduced with an interesting kind of regret: "We would have liked to be able to give some from all the provinces in the kingdom." Five years later, it was La Place who renewed this call and gave his own inflection to the taste for such songs: "Why do we have so few or, to put it better, practically none of these old *romances*, which are historical, tragic, or at all events interesting, whereas the Spanish, the English, the Germans, etc., have collections of them that are read with all the more pleasure because, while they recall more or less clearly to memory events designed to occupy the heart or the mind, they have the additional merit of depicting old customs."[32] Audible here is the echo of Herder, who had just released his collection, *Voices of the People in Songs* (*Stimmen der Völker in Liedern*) (1778–79); opening up here is the way for the Celtic Academy.

This academy published relatively few songs in the brief course of its activities, but its concern for historical song seems to have been confirmed twenty years later by the vogue for a genre associated this time with northern lands, the ballad. It was thought that the ballad should erect a new bridge between poetry's two riverbanks—the oral and the written, the ancient and the modern. As of 1770, had not Goethe himself, incited by Herder, gathered *Volkslieder* in the Alsatian countryside before later fashioning his great ballads from legend?[33] The years 1820–30 abounded in discoveries; in Paris, songs of Greek, Serbian, and Slavic origin were introduced, translated, and glossed. But could one really put the rare historical songs produced in France—for example, the one about the captivity of François I that Chateaubriand loved—on the same plane as songs of Hellenic *klephtes* (brigands) or fragments of epics from Illyria? Only romantic poets intertwined history and legend in their very erudite ballads. Only philologists hunting for medieval manuscripts tracked down those "chansons de geste" that they wanted to view as France's primitive poetry. It was in 1837 that Francisque Michel first published the integral version of *La Chanson de Roland*; thus appeared France's monument, the equivalent of the Scandinavian *Edda*, which was similarly deciphered from a codex manuscript in 1642. In consequence, only the fringes of French territory, the Basque country of the *Chant d'Altabiscar* (1837), the Brittany of the *Barzaz-Breiz* (1839), the Corsica of the *Voceri* (1840), could continue for a while to nourish—at the price of some picturesque packaging, indeed some clever forgeries—the demand for oral poetry born of historical events and devoted to the living expression of beliefs and customs from the past.[34] At the very same time that Elias Lönnrot, a young Finnish doctor, was publishing his 1835 *Kalevala* ("old Karelian songs from the Finnish people of yesteryear"),[35] France apparently had little to offer to the epic chorus of nations.

But for a long time already, there had been shadowy signs of a decisive reversal. As a matter of fact, the popular poetry that Montaigne celebrated did not a priori imply any rhetorical definition of genres, any obvious rule

of composition, expression, or content that the writer could adopt. One
could not simply decide to write a villanelle, any more than a *romance* or
a ballad: they arose from a milieu and its practices. An essential discontinuity separated "poetry according to nature" and "poetry according to
art." The scholar had to content himself with describing this difference
while forbearing to tame it or especially to reproduce it. That is what the
learned Mathieu-Antoine Bouchaud aspired to do from 1763 onward. In
his *Dissertation sur la poésie rythmique*, this encyclopedist defended the anteriority of the rhythmic melody with respect to the poetic text. The latter,
he argued, simply dressed up preexisting rhythms by making each syllable
correspond to a note. This genesis would explain the very particular al-
lure of such compositions: "A goodly number of our old songs for round
dances . . . have no rhymes or . . . have only a few by accident. One can
become convinced of this by listening to what people sing when they
dance in this manner. We also have *romances* in this style, and their number is fairly large."[36] So much for the rules of classical versification, those
that Malherbe established and that would lead to a view of popular songs
as mere bastardizations. Much later, in 1842, Nerval would hold the same
opinion and would use the same words when he published, in *La Sylphide*,
the first authentic collection of French songs.[37] For him, the inspiration
for oral song had not taken refuge in exotic dialects but was alive and
well throughout France, even close to Paris, "without concern for rhyme,
prosody, and syntax; the language of the shepherd, the sailor, or the passing cart-driver is just the same as ours, except for a few elisions . . . ; this
language has its rules, or at least its regular patterns, and it is irritating that
couplets such as those from the famous *romance*, "If I were a swallow," have
been abandoned—for having two or three oddly placed consonants—to
the vocal repertory of cooks and concierges." Further on, he speaks highly
of such resources as assonance and also the quasi miraculous concurrence
of language and thought, both stripped of all embellishments:

> Enfin vous voilà donc
> Ma belle mariée
> Enfin vous voilà donc
> À votre époux liée
> Avec un long fil d'or
> Qui ne rompt qu'à la mort.

> There you are at last, then
> My beautiful bride
> There you are at last, then
> Bound to your husband

With a long thread of gold
That breaks only in death.

Picturesque imagery is not absent from the sailor's song, "Ce sont les filles
de La Rochelle"; dramatic melancholy colors the laments of "Jean Renaud"
or "Saint Nicolas." There is no need to add "chivalrous romanticism" to
the dialogue of the king with his daughter:

Le roi Louis est sur son pont
Tenant sa fille en son giron
Elle lui demande un cavalier
Qui n'a pas vaillant six deniers!

King Louis is on his bridge
Holding his daughter to his bosom
She asks for the hand of a knight
Who does not own six deniers' worth!

Equally distant from the academicism that still surreptitiously limited the
taste of his contemporaries and from the platitudes of rhymesters churn-
ing out fashionable *romances*, Nerval defined and illustrated French oral
poetry. In the process, he set the tone for the proliferating research that
would subsequently blossom. Unlike the German-speaking countries, for
example, France has never made a methodical inventory of *everything* that
people sang, but only songs that, whatever their source, have been purified
and recreated in transmission. There has been a firm attempt to distinguish the popular from the popularized. Sociological learning has perhaps
suffered in this attempt; the notion of oral poetry of specific creation has
surely benefited. But, in this diversion, what happened to "the people,"
to whom some seem to attribute a continuing capacity for invention and
to whom certain others hope to restore what they "created"?

FROM THE POPULAR TO THE NATIONAL?

The very French preeminence granted to oral poetics was not without
effect on the very notion of "the people." At the beginning of the eighteenth century, Lecerf de Viéville attempted a definition that was afterward taken up and copied several times. Where music was concerned, he
set up an opposition between the *people*, who, with no "knowledge of the
rules," "often attend performances," and the *popular*, or those who "listen
to Pont-Neuf songs and do not go to the Opéra,"—which was to say, in
Paris, the world of servants, shopkeepers, and small artisans who adopted

tunes, reworked them, and shared them around by word of mouth.[38] The opposition took shape more clearly a century later. In the tradition of Montaigne, the popular was essentially everything elaborated apart from the written word, everything handed down by oral memory. This did not mean that the common people, as a body, authored the songs they sang. In 1824, when Claude Fauriel presented his *Chants populaires de la Grèce moderne* to the French public with a preliminary treatise that served for decades as a standard reference source on the subject, he admitted that "the spontaneous effusion of popular genius" was channeled through certain groups or individuals: the tanners of Iannina nurtured the repertory of Epirus, and beggars throughout Greece were dedicated to celebrating the exploits of bandits.[39] These authors signed their work frequently but anonymously ("Who made this song? / Three handsome young boys"), as if paying their debt to a tradition they knew they fleetingly incarnated. It was possible for some exchanges to cross the barrier of writing: as late as the Restoration, songs drawn from oral tradition were often noted in collections of dance songs, in chapbook librettos, and in certain of the *Key to the Wine Cellar* volumes that sociable singing placed in demand. But none of these replaced the powerful work of crystalization that oral tradition slowly accomplished. Then, too, in the wake of the Celtic Academy there arose the conviction that popular song never served as pure entertainment, as a completely separate, leisure-time activity. It was held to exist only as part of a ritual in which it played an efficacious role. If song narrated neither human history nor heroic legend, then it was thought that—in France, at any rate—it revealed customs, spelled out the intentions guiding them, uncovered what lay beneath them. Hence, from that time onward, the prestige of wedding songs that embroidered on all the circumstances of love encapsuled in such typical sketches as the meeting at a fountain, the stolen kiss, the gift of a sash, and, conversely, the imprisoned lover, the forgetful spouse, or the petty husband.[40]

To identify in this way a popular poetics and its ritual function led to the slightly bitter realization that its era was closed, that beyond the very end of the eighteenth century the treasures of the song tradition no longer increased. At least in regions where only French was spoken, people danced less and less often to unaccompanied vocal music, and rituals relied less and less on a necessary panoply of songs. This ineluctable death made the gathering of authentic songs difficult, as noted during the Second Empire by a noblewoman in a letter to Weckerlin, a famous musician and folklorist:

> You cannot know how difficult it has been for me to get anything really old, really naive. Yesterday, between mass and vespers, I as-

sembled all the youth of H . . . (a village in the Touraine). Here is
the result of my audition: 1) "Tu veux devenir ma compagne, jeune
Albanaise" (Labarre); 2) "Exil et retour" (Monpou); 3) "Je te bénis"
(Loïsa Puget), etc. All of this was sung with such singular variants
that I thought at first I was hearing something new. But then I had
the idea of calling for the cowherd, the old cook, the barnyard girl,
and two or three sexagenarian neighbors, from whom I gleaned a
genuinely popular song: "Su'l' pont du Nord."

The people of popular song—those who put it into action and are represented in it, those who choose it and pass it on—are thus the people of
the past.[41]

The French situation was very different from the German one. Between 1805 and 1808, the Heidelberg romantics published *The Youth's
Magic Horn* (*Des Knaben Wunderhorn*). Achim von Arnim saw it as the masterpiece of the age-old community of "soldiers of fortune" and "knights
errant." Attentive to this "university of art and migrant confraternity,"
he did not hesitate to draw heavily on old books and sheet music in order
to revive its songs. Meanwhile, Clemens Brentano, the other *Wunderhorn*
poet, took it upon himself to venture into the heart of Reformation liturgy, where he explored the vast forest of Lutheran chorales. The whole
collection immediately formed the charter for the defeated Germany that
was then partly occupied by Napoleonic troops. By singing, the German
people incarnated their suppressed nation. When that nation once again
took form, it persisted in identifying itself with those songs.[42] In France,
it was state policy, pedagogical concern, and intellectual ambition that
occasionally conspired to realize a dream: the metamorphosis of a few
traditional songs into national anthems.

Ministerial inquiries followed one upon another (Grétet, 1808; Sal-
vandy, 1845; Fortoul, 1852) with a view to establishing the *Recueil général*
of French songs. It was an enterprise that never achieved its goal, initi-
ating at the most a fruitful movement devoted to gathering songs from
the provinces.[43] In regard to schools, it was all very well for the Guizot
statute of 1833 to require musical training and for educators to praise
the moral and disciplinary merits of choral singing, but it was not until
the last few years of the nineteenth century that, under the guidance of
Julien Tiersot, popular *tunes* were heard in the classroom, always dressed
up with educational words.[44] As for the Orphéonic movement, launched
by Wilhem in 1819 and coming into its own during the Second Empire,
it abhorred traditional songs, oscillating instead between the eclecticism of
operatic arias and the vocal mimicry of comic entertainment.[45] If French
song was "nationalized" between 1815 and 1914, it was through the per-

sonal adulation received by singer-songwriters such as Béranger, Gustave Nadaud, Pierre Dupont, Loïsa Puget, Aristide Bruant, and others. They were all recognized by the greatest poets, a little as if they were peers of the realm who had succeeded in bending the ear of the people.[46] In this new world, where traditional transmission was definitively losing its foothold—petit bourgeois, domestic servants, tradesmen, soldiers, and students turned massively to modern songs—the old tunes had to carve out a space in which they became, only recently, the common property of the French people.

Everything began in 1843. A prolific author of vaudevilles, Théophile Marion, known as Dumersan, published a beautifully lithographed loose-leaf series, *Chants et chansons populaires de la France*, completed in 1846 with *Chansons et rondes enfantines*. In reading through these collections today, one realizes that amid a jumble of forgotten songs, they contain what has since been confirmed as shared knowledge. Who does not know "Il pleut bergère," "Cade Rousselle," "Le bon roi Dagobert," "M. de La Palisse," "Giroflé girofla," "Le Retour du conscrit," or "Gentil coquelicot"? All these titles have a known author, or else they have been definitively arranged and set down in writing. Added to them in 1860 were the *Chansons populaires des provinces de France* on which Champfleury and Weckerlin collaborated, the former choosing and introducing the texts, the latter arranging them for piano. Among them we find the traditional repertory known at that time, drawn from each of the former provinces but limited principally to the French language.[47] Once it was thus constituted, this corpus spread slowly and erratically. National singers undoubtedly played their part: Pierre Dupont loved these tunes, as did the litterateurs whom he frequented; and around 1920, Yvette Guilbert, a self-appointed defender of the old French song, repopularized "Le Roi Renaud." Since then, this movement of rediscovery has never stopped, all the more so because in the meantime schools have begun to teach so-called songs for children, and because all the youth movements have included a few tunes from the past in their repertories. Such songs still survive; for a while, Pétainism gave them a new lease on life.[48] But reduced in size and confined to separate regions, this recently invented tradition is known to everyone without being truly national.

One observation is thus essential: the French did not wait for the great European surge of romanticism in order to recognize the existence and begin the collection of works from oral tradition. They even called such works "popular" from very early on, thereby referring to a certain style and some particular social milieus: of peasants, tradespeople, women. In consequence, the erection of monuments to memory never occupied the place given to it by nations in search of selfhood: the Germany of Herder and the Grimm brothers, the Finland of Lönnrot, the Serbia of Vouk Karadjitch.[49] No oral work has ever been elevated into an emblem of French identity. There is nothing that recalls the Gallic hymns, the Balkan and Romanian ballads, the Iberian *romancero*, the patriotic anthems of Norway. At most, devolution to a small, regional homeland and its language has inspired a few belated songs of grateful recognition, often in French. There is thus no "folklore"—in the narrow sense of the term—that, chosen at a founding moment in French history, formed a pedestal for the homeland, bore witness to "the spirit of the people," and was thus transmitted, taught, and experienced as such.

The ways of speaking, storytelling, and singing that France's linguistic and cultural unification has widely disseminated are shared, certainly, but in a very personal manner. Held up in a haphazard jumble for children to marvel at, these works nourish no feeling of immediate communion, but rather serve as so many fragile traces marking the paths of memory. They do less to anchor a sense of belonging than to indicate a distance, a vision grown cloudy, a voice deserted by words. Hence their place in all recollection, their virtue with regard to biographical revelation. A "very old air, languishing and funereal" sufficed to make the colorful yet so far away picture of the *other existence* appear to Nerval. Similarly, the tales of Geneviève of Brabant or Bluebeard, projected by a magic lantern in a "vacillating and momentary stained-glass window," make a child feel, according to Proust, a disquieting enchantment that exiles him from his room and his body, dazzling him to the point of dizziness. It would be impossible to decide how this ambiguous charm arises: from personal memories attached to such moments or from the virtue inherent in these stories and tunes, the virtue that every transmission renews, that every listener recognizes.[50]

NOTES

Yvonne Verdier ought to have written this text; during the summer of 1989, she devoted the last weeks of her life to its preparation. At the time, we spoke together about it a great deal, and I hope I have not betrayed the thinking that she sketched out orally. These "Proverbs, tales, and songs" have been written not merely in her honor but—better—in the closeness of her memory.

1. Stéphane Mallarmé, *Richard Wagner: Rêverie d'un poëte français* (1886), in *Oeuvres complètes*, ed. H. Mondor and G. Jean-Aubry, Bibliothèque de la Pléiade (Paris: Gallimard, 1945), 544.

2. Reprinted in Ossian/Macpherson, *Fragments de poésie ancienne*, ed. François Heurtematte (Paris: José Corti, 1990), 202–6.

3. See the "discourse d'ouverture" of the Celtic Academy by Éloi Johanneau in *Mémoires de l'Académie celtique* 1 (1807): 29–64.

4. On the proverb and the locution, see Andreas Jolles, *Formes simples* (1930; Paris: Éditions du Seuil, 1972), 121–36.

5. On the medieval proverb and the description of manuscript collections, see Leroux de Lincy, *Le Livre des proverbes français*, 2nd ed., 2 vols. (Paris: Delahaye, 1859); and the introduction to Joseph Morawski, *Proverbes français antérieurs au XVe siècle* (Paris: Champion, 1925).

6. On Solomon the magician, see Leroux de Lincy; Pierre Saintyves, "Salomon: Son pouvoir et ses livres magiques," *Revue des traditions populaires* 28, no. 9 (1913): 410–25; and the various editions of the *Dialogue de Salomon et Marculf* presented by Natalie Zemon Davis, "Sagesse proverbiale et erreurs populaires," in *Les Cultures du peuple* (Paris: Aubier, 1979), 366–425 (here 410–11, n.1).

7. On this notebook and other "practical" manuscripts of proverbs, see Morawski.

8. For references concerning the ancient study of Occitan proverbs, see the "Présentation" by Josiane Bru and Daniel Fabre to Antonin Perbosc, *Proverbes et dictons du pays d'oc* (Marseille: Rivages, 1982), i–xxvi.

9. A preliminary list of proverbial citations in Montaigne is proposed by Katharine Elaine, "The Moral Force of Montaigne's Proverbs," *Proverbium* 3 (1965): 33–45. The quoted text is in the *Essais*, bk. 3, chap. 12.

10. On philological theories of the sixteenth century and on Pasquier's position, see Danielle Trudeau, *Les Inventaires du bon usage (1529–1647)* (Paris: Éditions de minuit, 1992). On these questions, see also Corrado Vivanti, "The *Recherches de la France* by Étienne Pasquier," in *Les Lieux de mémoire*, vol. 2, *La Nation: Héritage—Historiographie—Paysages* (Paris: Éditions Gallimard, 1986); and Marc Fumaroli, "The Genius of the French Language," in *Realms of Memory: The Construction of the French Past*, vol. 3, *Symbols* (New York: Columbia University Press, 1996).

11. The Jesuit compilers of the *Dictionnaire de Trévoux* did not follow those who rejected proverbs in favor of the classical style, but this rejection is found once more in the *Encyclopédie* of Diderot and d'Alembert.

12. Larade and Voltoire's work has been edited and presented by Jean-Claude Dinguirard, "*So ditz la gens anciana*: Recherches sur les plus anciennes collections de proverbes gascons," *Via Domitia* (Toulouse, 1982–2[sic]), 1–126; Oihenart, *Proverbes basques* (Paris, 1657; Paris: Franck, 1847); Jean Babu, "Proverbes," excerpted from his works by Léo Desaivre, *Revue des traditions populaires* 21 (1906): 149–55.

13. See Moisant de Brieux, *Origines de quelques coutumes anciennes* (Caen, 1676); *La Bugado prouvençalo* (Aix, 1660). Proverbs of a sprightly vein are very evident in Rabelais and in Béroalde de Verville (*Le Moyen de parvenir*, 1601); the adages of the latter are catalogued by Lazare Sainéan, *Problèmes littéraires du XVIe siècle* (Paris: De Boccard, 1927), 192–97.

14. Among the authors of such compilations, one might cite Pierre Lamésan-gère, *Dictionnaire des proverbes français* (Paris, 1821); and C. de Méry, *Histoire générale des proverbes*, 4 vols. (Paris, 1827–28).

15. We think here of parodies by the surrealists and the Oulipo group, as well as the recurrent reflections on proverbs in the work of Jean Paulhan.

16. Marcel Proust, *Du côté de chez Swann*, vol. 1 of *À la recherche du temps perdu*, ed. Jean-Yves Tadié, Bibliothèque de la Pléiade (Paris: Gallimard, 1987), 52–58 and 121–22 in particular.

17. Marcel Proust, *Le Temps retrouvé*, vol. 4 of *À la recherche du temps perdu*, ed. Jean-Yves Tadié, Bibliothèque de la Pléiade (Paris: Gallimard, 1989), 781–82.

18. See Michel Zink's introduction to the conference proceedings *Réception et identification du conte depuis le Moyen Âge* (Toulouse, 1987); and the anthology *Formes médiévales du conte merveilleux*, under the direction of Jacques Berlioz, Claude Bré-mond, and Catherine Velay-Vallantin (Paris: Stock, 1989).

19. Boccaccio, *Le Décaméron*, French trans. Jean Bourciez (Paris: Garnier, 1952), 7–25.

20. Some descriptions of storytelling evenings are usefully gathered in Éd-ouard Bonnafé, *Études sur la vie privée de la Renaissance* (Paris: L. Henry May, 1989), 152–68.

21. The first part, translated by Jean Louveau (1560), and the second, trans-lated by Pierre de Larivey (1563), were reedited by Pierre Jannet, 2 vols., Biliothèque elzévirienne (1857).

22. This period has been studied on several occasions: Mary Elisabeth Storer, *La Mode des contes de fées (1865–1700)* (Paris: Champion, 1928); Jacques Barchilon, *Le Conte merveilleux français, de 1690 à 1790* (Paris: Champion, 1975); Teresa de Scanno, *Les Contes de fées à l'époque classique (1680–1715)* (Naples: Liguori, 1975); Barbara Piqué, *Tra scienza e teatro, scrittori di fiabe alla corte del Re Sole* (Rome: Bulzoni, 1981); Raymonde Robert, *Le Conte de fées littéraire en France de la fin du XVIIe siècle à la fin du XVIIIe siècle* (Nancy: Presses universitaires de Nancy, 1981).

23. We refer here to the edition of Gilbert Rouger, *Contes de Perrault* (Paris: Garnier, 1967). The most essential study is that of Marc Soriano, *Les Contes de Per-rault, culture savante et traditions populaires* (Paris: Gallimard, 1968); see also Louis Marin, *La Parole mangée* (Paris: Klincksieck, 1985).

24. Excerpted from the announcement of the edition of Perrault's *Tales* in *Le Mercure galant* (January 1697); quoted in Soriano, 25–26. The text was doubtless writ-ten by Perrault himself.

25. Such chapbooks are studied by Catherine Velay-Vallantin, "Le Miroir des contes," *Les Usages de l'imprimé*, ed. Roger Chartier (Paris: Fayard, 1986), 129–85. The same work contains precise references to the illustration of tales by Perrault. On the study of images, see the example sketched out on the subject of "Tom Thumb" in Ségolène Le Men, *Livres d'enfants, livres d'images* (Paris: Les Dossiers du Musée d'Orsay, 1989), 23–26.

26. Soriano, 13.

27. Jean-François Bladé, *Contes populaires de la Gascogne*, vol. 1 (Paris: Maison-neuve, 1886), iii–iv. On the romantic movement's rediscovery of tales, see Nicole Belmont, *Paroles païennes* (Paris: Imago, 1986), 37–61.

28. Quoted by Andrée Denis, "Poésie populaire, poésie nationale: Deux intercesseurs; Fauriel et Mme de Staël," *Romantisme* 35 (1982): 3.

29. The essential works for our purpose are those of Patrice Coirault, especially *Formation de nos chansons folkloriques*, 4 vols. (Paris: Le Scarabée, 1953–63); Paul Bénichou, *Nerval et la chanson folklorique* (Paris: José Corti, 1970); Jean-Michel Guilcher, *La Chanson folklorique de langue française* (Paris: Atelier de la danse populaire, 1989), assembled from course notes. All have interesting critical viewpoints on Georges Doncieux's important *Le Romancero populaire de la France* (Paris: Bouillon, 1904).

30. The first edition of the *Romancero del Cid* was made by Escobar (Lisbon, 1601).

31. François-René de Chateaubriand, *Les Aventures du dernier Abencérage* (1826; Paris: Garnier, 1962), 316–24.

32. Quoted in Bénichou, 47–49.

33. Some specimens from Goethe's Alsatian collection are given in J. A. Bizet, *La Poésie populaire en Allemagne, suivi d'un choix de Volkslieder* (Paris: Aubier, 1959), 132–35 ("Die drei Grafen"), and 140–43 ("Der Herr Von Falkenstein").

34. On the *Barzaz-Breiz* by Hersart de la Villemarqué (1839), see the article by Jean-Yves Guiomar in *Les Lieux de mémoire*, vol. 2, *La Nation: Héritage—Historiographie—Paysages* (Paris: Gallimard, 1986), 569–97. We owe the first edition of the *Chant d'Altabiscar* to Francisque Michel in *La Chanson de Roland à Roncevaux* (Paris: Silvestre, 1837); it had been preceded by another false epic published by W. von Humboldt, *Le Chant des Cantabres*; it should be noted that J.-F. Bladé, the collector of tales already cited, battled against these fabrications. Prosper Mérimée was the first to edit some Corsican funeral songs, or *voceri*—authentic, this time—in his *Notes d'un voyage en Corse* (Paris: Fournier, 1840).

35. For a recent edition, see Elias Lönnrot, *Le Kalevala*, trans. and pref. Gabriel Rebourcet, 2 vols. (Paris: Gallimard, 1991).

36. Quoted in J.-M. Guilcher, 34.

37. See the critical edition in Bénichou.

38. Quoted in J.-M. Guilcher, 7–10.

39. This essential work by Claude Fauriel was published in two volumes (Paris: Firmin Didot, 1824).

40. The Celtic Academy was very attentive to the ritual of marriage and its punctuation by song; several articles are devoted to this in its *Memoirs* (1807–13). A. Lamarque de Plaisance works along the same lines in his excellent *Usages et chansons populaires de l'ancien Bazadais* (Bordeaux: Balarac Jeune, 1845).

41. This is the opinion of all the specialists cited here (in particular, P. Coirault and P. Bénichou), for whom there are no folkloric songs (or no songs rendered folkloric by oral transmission) in France after 1820.

42. On the composition and reception of the *Wunderhorn*, see Bizet, 33–37. For a brief anthology in French, see *Le Cor merveilleux de l'enfant* (Nantes: Éditions du Petit Véhicule, 1990).

43. On this movement, see Bénichou, 170–73; Jean-Jacques Ampère's "Instructions" on collecting popular songs in *Bulletin du Comité de la langue, de l'histoire et des arts de la France* 1 (1852–53) would henceforth constitute the basic reference work

on the subject. The unpublished results of the Fortoul inquiry are bound in six volumes in the manuscript department of the Bibliothèque nationale (*Poésies populaires de la France*, fonds français, nouv. acq., nos. 3338–43).

44. In 1893, Julien Tiersot launched a contest for the publication of a *recueil de chants* for the use of elementary schools in France; he proposed a choice of tunes—most of them popular—and solicited poems for them. It was Maurice Bouchor who won the prize and was published; on this subject, see *Revue pédagogique* 26 (Jan.–June 1895): 29–33.

45. On the Orphéons and their repertory, see Philippe Gumplowicz, *Les Travaux d'Orphée* (Paris: Aubier, 1987).

46. See, for example, J. Touchard, *La Gloire de Béranger*, 2 vols. (Paris: Armand Colin, 1968). On the tastes of Pierre Dupont, see Bénichou, 352; on the place accorded to traditional singing within newer social settings for songs, see scattered remarks in Marie-Véronique Gauthier, *Chanson, sociabilité et grivoiserie au XIXe siècle* (Paris: Aubier, 1991); and Concetta Condemi, *Les Cafés-concert* (Paris: Quai Voltaire, 1992).

47. The very muddled bibliography by Dumersan, his imitators, and his continuators is clarified in Bénichou, 165–70. Champfleury's preface to the volume *Provinces de France* is important from our perspective.

48. On the Pétainist promotion of folklore, see Christian Faure, *Le Projet culturel de Vichy* (Lyons: CNRS and Presses Universitaires de Lyon, 1989); and, for a wider perspective, our own article on Van Gennep's *Manuel* in *Les Lieux de mémoire* vol. 3, *Les France: Traditions* (Paris: Gallimard, 1992), 640–75. Numerous "songwriters" were published from 1940 to 1944 by the Compagnons and Jeune France movements; they took up and enlarged what would seem to have been already fixed repertory of the "old French song."

49. See Vouk Karadjitch, *Contes populaires serbes*, French trans. Ljiljana and Raymond Fuzellier (Lausanne: L'Âge d'homme, 1987).

50. We refer here to Gérard de Nerval, *Fantaisie*; Proust, *Du côté de chez Swann*, 8–9; and finally Stendhal, who ponders in *La Vie d'Henri Brulard* ([Paris: Garnier, 1961], 347) the secret of musical recollection.

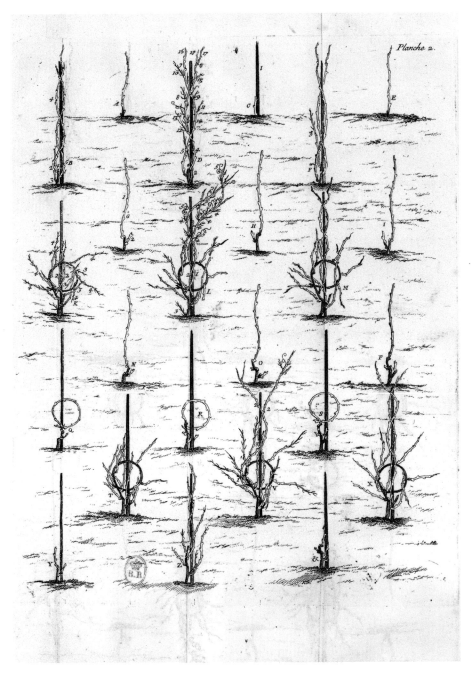

Figure 6.1
The vine is a domestic creeper; it is a creation of man and society. Durival, *De la vigne* (Paris, 1777).

$\mathcal{V}$INE AND $\mathcal{W}$INE

GEORGES DURAND

Some might be inclined to see wine, which intoxicates, as an agent of forgetfulness. But, in fact, every aspect of wine proclaims it to be a preserver of the past and a restorer of memory. To invest a particular moment with a special dignity, to make it memorable, the identifying stamp of some ceremony is called for: the presiding dignitary, having uttered a few solemn words appropriate to the occasion, will invite the assembled crowd to raise a glass to the felicity of the moment and the immortality of the project at hand. Wine is naturally associated with the unforgettable. An advertiser unconsciously borrowed from this custom when he wrote a piece of advertising copy for a series of placemats commemorating French vineyards. Indeed, he claims that the entire universe would be unable to celebrate any occasion without the assistance of the prestigious liquid:

> France, with its Wines,
> Immortalized the History of the World.
> For, throughout the World, at each historic event
> A French Wine was always present.[1]

Wine connotes commemoration and, thus, memory. This fact, which applies to everyday, trivial, as well as festive and solemn occasions, is consecrated in our Christian, Western culture by the central rite of Eucharist. Faithful to the Lord's tradition, the offering of a cup of wine transformed into the blood of the Savior establishes a memorial: "Do this in my memory."

What characteristics make wine, out of all the fruits of the earth and of man's labors, a locus of memory?

1. AN INTIMATE MEMORY

This memory rests at the heart of nature. Among the crops that, since the Neolithic period, we have developed into the vast range of what we consume, nature establishes a hierarchy of longevity. Green vegetables, which quickly wilt, contrast with grains, which can last a year or two without incurring any damage. The aging of wine sets it apart from all the rest: wine improves with the passing years, it acquires properties of taste and smell that, when the wine was first made, would have been impossible to detect or, perhaps, even to predict.

One sign of this ability to record a moment in time is the concept of vintage; indeed, the rare, if not the only, plant product to be marked with the year of its harvest, wine derives a double value from its vintage: age and identity. A wine's age is, first of all, an indicator of its quality. Years ago, before chemistry enabled us to stabilize and even to recover a wine threatened by one of the many hazards that could befall it, the distinction was made between "wine to be aged" (*vins de garde*) and the rest—which one was better off not keeping. This selection, according to a wine's ability to resist the ravages of time, forms the basis of its first hierarchy: old wine is a synonym for good wine—no doubt a simplistic equation, but never mind. Going along with this line of thinking, advanced age is matched by rarity, imagination takes over the market, the bidding gets out of hand, and we no longer buy a wine but a vintage. Thus—with a nod to the bicentennial of the French Revolution—the current record-holder is apparently a bottle of Château-Margaux 1787, purchased in its day by Thomas Jefferson.[2]

On this symbolic level, wine has become memory—but is it still wine?

It is—for several decades, at any rate—and it is during this time period that the alchemy of aging affixes its identifying seal upon the product. Open the bottle, fill a glass halfway, hold it up to the light, and examine the "robe" of your nectar; smell the intensity of the bouquet and sort out its complexity; then, finally, taste it, to appreciate its balance and enjoy its flavor! A sequence of tasting events such as this guarantees for the connoisseur the test of recognition. Distinctive features and nuances perceived by the eye, nose, and mouth reveal its personality. Identifying a wine by tasting it is a game, a sport that demands years of training. But the champion oenologist can spot, without too much risk, a 1971 Haut-Médoc or a 1969 Pommard. According to a unique combination and a subtle balance, each passing year leaves behind the richness of its aromas and the astringency of its tannins in the bottle. This composition is the summary of all the conditions obtained while the grapes grew and then reached maturity. Delayed blossoming, a gloomy spring, a torrid summer, a misty autumn: wine holds onto the recollection of the events that oversaw its birth. Each vintage is a story that is decanted into casks and matures in the bottle.

A year, a wine, of course; but, a wine, a grape variety, as well, and therein lies another secret of this special, intimate memory. Certainly, there are vines, and then there are vines, and vine growers prefer to speak of pinot and cabernet, of poulsard and chardonnay when referring to the object of their labors. A grape variety (*cépage*) may be defined as a collection of related clones, that is, a plant population, propagated by means of cuttings, from a single plant. Vines are never sown; a shoot is stuck into the ground to take root; it grows and becomes a vine plant identical to its neighbor. The grape variety is a single plant that is perpetuated in countless copies. The singular way in which vines are reproduced encourages the product's stability and the permanence of its characteristics. Once a certain vine has been planted in a specific place and the adaptation has been completed, the vine's qualities will be consistently reproduced. Thus, it is no surprise that a wine should build its identity on that vegetal permanence.

The choice of a vine is the founding of a tradition in a region. Pinot in Burgundy, cabernet in Anjou, gamay in Beaujolais all date back to the beginnings of the vineyards; indeed, the systematic selection of the best plants no doubt helped to particularize a wine that, from then on, strongly conformed to its own type. The grape variety took on qualities, tokens of the best adaptation of plant to soil and direction of exposure. This successful adaptation is, strictly speaking, what constitutes a vineyard. Beaujolais is the best example of this: at first, at the edge of the Burgundy region, Beaujolais deals in gamay, a mediocre grape from Burgundy, a grape favored by a populace more concerned with high yields than with quality. The slopes of Burgundy, with their chalky soil, do not form a harmonious relationship with the gamay grape. Indeed, the Dukes of Burgundy, staunch defenders of their wines' reputation, forbid the planting of these "very bad and very treacherous plants" (edict of Philippe le Hardi, 1395).[3] On the other hand, in the sandy, granitic soil of Beaujolais, gamay, specifically the variety known as "petit gamay," produces light, warm-bodied wines, which make the reputations of the hills of Juliénas, Chiroubles, and Brouilly. All of which doesn't stop the golden limestone of the southern slopes of Beaujolais from producing, from the same gamay, a somewhat rustic but well-structured wine with fruity flavors and a powerful, expansive bouquet. This close relationship between the properties of a *terroir* and the qualities of a grape variety is, in fact, the end result of a long history in which the intervention of human ingenuity wins out over every other factor. And so, here we are brought back around to the ultimate memory, that of the wine growers.

Without the memory of the various practices and methods, the culmination of a tactile, manipulative experience passed down through time, France's vineyards and their wines would never take their place among the (rather unusual) monuments of the French cultural heritage. Vine growers are to France's wines what architects are to our cathedrals. For the specific procedure of viticulture is the pruning of the vine; all the other tasks of the long annual cycle of work and time occur merely to prepare the ground or to go along with nature's rhythm: clearing, training, binding, lifting, hoeing, polling/pollarding, giving the soil a third tilling, or, for that matter, turning the soil, planting, and layering, according to this very precise vocabulary of operations that comprise the *métier* of vine grower. But all this work would be in vain without the truly creative act: pruning, which, by the way, is the single traditional procedure that chemistry and engineering are powerless to change or replace, the procedure that thus preserves the long history of this very particular specialization among agricultural workers.

Louis Liger, in his *Nouveau théâtre d'agriculture* (1640), comments: "Not all field laborers know how to grow the vine equally well: a good farmer could be a very bad wine grower, and to know his job well is what one would wish for in a man." Specifically, he continues, by way of advice to landowners in search of a good worker or smallholder, "a bit of genius in vine growing is quite necessary because there are many extraordinary little tasks that require his skill." Many portraits of the ideal farmer mention physical strength, moral honesty, and stamina for work as qualities valued by lords and masters; but an acknowledged intelligence in his craft is not typically found on the list of qualities required in a "field laborer." We can understand how the landowning class, conscious of its own interests, came to see viticulture as an aristocratic form of agricultural work. Indeed, as Roger Dion notes, "In the end, it is the wine grower himself, not the mineralogical composition of the soil, that determines the quality of wines. . . . It is possible that this fundamental truth would have remained present in everyone's mind, if, starting in the last years of the eighteenth century, the influence of Jean-Jacques Rousseau had not prompted some authors to see the earth's bounty as evidence of nature's generous disposition, and not the result of the accumulated toil of generations of peasants."[4] This fundamental truth applies twofold to viticulture, since the vine grower doesn't just create a plot of cultivated land, as all peasants do, but, in addition, he creates a plant; and for this, keen understanding is more important than peasant hardiness. Patiently, collectively, generations of wine growers have developed the "technique bearing on perfection" that is pruning.

Let us pause for a moment to contemplate the vine grower on a winter morning in the heart of his vineyard, bare of leaves.[5] His legs upright, his torso leaning a bit over the vine plant, sickle in hand, he has already decided at a glance where he will cut the vine branch. He has grasped the plant's overall appearance, he knows its age, he senses its vigor, he projects its future development, he counts the number of eyes needed, he decides where to make the cut, and he prunes. But he cuts in the way a tailor cuts cloth to make a custom-made suit, or the way a stonecutter cuts according to the grain of the rock. Cutting, almost sculpting: there is, in a well-pruned vine plant, a veritable sculpture in vegetation, not

Figure 6.2
Underlining the connection between town and vine, this miniature shows the essential task of pruning in the dead of winter. A precious plot of land, the vineyard is thoroughly fenced off.

Figure 6.3
Pruning vines today.

esthetic at first—it can be, in addition—but organic, practical, the result
of the harmony that exists between what remains of the previous season
and what will arise when it next comes into leaf. That is the work of the
vine grower's mind; if the gesture is quick, do not be misled into thinking of it as machine-like; or, if you must, then imagine a machine that is
sure, precise, and, what's more, intelligent.

To be convinced of the intelligence that is intrinsic to the job of pruning, go to a vineyard around mid-July. Study the architecture of the vine
plant and vine shoots. Compare three, five, ten plants; try, if you have
read and digested a treatise on vine pruning, to recapture the thought
process that has brought the vine to its present configuration. You will
be amazed. No vine plant is pruned exactly like its neighbor. O worth-
less schematism of pruning manuals. They set forth only basic principles,
from which the skillful vine grower draws only certain particular decisions in each instance. Pruning personalizes each plant. The aristocracy
of vine growing is an aristocracy of intelligence.

It is, without a doubt, this highly cerebral aspect that distinguishes the vine as a locus of memory. The vine contains the accumulation of years of know-how and tradition. The vine makes manifest, within the plant itself, the long collective memory of the vine-growing profession. Historians and sociologists have noted that vine growers can work only in a context of continuity, of stability, and of the passing-on of tradition. In this regard, it is enough to mention the customary length of the grower's lease, necessitated by the rate of growth for young vines, which generally take several years to mature: no harvest before the vine has produced leaves four times; and the longest time after that for the making of the wine. The aging of the harvests prolongs in the bottle the first period spent in the cask, where, after the decanting, the wine takes shape. Grape harvests come and go; each time, it takes four or five years: from planting to drinking, a full decade is required. The vine grower nurtures his wine while holding onto these time markers, which he ponders as he tastes. He'll tell you the—quite personal—history of the wine he shares with you: that spring's frost, that summer's dryness, the mists at harvest time, the slow pace of fermentation, the hesitations of the second fermentation, light north wind on the day of racking the wine, the fear of a hint of bitterness, and serenity recovered when the liquor acquires fullness and develops structure, when the specific character of the vintage became perceptible to the taste.

But stability and continuity extend well beyond mere decades to the succession of generations of vine growers on the same piece of land. These dynasties discovered by historians are evidence of a loyalty to the land, to the vineyard, to the family legacy. Hence the highly pronounced social endogamy characteristic of wine-growing families, who are not so much voluntarily closed off as they are simply isolated within a professional and cultural specialization. Thus, memory is reinforced by family lineage.

The dynasties and lineages of vineyard owners and vine growers form the foundations of vineyards—as manmade landscapes. For the vineyard puts its own particular stamp upon those places which it has taken over and divided up. Conditions of climate—or, more frequently, of microclimate, the further north one goes—and of the soil may indicate potentialities, but a vineyard is a human creation: without these communities of wine growers, there will be no vineyards. Not in the way that the prairie exists without the shepherd or the forest without the forester. Thus, it is appropriate to pause for a moment to consider this landscape and its creation, for it is accumulation, maintenance, conservation. It exists in space either as a present-day reality or as a trace of the past. Therefore, particularly in regions once planted with vines and now deserted by wine growers, we can detect the vestiges of an ancient dominion. In the same way that we can guess the layout of an early city, its center and ramparts, by looking at a town map from our own time, so too can a historian observe/perceive with certainty the signs of a defunct vineyard on a land survey. For this, the testimony of place-names—*les vieilles vignes* ("old vines"), *les clous* (in modern French, *les clos*, "the vineyards")—is not necessary. Noticeably smaller plots, a more highly concentrated network of roads, and the presence of low walls are the chief indicators of this former presence, along with a suitable exposure and, if need be, a noticeable slope. Everyone has been able to see, in several regions, the grooves in the earth that recall the former division of a hillside by means of low walls and terraces, indispensable not so much for the wine grower's convenience as for soil retention. Viticultural practices, especially the initial breaking up of the earth by digging and the biennial removal of its grassy cover by means of second and third dressings, make vineyards particularly vulnerable to soil erosion. Earth that slid down hillsides compelled earlier generations of wine growers to perform the task of earth-shifting. Load by load, on the backs of donkeys or of men, the vineyard was preserved thanks to a permanent bucket chain from the base of the slope to the summit. Hillsides fitted with a staircase pattern of retaining walls are among the characteristic features of many of these wine-growing areas. These vineyard terraces are footsteps written in space, durable if not indelible.

However, the conditions vary from place to place. A tour of the Bordeaux, Burgundy, or Champagne regions will enable us to sketch a sort of picture of wine-growing France. The features of the Bordeaux landscape go back to the beginning of the twelfth century and the privileges granted by the kings of England, rulers of Aquitaine, in order to ensure the supply to Britain. But starting in 1279 Edward I allotted his forest of Bordeaux and the uncultivated areas, on condition that those who cleared the land plant their holdings with vines. Almost the entire region was quickly divided into the vines of the alluvial plain along the Garonne River, the vines of the gravelly regions on the sandstone terraces of the left bank, and those on slopes on the opposite bank, around Lormont, soon extending into all of the Blayais. The hierarchy of wines corresponded to the social hierarchy: small, family-run plots operated by independent winemakers who took advantage of the northern European market; and large estates organized around the "chateau," where the master winemaker oversaw the work of the *prix-faiseurs*, workers who took a share of the harvested grapes. Hence the amazing diversity of Bordeaux vineyards, vineyards in plains and on hills, vineyards grouped into vast estates, these surrounded in turn by the mosaic of smaller landholdings; the fortified manor houses of Graves or Haut-Médoc and the wine-growing villages of the coasts or the plateaus. But first and foremost, Bordeaux is a paradoxical region—exposed to the

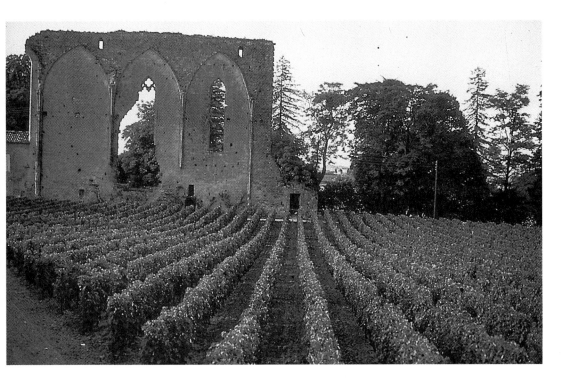

Figure 6.4
Vineyard at Saint-Émilion, Bordeaux region.

Figure 6.5
Vineyard at Andlau, Alsace.

Figure 6.6
Vineyard near Saumur, on the banks of the Loire.

Figure 6.7
Vineyards of Vosne-Romanée and Nuits-Saint-Georges, Burgundy.

moisture and cool temperature of the sea, a region where the grapes are slow to ripen, and where the atmosphere is certainly more important to the landscape than the topography or the soil.

And such a contrast to Burgundy! Here, the brutal overhang of the plateaus, which follows the fault line and limits the boggy trough of the plains along the Saône, makes each village a replica of the next, from Mercurey (if we include the Chalonnais slope) to Chenove, at the gates of Dijon. Each wine-growing area is a terraced rectangle extending from west to east, from wooded plateau to grassy plain. In between, on the foothills of the cliff, at the base of the limestone, wine growers have for centuries cultivated a narrow, select strip, twelve to fifteen hundred meters wide, planted exclusively with pinot noir for red wines and primarily with chardonnay for white, a bit more than a hundred hectares for each village. The population is concentrated in wealthy towns, whose heavy, octagonal church towers form a line from north to south. Seen from the plains below, the ridge unfurls the uniform succession and repetitive glory of its wine-growing villages, whose names are the names of wines: Gevrey-Chambertin, Vougeot, Vosne-Romanée, Nuits-Saint-Georges, Aloxe-Corton, Beaune, Pommard, Volnay, Meursault. A series of tiny plots, each enclosing a prestigious vineyard, all of Burgundy is in this marvelous strip of land known as the Côte-d'Or.

More arc than band, the wine-growing region of Champagne has slopes that face east; with indentations in the hillsides, formed by the transverse valleys of the Marne and Vesle Rivers, the sinuous garland of small plots unfurls from Reims to Epernay, and from Epernay to Vertus. The presence of a few large estates which guarantee the continued success of the great Champagne-making houses cannot mask the extraordinary fragmentation of the farming here, noticeable in the fine mosaic of the land under cultivation. Indeed, the vine grower of Champagne sells his produce "by the kilo," yielding all or part of his crop to the major wine-making or champagne-making brands. This region is, in fact, dominated by a technique, prized the world over, which, thanks to the bubbling, fizzing, and sparkling of the gasses incorporated into its juice, creates a dreamy effect that assures its value. But the realizing of this trick presupposes—apart from the great care taken in determining the proportions of its components, the main innovation of Dom Pérignon—a long maturation period in the bottle, "champagnization," and filtering, all of which is possible only for companies with a lot of capital. Brand holds greater sway in the cellars of the Champagne region and the power of the city of Reims than in a landscape or type of village resembling Burgundy more closely than Bordeaux.

Honor to whom honor is due, of course; but this tour of the great vineyards must not cause us to lose sight of other ones that, while more modest, are not necessarily inferior to their better-known counterparts. Thus, it is only fair that we direct our attention for a moment to the wines of the Jura; the particularities of this region, *vins jaunes* ("yellow wines"), *vins de paille* ("straw wines"), or the grape varieties—comtois, poulsard, savagnin—beckon us to explore this singular wine-growing area. Let us take note of its exceptional western exposure; its plantings on a Revermont fringed with blind valleys and crowned with wooded massifs; the predominance of marly soil; and the absence of a major urban center that would kick-start the demand for and promotion of the region's wines. All of these characteristics bear witness to the fact that for wine growing to take hold, paradoxically, against all natural local conditions is—here even more than anywhere else—the result of sheer will, nay, stubbornness, an act of pure creation that boldly flies in the face of all determinism. Here, too, the wine enjoys an exceptionally long maturation period in oak casks (a minimum of six years is the official requirement for a château-chalon) before its transfer to clavelins,[6] enabling the wine to be kept for two hundred years: a recently sampled bottle of arbois jaune from 1774 was still graced with all its original virtues. A scandal for wine experts, vin jaune partakes of the same mystery, or at least the same miracle, as the making of vin de paille; made in the month of February on straw mats, this wine spends the next six, or even twenty, years in small casks, a process that bestows upon it a smoothness and a warm bouquet rivaled only by its gorgeous burnt-topaz color.

With our quick tour of the world of French winemaking at an end, it should be clear that a history of the nation is rooted within it. Undoubtedly, plant and product harbor within their natures the ability to preserve a great identity and a strong personality to last through time; but more than this, the winemaker and his traditions maintain the continuity of a long-standing creation that is inscribed upon the land itself. Memory must bloom in history.

2. A National Memory

While not exclusively French—Italy and Spain are major players in wine production—wine growing, and, to an even greater extent, winemaking are strongly associated with the image of our country. If the French delight in this fact, foreigners recognize and proclaim it. Witness the edition of the television talk show *Apostrophes* (December 9, 1988) titled "The Civilization of Wine," in which Mrs. Jancis [*sic*] Robinson held her own alongside Emile Peynaud, master oenologist, and with Marcel Lachiver, doctor of the science of wine (*docteur ès sciences bachiques*). Witness also the

Wine Advocate, a bimonthly publication that reveals to its subscribers the momentary ranking of the world's nectars. Its author, Robert Parker, has become the undisputed oracle of American importers. When these international investigations are finished, French wine takes the top prize. But, more clearly than any words, sincere though they may be, the verdict on French wines can be found in our export statistics (orders of magnitude for 1984–87).

	Production Quantity	Export Quantity*	Export Value**
Total	70	12	17
AOC (wines of "guaranteed vintage")	17	4.5	14
Vins courants (wines for everyday drinking)	42	5	2

*Millions of hectares **Billions of francs

The predominance of high-quality wines (*Appellation d'origine contrôlée*, wines of "guaranteed vintage")—of which Champagne represents fully one third—associates France and its place in the world from the beginning with an image of high-end consumption. This association is based on a real, long-standing tradition, and serves as a kind of definition. It is no doubt in this connection that, consciously or otherwise, the conclusions of a recent poll on "The French and Their History" have their origins.[7] To the question, "To be French is, for you, first and foremost, . . . ?" the answer, "to love good wine" follows immediately after the most obvious ones, such as "to be born in France," "to defend our freedoms," "to speak French." To put it another way, after the territory, the Republic, and the language, wine assumes its place as the distinctive national point of reference. Let us once again savor the nuance: our Frenchman is not a "wine drinker," but a "wine lover"! Wine and our history, one and the same. Thus, it is fitting to weave together this double memory of the destiny of France and the invention of wine.

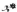

Although certainty would require that we choose the most probable hypothesis, the vine is apparently not descended from the selection of local wild grapes, but from the importation of grape varieties native to the Caucasus. The *vitis vinifera* arrived with Greek, and later Roman, colonization, as one of the hallmarks of the new civilization. *Orientalis proles* (of Eastern lineage) though it may be, the vine is no less, indeed perhaps all the more, contemporaneous with our beginnings as a nation; France, after all, has shown itself to be less the continuation of some Gallic destiny than the fruitful blending of defeated Celts and their Roman conquerors who imposed such institutions of proven worth as the Latin language, the *jus Quiritium*, and the classical virtues. In this legacy, greatly enriched by the contributions of the Greeks, vine and wine are at the forefront of the gifts derived from the integration of the Gauls into the Mediterranean sphere.

Archaeology and the written record emphasize the parallel advance of the Greco-Roman conquest and of viticulture. Suffice it to mention the innumerable remnants of amphorae alongside commercial roads and navigable rivers.[8] Craters such as the renowned Vase of Vix in Burgundy testify to the widespread use of wine beginning in the first centuries AD. Discovered in a treasure-filled tomb, brought to light at the foot of Mount Lassois and on display, since 1953, at the museum in Châtillon-sur-Seine, this bronze vessel, weighing 180 kilos, with a diameter of 1 meter 45 centimeters, and as tall as a man, recalls the ancient practice of mixing water with liqueur that had previously been brewed with a large quantity of aromatics. The Greek and Etruscan decorations reaffirm the origins of the vine grower's and winemaker's arts. Pitchers and *oenochoé*, also of bronze, and terra cotta drinking bowls complete this wine service.

The expansion of vine cultivation in Gaul dates back to the first century BC, that is, the time of the Roman conquest. At the time, vineyards were limited to the immediate surroundings of such Greek colonies as Marseille, Antibes, or Nice. Imported at first, wine was soon being produced on Gallic soil: beginning in the year 100, vineyards are noted at Gaillac, on the Tarn, at Tain, on the Rhône, like the vineyard of the Côte-Rôtie (Condrieu, Ampuis) connected to the city of Vienne— *Vitifera Vienna*, Vienne Rich in Vintage, as the poet Martial (Spain, ca. 40–104) put it.

The imperial era, and the Pax Romana that it fostered, enabled the expansion of wine growing far to the north; the *vitis biturica*, or biturige vine, prized by Columella (Cadiz, first century), exemplifies the conquest of Gaul's Atlantic-coast region by a grape variety resistant to the winds and rains of an area less hospitable than the warm, dry Mediterranean climate.

The origins of this biturige strategy are to be found, according to Strabon (58 BC–21 AD), in western Spain, and the Bordeaux wine-growing region is first mentioned in this context. Encouraged from the very beginning by the British market, a continuous presence ever since, the wines of Aquitaine abound in an ancient Burdigalia frequented by the *negotiator britannicus*, whose trading activity in the area, starting no later than the second century, is recalled in a contemporary inscription.

The vine's conquest of Gaul is marked by two imperial interventions. In the year 92, the edict of Domitian requires that half the vines be pulled up. This measure is justified by the unchecked expansion of vine growing into areas better suited to the cultivation of wheat, and by the concern on the part of wine producers to avoid a glut and a consequent drop in quality, as well as, certainly, a threat to a lucrative business. We don't know the extent of vine growing in Gaul at the beginning of the second century; at the end of the second century, on the other hand, the edict of Probus (276), which allowed all the people of Gaul, *Gallis omnibus*, to plant vines, shows that grape cultivation was, by that time, limited only by natural conditions. Indeed, many local witnesses confirm the planting with grapes of urban and suburban areas of such municipalities as Orléans, Angers, Auxerre, and even Laon, Soissons, and Épernay—at different dates, but by the beginning of the Middle Ages. Grégoire de Tours (ca. 538–594) and Fortunat (ca. 530–600) sing the praises of vineyards whose reputations suggest, if not antiquity, then at least anteriority. Elsewhere, the silence or the uncertainty of available texts demands caution in determining dates of origin. Burgundy and Alsace suffer from these lacunae, which make it impossible to show vine-growing activity in those regions at the beginning of the Middle Ages.

With the medieval period comes a new kind of evidence. By bringing together the information found in cartularies, privileges, and donations, we can sketch a social picture of vine growing: Bishops, monasteries, and princes compete to establish fine vineyards. Thus, episcopates are frequently moved away from their original locations in favor of a town more advantageously situated near vineyards: Langres, abandoned by Saint Gregory for Dijon; Saint-Quentin deserted by Saint Médard in favor of Noyon. A necessity for Eucharistic worship; an advantage of a town in a favorable location in terms of both nature and trade; the desire to control a production and an economic zone that is the foundation of an episcopal institution and of its role in the new society being established. Such were the apparent motives that brought the vine and the ecclesiastical authorities together just prior to the Carolingian Era.

To these reasons, the monastic orders add that of the hospitality owed to pilgrims. A monastery's vineyard was just as essential to the functions of monastic life as the cloister. The founding documents of every abbey and priory mention the *vineae* planted near the convent. Cluny in Burgundy, Jumièges and Saint-Wandrille in Normandy, cultivate grapes to enhance the reputation of the house. Visiting kings and princes, along with their retinues, are given lodging in the *cella hospitum*, where the best wine enhances the hospitality that leads to the bestowing of privileges and benefices. How many of the most famous wines can be traced back to monastic beginnings: Clos Vougeot, the jewel of the legacy of Cîteaux, or Château-Chalon, the vineyard belonging to the abbey of the same name?

Princes and kings imitated the clergy in the project of planting France with vines. Chanteau, in Orléanais, can be considered the first royal vineyard, established during the minority of Philip I by his tutor, Baudouin of Flanders. The vineyard connected to the castle benefits from its location on the hillsides that lead up to the castle walls and from the labors of the peasants assigned to the task. The *Très riches heures du Duc de Berry* (1340–1416) gives us a detailed account of the vineyard and of the noble ducal residence of the fief of Saumur.

It would be a mistake, however, to see wine growing during the Middle Ages merely as the shared passion of the important figures of the day. Wine was, primarily, a commercial product, and, to a large extent, a luxury item.

Indeed, the consumption of wine has long been a class signifier. The urban elites of all of Europe are fond of demonstrating their primacy, or even their supremacy, in the society of their time by engaging in an activity that is inaccessible to the average person: drinking wine. Apparently, the phenomenon of the bourgeois vineyard grows out of this tendency; every city-dweller, bent on having the pleasure of drinking the wine of his own vineyards, goes looking for a plot of land to plant and a vine grower to take care of it. The planting contract became the model for a system of exploitation that generated a structure particular to the economy of vine growing. At the behest of the bourgeois or the vine grower, the decision is made to break the soil and to plant a plot of land that is usually of mediocre quality but well exposed. Over the next five years, without yielding any grapes, the vine develops roots and vine shoots until the first harvest. From that point on, the fruits are divided up, with the bourgeois who owns the land conceding either half the land or half the harvest to the vine grower; the former retains control over the land but is also obliged to provide, in part, such needed accessories as vine props, fertilizer, casks, etc. This relationship leads to a production that is both bourgeois and of the people at the same time, whose distribution, in turn, determines a certain distribution of the market: the vine grower, burdened by taxes, immediate needs, even debts, feeds of necessity into the commercial flow. Paradoxically, but in fact quite logically, the wine is a product for the personal consumption of the bourgeois owner, who drinks the wine of his vineyards and sells off any surplus in the town under the privilege of the *vendans-vin* (wine sellers). This privilege, incidentally, varies according to the town: in Paris, the bourgeois sells his wine "à huis coupé et à pot renversé" ("with the door half opened and the drinking jug turned over"), meaning on the threshold of his home, while in Lyons, he receives the customer in his cellar and entertains him "sans assiette ni serviette" ("without plate or cloth") so as not to compete with the inn-keeper's trade. This set of institutions, including the contracts for plant-ing and winemaking, the bourgeois privileges of the *vendans-vin*, and the tax exemptions for vineyards in the country, was the foundation of the urban vineyard, that crown of vines that surrounded, and extended for some distance from, the cities. The extent of the Parisian vine-growing region is well known: down the Seine as far as Taverny and Chambourcy, or, on the road to Orléans, as far as Palaiseau, and, in the twists and turns of the Marne, as far as Dampmart, vines invaded every parish. Each one harvested more than a thousand hectoliters and, as in the case of Argen-teuil, up to fifteen thousand hectoliters. These impressive quantities were easily consumed by the bourgeois of the capital, in private homes or in one of the city's *guinguettes* (open-air cafés), from the neighborhood of La Courtille to that of Les Porcherons. In his admirable chapter 15, Roger Dion compounds notations and commentaries. Similarly, in his report on the district of Lyonnais, the administrator Lambert d'Herbigny noted in 1697, "One sees nothing but vines around Lyons . . . the biggest source of income for the people of Lyons is in wine."

By the time of the French Revolution, the vine had reached the geo-graphical limits of its possible area of cultivation. Its expansion was, as we have just seen, the joint accomplishment of the three estates, each one contributing, in its time and in its way, to the vine plant's conquest of the land. To this history, the nineteenth century adds several episodes that profoundly altered the map of wine growing in France, shaping it into the one we recognize today. The large table-wine vineyard area in Languedoc; the maintenance of high-quality vineyards on privileged land: Bordeaux, Burgundy, Champagne, Alsace; the move south of a line that extended from Nantes to Nancy, reminding us that, beyond it, vines had been cultivated outside the zone of the best climactic conditions for social reasons that no longer obtain. Four innovations contributed to this rebal-ancing between vine and earth: the democratization of wine consump-tion, the growth of railroads, the introduction of Pasteurian techniques, and, finally, phylloxera.

The consumption of wine by the popular classes is a by-product of the urbanization of the French population. Peasants, and even vine growers, drank wine only on Sundays and holidays; in 1833, Giron de Bazareingues could still note the following: "The day-to-day diet of vine growers and their families consists of rye bread, pork belly, vegetables . . . and, to drink, piquette, which is nothing more than water that has been poured over grape marc after all the wine has been extracted,"[9] an account confirmed by so many others. Meanwhile, Roger Dion comments that, with the end of the Middle Ages, "the customs imposed by the city upon its inhabitants, the examples it gave them, and certain types of self-respect that it developed in them all led them to refuse, even in straitened circumstances, to do without the everyday consumption of wine, which, of necessity, they sought out in its lowest-quality form."[10] It is thus clearly evident that a kind of social pressure and the customs of the day forged a connection between the consumption of (no doubt mediocre) wine and urban living. City and country were separated by a division that was alimentary and symbolic at the same time. The nineteenth century, by moving the demographic line and shifting the balance between rural and urban France, powerfully stimulated the demand on the wine-making market and for the most ordinary products. The France of *gros rouge* (inexpensive, undistinguished red wine) was replacing the France of *piquette*.

This profound change in habits of consumption depended, of course, on a revolution in transportation: the large urban centers of the north and east stimulated the supply in the south. The plains of Languedoc remained outside the zone of northern importation until the beginning of the eighteenth century; the disaster of the harsh winter of 1709, which, due to frost in the vineyards, reduced the production of the area that supplied Paris, opened the northern route to the vine growers of Béziers and Montpellier. Indeed, the controller general of finances, in a letter dated December 5, 1710, writes, "There is at the moment a considerable quantity of wines from Languedoc en route, whose arrival in Paris it is important to facilitate."[11] But shipping by water was, at that time, too slow and too costly to enable the regular transport of ordinary wines for popular consumption. "It was mechanical locomotion that ushered in the present vine-growing era in Languedoc."[12] In return, the establishment of railway lines between Languedoc, Paris, and the larger northern towns brought about a huge increase in production. Only a grape variety, the extraordinary aramon, whose yield can reach 300 hectolitres per hectare, made it possible for the supply to meet the demand. Over the course of the twentieth century, Languedoc laid claim to a superior position in the market for table wine, a position that no vine-growing area north of Beaucaire has ever been able to challenge.

Long-distance transportation was not without risks: temperature, mixing, and stocking often altered, and even spoiled, the wines transported by the railways, in particular the Paris-Lyons-Mediterranean and Paris-Orléans lines that served the Massif Central and the south. In this regard, the construction of the Halle aux vins in the vicinity of the Lyons and Austerlitz train stations was an unmistakable sign, in the very landscape of Paris, of the dominance of this north-south wine trade. The discovery by Louis Pasteur, a son of Arbois, of the phenomenon of fermentation, and the quick mastering by those that followed of the microbial causes of what was once called "degast," enhanced the security of commerce. Without the technological know-how of its engineers, as well as progress in chemistry and biology, the nineteenth century would never have brought the generalized use of table wine to the entire country.

And yet, everything was nearly called back into question by the attack of phylloxera. The insect known as *phylloxera vastatrix*, a plant-louse whose life cycle takes place alternately above and below ground, multiplies around the vine plant. The attack, in which sap is sucked from the root system, is slow and insidious: the first year, the damage is insignificant, but the phylloxera colonizes the rootlets; two years later, the plant dries up and dies. In between, the flowering is anemic, the leaves turn yellow, the seeds do not grow to normal size, the maturation is incomplete. The scourge spreads from plant to plant, from plot to plot, from village to village: the louse is carried by the wind, or transported by man, vehicle, or tool, stuck with the mud to its unconscious, involuntary vector.

Phylloxera was an American import:[13] the parasite made its first appearance in Gard around 1862–63; step by step, it overtook Provence and the Rhône River valley; it reached the Beaujolais region in 1871, with the first vines dying at Villé-Morgon in 1874. Burgundy was invaded, starting with Meursault in 1878, and soon, all of France saw its vineyards destroyed. Combating it was, at first, uncertain: pulling up and burning the vines; miraculous "phylloxericides" that soon proved useless; scalding, horse- or sheep-urine, depending on the region. Soon, the discussion narrowed to one between the "sulfurists," who hoped to kill the insect by treating the soil with long, expensive doses of carbon disulphide, and the "Americanists," who decided to pull up all the vineyards and replant them with American grape varieties, such as clinton, noah, and riparia, that were resistant to the parasite. These plantings yielded wine of mediocre quality; the taste was bitter, even nauseating. "This wine smells of fox urine: the phylloxera has gotten to it," was the judgment of good old Gnafron at Lyons.*

The restoration of the nation's vineyards succeeded thanks to the grafting of old French vines onto American ones, the latter reduced to the function of mere stocks. Around 1895–1900, requiring Herculean labor and at an exceptionally high cost, the vine was saved, but the traditional map of plantations and vineyards was only partially restored and sometimes greatly altered. Indeed, some old vineyards disappeared, limited to a few narrow, privileged microclimates, saved by their quality or by an uncom-

---

* Gnafron, the drunken shoemaker, was a popular character in the puppet theater of Lyons in the nineteenth and twentieth centuries.—Ed.

mon dedication on the part of the wine grower. Thus, Yonne, Aube, and Lorraine, regions henceforth reduced to chablis, to rosé des Riceys, pride of Morel and son, to Côtes de Toul, and to Moselle wines.

Meanwhile, the vineyards of Languedoc, the first to be affected by the parasite and, as a result, the first to be restored, benefiting from weak competition, moved down from the sud-cévenol hills to the plains of lower Languedoc. From this estimable sea of vines sprang the wines of the Midi, abundant and generous but lacking in tradition and limited in refinement, which set the tone for table wines and for everyday wine consumption.

From this cursory overview of two millennia of the history of vine and wine, we can judge to what extent the art of viticulture, and the attachment of the French people to a product of our land, make wine consubstantial with our destiny as a nation. The vine and its branches have woven a common history with our people. Gifts brought by the Greeks and by the Roman conquerors, vine and wine are contemporaneous with the origins of our civilization that make us a part of Greco-Latin Europe. The connection between wine and Eucharistic worship brings the symbol to life by making it holy; in their earliest sermons, the bishops and monks who evangelized the people of what would become France mixed into their message of hope and love the story of Jesus, whose own preaching is found between the Marriage at Cana and the Last Supper. As the subject of a Sunday-morning homily or of one of our paintings, vine and wine impress upon our culture the durable stamp of a reference point that is at once both familiar and solemn. The vineyard, first episcopal and abbatial, later princely and aristocratic, bourgeois and popular, completely takes over the society of old France. Once the vine had conquered the land, wine conquered a place and a role without equal among the French. It is they, after all, who naturally reply, in the same poll, "to be French is, first and foremost, . . . to love good wine." Now is a good time to explore the pathways, the places, and the monuments of this identification.

3. A Cultural Memory

Memory is, in fact, a process of identification. It is the judgment of consciousness, which identifies its contents with a reality from the past. To remember is to identify a past with a present. The same thing from the past is, once again, present in the mind. Quite apart from some history of vine and wine, complete with dates, well ordered, logically presented, and well supplied with commentaries, our culture identifies wine and vine with certain familiar images. This gallery of images requires an exploration of all the associations that life has established between a human activity, a life's work, a being, an outline, and vine and wine.

The festive is, without a doubt, the first of these associations. Drinking wine, even to the point of drunkenness, is one of life's pleasures. The Bible, in the book of Proverbs, articulated the adage that has been quoted so many times: "Vinum bonum laetificat cor hominum." In offering a glass of wine, we honor a guest by sharing something pleasurable. The popular imagination preserves the memory of collective libations given by municipal governments during times of celebration: the birth of a prince, the declaration of peace. Graciously, the town council dips into the treasury in order to distribute wine to the crowd. In this context, the praise of wine is often the subject of songs and rhymes. Let us borrow from a wild celebration at Lyons both this Bacchic exaltation and its more or-

Figure 6.8
The central rite of Christian worship. Wine becomes "the Lord's blood." *La Sainte Messe*, a miniature from *La Journée du Chrétien*, by the father of J.-K. Huysmans, 1852.

Figure 6.9
Poster for Paul Court
wine, 1900–1910.

dinary counterparts. In 1627, on the last Sunday before Lent, a procession of masked players, folksy and grotesque, made its way through the different neighborhoods of the city; dozens of carnival characters made up the retinue of Bacchus and his wife. At the head of the parade, Time bade the onlookers make no mistake about the licentious meaning of the masquerade:

> My journey has no end
> I march both night and day
> And if you want me to move along
> I'll need to have a drink or make love.

Opportunity chimes in, in a bawdy tone:

> I am Bacchus's faithful messenger
> I announce his arrival to all of his nurslings.

Like you, ladies, and not like the boys,
I'm best taken from the front, not from behind.

The regiment of the guards, apparently losing their warlike rage, would prefer to go

Rather to pillage
A maidenhead or a cask.

The Laughable One boasts of the consoling properties of wine:

I can easily polish off a quart of wine
Chasing away the sorrows of thwarted souls
And I'm as happy to see a bottle standing up
As I am to see the ladies on their backs.

Which recalls the grand master of the Knights of the Round Table, who

Fears neither glasses on the table
Nor women in the bed.

It seems, indeed, that the women themselves take pleasure in the same joys, if we are to believe the bacchantes:

Wine makes us run through the streets
And love keeps us in bed.

Which prompts the senators of Venice to reveal themselves to be more than bold in their plans regarding the women:

Though we in the Senate have grown old,
Though our brows are wrinkled and our beards gray,
At table we finish off a glass of Venetian crystal
Just as well as we do an affair of state in the Council.

Ladies, our flames are covered with ashes,
We wear a disguise to fool our jealous rivals,
White and red on the outside, but, inside, we keep for you
A piece that's just as red as it is green.★

★ To describe a man as "green," in French, is to call him vital, strong, or virile.—Ed.

Who would have thought the Venetians were so "Gaulois" (i.e., ribald)? It remains only to imagine the city's narrow streets filled with encouraging laughter at each of these off-color barbs, the broad jokes that prolong them, the rude gestures that illustrate them, and the mischievous thoughts that take hold of minds that have been inflamed by the public overturning of taboos, to the great horror of the Jesuit Menestrier. The tavern-keepers' idea having proved effective, the goal reached, the instincts aroused, we can assume that, with the masquerade at an end, people would then stream into the inns and cabarets, covering the town with the noise of a crowd let loose. Draining their glasses, the revelers all strive to echo this profane—and profaning—celebration of the rough, natural pleasures of the people of Lyons, as they forget, for a day, the harshness of work and the austerity of the coming Lenten season. This physical and mental heat causes the city to melt together. Festive wine has accomplished its integrating task. Unity is sealed in a glass enjoyed together; as liberty leads to intimacy, the Lyonnais discovers a fellow Lyonnais hitherto unknown to him.

However amusing the celebration, however, it does not account for the entire culture of wine. In the collective imagination, wine evokes other faces besides those of Bacchus and the Bacchantes. Of course, memory also shows its gratitude to those who, in a variety of ways, have served to advance the art of winemaking. A few names have become widely known, even becoming clichés in the form of verbs referring to various procedures of the winemaker's art: *chaptaliser, pasteuriser.* It is Dom Pérignon, however, who precedes both Chaptal and Pasteur in enjoying the gratitude of vine growers and wine consumers alike. Legend has generously attributed to Dom Pérignon all the techniques that have enabled champagne to achieve its present reputation. In fact, he deserves to be honored if only for his method of mixing grapes and grape musts from a variety of sources. When, in 1668, the Abbey of Hautvillers entrusted the direction of its vineyards, its winepresses, and its casks to Dom Pérignon, the quality of its products was already well known. During his long tenure (1668–1715), the famous monk's principal contribution was, thanks to his exceptionally refined palate, the practice of blending the products of outlying districts—Sillery, Ay, Avize—while delicately balancing the proportions. Always focused on making wines of great quality, Dom Pérignon apparently never wished to see his name associated with the fizzy variety that occurred naturally in the more ordinary local wines—wines that, when bottled under a full moon in March, were endowed with the sparkle that only became typical of the product some years later, compelled by popular demand, around 1720–30. Nonetheless, Dom Pérignon will be forever thought of as the benefactor of the champagne-growing region, even if he wasn't the sole

creator of champagne; the perfecting of champagne is a process extending over several generations of attentive, ingenious winemakers, each of
whom contributed, more or less anonymously, to the progress of the wine
of Épernay and Vertus.

Louis Pasteur was also one of the heroes of wine, although the immensity of his genius connects him to a multitude of discoveries, of which
the rabies vaccine was to make his image popular and immortal. Pasteur
had a unique connection to vine and wine. Very soon after his birth at
Dole, the Pasteur family settled in Arbois, a town that Pasteur always considered to be his true home. Each year, he went back to spend the summer among his compatriots, remaining into early September in order to
participate in the "Fête du Biou." On this final Sunday before the grape
harvest, the people of Arbois offer a giant bunch of grapes, made up of
many bunches of real grapes and weighing a hundred pounds, to their patron saint, Saint Just. The whole town accompanies the offering, carried
by four wine growers, in a procession, while dignitaries and musicians
express the joyful unity of the confraternity. This familiarity with local
popular celebrations was connected, in the scientist's mind, with a desire
to put his abilities at the service of the wine producers. His work led him
to develop practical aspects of his studies of microorganisms; thus, he was
able to protect the wine from ruinous diseases against which people had
been helpless until then.

Other benefactors of wine have not become household names, except
perhaps regionally. Nonetheless, let us evoke the name of Benoît Raclet,
a vine grower of Romanèche, who, after thirty years of damage, discovered an effective way to combat the *pyrale*, or vine leaf roller, a caterpillar
that was ravaging the local vines. Benoît Raclet had noticed that the vines
planted near the little stream into which his wife regularly dumped old
dish- and laundry water resisted the onslaught of the insect. Attributing
this positive effect to the high temperature of the used household water,
he recommended in 1841 that the vines be scalded. And so the Beaujolais
region was covered with kettles set out in the middle of the vineyards, their
fires fed with dry vine branches. Afterward, the vine growers carried in
large brass jugs heated by coals the boiling water that would save the vineyards. In a few years, the scourge was over. Collectors can still purchase
"pyralid jugs" designed by Benoît Raclet in local antique shops.

Dom Pérignon, Louis Pasteur, and Benoît Raclet bear witness to a
technical culture in which the consumer is not immediately engaged. For
this reason, we should now explore how drinking becomes a culture, and
even a cult—which serves to illustrate the group-forming function assumed by wine. The pairing of the soldier and his beloved *pinard* (slang
term for wine) can be held up in this context as the symbol of a typically

French sociopsychological construct. Certainly the ration of wine, along with tobacco and the possibility of borrowing money, constituted the amenities of military life. However, if we are to believe the refrains sung by the infantry battalions, it was more often the absence than the abundance of wine that held sway. The commissariat did not always follow.

While the refrain of the 30th Battalion laments:

> If I had some *pinard*,
> I'd gladly drink a drop.
> If I had some *pinard*,
> I'd gladly drink a quarter,*

That of the 13th Battalion had already given up hope, answering in advance:

> With no bread and no grub,
> In the Thirteenth we drink only water,

While, with courage and without illusions . . .

> We're the Twenty-ninth,
> We've got no bread,
> We've got no wine,
> We go on marching just the same.

And, of course, just to exhaust the subject of military folklore, we have to bring up the marching song which, to music by Georges Piquet, recites the famous words of Louis Bosquet:

> A song, authentic and bizarre,
> Whose refrain goes: Long live *pinard!*
> One, two!
> *Pinard* is plonk,
> Where it goes down, it warms you up,
> Go on, soldier, fill my cup,
> Long live *pinard*, long live *pinard*.[14]

Benefiting from such strong support, the French soldier of the First World War, though lacking heavy artillery, nonetheless held his position

---

★ *Un quart,* cup measuring about one-quarter liter, used in the army for rations of wine, coffee, etc.—Ed.

Figure 6.10
Wine means a feast; it marks the event and demands that it be remembered. *Fête de la nomination du maire,* engraving by Remhild, ca. 1850.

Figure 6.11
Wine, an element of
the national imagina-
tion, patriotic, almost
chauvinistic. "We had
it, your German Rhine!"
Engraving, illustrated
supplement to the *Petit
Journal*, 1895.

on the Marne, the Aisne, the Somme, and on the outskirts of Verdun
before eventually claiming victory. The discourse that has developed
around this theme (aside from the obvious pleasure of drinking, virtually the only pleasure available in the trenches) follows directly from the
image of a nation whose wine is, as we have mentioned earlier, inseparable
from its history. Wine the warlike, wine the glorious: history shows us
this phenomenon in an earlier manifestation, during that strange burst of
poetry and patriotism that the European crisis of 1840–41 unleashed on
both sides of the Rhine. The "Rheinlied" of Nikolaus Becker:

> They won't have it,
> Our German Rhine,

received an answer in the form of Alfred de Musset's "Le Rhin allemand."
Alluding to the German poet's phrase, "the wine of fire," the ironical
Musset recalled,

> We had it, your German Rhine,
> It held up nicely in our glasses

Figure 6.12
"Save wine for our soldiers," poster by
Suzanne Ferrand, student, Paris public
schools, aged sixteen, during World War I.

Before concluding with a threat:

> But take care, lest your drinking songs
> Awaken the dead from their blood-soaked slumbers.

Perhaps we should go so far as to include an example of an unambiguous, if brutal, symbolism connecting wine with blood in the context of war. Montéhus, in his elegiac "Red Hill," meditates with sorrow on that blood-soaked hill where, across the vineyards of Champagne, attacks and counterattacks left, in the heart and the mind of one who escaped the slaughter, the gloomy vision of spilled blood, smashed skulls, and the terrible echo of cries and sobs, for

> On that hill, we weren't having fun,
> The way you do in Montmartre, where the champagne flows.
> It's called Red Hill. The baptism happened one morning
> When whoever climbed up, rolled back down.
> There are vines today, and grapes grow there,
> But he who drinks that wine drinks the blood of my comrades.

This recollection shows the variety of bonds formed between wine and war, and the traces left in these cultural documents of poem and song are deeply rooted social and psychological signs of France. The iconography of the Great War has left us with the image of the foot soldier, who, like a Roman legionnaire, is weighed down by his pack, the well-known *barda*, in the middle of which, among the many pieces of equipment, his metal drinking cup and bottle are ever present, being just as essential to victorious combat as the grenade or the rifleman's Lebel gun.

A second theme, continuous and natural in our memories, associates wine with the phenomenon of the fraternal organization. The wine world, a kind of Bacchic freemasonry made up of secrets, ceremonies, and initiations, marks out a place for the elite among wine drinkers. The renown of a particular wine apparently cannot flourish without this place for consecration where the new knights are founders of a new noble order, a new race of men who guarantee to elevate and defend the reputation of both a piece of land and a treasure. We are obliged to list the many titles: from the Knights of the Tastevin (Clos-Vougeot), to the mysterious Judges of Pouilly, about thirty such brotherhoods attempt, through the use of evocative terminology, to accede to high rank, to prestige, to excellence. Saint-Émilion has its Magistrates, Chablis its Pillars, Bordeaux its Grand Counsellors, Arbois its Peers, Vidauban its Cup-bearers, Guyenne its High Constables, Bué-en-Sancerre its Berettes. More commonly, we find nine *chevaleries*, three *compagnonnages*, two *ordres* and two *commanderies*. The general flavor of these names brings to mind a somewhat conventional medievalism, a corps of dignitaries bound by oath to keep the secrets that are contained in some glorious charter. In these Bacchic societies, vine growing, winemaking, cooperage, and glassmaking are subjected to a religious conservation of the rites, traditions, and objects connected with those disciplines, handed down from the practices of a bygone age. They strive to create, or simply to elicit the feeling of, the prestige of a museum of local traditions. All of these qualities make these fraternal organizations into societies of memory in which the medieval titles reinforce the claim to ancient origins and to the noble ranking that ancient lineage guarantees.

This desire to return to a past—albeit perhaps more distant than authentic—would be nothing without the possibility of celebrating one's origins in a very old architectural setting. Gathering in wine cellars transformed into chapter houses, our knights or commanders consecrate the holy places of wine; in case real wine is in short supply, at least an evocation of same is expected from the devotees of wine legend. The storeroom is a place of the same great symbolic value as the wine cellar. The presence of an immense vat or of a majestic winepress imposes upon the (usually vaulted) room a solemnity, a majesty, a reverence bordering on the religious. The classic example is the city of Beaune; this old capital of the Dukes of Burgundy has transformed the former ducal residence into a museum of wine, while the Hospices, the charitable foundation of Nicolas Rolin, chancellor of Burgundy, and of Guigone de Salins, his wife, base their prosperity and, today, their international reputation on fifty-three hectares of a prestigious vineyard, planted with select vines and producing vintages of exceptional quality. On the third Sunday in November, in a public auction, following a venerable, immemorial tradition, the Hospices sell casks of burgundy to merchants from near and far, in accordance with the wishes expressed in the 1443 charter granted by Philip the Good to his clever counselor. Half a millennium later, when they acquired the château of Clos-Vougeot, the Knights of the Tastevin, a young order of wine chivalry barely ten years old, revived this master stroke of marketing. Proclaiming the opening of "Les Trois Glorieuses" at the end of the third week of November, the chapter brought together the most distinguished friends of Burgundy for a dinner for five hundred guests in the large storeroom, under the authority of the grand master and the grand chancellor.★ Places of memory, rites of memory, storeroom and wine cellar, grape harvest and grape pressing, all have found their priests to celebrate the glory of wine beneath venerable vaults, a jewel box of their imaginations.

To all of these capitulary celebrations, of knights, companions, and commanders, of the vine, Syrah, and Sacavin, would the drinking of commoners in taverns and pubs constitute an echo in a minor key? Let us not jump to the conclusion that their great numbers mean banality. The origins of the bistro, or pub, dedicate it as a place of disputation and, therefore, of liberty. Indeed, the frequenting of taverns, while tolerated during profane hours, was forbidden by canon law and by royal decree at ceremonial times. Mass, Vespers, and Holy Offices did not suffer competition; the drinker was obliged to defer the pleasure of conviviality, unless he was willing to run the risk of being arrested and having charges brought by the police. In repressing the modest leisure of the poor, the ancien régime's regulations concerning public morality were attacking a counterculture. The tavern was the place where the male workers of the village or the neighborhood savored the pleasure of being together, of momentarily escaping wife and children, and of discussing the news of

---

★ The Knights of the Tastevin borrowed the name of the three-day wine festival, Les Trois Glorieuses, from a somewhat more recent period of French history. The phrase refers to the three days of insurrection in July 1830 that brought Louis-Philippe to the throne and expelled the last of the Bourbon kings, Charles X.—Ed.

Figure 6.13
Labels for Château Mouton-Rothschild, featuring works of contemporary art by Henry Moore (1964) and Pierre Alechinsky (1966).

the day—public opinion in its embryonic state. It was the time when the workingman participated in a social life that was not limited to the storefront, the workshop, the home, or the church, when he attempted for a moment to be something other than a worker, a husband and father, or a follower—that triple function assigned by the three-pronged slogans of societies emphasizing order and duty: Work, Family, Fatherland. The slogan of 1789 was much more in keeping with the need for popular conviviality: the tavern, home of a liberty and a fraternity that were rudimentary but tangible, quite clearly conveyed a spirit of sedition. It was, for a time, a transgression, a revolt, or, at the very least, a rupture. Symbolically, it was doubtless more of a bastion of the working class; the poor man's salon, as it has been called, it pushed away the social elite, which felt ill at ease there. In the strategy of republicanism, the tavern played a decisive role in the nineteenth century. Often the home base of mutual aid societies, it has been a place in which to assemble, a center for ideological exchange. It was there that democracy became aware of its strength vis-à-vis the chateau, the presbytery, or the factory.

In the novels of Zola, the tavern holds a key place in the depiction

Figure 6.14
Labels for Château Mouton-Rothschild, featuring works of contemporary art by Joan Miró (1969) and Andy Warhol (1975).

of modest milieus; *Germinal*, with its meetings at the public house of the Bon-joyeux run by the widow Désir, shows clearly the evolution from unfocused discontent to the organization of the miners' collective struggle. The fact that the story's northern setting makes beer the drink of choice changes nothing. Elsewhere, in *L'Assommoir*, Zola presents us with his gallery of bars serving wine and spirits—wine once removed— the Veau à deux têtes, the Moulin d'argent, and his gallery of drinkers sliding into alcoholic ruin. Thus, literature brings, along with the mark of its curiosity regarding this social phenomenon, the imprimatur of a cultural consecration. These novelistic types add a new cohort of drunkards and tavern keepers to the pantheon of literary characters. But the realist novel is here simply bringing an older theme full circle, one first set in motion by Rabelais.

Realistically or symbolically, wine in its literary guise presents us once again with an infinite number of examples. At the dawn of the modern era bursts forth, enormous and fantastical, the celebration of wine that is the work of Rabelais. From the "Words of the Very Drunk" (*Gargantua*, chap. 5) to the oracle of the divine bottle (*Cinquième Livre*, chaps. 43–47):

"For Trinch is a panomphaean word, celebrated and understood in every nation, and to us it means: Drink!" rare is the page in which wine and thirst do not play a central, even if sometimes only metaphorical, role.

> All of a sudden . . . there came to him such an overheating of the throat, with an ulceration of the uvula, that his tongue peeled, and despite all the remedies they tried, found no relief at all, except by drinking without stopping, for as soon as he took the goblet from his mouth, his tongue burned. Thus, they did nothing but pour wine into his mouth with a funnel . . . and they all wielded the flagon to such an extent . . . each man in the army began to drink, to scoop up more, and to drink again in the same way. (*Pantagruel*, chap. 28)

This spectacle of the "Dipsodes" (from the Greek for "thirsty"), with their tumultuous use of wine, contrasts in the most extreme way imaginable with the delicate evocation of Calypso's caves, where, in the pleasant, cool atmosphere, hospitality offers, in addition to meats and fruits, "a wine sweeter than nectar flowing from great silver vessels into golden cups crowned with flowers" (Fénelon, *Aventures de Télémaque*, chap. 1).

More realistically, Boileau shows us bourgeois wine in the "Repas ridicule":

> Ah, sir, he said to me, I shall expect you tomorrow.
> Don't fail to come. I've got fourteen bottles
> Of an old wine . . . Boucingo has none like it.
> . . . .
> Thinking that, at least, the wine should make up for everything else,
> To understand better, I ask for some; and first,
> A Cheeky servant brings me a brimming glass
> Of murky Auvergnat, which, of mixed origins,
> Was sold at Crenet's as wine from the country,
> And, red and vermilion, but dull and sickly-sweet,
> Had nothing but a flat taste and a horrible aftertaste.
>
> (*Satire* 3.20–23 and 70–76)

And wine, the stimulant of the comic nocturnal escapades of *Le Lutrin*:

> Shadows, having meanwhile spread over the city,
> Descend from the rooftops to the streets below:
> Supper chases the chaplains from their choirs,
> And the taverns are filled with drinking choristers.
> The formidable Broutin, awakened by his duty,

Goes out immediately, carrying three bottles
Of a wine that Gilotin, who anticipates all,
Took care to give him at the end of the council meeting.
The smell of so sweet a juice lightens his burden.

(Canto 2.65–73)

Meanwhile, Rousseau evokes a peaceful domestic contentment:

In this setting, the window was our table, we breathed the air, we
could see our surroundings, the passers-by. . . . Who can describe,
who can fully understand the charms of this meal, which consisted
only of a hunk of bread, a few cherries, a little piece of cheese, and a
demi-setier [approximately a quarter-liter] of wine that the two of us
shared? (*Les Confessions*, book 8)

Baudelaire, in the group of five poems devoted to wine within his collection, *Les Fleurs du mal*, reveals his "Soul."

Through these few broad strokes, there emerges an infinitely nuanced set of feelings and responses; wine contributes to a multifaceted
pleasure, it becomes part of an art of living, and it reveals the true nature
of a civilization.

Apparently, the vine has not inspired poets or writers nearly so much;
nonetheless, let us mention Lamartine and his fine poem, "La Vigne et la
maison," which actually does not have much to say about domestic vine
growing. Let us also quote Mauriac, a native of Bordeaux:

Calèse slept without a breath beneath all the stars. And suddenly,
at about three o'clock in the morning, once again that squall, those
rumblings in the sky, those heavy, icy drops. They clattered against
the tiles to the point that I feared hail.

The vine has only just passed from blossom to fruit; the future
harvest blankets the hillside; but its presence there seems more like
one of those young animals that hunters tether and then leave out in
the darkness to attract wild beasts; grumbling storm-clouds circle the
vines that seem offered in sacrifice . . .

A whistling sound; then, a horrible din and, at the same time, a
flash of lightning, filled the sky. In the panicked silence that followed,
bombs exploded, thrown by the vine growers so that the hail clouds
would move away or rain out water. Rockets shot up from that corner of the darkness where Barsac and Sauternes tremble before the
scourge. . . . And suddenly, on the tiles, that noise, like a handful
of pebbles. Hailstones! . . . I've calculated, from habit: "one hun-

dred thousand francs gone." . . . A deep-seated peasant instinct was
throwing me forward, as if I'd wanted to stretch out and cover the
hail-strafed vines with my body.[15]

These selections on French wine, drawn from the most esteemed classics of our canon of great literary achievements and consecrated by talent
and genius, find their echo in the popular imagination in the many evo-
cations, allusions, and exaltations of vine and wine taken from the body
of (largely anonymous) French song.

The collection opens, with pleasure, on the jolly double silhouette of
Fanchon and Madelon.

> Fanchon, though a good Christian woman,
> Was baptized with wine,
> A Burgundian was her Godfather,
> A Breton woman her Godmother.

From the outset, we see France represented by the people of those provinces that have a strong tradition of wine consumption; we see also how
laughter, drinking, and singing are combined to chase away sadness and
to show one's pride.

> When I see the blush in my florid face,
> I'm proud to be from Burgundy.

Madelon awakens the same feelings and engages in the same practices;
she banishes the homesickness of the garrisoned soldier with that flirtatious banter that means she belongs to all:

> And why would I ever take a man
> When I love the whole regiment?
> Your friends will come
> You won't have my hand
> I'll need it to pour them some wine.

But wine is, first of all, the vine grower's business, and in order to
pluck up one's courage, there's nothing like a visit to the cellar before
climbing the slope of the vineyard.

> As soon as the morning light
> Has restored to the hillsides their golden hue,

I begin my rounds
By visiting my casks
Delighted to see the dawn,
A glass in my hand, I say . . .

. . . .

When I'm at table, nothing surprises me
And I think, as I drink,
If Jupiter thunders up there,
It's because he's afraid of me.

This drinking song, by Master Adam Billau, carpenter at Nevers in the seventeenth century, develops the theme of the challenge made by the drinker; death itself will be the drinking companion for a last, eternal libation.

If I die, I wish to be buried
In a cellar where there's good wine.

This is the last request of Valentin:

The spigot in my mouth
And the goblet in my hand,

whose tragic destiny is narrated by the singer:

Valentin had served to him
Five or six bottles of wine
The next day, he fell ill
And sent for the doctor.

But neither a prescription of abstinence nor the mention of death prevents him from proclaiming:

I've been drinking since I existed;
I'll drink until the end!

We could continue to gather quotations, but the subject matter is simple and the message clear. The song most often gives voice to a very materialistic, pagan philosophy of the pleasure of the drinker, and of a certain will to contravene that everyday morality which insists upon moderation and privation. It is based on a need to forget for a moment the hard constraints of work and of day-to-day life, and to express itself, it requires the collusion of a group; hence, the frequency of refrains encouraging fellowship.

> Let's drink together,
> And let's dance merrily, *Pécaïre!*

Or:

> Let's have a drink,
> Let's have two . . .

In the same way that songs of war endlessly repeat such phrases as "Let's march," or "Let us die," or "Let us be prepared to perish."

Feelings of serenity are rarely expressed in these songs, other than in marking the obvious cycle of flowering, pressing, and consumption in the famous litany:

> From the vine to the bunch of grapes,
> There they are, the pretty grapes,
> Grappi, grappa, let's grape the wine,
> There they are, the pretty grapes for wine,
> There they are, the pretty grapes.

And, following the route from the grape basket to the winepress to the glass to the mouth,

> There it is, the pretty mouth for wine,
> There it is, the pretty mouth.

At the end of our tour, we can understand that through its land, its people, its history, and its culture, whether it is manifested in customs, day-to-day life, literature, or song, France is closely bound up with vine and wine. Thus, among the various incarnations of France, there is one that combines the pleasure of the drinker, the pride of the hero, the courage of the workingman, the finesse of the vine grower as he prunes the vine, and the glory of its episcopates, its abbeys, its princely estates, or its major charitable institutions. But the foreigner is not excluded from our treasures: he, too, is capable of appreciating French wine and declaring his admiration for it. In this age of European unity, let us note the agreement of two great names. Friedrich Sieburg admitted, "French wines are of such variety and such splendor that tasting them is almost a spiritual act." Such praise would have been accepted by Paul Claudel, for whom "wine is the great teacher of taste and, by training us in the practice of focusing our attention within, it frees the spirit and illuminates the intelligence."

To your health!

NOTES

Readers familiar with Alain Rey's *Lieux de mémoire* article on "Les Trésors de la langue" (vol. 2, *La Nation: Héritage—Historiographie—Paysages* [Paris: Éditions Gallimard, 1986], 3: 638–39 and 642) will already be aware of the remarkable lexical data bank in the Institut national de la langue française. I would like to acknowledge my debt to that institution, pay homage to the memory of its founder, Paul Imbs, and thank deputy director Gérard Gorcy and his team of researchers for their gracious help. I would also like to express cordial thanks to my friends and colleagues, the medievalists Michel Rousse and Michel Stanesco, for their generous advice.

1. Written and produced by Bernard Douilly, Service de publicité pour la propagande des vins de France, Cazilhac, 34190 Ganges.

2. *Le Monde*, 26 June 1987.

3. Roger Dion, *Histoire de la vigne et du vin en France: Des origines au XIXe siècle* (Paris, 1959), 578.

4. Roger Dion, "Grands traits de la géographie viticole de la France," *Revue d'histoire et de philosophie* (1944): 43–44.

5. According to custom, the traditional time for pruning began on January 22, St. Vincent's Day. (St. Vincent is the patron saint of vine growers.) Autumn pruning was recommended in southern France in the eighteenth century; it was an agricultural innovation of the Enlightenment.

6. Bottle with a capacity of 62 centiliters, used for the wines of the Jura.

7. *L'Histoire* 100 (May 1987). Analysis and commentary by Jean-Pierre Rioux.

8. Eighty-four thousand amphorae dredged from the Saône at Chalon.

9. Dion, 474.

10. Ibid., 493.

11. Ibid., 326.

12. Ibid., 327.

13. The introduction of American plant varieties into French vineyards is documented as early as 1832: the first experimentation was performed near Frontignan by Cazalis-Allur, president of the Agricultural Society of Hérault. The identification of the "leaf-dryer" plant louse was the work of Riley, on the occasion of his visit to France in 1871. Refer to Gilbert Garrier's masterful synthesis, *Le Phylloxera: Une guerre de trente ans* (Paris: Albin Michel, 1989).

14. J.-E. Berthier, *Mille chants: Chansons d'hier, chansons sociales, hymnes nationaux* (Paris: Les Presses de l'Île-de-France, 1986), 276–77.

15. François Mauriac, *Le Noeud de vipères* (Paris: Livre de poche, 1932), 150–53.

Figure 7.1

Watteau, *Assemblée dans un parc* (detail).

"The high heels were fighting with their long skirts
So that in accord with the earth and the wind
Sometimes shone the bottom of legs, too often
Intercepted!—and we love this game of tricks."

(Verlaine, "Les Ingénus," in *Les Fêtes galantes*)

CHAPTER 7

GALLANTRY

❧

NOÉMI HEPP

"There is no longer any courtesy, nor any gallantry; the Revolution
has entirely destroyed these attractive qualities that distinguished our
nation from all the other peoples of Europe."

Such is the indirect reproach that I hear addressed to our young
people every day; I do not claim that it is without foundation in certain respects, but I reply that at least it is not new.[1]

Dated 1813, these few lines by the pseudonymous "Hermit of Chaussée
d'Antin" could easily carry any other date between the late seventeenth and the mid-twentieth centuries; giving them a contemporary feel
would merely require replacing the reference to the French Revolution
by another—liberal mores, English influence, democratization, feminism,
and so forth. Just as *la galanterie* was considered a trait specific to French
society ever since the term began to refer, in the early seventeenth century, to relationships between men and women, so *la galanterie française*,
as soon as it appeared, was regularly mourned—at least by those who set
great store by it—as an extinct quality. Constantly alleged to be thriving,
regularly lamented as dead, hailed as the epitome of courteous behavior, blamed as the site of all insincerity, valued as a sign of respect toward
women, despised as a mark of male fatuousness, admired as a structuring
force of civilized society, castigated as a socially destructive element: every
assertion has been made for French gallantry. The term, moreover, has
been used to cover everything from the most cultured manners toward

women to the most vulgar expressions of desire.* As the focus of every contradiction concerning its existence, nature, and value, *la galanterie française* assumes the features of a myth—it can never be entirely grasped nor, still less, dismissed.

No one, however, disputes the association of adjective with noun. As Charles Sorel wrote in 1644, "We, the Sovereign Masters of Gallantry, have decreed that only the French Nation can lay claim to the honor of excellently observing its precepts, and that it is Paris, a capital city in every regard, where its source must be sought."[2] A quarter of a century later, in a scene set in Sicily, Molière had a young Greek woman assert, "One must admit that the French have something courteous and gallant about them that other nations lack."[3]

The expression *galanterie française,* employed by Mme de Villedieu in 1675, entered the language somewhat later.[4] It became common in the following century, however: B. L. de Muralt, from Bern, made an attempt to define it;[5] a character in a Charles Duclos novel gave up trying to find "Spanish steadfastness" or "Italian passion" in Paris but "contented himself with French gallantry and levity";[6] and Rousseau himself employed the expression very often. Then, early in the nineteenth century, "the epochs of French gallantry" were the object of a kind of historical dissertation by the same "Hermit" who provided the opening lines to this essay. In 1835, the sixth edition of the Académie française's *Dictionnaire* admitted *galanterie française* as a full-fledged expression, while ten years later Bescherelle's *Dictionnaire universel de la langue française* included it along with the flattering comment that "French gallantry is famous throughout all of Europe."[7] This idea was pompously developed in 1853 by an obscure scholar named A. Vallet de Viriville:

> France is the classic land of gallantry. . . . The mere words *galanterie* and *culte des dames* [worship of ladies] suffice to evoke a more or less vague idea of romantic sentiments that are refined yet real, and this idea is intimately linked to our historical memories and national traditions. Such a conviction, such a presumption, is more than simple patriotic prejudice, for it is confirmed by the agreement of foreigners.[8]

That foreigners did indeed agree on the specificity of French gallantry was confirmed, to cite just a few examples, by the Swiss commentator

---

* By the late seventeenth century, the English word "gallantry" also came to connote flirtation and sexual sparring, just as in French; but whereas the primary definition in modern English now tends to refer to a noble display of courage, the French terms *galant* and *galanterie* still retain strong sexual connotations.—Trans.

Muralt, followed in the nineteenth century by Fanny Trollope in her *Paris and the Parisians*[9] and the German Karl Hillebrand, who observed, "The gallantry of Frenchmen contributes . . . to the charm of social life. . . . Gallantry gives society a stimulating charm and vivacity that we Germans replace, quite imperfectly, by the bottle."[10] As to the French themselves, they have generally looked upon *galanterie* as their private property. Sorel asserted it back in 1644, and Houdart de la Motte restated it at the end of that century by titling his popular ballet—which showed how love was conducted in France, Spain, Italy, and Turkey—*L'Europe galante*.[11] Even Stendhal's well-known penchant for Italy could not prevent him from writing that "passion is rare in any country, while gallantry has more grace and refinement and consequently greater felicity in France."[12]

It should be noted that the idea of *galanterie française* was not limited—after the Revolution, at least—to high-society circles. In Balzac's *Le Père Goriot*, Mme Vauquer is heard to exclaim, following a heavily ironic compliment paid to her by Vautrin, "he's fluent in French gallantry, that one!"[13] And in Courteline's *Messieurs les ronds-de-cuir*, an office bureaucrat preaches respect for "the healthy traditions of French gallantry" to one of his colleagues.[14] The national myth has therefore largely extended across social space as well as time.

Yet even as the myth was being trumpeted abroad, the pipes of funeral processions marking the death of French gallantry could be heard in counterpoint. As early as 1684, old Mademoiselle de Scudéry mused unrealistically on conditions that would encourage a resurgence of courtesy in society. "Courtesy would reign, a gallant tone would almost always follow, and true gallantry would shine once more in all its glory."[15]

Soon afterward, La Bruyère's literary sketches of the court were contrasting the immorality and impoliteness of young people with the gallantry of the old.[16] By the mid-eighteenth century, meanwhile, Diderot commented in the *Encyclopédie* that "truly gallant men have become rare,"[17] whereas Madame de Staël, in *De l'Allemagne*, accused the entire eighteenth century of having abandoned fine gallantry.[18] And the Revolution was hardly inclined to claim it back. Yet gallantry must have survived all the same, since Stendhal dated its death certificate from the time of the Restoration,[19] whereas Balzac associated its demise with the fall of Charles X.[20] So had it really expired by the mid-nineteenth century when Ernest Bersot asserted that "gallantry, that discerning game of wit, has been replaced either by easy pleasures, by earnest marriage, or by less extravagant conversation among men"?[21] Probably not, since Maupassant, in a famous short story set in 1870, describes a Rouen salon as being "the leading [salon] in the area, the only one where old-style gallantry was maintained."[22] Furthermore, at the end of the century, Courteline, quoted above, was still evoking the traditions of *galanterie française*; nor was he the last to do so, as will be seen below. In short, gallantry is like a dying man that continues to give tiny signs of life.

What, then, is to be made of this specifically French, dead-and-alive creature? How can its identity be established? It was back in the seventeenth century that it was first described, and in the eighteenth that its nature was first examined.

⁂

Although Sorel attributed "precepts" to it, *galanterie française* was no more than a vague fog of ideas when it was first employed in the sense discussed here.[23] In the mid-seventeenth century, grammarian Claude Favre de Vaugelas pondered how to define a "gallant" man:

> I formerly witnessed this question disputed by the people at Court
> and the most gallant persons of both sexes, who had much difficulty
> defining it. Some argued that it was a *je ne sais quoi* [an indescribable
> something] which differed little from *bonne grâce* [gracious manners],
> others that neither *je ne sais quoi* nor *bonne grâce* sufficed . . . but that
> both of them had to be accompanied by a certain air.

The fog still remained fairly thick, given the use of the term to be defined in the definition itself and the escalation of vague expressions, until Vaugelas offered a third, somewhat less insubstantial opinion that underpinned *je ne sais quoi* and *bonne grâce* with "a courtly air, wit, judgment, civility, courtesy, and gaiety, all without constraint or vice."[24] In short, early *galanterie* was the art of pleasing others by respecting the values then fashionable in high society. Some twenty years later, the Chevalier de Méré specified a few of those valued qualities—wit, inventiveness, adroitness, the art of "surprising twists," and the ability to "put a pleasant face on disagreeable things."[25] All of these could be learned at court, as Vaugelas suggested and Méré reiterated. Above all, Méré described the role of women in gallantry; women "know more expertly" than men "how to do things properly, either because the honor of pleasing comes more naturally to them, or because, sensing that it is their strength, they hone it like a craft right from childhood. . . . If there were no fame or pleasure in getting close to them, one would not seek so many little ways to make oneself agreeable."[26] Thus it is women who teach men the perfect social behavior incarnated in *galanterie* and, even more, it is to please them that men try to be gallant. Ladies, indeed, desire "refined manners, brilliant and spirited conversation; a pleasant and ever so slightly flattering complaisance; that stimulating *je ne sais quoi*, and the skill of bringing them to the fore without embarrassing them; that high-society manner which touches everything, bold yet modest behavior which has nothing low or crafty about it, nothing that might be unseemly."[27]

From Vaugelas to Méré, the fog of ideas began to cohere. Yet even though the relationship of *galanterie* to love became explicit, the limits of that relationship were clearly set by its nature as a social activity, which both commentators stressed. Since *galanterie* was to be displayed toward all women who might lay claim to male attention, it necessarily remained short of personal love. Gallantry developed within society gatherings, through them, and for them, reflecting the tone of those gatherings rather than of relationships between individuals.

Once *galanterie française* had been succinctly defined by a few basic precepts, its essence still remained to be grasped and judged—which is what the "philosophical century" set out to do. Diderot's thoroughly remarkable entry on "Galanterie" in the *Encyclopédie* addressed the sociological side of the issue. No gallantry is possible, he claimed, in an uncivilized state where love is a mere need, nor "in a state where everything is enslaved . . . because men have no freedom and women no empire." Free peoples may be expected to display great virtue, but their etiquette will never be more than "coarse and rough." Only "a government where a single individual is responsible for the affairs of all" will generate, among its leisured class, the desire for a pleasant social life; this encourages the tendency to please women and develop a gallantry that "sets an overall tone for the nation's habits and products of every type," such products gaining in delightfulness what they lose in power.

Whereas Diderot reasoned sociologically, some of his contemporaries were reasoning historically. They were not the first to do so; in the previous century, a Madame de Motteville had attributed Arabic roots to *galanterie*, claiming it had been transmitted to France via Spain.[28] Jean Chapelain, meanwhile, had discussed at some length the link between chivalry and gallantry in the days of courtly romance, although his text remained unpublished during his lifetime.[29] The idea of Arabic roots was not pursued in the eighteenth century, and only resurfaced, as far as can be ascertained, with Madame de Staël.[30] In contrast, the link between chivalry and gallantry was strongly highlighted. In *The Spirit of the Laws*, Montesquieu grounded that link in the romance imagination:

> Thus gallantry was born when one imagined extraordinary men who, upon seeing virtue joined to beauty and weakness in the same person, were led to expose themselves to danger for her sake and to please her in all the ordinary actions of life.

Our romances of chivalry flattered this desire to please and gave
to a part of Europe that gallantry that one can say was little known to
the ancients.[31]

Yet for a medievalist like La Curne de Sainte-Palaye, who delivered
a series of lectures on the subject of ancient chivalry to the Académie des
inscriptions beginning in 1746, gallantry originated not in the medieval
imagination but in social reality. Knights—by definition the protectors
and avengers of all victims of the unjust use of force—frequently found
themselves placing their own force at the service of damsels who, "without arms to maintain possession of their goods, devoid of means to prove
their challenged innocence . . . , would have often seen their lands and
fortune fall prey to an unjust and powerful neighbor, or their reputation
succumb to shafts of calumny, had knights not always been ready to take
up arms in their defense."[32] This led to a desire to please the protected
lady by reversing the situation: he who was given physical strength and
the mission to employ it convinced himself that all true power lay in
the hands of she whose only strength was moral. Love and prowess thus
formed an alliance—the development of highly virile qualities in order
to render homage to the delicate flower of femininity became the guiding
principle behind society life. In its day this principle was called *courtoisie*
rather than *galanterie*, but the newer term was unhesitatingly applied to
the former reality. This suddenly explains—at least in part—the varied
meanings of the term *galant*, for it indicates the passage from a courageous
and valiant man (or, later, a highly accomplished society gentleman) called
a *galant homme* (gentleman) to the man whose relationships with women
featured a discerning attention that earned him the epithet of *homme galant* (ladies' man).

The eighteenth century was equally interested, if not more so, in
judging gallantry as it was in ascertaining its origins. Was Montesquieu
being critical or complimentary when he asserted that the general desire
to please women—because loving and being loved is so delightful and
because women are good judges of personal merit—produced "gallantry
which is not love, but the refined, insubstantial, and perpetual fiction of
love"?[33] It is hard to tell. What is far clearer, however, is that Rousseau
intended to lead a crusade against gallantry. Take, for example, his *Letter
to d'Alembert*:

As for me, I find it hard to conceive how men can honor women so
little as to dare to address these stale amorous speeches ceaselessly to
them, these insulting and mocking compliments to which they do
not even deign to give an air of good faith. When we insult women

by these evident fictions, does it not amount to declaring to them rather plainly that no obliging truths can be found to say to them?[34]

Here, then, the fiction is a sign of contempt, which Rousseau was not the only one to assert. Muralt had already suggested it in less brutal fashion, describing French flattery of women as a way of treating them as "inferior, weak creatures toward whom one must make allowances."[35] In a more picturesque fashion, Madame de Staël would later compare gallantry to the behavior of a crocodile "who imitates the voices of children to attract their mother."[36]

In another, perhaps even more serious, reproach, Rousseau argued that by aping love, gallantry severed the roots of true love. For wouldn't men who were gallant with every woman "be vexed if they were thought to be seriously in love with a single one? Let them not be disquieted. It would require strange ideas of love to believe them capable of it, and nothing is so far removed from its tone than that of gallantry."[37] Nor, for that matter, did the diatribe stop there. Heretofore aimed at relationships between individuals, it was extended to considerations on an entire society subverted by the fact that "French gallantry has given women a universal power that needs no loving feeling to survive. Everything depends on them, things are done only by or for them; Olympus and Parnassus, fame and fortune are also subject to their laws."[38] Rousseau must have been appalled by the "highly gallant philosopher" in Montesquieu's *Persian Letters*, who declared to Rica that no natural law subjugates women to men and that the empire that men exercise over them is "absolutely tyrannical."[39] For his part, Rousseau thought it cowardly of men to obey a sex that they ought to "protect and not serve."[40]

Fortunately for French gallantry, however, Rousseau was not the only one to discuss the issue. It would be defended as well as attacked during the Enlightenment, in terms of individual relationships and society as a whole. Taking up Montesquieu's concept of perpetual fiction, Diderot's above-cited entry in the *Encyclopédie* neither developed nor disputed the idea; he quoted it, then inflected it in his own fashion: "But perhaps love only endures thanks to the aid of gallantry—it might be that love ceases because it no longer takes place between spouses." Whereas Diderot did not refute Montesquieu here, he did take strong issue with Rousseau, whom he called "the great sophist."

As to the respect shown women and the power conferred on them by gallantry, a viewpoint quite different from Rousseau's was suggested by David Hume, who, as a friend and connoisseur of France whose work was swiftly translated into French, merits mention here. Like Rousseau, Hume felt that the superiority and therefore authority of the male sex over women was incontrovertible, but this meant he thought it noble and entirely praiseworthy of men to display toward women "politeness," "respect," and "complaisance"—in short, gallantry. Since "nature has given man the superiority above woman, by endowing him with greater strength of both mind and body, it is his part to alleviate that superiority, as much as possible, by the generosity of his behavior, and by a studied deference and complaisance for all her inclinations and opinions."[41] No, retorted Hume to Rousseau in advance, gallantry is not false, but rather true respect of men for women; no, it is not cowardly abandonment by men of their natural prerogatives, but rather a civilized use of those prerogatives.

As to the question of the effects of gallantry on social life as a whole, Rousseau's viewpoints encountered equally serious dissenters. Describing the customs of medieval chivalry, La Curne de Sainte-Palaye stressed that the mere thought of a "Lady" contributed to valiance. "Even in war itself," he claimed, men retained "the image of courteousness and gallantry that governed tournaments. The desire to please his Lady and appear worthy of her was for a knight, in true as well as simulated combat, a . . . motive that spurred him to heroic action, carrying fearlessness to its highest pitch."[42] These comments clarify the complaint (cited by La Curne) made by Perceforest, the protagonist of a medieval romance bearing his name, that his knights, once victorious, covered in glory, and rewarded by their ladies, no longer did anything at all![43] It then becomes easy to understand La Curne's observations on "a policy [that] skillfully deployed love of fame and love of Ladies to sustain feelings of honor and bravura in the Order of Knights."[44] It could indeed be seen as a policy or scheme—although not attributable to a specific author—to insure the harmonious cohesion of society by developing in each of its members the loftiest potential. La Curne was writing of a society that no longer existed; it is therefore remarkable that in 1790 Edmund Burke felt that chivalrous gallantry still survived, at least until the dreadful days in October 1789, which prompted the following comment:

> Little did I dream that I should have lived to see such disasters fallen upon [Marie Antoinette] in a nation of gallant men, in a nation of men of honour, and of cavaliers. I thought ten thousand swords must have leaped from their scabbards to avenge even a look that threatened her with insult. But the age of chivalry is gone. That of sophisters, economists, and calculators, has succeeded. . . . Never, never more shall we behold that generous loyalty to rank and sex, that proud submission, that dignified obedience, that subordination of the heart which kept alive, even in servitude itself, the spirit of an exalted freedom. . . . On this scheme of things, a king is but a man, a queen

is but a woman; a woman is but an animal, and an animal not of the highest order.[45]

Such were the main lines of theoretical debate on *galanterie* during the Enlightenment. Philosophically speaking, it is easy to interpret: from Rousseau's standpoint, nature is good, so thwarting or being unfaithful to nature leads to personal and social evil; from the opposing standpoint, human nature is brutish and must be countered by education. "Philosophically speaking" might include "religiously speaking" if one agrees with Baudelaire that "Protestant countries lack two elements indispensable to the happiness of a man of good breeding—gallantry and devotion,"[46] and if one concedes that the High Anglican church is fundamentally more Catholic than Protestant. Yet this interpretation focuses on the people doing the judging, and therefore remains inadequate in terms of the object being judged, which is no less important. This raises the question of whether all the writers who discussed gallantry were discussing the same thing. What forms have been adopted over the centuries by what is commonly called *galanterie*?

It was in the first half of the seventeenth century that the term *galanterie* was used in the sense discussed here. Although it only progressively assumed a meaning restricted to the relationship between society men and women, the reality designated by that meaning was, as already noted, far more ancient—back in the Middle Ages, France had been the home of knights who bestowed studied politeness and attention on ladies. In a romance titled *Chevalier au cygne* (The swan knight), when Godefroi de Bouillon bowed before a Saracen princess she exclaimed in surprise that such "was not the custom in lands 'round here," only to hear Godefroi reply that back in his own country

> . . . n'y a prince ne duc ne per
> Qui ne face l'honneur es dames, c'est tout cler.[47]

> [. . . no prince, no duke, no peer
> would fail to honor ladies thus, 'tis clear.]

In *Le Chevalier au lion* (The lion knight), there are scenes of knights and princes being welcomed by girls or young women who hold their stirrups and take their weapons, after which the ladies charm the men with delightful conversation, naturally leading to an offer of service on the part of the knights.[48] Also worth citing is the fifteenth-century tale of a young Castilian noble, Pero Nuño, who travels through Normandy; he expresses delighted amazement not only at the gracefulness of ladies gathering flowers and participating in the hunt, but also at the proximity established between the two sexes by the alternate seating of men and women at the table during meals. Pero Nuño inevitably falls in love with the mistress of the chateau where he is offered hospitality.[49] All of this "collective gallantry"—entailing an overall social atmosphere—established the setting in which relationships marked by individual gallantry could emerge.

In the Middle Ages, a knight's "service" toward his dame was characterized, of course, by the exploits he accomplished for her. Savoir-faire involved wearing her colors in a tournament (which could not end without a final joust called *la lance des Dames*), wearing a ribbon or other favor of the courted lady when leaving for war,[50] and when returning victorious, attributing all the honor to her. Even better, according to La Curne, when entering the lists of a tournament, "Dames and damsels sometimes led these proud slaves onto the field attached by chains, which they only removed once in the enclosure of the lists or barriers, when [the knights] were ready to joust."[51] These customs—at least, some of them—were still current in the sixteenth century; Bayard modestly forbad himself to receive the prize at a tournament because the prize, he claimed, was due solely to the muff bestowed on him by a lady of Carignan, where the tournament was held.[52] And when courtier and memorialist Pierre de Brantôme wrote of the days of François I, it was with youthful ardor that he asked:

> What could gladden a gentleman more when he left Court to go to war or on a voyage, than to carry a favor from his mistress and to risk every peril in making good use of it for love of her and for his prince, and then to return to the satisfaction of receiving many lovely countenances and embraces from his Dame, after those of his King?[53]

Thus did people evoke that early form of gallantry whose fragrance would long linger over fair France.

⁂

Following the Wars of Religion, the first half of the seventeenth century featured major social transformations, including the founding of salons hosted by women,[54] and represented a key phase in what is being termed here collective gallantry. The idea that ladies were due special courtesy was henceforth strongly advocated; many manuals of etiquette, often in-

Figure 7.2
"The desire to please a woman and to appear worthy of her was for a knight a motive which carried him to heroic actions." La Curne de Sainte-Palaye, A tournament, miniature of *Roman du chevalier Tristan et de la reine Yseult*, fifteenth century.

spired by Castiglione's *Il Cortegiano* (The courtier),[55] as well as Honoré d'Urfé's *L'Astrée* and other pastoral romances, imposed this requirement, based either on the weakness of a sex that must not be offended because unable to defend itself,[56] or—more flatteringly—on the status of women as beings midway between human and divine (and therefore guides toward loftier ideas).[57] Chapelain waxed indignant over the "lack of consideration" shown to women by a gentleman who publicly expressed his suspicions of theft by a young lady;[58] La Rochefoucauld, in his self-portrait, thought it worth declaring that "I am scrupulously polite with women, and I do not think I have ever said a word in their presence that could have caused them embarrassment."[59] The comte de Bussy-Rabutin, meanwhile, referring to himself in his memoirs in the third person, wrote, "He was gallant with all the women, and highly civil; and the familiarity that he enjoyed with his best lady friends never caused him to lack the respect due them."[60]

Such was the gallantry defended above by Diderot, Hume, and Burke.

Figure 7.3
"The close proxim-
ity that the habit of
alternating men and
women around the
dinner table estab-
lished between the
two sexes." Miniature
of L'Histoire du grand
Alexandre, fifteenth
century.

Figure 7.3
"The close proximity that the habit of alternating men and women around the dinner table established between the two sexes." Miniature of *L'Histoire du grand Alexandre*, fifteenth century.

Yet the line is thin between showing respect for women and deferring to their tastes. It was crossed toward the middle of the century, when the novel triumphed over epic poetry, when the "minor genres" came to the fore, when "feelings" supplanted heroism on the stage, and when, somewhat later, the moderns appealed to feminine taste in defending their attacks on the cult of Greco-Roman tradition.[61] The cultural trait that so enraged Rousseau was becoming detectable.

As to personal relationships between men and women, the legacy of the Middle Ages had not been forgotten in the early seventeenth century. D'Urfé's early novel, *L'Astrée*, depicted lovers as knights errant—coming to the aid of the oppressed, notably all the helpless women they encountered—in order to become worthy of their damsels; similarly, in Corneille's *Le Cid*, Rodrigue invoked the need to "merit" her when explaining to Chimène why he provoked a duel with the count.[62] In another Corneille play, Cinna perpetuates the tradition of a knight who is a "slave" to his lady when he betrays his own conscience by joining Emilie's conspiracy against Augustus.[63] All of this was not mere literary conceit, as demonstrated in 1643 by the death of Coligny in a duel designed to defend the reputation of Madame de Longueville.[64] An even more surprising demonstration was the passage in La Rochefoucauld's memoirs where, after having praised Madame de Longueville as a perfect individual, he pointed out that she had "a flaw never seen in a princess of such merit," namely that "far from laying down the law to her admirers, she entered into their feelings to the point of no longer recognizing her own."[65]

This medieval legacy should not, however, mask the most specific traits of early seventeenth-century gallantry, which are to be found elsewhere. In the *Dialogue* quoted above, Chapelain sums up rather well—if rather harshly—the opposition between medieval gallantry and that of his own day: in the Middle Ages, passion was demonstrated by a quest for danger, blood, and victory; latterly, it could be demonstrated "only by flirtatiousness and persistent attentiveness or, at most, by light suppers, music, and tilting at the ring."[66] And, it might be added, by the art of speech, which counted even more. Henceforth, chatting to ladies became an essential part of savoir-faire. And what else could one talk about, if not love?

> . . . le joli passe-temps
> D'être auprès d'une Dame et causer du beau temps
> Lui jurer que Paris est toujours plein de fange,
> Qu'un certain parfumeur vend de fort bonne eau d'Ange![67]

> [. . . the pleasant pastime
> of sitting near a Lady, chatting of the weather,
> bemoaning Paris—full of grime—
> yet praising one perfumer's Angel water!]

Unthinkable! Obviously, even though one should not "make public profession of saying sweet nothings to every woman, there is no great danger in behaving with all pretty women in such a way as to let them think that even if one does not love them, one could."[68] Praising the woman to whom one is speaking was therefore the first step to take—and refusing to take it was a type of provocation.[69] When Anne of Austria, on perceiving the poet Voiture (walking in the gardens of Rueil, deep in thought, as she passed in a carriage), laughingly asked him what he was thinking, she received lines addressed to:

> . . . la plus aimable
> Qui fut jamais dessous les cieux,
> À l'âme la plus adorable
> Que formèrent jamais les Dieux.

[. . . the kindest of all
under these heavens,
the most adorable soul
the gods ever fashioned.]

The poet went on to vaunt not only the queen's waist and mouth
but her feet "so sweet and well turned," her "two incomparable hands,"
and her "two eyes full of flame," not to mention her "hundred thousand
secret charms."[70] Even though these lines referred to the queen regent,
every Chloris, Iris, or Sylvie heard the same thing said to her by the likes
of Voiture, Sarasin, Malleville, Benserade, and others. They provided a
great deal of wood for the bonfire on which Rousseau hoped to burn
mendacious compliments.

More interesting was the requirement, expressed early on, that gallant comments contain piquant wit. "It is difficult," wrote Chapelain,
"for there to be gallantry where wit plays no role, where grace is completely absent."[71] Poets therefore delighted in including unexpected and
paradoxical comparisons in their praise. One of them, deploring the in-
constancy of his mistress, addressed a sonnet to Cupid to entreat to him
to perform alchemy.

Comme ce coeur constant me serait un trésor,
Je ne demande point que tu fasses de l'or,
Travaille seulement à fixer ce mercure.[72]

[If her heart were constant, a treasure would I hold!
Thus I beseech you not to fashion gold—
Just steady mercury with your art]

A second poet asked the sun to disappear in the presence of his ebony-
haired Parthenice, who was herself another sun:

Un autre qui pourvu d'un plus riche partage
Porte la nuit au front et le jour dans les yeux.[73]

[Another who, endowed with richer share,
Bears the day in her eyes, the night in her hair.]

Everyone was familiar, at least through hearsay, with the gallant pastimes invented in fashionable salons in the mid-seventeenth century. Regular visitors to the residence of the Marquise de Rambouillet, charmed by

her eldest daughter, composed the *Guirlande de Julie*, a "garland" of poetry in which each poem adopted the identity of specific flower in order to extol Julie in a form appropriate to that flower. In Madeleine de Scudéry's salon, meanwhile, a game called the *Carte du tendre* (Map of affection) plotted the complex obligations (and fatal temptations) of players who hoped to reach towns like Tendre-sur-Estime or Tendre-sur-Reconnaissance, the marvelous city of Tendre-sur-Inclination being accessible only by virtue of a *je ne sais quoi* that defied all rules.

Given such fashion, it is quite clear that the feelings declared by every man to every pretty woman—revealed to all and sundry by poets, then recited, set to music, and sung in salons[74]—had precious little to do with love, and nothing whatsoever with passion. An anthology of letters purporting to provide models of epistolary art soon carefully distinguished "passionate letters" from "gallant and amorous letters."[75] Thus at almost the very moment that people began to use the term *galanterie*, they quickly distinguished it from what it fraudulently mimicked—true love. Mademoiselle de Scudéry conceded somewhat coyly that "extremely few men who are extremely enamored are extremely gallant,"[76] whereas La Rochefoucauld's verdict was more direct: "The last thing to be found in gallantry is love."[77] Everyone recognized this more or less distinctly, for in novels contemporary with the blossoming of gallantry—those by Madame de La Fayette and, earlier, those by Madeleine de Scudéry—a man truly in love could be indentified by his trembling, respectful silence.

Gallantry as practiced in the mid-seventeenth century was defined by traits that intersected in varying ways: the habit of always behaving respectfully toward women; affecting, when in public, to bow to their taste; and the art of pleasing women by praising them wittily (hence concerned less with the object of praise than with the quality of that praise). None of these traits would vanish completely, which not only explains the extreme ambiguity riddling the term but also sheds light on the controversies of the following century. Furthermore, this ambiguity was intensified, starting around 1660, by the development of the *playful* side of gallantry.

In fact, this purely playful or sporting aspect had surfaced earlier. Voiture (died 1648) and Sarasin (died 1654) alternated love-struck poems with thoroughly flippant pieces. Voiture composed songs in which successive stanzas praised, as peerless, a whole succession of "divinities." He also penned highly racy verses to a certain Philis, "whose skirt rolled up while overturned in a carriage in the country."[78] Sarasin, meanwhile, declared in a single poem that he "loved Cléon, Sylvanire, and Chloris," and he assured a Phyllis who promised to be faithful but had an "Indian-giving heart" that he would not die of sorrow at losing her:

Figure 7.4
Frontispiece of *La Guirlande de Julie*, by Nicolas Robert, book offered by Charles de Salles, future Duke of Montpensier, to Julie d'Angennes, eldest daughter of the Marquise de Rambouillet, January 1, 1642.

Si je n'ai que ce mal, je vivrai longuement.[79]

[If that's all that afflicts me, I'll live a long time.]

These signs pointed to a new conception of gallantry in which respect for women no longer played a part—although appearances were
maintained—and in which men would henceforth seek only their own
pleasure or advantage via ritualistic compliments, confessions of love,
and submission. As an anonymous poet declared in 1664 in *Délices de la
poésie galante*:

Pour toute Loi d'Amour pratiquons l'enjouement
N'admettons de ses Lois qu'une Loi si charmante
Et ne brûlons jamais que d'une amour galante.[80]

[The sole Law of Love we admit is enjoyment
Only this Law so charming we'll warrant
and the only love that consumes us is gallant.]

Two years later, Molière's *The Misanthrope* powerfully depicted this
gallantry dedicated solely to personal satisfaction. Although Oronte declared to Phyllis-Célimène in act 1 that "death would be [his] recourse"
if she did not respond to his entreaties, he was one of those who show-
ered their contempt on that same Célimène in act 5. As to Molière's two
aristocratic fops, whose characters are more developed, in act 2 they are
all sweetness and light, declaring that they could delight in her company
all day long, thanks to her faultless "charm and grace." Yet when they are
alone in act 3, they make it plain that Célimène is nothing more than a
good financial prospect. If she lets them languish, they will abandon the
chase; if she chooses one of them, the other will easily console himself—
without even needing to find a new lover—with the thought of his own
worthiness.

Quelque rare que soit le mérite des belles,
Je pense, Dieu merci, qu'on vaut son prix comme elles.

[However rare the merits of that sex so fair
I think, thank Heaven, our value matches theirs]

In act 5 these same fops, who discuss love like an economic transac-
tion, join Oronte in condemning Célimène.

Leaving the realm of fiction, real life provided similar scenes. In
the 1660s, in order to gain favor with the king, the young and brilliant

Marquis de Vardes used confidences he had extracted from Madame (as Louis XIV's sister-in-law was called) by feigning attentive love for her.[81] And Madame de Sévigné recounted a visit that the Chevalier de Lorraine paid to Mademoiselle de Fienne after having ignored her for some time; on seeing her long face, the chevalier reportedly commented: "What's wrong with you, mademoiselle? Why so sad? What is so extraordinary about what has happened? We loved each other, we no longer do; faithfulness is not a virtue of people of our age. . . . Now, *there's* a nice little dog—who gave it to you?"[82]

Behavior like that of Vardes could have occurred during any era, whatever the reigning ideas on personal honor, respect for women, and morality in love. The tone adopted by the Chevalier de Lorraine, however, is truly revealing of the flippant *galanterie* that supplanted the original version. As gallant poetry of the day repeatedly demonstrated, a man who courted a woman owed her neither self-control nor faithfulness nor secrecy (though this latter was still favored)—which was the logical outcome of a denial of all duty.[83] When it came to women they were *not* wooing, French courtiers, according to a young Englishwoman, "make jokes about them and often ridicule them . . . if [such women] do not have enough charms to merit their attachment."[84] The previously cited complaints by Madeleine de Scudéry and La Bruyère on the absence of *galanterie* among the younger generation thereby become comprehensible. Young people were no longer *galant* according to the canons of the first half of the seventeenth century—yet they couldn't have cared less, for they had their own gallantry. And if the latter contradicted the former, that was just too bad.

The eighteenth century would stress and even considerably extend one facet of old-style *galanterie*—the influence of women in social life—all the while developing the newer version by distilling a method or "art" from what initially, under Louis XIV, had been just exuberantly youthful dissipation. Yet every aspect of gallantry that had fallen more or less by the wayside would nevertheless survive in the form of passing allusions or even, on occasion, as the basis of social analysis.

The power of women at court and in society was one of the major characteristics of the eighteenth century. Almost nobody remembers whether or not Madame de Lambert, Madame de Tencin, Madame Geoffrin, Madame du Deffand, Madame d'Épinay, or even the Duchesse du Maine actually had husbands, but everyone knows that they hosted a salon or minor court and that they nurtured fruitful encounters, supported intellectual movements, and helped beginners to get along in the world. Other women such as Madame de Prie, Madame de Châteauroux, Madame de Pompadour, and Madame du Barry often played a key role in state affairs as mistress to king or minister.[85] This feminine power became well established and functioned in every sphere. Muralt commented that women imposed their taste in France; whether their dresses were "decorated with flowers, or with dragons and Furies," everything "turned equally to their advantage."[86] Sébastien Mercier described how they always benefited from favorable bias in public opinion; if there was a row between husband and wife, "the husband starts out by being wrong, and three days later is being painted in the most dreadful tones."[87] Montesquieu noted that women governed everything. "A man who watches the actions of ministers, officials or prelates at court, in Paris or in the country, without knowing the women who rule them, is like a man who can see a machine in action but does not know what makes it work."[88]

Mercier, meanwhile, claimed that women shaped public opinion.[89] To conclude, it is perhaps worth quoting a poet who clearly attributed all of the above to the dominion of gallantry governed by the "fair sex":

Il sait régler, il sait proscrire
Les modes, les goûts et les moeurs;
Pour des lois donne des erreurs,
N'aime, ne répand que des fleurs
Communique un brillant délire,
Orne le frivole et le faux,
Reçoit l'encens des madrigaux,
Et soumet tout à son empire,
Les grands, les sages et les sots.[90]

[It knows how to dictate, to rule
All fashion, taste and manners;
As law, it lays down errors,
For it loves and bestows only flowers,
Conveying ecstatic abandon
By rewarding frivolity with jewels,
Receiving the praise of madrigals,
And extending to all its dominion:
Great men, wise men and fools.]

That is precisely what outraged Rousseau.

Everything indicated, meanwhile, that the new gallantry was well established. Soulavie, the biographer of the Duc de Richelieu, referred in passing to another duke at the court of Louis XV who had the "habits and tone of the old court; his gallantry was of a pleasant yet respectful type concerning women, whose esteem he valued."[91] That *yet* reveals awareness of an evolution henceforth considered definitive. Soulavie was more explicit elsewhere, asserting that the regent's extremely bawdy conduct "set the tone for the nation, and made manners less strict and love less decent, or rather it abolished all the preliminaries and accouterments of love, depriving women and society of the customs of our old gallantry that had such special charm and that Louis XIV had the skill to preserve."[92] The phenomenon was explained differently—though with no fundamental discrepancy—in a dialogue that Marivaux invented for the characters of Cupid (representing fashionable gallantry) and Eros (the vestige of the previous century). Both plead their case before the gods on Olympus. Eros vaunts the changes he had wrought on men in his day; nature made them coarse, but he instilled politeness, humaneness, and a desire to cultivate talent. "In my day, people blushed when they were unkind. The desire to please, and the impossibility of doing so other than virtuously, obliged their souls to become estimable."[93] Cupid's language, obviously, is quite different. He describes the lovers of yore as simpletons:

> All they did was languish, utter sighs, and recount their sorrows to the echoes. Good heavens! It's no longer like that. I've done away with the echoes, I have. I wound—ouch! So up with a remedy, quick! Go straight to the source of the pain. "There now," they say, "I love you—so let's see what you can do for me, because time is short."[94]

Those are indeed the precepts followed by the most famous "gallants" of the eighteenth century, starting with the regent, who "never applied himself to difficult conquests or to women who required a certain perseverance."[95] Meanwhile, the Duc de Richelieu, according to his biographer, was "so famous for his talents in the art of gallantry" that, thanks to "the thorough study he had made of the nature of women, always at their expense," he had acquired "the art of knowing them and making them act"; he placed this art at the service not only of his own pleasure but also that of others, notably Louis XV.[96] Later in the same century came the Maréchal de Saxe, a notorious skirt chaser who firmly advocated—on behalf of his troops as well as himself—"a warrior's rest and relaxation," which earned him the reputation of being the most "gallant" of great soldiers.[97]

Three major traits characterized the new *galanterie*, which, although libertine, was not totally licentious and dissolute. The first feature was vanity. A character in Claude Crébillon's *Sopha* asks what men want from the world: "Love? Probably not. We want to satisfy our vanity, want people to talk about us constantly; go from woman to woman, not missing a single one, making conquests, even the most contemptible . . . constantly seeking them yet never loving them."[98] This attitude is confirmed by the Baron de Besenval's *Mémoires*: "At the beginning of the King's reign, men were concerned solely with authentically extending the list of their mistresses, and women with publicly snatching lovers from each other."[99]

A sorrowful Mademoiselle de Lespinasse, meanwhile, offered this diagnosis on Mora, whom she adored: all his attempts to seduce honest and virtuous women were designed only to satisfy his own pride, "so much so that he could not suffer resistance. Not because it would wound his heart, but because it offended his vanity, yes, his vanity! . . . For he sought to subject rather than to move."[100] The coxcomb in Marivaux's *Le Petit-maître corrigé* displayed similar behavior prior to receiving "correction," as indicated by a knowing maidservant who, when questioned on the hero's past, answered that "he was only in love with the reputation of being lovable."[101]

Being on such poor terms with true love, this kind of *galanterie* was cerebral instead, which constitutes its second characteristic trait. It was closely related to military strategy, as already glimpsed in the Duc de Richelieu's behavior. More analytical is Besenval's sketch of a young German noble who lived in Paris, "where he captivated women all the more easily since, not having a single principle, he paraded them all, and not being dominated by desire, he replaced it with rage and sang-froid, praise and disapprobation," thereby turning against women the weapons that were ordinarily their own.[102] Novels reflected this state of affairs, notably those by Crébillon—one thinks immediately of Versac's long speech to the young Meilcour in *Les Egarements*.[103] Obviously, however, it is Laclos's *Les Liaisons dangereuses* that shed the sharpest light on gallant stratagems. Without repeating the stages of Valmont's conquest of Madame de Tourvel, so familiar to everyone, it is worth quoting the proud note of victory he addressed to Madame de Merteuil:

> You will see that I departed in no respect from the true principles of this war, which we have often remarked is so like the other. Judge me then as you would Frederic or Turenne. I forced the enemy to fight when she wished only to refuse battle; by clever manoeuvres I obtained the choice of battle-field and of dispositions; I inspired the enemy with confidence. . . . I was able to make terror succeed confidence before joining battle.[104]

Figure 7.5
Watteau, *L'Indifférent*, 1716. "He was still only in love with the reputation of being pleasant" (Marivaux, *Le Petit-maître corrigé*).

The "divinity" of the previous century was henceforth called nothing less than "enemy."

But the most surprising thing about this vain, cerebral, and therefore cynical *galanterie* is that—and this is its third distinctive trait—women seemed to adapt to it admirably. Besenval, quoted above, has them matching a man's lists of mistresses with their own hunt for lovers (stolen from one another, to add to the pleasure); in one short story by Marmontel, a man took great care to behave "as forward as etiquette demanded,"[105] while in another, a young widow faced with two suitors preferred the one who "made himself desirable by a slightly ribald gallantry that apparently aspires to nothing" over the one who, simple and natural, was sincerely in love with her.[106] Marivaux made the same diagnosis of female reactions, as witnessed by the Parisian woman who, after spending two hours in a provincial salon, is exasperated at having been the object of "an ingratiating [gentleman] who spoke to me in flowery language. Such language! Oh so perfect! He made a declaration of feelings he dare not reveal to me; those feelings so refined, accompanied by that respect I find so bland! So bland!"[107] Then there is Marivaux's Minerva, who, in *La Réunion des amours,* admits that Eros needs to alter his approach; in the same play, Virtue even takes pleasure in allowing her hand to be kissed by Cupid.[108] By way of counterexample, mention could be made of the old clergyman who, meeting in a country château a charming young woman who is the object of sarcasm from the entire dazzling company, advises her: "If you want to live in peace around here, disguise your love for your husband better; marital love is the only kind not tolerated in these parts."[109]

Nevertheless, the agreement between the sexes on this casual morality, on a new gallantry henceforth unburdened of everything except pure appearances, gave rise to an incomparable grace absolutely specific to the eighteenth century. That is exactly what Verlaine had in mind when he titled his exquisite—perhaps his most exquisite—volume *Les Fêtes galantes.* He was thinking of Watteau, Boucher, Fragonard. and countless prints with titles like "How Awareness is Awakened in Girls," showing delightfully dressed, flirtatious adolescents in flowing, relaxed poses against a backdrop of enchanting woods or refined silks. Such figures took pleasure in the moment, intoxicated by its heady scent. That is how one pictures Chérubin in Beaumarchais's *Le Mariage de Figaro*—irresistible with his pretty face, his ribbon (stolen from the countess), his love song.

Yet the realm of this cynical—or graceful, or perhaps gracefully cynical—gallantry should not be made too universal. Diderot's correspondence with Sophie Volland, his "kind and solid friend,"[110] reveals a kind of amorous camaraderie that does not exclude compliments but leaves no room for vanity or deceit. "Love me always then, so that I shall always shrink from vice."[111] In Rousseau's *La Nouvelle Héloïse,* Julie's relationship with Saint-Preux displays the same quest for true love and the same rejection of gallantry that their creator professed on his own behalf. The praise for gallantry that came from the pens of Diderot, Hume, and Burke would be inexplicable unless it referred to the form practiced earlier. As far as they were concerned, the original gallantry was still alive. Just as it was for charming young characters portrayed in fiction, like Marmontel's Lindor, who fears surrendering to his beautiful cousin's request to postpone his departure for the army, lest he miss a great battle and therefore be unworthy of her.[112]

On the whole, however, it must be acknowledged that the eighteenth century, sustaining a movement begun in the seventeenth, saw *galanterie* become the opposite of what it had been originally. It had been polite and respectful, was henceforth flippant; it had been principled, was henceforth sly and calculating; it had been patient, but now sought only immediate gratification; it had banked on the reserve of females, it henceforth banked on the pleasure taken by women in succumbing, indeed in provoking; it had been dutiful, yet became domineering. How could a single term apply to attitudes that are so completely contradictory? The only shared trait, albeit an important one, was a certain elegance, a certain grace, a certain conviviality that marked a man of good breeding—a cad, perhaps, but one who was well trained, graceful, able to converse with women, and anxious to please them even if he denied it. Gallantry was a question of high society, of gentlemen who liked women, gentlemen with wit.

⁂

These "society people" were the very ones that the French Revolution forced into hiding or exile (when it spared their heads). It might be expected, then, that the history of *galanterie française* would end along with them, its meager source of sustenance being the makeshift salons in Brussels and London. That was not entirely the case, however.

It would seem that the best picture for studying its fate during the subsequent era is provided by the magnificent fresco that Chateaubriand composed around his own life. He depicted not only the world in which he was born and raised (the ancien régime) and the world in which his political and literary careers developed (the rapidly shifting scene from the Consulate to the July Monarchy), but also—because he was a visionary—the world of the future. Although he employed the term *galanterie* just three or four times, Chateaubriand discussed, or at least mentioned, all the main aspects of the matter in the long century that lasted from the aftermath of the Revolution to the eve of the First World War.

Figure 7.6
Watteau, *L'Embarquement pour Cythère* (detail).
    Their short silk vests
    Their long-tailed dresses
    Their elegance, their joy
    And their soft blue shadows

               (Verlaine, "Mandoline," in *Les Fêtes galantes*)

What immediately emerges from a reading of the *Mémoires d'outre-tombe* is that French society remained incomparably sociable compared to other European countries, thereby providing one condition favorable to the survival of gallantry. In England, Chateaubriand described the dandy of 1840 as a man "who discloses the haughty independence of his character by keeping his hat on his head, lolling on sofas, and stretching his boots under the noses of ladies seated in admiration on chairs before him."[113] What a man! And what women! thinks a French eyewitness or reader. In Rome, Chateaubriand mentioned a palace with a "kind of gynaeceum" for the noble ladies, with whom there was no question of having a conversation.[114] During a dinner in Prague, he met a woman who reputedly represented the flower of Viennese high society—Chateaubriand found her "shrill and stupid."[115] A passage in which he labels England and various Central European countries as places "where you can feel yourself dying" follows the affirmation that "France is the heart of Europe; as one gets farther away, social life withers."[116] A social life in which the relationships between men and women were relaxed and charming existed only in France. And it survived the Revolution.

Not limiting discussion to Chateaubriand alone, it is worth noting that French society was highly aware of the traditions of *galanterie française*, as testified by the two nineteenth-century treatises cited at the outset of this article.[117] Furthermore, a character from Balzac's *La Maison Nucingen* admiringly recalls "the [Duc] de Richelieu, who knew a thing or two about gallantry,"[118] while Proust described "the clever women of the Faubourg [Saint-Germain]" as being scandalized that the Duc de Guermantes could present himself at the stage door of the Comédie-Française "with a gallantry that would have done credit to the Maréchal de Saxe" in order to invite an actress to come and recite poetry at his salon.[119] All forms of gallantry from previous eras were resuscitated in works of fiction—the king in Musset's *Carmosine* incarnated medieval gallantry in a charming, heartfelt way,[120] whereas Balzac's Cousin Pons was a worthy representative of assiduously polite gallantry.[121] At the dawn of our own century, gallantry could be conveyed in various manners: announcing first to a woman the promotion that has just been granted her husband (in Anatole France);[122] feigning fear of suffering to excuse oneself for not seeing a woman as frequently as she might desire (in Proust);[123] being a man on whom one can count not to reveal that a young widow who will soon remarry was once his mistress (in Henry Bernstein).[124] And, naturally, brazen *galanterie* also had its place—it was out of principle that Stendhal's Lucien Leuwen felt he was obliged "to take a bold and almost passionate tone" in addressing Madame d'Hocquincourt.[125] Several of Balzac's young characters, like Canalis[126] and Rastignac,[127] were not necessarily brazen but merely self-seeking when they obeyed every whim of the woman ostensibly being courted so that another love affair could be successfully pursued or disguised—or both.

It is therefore quite clear that French society, despite all its changes, remained marked by the recollection, at least, of gallantry. Yet Chateaubriand draws attention to a second element that was even more important to the survival of the original spirit of gallantry—the worship of women. This worship was obviously reserved for certain women who aroused it through their beauty, charm, cultivation, wit, conversational skills, and considerateness (or who displayed at least a few of those traits), but it also

Figure 7.7
"If it were possible for me to envy that which I love, I would give all that I am for you" (Madame de Staël to Madame Récamier). *Madame Récamier à l'Abbaye-aux-Bois,* by François-Louis Dejuine, 1826.

colored all of society life. Among such women, Chateaubriand's *Mémoires d'outre-tombe* includes the fragile and moving Madame de Beaumont[128] and above all Madame Récamier. One day the latter gave to General Masséna, at his request, a blue ribbon she was wearing, a ribbon "that never left the general and constantly favored his victory," he informed the beautiful lady,[129] while in London "the Prince of Wales proudly wore her shawl."[130] These examples admittedly occurred quite soon after the ancien régime, but they nevertheless bear comparison with the fervent personality cult devoted to women like Madame de Noailles one hundred years later.

Works of fiction also echoed this theme—certain women became a kind of goddess to their milieu, such as Balzac's Duchesse de Langeais or Proust's Duchesse de Guermantes and Princesse de Parme. There were also women who aspired to that rank, like Balzac's provincial Madame de Bargeton, who thought that Lucien de Rubempré would be a worthy bard in spreading her cult.[131] In addition to public worship there was secret devotion, like Flaubert's Frédéric, in thrall of Madame Arnoux— "my heart, like dust, rises behind your every step."[132] There was even gallantry that lacked a specific object, exemplified by the young Guillaume in Zola's *Madeleine Férat*: "He placed women on a pedestal, turning them

into idols before which he chanted an eternal hymn of faith and love."[133] In this sphere where gallantry was once again associated with love, it is worth remembering the chivalrous Stefani in Musset's *Bettine*, who, on learning of the heroine's forthcoming marriage with the Baron de Stein-berg, offers her a priceless set of diamonds and who, on discovering that the engagement has been broken off, offers to marry her as soon as she can recover enough to consider it.[134]

The above examples show that traces of ancien régime gallantry sur-vived, with nuances that occasionally updated it. The *Mémoires d'outre-tombe*, however, also demonstrate that new forces were at work, under-mining gallantry. In this respect, Chateaubriand's portrait of the actor Talma merits attention:

Talma was oblivious to the mediating world: he had not known *gentlemanly* behavior; he was unfamiliar with our old society; he had not sat at the table of the mistress of some Gothic chateau set in the

woods; he was unaware of the flexibility, the varied tones, the gallantry, the apparently frivolous manners, the naiveté, the affection,
the honor-bound heroism, the Christian duties of chivalry. . . . Dark
ambition, remorse, jealousy, a melancholy soul, physical pain, god-
inflicted madness and adversity, human affliction: that is what Talma
had known.[135]

It would be hard to find a better way of indicating that gallantry existed within a closed system or society defined by a whole set of codes
and references, and that it had no place as soon as one entered the world
of violence—emotional violence and outward violence. A musical image,
however, might be risked: *galanterie* was at home with Mozart, whereas
Chateaubriand's Talma called for Beethoven. The rejection of gallantry
after the Revolution was not Talma's doing alone. Stendhal was pleased to
see the French caught up in political passions that freed them from "stu-
pidities" and conventional attitudes, including "vanity-love" and gallantry,
which he identified with "mannered love."[136] In Stendhal's novels, gallantry meets with disapproval. Julien Sorel by no means practices it, and
Mathilde likes him precisely insofar as he differs from the bland young
men who court her in her father's salon—Julien reminds her of Danton.[137]
Similarly, in Clélia's eyes Fabrice appears to be the opposite of all the
flattering little fops in her usual circle.[138] Julien's dark and vehement side
and Fabrice's bright freshness exclude them from the worldly character
of gallantry. And when writing in his own name, Stendhal stressed that
"this should clearly mark in the eyes of women the difference between
passionate love and gallantry, between a sensitive soul and an unimagi-
native one."[139]

Henceforth young men in love might disclaim gallantry as proof of
their sincerity; such was the case, in real life, with Balzac and Madame de
Berny,[140] and in fiction with Madame de Duras's Edouard and Madame
de Nevers.[141] Victor Hugo set a number of encounters between heartfelt
lovers Marius and Cosette in a garden that, a century earlier, had been
"shaped, clipped, crinkled, decked out, and fashioned for gallantry; nature
had claimed it back, filled it with shade, rearranged it for love."[142] Not only,
then, was the disavowal of *galanterie* dictated by the broader and more serious concerns that henceforth occupied men's minds but, following Rousseau, that disavowal was associated with true, powerful love.

Musset's plays express this new attitude in a bantering tone—Mi-
nuccio, the court musician and poet in *Carmosine*, describes his profession thus: "I have general charge of birthday odes and serenades, I dispense passion and ardor, intoxication and transport, arrows and darts."[143]
In *Barberine*, meanwhile, Baron Rosenberg, taught by the Chevalier to

please women by treating "them all (without exception) as nothing less than divinities," paid assiduous court to the charming Barberine, who wittily mocked him.[144] A similar, if less elegant, irony is found in Romain Rolland's *La Foire sur la place*, when a writer of "bland social correspondence," is described as "the champion of fine French style, French elegance, French gallantry, French wit."[145]

A taste for grander feelings, a craving for "tempests," and a desire for a type of love free from all codification were not the only potential reasons for rejecting gallantry. Others existed, including one that Chateaubriand raised almost obliquely, though at a crucial point, when sketching the portrait of George Sand at the end of his *Mémoires*—namely, feminism. Full of admiration for her talent as a writer, Chateaubriand remained puzzled and dismayed at the idea of Madame Sand "dressed like a man or wearing a mountain dweller's jacket and metal-tipped alpenstock," drinking "from the revelers' cup," and smoking.[146] Such a woman might spark amorous adventures and passion, but certainly not *galanterie,* which her entire lifestyle rejected in advance. Feminism would not have much impact on society life prior to the First World War despite the likes of Flora Tristan, Louise Michel, and a few others, but another trend also threatened *galanterie*: the mid-nineteenth-century introduction into France of English customs, that is to say, conversation among men, alleged to be destructive of gallantry in the passage by Ernest Bersot quoted above, and illustrated by the spread of male clubs and even all-male dinners as described in Flaubert's *L'Education sentimentale*.[147] Obviously, the most important trend challenging gallantry was the growing social equality and the increasing rarity of exclusive circles. The final book of Chateaubriand's *Mémoires d'outre-tombe* speaks eloquently of that development, but it is from Proust that a few lines will be cited as touching most directly on the subject. Although referring to etiquette, these lines apply equally, at least to a certain extent, to *galanterie*:

> It would seem that in an egalitarian society social etiquette would vanish not, as is generally supposed, from want of breeding, but because on the one side would disappear the deference due to a prestige which must be imaginary to be effective, and on the other, more completely still, the affability that is gracefully and generously dispensed when it is felt to be of infinite price to the recipient, a price which, in a world based on equality, would at once fall to nothing like everything that has only a fiduciary value.[148]

Many hostile factors therefore allied themselves against gallantry. Yet Chateaubriand noted that during the empire, Napoleon's court "sought to acquire old world manners, in the hope of masking its recent origin."[149] This comment applied not only to the court, nor only to the First Empire. The role assigned to *galanterie*—or at least, the term—by writers like Zola and Maupassant is striking in their depiction of milieus with no tradition of gallantry, where it therefore appeared as a recent, status-enhancing acquisition. In Zola's *La Curée*, it was Saccard who "prided himself on his extreme gallantry toward his wife," which consisted in particular of paying the monumental bills of her fashionable dressmaker and giving her the receipts himself—woman decides, man executes in chivalrous manner.[150] In *L'Argent*, a similar attitude is expected of Mazaud by the Baronne Sandorff when she asks him to reduce her debt to him; here, however, the businessman was wary of "an excessively stiff assault on his gallantry" and therefore avoided meeting the lady by delegating an inferior to inform her that he could not "concede a penny."[151] Courte-line, meanwhile, in *Boubouroche,* puts perfectly chivalrous if incongruous words in the mouth of Boubouroche's rival when the latter is discovered hiding in Adèle's apartment: "A gallant man is always a gentleman, even the day when certain circumstances of life force him to hide in a ward-robe." The rival then performs "the least of [his] duties" by demanding Boubouroche's "word of honor" that "not a single hair" of the unfaithful woman's head will be touched.[152]

There was also that gallantry which, without costing the man a thing, indicated his intense pleasure at being near women; in Zola's *Au bonheur des dames*, the seated women chat among themselves while "Monsieur de Boves, standing behind them, would lean forward every now and then and offer a comment with his fine civil-servant's gallantry."[153]

Maupassant, meanwhile, described an unexpectedly long voyage during which a group of travelers had nothing to drink except the wine and metal cup offered by Boule-de-Suif. They passed the cup among themselves "after having wiped it. Only Cornudet, probably out of gallantry, put his lips on the spot still damp from his neighbor's lips."[154]

Gallantry as a method of systematic conquest and long-term strategy was practiced by Octave Mouret, the founder of the department store in Zola's *Au bonheur des dames*, not only toward the women whom he hoped would make his fortune but also toward the entire female sex that his store was designed to entice and ultimately conquer—the term *galanterie* figures in both instances.[155]

Finally, the term sometimes embellished the straightforward practice of taking women for one's own pleasure, if the man conducted the operation with a certain panache and was driven by vanity as much if not more than sensual satisfaction. Zola's Antoine Macquart, overly interested in his son's young female friends (even going so far as to appropriate one of them), was described by the novelist as an "old rascal [who] prided himself on his gallantry."[156]

Every form of the old aristocratic gallantry was thus recuperated by the nouveau riche, the petite bourgeoisie, and even the working class. Given the period when the literature under discussion was written, it might be wondered whether there was more at stake than Chateaubriand's observation concerning the Napoleonic court. That possibility is suggested by a short dialogue in Maupassant. To a man who has just asserted that although certain woman are intelligent, females in general are not, "Monsieur Patissot—offended in all his primal, chivalrous instincts—declared, 'You're not French, monsieur. *Galanterie française* is a form of patriotism.'"[157] This perhaps indicates a need to soothe French national pride after the military defeat of 1870. And perhaps nothing could serve that purpose so well as a trait of civilization to which the Prussians could never lay claim.

Whatever the case concerning this simultaneous resurgence, transplantation, and distortion of *galanterie française*, it hardly needs to be pointed out that the forces of destruction gained the upper hand after the First World War. The ranks of these destructive forces were swelled by the oeuvre of Montherlant; his fanatical attack, in the name of male supremacy, on everything that might resemble male submission to women was a paean of male pride. Such literature, however, was not the sole nor even the main ally of the forces under discussion. In the realm of social behavior, separate but equal education for both sexes (while awaiting coeducation), plus the entry of women into professions formerly reserved for men, produced females who were everyday colleagues, financially independent, and sometimes politically committed; this trend significantly reduced men's feeling of the otherness of women, and subsequently men's tendency to worship them (the ultimate root of gallantry). It should be added that the elimination of domestic servants placed the burden of household tasks on nearly all women—which is hardly becoming for a goddess! The female wreathed in leisure, dreams, and mystery ceased to exist. Real women will generally have nothing to do with the gallant behavior directed at them, for they no longer seek—at least explicitly—the protection of a man, nor do they wait for a man to make advances, preferring to make their own choice. They simply expect friendship from men, friendship potentially leading to love or surviving through love, as already suggested by the relationship between Diderot and Sophie Volland. The couple formed by Sartre and Simone de Beauvoir is typical in this respect—"Castor" was in no way a goddess.

Has *galanterie française*, then, completely and permanently vanished? Looking strictly at the destructive trends listed above, the answer is yes— all are more operative than ever in today's world. The term is used less and less, and when used is applied either to behavior considered inappropriate or to simple anonymous politeness, with no amorous connotation at all. The 1983 *Grand dictionnaire encyclopédique Larousse* illustrates these two definitions: for the former, the example given (without reference) reads, "He spouted questionable gallantries at a serving girl"; while the latter is illustrated by "offering, out of gallantry, to carry a lady's bag." Although aimed at a more educated public, the *Encyclopédie universalis* does not even have an entry for "galanterie" nor does it mention the term among the various cross-references listed under the entry for "love." So much for the term. As to the behavior itself, a study carried out some ten years ago by Theodore Zeldin, titled *The French*, hardly offers a better image. Zeldin quotes a teenage girl as saying that "the boys play at being hard. It is out of date to court, to show one's feelings. Everything moves too fast: three compliments, a non-alcoholic mint drink, and immediately they get to the point."[158] A recent advertising campaign while this was being written featured a street poster selling a car with the exclamation "Hot stuff!" followed by the commentary, "There's never been a better way to say, 'I love you.'"

So is that the last word? No. A third dictionary, published by Quillet in 1977, refers to polite and pleasant manners and attitude, to constant attentiveness to women, and to delightful compliments—in short, to pure mid-seventeenth-century gallantry. As to behavior, meanwhile, many interesting things emerge from Zeldin's study. On the feminine side, he quotes Brigitte Bardot as saying, "I believe that women, in wanting to liberate themselves too much, are going to be increasingly unhappy. Because a woman is not made to live a man's life. A woman has her weaknesses, and is so very vulnerable. . . . A woman is a gentle creature."[159] Shifting from stars to statistics, Zeldin also asserts that "out of every ten women, nine believe that men should take as much care of their appearance as women. . . . Three-quarters like men to court them. . . . And since men do not court enough, seven out of ten have in practice taken the initiative in courtship and most say they like doing that."[160]

It is this type of statistic that inspired a recent advertising campaign by a lingerie manufacturer who hoped to attract female buyers by using floral prints and addressing them in caressing tones—"You like being offered flowers, right?"

On the male side, one of the illustrations in Zeldin's book is a cartoon by Wolinksi that shows a man and a woman engaging in the following dialogue:

MAN: I'd like to flirt with you the way we did when we were young.

WOMAN: Listen Georges, if you want to make love say so straight away, because I've got to be in Melun in an hour's time.[161]

Perhaps a fair number of people today, both men and women, feel an almost obscure regret for lost gallantry, a secret aspiration to rediscover a marked differentiation between the sexes, and, along with all that, time to really live—time when beings are more important than things—leading to a savoir-faire that would include disinterested gestures like flowers, polite manners, playful smiles, and refined conversation. Yet it must be recognized that if such aspirations do exist, they remain well buried. And that the context of public life, both here and abroad, seems in no way conducive to their development. In order to foresee the future, however, one would have to be a Chateaubriand. Since I'm not, I prefer to let readers muse, as I do myself, on the contradictory signs given here.

NOTES

Readers familiar with Alain Rey's article "Les Trésors de la langue," in *Lieux de mémoire*, vol. 2, *La Nation: Héritage—Historiographie—Paysages* (Paris: Éditions Gallimard, 1986); 3:638–39 and 642, will already be aware of the remarkable lexical data bank in the Institut national de la langue Française. I would like to acknowledge my debt to that institution, pay homage to the memory of its founder, Paul Imbs, and thank deputy director Gérard Gorcy and his team of researchers for their gracious help. I would also like to express cordial thanks to my friends and colleagues, the medievalists Michel Rousse and Michel Stanesco, for their generous advice.

1. [E. de Jouy], "Les Epoques de la galanterie française," *L'Hermite de la Chaussée d'Antin, ou Observations sur les moeurs et les usages parisiens au commencement du XIXe siècle* (Paris: Pillet, 1813), 3:3.

2. Charles Sorel, *Les Lois de la galanterie* (Paris: Aubry, 1885), 1.

3. Molière, *Le Sicilien ou l'amour peintre* (1668), sc. 13.

4. Mme de Villedieu, *Les Désordres de l'amour*, republished in, *Textes littéraires francais*, ed. M. Cuénin (Geneva: Droz, 1970), 22.

5. B. L. de Muralt, *Lettres sur les Anglais et les Français* (Cologne, 1725). Letter 3.150–51: "*La galanterie française* is the fruit of kindheartedness combined with attentiveness to little matters. . . . In conversation, they use *galanterie* to mean a fine wit that adroitly turns the tiniest subjects to flattery."

6. Charles Duclos, *Confessions du Comte de ✱✱✱*, ed. L. Versini (1741; Paris: Didier, 1969), 44.

7. *Dictionnaire universel de la langue française* (Paris, 1845–46), entry for "Galanterie."

8. A. Vallet de Viriville, "De l'amour et des sentiments chevaleresques: Étude historique de moeurs," *Revue de Paris* 18 (1853): 191.

9. Fanny Trollope, *Paris and the Parisians* (1836; New York: Hippocrene Books, 1985). The French approach to gallantry features in letter 66.456–52, which recounts a conversational joust between an Englishman ("Saint-George") and a Frenchman ("Saint-Denis").

10. Karl Hillebrand, *La France et les Français pendant la seconde moité du XIXe siècle* (Paris: Dreyfous, 1880), 54.

11. A. Houdart de la Motte, *L'Europe galante* (Paris: Ballard, 1697).

12. Stendhal, *De l'amour* (1822), chap. 43.

13. Honoré de Balzac, *Oeuvres complètes* (Paris: Michel Lévy, 1875–87), 4:159.

14. Georges Courteline, *Messieurs les ronds-de-cuir* (1893), act 4, sc. 2.

15. Madeleine de Scudéry, *Conversations nouvelles* (Paris: Barbin, 1684). Scudéry was born in 1607.

16. La Bruyère, *Caractères* (1688), 74.

17. *Encyclopédie*, entry for "Galanterie."

18. Madame de Staël, *De l'Allemagne* (1814), pt. 1, chap. 4.

19. Stendhal, *Le Rouge et le noir* (1830), pt. 1, chap. 7.

20. Balzac, *La Cousine Bette*, in *Oeuvres complètes*, 10:89.

21. Quoted in the *Dictionnaire Larousse du XIXe siècle*, entry for "Galanterie."

22. Guy de Maupassant, "Boule-de-Suif," in *Oeuvres complètes* (Paris: Librairie de France, 1934), 1:12.

23. The noun *galanterie* appeared in French in the second half of the sixteenth century. Two centuries earlier, it had been preceded by the adjective *galant*, potentially used as a noun. The etymology stems from the Old French verb *galer*, which means "to make merry, amuse oneself, have a good time." That led to the first meaning of *galant*, namely (1) "lively, alert, spirited, playful." Given a positive turn, this vivacity yielded (2) "courage, elegance, distinction," whereas a negative turn produced an inclination toward misdeeds such as (3) "banditry, larceny, and sundry trickery." *Vert galant* originally referred to a bandit who hid in the woods (whence *vert*, green) but came to mean a lustful old man. So whether given a positive or negative turn, *galanterie* entailed (4) "daring behavior" toward women. The shift from meaning (3) to meaning (4) occurred easily, as the semantic evolution of the expression *vert galant* demonstrates.

In the sixteenth century, then, *galanterie* referred to a "gallant" act—a joke, a trick, or bold, flirtatious move. By the early seventeenth century, the term began to encompass a quality as well as an act, the quality being related to meaning (2) above, although that use of the term did not become common until roughly 1640. In this article, *galanterie* is discussed only as a quality, and only when it is associated with social prestige; excluded, therefore, is feminine *galanterie*, which has always had a pejorative connotation in France.

24. Claude Favre de Vaugelas, *Remarques sur la langue française* (1647; Paris: T. Jolly, 1664), 349.

25. Antoine Gombaud, Chevalier de Méré, *Oeuvres complètes*, ed. Charles Boudhors (Paris: Roches, 1930), 2:42–43, 1:19.

26. Ibid., 1:18.

27. Ibid., 1:20.

28. Madame de Motteville, *Mémoires*, ed. F.Riaux (Paris: Charpentier, 1855), 1:13.

29. Jean Chapelain, "De la lecture des vieux romans," *Opuscules critiques*, ed. A. C. Hunter (Geneva: Droz, 1936), 206–41. Written in 1646–47, Chapelain's dialogue was first published in 1728.

30. Madame de Staël, *De la littérature* (1800), pt. 1, chap. 18.

31. Montesquieu, *The Spirit of the Laws*, trans. Anne Cohler, Basia Miller, Harold Stone (Cambridge: Cambridge University Press, 1995), bk. 28, chap. 22, p. 652.

32. La Curne de Sainte-Palaye, *Mémoires sur l'ancienne chevalerie* . . . (Paris: Veuve Duchesne, 1781), 1:75.

33. Montesquieu, 561 [slighty adapted by this translator].

34. Jean-Jacques Rousseau, *Politics and the Arts: Letter to M. d'Alembert on the Theatre*, trans. Allan Bloom (1758; Ithaca: Cornell University Press, 1973), 104 [slightly adapted by this translator].

35. Muralt, 19.

36. Madame de Staël, *De l'Allemagne*, pt. 1, chap. 4.

37. Rousseau, 104.

38. Jean-Jacques Rousseau, *La Nouvelle Héloïse* (1761), 2:21. This attitude was echoed by Louis-Sébastien Mercier, *Tableaux de Paris* (Amsterdam, 1782), vol. 2, chap. 28, and by the highly brilliant commentary made by Edmond and Jules de Goncourt in *La Femme au XVIIIe*, chap. 9.

39. Montesquieu, *Persian Letters*, trans. C. J. Betts (London: Penguin, 1973), letter 38.93.

40. Rousseau, 101.

41. David Hume, "Of the Rise and Progress of the Arts and Sciences," in *Of the Standard of Taste and Other Essays*, ed. John W. Lenz (1741; New York: Bobbs-Merill, 1965), 91. A French translation of Hume was published in Amsterdam as early as 1752.

42. La Curne de Sainte-Palaye, 1:218–19.

43. Ibid., 1:158–59.

44. Ibid., 1:224.

45. Edmund Burke, *Reflections on the Revolution in France* (London: J. M. Dent & Sons, 1960), 73–74. The phrase "a nation of gallant men" was translated into French in 1790 as *une nation de galanterie*, and although P. Andler's 1989 translation (Paris: Hachette/Pluriel) gives a different version (p. 96), this was how it was known to French readers during the period in question. [Whereas Burke's use of "gallant men" might remain slightly ambiguous in this context, his 1791 discussion of "gallantry" in an attack on Rousseau ("Letter to a Member of the National Assembly," Ibid., 266) suggests that he was alluding not to bravery but to refined behavior toward women. Interestingly, Andler's recent French translation (*un peuple composé d'hommes d'honneur*) reflects the evolution of the modern meaning of "gallant" in English.—Trans.]

46. Charles Baudelaire, *Fusées* (Paris: Gallimard, 1986), 78.

47. Anonymous, *Chevalier au cygne* [thirteenth century] (Brussels, 1848), lines 14,807–12.

48. Chrétien de Troyes, *Yvain ou le chevalier au lion*, ed. M. Roques (late twelfth century; Paris: Champion, 1960). See, for example, the episodes recounted in lines 173–259 and 2361–2467.

49. Alfiérez Gutierre de Games, *El Victorial*, Vol. 1 of *Collección de Crónicas españolas* (Madrid, 1940).

50. A vestige of this use can be seen in the small ribbon still called *faveur* in France and found not long ago in haberdasheries .

51. La Curne de Sainte-Palaye, 1:91.

52. Ibid., 1:97.

53. Pierre de Brantôme, *Vies des hommes illustres et des grands capitaines français*, Discourse 55.

54. On this subject see the major book by Maurice Magendie, *La Politesse mondaine et les théories de l'honnêteté en France au XVIIe siècle* (Paris: PUF, 1925), pt. 1, chap. 9; pt. 4, chap. 9. See also Noémi Hepp, "Dames en leur hôtel," *Dix-septième siécle* 162 (1989): 67–76.

55. See Magendie, vol. 1, pt. 2, chap. 8.

56. Ibid., 344.

57. Ibid., 188.

58. Ibid., 92–93.

59. La Rochefoucauld, *Maxims*, trans. Leonard Tancock (Harmondsworth, Middlesex: Penguin, 1981), 29.

60. Quoted in Magendie, vol. 1, pt. 2, p. 852.

61. The *Mercure galant*, a society monthly published in the form of a letter addressed to a lady, adopted positions very hostile to the supporters of Greco-Roman antiquity in 1687, the year that the dispute between the ancients and the moderns erupted, and again in 1715, the year that the quarrel over Homer came to a climax. Charles Perrault, in his *Parallèle des anciens et des modernes,* which he began publishing in 1688, invoked feminine sensibility in order to discredit Pindar, Plato, and the Greek anthology (Munich: Eidos Verlag, 1964), 27–38.

62. Corneille, *Le Cid,* 3.4.871–96.

63. Corneille, *Cinna,* 3.4.

64. La Rochefoucauld, *Mémoires* (Paris: Hachette, 1874), 82–92.

65. Ibid., 525. Long attributed to La Rochefoucauld, this assessment was in fact by his contemporary Vineuil, as can be seen in the edition cited above.

66. Chapelain, 239.

67. Corneille, *La Veuve*, 1.1. The same idea was expressed in Mademoiselle de Scudéry's *Clélie: Histoire romaine* (1654–1660; Slatkine reprints, 1973), 2:1140–41; and by Muralt, 151.

68. Scudéry, *Clélie*, 6:1366. The quotation is one of the "gallant maxims" uttered by the character Térame to a whole series of interlocuters.

69. La Bruyère's *Caractères* described how wounded Emire was when a young man to whom she was introduced and whom she liked did not take that first step:

"But since he gazed at her little, and spoke still less of her and her beauty, she was surprised and almost indignant that a man so fine and witty should not be gallant." ("Des femmes," 81).

70. Vincent Voiture, *Poésies*, ed. H. Lafay (Paris: Didier, 1971), 1:64.

71. Chapelain, 237.

72. A sonnet by Georges de Scudéry in J. Rousset, *Anthologie de la poésie baroque française* (Paris: Armand Colin, 1968), 1:105.

73. A sonnet by Malleville, Ibid., 2:66.

74. A recording of *Airs de cour* by Michel Lambert (1610–96), a fashionable composer and singer during the reign of Louis XIV, was released by Harmonia Mundi in 1981. All the poems set to music in this collection speak of love, and all concern an unrequited lover's complaint, even when the poet is a lady.

75. P. Richelet, *Les plus belles lettres des meilleurs auteurs français* (Lyons: B. Bailly, 1689).

76. Madeleine de Scudéry, *Le Grand Cyrus* (Paris: Courbé, 1656; Slatkine Reprints, 1972), 10:529.

77. La Rochefoucauld, *Maxims*, maxim 402, p. 88.

78. Voiture, 1:83–86 and 53–54.

79. J. F. Sarasin, *Ouevres*, ed. P. Festugière (Paris: Champion, 1926), 1:311 and 309.

80. Quoted in Jean-Michel Pelous, *Amour précieux, amour galant* (Paris: Kincksieck, 1980), 205. Pelous's book is a key work on the subject discussed here.

81. Madame de La Fayette, *Histoire de Mme. Henriette d'Angleterre* (Paris: Mercure de France, 1965), 68.

82. Madame de Sévigné, *Correspondance* (Paris: Gallimard, 1972), 1:469, letter dated April 1, 1672.

83. See Pelous, 199–204.

84. J. de Préchac, *Le Voyage de Fontainebleau* (Paris: Cie. des Librarires, 1678), 147–48.

85. This subject is fully and admirably developed by Edmond and Jules Goncourt.

86. Muralt, 131.

87. Mercier, vol. 2, chap. 28.

88. Montesquieu, *Persian Letters*, letter 107, p. 197.

89. Mercier.

90. N. T. Barthe (1734–85), "Epître à Mme du Bocage," ed. M. Allem, *Anthologie poétique françiase, XVIIIe siècle* (Paris: Garnier, n.d.), 300.

91. Soulavie, *Mémoires du Duc de Richelieu* (Paris: Firmin-Didot, 1858), 1:244.

92. Ibid., 20.

93. Marivaux, *La Réunion des amours* [1731], sc. 10.

94. Ibid., sc. 1.

95. Soulavie, 20.

96. Ibid., 388.

97. See Jean-François Marmontel, *Mémoires* (Paris: Firmin-Didot, 1846), bk. 4, p. 137.

98. Claude Crébillon, *Collection complète des oeuvres de M. de Crébillon fils* (London, 1777; Slatkine Reprints, 1968), 1:271.

99. Pierre-Victor, Baron de Besenval, *Mémoires* (Paris: F. Buisson, 1805), 1:204.

100. Julie de Lespinasse, *Lettres de Mademoiselle de Lespinasse*, ed. Jules Janin (Paris: Amyot, 1847), 109.

101. Marivaux, *Le Petit-maître corrigé* [1734], act 1, sc. 9.

102. Besenval, 254–55.

103. Crébillon, 1:196–201.

104. Choderlos de Laclos, *Dangerous Acquaintances*, trans. Richard Aldington (New York: New Directions, n.d.), letter 125, p. 278.

105. Marmontel, "Le Scrupule," *Contes moraux* (Paris: Née de la Rochelle, 1787), 1:116.

106. "Tout ou rien," ibid., 1:338.

107. Marivaux, *Le Petit-maître*, act 2, sc. 2.

108. Marivaux, *La Réunion des amours*, scs. 14 and 12.

109. Charles Nicoullaud, ed., *Mémoires de la Comtesse de Boigne* (Paris: Plon, 1907), 1:43.

110. Denis Diderot, *Lettres à Sophie Volland* (Paris: Gallimard, 1978), 41, letter dated June 4, 1759.

111. Ibid.

112. Marmontel, "Le Scrupule," 120.

113. René de Chateaubriand, *Mémoires d'outre-tombe* (Paris: Flammarion, 1948), 3:101–2.

114. Ibid., 3:435.

115. Ibid., 4:243.

116. Ibid., 4:193.

117. See above, notes 1 and 8.

118. Balzac, *Oeuvres complètes*, 8:601.

119. Marcel Proust, *Remembrance of Things Past*, vol. 2, *The Guermantes Way*, trans. C. K. Scott Moncrieff and Terence Kilmartin (New York: Random House, 1981), 446.

120. Alfred de Musset, *Carmosine*, act 3, sc. 8, in *Comédies et proverbes* (Paris: Charpentier, 1853), vol 2.

121. Balzac, 10:409.

122. Anatole France, *Le Lys rouge*, in *Oeuvres complètes* (Paris: Calmann-Lévy, 1927), 9:357.

123. Proust, *À la recherche du temps perdu*, vol. 1, *Du côté de chez Swann* (Paris: Gallimard, Bibliothèque de la Pléide, 1969), 246.

124. Henry Bernstein, *Le Secret* (1913), act 1, sc. 7.

125. Stendhal, *Lucien Leuwen* (Paris: Gallimard, Bibliothèque de la Pléiade, 1952), 1003.

126. Balzac, *Illusions perdues,* in *Oeuvres complètes,* 7:285.

127. Balzac, *La Maison Nucingen,* in *Oeuvres complètes*, 8:599.

128. Chateaubriand, pt. 2, bks. 1 and 3.

129. Chateaubriand, pt. 3, p. 334.

130. Ibid., pt. 3, p. 329. On the worship rendered to Madame Récamier by Chateaubriand himself and his contemporaries, see pp. 308–9.

131. Balzac, *Illusions perdues,* in *Oeuvres complètes*, vol. 7. The entire first part of the novel is driven by this shared illusion.

132. Gustave Flaubert, *L'Education sentimentale*, pt. 3, chap. 6.

133. Emile Zola, *Madeleine Férat,* in *Oeuvres complètes* (Paris: Cercle du livre précieux, 1966), 1:730.

134. Musset, *Bettine,* scs. 15 and 18, in *Comédies et proverbes*, vol. 2.

135. Chateaubriand, 2:38.

136. Stendhal, *De l'amour*, chap. 40.

137. Stendhal, *Le Rouge et le noir,* pt. 2, chap. 9.

138. Stendhal, *La Chartreuse de Parme,* chap. 15.

139. Stendhal, *De l'amour,* chap. 24.

140. Honoré de Balzac, *Correspondance,* ed. R. Pierrot (Paris: Garnier, 1960), 1:168.

141. Madame de Duras, *Edouard* (1825; Paris: Stock, 1950), 129.

142. Victor Hugo, *Les Misérables* (Paris: Garnier, 1957), 2:82.

143. Musset, *Carmosine,* act 2, sc. 2.

144. Musset, *Barberine,* act 1, sc. 4; and act 3, in *Comédies et proverbes*, vol. 1.

145. Romain Rolland, *Jean-Christophe* (1908; Paris: Albin Michel, 1932), 5:28.

146. Chateaubriand, 4:555–56.

147. There is a men-only dinner in pt. 2, chap. 4, and a passage on the "Club de l'intelligence" in pt. 3, chap. 1.

148. Proust, 2 (*The Guermantes Way*): 472.

149. Chateaubriand, 3:353.

150. Zola, *Les Rougon-Macquart*, 1:403 and 460.

151. Ibid., 5:88.

152. Georges Courteline, *Boubouroche,* in *Théatre complet* (Paris: Flammarion, 1961) act 2, sc. 3.

153. Zola, *Les Rougon-Macquart*, 3:448.

154. Maupassant, 19.

155. Zola, *Pot-bouille* and *Au bonheur des dames,* in *Les Rougon-Macquart,* 2:98 and 461.

156. *La Fortune des Rougon,* Ibid., 1:127.

157. Guy de Maupassant, "Les Dimanches d'un bourgeois de Paris: Un dîner et quelques idées," 1:228.

158. Theodore Zeldin, *The French* (London: Flamingo, 1984), 108.

159. Ibid., 137.

160. Ibid., 151.

161. Ibid., 113.

Figure 8.1
Watteau, *Étude de deux hommes conversant*. The peak of French-style conversation reflected in gesture: the grace of a dance, the ease of improvisation, the total convenience of others.

---- C H A P T E R 8 ----

CONVERSATION

MARC FUMAROLI

> The history of conversation . . . seems to me impossible, as is true of
> anything that is essentially relative and fleeting and which depends
> on mere impressions.
>
> Augustin de Sainte-Beuve*

Proposing to establish, even very informally, a history of French conversation might seem as foolish as attempting a history of tears, fare-
wells, or first encounters. *Scripta manent, verba volant.* Is not conversation
after all an exchange of fleeting and futile words, in short a trivial bourgeois game? Of late, it would seem, France has fallen victim to a terrible
prejudice with regard to words and things. In a few short years, a swarm of
metaphysical coleoptera have ruined the relationship between the two in a
buzzing of insect wings in which one dimly discerned words and phrases
such as "incommunicability," "absurdity," "suspicion" and "language as
snare, veil or prison." Nor did sociology, aided and abetted by linguistics, lag behind: on the ruins of conversation, communication was made
king. This new plague of Egypt (prophesied by writers from *La Peste* to
La Jalousie) did not however eradicate either the natural inclination of the
French to talk and gossip or the old article of faith of our national religion
according to which "il n'est bon bec que de Paris" (Villon). This proud old
French heritage, this sunny confidence in the *genius loci* to foster through

---

* The translations for all cited French editions are my own.—Trans.

shared speech not only social but philosophical and literary well-being, has both illustrious classical antecedents and solid contemporary exponents. People talked, people conversed orally and even in writing, in Athens and other places before Plato. But true conversation could be found only in Athens, the birthplace of theater, and one could appreciate the elevation of conversation to an art form—Atticism—only in the written accounts of Athenian conversation contained in Plato's dialogues.[1] While the word *conversation,* from the Latin, did not in all probability come into common usage in French until the sixteenth century, its referent had been waiting, so to speak, in those Greek texts since the end of antiquity. In modern Europe, it was revived, in Italy initially, after the dialogues of Plato and his Latin emulator, Cicero, were rediscovered in Venice and Florence.

How, in a few words, can one characterize the particular form of oral collaboration that the Platonic dialogues stylize and imitate in written form? The talk involved free men, who gathered in settings unconnected with the business of the city (frequently the homes of friends but sometimes outdoors in the countryside around Athens, or its streets). These citizens were brought together by a natural inclination to talk, as if they found in conversation a fascinating game, a supreme form of sport, worthy of the gods. Naturally, the almost constant presence of Socrates and the mordant irony of his frequent interventions gives these playful exchanges an unparalleled degree of vivacity and complexity. But since Socrates appears at ease and very much himself whatever the circumstances, it is the different personalities of his interlocutors that make the verbal games he arbitrates so varied: in each instance, the subject of the conversation is different. No subsequent writer ever succeeded in representing as effortlessly as Plato, with his incomparable directness and delicacy the meandering, shifting quality, the varying tonalities—in a word, the music—of conversation. In this regard, the history of literary dialogue in prose is similar to that of printing, photography, and film: no sooner was it invented than it achieved perfection. This perfection is all the more miraculous in that these dialogues, conceived for the purpose of teaching philosophy in the Academy, confront the reader with exchanges that seem initially uneven in quality, by turns pedestrian and lively, but that suddenly, without warning, take flight to tackle the most difficult questions the human mind can conceive: happiness, truth, the good life, poetry, art, music, theology, and cosmology. From its earliest beginnings, conversation—a superior form of recreation among free men—presented itself as the most subtle of pedagogical methods and, despite its discontinuity, as the most encyclopedic of forms. It is, of course, Socrates and his irony that act as the yeast, transforming a relaxed exchange of opinions into a breathless struggle between two or more combatants from which divine sparks fly.

Yet even this yeast would achieve nothing without the very dough of human nature in all the diversity and singularity of its representatives, in all the reality of its psychological and social types, perfectly blended to provide a delicious and subtle feast of speeches, emotions and thoughts. Socrates, transformed by these dialogues into the immortal master of the Academy, is the agent that reveals not only the philosophical vocation of conversation, but also its roots in human nature. In and of itself, the naive and elementary enjoyment of this friendly wordplay among free men constitutes an exhilarating liberation from physical, social, political, and economic gravity. A space opens up that the presence of a teacher can transform into a launching pad. From the diversity of his interlocutors, their particular traits and disagreements, Socrates succeeds in making a rose window where something resembling the inaccessible unity of truth is revealed and with it a sense of fulfillment that no sensual pleasure or worldly acquisition can match.

Indeed, the Platonic dialogue (contemporary with the comedy of Aristophanes and the tragedy of Sophocles) is not the origin of the history of conversation; it is the center, the source. Conversation begins when Socrates and his animated company of Athenians come together, and ends when they part. People in all times and places have known how to argue, chat, exchange words, gossip, discourse, and negotiate—but since Plato, to converse has meant to abandon these colloquial forms of discourse for the naturalness of human speech, to bathe once more in the light of the Academy. In this way, without effort, we glimpse sparks, at least, of the great blaze of the Socratic spirit and experience the philosophical ascent that is achieved at home, when a number of people gather for the purpose of contemplation, in the hope of moving a little closer to unity, truth, and happiness.

Is France, and more particularly Paris, the Athens of the moderns and thus, at times, its Academy? That is, at any rate, what Emmanuel Kant was suggesting when, in 1798, he felt able to write in his *Anthropology* :

> The form of well-being that seems best suited to humanity is a
> good meal in good company (varied, as much as possible). Chester-
> field used to say that a party at table should never number less than
> the Graces or more than the Muses. . . . The French nation sets it–
> self apart from all others by its taste for conversation; in that respect
> France is a model for other nations, courteous above all to foreign
> visitors, even now when courtly manners are no longer fashionable.
> The French are forthcoming, not out of interest, but by virtue of
> the dictates of their taste. Since taste is determined in large part by
> women from the most elegant social circles, their conversation has

become the accepted language of that milieu. There can be no doubt that such a tendency must exercise no small influence on the readiness to be helpful, the willingness to lend aid, and little by little, on a universal philanthropy grounded on established principles which makes a people on the whole very likeable.[2]

Was France specially selected for this supreme delight of free men: conversation, good company, the pleasures of the table? If France might be considered another Athens, it was in no way Plato's Academy. Reformulating Thucydides' moral judgment on the Athenians, this time to the detriment of the French, Kant adds:

> The other side of the coin is a vivacity insufficiently tempered by considered reflection, a frivolity accompanying a clear-sighted gift of reason that dispenses with certain forms for no other reason than that they are old or have been taken up with too great an enthusiasm, even if they have proved entirely satisfactory. Moreover, the spirit of freedom is contagious and subordinates in its play reason itself, provoking in the relationship between this people and their nation enthusiasms capable of overturning everything, of going beyond the wildest excesses. The characteristics of the French, seen in their worst light, but in accordance with the living reality, can be represented without further description, as fragments thrown out at random, as pieces for a portrait.[3]

The shadow threatening conversation, when Socrates is not there and the Sophists have taken over, is the French sickness, anatomized and anthologized by Alain Peyrefitte: sufficient detachment to permit the play and pleasures of conversation, but not enough logical stamina to create durable institutions (Plato's Academy endured for almost a thousand years) and so transform this refined form of sociability into a persistent philosophical quest and an evolving tradition of lived experience.

The testimony of Madame de Staël, a Frenchwoman from outside France, is not as profound, though better known. It is also more flattering for France's self-esteem and did a great deal, after the tragedy of the years 1792–94, to reassure France of its sociable vocation and set it back on the path of conversation:

> I believe it is generally recognized [she writes], that in the entire world, Paris is the city in which the spirit and appreciation of conversation are most wide-spread; and what we call home-sickness, that indefinable yearning for one's native land, which is independent even

of the friends one has left there, has to do above all with the pleasure of conversing, which the French find nowhere so fully developed as in their own country. Volney tells us that during the Revolution, French émigrés sought to clear the land and establish a colony in America. From time to time, however, they would drop everything in order, as they said, to renew the delights of social, urban conversation. And the town to which they repaired, New Orleans, was six hundred leagues from where they lived. The need to talk is felt at every level of French society: speech is not always, as it is elsewhere, a means of communicating one's ideas, feelings and business; it is also an instrument on which one loves to play and which has the same delightful effect as music for some nations and strong liquor for others.[4]

After thirty years of existentialism, the nouveau roman, and the "class-struggle," during which frivolity and fashion fed the flames of terror, studies reach us from abroad on "civilization and manners" (Elias), "pragmatic discourse" (Goffman), "the optimal conditions of oral cooperation" (Grice). And quite apart from these learned studies, a Danish film, *Babette's Feast,* based on a short story by Karen Blixen, turned out to be for today's French audience what Madame de Staël's "On the Spirit of Conversation" had been for the public of the Napoleonic empire—the reminder of an ancient delight. We see a group of Danish dinner guests discover the pleasure of talking, through the agency of a banquet, lovingly prepared by a Parisian woman, an exiled *communarde.* Despite being the victim of French political tragedy, this woman has nonetheless remained faithful to the wellspring of humanity and benevolence that France has always fostered through good food, good wine, and conversation. Babette was one of the great cooks of the Second Empire. To thank her hostesses, she has initially arranged to have shipped from France, and then prepared with her considerable skill, all the things that in France contribute to the euphoria of the mouth, the loosening of tongues, the suspension of disagreement: gastronomy, great vintages, the complete art of the table. Conversation is inseparable from its comforts; it loves luxury. For this one transcendent evening, frozen reticence melts under the influence of this splendid convivial rite: men and women, villagers and dignitaries discover together the sensual pleasures of the table and the joy of verbal exchange. The earnest, close-knit community described by Dreyer and Bergman, partakes for a few well-filled hours of the French gospel of Brillat-Savarin and Rabelais.

With nothing more than the compelling example of the Parisian salons, without the slightest recourse to political or military intimidation or any particular cultural policy, the France of the ancien régime conquered all of Europe's courts and social elites, creating beyond its frontiers a society in which any citizen, speaking French, could claim a superior spiritual homeland. In the chapter of *De l'Allemagne* already mentioned, Madame de Staël, even as she was enlarging on themes derived from Rousseau, was combining them with recollections from Montesquieu showing how in French conversation, which he by no means condemns, sophistry tends to prevail over the Socratic spirit:

> The spirit of conversation [he writes in his *Pensées*] is what the French call *esprit*. It consists of a dialogue, generally light-hearted, in which each participant, without paying much attention to what anyone else is saying, speaks and replies, the whole business proceeding by fits and starts in a brisk and lively fashion. The style and tone of good conversation, that is to say, the style of dialogue, must be learned. There are countries where the spirit of conversation is quite unknown. Such is the case in nations in which people do not live communally, or those where manners are dominated by serious concerns. Thus what the French term *esprit* is not just wit but a particular form of wit. By its nature, *esprit* is the combination of good sense and discernment. Good sense is the just comparison of one thing with another and even the distinction between things in their definite and relative states.[5]

Even though it was spontaneously diffused throughout the whole of French society, a natural taste for conversation was always associated with a certain "art"—an art better articulated and more suited to serve as a model at the summit of the social edifice, in Paris, in "good society." In *Dix années d'exil*, Madame de Staël defines conversation in France *a contrario*, in terms of two characteristics seen as essential to exemplary conversation: "education" on the one hand, "confidence" on the other, from which both "enjoyment" and "intimacy" are derived, for without these two, *esprit*, the flame lit by conversation, could never ignite.[6] By concentrating their attention on a small Parisian elite as a model—both the source and the inspiration—for the bourgeoisie, the provincials, and the foreign courts, neither Montesquieu nor Madame de Staël reveals a partiality born of privilege. They acknowledge a fact that Plato and Kant also recognized: conversation can take place only among a small number of people. By its very nature, it is associated with an elite. In the Parisian society of the ancien régime, conversation achieved one of its most highly developed forms: a superior game played in front of a European public which in turn tried to emulate its elite players. These players were "noble," but also erudite, and they enjoyed, in their liberty and leisure, the kind of contagious confidence that the spirit of conversation demands.

Both Montesquieu and Madame de Staël suggest that despotism, the arbitrary exercise of power that was in other respects so ubiquitous in France, was halted at the threshold of these nobles' private lives, and it is precisely at that point that the elegant verbal saturnalia began. Montesquieu does not deal with conversation in *L'Esprit des lois*, but Madame de Staël works to establish the connection between the political and social aspects of the ancien régime and this distinctive trait of French society:

> Relations between the different classes were likewise well calculated to develop in France a certain intellectual maturity, a sense of proportion and a feeling for what was appropriate to the spirit of society. Rank was not rigorously defined, nor individual ambition clearly circumscribed within an uncertain social space in which individuals might either make their mark or fail. The rights of the Third Estate, the parliaments, the nobility, the power of the king himself, none of these were inalterably laid down: everything was made subservient to conversational address. Grave difficulties could be successfully navigated by delicate nuances of speech and manner and it was rare that participants either clashed or were forced to yield, so much care was devoted to avoiding either contingency. Great families, likewise, harbored undeclared or understated pretensions among themselves and this very vagueness excited more vanity than clearly indicated distinctions of rank could have done. It was necessary to study every detail of a man's or a woman's existence to know what respect was due to him or her. Arbitrary factors, of every sort, have always been part of the French way of life and that is why the French have, so to speak, so pedantic an attitude toward frivolity. Since the principal layers of social demarcation were never firmly established, they sought to give consistency to the slightest details. In England, the privilege of originality could be granted to individuals since the social mass was so thoroughly under control. In France it was as if the spirit of imitation formed a kind of social bond and that confusion would reign everywhere if this bond were not there to compensate for the instability of French institutions.[7]

An art, a diplomacy of the privately spoken word, appears to compensate for the unstable, arbitrary, wounding character of France's administrative and political institutions. In turn, these institutions implicitly respect the regulatory and amending role played by this particular form of free speech operating on their fringes, fighting back effectively against the arrogance and conformism of officialdom. This analysis even makes it possible to understand exceptional occasions: the "revolutionary moment" (the Fronde, the Convention) when this extremely delicate balance is upset, when institutions collapse at the same time as conversation gives way to the vehemence of orators. Mme de Rambouillet (the wife of one of Louis XIII's best diplomats) was silenced by the tribunes of Retz; Mme du Deffand and Mlle de Lespinasse were obliged to yield the floor to Mirabeau and Marat. The same political philosophy of conversation still holds today, in our neomonarchical institutions whose weightiness, rigidity, and crushing intrusions are felt to be endurable only thanks to the tireless mediation, however too often self-indulgent, of the colloquia, debates, and private dinner parties of Paris. Without suppressing the natural roots of French conversation, Madame de Staël helps us understand why it was in France that conversation took flight and soared in such an exceptional way. From its natural origins as one of the great pleasures of private life, it took on a political function as a source of compromise, indispensable to the proper functioning of institutions that were both awkward and by their very nature, an irritant. As a result, the cacophony of French public life has its counterpart and counterbalance: the luxuriousness of French manners, the vocal music which, like Orpheus, softens the ferocity of predators, the egotism of rank, birth, fortune, and appearance. But the voice of Orpheus is the price of Euridice's demise. It is the misfortune of the *castrati* that creates the magic of their voices. The pleasant conversation among the guests at Clarens, in *La Nouvelle Héloïse*, is a kind of chamber music in which absent passion is effectively sublimated. Madame de Staël can write on one occasion, "It has been said by a lady of some wit that Paris was the best place in the world for doing without happiness." And what is true of its people holds even more true for the nation. It is the misfortunes and jolts of French public life (especially dramatic at its center, Paris), the cruel frictions of French social life, familiar in appearance, harsh in reality, which make conversation indispensable and give it both its brilliance as a supreme sublimation of failure, and also its corrective capacities, in rare moments of grace.

Since we cannot conjure up every French conversation—the chitchat around every village dinner table and newborn's crib, the evenings of gossip in front of the fireplace, or the exchanges in offices and cafes—we are obliged to focus our attention, like Montesquieu and Madame de Staël, on the conversation of good Parisian society, the form of conversation that inspired a vast normative literature, both rhetorical and ethical: treatises simply entitled *On Conversation,* or alternatively, on the art of living in society, *On Civil Society,* but also dialogues and exchanges, plays and novels in which dialogues and conversations intermingle with the narrative text. One can see in all these written genres claiming to set out the rules of conversation or put it on stage the innumerable successors and imitators of Plato's dialogues and Greek theater; and attempts have been made, using this normative literature (which still remained abundant in the nineteenth century), to establish a "rhetoric of conversation."[8] But one has first to distinguish between "eloquence" on the one hand—for which rhetoric was invented and where it openly deploys its resources—and on the other, the "art of talking" among equals, at leisure, a context in which rhetoric must remain unseen and be transformed into improvisation, serendipity. Eloquence is the premeditated art of addressing oneself *in public* to an assembly, or else addressing oneself officially to public personages. In a democracy it governs three genres: the deliberative, the judicial, and the epideictic (the praise of great men and of virtue); in a monarchy it is cloaked in secret deliberations between the king and his councilors or flowers into its only public form, the eulogy: the secular eulogy of a prince, or the clerical eulogy of God, his saints, or the Christian doctrine. These official genres are not propitious for conversational exchange. In Plato, to whom one must constantly return, the professors of rhetoric (the sophists) do not shine in the very dialogues in which Socrates by contrast attracts universal acclaim. Even at the time of the Renaissance, the discrepancy between the rhetoric learned in schools and the talents required by the art of conversation among adult friends or social acquaintances was acutely felt.[9] Similarly, a notable difference was seen between the art of writing in a professional context and the art of the private correspondent, which remained very close to familiar, oral improvisation. On the one hand, utility, efficiency, and a specific aim were emphasized; on the other, ease, leisure, and play. Here we encounter the basic difference at the ethical if not the ontological level between noble and fashioned language. Paradoxically, the former can allow itself the luxury of simplicity, while the latter needs recourse to the entire arsenal of oratorical technique with a view to turning them to account. In switching from one register to another, rhetoric changes not only its meaning but its essence. To know how to persuade, to have learned that particular art, is an acquired skill and a skill that seeks certain ends. To take part in a conversation, sophisticated or naive, is to engage in a game with partners one accepts as one's peers and from which one expects nothing more than the pleasure of playing well. One is not judged in terms of technique or results achieved but on the degree of art and wit deployed. Whereas professional speech, since its intention is to persuade, is to a greater or a lesser extent prepared and certainly premeditated, spontaneous conversation favors the unforeseen, and therefore improvisation. Speed of reply and readiness of wit upset the calculations of the professional orator. If there is such a thing as a rhetoric of conversation, it is what remains when everything relating to technique has been forgotten: felicity of expression, quickness, clarity, vivacity. Is it by chance that these qualities, for four centuries, from Montaigne to Cocteau, have been seen as the special mark of grace investing the language of our most "French" writers? These traits, throughout the ages, were fashioned not from manuals and text-books, but from experience, by example, through taking part in the closed circles of conversation that flourished more widely in Paris than anywhere else. Athens was a democracy that Socrates and Plato accepted only insofar as it was subject to scrutiny: a dialogue such as *The Republic* is not far from being subversive. There was nothing democratic about the ancien régime. And yet, at the fringes of the court and the institutions of the régime, the kind of conversation carried on in Paris by a fair number of private groups assumes quite naturally the status of a counterinstitution, a private system of implicit conventions, with its own rules of play, its ethics and rituals, its style or styles. It is "egalitarian" to the extent that within its play, rank, and titles, fortune and power count for very little. Only personal merit, as manifested in this verbal sport, determines the rank of each participant in each assembly. In this elite group, a man of letters with neither birth, rank, nor fortune such as Voiture can joust on equal terms with a Prince de Condé, as long as the prince proves capable of holding his own.[10] This intoxicating game is so important in the life of Paris that it rivals even such pastimes as the *jeu de paume* or games of chance.

The influence of conversation extends to domestic architecture and decor: a learned "correspondence of the arts" (to which the finishing touches were still being put in 1789) draws parallels between the layout of the great Paris houses, their decoration and furnishings, their household staff of servants, and a social life which sees conversation as its liveliest source of pleasure and finds ingenious ways to facilitate and stimulate it. An arrangement quite different from the enormous *saloni* of Italian palaces which were created for mass receptions or the "comfort" of English clubs designed for small talk among men. In this euphoria of private speech, the decorative arts, the art of the table, the art of the sommelier, the chef, the pastry-chef, the musician, to say nothing of the tailor, the coiffeur, the "philosophy master," and the "dancing master" so dear to the bourgeois gentilhomme, all contribute to the success of these endless Olympiads among the Socrates, the Gorgias, and the Diotimas of France. In Molière's *Bourgeois gentilhomme*, philosophy is first and foremost an art of diction, the elegant simplicity of the spoken word. It is the philosophy of Isocrates, mocked but not condemned by Molière-Socrates; as for dancing, in the seventeenth and eighteenth centuries the dance is above all the art of walking and turning gracefully, of presenting oneself well. It is a bodily discipline very different from the *actio oratoria* of ecclesiastics and lawyers, which retains from the art of the dance only the elements that

raise to the status of an art the grace and ease of manner that come naturally to a man of breeding, a man whose personal freedom and extensive
leisure best suit him to conversation. Bodily *sprezzatura* (effortless grace
without affectation) is as indispensable in these verbal championships as
the incisive wit and Attic playfulness of an independent spirit.

Conversation is to communication what the Marguerite Long–Jacques
Thibaud music competition is to the Muzak of supermarkets. And like all
great competitions, it maintains its legends in innumerable books crammed
with delectable stories, anecdotes, incidents, and *bons mots*. Conversation
has its "stars," both male and female, noble and other, from Mme de Rambouillet to Louise de Vilmorin, from Voiture to Paul Morand. It has its
celebrated "stadiums," from the Chambre bleue at Verrières or the Hôtel
de Lambert to the home of Florence Gould in Neuilly.

But conversation, understood in this highly selective sense, is also
contained in both manuscript and print archives, which remain abundant
in France. Oral and ephemeral though it may be, conversation has, until
very recent times and the telephone, managed to spread itself abroad and
to prolong its existence in writing, in correspondence—that most French
of literary genres—to the precise extent to which conversation as a sport
abandoned its Athenian origins and was naturalized French. Letters allow
a conversation, interrupted by absence or distance, to be continued and
leave its tone unchanged. Like the dialogues of Plato, the more they cling
to the spoken word, the more successful they are. This spoken work aims
at being both natural and artistic, and in its literary transposition it retains
its freshness and happy turn of phrase. *The Thousand and One Nights* of
French literature is made up of a series of uninterrupted correspondences
which, regrettably, have never been collected in an anthology. *Mémoires*
are another literary form derived from conversation, often written by
virtuoso conversationalists (Retz, Mlle de Montpensier, Saint-Simon,
Morellet, Mme de Boigne) in the evening of their lives. They are oral
improvisations *written down*; they do not so much tell the history of the
author or his time as sum up the reflections, commentaries, things seen
and heard, portraits, and characters that a lifetime of conversation has
accumulated, like the prose chorus in a Greek tragedy in the margins
of the public and historical life of the narrator. In that sense, *Mémoires*
are the work of a collective group—*Maximes* too—a product of the groups
that surrounded Madame de Sablé and La Rochefoucauld; and so, for that
matter, were the novels attributed to Madame de La Fayette. If we add
to this already imposing library the collections of poetry composed for a
society steeped in conversation (La Fontaines's *Fables* are the masterpiece
of this genre), the plays, the individual poems which were read, judged,
and discussed first of all by "good society," there is no denying that this

oral milieu was simultaneously the foyer of invention and of reception for whole chapters—and some of the most brilliant chapters—in French literature.

These remarks bring us back to Madame de Staël's comment about the indispensable prerequisite for French conversation: its exemplary practitioners are "educated." They treat conversation as one of the "liberal arts" because they also regard reading as a liberal art in itself. These elite conversationalists are neither orators nor writers nor professionally learned readers. The spirit that presides over their exchanges is incompatible with the pedantry of the specialist. And yet they are not amateurs. "Nothing can equal," writes Madame de Staël, "the charm of a story told by a witty and well-bred Frenchman. He anticipates every contingency and is careful not to offend, and yet will not sacrifice an iota of whatever may stimulate his listeners' interest. His physiognomy, less pronounced than that of Italians, indicates lightness of heart but sacrifices nothing of his dignity of bearing and manners. He stops at just the right moment and never tires even an amused audience. . . . Soon, his listeners are induced to join in the conversation and he is careful to direct attention to the merits of those who have just been applauding him, he never lets a happy turn of phrase go uncomplimented, or a piquant pleasantry pass unacknowledged, and at least for a while, regard is mutual, and all take equal pleasure in each other's contributions, as if concord, unity and sympathy reigned throughout the world."[11]

These artists of the spoken word do not speak like books, but with all that they have heard, they are widely read, and it is on the basis of that social and musical resonance that they judge books. Although they are immersed in a society of the written and printed word, their oral usage of language is still more exacting, more concerned with the precise turn of phrase, than professional writers may be at their writing desks. The pleasure of listening in a society full of gourmets of the spoken word takes precedence over any "pleasure of the text." In order to survive, the French literary text had to borrow an overt oral quality, the harmonious sound of the spoken work addressed to someone and "heard" by the reader as if he were involved in an absorbing verbal discussion.

One is led, as a result, to consider conversation no longer from the viewpoint of political philosophy, as did Madame de Staël, but in terms of a literary poetics and rhetoric. But how exactly do the latter differ from their counterparts in oratory? The true poet, like the true writer, never addresses himself to a crowd (Hugo does, alas!). Both create with their reader a singular and personal intimacy, and what becomes wonderful about reading in such cases is the certainty for so many readers that they have entered into a private conversation with a partner who speaks personally to each one of them. In that sense, the boundary between literature and various oratorical genres reflects the dividing line between conversation and eloquence, between official and private life. What is true of all literature is especially true of France which, in spite of Proust and to Sainte-Beuve's credit, is more deeply rooted than any other in conversation and conversational groups. That is why one is tempted, in France, to remain faithful to the platonic form that we assigned to conversation, to consider conversation as a literary genre encompassing a host of oral microgenres (the epigram, the lively anecdote, the stichomythic exchange of repartee) and written genres (correspondences, memoirs, novels set in the framework of a dialogue or marked by the tone of the spoken word—even the various genres of occasional poems). But conversation is also an *amphibious* genre, since it plays on two registers, the oral and the written: verbal improvisation and reading and writing. In short, it is an *encyclopedic* genre, for conversation in the platonic tradition, like true literature, treats *de omni re scibili et quibusdam aliis,* from grammar to criticism, from politics to metaphysics, from news or gossip items to moral philosophy. To bridge the gap between the *Symposium* or the *Phaedra* on the one hand, and *The Courtier* of Castiglione or the salon of Madame de Rambouillet on the other, let us propose Montaigne's *Essais* as a modern French model for conversation. Through all its vast improvisation, whether dictated or written down, the *Essais* retain the spontaneity, the friendly tone, the unpredictable rambling of a familiar Socratic conversation, not just with the reader, who is already for Montaigne, "my double, my brother," but with the noble society of the ancients: the philosophers, poets, and heroes, who, thanks to Montaigne, are no longer books but participants in a wide-ranging and quite fascinating conversation. The *Essais* are made up of a multiplicity of genres (moral, educational, poetic, and theological treatises, textual commentaries, portraits and epigrams, reflections on language and style) which transport the reader into a "lecture" and an "experience" replete with humanity, a symposium of wisdom from which he will emerge less unhappy and more mature. As a collection of readings that unfold like an uninterrupted conversation, the *Essais* anticipate the discussions of the seventeenth century "honnêtes gens" for whom they will serve as a breviary. And there is another model at the other end of the century: Bayle's *Dictionnaire,* masterpiece of the Republic of Letters, an international community of men of learning who through travel, encounter, correspondence, and exchanges with peers keep the European literary community alive and fertile. Every article in the dictionary is an essay in which notes and notes to the notes proliferate in a concentric fashion, introducing the reader into a vast council of skepticism where sages, philosophers, theologians, and philologists, from antiquity to the age of humanism, are assembled and engage in lively discussion. Bayle has constructed an immense shell filled with learned conversation in which a transhistorical library of Alexandria finds its voice again in a *Concordia discors* that is fated never to conclude its debate. The Republic of Letters found in Bayle its Montaigne just as fashionable, modern, and literate society had found in Montaigne its Bayle. The two great works present certain analogies. Out of a spiral of conversation, they fashion the interpretative funnel through which all the resources of speech are brought together to reward and harmonize the recurrent aporia of thought and action. Their authors are the scribes who, summarizing this collective meditation and concentrating it in written form, allow it to be both preserved and renewed. Just as the *Essais* were the model for superior conversation in France throughout the classical age, Bayle's dictionary serves as a cornucopia for superior conversation in the Europe of the Enlightenment.

For the purposes of analysis, the political and literary aspects of conversation and the circles in which it flourished can and should be studied separately. In fact however, the two cannot really be dissociated. Simultaneously heuristic, eristic, and hermeneutic, conversation allows politics access to the diplomacy of mind and spirit that we call literature, a comprehensive critique of human language and behavior, an all-encompassing *confrontation* of thoughts and passions. It introduces into politics the interpretative distance, the finely tuned perspective which alone can make it in some way liberal. Conversely, the proximity of politics keeps conversation alert, in perilous contact with human drama while at the same time distanced enough to be reflective and recognize its precedents. Functioning as a seamless literary genre in which the written and the spoken word, current events and collective memory are intertwined, conversation, both in Paris and in Europe, is simultaneously civilization's political gyroscope and its raison d'être.

I. The Advent of French Conversation

Conversation. Neither the word nor the phenomenon has been French from the dawn of time. At least, not in the form in which they became legendary and attracted the scrutiny of Madame de Staël in *Dix années d'exil*: "There have been men who owe their entire education to the lively and serious discussions in which noblemen and men of letters took part."[12] And again, in *De l'Allemagne*: "The truly liberal object of conversation is to be found in the ideas and facts that are of general interest. . . . A pleasant chat, even if it is about nothing in particular and which owes its charm simply to the elegance of its expression, still gives a great deal of pleasure; one can assert without undue presumption that the French are almost alone in being capable of such an exchange. It is a perilous but exciting exercise in which one has to play with every subject as with a ball that, when thrown, must be returned in time to the hand of the player who threw it."[13]

When did these conversations between nobles and men of letters, this *jeu de paume* of the mind become part of the Parisian way of life? We know the answer: under Louis XIII. The first Parisian "salons"—of the Calvinist Madame des Loges and the Catholic Madame de Rambouillet—were formed as early as 1615. But one should not be in too much of a hurry to limit Parisian conversation to fashionable society. In many ways, conversation among men of learning—which excluded members of the *noblesse d'épée,* simply because they were not erudite—continued in Paris a tradition that goes back to the *sermo convivialis* of antiquity[14] and the *politia literaria* of the Renaissance.[15] The circle formed by the Dupuy brothers, which met every day in the library of the Président de Thou, was frequented by Parisians and by their provincial peers as well as foreign visitors passing through the French capital. Superior magistrates and diplomats, men of the stature of Peiresc or Grotius, could also be found there, the nerve center of the erudite Republic of Letters for the whole of Europe and the focal point of a network of correspondence which allowed Dutchmen and Italians, Englishmen and Germans, to meet and mingle. Using channels opened up by the Jesuits and their missionaries, seconded by Peiresc and his correspondents, this encyclopedic network reached out beyond the frontiers of Europe to become its living, working memory. The conversations of these learned men who frequently held offices at court were as well regulated and civilized as those of the noblest society, and as free of ceremony and pedantry. If they lacked some of the refinements of gallantry, they were armed against the sophistries of fashion. This erudite tradition, alien to the spirit of the salon, would be maintained under Louis XIV and throughout the eighteenth century. In the nineteenth century, it was reborn with Delécluze and in the coterie surrounding Sainte-Beuve, Taine, or Renan.

It is however undeniable that for Europe as a whole, French conversation became identified with its most fashionable version. As early as 1700, the triumph of the moderns put the crowning touches to its dominion. From then on, in place of the learned conversation which would always escape its grasp, the fashionable sphere would annex the conversation of the "modern thinkers" that the Fontenelles, the d'Alemberts, and the Buffons had no scruple according it.

The birth of that empire, under Louis XIII, coincides with the emergence of a stable court in Paris and a new language, "reformed" by Malherbe, the poet who had conferred on Madame de Rambouillet her

Figure 8.2
Angelo Decembrio, *De politia literaria*. On this wood engraving from 1540, the ideal of the cooperation of spirits in humanist studies, a Last Supper in which the Eucharist is the book.

pastoral name, Arthénice, and whose *Oeuvres* were published in a collection by Godeau in 1630. The *Lettres* of Guez de Balzac, marking the reformed "Malherbian" prose epistle, had appeared in 1624. The word "conversation" itself, borrowed from the French translation of the *Civil conversazione* of Stefano Guazzo, which first appeared in 1579, began to be used in fashionable circles in a modern sense very different from that of the Latin *conversatio*.[16] The town residences of the aristocracy adopted an interior plan better suited to entertaining society. The arts and manners of the table reflected the ordered splendor of these hospitable dwellings. But does it necessarily follow that the court was the origin and the model for this new "civility of manners"? It kept, to be sure, the higher ranks of the nobility in Paris, and it was from the ranks of this court aristocracy which had read *L'Astrée* and Montaigne's *Essais* that Madame de Rambouillet, the Princesse de Condé, the Comtesse de Soissons chose their guests. But under Louis XIII, the court was still subjected to turbulences not entirely suited to the verbal *jeu de paume* between nobles and men of letters which, according to Madame de Staël, constitutes the essence of true conversation. Such conversation was the province of the town, not the court. It was not the king, Louis XIII (whom Madame de Rambouillet found both coarse and dull), nor court protocol—traditionally very lax in France and destined to remain so until Louis XIV—that could serve either as arbiter or model for this elegant sport. It took a few great ladies, in their own residences, to inculcate into a number of handpicked guests the ethics, the tone, the *fair play* of conversation; it took their authority and the gallantry that was their due, modeled on the nymphs in *L'Astrée*, to per-

Figure 8.3
Abraham Bosse, *L'Ouïe*. Polite conversation, under Louis XIII, is a quest for harmony between spirits. The chamber concert, with no listeners other than the instrumentalists, is one of the most precise metaphors.

suade the two "teams" of this great game—nobles and men of letters—to agree in fictitious equality to compare their talents and vie with each other in the art of great conversation. The court remained close at hand, but it figured as the object of conversation and not its venue. Admittedly, the practice acquired at leisure on private ground would have its uses both in the exchanges and the negotiations at court. Every treatise on the courtier includes a chapter on how to speak well at court, how to flatter gracefully, and how, tactfully, to make a good impression.[17] But this combination of rhetoric and vested interest did not constitute conversation, which could flower only outside the world of business. Its true climate, liberated and relaxed, was to be found only amid the leisure and the delights of private dwellings, where one became simply part of a group chosen by a hostess more concerned with harmony than hierarchy. All the literary myths that form the symbolic architecture of these conversational assemblies— the Happy Isles, Arcadia, the Platonic Symposium—are myths of a life of noble leisure, at some remove from the worlds of commerce and public life. Town and country, each in its own privileged sites, provided a counterpoint to the court. But private life was not a hidden life. It was still a stage, though of a different order from that of the court. To be numbered among the elect of the Hôtel de Rambouillet was a greater honor for a nobleman, even a great nobleman, than recognition at court, from as early on as the reign of Louis XIII and the Regency of Anne of Austria. In the same way (but how much more!) for men of letters, this distinction was felt to be a privilege beyond price: from its inception, the academy was stocked with familiar guests of the Chambre bleue.

For a young man intent on his career—even in the church—his presentation in the marquise's salon counted for just as much as his presentation at court. It was in that salon that Bossuet would preach the first sermon of his brilliant Parisian career, even before preaching the Lenten sermons at the Louvre. As Bossuet delivered the sermon in question well into the night, Voltaire quipped, "I have never heard anyone preach either so early or so late." For her circle, Madame de Rambouillet exercised a kind of royalty that Madame de Lambert would rediscover in 1690, but that both Madame du Plessis-Guénégaud and, to a lesser extent, Mademoiselle de Scudéry had already inherited from her in the days of Fouquet and Colbert.

The setting for fashionable conversation was thus established: the reception rooms, or possibly the garden, of a private residence. Its moment was established too: the leisure hours. This game between equals also had a referee: its hostess. Fashionable conversation projected into the private urban setting of the salon, the alcove, the supper, a literary scenario—that of Petrarch and Laura, the "lovers" of the pastoral novel, distant heirs of the Socrates-Diotima couple in *The Symposium*—and attributed to the noble hostess a role as *compass* for the speech and behaviour of the men who "submit to her authority." The *Introduction à la vie dévote* by François de Sales, published in 1607, adopted this Neoplatonic scenario, gave it a name, and made it a model for the ladies of the Catholic aristocracy.[18] The "Philotée" whose spiritual director was the Bishop of Geneva (and Mme de Rambouillet was a "Philotée") is a wife and mother, an active participant in society, but thanks to her inner life (prayer, meditation, reading), she escapes its vices. Indeed, she even sees her worldly existence as something of a mission. Her charm, her smile, her words are a means to raise up those about her—and above all the men she has chosen for her circle—to Christian civility. In other words, just like the nymphs and shepherdesses of *L'Astrée,* she imposes moral and aesthetic rules on the conversation that circulates around her.

It is worthwhile pausing a moment to consider the influence exercised by a number of women from the highest ranks of the nobility on the development of a truly Parisian social scene. French conversation was

CONVERSATIONS.

Figure 8.4

Frontispiece of the *Conversations* of Mademoiselle de Scudéry (new edition, 1710), engraved by Sébastien Leclerc. The "galerie," largely open on the outside, garden and park, was one of the favorite places for conversation and literary leisure during the Renaissance. The "salon" was a version of it.

not satisfied with merely bringing together for the purposes of verbal exchange nobles and men of letters in accordance with Mme de Staël's definition. These exchanges were made possible only by the presence of a third party: the feminine equivalent of the *honnête homme*. In the great families of France, the noblewoman enjoyed the advantage of an authentically feminine tradition in education whose roots extended far back into the past: Christine de Pisan's *Cité des dames*, to cite one worthy example, or the *Instruction* devised by Anne de Beaujeu for her daughter's edification.[19] Reinvigorated by the Italian Renaissance, this tradition found in seventeenth-century France a favorable terrain enhanced by the zeal of the Catholic Reformation and the women's religious orders that it revived or created. Feminine pride, so roundly attacked by both learned and scurrilous opponents, found in this tradition a means of justifying itself. On the one hand, it claimed the certainty of a distinct feminine nature whose model was the Virgin. On the other, it fostered the habit of translating into specifically feminine terms arts which gave form to that nature. Rhetoric, ethics, moral theology, spirituality—the entire encyclopedia of Christian humanism was absorbed by the feminine educational milieu and adopted, with an infinite number of nuances, by women for the benefit of other women. Exceptional mothers in the great families of France became involved in an educational task which was almost always secret, or at least much less explicit than the education of boys. Jeanne de Schomberg, Duchesse de Liancourt (whose fashionable literary circle flourished under Louis XIII and the Regency) was the author of a handwritten *Règlement,* written for her granddaughter, the future wife of La Rochefoucauld.

A number of the women who presided over the noble households of the ancien régime such as Mme de Lambert, author of *Avis d'une mère à sa fille*; Mme d'Épinay, author of *Conversations d'Emilie*; and Mme de Genlis, author of *Adèle et Théodore,* also undertook the education of their daughters. Mme de Rambouillet and Mme de Sévigné were tied to their daughters by the strongest of all bonds: pedagogy. Mme de Necker made her daughter, Mme de Staël, her unquestioned masterpiece. All of these mothers were also—and the two are not unrelated—incomparable partners in polite conversation. In the concert of the great Parisian salons, these women's voices, formed by women, take their part equally and harmoniously with those of noblemen and men of letters. Taking different paths, Natalie Zemon Davis[20] and Paule Constant have drawn attention to these feminine sodalities as a feature of the ancien régime, which served as a testing ground for young ladies about to enter into matrimony or make their entry into society. One of the subtlest traits of François de Sales's *Introduction*, and of Honoré d'Urfé's *L'Astrée,* is the exquisite sense that the great spiritual advisor and the novelist had of feminine modesty, the refinement of manners from which it naturally evolves and from which men profit by mere proximity. The priest in Saint-François, the courtly nobleman and Platonist poet in d'Urfé, feel a profound sympathy for this feminine delicacy in which they rightly see a major civilizing force. French conversation is a space for play, which makes possible the *repons* between masculine and feminine voices and fashions from what we call *esprit* the point at which they sound a perfect chord. It is highly probable that this masterpiece of nature allied to culture owed its harmony to the musical element of its composition, freeing it from any asperity it might otherwise have had. This social art, like the garden of Akadémos, is not without its Muses.

Malherbe's pedagogy completed the groundwork established by François de Sales and Honoré d'Urfé, taking as its subject the language of polite conversation itself, where women found themselves in their element. Even when their education extended to reading and writing or to the rudiments of humanism, it was rare for women to have had any instruction in Latin or Greek. In a sense, it was to them that the tradition of the mother tongue became entrusted, since it was often clouded for men of letters by their cult of the learned languages; and as for noblemen, their language was more readily corrupted by the familiarity of the countryside and military encampments. Malherbe, the "court grammarian," raised to the status of rules the decency and delicacy of speech so dear to the shepherdesses of *L'Astrée* and the devout ladies of Saint-François. Out of the choice of words and their euphony he made both a law and a subject of fashionable conversation.[21] The "Malherbian" man of letters (reestablishing the link with Guillaume de Lorris and Marot) became in his way the accomplice and privileged partner of the "honnête femme" as an arbiter of the very terms in which French conversation was conducted. After Malherbe, it was Voiture who set the tone in the Chambre bleue, in perfect harmony with Arthénice/Mme de Rambouillet. But this duo allowed room for all sorts of variations and vocal harmonies. Other men of letters, with different temperaments and styles, vied with Voiture: the Chapelains, the Racans, the Godeaux, spoke in their own voice, the register deeper or higher, the tempo slower or quicker as the case may be, but always in tune with their hostess. She, in turn, drew into the company her daughters and female friends, who supported and modulated her own voice. All these participants were musicians, and one of the beauties of Mme de Rambouillet's salon, the "lioness," Mlle Paulet, a repentant sinner, was also one of the great singers of the period.

The noblemen, her guests, played the lute, danced, sang every bit as well as they handled a sword: they too had read *L'Astrée* and could recite

Malherbe or Voiture by heart. In this setting, they found themselves in a
magnetic field whose two poles were exceptional women and equally exceptional men of letters. They educated and reeducated each other. This
high academy of French *esprit* was the best possible training ground for
the various ambushes, devious intrigues, and conflicting ambitions they
would encounter at court. It trained the most formidable courtiers and
thus contributed, perhaps, to the subordination of the higher nobility to
absolute monarchy. But let us not digress: "fashionable society" and its
conversation were no more the court than the conversation of Socrates
was the agora. Born of the leisure enjoyed by the nobles, the salon was a
leisure society, steeped in a utopia at once Arcadian and academic. It was
social intercourse detached from family ties, rank, or profession, an intense acting-out of literary roles. And thus the conversation of the Hôtel
de Rambouillet (and the most distinguished of its satellites) quickly became a laboratory for literary language, its *bon usage* first established orally
and by reciprocal correction. It speedily gained recognition as the tribunal
of "good taste," whether in matters of poetry, prose, or the theater. The
value of words, like that of books, was determined first and foremost in
the community of fashionable conversation, which was thus granted the
privilege of testing both their wisdom and their power. Under Louis XIII,
we are still talking about books in French, Italian, or Spanish. Ambition
and scope are still modest. Discussion rarely goes beyond matters of utility and enjoyment. But Cartesianism, Jansenism, and even the Epicur-
ism of Gassendi brought before the tribunal of fashionable conversation
philosophical, scientific, and theological works written in French as early
as the Fronde. The privilege claimed by erudite circles, which held fast
to their monopoly as supreme arbiters of works of learning and science,
began to be eroded, and men and women of fashion, undeterred by their
limitations, began to insist on having the last word. Descartes, in his *Discours de la méthode* (1637) actually invited them to do so,[22] and since they
were the guardians of good oral usage, their opinions, elegantly formulated, held sway.

These opinions even end up in the eighteenth century being regarded
as authoritative in matters of economics and politics. But we should not
forget that this community, whose judgments issued from its exchanges,
was above all a pedagogical community of a very unusual type, very effective and yet not without grave defects. Conversation was not only the
principal practice for the "school of fashionable society"; it was also its
method. In that sense, this community was both a remote descendant of
the Platonic Academy and a close relative of the Académie française. What
it taught above all was proper usage in the spoken word. Vaugelas in his
Remarques sur la langue française defined proper linguistic usage in terms of

a restricted number of speakers: "the most reliable part of the court." One can, with some confidence, delineate quite clearly the frontiers of this legislative linguistic body: the Hôtel de Rambouillet and its allies, the Hôtel de Condé, the Hôtel de Soissons, the circle about Henriette d'Angleterre, in short, the conversation of the most distinguished social sphere. In relation to this legislative body, the academy acted as a kind of court of registry or appeal. In the highest society, in the most select circles, good usage was both learned and determined. It was a self-regulatory critical movement but primarily an oral movement. The men of letters, those who wrote professionally, were active conversational participants. It was this verbal participation of literary practitioners that gave rise to the asymptote peculiar to French letters between what was deemed "natural" in the spoken French of high society and what was felt to be "natural" in the written language of literature. Such at any rate was the tone of French classicism which one readily detects in the first comedies of Corneille, in Pascal, Racine, and La Bruyère, and which is also documented in the *Mémoires* of Retz and the *Lettres* of Mme de Sévigné. This refinement of speech and elegance of style, midway between what one hears and what one reads, bespoke continuous exchanges regulating and relating the spheres of conversation, theatrical dialogue, poetry and prose readings, all subject to the test of being read aloud in public.

The test was all the more severe in that the conversation of the best society, because its partners were members of the French noblesse d'épée, was a verbal sport modeled on the nobles' favorite sports: hunting, fencing. These virile games were characterized by liveliness, terseness, variety, and surprise. "If I'm engaged in debate with a partner of strong will and robust jousting skills," writes Montaigne, "he puts pressure on my flanks, lunges to my right and to my left; his power of imagination fans mine. Jealousy, fame, competitiveness urge me on and raise me to heights I could not have reached on my own. And this kind of unison is not unwelcome in debate."[23]

This keenly fought tournament, this dialectical duel which assumed a sporting model, was merciless on the mediocre. It raised champions, schooled by the *moralistes*. La Rochefoucauld, the Molière of *Le Misanthrope*, La Bruyère, to mention only the most celebrated among them, tracked down the vices and spiritual falsehoods which perverted the sporting nature of the dialogue and undermined its success: *esprit*. "Our mistrustfulness," writes La Rochefoucauld, "justifies the deception of others."[24] "Love, delightful as it is, endears itself more by the manner in which it is made manifest than for its own sake."[25] Knowing oneself and those against whom one was matched was essential to the proper conduct of these duels. Weaknesses in conversational style—obscurity, ponderousness, pomposity,

contrivance, affectation—were also seen as symptoms of a deficient mind. "Naturalness," the ideal to which classical discussion aspires, supposed robust moral health and a readiness to interact with others. This affinity with the true was the basis of the concept of *gens d'esprit*.

But the school of high society, precisely because of its liberal character, because it relied on the self-criticism and self-discipline that an entire milieu required of its members, was exposed to the dangers of excess or divagation. Among these the most famous was "preciosity." It is difficult to know where "precious conversation" began and where it ended. There is abundant testimony on the subject but its interpretation is still a matter of dispute. The temptation is there to give preciosity (the absence of naturalness, the jargon of a clique) a narrow sociological basis. In the milieus of the higher judiciary and the upper middle class, the privilege of social leisure, outside the domestic circle, was restricted to men. This was true of Paris and it was still more true in the provinces. At the point at which the impact of the aristocratic salons became widespread, sisterhoods of women stifled by their narrow milieu claimed for themselves the same liberty as the ladies of the nobility and found male sycophants and boudoir *abbés* to support them. Absolute mistresses of conversation in their own homes, they defiantly cultivated, some have suggested, an exclusively feminine art of sophistry, featuring ethereal affectation of expression, drawn-out metaphor, hyperbole, and the allegorization of emotion. These first femi-

Figure 8.5
Rubens, *Le Jardin d'amour* (detail). In this composition, Rubens depicted the myth of "gallant conversation" in French, which Watteau recaptured in *Embarquement pour Cythère*. The gods of love and creativity, in a park that is always green, accompany the choreography of a wedding dance.

nists, in other words, sought to make their mark by prudishly annexing stylistic expression. They upset in their favor the natural classical triad of the conversational circle: great ladies, noblemen, and men of letters.

That triad brought women into its jousts. In the early comedies of Corneille, in the *Maximes* of La Rochefoucauld, in the *Mémoires* of Retz, in the *Mémoires de Gramont* of Anthony Hamilton, one can still hear the quick sounds of cut and thrust, charged with irony, to which women were potentially attuned. It is to this boldness that the *Lettres* and the poetry of Voiture owe their value, and it is to be supposed that the *Rey chiquito,* the favorite of the Marquise de Rambouillet, set the tone in her salon in harmony with the warlike spirit of noblemen who were off campaigning with the start of spring, and who even in their winter leisure in society looked for trouble and dangerous games. The tone of high society under Louis XIII and Louis XIV was sharply competitive. But even in Mme de Rambouillet's circle, the Marquis de Montausier submitted to the lengthy bondage that preceded his marriage to the *précieuse* Julie d'Angennes, Arthénice's eldest daughter, and took care to collect the chapelet of vapid gallantries which became in 1634 the *Guirlande de Julie.* In reality, preciosity was as much an essential element of fashionable conversation as sophistry had been of the Platonic dialogues, exaggerated rather than invented by other circles outside the aristocracy. Significant traces can be detected in the "Marguerites" that had flourished at the court of Nérac among the en-

tourage of the Queen of Navarre; they reappear at the martial court of
Henri IV. Nevertheless the *Mémoires* of Marguerite de Valois were seen,
quite rightly, in the seventeenth century as a masterpiece of natural, truly
elegant prose. Preciosity appeared and reappeared every time the duel between male wits, fiery-spirited noblemen, and well-read men of letters
ceased to provide the scaffolding for conversation and had to give way to
the ingenious artifices and conventions of gallantry. It is difficult, in these
lively exchanges from Corneille's *Mélite* to distinguish between the part
played by male fencing and the part played by the *comédie galante*:

> TIRCIS
> Si le Coeur ne dédit ce que la bouche exprime,
> Et ne fait de l'amour une meilleure estime,
> Je plains les malheureux à qui vous en donnez,
> Comme en d'étranges maux par leur sort destinés.
>
> MELITE
> Ce reproche sans cause inopiné m'étonne,
> Je ne reçois d'amour, je n'en donne à personne.
> Les moyens de donner ce que je n'eus jamais?[26]

Saint-Evremond, taking up an expression of Ninon de Lenclos, called
the *précieuses* the "Jansenists of Love." It was women above all who forced
his men to submit to the *carte du Tendre* and to lace their speech with sentiment. The opponents of preciosity, such as Molière or Boileau, were
resolutely antifeminist. Both aspired to be the Socrates of conversation.
For them, even amid the gallantry and politeness of a society in which
women were loved and appreciated, the "natural," the "true" in language
and style implied a substantial dose of "manly vigor." The feminization
of conversation and fashionable writing would resurface under the Regency as *marivaudage*. And the Revolution provides a striking revenge of
manly virtue and male eloquence over the supple graces of the sopranos
and the high-pitched chatter that marked salon conversation during the
ancien régime. Even Mme de Staël, the great restorer of conversation after
Thermidor, set herself sharply apart from the delicate *douceur de vivre* of
the prerevolutionary salons by an almost male amplitude of voice as well
as the power of her eloquence. Learned conversation, successor to the
conversation and banquets of antiquity among men, sought its harmonies
of discourse in a deeper bass register. Aristocratic conversation, caught
between the perils of pedantry and preciosity, inclined toward the latter.
The conservative authority of noble society, reinforced by the greatest
"sages" among the men of letters, struggled to limit the peril and keep it

contained within marginal circles. And by no means always successfully. *Animus* and *Anima*, the masculine and the feminine, meet in battle on the field of noble leisure, where *Animus* is obliged to lay down his arms and yield to the insidious lures of *Anima*. Off the battlefield, aristocratic principle, weakened by fashionable manners, oscillates between honor and gallantry. This is the conflict that illuminates the drama of French letters, wavering between competing feelings for the language: the first, vigorously "paternal," is inspired by its Latin ancestry, the other by the "maternal" qualities of French, a language deemed by Montaigne to be wanting in the vigor of the ancients and established even by Malherbe as a melodious *douceur* that could easily degenerate into vapidity and affectation. One of the stakes of French conversation under the ancien régime was its musical key, which determined not only word and gesture but also the *tempo* of the dialogue. Brought up to admire the "naturalness" of the great French classical writings, we are apt to forget that they represent a rare conquest, a hard-won equilibrium in a world in which fashion inclined toward precious sophistry. The abbés Cotin, de Villiers, and their kind, ladies such as Mme Deshoulières and Mme de Villedieu, and writers like Pradon and Benserade were more attuned to the spirit of the age than Pierre Corneille (who yielded to it on occasion) or Molière, Racine, and La Fontaine (who was not impervious to the sirens' song). The classical period echoes with the harsh or bitter reproaches that writers like Ménage and Furetière, or even Bussy-Rabutin and Saint-Evremond (the real sages and arbiters) address to the "foibles of the age"—the invasion of the French academy by favorites of the fashionable *marquis, abbés de cour,* and *précieuses*. An amphibious genre, conversation regulated both verbal sociability and the written and printed works which secured its approval or alternatively, provided its sustenance. Precious conversation, in spite of the counterattack of the *Précieuses ridicules,* was excessively common in the seventeenth century, both in Paris and in the provinces. Molière himself admits as much in his *Critique de l'école des femmes*. Natural conversation and the works it endorsed and which sustained it were the exception, not the rule.

II. FROM THE AGE OF ENLIGHTENMENT TO THE REVOLUTION

At the beginning of the eighteenth century, a school of fashion—with its distinctions and its champions of both sexes—held sway in Parisian society. It was an extremely strange school, judged by the criteria that have prevailed for so long in our culture. Its sole aim was to train what it called *esprit* and to exercise it through play. *Esprit* supposed intelligence, and even a kind of genius, for the Latin word *ingenium* (which is related to *ingenuus,* well-born, of free birth) confers on both a common semantic origin. In a *Discours* addressed to a lady, the Chevalier de Méré defined *esprit* as a gift and as an art of thinking and speaking that is simultaneously precise and pointed, spontaneous and playful, whatever the circumstances or the conversational partners.[27] Socrates' particular *daimon* was more indebted to his inspired sense of this art than to all of Gorgias's rhetoric. This social ideal, the most difficult of all to attain, lost none of its relevance in the eighteenth century. Toward that end, nurtured by both natural and artistic components, the school of fashion added the finishing touch to a small elite of literary figures and nobles, completing their preparatory education at the *collège* and the *couvent.* On the feminine side, the education of young ladies of noble birth had never demanded or received so much care. Fénelon devoted a treatise to it. Mme de Maintenon, who was well aware of the role of women in the school of fashion, added Saint-Cyr, a semi-lay institution, to the convents of the Ursulines and Visitandines in which well-born young ladies were educated. As for men of letters, the academy system, established or perfected by Louis XIV and Colbert, mapped out a path to honors accessible to a wide range of talents. For nobles and those aspiring to nobility, the court of Louis XIV and Louis XV taught boldness in the use of language. Men of letters, noblemen, and male members of the upper middle ranks all received to a greater or lesser extent the education dispensed by the Jesuits of the Collège Louis-le-Grand, who were simultaneously masters of dramatic art and dance and professors of rhetoric. Example and worldly symbiosis effected the transition from learned eloquence to spontaneous wit. Neither convent, collège, nor court, the school of fashion (the word "school" should be understood in the sense that Molière gave it in *L'École des femmes,* that of the Greek *scholé,* a leisure milieu conferring freedom) brought together in genuine conversation, far from the constraints of court, institutes of learning, or the church, the "well-born" men and women—by blood, talent, or fortune—of every profession and of every age. Ease of manner and variety, the *beau feu* kindled by each in turn to dispel even the merest hint of boredom—these were the agreeable dictates of this co-opted society. Mme de Maintenon may well have reigned at court and at Saint-Cyr, but it was Mme de Lambert, whose salon opened its doors as early as 1690, who reigned over the school of good society. The Chambre bleue was a rough and ready affair compared with Mme de Lambert's *hôtel.* But much the same can be said in comparing the academy where Fontenelle was the permanent secretary to that of Valentin Conrart.

The formal progress was quite dazzling, as was the harmony among the various cogs of a delicate mechanism devoted to the selection and exercise of an intellectual and spiritual elite. Though it may well have been politically and economically a monster, the ancien régime turned ever more perfectly around its apex, which was not royalty but *esprit*. The latter extended to the court, but its true flint was the school of good society, where it created sparks only for its peers and their pleasure.

Adorned by the presence of illustrious prelates and great nobles, enjoying the patronage of the king, the Académie française published its *Dictionnaire* in 1691, and in spite of Furetière, established its authority as an arbiter of good linguistic usage. Good and elegant linguistic usage is of course one of the proofs of cultural development, one of the principle criteria of its superiority. Closely cooperating with the academy, the salon of Mme Lambert was a veritable fishpond in which men of letters learned elegance of language from the nobles and the ladies of fashion and in return nourished their conversation. It is there that literary reputations were tested, before being consecrated by the academy. A dominant figure of the school of fashion, spiritual mother to the literary church, Mme de Lambert would maintain her de facto authority for nearly half a century, until her death in 1723. Mme de Tencin then became her almost official successor, and after her, a kind of dynasty, revered throughout Europe, viewed as rivals and successors Mme Geoffrin and Mme du Deffand, Mlle de Lespinasse and Mme d'Épinay, the Maréchale de Luxembourg and the Maréchale de Beauvau, Mme Helvetius and Mme Necker. It was a kingdom within a kingdom. We imagine it as something familiar, but in reality it is as mysterious for us as the courts of ancient China or Japan. The eighteenth century's most complete artists came from its circles: the others, together with the finest craftsmen of luxury, were there for their recreation. Nor should we forget the literary and philosophical cafés in which men met each other: there is still nothing of the bohemian nineteenth century about these encounters. Both in manners and in their cult of wit and intellect, they remain within the orbit of the most polished conversational circles, the wonder of Europe, with nothing prudish, constrained, or conventional about them.[28] Mme de Lambert knew that she had become, as she had always wanted to be, the *Diotima* of the school of fashion, heir to Mme de Rambouillet and Henriette de France. She writes in her *Réflexions*: "One emerged from these houses as from some Platonic banquet which nourished and fortified the soul."[29] In her eyes, conversation represented a communal search for perfection, a way of gaining knowledge about oneself and others, about manners and customs, language and gesture. For so grand and exhaustive an enterprise, no effort was too great when it came to the selection of its finest exemplars.

The teachers taught each other by example and by symbiosis, not by formal lessons. And what they taught was an indefinable something which conveyed the atmosphere and taste of the best society and which therefore supposed, even among debutants and foreigners, an already remarkable degree of polish. It was a school of higher learning where teachers and pupils, both past and present, were provisionally admitted as equals; the "recycling" was permanent. Mme de Lambert received guests two days a week, Tuesdays and Wednesdays. For each of these days, the program was different and the guests not always the same. In its time, her salon represented a veritable institution as harmonious as—though less formal than—the privy council or the academy. Hénault, who was present on both days, recalled in his *Mémoirs* the timetable of the Tuesday gatherings, to which only persons of the highest distinction (less in terms of rank than of literary authority or social prestige) were admitted:

> It was the obligatory path to the Académie française; works about to be published were first read there. On one day a week there was a dinner, and the whole afternoon was employed in academic discussion. But in the evening, the *décor* would change as well as the actors. For the most gallant company, Mme de Lambert would give a champagne supper.[30]

On such occasions, men and women of the best social circles would take their places at table beside the academicians and future academicians. Around a candlelit banquet, with all the trappings of luxury, men of letters moved from academic to more gallant conversation. The Wednesday suppers included, in addition to some of the Tuesday set, artists, foreign virtuosi and scholars of lesser eminence.

Fontenelle was to Mme de Lambert what Voiture was to Mme de Rambouillet, but this time the poet, author, and conversationalist was also a representative of "the new science," the permanent secretary of three academies, including the Academy of Sciences. In his *Entretiens*, this champion of the moderns displayed to the full his talents as a teacher of Cartesian science to the great ladies and the good society over which they reigned. He was at the center of a new encyclopedia, from which humanistic erudition had been trimmed and which tempered the Cartesian method and cosmology with lively literary wit and elegance. Fontenelle reconciled the precious *églogue* and the *Discours de la méthode*. But language and literature, even as they served as mediators between the new science and fashionable society, were still the principal concern of Mme de Lambert's salon as well as the primary educational bond of its society. Père Bouhours, the oracle of good French usage and an expert on literary taste and wit, had frequented Mme de Lambert's salon from 1698 to 1702 and had found gathered there that "soundest kernel of the court" which, according to Vaugelas, was the living oral arbiter of good French taste.

The "chosen few" taking part in the conversations in Mme de Lambert's salon were selected instinctively with a care which, by calculating the mix of attributes (age, sex, rank, profession) of good Parisian society, cut down the margin of error with greater subtlety than present-day methods of opinion polls. The opinion at issue here was the judgment to be pronounced on literary and artistic merit and the reputations of their authors, but also on the words, the turns of phrase, the forms of expression, the style befitting the best spoken and written French. This informal school was also a tribunal, and it is precisely because it functioned as a tribunal that it was so effective a school. But however much subtlety was employed to facilitate this conversation, its subtlety introduced a margin of error. It was Mme de Rambouillet's salon that begat "preciosity." The salon of Mme de Lambert (who was herself well aware of the danger) engendered a variant which was denounced in 1726 in Desfontaines's *Dictionnaire néologique*, a work which was very favorably received.[31] Members of Mme de Lambert's circle—Fontenelle, Houdart de la Mothe, the young Marivaux—were to be counted among the vanguard of the *nouveaux précieux* denounced by Desfontaines. The very crucible of good linguistic usage became itself a source of corruption, threatening the health of the language and by extension, the foundations of thought itself. Even so, we can appreciate the extent and the limit to which a single salon could wield so much authority, since the linguistic mannerism that had taken root there—together with the literary works governed and approved by it—were seen as a source of considerable harm and inspired, as did the original preciosity, a Socratic form of criticism attracting strong support. However great the authority of any one salon, even one championed by Fontenelle, it could not impose a dogma accepted without question. This *querelle* was sufficiently fierce to force Marivaux on the occasion of a new edition to correct, as too full of "neologisms," the prose of his *Spectateur*.[32] Such self-criticism is not without precedent. When La Fontaine wrote in 1660:

> Now not one step away from Nature
> *Is to be taken*

he was disavowing his earlier "precious" ventures. Marivaux's conversion was less complete. Voltaire, faithful to Boileau, detested not only Marivaux's manner, but also the conversational school from which it had evolved. Voltaire's irony was the counterpart and complement to the grand style of his tragedies. The delicate humor of Marivaux's web-like analyses, much less naive than the hyperbolical earnestness of the original preciosity, was no less scrupulously attentive to the sophisticated complexities of a femininity which Voltaire was willing to acknowledge but not to serve.

Marivaux was on the side of women and the moderns. Even if we cannot hear the voices and the remarks exchanged in Mme de Lambert's salon, we encounter them in their theatrical form in the stylized exchanges of her guest's comedies or in the subtle analyses of his novels. This is the spirit of the conversational "school," interpreted by its greatest and most original master.

> THE COUNTESS: That's a most unruly love you have there. It is in quite a hurry.
>
> THE CHEVALIER: That is not my fault; it is as you gave it me.
>
> THE COUNTESS: Well then, let's see. What is it that you want?
>
> THE CHEVALIER: You to love me.
>
> THE COUNTESS: Well, well! You'll just have to live in hope.
>
> THE CHEVALIER: Not me! I'll not embark upon hope. I am not going to be stranded in a unfamiliar country. I shouldn't know in which direction I was walking.
>
> THE COUNTESS: Just go on walking; you won't be led astray.
>
> THE CHEVALIER: Let your heart go with me on my journey and then I'll set off.
>
> THE COUNTESS: Mmm. I don't know that we should go very far together.
>
> THE CHEVALIER: Ah! And what leads you to that conclusion?
>
> THE COUNTESS: It's because I think you fickle.
>
> THE CHEVALIER: For a moment there, I felt some apprehension. I thought you suspected me of something far more serious. But the cause your concern is merely fickleness, then let us be on our way; when you know me better that's one defect of which you won't have to complain. (*La Fausse Suivante* 3.8)

Allegorized sentiment, as in the *Roman de la rose* (*amour, mutin, pressé*), bold metaphors linking the abstract with the concrete (*me jeter dans l'espérance*), metaphors sustained from one exchange to the next (*marche, voyage, embarquement pour Cythère*), all these are what Desfontaines derides as "neologisms" and that Voltaire describes in a celebrated formula as "metaphysics of the heart," or still more cruelly, referring to the *Serments indiscrets*: "A great deal of metaphysics and little that is natural: the café crowd will applaud while people of sense will find it meaningless." The world of Marivaux is exactly that of Shakespeare's *Love's Labours Lost*, which is set in a French court, and in which the "heavenly rhetoric" (4.3.57) inspired by women's eyes triumphs over the Platonic "Little Academy" (1.1.13): a place of peace and contemplation, that the noblemen and the King of Navarre would have liked to find in the world of men. To listen to Marivaux is to hear once again the harmony, the melody, the ingenuity of voices now stilled: the talk of the more "gallant" guests at Mme de Lambert's suppers. To listen to the *Fables* of La Fontaine is to hear once more the tone and turn of phrase, the tart Epicureanism and courtly charm of conversation at the home of Mme de La Sablière. It is thus that the high fidelity of literary texts preserve, if not the letter, at least the spirit of these circles, which sought indeed to be "islands of the blessed," with a Muse at their center who conducted the choir and kept the voices in harmony. None of them exhausted the music of the language; each made a choice which quite properly attracted its critics. All the same, they did each invent a "school of music" ("music," for the Greeks was a word used to sum up the highest form of liberal education) in which moral insight, delicacy of manners and politeness, the art of speaking well formed a "style" of being that several masterpieces have, here and there, fixed on the page for all time. In these works, the Sophists and Socrates continued their dialogue in the language of Malherbe.

Every family, every milieu, under the ancien régime had its own linguistic tradition and its own style of conversational French. The language was alive, full of variety, unlike the Latin used by scholars that teaching and the *collèges* had standardized and ossified. The fashionable salon, unlike the assemblies of humanists brought up on Latin, was a melting pot in which various styles of a living language sought in dialogue a superior harmony, particularly between feminine and masculine styles, between heart and mind, a polarity quite unknown to the learned. Paris perfected a kind of parliament regulating speech throughout the kingdom. This parliament was held in check by two different bodies: the Académie française, which took on a senatorial role, and the moralists and grammarians excluded by these two "rhetorical chambers" who knew how to appeal to public opinion. The regulation of French language and style under the ancien régime, even if centralized in Paris, was never absolutist: the linguistic parliament resembled the English parliamentary institution that Montesquieu and Voltaire admired, and like its English model, it was customary law. From the reign of Louis XIV, stylists like Ménage and Furetière, the former shunned by the Académie, the latter excluded in 1690, countered the fashionable and erudite norms by invoking language's "memory," its etymology and its "good sense" established by a much greater host of practitioners throughout the kingdom, both past and present.

Ménage used to say, "One is always a child in one's language when one reads only contemporary authors and speaks only the language of the nursery. More clarity and sublimity are granted speech when one can follow the genealogy of the terms one is using. And how is that possible unless one reads the Ancients in their own tongue?"[33] The *mercredis* of Gilles

Ménage, gatherings of men and of philologists, thus became the critical observatory of the fashionable usage which the academy confined itself to recording. The *Observations sur la langue française* published by the great linguist in 1671 are a safeguard against the narrowness and fallacies of a purely fashionable conception of good usage. The "ana" collections (Scaligerana, 1666; Menagiana, 1693; Furetierana, 1696; Santoliana, 1708; Huetiana, 1722) gather together the remarks and recommendations made during these learned discussions; these often deal with questions of language, of style, and thus constitute in print a counterweight to fashionable conversation.[34] Not a very effective counterweight: learned philologists of the stature of Étienne Pasquier, Gilles Ménage, Pierre-Daniel Huet, and their like became scarce, and the "ana" ceased in the course of the eighteenth century to count as learned works, becoming little more than amusing compilations.

Historical, erudite philosophy, which favored a memory for good usage, ceded its place to another kind of learned grammar, whose teachings the logicians of Port-Royal, Arnauld, Lancelot, and Nicole had established as early as the reign of Louis XIV. It is this "general" grammar that informs the *Encyclopedia* of Diderot and d'Alembert and would be dogma for the Ideologues and the *doctrinaires*.

It separates premeditated written style from that collective and oral improvisation which, for Vaugelas and for Bouhours, for Ménage as for Furetière, was still the ultimate test of elegant language and natural style. Port-Royal (but without Pascal) was responsible for the intellectualization of speech, for the loss of the lively oral naiveté of French conversation. But in the eighteenth century, conversation's empire was still so great that the flashes of inspired wit, even in the case of the encyclopedists Diderot, Suard, or Morellet, triumphed over the Cartesian theory of rational grammar and logic of the Solitaires. The bons mots, the quips that neatly capture a sudden inspiration, which arise spontaneously from the stimulating sense of well-being sparked by a society of keen talents, which strike the memory and excite the imagination, contribute to the slight feeling of intoxication without which there is no real conversation. The eighteenth-century aphorisms, collected in the form of ana, repeated all over Europe, fill entire volumes. Fontenelle, learning that his opera was in danger of being banned by the Archbishop of Paris because it contained a chorus of priests, retorted, "I don't interfere with his clergy, why should he interfere with mine?" To M. de Chaulnes, wondering aloud how to have his portrait painted to match his wife, portrayed as Hébé, Mlle Quinault quips, "Have yourself painted as hébété" (bewildered). Montesquieu, referring to a friend with whom he has quarreled, warns, "You must never believe me when I speak ill of him." These deft plays on meaning turn a figure of speech, a word, a syllable into an epigram, invariably piquant and sometimes attaining a genuine moral propensity, even at the expense of the person who formulates it, which is the ultimate elegance.[35] The political skirmishers moved quite naturally onto this terrain, both the great nobles and the common people, who clearly loved their satirical *chansons*. The Maréchale du Luxembourg provides a case in point: hearing of some new favors granted by Louis XV to Mme du Barry, she whispered an even more ingenious string of puns into the ear of the Prince de Ligne: "There are obviously only three virtues in France, vertuchou, vertubleu, and vertugadin." These private witticisms made their way to the court and played a part in the affairs of state. Louis XVI, whose love of the chase is well known, affected to mistake the names of "all these economists Turgot, Mirabeau, Baudeau," for those of his hounds, whose names "Miraut," "Briffaut," and so forth rhyme with theirs.[36]

But this attic salt is more at home or more dangerous in the city, and Rousseau himself felt obliged to pay tribute to the quality of Parisian conversation, to the harmony created out of the various ingredients which gave it its savor: "The tone of the conversation flows naturally. It is neither heavy nor frivolous, it is learned without pedantry, lively without being strident, polite without affectation, gallant without fatuity, playful but not dubious. One hears neither dissertations nor epigrams. Reasoning is free of arguments and humor from wordplay: wit and reason are skillfully united together with maxims and witticisms, pointed satire, adroit flattery, and austere morality."[37]

Naturalness as Boileau, Molière, and Voltaire understood it would appear then to have triumphed, in spite of the temptations of preciosity, thanks to the subtle play of checks and balances that regulates the forms of discussion among men of letters and men of fashion. A vast normative literature, already abundant in the seventeenth century with writers like Méré, Scudéry,[38] Vaumorière,[39] sustains the rules governing the art of conversation, which the ambient philosophy transformed into a discipline for ensuring social well-being.

And yet this school of fashionable society, which all of Europe imitated or dreamed of frequenting, is exposed to one dissenting voice. Rousseau was not content to be the Molière, or even the Socrates, of French conversation: after having himself excited the curiosity of the Parisian salons, he became their Diogenes. Not that the citizen of Geneva, except in his final *Rêveries*, challenges the fundamental principles of conversation or its educative function, in keeping with the nature of man who is born for society, born for speech. But he saw how conversation had become institutionalized in Paris, an artificial construct, harmful alike to genuine political life and the truth of private feelings—indeed to truth itself. For the

French moralists, preciosity was no more than a deviation to be corrected. For Rousseau, Parisian society and its conversation were essentially pure sophistry. His criticisms are first sketched out in the two *Discours* (1750–55) in which he aligns himself with the position adopted by the *anciens* in their famous quarrel with the *modernes*, but using a new and far more radical line of reasoning. The whole of "modern" civilization, seen as a betrayal of both nature and virtue, is called to account before a tribunal constituted by an antiquity which Rousseau rejuvenated by associating it with the "noble savages" made prominent by the new science of ethnology. These two impassioned attacks revived the memory, dormant since the sixteenth century, of Cato the Elder's eloquence and the Peasant from the Danube. And even before proposing, in *Émile* (1762), a program of education which would be a preparation neither for court nor for society, but for a life of natural virtue uncorrupted by those foyers of modernity, Rousseau used the device of fiction to destroy the prestige of French conversation even in the minds of the ladies who believed they reigned there as its queens (*La Nouvelle Héloïse*, 1761). Modern society was corrupt, but man was naturally good. The charm that Rousseau was prepared to acknowledge in the manners of modern society par excellence, French society, was thus in his eyes all the more corrupt and corrupting. Until society was regenerated by the *Contrat*, no real health or happiness was to be found outside of small groups of uncorrupted but informed friends far from Paris, far even from any town. Rousseau was rediscovering here the great myth at the origin of conversation: Arcady. *La Nouvelle Héloïse* sets out for us the genesis, at the margins of corrupt modernity, of a little Arcady. It was to be sought halfway between Paris and Geneva. In Paris, Saint-Preux discovers the French style of conversation: "The French," he writes, "are naturally good, open, hospitable, charitable."[40] Good French society seems to him at first to be a kind of flowering of those natural virtues. A more careful analysis reveals to him, underneath the appearance of harmonious cooperation, a rigged stage for versatile and hypocritical sophists. In France the community of speakers betrayed nature, drew a veil over the ferocity of a war in which everyone was opposed to everyone else, and encouraged its perpetuation.

In Geneva, on the other hand, as Claire, another character in *La Nouvelle Héloïse* observes, the natural goodness of the inhabitants goes hand in hand with the most direct candor. The corruption of nature by society assumes more naive, more rough-edged forms until one finds oneself missing the outward politeness of the French. In Geneva, one feels the influence of the trading nations of the North, which, like England, separate men from women, making conversation substantive but at the same time pedantic and slow. "Whereas the French write as they speak, the citizens

Figure 8.6
Watteau, *La Conversation*, 1712–13. Watteau made "gallant conversation" a genre in itself, a common pictorial place. Dance, music, greenery, hazy atmosphere, many visual metaphors in that delicious but fleeting harmony between young friends and lovers.

of Geneva speak as they write. They hold forth instead of conversing."[41] In Claire's eyes, they have no feeling for correct usage or tone, and the language they speak lacks the melody that the Parisian sophists are able to give theirs. Decline is thus everywhere, even if it is more seductive in Paris. In the little Arcady of Clarens, the heroes of *La Nouvelle Héloïse* finally succeed in weaving, through trial and error, a web of conversation which is authentically of their own creation and not an artifice forced on them by social custom. This success is achieved at the price of wrenching sacrifices in the domain of both the senses and the heart. A tragedy, the death of Julie, will bring it to a close. But in certain letters of Saint-Preux to "milord Edouard," in the fifth book, some sort of ideal is momentarily reached. In this ideal conversation, the contemplative silence of mornings spent in the English fashion "sharing in the silence, savoring at the same time the pleasure of being together and the tranquillity of meditation" alternate with long discussions in which Julie, Saint-Preux, and M. de Wolmar think aloud and by means of shared reflection tackle the great problem so dear to Rousseau's heart: the moral education of children and the way to preserve their naturalness without making them unfit for society as it is. Julie, an exemplary mother, warming to the subject, forges a personal eloquence which seeks equally to avoid the pedantry of Geneva and French *esprit*: "The organ of truth," she says, "the worthiest organ in man, the one that distinguishes him from the animals, was not given him for him to fail in making better use of it than they do of their cries. He puts himself beneath them when he speaks to say nothing and man must remain true to himself even in his less public moments. The proper way to behave in society, the way that makes us cherished and sought after, is not so much to shine ourselves as to make others shine and by our modesty to give freer rein to their sense of pride."[42]

It is as if we were already listening to the warm, enthusiastic voice of the nineteenth century's schoolmistress, Mme de Staël. Julie's doctrine does indeed seem, at first sight, to coincide with that of the classicists and to confront once again the sophistry of Paris in the name of "the natural" and "the true." On closer examination, one sees that its aim was to perfect citizens who would be both virtuous and thoughtful, even in their moment of relaxation, citizens of a primitive Rome, in which no distinction would be made between private and public life. Paradoxically, this was a project that could only take root in the small circle of Clarens—as private and sheltered a group as ever was. As a force for regeneration—as Rousseau himself was well aware—the fiction of *La Nouvelle Héloïse* could not supplant the *Contrat social*. The premature utopia of Clarens ends in tragedy. And yet the philosopher wrote these pages during one of the happiest and most fertile periods of his life, at the Hermitage in the grounds of La Chevrette, where he was the guest of Mme d'Épinay. "It is there," wrote Diderot, "that one finds peace, friendship, gaiety, freedom, pleasure, happiness."[43] The latter himself, according to Mme d'Épinay, was the "creative genius" of the circle that gathered around her in the countryside. "He shakes his torch over our heads and the result may be one thing or another depending on whom the sparks fall."[44] Duclos and Grimm, Saint-Lambert and his friend Mme d'Houdetot (with whom Rousseau fell passionately in love) were members of her circle.

Mme d'Épinay was a musician; Jully, her brother, a painter, engraver, and collector of antiques with which he decorated the château. The châtelaine maintained a copious correspondence with the Abbé Galiani and with Catherine the Great, and it was under her roof that the first oral drafts of many of the articles for the *Encyclopédie* were formulated, as well as many of the installments of Grimm's *Correspondance littéraire*. Diderot, who was often present, enlivened the salon: "One yielded to the seduction of his conversation for hours on end" wrote Abbé Morellet, "as if carried on a clear and gentle stream, with banks in a rich countryside adorned by handsome dwellings."[45] In his letters to Sophie Volland, the philosopher gave the following description of an afternoon at La Chevrette:

> Over by the window which looks out on the garden, Grimm was having his portrait painted and Mme d'Épinay was leaning on the back of the painter's chair. Seated lower on a stool someone was sketching his profile in pencil. In one corner, M. de Saint-Lambert was reading the latest brochure I sent you. I was playing chess with Mme d'Houdetot. That kind and venerable lady, Mme d'Esclavelles, Mme d'Épinay's mother, was surrounded by her children and was chatting with them and their tutors. Two sisters of the person who was painting my friend were doing embroidery, one with the cloth in her hand, the other using a frame. And a third was trying out a piece by Scarlatti on the harpsichord [. . .]. After dinner, we had a little music.[46]

The gracious simplicity of this scene is perhaps the most enchanting legacy left us by eighteenth-century France. In a leisured existence, in music, in beauty, the conversation of Diderot and his friends became a verbal literary workshop, a cornucopia of letters, essays, articles, books. Rousseau is absent from this tableau. He was not far off, however, when he conceived the ideal society of Clarens. The Swiss genius, profoundly imbued with northern pietism and in love with the music of Italy, found his style cramped in Parisian conversation—even when it was transported to the countryside.

Nor was he to be seen at the home of his fellow citizen of Geneva, Suzanne Curchod, who after her marriage to Jacques Necker in 1765 opened a salon in Paris, rue Michel-le-Comte in the Marais. This salon became as famous as those of Mme Geoffrin or Mme du Deffand. Diderot, Grimm, Marmontel, d'Alembert, Suard, Morellet were frequent guests. It also welcomed foreign politicians and diplomats when Necker, first at the "hôtel Le Blanc," then as controller-general of finance, became one of the most important people in the kingdom. Mme Necker's salon coincides with the period when *La Nouvelle Héloïse*, published in 1761, was having its greatest impact. One of the most intimate members of the circle was Antoine-Léonard Thomas, who, when elected to the Académie française in 1766, introduced to that body a version of the noble civic rhetoric re-invented by Rousseau, attenuated only by the majesty of its eulogy.

That acceptance speech, which provoked a scandal, was entitled "De l'homme de lettres considéré comme citoyen," and it took place in the same year that Germaine (future Baronne de Staël) was born. The major works that were "launched" by readings in Mme Necker's salon—Bernardin de Saint-Pierre's *Paul et Virginie*, Buffon's *Époque de la nature*—bear the imprint of Rousseau's genius. In her *Pensées et mélanges*, which were to be published in 1798, Mme Necker proves to be a faithful disciple of the ideas on conversation found in *La Nouvelle Héloïse*. She writes, for example: "I admit that there is more virtue in Switzerland than in Paris, but it is only in Paris that virtue is spoken of with elegance and wit. Virtue is like the Delos Apollo who pronounced his oracles only from a cave into whose depths no ray of sunlight had ever penetrated."[47] This Geneva-born reformer of Parisian conversation brought up her daughter in the spirit of Jean-Jacques and it was Germaine de Staël, an indefatigable traveler and cosmopolitan, who was destined to invent what one might call romantic conversation, simultaneously literary, philosophical, eloquent, and militant, born of the conversation of the Encyclopédistes, but above all marked by Rousseau. This is the oral genre that dominated the Europe of the Holy Alliance, that allowed it, with the help of music, to sustain a dialogue in spite of the nationalist passions that stirred and divided it. The common point of reference was no longer wit and decorum in the French fashion, but the natural "I," full of the conviction that an inspired assembly of noble spirits would regenerate by the spoken word the corrupted cities around them. From the world of Fontenelle, we have passed to that of Rousseau.

III. The Nineteenth Century

1. Conversation: A Nineteenth-Century Myth

In her slapdash *Histoire des salons de Paris*,[48] a repository nonetheless, like Tallemant's *Historiettes*, of a vast oral tradition, the Duchesse Abrantès created one of the great motifs of the romantic narrative, taken up in turn by Balzac and Barbey d'Aurevilly: the negative aspect of conversation, conversation as terror. She devotes to it two of her best chapters, which read like genuine news items, "Une lecture chez Robespierre" and "Le Salon de Robespierre." From antiquity until 1793, conversation, whether it was philosophical or sophisticated, learned or purely social, always had something in common with the banquet: the pleasure of being in company. Mlle de Scudéry had even invented the expression *esprit de joie* in order to define simultaneously the atmosphere and the ultimate goal of conversation in the context of aristocratic leisure. Mme d'Abrantès tells of a pleasant dinner at the home of Robespierre on June 18, 1794, with Danton and Saint-Just; the lively cut and thrust of argument and counterargument seems, almost as an oversight, to fuse with the decision to arrest and execute the very worthy Mme de Saint-Amaranthe and her daughter, the very lovely and very young Mlle de Sartines. The Duchesse d'Abrantès names Tallien as the source for a story of another evening at the home of the Incorruptible. Among those present were Hébert, Danton, David, Mme Lapalud, and the enchanting Mme Desmoulins. Camille Desmoulins was reading his play *Emilie ou l'Innocence vengée*, in accordance with a literary rite that dates back as far as the Hôtel de Rambouillet. "This gathering of men steeped in blood, listening to a work of art, and smiling at the voice of one of their number as he spoke of daybreak, the peace of the countryside, and the tranquillity of a clear conscience. A curious spectacle that was. What thoughts must they not have harbored in their souls as they listened to these peaceful words, worthy of Arcady, spoken in the Tiger's den, while his lips were still red from gorging on the human blood he had shed in the course of the day. . . . This reading took place shortly before the tragic end of the hapless Camille [. . .]. The monster touched his forehead with a bloody finger and his head had to fall."[49]

The Happy Isle of conversation was now a dreadful trap. Arcady itself was employed by Hell as an alibi and a bait. Mme d'Abrantès ends with a nightmare vision:

> No doubt during the reign of the Terror, there was no longer in
> France what we call "Society," but the elements of which it was
> made were not quite lost. During this period when the town houses
> were deserted, when mansions were barred at eight in the evening,
> the only surroundings for people to chat, for laughter, were the Lux-
> embourg prisons, the Carmelite monastery, or Saint-Lazare, where
> the only people who were able to talk and who understood the art of
> conversation could be found.[50]

This was the story of Acis and Galatea, of Paolo and Francesca, recast on the scale of an entire city, an entire civilization. Conversation was confined to a dungeon, where heads destined for the guillotine, where wit, elegance, and leisure nobly employed, were buried in the *Carceri* of Piranese. In a few months, in a few words, the disciples of Rousseau, erecting the scaffolding of a new modernity that their master had not foreseen, cut down the last practitioners of the great leisure art, however "modern" in its day. The curtain fell in a rain of blood (Barbey's *Rideau cramoisi*) both on the stage depicting *la douceur de vivre* and on the actors themselves. It is true that the nineteenth century, a century of politics and industry, would attempt to reconstitute "society," to revive conversation, but against an overpowering background of doubt, of mourning, of *what's the use?* Or even worse, with an effort of will and a sense of duty which put the finishing touches to the abolition of charm. The two mainsprings of conversation, apart from the natural human propensity to speech and to dialogue, were the two orders of leisured aristocracy: the nobility and the clergy. The nobility then had to struggle to survive politically and economically. The church after the Revolution was mauled, hurting, and embittered. Its figurehead was no longer François de Sales, but Mennais. The nineteenth century middle-class for its part had no gift for leisure. The conventions of "respectability" made it dull and ponderous. On every side, grace vanished without trace. The sense of play, the sense of equality among the players was difficult to find in a society driven by egalitarian resentment. Looking for conversation, the ordinary bourgeois everyman at best encountered discussion. He was afraid of wit, he preferred genius, which, though different from middle-class respectability, was not playful either. The nineteenth century, even in France, was dreadfully serious.

It is at this point that conversation became a place of memory, a somewhat funereal object of reverence and hagiography. It ceased to be an art, which calls for ease and grace; it was in the process of becoming a commemoration, a perpetual anniversary mass. In 1825, Count Roederer, a former representative of the revolutionary convention but in no way a regicide, published a historical study in honor of the Marquise de Rambouillet and the Chambre bleue: *Mémoires pour servir à l'histoire de la société polie en France.*[51] This was a ponderous act of reparation, dealing not with the eighteenth century (still banished from the public mind, as it would be until the time of the Second Empire and the Goncourts) but with the period of Louis XIII, which the Restoration looked on with favor. It was the start of a vast literary enterprise under the July Monarchy, at which Victor Cousin (an indefatigable apologist for the conversational muses of the *Grand Siècle*), Mlle de Scudéry, Mme de Longueville and above all Sainte-Beuve would excel. As early as 1829, in a portrait of Mme de Sévigné, the great critic articulated the central theme of all his works: literary France was inseparable from the spirit of conversation. He writes:

> Our critics and especially those from abroad, who have lately been passing the harshest of judgments on our two centuries of literature, are unanimous in recognizing that the dominant factor throughout that period, reflected in a thousand different ways, what provided its splendor and its adornment, was the spirit of conversation, the feel-

ing for society, the harmony between men and the world, the acute
awareness of what was acceptable in society and what was ridiculous,
the rarified delicacy of sentiments, the grace, the piquancy, the refined polish of language. Such is, indeed (with the reservations that
everyone makes, two or three names such as Bossuet and Montesquieu that are taken for granted), the distinctive characteristic, the
defining feature of French literature among the literatures of Europe.
That glory, with which our nation has almost been reproached, lacks
neither fecundity nor beauty for anyone who can understand and interpret it.[52]

Mme de Sévigné provided the crowning moment of this French
trait. But Sainte-Beuve refused to bury beneath her example the merits
of Mme Necker and her daughter Mme de Staël, the mothers of conversation in postrevolutionary "society." "Mme de Staël," he writes, "represents
a whole new society, Mme de Sévigné a society that has vanished, hence
the enormous differences between the two."[53] And he adds: "Today, noble
society, which has best preserved the leisurely habits of the last two centuries, seems to have been able to do so only at the expense of remaining
a stranger to the manners and ideas of the present day." "One is all the
more delighted," he writes in a note, "to revel in these postseasonal rarities
which have the flavor of a second coming, and a mystery."[54] In a portrait
of the Duchesse de Duras, published in 1834, he focuses on the contrast
between such exquisite but autumnal survivals and the high-mindedness
of a new conversational regime in Paris:

> There existed [during the Restoration] between the studious and
> doctrinaire circles—thoughtful, high-minded and above all pro-
> ductive—and those that were purely aristocratic and irresponsible,
> a very distinct gap, a divorce as stubborn as it was complete: on the
> one hand, enlightenment, modern ideas and on the other, the charm
> of days gone by separated by differing pretentions and reciprocal
> disdain.[55]

On both sides something was grating. The old chamber music (which
sounded false and modern to Rousseau's ears) had fallen silent. And for
that very reason the process of mythologizing it had become more nostalgic and more idealized. In 1842, Mme Ancelot dedicated to Mme Récamier a comedy entitled *L'Hôtel de Rambouillet,* performed at the Théâtre
du Vaudeville that her husband directed. The play recounts the origins of
the Chambre bleue. Mme Ancelot took as many liberties with chronology and historical verisimilitude as Dumas did in *The Three Musketeers.*

She was less concerned with history than with the myth that had haunted Parisian society since Roederer and condensed and schematized in order to idealize more effectively. Tallemant des Réaux (who in fact knew the marquise only in old age and retirement) is presented as the inventor of a project for creating a salon, to which Mme de Rambouillet finally gave her assent as a last resort. We recognize here the theme so dear to Mme de Staël: "Fame for a woman is mourning for happiness." Here is the project as expounded by its "inventor" in Mme Ancelot's play:

> An exclusive salon where wit is to be appreciated, talent recognized, and good taste promoted will serve the interests of every person of distinction and make French society the model for all others. But an empire of the intellect requires a queen. And that queen has to be witty, for no one reigns long anywhere without wit. She must be elegant and gracious since, in France, no lady finds more than momentary favor if her taste is suspect. She has to be as wise as she is beautiful, for otherwise she would be carried away by love. Love occupies so much room in a woman's life that it does not leave much for anything else! Young, virtuous, and witty, the Marquise de Rambouillet is perhaps our only hope.[56]

This Louis-Philippe version of Arthénice was nevertheless tempted by a disreputable young man, the Marquis Henri de Sévigné. It was not until the very young Marie de Rabutin-Chantal has married the marquis that Mme de Rambouillet could make up her mind to prefer the innocent pleasures of organizing a salon to a passion she rejected. In this way, three great myths: the Chambre bleue, the great epistolary writer Mme de Sévigné, and Mme de Lafayette's *Princesse de Clèves*, were fused into a single plot in order to create the model Parisian hostess. Sung interludes (the *vaudevilles*) introduced an element of fancy into this sentimental comedy, which foreshadowed, from a considerable distance, the period pieces of Sacha Guitry. Mme Ancelot, moreover, joined Mme d'Abrantès in the task of chronicling the salons of the Restoration in a book, *Les Salons de Paris: Foyers éteints* (1835), that even the austere Tocqueville enjoyed. With a talent for painting later to be shared by Madeleine Lemaire, she exhibited in the Salon of 1828 a group portrait entitled *Une lecture de M. Ancelot*. In another book published in 1866, *Un salon de Paris, de 1824 à 1864*, she relied on the reproduction of four of her group portraits (depicting her own salon under four different regimes: the Restoration, July Monarchy, Second Republic, and Second Empire) to represent "bouquets" of personalities and proffer moral reflections on conversation. The nostalgic evocation of the Restoration is particularly fervent:

A host of houses opened on a given day, once a week, made it possible to meet with the same persons, so often that life was one great
succession of conversations in which ideas were suggested and discussed. Business was never mentioned and the word money was not
admitted [. . .]. A Pléiade of great poets, great painters, great writers
of every kind lit up the intellectual world in which we lived and in
which we thought of nothing but our happiness.[57]

The tableau that deals with the July Monarchy represents Rachel reading aloud the part of Hermione in *Andromaque* before an invited audience
of guests which included Chateaubriand and Mme Récamier. The revival
of the *douceur de vivre* is decidedly compromised: "Who would contribute,
in the homes of the few cultivated women who still find a certain pleasure in interesting conversation, these too rare elements of society, if not
men of learning accustomed to an austere and studious life?"[58] And Mme
Ancelot cited Jouffroy and Tocqueville among the most indispensable participants, during Guizot's ministry, in the life of a salon.

The salons had apparently returned to life and with them conversation. To former legends, piously revived, new ones were added, with
Mme d'Abrantès, Mme Ancelot, or Sainte-Beuve serving as enthusiastic
or learned commentators: Mme Duras's salon, the Arsenal of Charles Nodier and his daughter Marie, even the salon of Mme Guizot (Pauline de
Meulan), studied at length by Sainte-Beuve. Sainte-Beuve analyzes with
notable finesse the correspondence between the tone of these salons and
the style of the literary works which proliferated during the Restoration
and were conceived or at least appreciated in them. He rightly sees the
fiction of Mme de Duras, like the moral essays of Pauline de Meulan, as
efflorescences of the spirit of conversation that, thanks to them, prevailed
in their own salons. Sainte-Beuve was swimming against the tide and
knew it. He never yielded, however, on the principle which for him was
France itself and for which Proust would so roundly denounce him: "At
no moment in his life does Sainte-Beuve appear to have had any profound
conception of literature; he situates it on the same plane as conversation."[59]
More precisely, for Sainte-Beuve, a French book was literary because it
was the written and thus durable echo chamber of a lettered society and its
voices, the spirit of which it preserved. It was up to the critic to rekindle
that spirit by reconnecting the written work to the milieu that gave birth
to it. Sainte-Beuve was never willing to admit that the communicating
vessels between literature and conversation had finally broken down. He
was caught in a trap. In conversation, *l'esprit de joie* and *l'esprit* pure and
simple were caught up together in the plenitude of the instant, here and
now. Capturing them on the page involved a repetition in the Kierke-

gaardian sense, a reflowering in the mind of the reader, not a melancholy commemoration. Sainte-Beuve was well aware of this, and that is why he took such pains to discover in his own era examples of what he took to be the essence of French literary felicity. Unfortunately for him, his era let him down, and to mask its shortcomings, he had to pass off as *esprit* what was all too often a spirit of earnestness, pedantry, or sentimentality. He became the principal witness of the nineteenth century's persevering but luckless quest for a conversation that continually escaped it. This quest kept the salons busy; it is active in the novel from Balzac to Bourget. It became the Holy Grail for a few unusual men who occasionally realized their aim: Talleyrand and Custine, Beyle and Mérimée. But the ancient caduceus was broken. The quest itself and the poor substitutes it accommodated are the object of increasing derision, visible in Flaubert and in Baudelaire and reaching truly Aristophanic proportions in *À la recherche du temps perdu,* which is simultaneously a web of conversations and an engine of war directed against conversation itself, the site of camphor-scented memories of a phantom aristocracy.

The genius of romanticism, so faithful to Rousseau, had defined itself from the outset in opposition to the spirit of conversation. Mme Ancelot, on Sainte-Beuve's side, tried in *Un salon de Paris* (1866) to restore the balance in favor of that spirit. She portrays Balzac—genius incarnate, holding forth in the salon of Mme d'Abrantès—as an overweight nincompoop, completely absorbed in himself, oscillating between lamentations and tirades. Unfortunately for her, whom can she propose as a corrective to Balzac? "M. Gozlan possesses what Balzac lacked, a capacity for conversation, full of charm, wit, and gaiety, squandering subtle and original ideas with a prodigality born of the confidence that he will always have riches to dispense without risking impoverishment."[60]

What adds yet more spice to the comparison, which Saint-Beuve might quite well have made, is the fact that Balzac himself had already made it: it was to Léon Gozlan that, in 1842, he dedicated the definitive version of *Autre étude de femme,* one of the *Scènes de la vie privées* devoted to the myth of Parisian conversation and constructed as long, nested conversations. Balzac is the most complete case in the nineteenth century of "genius" devoid of wit, although he devoted huge sections of his work to evoking with indefatigable enthusiasm the very aristocratic wit that he himself lacked. Masterpieces like *Une passion dans le désert* or *Les secrets de la princesse de Cadignan* succeed in communicating to the reader the fictitious experience of an intense conversational happiness beside which the letters of Mme de Sévigné or the *Contes* of Voltaire seem almost insipid. But it is the daydream of a starving man:

During that evening, chance had brought together a number of people whose undeniable talents had won them European reputations. This is by no means a piece of flattery addressed to France, for there were a number of foreigners among us. The men who shone most brightly, moreover, were not the most famous among them. Ingenious repartee, shrewd observations, delightful teasing, description drawn with dazzling clarity, sparkled in profusion and without contrivance, proliferating neither casually nor with conscious determination, but deliciously perceived and delicately savored. Those who belonged to the best society were conspicuous above all for a certain grace, a quite artistic verve. Elsewhere in Europe, you will encounter elegant manners, cordiality, warmth, learning, but only in Paris, in this salon and the others I have mentioned, will you find in abundance the kind of genius that makes an irresistible whole of all these social accomplishments, an impetuous flow that carries downstream this profusion of thought, formulation, anecdote, and documented history. Only Paris, the capital of taste, understands the skills involved in transforming a conversation into a joust where every kind of wit is condensed into an aphorism, in which each finds his own turn of phrase and converts his experience into a telling word, in which every one enjoys himself, relaxes and contributes [. . .] There, to sum up, everything is about wit, brilliance, and thought. Never before had I been so completely bewitched by the spoken word, which, when well studied and well managed enhances both the actor and the storyteller . . . As the conversation became anecdotal, it swept among in its tumultuous current strange confidences, a number of portraits, a thousand follies which made this enchanting improvisation altogether untranslatable while preserving the freshness of all these things, their abrupt spontaneity, their deceptive sinuosities, perhaps you can understand the charm of a French *soirée*, captured at the moment when its most congenial familiarity allows each participant to forget his interests, his particular conceit, or, if you will, his pretentions.[61]

Nothing is missing, in one of the most complete and profound descriptions ever given of the supreme French art; the purest aristocratic leisure, the confidence, the game both free and rigorously governed, *l'esprit de joie*. Within this magnetic field, Balzac conjures up the person and the voice of De Marsay, the prince of wit, the Talleyrand of the *Comédie humaine*, and this is the mask that Balzac the novelist puts on to give life, suspense, irony, and intoxication to his story. But it is clear that the novelist

Figure 8.7
Parceval de Grandmaison lisant des vers de son poème de Philippe Auguste, 1824, in *Madame Ancelot: Un salon de Paris*. This scene, painted by Madame Ancelot to illustrate her salon under the Restoration, shows Baour-Lormian, Victor Hugo, Alfred de Vigny, Delphine Gay (later Madame de Girardin). The "right" bourgeois stiffen romantic conversation.

Figure 8.8
Rachel récitant des vers du rôle d'Hermione dans la tragédie d'Andromaque, in *Madame Ancelot: Un salon de Paris*. In this group of celebrities assembled at the house of Madame Ancelot, under the July Monarchy, is Chateaubriand, de Tocqueville, and Madame Récamier. With Delphine Gay, Madame Ancelot was the most informed animator and chronicler of the "good society" of Paris under the Restoration and the July Monarchy. The salon conversation became, with these women, a conversation of good company.

himself as well as the reader he is addressing are exiled from paradise and must watch, as if through a window, like fascinated spectators, this feast of the gods.

Under the Second Empire, a gala regime for Parisian society, more homage than ever was paid to the myth of conversation. Every week, the *lundis* hosted by Sainte-Beuve revived its ceremonies. Describing its most modern version, Jules Janin recapitulated those of Mme de Staël, Sainte-Beuve, Balzac, and Mme Ancelot, while at the same time reducing, hardening, and vulgarizing them:

> To trace the history of conversation would be to write a universal history. Not every word issuing from the mouth of man qualifies as conversation. Conversation is the spoken word carried to a point of perfection, erudite and delicate; this is the speech of men in society, but a refined, elegant, well-ordered society; conversation is all that is superfluous in human speech. It is every word not uttered out of anger, ambition, vanity, or base passion; it is not a cry, it is not a threat, it is not a lament, it is not a request nor a prayer. Conversation is a kind, if capricious, murmur; erudite, amiable, caressing, mocking, poetic, always flattering, even in its sarcasms; it is a reciprocal courtesy extended by men toward one another; it is a separate language within a universal language, which uses many more vowels than consonants. It is a language everyone thinks he understands and speaks but that very few know how to understand and fewer still how to speak [. . .] It is in France above all that conversation is a feature of national pride.[62]

This definition appears to be general and even something we have heard before. It was in fact new: a Flaubertian platitude had been born. With this definition, conversation lost its natural foundation, on which all of Janin's predecessors insisted. If still a feature of national pride, conversation was now reduced to a social privilege. Not once does the word *esprit* appear in this article. Everything is geared to a code rather than to a game of words. The participants in the conversation are now no more than members of a clique, showing off to each other and knowing just how far they can go. Women and gallantry are no more in evidence than *esprit*. We are right in the middle of the nineteenth century, and artists and poets alike were on the verge of breaking definitively with a society capable only of poses which they found repugnant. The sense of pure leisure, the contemplative essence of conversation, forgotten or derided by the ambitious and the pretentious, found a refuge in the arts; formerly servants of the supreme Art, leisure and contemplation were now its last resort,

silent and spiritual. This is the significance of Manet's *Balcon,* Baudelaire's
L'Invitation au voyage. Fashionable conversation, powdered and mummified
by Jules Janin, was no longer a liberal art that made witty improvisation
a feast for aristocratic and cultivated natures, their "dance" as it were. It
was one speciality among others, at the service of all the others, a distinction proper to men of importance, to men of sound principles. The very
collection for which Janin's article was written, the *Dictionnaire de la conversation,* was a gross heresy. Bouvard and Pécuchet were not far off. This
"fat Plutarch" of the drawing room, in sixteen volumes, consecrated the
alliance between fashion and pedantry. It put the seal on an era of "stuffi-
ness" in conversation. Genuine wit would want no part of it, taking its
cue from context and improvisation. Janin himself noted the decline in
vivaciousness and, journalist that he was, saw its explanation in the ever-
widening scope of the press:

> Deprived from then on of its initial attractions by the newspapers:
> learning the political news, the latest from the world of literature,
> theatrical reviews, the most common incidents of life, even a street
> accident, conversation in France has struck out along new paths. It
> has become more serious, more settled, more learned. It has become
> concerned with all the progress and novelty that exceed the news-
> paper's grasp. It has found a formula all of its own, for judging, ap-
> proving, blaming, or applauding. Conversation, which is now both
> less rigid and less frivolous, has sought to find some of its daily nour-
> ishment in history and in science.[63]

Small wonder then if, as early as the Second Empire, artists, poets,
free spirits shunned the salons to gather in the cafés,[64] studios, or the kind
of indoor settings dear to Vuillard. This page of Léon Daudet sums up
the divorce:

> I propose this axiom: the café undoes the glories of the antecham-
> ber and the salon. The salon does not undo reputation, consecrated
> by the café [. . .] None of the *habitués* of the Café Weber in the rue
> Royale would have put up with Claudius Popelin or General Gallifet
> for five minutes, or, closer to our own time, the Vicomte d'Avenel,
> Gabriel Hanotaux, or Victor Du Bled. The café boor appears less
> scrubbed, soaped, and varnished than the salon boor; he retains his
> sharp edges, his highlights, his acerbities. Frequently, like a Roman
> victor, he hears himself saying: "You are a boor." Wit in the cafés is
> the real article and promptly rewarded by boisterous ringing laughter,
> whereas in the salon, it is still too often a pale imitation, a scrap of

tawdry finery, applauded, passed on, and drawn out by routine, conventional smiles. A counterfeit talent has no more currency in a café than a counterfeit coin. In short, the café is the school of frankness and spontaneous fun, whereas the salon, in general, is the school of pomposity and brainless fashion. The café has given us Verlaine the exquisite and Moréas the pure, the salon Robert de Montesquiou and countless Muses, as futile as they are laughable. I have no difficulty seeing Immortality as a lady behind the bar, making benevolent little signals to a few chosen customers.

At about half-past seven, a pale young man with doe eyes would arrive at Weber's, sucking at or chewing one half of his dark drooping moustache, wrapped up in woolens like a Chinese bibelot. He would ask for a bunch of grapes and a glass of water, declare that he had just got up, that he had a cold, that he was going back to bed, that the noise made him feel ill. He would cast around him anxious glances which soon turned mocking, and in the end he would burst into delighted laughter and stay. Then from his lips there would issue, in hesitant and breathless tones, remarks of extraordinary originality together with insights full of diabolical finesse. His highly original images reached the summit of people and things and enveloped them, like great music, just as they say used to happen at the Globe tavern, among the companions of the God-like Shakespeare. There was something of Mercutio about him and something of Puck as he pursued several lines of thought at the same time, dexterously apologizing for his amiable displays, tormented by ironic scruples, naturally complex, throbbing with energy and brimming with *joie de vivre*. This was the author of that highly original book, disconcerting at times and full of promise: *Du côté de chez Swann*. This was Marcel Proust.[65]

Mlle de Villeparisis and Mme Verdurin, exposed to the irony of Ariel, had already been annihilated and along with them, the myth of Mme de Rambouillet.

2. Two Muses of Romantic Conversation

Two extraordinary women, legends in their lifetime, had nevertheless done their best to bring back Parisian "society" and conversation after the 9th Thermidor: Mme Récamier and Mme de Staël.

The Revolution was the province of lawyers and orators before it became a military affair. The civic speech and heroic virtue it featured were a mortal challenge to the power of the idle ladies of the aristocracy and to the spirit of conversation which, around them and because of them, inspired both men of letters and men of fashion. Napoleon embodied more effectively than Robespierre this masculine genius, scornful of the feminine character of the ancien régime and its finesse. While he was boldly embarking on the restoration of court manners and protocols around his person, he persecuted Mme Récamier and Mme de Staël, who were trying to revive both salons and conversation in the capital.

The contrast between these two women, friends and allies though they were, was considerable. They had however certain traits in common. Both were from the provinces, one from Geneva, the other from Lyons; both were born into the bourgeoisie, one the daughter, the other the wife, of a banker. Though they both saw themselves attempting to link up with an earlier tradition, they created, each in her own way, two very different traditions that were in fact far removed from the ancien régime's art of noble leisure. That tradition, even in the most brilliant salons of the great ladies of the Restoration, was struggling to revive itself and found no afterlife except for a few isolated and gifted individuals, never at the level of an entire society. The companionable spirit of conversation had died in France with the fall of the two orders of aristocratic leisure: the nobility and the clergy. Mme Geoffrin was much less "middle class" than Mme Récamier; she was a bourgeoise in the mode of M. Jourdain, with a deep and intimate sense of what is to "live nobly," contributing to that vocation all her money, tact, and wits. Mme de Staël was opposed as a matter of principle to this humility of the bourgeois ego under the ancien régime.

The beauty of Juliette Bernard, who became Mme Récamier at the age of sixteen, on the fourth of April 1793, had as the story goes, attracted the attention of Marie-Antoinette as early as 1784.[66] Mme Récamier very cleverly turned to account the classic perfection of her figure, which conformed admirably to the taste of Louis XVI at the end of his life, and became a model for David while winning the admiring affection of Canova. A masterpiece of convent education: pious, precious, and a virgin in spite of her arranged marriage, she could play the part of a martyr in the cause of Christian virtue which had come back into fashion with the empire and which became obligatory under the two following regimes. Mme Ancelot, less naive than many of Mme Récamier's hagiographers, saw in her the embodiment of calculating femininity and concluded that she could have had no vocation for reestablishing a conversational art based on naturalness, gaiety, and open-heartedness.[67] A carefully orchestrated mirage, Mme Récamier appeared during the Directoire and Consulate years as a living Saint Cecilia, gathering about her an assortment of worshippers as varied as Adrien and Mathieu de Montmorency, the Bernadottes, the Massénas,

Eugène de Beauharnais, and even Bonaparte's brothers, Lucien and Louis. This resurgence of preciosity, thinly veiling political intrigues, irritated Napoleon. Mme Récamier was obliged on a number of occasions to remove herself from the capital. M. Récamier paid for his wife's intrigues: the emperor took steps to ruin him in 1806. In 1811, Juliette was formally exiled. In Lyons, before reaching Rome, she met Ballanche and found in him her duly accredited evangelist: under the names of Antigone and Eurydice, he did not cease singing her praises. In 1815 she reopened her salon in Paris, at the same time as Mme de Staël (whose exile at Coppet she had shared for a time), and it was at the bedside of her dying friend that, in 1817, she met Chateaubriand. In the course of the following year, she took up her final residence at the *Abbaye-aux-Bois,* a convent devoted to the education of young ladies since the days of the ancien régime.

In the reception room, Gérard's painting showing Mme de Staël as *Corinne au cap Misène* occupies the pride of place. There, in 1829, Chateaubriand read his *Moïse,* his only—but unsuccessful—attempt at a dramatic work. Antigone, who was about to go blind, had found her Oedipus. Under the July Monarchy, the main business of the abbey was reading aloud, installment by installment, the *Mémoires d'outre-tombe.* In this romantic foyer of the sublime, conversation was tuned to a concerted note of languishing melancholy. Ladies were not especially welcome. "At Mme Récamier's," wrote Mme Ancelot, "one was absolutely obliged to talk of fame and glory: the salon was a temple, where honors were divided between its hostess and Chateaubriand. One was perpetually burning incense for both of them, a obligatory incense if one wished to be well received, but whose fumes came to resemble the natural atmosphere. One received no gratitude for contributing to it; there were even days on which Chateaubriand seemed disdainful and world-weary, so that in his vicinity one felt positively discouraged."[68]

The greatest writer of the century, the idol of the *Abbaye-aux-Bois,* did not care for conversation. He even felt a violent aversion toward it. Of Mme de Staël, seeking to pay tribute to her, he writes, "Had she shone less in conversation she would have been less attached to society and so known nothing of petty passions."[69] The *Mémoires d'outre-tombe* have a choral amplitude in which multiple voices are perceptible, but as in the Nekuya of the *Odyssey,* they form a spectral symphony. Mme Récamier was able to arrange a *chapelle ardente* for the inner voices of this *Miserere.* On a less grandiose scale, the pious salon of Mme Swetchine, the egeria of Montalembert, Ozanam, Lacordaire, and Falloux, was no less sinister.[70] Later still, the turning tables at Guernsey, a funereal banquet presided over by Hugo and another Juliette, bring us into contact with the depth of the haunted melancholy of the nineteenth century, weighty and damp in its farthest place of exile from *la douceur de vivre*. The portraits of Flandrin, Bonnat, Gérôme give some ideas of the bituminous affectation and the meticulous conventions predominating in these indoor scenes overloaded with historical knickknacks like boudoir museums. Even the *Journal* of the Goncourt brothers, those spies of the social life of Paris, is filled with so much bile only because they did not believe that there had been any conversation in society since the days of the Revolution. It was a secret only the eighteenth century possessed. It was a spurious eighteenth-century spirit that invaded the desirable areas of the city.

A very different vitality inspired the generous Mme de Staël, eleven years Mme Récamier's senior.[71] In her mother's home (the first Calvinist salon in Paris since Mme des Loges), she had met the encyclopedists and the upper crust of Parisian society. She herself, married in 1786 to the Swedish ambassador, held her own salon with La Fayette and Barnave, Condorcet, Sieyès, Talleyrand, and Broglie among her guests. In accordance with her own early experience, the salon was for her, from the very outset, an instrument of political action, a rival for the "club" when it came to preparing and manipulating the votes of the Assembly. Driven into exile during the Terror, she reemerged during the Consulate as an associate of Benjamin Constant, working with him for Bonaparte and then against the first Consul. The latter exiled her in 1803. She traveled from one end of Europe to the other, stopping in Weimar and then in Rome, always *en mission* against tyranny and despotism. She was a militant to a degree that would have made Voltaire smile. She traveled with her troupe of friends and sidekicks, appearing, whenever possible, with Benjamin Constant: together, the two were a star duet of intellectual *bel canto*. "According to witnesses," writes Sainte-Beuve, "nothing was so dazzlingly superior as the conversations they engaged in among their chosen circle, each of them wielding a magical racquet with which for hours on end they send back and forth shot after shot of elegant argument without ever missing the shuttle cock of a thousand intertwining ideas."[72]

From 1807 onward, Coppet was the Wimbledon of these two stars of sublime discussion. Sainte-Beuve has no hesitation in comparing the Necker family mansion favorably to Ferney:

> Coppet counterbalances Ferney and at least partially dethrones it. All of us who belong to the early years of the century judge Ferney from the starting-point of Coppet. Life at Coppet was like life at any château. Often as many as thirty people, strangers and friends, would be gathered there. The most frequent guests were Benjamin Constant, M. Auguste Wilhelm Schlegel, M. de Sabran, M. de Sismondi, M. de Bonstetten, the barons de Voght and de Balk. Each year would

bring with it one or more visits from M. Mathieu de Montmorency, M. Prosper de Barante, the Prince Augustus of Prussia, Mme Récamier, and a host of people from the best society, acquaintances from Germany or from Geneva. Conversations, philosophical or literary but always intriguing or elevated, would get under way as early as eleven o'clock in the morning at the breakfast table: they would be resumed over dinner and in the interval before supper, which was usually served at eleven o'clock, and after that continue on until after midnight. Benjamin Constant and Mme de Staël figured prominently.[73]

Constant, beset by ennui and by spleen, possessed to a remarkable degree the aristocratic sense of the gratuity of things, even including his own gratuity—something Chateaubriand never experienced. Mme de Staël, for her part, was all activity and endless enthusiasm, the finale of Beethoven's Ninth Symphony. She was the alcohol, odious, but indispensable, that Constant needed. For her, he provided the framework that allowed her great but vague ideas to take shape. The term *homme d'esprit* in the sense that Méré gave the term fits him to perfection. Chênedollé describes him in these terms:

> Nothing was more lively than his conversation. Perpetually in epigrammatic vein, he would counter the loftiest political questions with clear, sharply focused, urgent logic, in which the sarcasm was always hidden under the surface of his reasoning; and when with admirable if perfidious skill he had led his adversary into the trap he had set for him, he would leave him there not only beaten but thunderstruck under the impact of an epigram from which nobody could recover. And no one was better than he was at letting loose with both barrels at once."[74]

Constant was all the more worthy of Mme de Staël because he was in every way her opposite. Gifted as a singer, as an actress, the alter ego of Mlle Mars, Germaine Necker had the good fortune to meet up with Benjamin. A Talma would have laughed at her. Her genius was entirely oratorical, her voice made for public speaking rather than conversation, and Coppet, without Benjamin, would have been the first Strasbourg parliament. The real discussions and decisions took place elsewhere. Nevertheless, as the female Cicero of Coppet understood it, conversation was neither a game nor an entertainment, nor even an exercise: it was always, she believed, a task, an action, a conversion to be effected. She had no sense either of playfulness or repartee. This inexhaustible improviser, who thought while speaking, who wrote as eloquently as she spoke, was determined to convince her readers as she had convinced her listeners. The conversations in *Corinne ou l'Italie* (1807) transpose into the fictional narrative her experience of enthusiastic and imperious speech. In that sense, she renewed in France the characteristic link between literature and conversation. Sainte-Beuve saw that clearly and let her know of his gratitude. But on one point she renewed it in a way that was in no way characteristically French: the confusion of eloquence and conversation that she maintained is precisely the lapse of taste and esprit from which French literature was preserved by Méré and Montaigne, by Voltaire as well as Marivaux. Even Rousseau, in so many respects Mme de Staël's mentor, was able on occasion to come down from his neo-Roman tribune and the eloquence of a Cato to capture, at the right moment, the tone of simplicity, of smiling intimacy, of which Mme de Staël had not the slightest idea. She taught many of the journalists and publicists of the nineteenth century their trade: enthusiasm for grandiose ideas and the demagogy of the purple passage. The genius of Balzac came from that school. Because of her immense influence, in tandem with modern subjectivity, she contributed significantly to burying deep the secret of *l'esprit*. With her, the reign of the intellectuals began.

Having returned, *in extremis*, to inaugurate the Restoration, Mme de Staël bequeathed her daughter Albertine to it as well as to a host of political-literary salons. The unacknowledged daughter of Benjamin Constant, Albertine almost married Astolphe de Custine, who in many ways resembled her father. She had to be satisfied with becoming Duchesse de Broglie at Pisa in 1816 (during the Hundred Days) and also, according to Charles de Rémusat, "muse, guardian angel, magician, and genius" of the doctrinaire salons of the liberal opposition. "She appeared to me," he adds, "like an allegorical figure, a living and personal embodiment of the True and Beautiful."[75] The tone that prevailed in these salons is described by Sainte-Beuve—more straitlaced than you might think—as "above all serious; the tone of general discussion was lengthy, sustained, political, or literary, with psychological asides, a certain air of studiedness even in private conversation, and preaching even in moments of relaxation."[76] Guizot, Royer-Collard, Barante, and later Victor Cousin are the key figures in these clubs for the promotion of considered reflection.

Between these and the purely Legitimist salons, Mme de Duras under the Restoration and Mme de Boigne under the July Monarchy created a middle ground of understanding and compromise. At the home of the Duchesse de Duras, one found "a combination of aristocracy and affability, gravity without pomposity, an atmosphere that was brilliant but never vulgar, semi-liberal and imperceptibly progressive."[77] Chateaubriand was this group's political representative. But Sainte-Beuve penetrated more deeply still into the conversational tone of Mme de Duras, Mme de Staël's friend—but not her imitator—when he analyzed the style of her novel, *Édouard*:

> The style of Mme de Duras, who took up writing so late in life without any thought of becoming a writer, shows no sign of either tentativeness or of carelessness. It was *born* natural and already perfected: simple, brisk, yet reserved, a style in the manner of Voltaire, but belonging to a woman; no affectation, unfailing tact, no dubious coloring and yet no lack of color, at least in its choices of background and accompaniments, and finally a great purity of line. Everywhere passions more profound than their expression, and no more extravagance or exuberance than in a polite conversation.[78]

With more dryness of manner, but no less adept in a simple, unaffected style, Mme de Boigne retained all the same from Mme de Staël the notion that a modern salon was absolutely obliged to be a center of influence and therefore a forum for discussion among the representatives of differing opinions:

> I saw her often. In my house, she expressed herself in terms congenial to my heart. But in hers, I was often scandalized by the things uttered by her guests. She entertained every viewpoint and style of speech, and though she did uphold with the utmost vigor the cause that she supported, she would always end up with a polite skirmish, for she had no wish to deprive her salon of any of the vocal fencing champions who might introduce an element of variety into the debate. She loved all celebrities, those remarkable for their wit, or rank, even those whose celebrity rested on the violence of their opinions. For people like myself who lived with the more restricted notions conforming to group opinion, that seemed highly shocking. And I often left her salon filled with an indignation provoked by the views that were expressed there, saying, using the language of my own set, that it was *really too much*.[79]

The lesson was retained. Under the July Monarchy, banished from the hub of political activity, Mme de Boigne maintained her position by concerting exchanges between Legitimists and Orleanists, making her salon a "chamber of reflection" and herself an indispensable mediator.

> From time to time, I would entertain guests at these soirées, which had become rather fashionable. My invitations were by word of

mouth and supposedly addressed at random to people I chanced to meet. All the same, I took great care that chance should place in my path the persons I wanted to bring together and whom I knew would find each other congenial. I thus avoided having too great a crowd and escaped the necessity of receiving the mass of bores, whom good taste bids us shun, but who never fail to swarm around us at the slightest sign. I would look them over carefully, in the course of the winter, a few at a time, so as not to be trampling them underfoot in my drawing room. The uncertainty of being invited gave these evenings a certain cachet and contributed more than anything else to their being much sought after. I saw people of every opinion. The Ultras predominated in the private gatherings because my family and social connections led naturally to them, but the usual guests on the other evenings were made up of persons holding a quite different assortment of viewpoints.[80]

Salon conversation had become a cog in the political machine, a kind of preliminary diplomacy preceding the maneuvers of the Assembly or the Cabinet. The *Mémoires* of Mme de Boigne, poor in general ideas, but rich in things seen and heard, in a moralist's observations, sum up her experience as a "stateswoman" for whom conversation is action. Their style conveys some idea of the sharp-edged propriety which was her chief characteristic, "attic salt" compared with the diplomatic reserve which held sway in the salon of the Princesse de Lieven, the friend and ally of Guizot.

An enemy of the overly respectable gravity of the *doctrinaires* and disinclined to the pomposity of Chateaubriand and Mme de Staël, Stendhal rediscovered *le naturel* in Italy, along with gaiety, insouciance, music, and love. In Paris he found *esprit* only in the fictitious society he assembles around the banker Leuwen:

> The dinners given by M. Leuwen were famous all over Paris, for they were often perfect. There were days on which he invited men of fortune or ambition; but these gentlemen were by no means admitted to his wife's circle. In this way, that circle was not spoilt by M. Leuwen's profession. Money was not the only merit there and moreover—incredible as it may seem—it was not even considered to be the greatest advantage one could possess. In this salon, the furnishing of which had cost a hundred thousand francs, no one was hated (a strange contrast); but the company loved to laugh and there were moments at which they made fun of every affectation, starting with the king and the archbishop. As you can see, the conversation

was not directed toward securing advancement or achieving important posts. In spite of that drawback, which drove away a number of people who were not missed, quite a crowd vied for admittance to Mme de Leuwen's circle. She would have been fashionable if she had been willing to make her salon more accessible, but several conditions had to be met before one could be received there. Mme de Leuwen's only aim was to provide diversion for a husband twenty years older than herself and said to be on familiar terms with the dancers at the Opera. In spite of that drawback and however agreeable her salon might be, Mme de Leuwen was never completely happy unless her husband was present.[81]

A little like Montaigne, Stendhal was a brilliant conversationalist who never encountered a more congenial conversational partner than himself; he made unfailing progress in the *esprit de joie* which sprang from his close association with his own *moi*. A period of respite in Italy under the July Monarchy led him to the discovery that in a utilitarian modern society, dominated by commercial and political considerations, the artist's life was the sole surviving form for the noble lifestyle of the ancien régime for which conversation was an art of living that provided fulfillment and happiness. His *Promenades dans Rome* are delightful, lively gossip, while exuberant improvisation and unerring audacity characterize *La Chartreuse de Parme*. Stendhal overcame the evil spell that lay over the age of the Fisher King. Through literature, he set his spirit free. Mérimée, an excellent raconteur, pressed hard on his heels and would end up brilliantly— if a little sadly—in the circle surrounding the empress at Compiègne. Beyle and Mérimée had been frequent visitors to "Delécluze's garret," where their host was as irritated as they were by Mme de Staël: "In spite of her constant claims that she is not prosaic, she is the least poetic writer I know: she never paints her subject, she spends all her time arguing."[82] Delécluze does however concede that she is a gifted moralist, "as can be proved," he writes, "by her chapter on conversation in *De l'Allemagne*." A pupil of David, and exceptionally well read, Delécluze was perhaps the nineteenth-century figure who best understood both Delille's poem "De la conversation"[83] and the teachings of the Abbé Morellet on the same subject.[84] His ideal was more literate conversation than social brilliance, however harmoniously enjoined the two had been in the seventeenth century. It was the educated taste made up of a blend of Atticism and *astéisme*, whose unerring insights applied equally to texts, works of art, and people. His *Journal* for the years 1824–28 is like a ball of yarn into which have been wound the fruits of its author's wide reading and the limitless conversations he carried on with some of the acutest minds in Paris and with the most refined of ladies, Mme Récamier and the niece she brought up, Amélie Cyvoct (Mme Charles Lenormand), Mme Ancelot. In love with Amélie, though with neither hopes nor illusions, Delécluze found a kind of happiness in this close alliance of literature and conversation, free of ambition, pretension, and haste. This unfrocked painter invented a way of living that, thirty years later, the Morisots and the Rouarts, the Manets and the Mallarmés would all adopt. The *Journal* is the shell containing the day-to-day pleasures—in the seventeenth century it would have been called a *virtuose*—allowing us to hear shorthand accounts of conversations which often amount to regular scenes of comedy.

Less sedentary than Delécluze, Delacroix, in his *Journal* combines reflections on his *atelier*, readings, travel stories, and dinners. Politics and ambition play no part in it:

> 17th of June 1855: Dined at Halévy's with Mme Ristori, Janin, Laurent Jan [. . .] a certain M. Caumartin made famous, so I was told, by a cruel adventure [. . .] Laurent Jan was passably unbearable, as he generally is, holding forth in his usual way and attempting to be witty by taking up the contrary position of every reasonable argument. His verve was inexhaustible. And yet, however little sympathy I may have for his continual sallies and the noisy outbursts that leave one mute and almost saddened, I was glad to see him. At my age, there is no greater pleasure than to find myself in the company of intelligent people who understand everything one says without having it spelled out for them. He was telling the little blond Roman prince, who was next to him at table, that opinion in Paris sets the seal on reputations and consists of five hundred persons with the wit to judge and think for the mass of two-legged animals who live in Paris but are Parisians in name only. It is in the company of one of these thoughtful men of judgment with, above all, the capacity to think for themselves that one really enjoys oneself, even if one should quarrel for the quarter of an hour or even the whole day one spends with them. When I compare this Sunday society with that of the night before, I can easily overlook the eccentricities of my Laurent Jan and think only of the unexpected insights, the artistic sense he shows in everything that make him a priceless original.
>
> Those who title themselves society people par excellence have no idea just how deprived they are of real society, that is to say, truly sociable pleasures. One does see a few members of high society capable of finding amusement after the fashion of artists—I use this word with all its associative resonances—who take real pains to attract art-

ists into their circle, and who take genuine pleasure in their conversation.[85]

The artist is clearly beginning to succeed the aristocracy as the salt of the earth, the man of accomplishments as well as the man of genius, who, even in society, when he ventures into it, is the best guarantee against pedantic platitude and boredom. The ascent of art in the scale of modern values is due first of all to the fact that art—and the artist himself—presupposes a certain freedom, a naturalness, an indifference to the conventions and prejudices of "bourgeois" society. It is the final refuge, here and now, of the supreme art: *combining genius and leisure.*

In this respect, the narrator of *La Recherche* managed to compensate for this modern rise in the stature of the artist by forging an equivalent myth for the writer and the act of literary creation. At any rate, as soon as the aristocrat and the ecclesiastic faded away to be lost in the penumbra of the business class, a vacant space was created—Socrates' place in the *Symposium* around which "real life" was to be found, the "real society" that modern utilitarianism and earnestness had made more remote but all the more desirable. There was no lack of impostors for his role. All the same, in the nineteenth century, nostalgia for the aristocratic conversational community remained intense for a long time. Nowhere does one find it in a purer state than in Jules Barbey d'Aurevilly. He was born for it, and in him the writer is inseparable from the conversationalist. "Conversation is my game of whist, deprived of which, I languish."[86] "I write as I talk and I talk better than I write when the Angel of conversation seizes me by the hair like a prophet" (ibid.). Barbey the letter writer improvises in the same way, moving from speaking to writing, but always addressing himself to someone in a vivacious dialogue to which he commits his whole being in search of incandescence. "My letters, in the rapidity of their execution, like the wind from a cannonball, are worth more than all my other writings. Do you know why? It is because I come closer in them to conversation, and conversation, when my overwhelming disdain of everything allows it, is for me the full tide of thought beating on the shore"(ibid). He praises Balzac for having put "stories, entire novels, into conversations." Like Stendhal's, like Mérimée's, Barbey's grail is that society of kindred spirits, who, on the spur of the moment, shake off time to become its master—to become like gods. Other than in friendship it is useless to look for it in literature. Barbey speaks of his short stories in *Les Diaboliques* as "conversational sonatas" or "sonatas for four hands." The narrative emerges from the clash of dialogue, from questions, from diverse reflections, from a conversation carried on during a journey, at supper, or in the course of a walk. What one remembers of what has taken place becomes the bread and wine of a Eucharistic feast, here and now, amid the bitter satisfaction of a remembrance extended by the novelist to his readers "by lamplight."

This satisfaction is knowledge. Tragic knowledge in the case of Barbey, or comic (in Dante's sense of the word), from Boccaccio to Diderot. It is at this elevated level that it rejoins the Platonic dialogue which the great literature of Europe has always sought after to lead it back to conversation. Conversation, which the ancien régime, to its credit, had seen as a major liberal art which then achieved recognition throughout Europe, had its dangerous side. After the La Bruyère of the *Caractères* and the Montesquieu of the *Lettres persanes* (two *anciens*), Rousseau drew up the sternest indictment of Parisianism in conversation, condemning its philosophical and political frivolity, its sterile spitefulness. Sainte-Beuve on the other hand, following Mme de Staël, made himself the apologist of a reformed conversational model, European rather than Parisian, nurtured by the classics and capable in its turn of nurturing new ones. In the twentieth century, Proust's point of view became dominant: conversation is the antithesis of the literary ascesis which alone can give literature, retrospectively and ironically, a meaning. It is clear that in the margins or at the heart of this French institution, an endless debate has held sway: at stake is not only the status of conversation in general—whether it is to be the frivolous pastime of an idle few or a Socratic learning device—but also how a French model of conversation is to be judged. Is it a facet of Parisian, or even of national folklore, or is it an intersection of minds ancient and modern, French and foreign, the live verbal manifestation of a literature whose scope is universal? The seriousness of this debate throughout the Age of Enlightenment as well as in the nationalistic and romantic nineteenth century has perhaps been underestimated. Today it appears much more evident.

Why? Like Proust, we no longer believe in conversation. Beckett and his theater of aphasia sum up our skepticism, if not our hostility. We have set our face against idle chatting, but we cannot help dreaming, along with Mme de Staël and Sainte-Beuve, along with the whole of European literature, of a conversational circle set above the chattering, quarreling masses, a concilium of the world's best minds which, smilingly, would give simply by virtue of its coming together a meaning and a justification to our chaos. In place of that ideal which no one dares formulate, all that we have to sate our hunger is the ideology of communication. True conversation supposes equality both in principle and in fact among a small group of voluntary participants. It also requires the invisible, living presence of absent voices: those of the classics, our eternal, universal friends. Communication, on the other hand, presupposes an egalitarianism in principle between contemporary receptors and transmitters, in unlimited numbers. To gain admittance to the network, these interchangeable interlocutors divest themselves of every personal quality, pledge, and raison d'être of their individual freedom. They consent at the same time to renounce the rhetorical dimension of language, its energy, its irony, its wit, without which their personal freedom is left without a voice.

One enters into communication as one enters into a concentration camp, with a serial number: one is there to receive and to transmit information with no regard for truth, beauty, or happiness. In return for this docility and abstraction, the dreamworld of technology dazzles us with the prospect of cognitive omnipotence: seated in front of their screens and keyboards, our modern Pico della Mirandolas can promise themselves that they will ultimately be able to juggle and combine all the information in the world and resolve every question put to them. Literature, now marginalized, has become no more than a province of this impersonal empire. Politics has become superfluous. An "invisible hand" controls and homogenizes the impersonal circulation of signs and images. By a quite significant irony, the word "conversation" has been adopted by cybernetics and the sociology of communication to designate—in their specific jargon—both the dialogue between computers and exchanges of information in everyday life. In fact the criticism leveled by Rousseau against Parisian conversation, which, according to him, confuses examined truth with an irresponsible, purely discursive game, could be invoked with even greater justice against a "communicational society" which finds in its own functioning its own goal, shutting out simultaneously the joys of speech and political and philosophical choice. Is it by chance that the fashionable conversation that Rousseau chastised and that Proust mocked should find in its capital today the celebrants and temples of the ideology of "communication"?

All the same, the question still remains whether conversation as understood by Plato, by Montaigne, by Mme de Staël and Sainte-Beuve, a conversation carried on among free and distinguished individuals, among men of letters, does not obstinately persist in seeing France as its home? Europe is once again calling on France to be the source of that conversation. For if Europe really exists and if it has any precedents, they are surely to be sought in that republic of cultivated conversation whose preferred meeting place was Paris but whose participants included Cicero as well as Plato, Heine as well as Walpole, Turgenev, and Mickiewicz. A myth perhaps, but a myth rooted in nature and in reason and carrying with it one of the European vocations of France. Communication is not addressed to anyone, any more than are circuits or computers. Conversation is a luxury of mind and spirit, inseparable from the genius of certain places and it has to be loved, understood, cultivated, even with a certain amount of obstinacy if it is to be rediscovered. To rediscover it is also to rediscover freedom.

NOTES

1. On the Platonic dialogue, see Victor Goldschmidt, *Les Dialogues de Platon: Structure et méthode dialectique* (Parionne: Monfort, 1984); Monique Dixsaut, *Le Naturel philosophe: Essai sur les dialogues de Platon* (Paris: Les Belles Lettres, 1985); M. C. Stokes, *Plato's Socratic Conversations: Drama and Dialectic in Three Dialogues* (London: Athlone Press, 1986); Kenneth Seeskin, *Dialogue and Discovery: A Study in Socratic Method* (Albany: State University of New York Press, 1987). Aristotle too has a theory of conversation (see "Les Sanglots d'Ulysse" in *Mercure* [Paris: José Corti, 1990], 169–83).

2. Emmanuel Kant, *Anthropologie du point de vue pragmatique* (Paris: Vrin, 1964), pt. 1, bk. 3, p. 128; and pt. 2, p. 155.

3. Ibid., pt. 2, p. 156.

4. Mme de Staël, *De l'Allemagne,* ed. S. Balaye (Paris: Garnier-Flammarion, 1968), pt. 1, chap. 11, "De l'esprit de conversation." The whole chapter should be read; according to the exacting standards of Etienne Delécluze, it was the author's masterpiece. In fact, it is a dazzling and intelligent variant of Saint-Preux's letters to Julie in *La Nouvelle Héloïse.*

5. Montesquieu, "Mes pensées," in *Oeuvres complètes* (Paris: Gallimard, Bibliothèque de la Pléiade, 1949), vol. 1, p. 1417, no. 1740.

6. Mme de Staël, *Dix années d'exil,* ed. S. Balaye and P. Gautier (Paris: U.G.E., 1966), 213: "The whole company in Russia has impeccable manners but there is not enough instruction for the nobles, nor enough confidence among people who live under the influence of a despotic court and government for anyone to discover the charms of intimacy."

7. In *De l'Allemagne,* pt. 1, chap. 11, pp. 105–6.

8. Christophe Strotzeski, *Rhétorique de la conversation: Sa dimension littéraire et linguistique dans la société du XVIIe siècle,* trans. Sabine Seubert (Paris-Tubingen-Seattle: Biblio 17, PSCL, 1984).

9. See, among others, Antoine Gombaud, Chevalier de Méré (*Oeuvres,* ed. Ch. Boudhors [Paris: Roches, 1930], 2:102–3), who avoids even mentioning the oratorical and dissociates his definition from the "Conseils et Conférences" of deliberation and discussion "where generally neither laughter nor lightheartedness is permitted."

10. In his discussion of Voiture's posthumous *Oeuvres,* published in 1648, Tallemant des Réaux cites the following exchange between Mme de Rambouillet and one of her noble guests: "Monsieur de Blairancourt remarked to Mme de Rambouillet that since nobody was talking of anything else but this book, he had read it and found that Voiture was not devoid of wit. 'But Monsieur,' replied Mme de Rambouil-

let, 'did you think that it was on account of his nobility or fine figure that he was received everywhere, as you saw.'" *Historiettes,* vol. 1, *Voiture,* ed. Adam (Paris: Gallimard, Bibliothèque de la Pléiade, 1960), 1:499.

11. Mme de Staël, *De l'Allemagne,* pt. 1, chap. 11, pp. 109–10.

12. *Dix années d'exil,* chap. 16, p. 214.

13. *De l'Allemagne,* pt. 1, chap. 9, pp. 93–94.

14. The Italian and European Renaissance paid special attention to the dialogues of late antiquity, which compiled conversations between scholars and brilliantly summarized the encyclopedia of the "last" men of learning before the barbarian age. Aulu Gelle's *Nuits attiques,* Plutarch's *Banquet des Sept Sages,* Athénée's *Deipnosophistes,* Macrobe's *Saturnalia* are to be counted among the favorite readings of Renaissance humanists (see Michel Jeanneret, *Des mots et des mots: Banquets et propos de table à la Renaissance* (Paris: José Corti, 1987).

15. One of the great neo-Latin dialogues of the Italian Renaissance, written by Angelo Decembrio in about 1450, printed only in 1540. *Politia* (the latinized form of *politeia*) means "good society" or "refined society" here, suggesting the decorum to be adopted by men of letters in their exchanges. On Italian conversation in the sixteenth century, see Carlo Ossola, "L'homme accompli: La Civilisation des cours comme art de la conversation," in *Le Temps de la réflexion* 4 (October 1983): 77–89.

16. The Latin word that best corresponds to our "conversation" is *sermo. Conversatio,* which is not a Ciceronian word, appears in the first century, not as exchange, but as "mode of being together," "way of communal life," among friends or soldiers. It is the Italian *conversazione* which oriented the French *conversation* toward the more specialized sense of verbal exchange, and even exchange in good society. Conversation is general. Exchanges focus on specific subjects.

17. Here we encounter the difference between a treatise like René Bary's *L'Esprit de cour ou les conversations galantes* (dedicated to the king, 1662) and the *Essais* of the Chevalier de Méré on conversation, wit, and refined leisure (1677), or again the chapter on "La conversation" from the *Testament* of Fortin de la Hoguette (1648), which dissociates the court from the spheres of society where one converses with pleasure and *esprit.*

18. François de Sales, *Introduction à la vie dévote,* bk. 3, chap. 17, "De l'honnesteté des paroles et du respect que l'on doit aux personnes." See Ruth Murphy, *Saint François de Sales et la civilité chrétienne* (Paris: Nizet, 1964), 123–42, 171–97.

19. One can profitably consult Paule Constant's fine book, *Un monde à l'usage des demoiselles* (Paris: Gallimard, 1987), which offers an extensive background to the studies of Carolyn C. Lougee, *Le Paradis des femmes: Women, Salons, and Social Stratification in 17th Century France* (Princeton: Princeton University Press, 1976); Paul Hoffman, *La France au 17e siècle* (Paris: Ophrys, 1977); and Ian McClean, *Women Triumphant: Feminism in French Literature, 1610–1652* (Oxford: Clarendon Press, 1977).

20. See Natalie Zemon Davis, in *Histoire des femmes en Occident,* edited by Georges Duby and Michelle Perrot (Paris: Plon, 1991), vol. 3, chap. 6, "La femme 'au politique,'" pp. 175–92.

21. See Ferdinand Brunot, *La Doctrine de Malherbe d'après son commentaire sur Desportes* (Paris, Armand Colin, 1969; orig. Paris: Masson, 1891), and the chapter he devotes to Malherbe in his *Histoire de la langue française des origines à nos jours,* vol. 3,

La Formation de la langue classique (Paris, 1966; orig. 1905; vol. 3 in two parts appeared in 1909 and 1911), pt. 1, bk. 1, chap. 1.

22. Descartes's elegant flattery of important society figures is well known: "Le bon sens est la chose du monde la mieux partagée." In his biography of the philosopher whose correspondence with the princess Elisabeth is a masterpiece of galantry, foreshadowing the *Entretiens* of Fontenelle, Adrien Baillet evokes Descartes's concern to "convert" the language of women, more specifically, of prominent ladies in society. His wish is amply fulfilled: from Madame de Bonneval to Madame du Châtelet, Cartesianism would be diffused and discussed by many "learned ladies" (*La Vie de Monsieur Descartes* (1691; abridged, 1692; Vanves: La Table ronde, 1946), 291.

23. Montaigne, *Essais,* ed. A. Micha (Paris: Garnier-Flammarion, 1969), vol. 3, bk. 3, chap. 8, "De l'art de conférer," p. 137.

24. La Rochefoucauld, *Maximes,* ed. Truchet (Paris: Garnier, 1967), 26 (no. 86).

25. Ibid., 112 (no. 501).

26. Corneille, *Mélite*, 1.2.153–59, in *Théâtre complet*, ed. Georges Couton (Paris: Garnier-Flammarion, 1971), 1:93–94.

27. Chevalier de Méré, "De l'esprit," in *Oeuvres*, 2:57–95.

28. See "Le café," by Benoît Lecoq, in this volume.

29. Anne Thérèse de Lambert, *Réflexions nouvelles sur les femmes* (1727; Paris: Côté-femmes Editions, 1989), 41–42.

30. See *Mémoires du président Hénault,* ed. Fr. Rousseau (Paris, 1911; Geneva: Slatkine Reprints, 1971), 120.

31. See Frédéric Deloffre, *Marivaux et le marivaudage* (Paris: Les Belles Lettres, 1955), 16.

32. Ibid., 69.

33. *Menagiana, ou les bons mots: Les Pensées critiques, historiques, morales et d'érudition, de M. Ménage, recueillies par ses amis*, 2nd ed. (Paris: Delaulne, 1694), 1:374.

34. See Bernard Beugnot, "Forme et histoire: Le Statut des ana" in *Mélanges Couton* (Lyons: Presses universitaires de Lyon, 1981), 85–101.

35. The "line," the "epigram" is the rhetorical figure par excellence of wit. Its great theorist was the Spaniard Baltasar Gracián, *La Pointe, ou l'art du génie,* French trans. M. Gendreau-Massaloux and P. Laurens (Lausanne-Paris: L'Âge d'homme, 1983).

36. I am borrowing these "characteristics" from the assortment compiled by Marguerite Glotz and Madeleine Maire, *Salons du dix-septième siècle* (Paris: Hachette, 1945).

37. Jean-Jacques Rousseau, *La Nouvelle Héloïse,* pt. 2, letter 14, in *Oeuvres complètes,* ed. B. Gagnebin and R. Raymond (Paris: Gallimard, Bibliothèque de la Pléiade, 1964), 2:232–33.

38. Beginning in 1680, Mademoiselle de Scudéry published several volumes of *Conversations* taken from her novels, which had become unreadable because of their excessive length. These compilations were immensely successful and were translated into several languages. They constitute one of the best seventeenth-century treatises on the subject.

39. Pierre d'Ortigue, sieur de Vaumorière, *L'Art de plaire dans la conversation* (Paris, 1688), various editions.

40. Rousseau, pt. 2, letter 14, 232.

41. Ibid., pt. 6, letter 5, p. 659.

42. Ibid., pt. 5, letter 3, p. 577.

43. Denis Diderot, letter of September 16, 1761, to Mme d'Épinay, in *Correspondance,* ed. G. Roth (Paris: Éditions de Minuit, 1957), 3:305.

44. Quoted by Glatz and Maire, 248–49.

45. André Morellet, *Mémoires de l'abbé Morellet (. . .) sur le dix-huitième siècle et la révolution* (1821; Paris: Mercure de France, 1988), 58.

46. Diderot, letter of September 15, 1760, to Sophie Volland, in *Correspondance,* 3:67 (or *Lettres à Sophie Volland,* ed. J. Varloot [Paris: Gallimard, 1984], 113–14).

47. *Mélanges extraits des manuscrits de Madame Necker* (Paris, 1798), 1:112.

48. Madame d'Abrantès, *Histoire des salons de Paris, tableaux et portraits du grand monde, sous Louis XVI, le Directoire, le Consulat et l'Empire, la Restauration et le règne de Louis-Philippe* (Paris: Garnier, 1893), 2:167.

49. Ibid., pp. 177–80.

50. Ibid.

51. Comte Pierre-Louis Roederer, *Mémoires pour servir à l'histoire de la société polie en France* (Paris: Firmin-Didot, 1825).

52. Sainte-Beuve, *Portraits de femmes* (Paris: Garnier, 1886), 3.

53. Ibid., 16.

54. Ibid., 10.

55. Ibid., 54.

56. Madame Ancelot, *L'Hôtel de Rambouillet: Comédie en trois actes mêlés de chants* (Paris: Beck, 1842), dedicated to Madame Récamier, for the inauguration of the Théâtre du Vaudeville, act 1, sc. 9.

57. Madame Ancelot, *Un salon de Paris, de 1824 à 1864 (Et in Arcadia ego)* (Paris: Emile Dentu, 1866), 95.

58. Ibid., 250.

59. Marcel Proust, *Contre Sainte-Beuve,* ed. P. Clarac (Paris: Gallimard, Bibliothèque de la Pléiade, 1971), 225.

60. Madame Ancelot, *Un salon de Paris,* 265.

61. Honoré de Balzac, *Autre étude de femme,* ed. P.-G. Castex (Paris: Gallimard, Bibliothèque de la Pléiade, 1976), 675–76.

62. See Jules Janin's article "Conversation" in *Dictionnaire de la conversation et de la lecture,* 2nd ed., ed. W. Duckett (1832–51; Paris: Firmin-Didot, 1867–68), 6:455–58.

63. Ibid., col. 457.

64. On the importance of the café in the social life of artists and men of letters in the nineteenth century see Benoît Lecoq, "Le café," in this volume; and more generally, Jerrold Seiger, *Bohemian Paris: Culture, Politics, and the Boundaries of Bourgeois Life* (New York: Viking Penguin, 1986); French translation: *Paris bohème, 1830–1930* (Paris: Gallimard, 1991).

65. Léon Daudet, *Salons et journaux* (Paris: Grasset, 1932), 253–55.

66. On the subject of Juliette Récamier, consult Pierre-Emile Buron, *Le Coeur et l'esprit de Madame Récamier* (Saint-Malo: Combourg, 1981); and Françoise Wagener, *Madame Récamier, 1777–1849* (Paris: J.-Cl. Lattès, 1986).

67. Madame Ancelot, "Salon de Madame Récamier," in *Les Salons de Paris: Foyers éteints* (Paris: Tardieu, 1857), 167–205.

68. Ibid., 189.

69. Chateaubriand, *De quelques ouvrages historiques et littéraires,* in *Oeuvres complètes* (Paris: Ladvocat, 1826), 12:399.

70. *Madame Swetchine: Sa vie et ses oeuvres,* by the Comte de Falloux (Paris: Didier, 1861).

71. See Simone Balayé, *Madame de Staël: Lumières et liberté* (Paris: Klincksieck, 1979); and Ghislain de Diesbach, *Madame de Staël* (Paris: Perrin, 1983).

72. Sainte-Beuve, *Portraits de femmes,* 146.

73. Ibid., 145–46.

74. Chênedollé in an unpublished note quoted by Sainte-Beuve in *Chateaubriand et son groupe littéraire* (Paris: Garnier, 1861), 1:189.

75. Charles de Rémusat, *Mémoires de ma vie* (Paris: Plon, 1958), 1:449.

76. Sainte-Beuve, *Portraits de femmes,* 63.

77. Despite his Rousseauist hostility to salon conversation, Chactas, in Madame de Duras's home, was obliged to submit to the school of fashion.

78. Sainte-Beuve, *Portraits de femmes,* 74.

79. Comtesse de Boigne, *Mémoires,* ed. J.-Cl. Berchet (Paris: Mercure de France, 1986), 1:271.

80. Ibid., 2:6.

81. Stendhal, *Lucien Leuwen,* ed. H. Debray and M. Crouzet (Paris: Flammarion, 1982), 96–97.

82. Delécluze, *Journal (1824–1828),* ed. R. Baschet (Paris: Grasset, 1948), 372. All these pages by Delécluze give us a sense of French literature from the seventeenth to the nineteenth century that is worthy of Sainte-Beuve.

83. Abbé Delille, "De la conversation," in *Oeuvres,* ed. Michaud (1806; Paris, 1824), vol. 12. The notes of this edition are extremely valuable. Contemporary with Roederer's volume *La Société polie,* their considerable erudition helps found the historiographic myth of conversation that haunts the nineteenth century.

84. Abbé Morellet, "De la conversation," written in the wake of *Éloges de Madame Geoffrin, contemporaine de Madame du Deffand, par MM. Morellet, Thomas et d'Alembert, suivies de lettres de Madame Geoffrin et à Madame Geoffrin* (Paris: Nicolle, 1812). This essay is one of the maserpieces of the genre.

85. Eugène Delacroix, *Journal, 1822–1863* (Paris: Plon, 1980), 516–17.

86. Jules Barbey d'Aurevilly, "Le Récit-conversation," in *Les Diaboliques,* edited with a preface by M. Crouzet (Paris: Imprimerie nationale, 1989), 13f.

CHAPTER 9

THE CAFÉ

☙

BENOÎT LECOQ

Regularly evoked by memoirists and columnists, praised by poets, celebrated by painters and writers, the café—in the mind's eye of the French as well as in their social reality—holds a place that neither the aristocratic salons nor the official academies nor the social circles of the bourgeoisie could match. Yet we must distinguish between cafés. The tavern, the grogshop, the bistro, the wine seller's, all of these gave rise to an imagery spread by the serialized story, by the popular novel, by realist painting, and by films. Their evocative power is all the more diffuse because they are part of a world so familiar to us. At an opposite pole were those cafés where the best minds of the eighteenth century met, the places where aesthetic or political movements formed, where men promised to glory, or at least to notoriety, chose to live—such cafés were soon felt to be not merely specifically French but characteristically French, and even, do we dare to say, one of the multiple elements that compose the City of Light.[1] "Without cafés and newspapers, there would be no Paris," exclaimed Félix Mornand in 1855.[2] Twenty years later Philibert Audebrand went even further: "For nearly two centuries now a real Parisian café has been the symbol of the city!"[3]

These cafés and their coffee are, then, recent inventions. When sixteenth- and seventeenth-century society wanted to drink, smoke, and talk business, it had only the tavern and the cabaret, places of ill repute where the wine was mediocre and the elite rarely ventured.[4] So of course the

Figure 9.1
By the end of the eighteenth century the café had become one of the places of choice for political emancipation: the Café de Foy, July 12, 1789, when Camille Desmoulins made his motion at Palais-Royal. Gravure by Berthault, from Prieur.

introduction of coffee in the eighteenth century was generally interpreted as a sign of progress, a triumph of civilization over barbarism: with the reign of the mind came also that of elegance. From this time on it was permissible for persons of good breeding to meet over a beverage deemed intellectually stimulating, to play chess, discuss a point of metaphysics or even politics, or pass judgment on the latest play. This idealized vision, far though it may be from ordinary reality, is the one dear to literary history textbooks and popularized by the press.[5] One need only invoke the names of the most famous cafés to see whole sections of the capital suddenly appear, generations of intellectuals rise up again, and scenes from our history set in motion. Of course imperial Vienna also had its prestigious establishments which fascinated all of Europe.[6] But, while "café life" in Paris has above all the tang of a sentimental or political engagement, in the Austrian capital it is, far too often, merely an ingrained habit. The café was bourgeois before it was ideological.

"Factories of wit" for some, "salons of democracy" for others, the veritable "legislative force of France" for yet others, the definitions of the café all have symbolic connotations. It is by measuring the distance that separates the Procope from the Flore and then examining the different functions of the café that one may tease out some sense of whether or not this high temple of Parisian sociability really does possess all the virtues attributed to it.

I. Procope's Fortunes

Tied as it is to the economic and social changes of Paris and to the caprice of fashion, the vogue of cafés is subject to endless modulation. It cannot count on lasting in any neighborhood—the heart of the capital never ceases to change location. Even the intensity of café popularity fluctuates with the times. Finally, the way the café as place is seen is actually transformed by the intellectual and political effervescence of the day. And so to each great historical period there corresponds a characteristic typology and topography. The cafés of the Palais Royal evoke the rebellious, libertine Paris of the end of the ancien régime; those of the boulevards symbolize the imperial celebrations of Napoleon III. Montmartre cabarets share the glory of a certain bohemianism; the cafés of Saint-Germain-des-Près stir memories of the occupation and liberation. But, beyond their apparent differences and their passing glamour, they all share a connection to the tradition christened at the end of the seventeenth century by the celebrated Francesco Procopio.

Procope

First known and appreciated in Abyssinia, the cultivation of the coffee bush was carried to Arabia in the thirteenth- and fourteenth- centuries and from there spread throughout Asia in the course of the following century. Only between 1570 and 1650 did the plant and its use begin to penetrate Europe, thanks to the intense new maritime trade with the Levant: Venice and then Marseille were without a doubt the first Western ports to sell coffee beans. A few merchants took it on themselves to explain their preparation and to praise their stimulating properties, and from the beginning of the reign of Louis XIV, coffee was known in Paris. At about the same time, Vienna would take it up in the aftermath of the Turkish invasion.[7]

The success of the new beverage was blunted by medical controversies associated with it and by the Parisians' traditional attachment to wine.[8] It was, then, in the liveliest neighborhoods of the capital that the first coffee merchants, often of Armenian descent, sought to set up shop: within the walls of the Saint-Germain Fair, along the quai de l'École, on the rue de Buci, rue Mazarine, and elsewhere. These coffee houses were no more than humble stalls with an atmosphere not so very different from the cabarets and taverns. The genius of the Sicilian Francesco Procopio dei Coltelli was in understanding that only a sense of the theatrical and a distinctive decor would assure him an elegant clientele of regular customers. In the premises in rue Saint-Germain-des-Prés where he opened in 1686, he hung the walls with mirrors, suspended crystal chandeliers from the ceiling, and installed marble tables throughout. Not content merely to serve coffee, he also offered liqueurs, candied fruits, and ices: his café took on the appearance of what we would today call a tearoom. In 1689, the theater troop of Comediens-Français moved to a nearby town house, enhancing Procope's ambitions. Even before the encyclopedists gathered in the 1750s, his establishment became the rendezvous of theater people and writers. This was the place for making or breaking reputations. This was the place one came looking for the latest news.

Procope's success doubly and durably orients the history of the literary cafés. Decor became an essential element of the café's seduction. Whether one has a—sometimes exaggerated—taste for the luxurious and for refinement (which would be the case of Second Empire cafés) or one seeks a certain primitive simplicity (as would the bohemian cafés), the choice of establishment becomes one way the people who frequent them proclaim their cultural identities. Above all, Procope became the point of reference. Its reputation was such that it sometimes eclipsed those of its immediate rivals, Widow Laurent's Café (rue Dauphine), and Café Gradot (quai de

l'École), even though they had similar clienteles. The Procope "phenomenon" was perceptible already in the eighteenth century. When Voltaire
wrote *The Scotswoman or The Café* in 1760—a pretext for satire at the expense of Abbé Fréron—he set the first act in a London café. In fact it is
quite clear he had in mind the Procope.[9] It was also in the Procope that
the anonymous author of an odd antiparliament pamphlet that appeared
around 1770 chose to place his characters.[10] The café, beneath his pen, became a genuine allegory of society. It is comprised of three rooms, he explained: one for the lawyers (*Bazoche*) which brings together the outsiders;
the "House of Lords," with the nobles who "treat matters of State"; and
the "House of Commons," where only "reasonable men" are admitted
(that is to say, monarchists). In the nineteenth-century, allusions to the
Procope became more and more abundant. Philibert Audebrand, evoking
the denizens of a journalists' café under Napoleon III, observed that "all
spoke like cultured men and the ripples of their conversation could put
one in mind of the Café Procope that history showed us in the days when
the author of *Le Neveu de Rameau* was there talking to Piron."[11] A disillu-
sioned student, believing he had found at the Procope what he'd searched
for in vain in Latin Quarter cafés, discovered in 1860 that the place was
filled "with the elegance that had, ten years or so before, replaced wit."[12]
But, while the Procope continued to disappoint or to charm, the literary
cafés multiplied, proof of the rich possibilities of the institution.

The Cafés around Palais-Royal

Until the 1730s the Left Bank neighborhoods were the liveliest. As the
century progressed, though, the Palais-Royal area slowly took precedence
over them. It was a financial center—the stock exchange and the headquarters of the Compagnie des Indes were nearby—and it was a business
center stimulated by the proximity of the market district of Les Halles. Its
parks, the presence of a Chinese shadow theater, the Opera, the Comédie-
Italienne, and the Théâtre des Variétés made it a leisure center as well. The
Duke of Chartres, who owned the Palais-Royal at the end of the eighteenth century, was quick to understand how he could profit from this
exceptional situation. He renovated it between 1781 and 1784. Under his
guidance Palais-Royal soon became—as would the zone of the boulevards
in the nineteenth century—a city within the city, where one was sure to
find, in the words of Restif de la Bretonne, "all the advantages and . . .
all the abuses of sociability."[13] There were no fewer than seven cafés in
Palais-Royal on the eve of the Revolution and as many along the nearby
rue Saint-Honoré.[14] We knew that the author of *Le Neveu de Rameau* had
the habit "in fair weather or foul" of appearing at five o'clock at Palais-

Royal; if the weather was "too cold or too rainy," he liked to take refuge in the Café de la Régence and observe the strategies of the most celebrated chess players, "Legal the Profound," "Philidor the Subtle" and "Dependable Mayot."[15] But, even more than the chess players, it was the *nouvelliste*, the "news garbler," a character that began to appear in the early part of the century and became an object of derision for Lesage in *Valise trouvée* and for so many others, who made the reputations of these cafés.[16] The nouvelliste's presence was a promise of success to a café. The proprietors of the Café de Chartres, the Café du Caveau, the Café des Aveugles, the Café Février, the owners of the Café de Foy and the Café Corazza quarreled over these men who, to make themselves indispensable even after newspapers were read, didn't hesitate to misrepresent the facts of the stories. As for the Café Méchanique, it was especially appreciated for the ingenious dumbwaiters hidden in the bases of its tables.

Palais-Royal was the private property of the future Philippe-Égalité. Therefore access to it was barred to soldiers and uniformed policemen. That is how it came to be a place that was both fashionable and scandalous. Con men, libertines, courtesans with their wealthy clientele, nouvel-

Figure 9.2
Emblematic of the philosophic spirit of the Enlightenment figures, Procope inaugurated the tradition of the literary café in the eighteenth century. In the insets above (from the left): Buffon, Gilbert, Diderot, d'Alembert, Marmontel, Le Kain, J. B. Rousseau, Voltaire, Piron, d'Holbach. Nineteenth-century engraving by Badoureau.

Figure 9.3
Readings of the gazettes with commentaries, luxurious decor—such were the attractions of most Parisian cafés at the beginning of the nineteenth century. Interior of Café Lemblin in the galleries of the Palais-Royal in 1817. Engraving by Motte from Boilly.

listes, players and pleasure seekers made up the strange fauna that became the object of curiosity. Mrs. Cradock, an English lady of the upper class who was passing through Paris in 1785, noted in her appointment book a visit to a café of the Palais-Royal.[17] The freedom that ruled there, which one found no where else in the capital, partly explained how the cafés of Palais-Royal became the theater of the first scenes of the Revolution: it was at the Café de Foy, standing on a table on July 12, 1789, that Camille Desmoulins called the crowd to arms. Palais-Royal was to be deeply marked by this first encounter with politics. The Café du Caveau soon became the rendezvous of the provincial Fédérés, the Feuillantine Club members preferred the Café de Valois. Under Louis XVIII and Charles X, the Café Lemblin, opened in 1805, continued to harbor partisans of Napoleon's empire and its pensioned-off soldiers, while monarchists remained faithful to the Café de Valois, whiling away the time "with the soporific *Méditations* of Monsieur de Bon(ald)."[18]

Procope had founded the tradition of the literary café; the galleries of the Palais-Royal gave the café its political dimension. Certainly politics had been introduced to the Procope, but in a controlled, censored form. In the cafés of Palais-Royal, politics entered and made itself comfortable:

they knew at that moment that the café could turn into the club. Palais-Royal managed to preserve its vogue until the last years of the reign of Louis-Philippe. But the suppression of the gambling houses in 1837 and the police's harshness toward courtesans hurt the place. It entered a period of decline, and as the years passed, took on the air that it must have had at the time of Colette: that of a peaceful, retiring neighborhood.

The Reign of the Grands Boulevards

More people, more profit. Result, improve the space, ladies' toilet fancier. Hooray for business! More regulars, new mirrors, gilt on the paneling, toilets more decorated. Hooray for business! Crowded café, mirrors and gilding throughout, bronze and mahogany bar, pearl tiaras with diamond spares, fine wool dresses, cashmere shawls. Hooray for business!"[19]

This celebration of the commercial virtues of the café, which in 1819 inspired the establishments that opened along the rue Saint-Honoré, could be applied even more to those who, throughout the century, set up along the Grands Boulevards. The center of pleasure had been progressively shifting to the Grands Boulevards from 1780 to 1830. Theaters proliferated there; it was swarming with cafés. On boulevard du Temple and boulevard Saint-Martin, each theater had its café and each café had its population of out-of-work actors and authors, who mixed with a working-class clientele: the Café Goddet, the Café du Cirque, the Café de la Porte Saint-Martin, and others. From the First Empire of Napoleon to the end of the Second Empire of Napoleon III, luxury commerce and the grand café-restaurants came to line, in ever increasing numbers, both sides of the boulevard Montmartre, boulevard des Italiens—called "de Gand"—and boulevard des Capucines. They soon formed an unbroken chain, a veritable pleasure belt, where dandies, "young lions," and "kid gloves" strolled from the Chaussée d'Antin to the Théâtre des Variétés. Aware of the boulevard's *à la mode* status, journalists, well-known men of letters, and consecrated artists lost no time following. Never before had a century been so curious about itself as was the nineteenth century, and thanks to an eyewitness of genius like Balzac and to those less famous witnesses, among them Edmond Texier with his remarkable *Tableau de Paris*,[20] these immediately took their place in legend: Frascati, the Maison-Dorée, the Divan de la rue Lepelletier, that "Café Procope of the nineteenth century,"[21] the Café de Paris, the Café Anglais, the Café Riche, and, above all others, Tortoni, with a reputation for its ices, "besieged by all of Europe, one could not say why,"[22] its front steps the place to watch the passing parade of the harbingers of romanticism, the well-heeled bohemians,[23] and the supporters of the new school of naturalism.

If the path of the Grands Boulevards owed nothing or nearly nothing to Second Empire urbanism, the boulevard life of which café life was the microcosm, was, nevertheless identified with imperial glory. "Everything in this neighborhood calls up memories of the Second Empire," notes August Lepage in 1888.[24] The taste for luxurious interior decoration that became apparent among café proprietors under the Directory reached its zenith between 1850 and 1870, before it was pushed to the point of excess. The elegance of the time blended easily with the flashy. Gilding, marbling, bronzes, columns, chandeliers, velvet settees took over the salons of most establishments.[25] Moreover, cafés were no longer mere places one went to drink the liqueur of the East. They had become what Léo Larguier would later call "the steamships of the business of beverage,"[26] where the beer ran freely, where sherbets and ice cream concoctions were served in profusion. One went there to lunch, to dine, and late in the evening, to sup. It was the time of the private dining rooms which inspired so many pages of Zola and Maupassant on the peculiar sensuality those confined places stimulated. In 1855, there opened on the boulevard du Temple, with a great flourish of publicity, the Grand Café Parisien, which the architect, Charles Duval, intended to be "the biggest café in the world."[27] It was destroyed the following year to build the Château-d'Eau barracks. But the architect didn't give up and successfully concluded an even more gigantic project: a room fifty meters long, twenty wide, and fifteen high, equipped with twenty-four billiards tables. It was no longer a café but a temple. Its main door was supported by two caryatids, one representing industry and the other commerce. The architecture of cafés was ostentatious and their customers were no less a spectacle. In the unanimous opinion of contemporaries, one went to the café, from the Riche to the Tortoni, essentially to see and be seen.

The excess and splendor that characterized these cafés accentuated, during the Third Republic, the image of corruption left by the imperial regime. Tortoni, which had become a symbol, evoked for some a period of decadence, even degeneration, and for others a vanished golden age. The latter, by their incurable nostalgia, annoyed the young. Marcel Boulenger, in *A Course on Parisian Life for Foreigners*, sketched the type of silver-haired and mustached old gentleman for whom the boulevard, around 1910, was no longer what it had been: "There had been, if you could believe it, the extraordinary, the fantastic and the dazzling Tortoni, with its marble tables behind which fierce and sparkling Parisians found themselves constantly ambushed, firing off epigram after epigram followed tit for tat by the retort, the whole exchange delivered in that propitious half-silence

Figure 9.4
In the course of the nineteenth century decoration of the Grands Boulevards cafés became increasingly rich: luxury became ostentatious. Café Frascati, drawing and engraving by Debucourt.

and followed by a jovial uproar which was nothing less than flattering; it's an effective form one appreciates in the theater." And the cynical author concludes, "But really, Tortoni was no more than a café on the mall."[28] Once Tortoni was closed (1893), only the Napolitain, the "Napo," fossil of a time passed, perpetuated the authentic boulevard tradition thanks to the assiduousness of Catulle Mendès and Ernest Lajeunesse.

From the "Latin Country" to Montmartre

With the primacy of the boulevards came the beginning of what would soon become the war of the two banks of the Seine: an elegant Right Bank, splendid, frequented by people of wealth and successful artists; a more working-class Left Bank, sometimes poverty-stricken, but also younger, which attracted students, second-rate painters, and third-rate writers and musicians. "Compare the boulevart [sic] café to the café of the Latin Quarter, you might as well compare the noble lady of the Chaussée d'Antin to the poor working woman in the rue de la Harpe," the author of *Physiologie des cafés de Paris* explained in 1841.[29] It was true; everything separated the boulevard temples from the modest public houses of the other bank:

Figure 9.5
Boulevard des Italiens, Café Tortoni at four o'clock in the afternoon, by Guérard (next to it is the Café de Paris).

decoration, drink, conversation, customers' wardrobe, etc. Here, the pipe replaced the panatelas, and bock was the choice of men and women customers. The brasserie Andler-Keller, rue Hautefeuille, where partisans of realism gathered around Courbet to feast, had a German air about it, with neither mirrors nor divans but a long cobbled room lined with benches and wooden tables and whitewashed walls.[30] Every literary or artists' group, even the smaller cliques, soon had their café. In the Café de Buci, the Café de la Renaissance, in the Café Soufflet, the Sherry-Cobbler, the Café de l'Union,[31] in the Estaminet de Bobino (Bobino Pub)—to name just a few—interminable debates on political or aesthetic questions were held amidst a hubbub that frightened passers-by. "The bocks flowed, waiters hopped to it, discussions became more and more heated; they shouted, raised their arms and shook their manes of hair," Alphonse Daudet recalled in 1888.[32] Nevertheless the Latin Quarter also had its establishments of great formality. The Café Voltaire, the Café Tabourey, and the Café d'Orsay were frequented by a few celebrities from the other side of the Seine. There was, in fact, a bohemian pose, and its affectation was confined to the dandies. This could explain how a figure as complex as Jules Barbey d'Aurevilly could never have been satisfied with Tortoni or Tabourey alone: each expressed one aspect of his personality.

The attraction of the Latin Quarter remained intact until 1860–70. Émile Goudeau, an avid reader of *Scènes de la vie de bohème*, newly arrived and set up in Paris, explored all the cafés[33] in the hope—soon dashed— of finding the atmosphere of the Café Momus exactly as Henry Murger had described it.[34] A few years later, he would be setting the tragicomic farces of his *Cercle des hydropathes* in a good many of these same establishments.[35] But around the eighteen-seventies, the Latin Quarter began to lose some of its habitués. Crossing the boulevards, the artistic and literary bohemia, led by the doctrinaire of "brutalism," Jean Richepin, betrayed Café Momus and emigrated to the foot of the hill in Montmartre. Manet and the defenders of the impressionists had already abandoned the Batignolles neighborhood and the Café Guerbois to set up La Nouvelle-Athènes. Daudet, Gill, and Murger went to the Brasserie des Martyrs to steep themselves in the latest change. The atmosphere in these first Montmartre cafés was close to that of the Latin Quarter coffee houses. But by conquering the heights of the "Butte" and by making Montmartre the capital of a liberated nation, bohemia slowly changed its behavior and its state of mind. The Cabaret des Assassins, commonly known as Lapin Agile, and especially La Grande Pinte, later nicknamed l'Âne Rouge, opened the era of the Louis XIII-style cabaret.[36] This new kind of café "in contrast to the white and gold of Procope-style cafés . . . gave itself stained glass and, to keep the clientele it coveted, the bric-a-brac of artist studios."[37] Being a bohemian was no longer a simple fact of life; it had become a "requirement." Raoul Ponchon, Maurice Bouchor, Jules Jouy, and even the sinister Maurice Rollinat understood the advantage of the publicity, the staging, and the show. At the Chat-Noir in its first incarnation, founded in 1881 by Rodolphe Salis on an original idea of Émile Goudeau's, the "gentleman tavern keeper" didn't hesitate to shock the bourgeois by shouting at them mercilessly. Bruant was his successor in insolence and street humor at the Chat-Noir in its second incarnation (with the help of a shadow theater), then at the Mirliton. Through his songs and thanks to the poster by Toulouse-Lautrec, he has remained alive in the collective memory of the French.

And so, dotted with these legendary places, Montmartre kept the power to fascinate until the eve of the Great War. Its most glorious time was the days between 1900 and 1910 when the avant-garde painters moved in. But the success and laziness of some led them to desert a neighborhood that had remained poverty-stricken. In the future only a hill could gather around it the Montmartre heritage. "Bohemias must follow each other and each must be different; one generation has a jovial bohemia, the next has a sad one; I have a hunch that future young bohemians will be more and more pessimistic."[38] This prophecy of Émile Goudeau, colored perhaps

Figure 9.6

Merwart, *The Cabaret du Chat-Noir [Black Cat Cabaret]: The first of the projected shadows of "EPIC"* drawn by Caran d'Ache (1886). We recognize, from left to right, Armand Silvestre, Francisque Sarcey, Litvinne, Alphonse Daudet, Syamour, de Mun Račsy, Paul Merwart, Émile Zola, Mac-Nab (standing), Juliette Adam, Albert Wolff, Augusta Holmès, Ernest Renan, Carolus Duran, Ferdinand de Lesseps, Rodolphe Salis, Henri Rochefort, Clovis Hughes, General Boulanger, Reichemberg, Coquelin Junior, and Coquelin Senior. On the screen: "Napoleon by Caran d'Ache."

by the spirit of a time that was abandoning itself to Schopenhauer, would, for the time being, be belied by Montparnasse and its cafés.

Montparnasse

The end of the boulevards' reign had coincided with Montmartre's decline; it restored some life to the old Latin Quarter. The new generation, which Jean Moréas and Maurice Barrès would depict, was happy enough to frequent Le François Premier, still soaked with the memory of Verlaine, and, most of all, Vachette, where the author of *Stances* composed a few of his *Vers de café*.★ But this latest rejuvenation of the Latin Quarter was only a quick transition. The point of junction called "the angle of the diamond's cut"[39] between boulevard Saint-Michel and the Vavin intersection, the Closerie des Lilas—already made famous by the end of the nineteenth century by

★ *Vers* is both a line of poetry and a possible pun on *verre* (a glass) and on *ver* or *vers* (worm).—Ed.

Figure 9.7
Montmartre, Le Lapin A. Gill, around 1872: the Lapin Agile sign painted by André Gill is visible on the facade.

Richepin, Bouchor, Ponchon, Manet, Baudelaire, Jongkind, and Whis-
tler—became a universal meeting place for writers and painters from 1905
to the end of the Great War. The Closerie saw them come, in turn or sometimes together, the literary and artistic "schools," Parnassians, naturalists,
symbolists, unanimists, futurists and even, at the end, dadaists. And then
began the Montparnassian epic. Even more than Montmartre, more what
Saint-Germain-des-Près would be forty years later, Montparnasse sprang
from nothing. The initiative came first from Paul Fort, then from Andre
Salmon, from Guillaume Apollinaire and Stuart Merill.[40] From La Closerie, where he was chosen "Prince of Poets," Paul Fort directed *Vers et prose,*
an anthology revue of symbolist poets and prose writers. Every evening,
but especially on Tuesdays, he held meetings of the authors of *La Plume.*
It was for him a question of turning La Closerie into a vast international
brotherhood of the new spirit. In his *Mémoires,* he insists that he had more
than ten thousand letters written with the purpose of reaching the artistic
and literary milieus of the entire world. And so it was that Paul Fort had
imprinted Montparnasse with the characteristic that would become, after
the war, its most important feature: cosmopolitanism. Under the auspices
of good-natured café "patrons"[41] and indulgent waiters, Scandinavians,
Brazilians, Mexicans, Spaniards, Russian exiles, oddballs (*louftingues*) and
"montparnos" invaded the cafés—the inside tables and the sidewalk *ter-*

rasses—from morning till night. The principle came to be accepted that one needn't order more drinks after the first one. To this medley of nations and languages was soon added an intellectual and aesthetic mix. From the Dôme, from La Rotonde, the Café du Parnasse, from the Caméléon, where they showed their work, Foujita, Kisling, Modigliani, Roger Wild, and so many others made a "stock exchange of artistic values."[42] However, the economic crisis and the disturbances of the prewar period began to threaten the beautiful confusion that the cultural life of the neighborhood thrived on. Through the Montparnasse cafés, genuine annexes of the neighboring artists' studios, Paris was able to attain one of its mythic dreams: it became the universal capital of the mind. That colossal fair the Vavin intersection had been for twenty years, that noisy celebration everyone pretended they never wanted to end, at last bred a kind of weariness that sent some running and made others withdraw into themselves. From 1935 on, nostalgia prevailed over exuberance, a nostalgia which Paul Fort echoed: "Dear Closerie des Lilas, you seem bereft of your poetic glow today! And it's winter. Have you been murdered by La Coupole, La Rotonde, Le Dôme? If they did that they have killed their own mother."[43]

Saint-Germain-des-Prés

Those who write memoirs and columns are unanimous: at first Saint-Germain-des-Prés was popular because of its nearly provincial calm. At the very beginning of the century Café Caron, at the corner of the rue des Saints-Pères and the rue de l'Université was "completely of the old style, more a salon than a café,"[44] where pipe and conversations were forbidden. Around 1903, Léo Larguier frequented the Flore, where the domino players provided an old-fashioned charm. However, well before the era of the zoot-suiters (*zazous*), from the early 1920s, the neighborhood began to experience a certain effervescence. The nearness of publishers and booksellers in the sixth arrondissement and the proximity of the Chamber of Deputies attracted a clientele of politicians and intellectuals. Léon-Paul Fargue went regularly to "poison himself" at the Brasserie Lipp, where his father had designed the interiors, and he could watch Gaston Gallimard, Louis Jouvet, André Gide, Derain, or Patrice de La Tour du Pin.[45] Charles Maurras and the members of Action française were headquartered at the Flore. Surrealist dissidents (Leiris, Desnos, Ribemont-Dessaignes, and others) and then even André Breton himself convened at the Deux-Magots. But this activity was still not enough to compete with Montparnasse. It was "the Prévert gang," those of the October group, that launched, around 1938, Flore's good fortune and at the same time, that of the fifteen other cafés that clustered around it. During the occupation, the tightening of conditions, the general lack of comfort, and the difficulty of finding supplies made these cafés the permanent refuge of intellectuals, their natural sanctuary. It was at the Flore, as we all know, that Sartre and Beauvoir went to write, under the paternal eye of Paul Boubal. As much kept alive as it was distorted by the press, the fashion of Saint-Germain-des-Prés was identified at the liberation with the budding vogue for Jean-Paul Sartre: the entire neighborhood became the symbol of a popularized existentialism. It was entirely normal that when Juliette Greco and Anne-Marie Cazalis were interviewed by a journalist about "what they were," they would reply "existentialists, partly because they were rather literary, partly because . . . this philosophy was à la mode at that time among the snobs."[46] But the obtrusive publicity around what was really neither a school nor a movement forced its young creators to search out increasingly obscure and secret meeting places. Montmartre had had its cabarets; Saint-Germain-des-Prés would have its basement *caves*. Even more than the Flore or the Deux-Magots, it was the Bar Vert, the Tabou, and the Mephisto which gave Saint-Germain-des-Prés its "face" in the postwar period.

The Germanizing (*germanopratin*) phase, in its short-lived authentic stage, remained a determining factor in the image, not to mention the imagery, of the café. As in the Procope era, the cafés' literary, artistic, philosophic, and political vocation was vigorously confirmed. There they were, then, elevated to the rank of intellectual laboratories or, to use the language of the *Encyclopédie,* "factories of thought, as good as they were bad."

II. A "FACTORY FOR THOUGHT"

Never had France spoken more nor better. There was less eloquence and rhetoric than in 1789, they were missing a Rousseau. They had nothing to quote. Wit spurted spontaneously, as best it could. There is no doubt that this sparkling explosion owed much to the fortunate revolution of the time, to the great fact that created new habits and even changed temperaments: the coming of coffee.

Michelet continues his evocation of the influence of coffee on eighteenth-century society:

Coffee, the sober liqueur, powerfully cerebral, which, contrary to spirits, increases the sharpness and lucidity of thinking, this coffee, which suppresses the vague and heavy poetry of a smoky imagination; which from reality unflinchingly observed, brings forth sparks and bolts of truth; the strong coffee of Santo Domingo drunk by Buffon, by Diderot, by Rousseau, added its heat to souls already hot, to the

piercing vision of the prophets assembled in that lair, Procope, who
saw, in the depths of the dark brew, the future ray of light of '89.[47]

Coming from Michelet's lyrical pen, this praise of coffee and cafés is not
surprising. Visionary, always quick to associate economic and social phenomena with intellectual, ethical, and political events, Michelet pulls together in just a few lines the features that give coffee its symbolic impact.
If they needed a school for liberty, the café would be the place par excellence for critical minds to do their work and for new ideas to ferment.
Early on it would also be a kind of political and ideological club. Beneath
the exaggeration of his remarks and despite a highly rhetorical "retroactive prophecy," his fundamental intuition is not mistaken. It was in the
course of the eighteenth century that the writer and the thinker stopped
behaving as simple subjects to become citizens as well: citizens of a modern republic, whose competence extended well beyond letters; citizens
who appropriated for themselves a domain until then reserved for others.
Even if they did not yet know the name that would describe them, the
"intellectuals" were born. It was at the café, in particular, that one could
find the apprenticeship and the experience of this new condition.

A Counteracademy?

With the rise of cafés in France of the ancien régime, there appeared a sociability which opened the way to hitherto unexpected social relationships
and intellectual exchanges. Elitist, often inaccessible, the salons offered
encounters that were charming as well as affected. Constraints were all
the more strictly enforced because rules of urbane behavior were taken as
understood. One went to converse, certainly, but discussions were subject to the despotic laws of gallantry and courtesy. Another structure of
eventual hospitality, the academies, in fact formed a closed world. The
system of learned co-optation upon which they reposed made them fortresses of knowledge that shut out new men and more than one independent talent:[48] the misfortunes of Gilbert, the "unhappy poet," who
predated Chatterton, are instructive.[49] In this context the café, theoretically open to all, is quickly perceived to be antisalon, a counteracademy,
and even, to some, a counterchurch. As he evoked the regular sessions at
the Café de la Veuve Laurent where Fontenelle, Boindin, La Motte, and
also Jean-Baptiste Rousseau and Rochebrune went to compose quips and
to mock (more than judge) the current literary production, Voltaire observed: "It was a school of thought that allowed a little liberty."[50] Several
scattered remarks by his contemporaries echoed this thought. In a "Note
for Foreigners Who Know Nothing of Paris," the author of an anony-

mous pamphlet presented Procope as a place where "each has the right to speak and argue as he wishes"; the man who goes there, the author adds, has "full and complete permission to talk nonsense, for the rest of his life if he chooses."[51] A comedy that appeared in 1785 compared the literary cafés to the "museums" and "clubs" the "newspapers are talking about."[52] The play's main character, a café owner, defined his establishment (in La Fontaine's wry style) as "the casual, daily assembly" of a "literary breed that's swarming more than ever."[53]

By the freedom they offered, the cafés attracted a very diverse clientele that was not at all confined to the narrow coterie of the *philosophes*. Throughout the century—and in particularly obvious fashion in the seventeen-eighties—the cafés siphoned off the literary bohemia that Robert Darnton has demonstrated was a determining role in the preparation for the Revolution.[54] Numerous enough to make belief in a Republic of Letters, of which Voltaire, Diderot, and d'Alembert were the fascinating symbols, plausible, indeed rushing to it in the hope of rising in the social hierarchy by sheer force of talent, young authors saw themselves eliminated from the "world" by the elitist play of a corporate social system. At best they could hope to band together in the "museums," the lyceum, and the "clubs" that made official the function of the cafés. More often, however, they landed in the boulevard cafés that were the refuge of con men, spies, and prostitutes. There, they were able to spill out their hatred of an ancien régime too exclusive to include them. We see then, that at the same time they were multiplying, the cafés were defining their own hierarchy.[55] There was at work a split among the cafés that distinguished the *bureaux d'esprit* (offices of thought) from the cafés where one would find only "hangers-on [*raccrocheurs*], inoffensive saps, and the beautiful boys [*bardaches*]."[56] Even if it happened that someone sneered at the church and that someone else made unflattering comments about royal policy, Procope, Café Gradot, and the Café de la Veuve Laurent were branches of the academy and not of the counteracademies. Like the salons, they were the private preserve of protected *philosophes*. Rather, it was in the cafés of Palais-Royal and in those on the boulevards, where the obscure writers assembled, that one went looking for those who truly opposed the established power.

Schools of thought and of freedom, the cafés quickly awakened the authorities' suspicion. As early as 1685, at a time when Paris had only a very small number of cafés, Secretary of State Seignelay wrote to La Reynie, the lieutenant of the police: "The King has been informed that, in several places in Paris where they serve '*caffé*' [sic], there are gathering together all sorts of people, and in particular foreigners. Upon which, His Majesty orders me to write you to send me a memorandum about all those which sell [coffee] and to ask you whether you believe that it would be appropriate to prevent them from so doing in the future."[57] Naturally, in light of the success of the new beverage, the royal suggestion was not effectively followed. But it did begin a tradition of mistrust which in 1721 Montesquieu chose to interpret: "If I was the sovereign of this country, I would close the cafés; because those who frequent these places heat up their brains to a dangerous degree. I would prefer to see them intoxicating themselves in cabarets. At least then they would only harm themselves; otherwise, the drunkenness that coffee confers on them makes them dangerous for the future of the country."[58] From then on, officialdom's worst fears were confirmed.

Along with that of the salons and the public thoroughfares, the surveillance of cafés was part of the regular work of the police spies who, daily or weekly, delivered their reports to the lieutenant general, detailing conversations they had heard or overheard. Of course for the most part, these remarks had nothing subversive about them; often they were trivial chat or malicious society gossip.[59] In regard to this, the *Entretiens des cafés de Paris et les diférens qui y surviennent*, published in 1702 by the Count de Mailly, an excessively modest author, speak volumes: they are no less than the account of amorous adventures, quarrels about the respective qualities of the wines of Champagne or Burgundy, spats on the merits of this or that play and, much more rarely, controversies between the disciples of Gassendi and those of Descartes.[60] We know, however, that the habitués of Procope felt a need to thwart the attentiveness of spies: to carry their discussions of theodicy, the *philosophes* were accustomed to using a coded language. God was called Mr. Being (Monsieur de l'Être), Javotte's religion, and Margot's soul. Moreover, as it became more pronounced, the democratic character of cafés made them places increasingly difficult to monitor and rendered them even more disturbing. It is thus understandable that from the eve of the Revolution until the great laws of the Republic in the eighteen-eighties, these establishments became the object of increasingly active surveillance: in each period of crisis a repressive policy was adopted that tended to prevent the café from veering into another form: the political club.

This process, which was already apparent in Paris in the early seventeen-fifties, was responsible for the double image that the café has projected since the end of the eighteenth century. For some, the café was the ideal place for intellectual exchanges: it offered that slight disorder and gaiety of genuine quality, "that moderate tumult which perfectly suits the mind."[61] For others, on the contrary, it was the center of all vice: unhealthy and unproductive idleness hid there; it was there, in the café, that the failed writers and artists went to drown their disillusionment in drunkenness. An enlightened and moderate-minded man, Louis-Sébastien Mercier, seems to have been sensitive to both aspects; he would be ready to acknowledge some of the café's merits were it not for the degradation he thought it had suffered: "It is no longer respectable to linger in the café, because it indicates a dearth of knowledge and an absolute vacuum of social contacts; nevertheless a café where educated pleasant people gather would be preferable, by the fact of its freedom and gaiety, to our sometimes boring social circles."[62] Still ambiguous in the seventeen-eighties, café commentaries during the nineteenth century became more trenchant. That was when they became colored with ideological and political passion. For those with nostalgia for the salons, the café's success signified a debasement of the social forms. As it developed it had opened the way to a corrupting egalitarianism. By becoming more democratic, it had become vulgar. By becoming political it had contributed to dividing the country into factions. Such was, for example, the partisan opinion that colored Auguste Lepage's 1882 book on artistic and literary cafés. In a fit of resigned pessimism he remarked: "Each group, then, had its own café and one simply knew that the realist democrats met at one establishment, that the reactionaries, that is the sincere and non-partisan admirers of everything beautiful, were to be found in another."[63] Writers like Lepage notwithstanding, others, whether they were republicans, bohemians, or democrats, congratulated themselves on the revolution of social behavior that brought the café into prominence. "It is the café and the café alone that has enlightened minds, brought about the fusion of castes and provoked the most energetic demonstration of the people's will!" exclaimed the author of one of the *Physiologie des cafés de Paris* in 1841. The café is "democracy's salon" was the slogan that democrat publicist Hippolyte Castille soon launched.[64] Gambetta took it up, and this expression was so successful that it quickly passed into banality. When at a dinner in 1891 Eugene Spuller celebrated the café as "the salon of those who don't have one" it was acknowledged that this homage was thought suitable by those present.[65]

And so, as the salons' prestige—if not their number—diminished, and as an entirely new kind of bourgeois sociability asserted itself through the circle,[66] cafés became the stakes in an ideological debate. In the image he develops of "the upper crust at the café" (*Tout-Paris au café*) in the second half of the nineteenth century, journalist Maxime Rude dedicates his last chapter to "those who have never gone" and to "those who have stopped going."[67] He is not impartial when he distinguishes the men whom an early popularity has exempted from using the café as a forum from those once and for all dissuaded by their rank, fortune, or moral and political convictions from giving themselves over to a leisure activity they consider futile or vulgar. Among the former were Gambetta, who, after the impact of the Baudin trial no longer had to practice his oratorical talent before Procope's student audience; Thiers, who, already a minister in his thirties, could stop playing part of the smart set on the steps of Tortoni; and Carolus-Duran, who, full of his celebrity at the Cercle des Mirlitons, gave up his habits at Café Molière. Among the latter: the puritan Jules Favre, the ultramontane papist Louis Veuillot, the Duke de Broglie, "too much a lord," and Camille Doucet, life secretary in the Académie. As for men of letters and artists, they determined their form of sociability according to the answer they had for the question that was latent in each of them: what example of life should one prefer, the one Henry Murger proposes with so much good-naturedness, or that life, on a higher plane, from the hermit of Croisset? Around 1875, Paul Bourget didn't mind taking part in the merry drinking parties that brought Richepin, Bouchor, Ponchon, Coppée, and Mendès around the tables of the Sherry-Cobbler. But some years later, his friends watched him keep his distance, as if drawn into the orbit of the salons. Soon after that he preferred the life of a recluse and in one of his poems denounced the softening of resolve that was in store for café regulars:

> I sat down in a far corner of some café.
> I watched through thick and overheated air
> as they leaned over glasses where absinthe clouded,
> Men not past thirty, eyes without light,
> Already bald, they smoked and they read the paper.[68]

Just out of the École Normale Supérieure, Francisque Sarcey's literary debut was a virulent article in which he sneered at bohemians and branded them "brasserie melancolics."[69] Nevertheless, by midcentury everyone went to cafés, so it was less important to take sides with those for or against cafés than to say what kind of establishment one looked for. As an already fashionable and distinguished young man, Sarcey set his sights on Momus; he wouldn't have dared take on Tortoni. Fernand Vandérem showed in one of his novels how Paris had progressively broken into two antagonistic castes symbolized by the two banks of the Seine.[70] The narrow classicism of the academy and bourgeois good taste triumphed on the Right Bank. On the Left Bank, one only accepted that which was on the Left.[71] In the boulevard cafés middle-aged men would fret about the next Académie election. In the Latin Quarter cafés—and, soon, in those of Montmartre/ "free city"—youth raised statues to writers that had none and demolished those of consecrated authors. Philibert Audebrand told about the time in the eighteen-sixties when the fellow diners of the Brasserie des Martyrs, whose rallying cry was "It's youth's turn," sometimes went to the Café de Robespierre to insult the "dolts" (*ganaches*) and "Methuselahs."[72] As for Charles Virmaître, he complained in 1888 of ridiculous statements one would hear in the "so-called artistic dives": this or that apprentice musician dared question the musical science of Meyerbeer, or some little upstart rhymer insisted from his high horse that Lamartine was a mediocre poet: "In these brasseries it's a perpetual disparagement of anyone successful and as soon as you have a little talent you're a good-for-nothing; nothing exists outside of their own circle."[73] Rivalries like these reflect the traditional cleavage that opposed well-to-do and poor, celebrities and unknown artists, conformists and bohemians. Most of all they illustrate the different use each made of the café. For the former, the café was no more than an agreeable pastime, an opportunity for a convenient interlude; it was a kind of circle where one chatted instead of gambling. For the latter, who had been shut out of not only the salons, but also the theater companies and the editorial offices of newspapers and publishers, the café took the place of everything. It was part of the public arena and the salon. It was an extension of the Paris street, the forum where one could test one's eloquence and wit, strengthen one's hopes, and heal a measure of bitterness. Here, then, is the start of an outline for a kind of typology of intellectuals that derives from the place for sociability they frequent. One can compare intellectual types: the overeager social climber tempted by academic ambition, Abel Herman, for example; or the meticulous university type, often seen as haughty, a Romain Rolland. The jolly, intellectual bohemian typified by Léon-Paul Fargue rose up among them in the twentieth century.[74]

It is, of course, obvious that not all cafés were centers of intellectual agitation or political opposition; nor had all played the role of the "anti-academy." Nevertheless this was the image that finally captured the collective memory of the French, a memory that was by its very essence forgetful and selective. In a leap of hospitable generosity, that memory had assembled into the pantheon of nonconformity and avant-garde ideology Procope and its *philosophes*, the Brasserie des Martyrs and its bohemians, Montmartre and its second-rate painters, Montparnasse and its oddballs, Saint-Germain-des-Près and its "zoot suiters," not to mention the Odéon brasseries and their sixty-eighters. Such an amalgam, while shocking at first glance, seems ascribable to the fact that each time, with each new generation, the café contributed to the spread of a mentality that was typical of a time and a society. In that sense it would be a kind of laboratory where the French spirit, or at least certain fragments, would come in search of itself, sometimes to flower.

An Intellectual Laboratory?

By peddling the banal idea that the café occupies an eminent place in French literary history, textbooks, newspapers, and popular magazines have insured the success of a debate that is not only minor but also has obscured the real question.[75] Instead of examining the role the café might have had in the elaboration and diffusion of ideas, some have been satisfied simply to distinguish between a high literature conceived in solitude and a literature called "café literature." Apart from the fact that this division assumes it is easy to define the place where a work of art takes form, it has the further defect of artificially opposing the Republic of Letters and the Republic of Arts. On one hand there would be authors worthy of that title, enemies of frivolity, and on the other hand superficial minds. As for Verlaine, he would be the exception that confirmed the rule, the one who would have deliberately traded the merest hope of a fortieth chair in the academy for the very real imitation leather of a café seat. But the cliché is firmly imbedded in the thinking of those days. Disgusted by the show the Montmartre of the nineteen hundreds had put on for him, an English tourist became annoyed at what she took to be the undeserved reputation of the artistic and literary cafés: look at Hugo, look at Leconte de Lisle, François Coppée, Sully Prudhomme, she tells us; none of them needed to go to a smoky brasserie for his inspiration.[76] Léo Larguier reported that brief but frequent appearances at the Cluny nearly cost André Bellesort his chair in the French Academy, his rivals repeated to all and sundry that it would be difficult to justify admitting a pillar of café society into the holy of holies.[77] Finally, in a withering diatribe that appeared in 1934, a journalist condemned café literature, which he saw fit to oppose to a literature of "the cell," in the sense of monastic isolation: "There really is a café literature; but only one . . . , it is quite simply literature about the café; nothing more. Pages have their smell. From a distance we can identify a 'page of café' . . . What are we waiting for to describe the influence of nicotine and caffeine on the progress of art and thought? . . . The café, that's real. But it is a reduced reality . . . with such a low ceiling!"[78]

Despite the glorious exception of Verlaine—to whom we might add Moréas—the image of the author who writes in the café is tinged with the legendary, no matter how deeply rooted the image might be. It was only periodically and as a result of imperious necessity that the café became a study. In the nineteenth century the discomfort of the rooms in the Latin Quarter made Champfleury and his companions spend entire days in the café.[79] During the occupation, Sartre and Beauvoir went to write at the Flore for analogous reasons. As for the surrealists, if they asked the waiter

Figure 9.8
Paul Fort (at right) on the terrace of the Closerie des Lilas around 1920.

Figure 9.9
Simone de Beauvoir at the Café des Deux-Magots.

for paper and ink so often, it was because the writing games they played
came out of a collective thought process. We shall let Louis Aragon tell
us where and how "words took [him] by the hand":

> There had been the season of the Rotonde and that
> of some bistro or other over by Courcelles
> There had been that café in the Passage Jouffroy
> The Excelsior Porte Maillot that narrow bar
> rue du Faubourg-Saint-Honoré
>
> . . . .
>
> There were three or four of us at the end of the day
> > sitting
> Coupling sounds to reshape things
> Endlessly moving to metamorphoses
> And we made strange animals leap out
> Because one of us had invented to use on words
> > a kind of wolf-trap but for speed
> Waiter something to write on And born in our steps
> The antelope-pleasure the compass gulls
> > Great anteater eating sadness
>
> Pictures reversed as if painted on ceilings
> Varieties of sleep unknown to Buffon.[80]

But, in general, it was anything but the occasional editorial office that
men of letters and artists came looking for in the café. Let us not forget
that the café and the gazette were born at the same time. When the old
social form of the evening gathering faded, it was the café that took its
place: to the attraction of drink was added more and more often the seduction of the reading of the newspaper with commentary. By the middle
of the nineteenth century, and especially in the north of France, many
coffee houses had taken to the habit of subscribing to several periodicals,
as a courtesy to their customers. In Paris this phenomenon was general.[81]
When the writer went to the café, Auguste Lepage observed in 1882, "it
is to read the papers, the magazines, to write a letter or answer one, to see
a colleague, to meet with those too irksome to see elsewhere, but rarely
to have a good time."[82] Thus that space for freedom soon played a role
analogous to that of a laboratory for ideas and experiments: in the dialogue there one tested opinions; it was there that doctrines appeared in
outline, there that esthetic, ethical, and political choices became clearer
and that affinities and discords were born. The café's function was close,
therefore, to that of a magazine. But its characteristic was to be a spoken

and contradictory magazine from which the new spirit burst forth to be subsequently expressed in books, periodicals, or even manifestos or on the walls of galleries and museums. With this in mind it is probably not too bold to assert that the Brasserie Andler was the den of realism and Café Guerbois, even more than the Durand-Ruel Gallery, was the cradle of impressionism. In the eighteen-fifties, critics, painters, and young writers rushed to rue Hautefeuille to receive "the baptism of 'Reality.'"[83] About twenty years later Zola and Antonin Proust went to Café Guerbois to support those the quiet bourgeois of the neighborhood called "these gentlemen from the Batignolles School." But the esthetic, not to mention the ideological commitment of these cafés, also threatened their fortune. When the legitimacy of realism was no longer in question, Brasserie Andler slowly lost its clientele of reformers. As soon as bohemians achieved notoriety or fame, the Brasserie des Martyrs returned to its earlier state: that of a neighborhood public house. As soon as impressionism no longer raised controversy, Café Guerbois and Le Rat-Mort attracted a more mixed clientele.

Besides, what is true of magazines is also true of cafés. Some form only tiny coteries and are, by their nature, ephemeral. By contrast, others open themselves to all trends and enjoy a more durable popularity. If Montparnasse was, for twenty years, regarded as "the great university of the world,"[84] it is because its cafés knew to welcome and mix all the avant-gardes. This eclecticism was a promise of longevity. But, by reason of the very fascination they held, artistic and literary cafés soon saw those who had made their celebrity withdraw. Deserted battlefields, they then entered into legend.

"The Cafés of Paris"

One day as Léo Larguier sat daydreaming at the village sidewalk café, the café owner went up to him and, thinking he should console him, murmured: "Don't be bored . . . you'll be back soon enough in your big Paris cafés!"[85]

"The cafés of Paris!" This innocent expression was like magic words to Léo Larguier. All at once it gave him his first visit to the Café Napolitain, to the sidewalk tables of Deux-Magots and the muffled interiors of Lipp. For nearly three centuries the café's seductive power over the imagination has not ceased to increase Paris's legend. For the provincial as for the foreigner, frequenting cafés is one way to become initiated into the mysteries of the capital, to take for oneself this "Parisine" which Nestor Roqueplan distilled into its charms and defined as a kind of antidote: "We say strychnine, quinine, nicotine, aniline . . . I say: Parisine."[86] Also, few accounts of trips to Paris fail to devote a few lines or even an entire chapter to the recreation of the most famous establishments. At the beginning of the eighteenth century the tutor Joachim-Christophe Nemeitz endeavored to describe the "cafés of bright minds" which he saw as one of the capital's original features.[87] Around 1880 Edmondo de Amicis, the successful author of *Souvenirs de Paris et de Londres,* observed indulgently that "Tortoni is more famous than many of the immortal monuments."[88] After the liberation, when articles in *Samedi-Soir* and *Life* had let the whole world know that Saint-Germain-des-Près had become the center of intellectual life, Americans rushed to the Flore and to Deux-Magots, thereby chasing away the original habitués.[89]

If tourism occasionally corrupted the very places it set its heart on, it also helped to perpetuate their memory. Beyond the passing prestige that this or that political or artistic circumstance had gotten them, cafés have often had the good luck of a second life. Once the players are gone and the effervescence is flat, they remain: witnesses miraculously rescued from a bygone time. As they become sites of pilgrimage, we visit them as we would a museum, in the secret hope of finding something there from a lost time.

NOTES

1. On the myth of Paris see Pierre Citron, *La Poésie de Paris dans la littérature française de Rousseau à Baudelaire,* 2 vols. (Paris: Éditions de Minuit, 1961).

2. Félix Mornand, *La Vie de Paris* (Paris: Librairie Nouvelle, 1855), 24.

3. Philibert Audebrand, *Un café de journalistes sous Napoleon III* (Paris: E. Dentu, 1888), 8.

4. There are however some notable exceptions: for example the Cabaret de la Pomme de Pin (The Pine Cone Cabaret) was frequented by Villon in the fifteenth, by Rabelais in the sixteenth, by Guillaume Colletet et Saint-Pavin in the seventeenth century.

5. To be convinced of this it is enough to leaf through the "Actualités" dossiers in the collection of the history library of the City of Paris (series 77, Cafés, "Généralités").

6. In Vienna of 1900 there were more than six hundred cafés. Among the great arts cafés we can name: Café Griensteidl, Café Central, Café Herrenhof, Café Museum, Café Imperial, and Café Sperl. On Viennese cafés see Ulla Heise, *Histoire du café et des cafés les plus célèbres* (Paris: Belfond, 1988). There is also some information in Heinrich Eduard Jacob, *L'Épopée du café* (Paris: Édition du Seuil, 1953): 208–21.

7. On the spread of the uses of coffee, cf. especially Alfred Franklin, *Le Café, le thé et le chocolat* (Paris: Plon, 1893). See also Auguste Chevalier, *Le Café* (Paris: PUF, 1944), and particularly the very recent *Histoire du café* by Frederic Mauro (Paris:

Desjonquères, 1991); from 1723 (year of the monopoly concession) to 1769 (the year it was suppressed), commerce in coffee was a lucrative source of profit for the French East India Company. Established as early as 1720 on Île Bourbon, Île-de-France, and in the French West Indies (Antilles), coffee-growing rapidly prospered. For nearly a century it was the French colonies that supplied Europe in coffee. More than thirty thousand tons of it were produced annually up to the eve of the French Revolution.

8. The wine merchants' hostility to coffee gave rise to a campaign of libel. Again at the beginning of the eighteenth century there appeared a *Manifeste de Bacchus contre les cafés et vendeurs de bière, avec ordonnance pour la réforme des moeurs et la conduite de ses sujets* (Paris: G. Valleyre, 1711).

9. *L'Écossaise ou le café: Comédie en cinq actes par Voltaire, représentée pour la première fois au Théâtre-Français le 26 juillet 1760* (Paris: Veuve Dabo, 1822).

10. *Discours de M. le Premier Président de la Chambre des Communes du Caffé de Dubuisson, successeur de Procope, sur les affaires actuelles de l'État* (N.p., n.d.).

11. Audebrand, 7.

12. *Confessions d'un étudiant: Estaminets, bouges et ruisseaux par un Bohème* (Paris: Lucien Marpon, 1860), 52.

13. Nicolas Restif de la Bretonne, *Les Nuits de Paris* (London, 1788), 1:470.

14. On the role of Parisian cafés in the eighteenth-century, it is useful to consult the master's degree thesis of Chantal Grell: *Les Cafés parisiens au XVIIIe siècle: Étude sociale, politique et intellectuelle* (University of Paris-IV, 1977). The use of *gazetins*, those reports sent by spies to the lieutenant general of police, provides the original contribution of this work.

15. Denis Diderot, *Le Neveu de Rameau,* critical edition with notes and lexicon by Jean Fabre (Geneva: Droz, 1963), 3.

16. Here is what the character, the nouvelliste, becomes under the incisive pen of Lesage: "What is amusing to think about is that this eccentric wanted to appear knowledgeable about all the news, and if he heard someone talking about something that was new to him, he would—quite rudely—interrupt whoever was announcing it and shut him up by telling him: 'you don't have the right gloves for it' . . . I admired that nouvelliste's impressive air and had to laugh to myself." From Alain-René Lesage, *La Valise trouvée* (N.p., 1740), 67f.

17. *Journal de Madame Cradock: Voyage en France (1783–1786),* translated from the original unpublished manuscript by Mme O. Delphin Balleyguier (Paris: Perrin et Cie., 1869).

18. E. F. Bazot, *Les Cafés de Paris ou revue politique, critique et littéraire des moeurs du siècle par un flâneur patenté* (Paris: Lécrivain, 1819).

19. Ibid., 70–71.

20. Edmond-Auguste Texier, *Tableau de Paris,* 2 vols. (Paris: Paulin et Le Chevalier, 1852–53).

21. Mornand, 21.

22. Jules Barbey d'Aurevilly, *Une vieille maîtresse* (Paris: Gallimard, 1979), 3.

23. In their *Journal* the Goncourt brothers stress this phenomenon in October 1857: "Murger, with whom we dined [at the Café Riche] makes his act of faith to us. He renounces Bohemia and crosses lock, stock, and baggage over to the side of worldly men of letters."

24. Auguste Lepage, *Les Cafés artistiques et littéraires de Paris* (Paris: Martin-Boursin, 1882), 194.

25. With the notable exception of the Café Anglais, which remained loyal to the tradition of a certain sobriety.

26. Léo Larguier, *Au Café de l'Univers* (Avignon: Aubanel, 1942), 72.

27. See J. A. Luthereau, *Charles Duval architecte* (Paris: Chaix, 1856); and *Le Grand Café parisien, le plus grand café du monde* (N.p., n.d.).

28. Marcel Boulenger, *Cours de vie parisienne à l'usage des étrangers* (Paris: Paul Ollendorff, 1913): 185–87.

29. *Physiologie des cafés de Paris* (Paris: Desloges, 1841), 103.

30. Champfleury, *Souvenirs et portraits de jeunesse* (Paris: E. Dentu, 1872), 186.

31. For the Café de l'Union, see Charles Virmaître, *Paris oublié* (Paris: Dentu, 1886), chap. 2, 53–84.

32. Alphonse Daudet, *Trente ans de Paris* (Paris: Marpon et Flammarion, 1888), 253.

33. Emile Goudeau, *Dix ans de bohème* (Paris: Librairie Illustrée, 1888): 1–15.

34. Henry Murger, *Scènes de la vie de bohème* (Paris: Julliard, 1964), chap. 11, 165–75, and passim.

35. First heard at the Besselièvre concert, *l'Hydropathen-valsh,* attributed to a certain Gungl', gave Goudeau the idea for this group.

36. On one of the shutters of the Cabaret des Assassins, André Gill had drawn a rabbit escaping a pot and carrying a bottle, whence the name "Lapin à Gill" (Gill's rabbit) and soon after the "Lapin Agile" (Agile Rabbit). La Grande Pinte (the Tall Pint) was called L'Âne Rouge (the red ass) because of a drawing by Wilette showing Rodolphe Salis's brother as a red ass.

37. Georges Montorgueil, *La Vie à Montmartre* (Paris: G. Boudet, 1899), 147.

38. Goudeau, 282.

39. Paul Fort, *Mes mémoires: Toute la vie d'un poète (1872–1943)* (Paris: Flammarion, 1944), 91.

40. See Fort; and André Salmon, *Montparnasse* (Paris: Andre Bonne, 1950). See also Gustave Fuss-Amoré and Maurice des Ombiaux, *Montparnasse* (Paris: Albin Michel, 1925); and Jean-Émile Bayard, *Montparnasse hier et aujourd'hui: Ses artistes, ses écrivains étrangers et français les plus célèbres* (Paris: Jouve et Cie., 1927).

41. Libion at La Rotonde; Lafon at La Coupole, opened December 20, 1927.

42. Salmon, 129.

43. Fort, 92.

44. Remy de Gourmont quoted by Larguier, 131.

45. For the history of the Brasserie Lipp, see Marcelin Cazes, *Cinquante ans de Lipp* (Paris: La Jeune Parque, 1966).

46. Jean-Paul Sartre quoted by Anne-Marie Cazalis, *Les Mémoires d'une Anne* (Paris: Stock, 1976), 76. For life in Saint-Germain-des-Près at the liberation, the best informed document is still Boris Vian, *Manuel de Saint-Germain-des-Près* (Paris: Chêne, 1974).

47. Jules Michelet, *La Régence* (Paris: Chamerot, 1863): 174–75. Alluding to the progressive incursion of the café in the West, particularly in France, Michelet

adds: "The three ages of the café are those of modern thought; they mark the solemn moments of the mind's brilliant century."

48. On academic milieus of the eighteenth century, we return to that reference, Daniel Roche's thesis: *Le Siècle des lumières en province: Académies et académiciens provinciaux (1660–1789)*, 2 vols. (The Hague: Mouton, 1978).

49. Laurent Gilbert (1751–80), born into a family of poor farmers, tried in vain to break into the academies. He symbolizes the *poète malheureux* (the unhappy poet), which is also the title of one of his first plays.

50. *Oeuvres de Voltaire, avec préfaces, avertisssements, notes par M. Breuchot* (Paris: Lefevre, Werdet et Lequien fils, 1929), 37:491.

51. *Discours de M. le Premier Président*, 4 and 23.

52. We have known since the pioneer work by Daniel Mornet, *Les Origines intellectuelles de la Révolution française (1715–1787)* (Paris: Armand Colin, 1934), the role the "museums," the "lyceum" and the "clubs" played in the preparation for 1789: these institutions, which proliferated beginning in 1787, strongly contributed to the popularization of the Enlightenment spirit. We might add that Roger Chartier has taken up this subject in his work, *Les Origines culturelles de la Révolution française* (Paris: Éditions du Seuil, 1990).

53. A. Carriere-Doisin, *Le Café littéraire ou la folie du jour, comédie-prologue sans préface représentée tous les jours et selon les circonstances* (Athens and Paris: Leroy, 1785).

54. Robert Darnton, *Bohème littéraire et Révolution: Le Monde des livres au XVIIIe siècle* (Paris: Gallimard-Éditions du Seuil, 1983), 23 and passim.

55. According to A. Franklin in *Le Café, le thé et le chocolat,* there would have been 380 cafés in Paris in 1723 and 1800 on the eve of the Revolution.

56. François-Marie Mayeur de Saint-Paul, *Le Désoeuvré, ou l'espion du boulevart [sic] du Temple* (London, 1781).

57. Archives nationales, Registres du Secrétaire d'État de la Maison du Roi, D1 29, f. 568, December 27, 1685.

58. Montesquieu quoted by François Fosca, *Histoire des cafés de Paris* (Paris: Firmin-Didot, 1934), chap. 2, "Les Cafés du XVIIIe siècle."

59. Grell, 85–86 and passim.

60. Comte de Mailly, *Les Entretiens des cafés de Paris et les diferens qui y surviennent* (Trévoux: Étienne Ganeau, 1702).

61. Bazot, 144.

62. Mercier, vol. 1, chap. 71.

63. Lepage, 235–36.

64. Hippolyte Castille quoted by Alfred Delvau, in *Histoire anecdotique des cafés et cabarets de Paris* (Paris: E. Dentu, 1862), 7–8.

65. *L'Éclair,* January 19, 1891, "Le règne des cafés" (anonymous article).

66. Of course this sends us back to Maurice Agulhon's work, *Le Cercle dans la France bourgeoise (1810–1838): Étude d'une mutation de sociabilité* (Paris: Armand Colin, 1977).

67. Maxime Rude, *Tout Paris au café* (Paris: Maurice Dreyfous, 1877), chap. 29, 293–99.

68. Paul Bourget quoted by Goudeau, 56–57.

69. The episode is retold by Alphonse Daudet in *Trente ans de Paris,* 249.

70. Fernand Vanderem, *Les Deux rives,* 2 vols. (Paris: P. Ollendorff, 1897).

71. On the subject of Left Bank writers, Marcel Boulenger (op. cit., 212) jeers: "They decided that Art was on the left and nowhere else and that whosoever set foot in a salon could not know how to write. Finally they declared the law of suspects: 'Thou shalt not scoff, nor smile, nor have a tailor nor a horse nor even a dog. . . . And thou shalt never feel at home in you know which despicable brasseries.'"

72. Audebrand, 89–90.

73. Virmaître, 133–34.

74. Along with others, the author of *Refuges* had the presentiment that the decline of the salons was the prelude to the café's rule: "When Léon Daudet, an old Parisian who knew value, said that as far as reputation was concerned the café had had the salon beat for some time, he was telling the truth, he was accurate. Why? Well, because in France, and in the provinces as well as in Paris, the café was conceived for the conversations of individuals or groups since, for far more than two hundred years those who have something to say, to defend, to fight for, need to meet and put their concepts to the test; because, if I may say so, cafés were always the cradles of clubs and schools of thought [*chapelles*] and it was from these that schools arose and from the schools that men of talent, accomplishment, and genius arose"; from Léon-Paul Fargue, *Refuges* (Paris: Émile-Paul Frères, 1942), 100.

75. Thus, in his account of François Fosca's *Histoire des cafés de Paris,* Edmond Jaloux states, "For three centuries a very important part of the history of France has been prepared and discussed in the café"; "Des cafés," *Le Temps,* March 23, 1935.

76. Mrs. Richard Whiteing, *The Life of Paris* (London: John Murray, 1900): 210–11.

77. Larguier, 181.

78. "Le café et le réel," June 16, 1934, signed R.K., "Actualités" files in the historical library of the City of Paris (series 77, Cafés, Généralités), unidentified newspaper.

79. Champfleury observes in his *Souvenirs et portraits de jeunesse* (122), "The truth is that until 1848 our study was more located in hospitable cafés where the gang pulled in at nine o'clock in the morning with raging appetites and didn't leave before midnight. Some read, others played; some wrote for want of anything else to do, and it was a big surprise the day Fauchery came with his engraving tools and tried to practice his trade."

80. Louis Aragon, *Le Roman inachevé* (Paris: Gallimard, 1966): 80–81 (*Les mots m'ont pris par la main*).

81. On this subject see Frédéric Barbier, "Libraires et colporteurs," in *Histoire de l'édition française* (Paris: Promodis, 1985) 3:243.

82. Lepage, *Les Cafés artistiques et littéraires,* 4.

83. Champfleury, 187.

84. Fuss-Amoré and des Ombiaux, 11.

85. Laguier, 36.

86. Nestor Roqueplan, *Parisine* (Paris: J. Jetzel, n.d.).

87. Joachim-Christophe Nemeitz, *Séjours de Paris c'est à dire instructions fidèles pour les voyageurs de condition* (Leide: Jean van Abcoude, 1727). See chap. 13, "De la fréquentation des caffez, comme aussi des jeux de paume et de billard."

88. Edmondo de Amicis, *Souvenirs de Paris et de Londres* (Paris: Hachette, 1880), 245. This work has had many editions and translations.

89. Anne-Marie Cazalis comments (90), "It was the Americans who really launched Saint-Germain-des-Près in 1947. The myth was neither born in existentialism nor even in the neighborhood basement 'caves,' but in the columns of the international press."

CHAPTER 10

NOTRE DAME OF PARIS

❧

ALAIN ERLANDE-BRANDENBURG

Encircled by the arms of a powerful river which half parts to better present an audacious and proud apse and thereby better enhance
it, Notre Dame of Paris seems to receive with noble disdain this homage rendered by water to so superbly moored a monument. It appears to
be unaware of all that moves at its feet, so strong is the vertical tension
which animates it. It effortlessly continues the long dialogue it has engaged in with eternity since the twelfth century. So it appears to someone
going down the Seine. Completely different is the impression one gets
when approaching Notre Dame from the west. The long distance that
one must cover before reading the base of its façade appears as dwarfing
as the splendid isolation makes it appear immense. How can one attempt
to revive the former dialogue between the city and the edifice, once so
intense when the cathedral was surrounded by the teeming life that Victor Hugo knew just how to revive in his 1831 *Notre-Dame de Paris*? The
evocation proved, at that time, easier than it would be today, the Île de la
Cité having not yet been gutted. The present reality belongs entirely to
the nineteenth century, which succeeded in tailoring Notre Dame little
by little to its own vision. Notre Dame lost its original meaning to a new
one given to it by the crowds that invade the church without wishing to
find a place of contemplation there. Notre Dame is no longer the pro-
jection of a vaster reality: it is satisfied today to be itself. In the collective
unconscious, it belongs to those *monstres sacrés* that are symbols of Paris,

Figure 10.1
Notre-Dame de Paris, photo by Marc Gantier.

rivaling the Eiffel Tower, the Centre Georges-Pompidou, the Louvre, and the tomb of Napoleon I. It is a memory of a history; although barely perceived, it testifies to one of the great moments of architecture. The religious meaning, which it had since its inception, has been followed by a new symbolism which belongs to our time. This strange bond that the modern world has forged only appears renewed. In this respect, the destiny of Paris's cathedral is unique because each era has created its own vision, loading the edifice with a particular dimension. During the nineteenth century, this was of a political nature. Are the millions of visitors who walk through and around the church each year conscious of this? In the end they retain only the aesthetic aspect, which affects them more or less deeply. How could they understand today the magnitude of Louis XIII's vow in a nineteenth-century presentation which, with its urge toward the ordinary, suppressed all symbolism? It is this same discouragement which takes hold of the historian when he endeavors to understand the bond that was established between the monument and men.

CLOVIS, OR THE SUCCESSFUL BET

The history of the origins of the cathedral of Paris still presents many difficulties attesting to the absence of documentation which would allow for an answer to a delicate question. Without getting into an analysis of the different theories, let us say by way of summary that it is generally acknowledged that the foundations of the edifice excavated in the middle of the nineteenth century[1] and again in recent years which stand on the *parvis* date to the Merovingian era—and more precisely to the reign of Childebert.[2] We will see later that this very old thesis[3] could not predate the twelfth century, and was elaborated during an era which sought to exalt the memory of the first line of kings. In fact, the fundamental revival of studies dedicated to this period, and above all, its different approach, obliges us to frame the Merovingian question in other terms.[4] Whereas, until fairly recently, historians insisted more on the "barbarous" aspect of the invasions, they seek today to show not so much the rupture as the continuity between the new era and the world which immediately preceded it. Henri-Irénée Marrou endeavored to shed light on this complex period by insisting on the birth of a unique civilization prior to the invasions: a "late antiquity," into which the Germanic peoples were integrated without great difficulty.[5] It was distinguished from others in the new area of religion by a profound change: the appearance of a "new religiosity" which made paganism obsolete. God invaded the Mediterranean world, reducing the gods to deceitful idols; man thought of himself above all with reference to God. Christianity participated in this movement, of which it was the most illustrious manifestation, and would triumph, thanks to its ecumenism.

While this revolution was taking place in hearts and minds, the secular world underwent an upheaval with lasting effects. The ancient town was an open unwalled town, a fact explained by the Pax Romana. The dangers of invasions made it necessary to establish a stone protection around the political and administrative heart of each of these, in order to take care of these sorts of *castra*. But life continued *extra muros*.[6] It was within these walls that the cathedral complex was to take root: the double cathedral, the baptistery, the *domus episcope*, and the annexes.[7] At the moment when the Germanic peoples crossed the *limes*, the Christian administrative network was thus perfectly organized, and the modifications made to it later on proved to be fairly minor. The Germanic tribes were to discover towns protected by strong stone walls, within which the religious life was forcefully asserted. One appeared inseparable from the other: the urban world was a Christian world, which is not to say Catholic. Recent research in this area has revealed that all cathedrals had been constructed from the very beginning inside the closed town and that certain ones took up a substantial part of their towns' areas.[8] What is the place of Paris in this general panorama?

Clovis's choice of this town as the kingdom's capital was made to coincide with his baptism. They appear as major events that go beyond the limited framework of a simple biography; both were to determine to a great extent the history of the country. The notion that they had been united, belonged to the "political" arena, and had even been tightly linked should not be entirely ruled out, even if the dates do not overlap: 498 or 499 for the baptism at Reims, 508 for the choice of Paris as capital.[9] We know that the sovereign's conversion brought Clovis approval: the Gallo-Romans must have been happy to say that a barbarian king had embraced the Catholic faith and not the Arian one like so many others henceforth considered to be odious heretics. Although Clovis's seemingly extraordinary luck smacks of a premeditated act, it must be added that Paris was known as a town where Catholicism was particularly developed. The archaeological discoveries of the last century and of recent years have been particularly eloquent in this regard:[10] the number of necropolises unearthed compels us to imagine numerous sites of worship. This seems to indicate a profoundly Christianized town, fully developed and prosperous, amid the fairly loose urban fabric, but sufficiently tied to the nucleus of the island, enclosed by a stone defensive wall, to form a true town. Without great risk of error, one can affirm that the reign of Clovis fits into this continuity. The sole contribution by the king was the foundation of the Apostles, on the summit of the hill which would become the "Montagne Sainte-

Geneviève."[11] In doing this, Clovis renewed Constantine's legacy: he put his new capital under the protection of Christ's disciples as well as under his own when he decided to have himself buried there.

The Merovingian king did not have the leisure to carry out his plan, which gave full meaning to his course of action; it was left to Clotilde, who took care to lay the body of her royal spouse to rest there.[12] To the religious reasons which prompted the king to make such a choice we must add others related to the quality of the site, remarkable not only for strategic reasons but also for its convenience in terms of defense, ease of communication across the Seine—thanks to the island—and the waterway represented by this superb river. Indeed, the swampy right bank seemed unfavorable for any such development. The left bank, on the other hand, offered the possibility of some comfort: the tiered public buildings that rose up along the slopes of the promontory, and the villas to the west assured it. Finally, the island, naturally protected by the river, was reinforced by a recently built powerful stone wall. It enclosed, among other buildings, the palace which would become the royal residence as it had been in the days of the emperors Julian (357–58 and 359–60) and Valentinian (365–66). Ultrogothe, Childebert's wife, enjoyed cultivating a garden which Venantius Fortunatus could not stop praising.[13] The island was divided by a transversal road, the *cardo*, thus creating a bipolarization which only became more apparent over time: political authority to the west, religious authority to the east. With its ten hectares, the island equaled some ancient cities in size (Rouen, Nantes, Strasbourg), and was smaller than others (Autun, Nîmes). Its fate differed fundamentally from theirs because of the role that it played in the political life of the country. It seems inconceivable that Clovis had not found in Paris the qualities that he had found in each of the royal cities he created, which had this same bipolarity. The absence of a cathedral in the city chosen as capital was hardly within the realm of possibility. Without tackling the delicate question of the chronology of the edifice discovered in front of the west façade of the Gothic cathedral, let us say that a number of reasons argue in favor of a date before Clovis's reign.[14] Indeed, at first, only the westernmost part was unearthed in 1847 and from 1962 onward, while the rest remained forever engulfed by the twelfth-century construction. The plan could nevertheless be determined, as well as the quite exceptional dimensions. With its five naves, it covers a width of thirty-six meters; it is the only one of its kind in Gaul—if one excludes Trèves. But Trèves, with its double cathedral and baptistery, is explained by the fact that it was one of the capitals of the empire: Constantine's mother was no doubt familiar with its foundation. We know that the emperor took a personal interest in the design of worship sites intended for Christians: the basilica had the advantage of being an enormous mass terminated in the east by an apse, with or without a transept, in which the faithful could celebrate the Eucharist. The abandonment of the arch in favor of a wooden frame allowed for a very light construction, with thinner walls to support it; it could have as many as five large openings between the different naves, with bays inserted at narrow intervals to let air and light circulate. This luminosity was accentuated in the east by even more numerous perforations. Light thus introduced into the house of worship reflected off walls covered in mosaics and floors inlaid with marble. Thus enveloped by light, the believer neared divine contemplation, God being light. The Parisian cathedral must have offered an identical picture, if one can trust the few vestiges discovered: marble columns and capitals, and mosaics. They are evidence of the care put into its realization, and the desire to rival the most remarkable basilicas built in Trèves, Rome, and Constantinople, which had benefited from the empire's exceptional financial resources. It is in this context that the cathedral of Lutèce's foundation must be resituated; its presence underscores the degree to which the town was Christian. It is likely that Clovis was aware of this, and that, in choosing Paris, the presence of such an exceptional house of worship carried weight. More than anything else—more so, in any event, than the palace—it could have meant the affirmation of his own power, one of the poles of which, as has been said, was the Catholic faith. The cathedral henceforth became part of the Merovingians' collective imagination. The Apostles, destined to guard the founder's tomb, only reinforced the association between the Catholic faith and the Merovingian monarchy.

PATRONAGE

This initially close connection between the dynasty and the church became stronger or weaker depending on political events. The cathedral, the major center of religion, could not remain unaffected by fluctuations in civil power, symbolized by the palace a few hundred meters away. At its inception, the cathedral was distinguished, as was typical of the era, by the word *ecclesia*: it designated the church of the diocese, the bishop's see. The first mention of a *titulus*, Saint Stephen, appears in the seventh century in Sens, where the Bishop of Paris was suffragan.[15] In 425, the relics of the martyred saint had been discovered and quickly passed around the Christian community. Paris was thus not at all unique in this respect. Things were particularly complicated when to this first name was added a second, the Virgin, in a charter of Charlemagne (775). Certainly, since the

Council of Ephesus in 431, the cult of the Virgin had spread throughout Christendom; she had been solemnly proclaimed Mother of God. From this double patronage, one came to the conclusion that one was in the presence of a double cathedral: Saint-Stephen, discovered in 1847, and Notre Dame, the apse of which was to be discovered by Viollet-le-Duc in 1856 when he built the archbishops' burial vault in the Gothic cathedral's choir. Paris would have thus adopted a common arrangement. In fact, this hypothesis, seductive as it is, faces several obstacles: the first concerns textual analysis.[16] The texts never refer to a dual edifice when they mention the cathedral as a building. The oneness of the building is explained by the exceptional dimensions of the monument itself. The second obstacle involves the island's topography: this apse was in fact outside the ancient wall, the layout of which was discovered in 1711 in the second bay of the choir, and for this reason was not part of the group. The third concerns the edifice's dimensions, so scaled-down that it could only have been an oratory. The last, finally, concerns the fact that to these two titles was added a third, Saint-Germain, as evidenced by the will of Count Stephen in 811.[17] In fact, Paris, as can be said on many other counts, is a unique case, even if we are assured of the existence of a baptistery, which disappeared in 1748. It was found standing along the length of the north wall of the ancient cathedral.

A Common Destiny

History adequately explains the long neglect of the cathedral over the course of succeeding centuries. Except for a short period at the end of the ninth century, it followed the usual route. Paris felt the effects, at least after the death of Caribert (567), of repeated divisions. The sovereigns sought to maintain the fiction of the unity of the kingdom by refusing to divide Paris, since one sovereign could not surrender without the agreement of the others. Paris maintained a prestige which no other town succeeded in wrenching from it; it was of a moral nature. Things were hardly better under the Carolingians. Life was no longer urban: the enlargement of the Carolingian empire forced Charlemagne to situate his favorite residence in Aix, which was, in fact, a country palace.

A major event was to challenge this slow torpor. The town abandoned by the sovereigns was in the hands of powerful lords. The siege begun by the Normans on November 26, 885, would raise Count Eudes, son of Robert the Strong, and Bishop Gozlin to the first ranks. The heroic defense that they organized lasted two years and gave the town a new prestige attested to in the epic poetry written by Abbon, the monk of Saint-Germain-des-Prés. The provisional alliance between the two men would have a staying power they could not have anticipated. Eudes became king, the first of a new line, the future of which was to be assured by his great-nephew, Hugh Capet.

THE TWELFTH CENTURY AND THE MEROVINGIAN "REVIVAL"

The Norman siege of Paris had sucked the town dry. It had to be reconstructed, toward which end the sovereigns worked. A shift can be observed toward the right bank which, since the very end of the ninth century, offered proof of a renewal that was hesitant at first, but that had to be expressed. The Roman left bank was ruined for good. It was not until the twelfth century, however, that Paris regained its status as capital of the kingdom.[18] This revival was manifested in a tentative manner under Robert the Pious (996–1031), who undertook the reconstruction of the palace at the end of his reign.[19] The involvement of Abbot Suger was to be decisive. During his regency in 1147, he gave Paris capital status. In 1190, at the time of Philip Augustus's departure for the Crusade, the most important organs of government were concentrated there. The cathedral could not escape this movement, which was to take shape in 1160 with the reconstruction of the monument, thanks to the initiative of Bishop Maurice de Sully. But, even before this date, a spate of work on the ancient, half-ruined cathedral had very recently shed light on peoples' conception of its origins.

The Saint Anne portal, dismantled in order to be reassembled as part of the west façade of the Gothic cathedral, had been designed around the year 1150 for the ancient cathedral.[20] Along the tympanum on either side of the seated Virgin holding the Child are represented the Bishop Saint Germain (d. 576) on her left and King Childebert (d. 558) on her right. Saint Germain, twentieth Bishop of Paris and one of the most famous, owed his Episcopal throne to Childebert. Together they unroll a long banner (*phylactère*) which has an inscription, enabling the viewer to grasp their importance in the founding of the cathedral. In his poem *De ecclesia Parisiaca* (On the Church of Paris), Venantius Fortunatus, Bishop of Poitiers and a contemporary of Saint Germain, attributed construction of the early cathedral to Childebert.[21] In the middle of the twelfth century, people did not hesitate to invoke the Merovingian era for the purpose of finding letters patent of nobility on the edifice. The movement was not isolated and, to speak only of Paris, it was enough to evoke the execution of four effigies of Merovingian kings intended for the choir of Saint-Germain-des-Près: Childebert, Chilpéric, Childeric, and Frédégonde.[22] Although tombs dedicated to sovereigns could be acceptable, one still remains perplexed by the audacity of depicting secular beings on either side of the Virgin on the tympanum. This Merovingian self-promotion was echoed in the piers by the representation of Saint Marcellus. The presence of this fifth-century bishop appears quite odd.[23] His life, even then, was in no way noteworthy; when Saint Germain, Bishop of Paris, asked Venantius Fortunatus to write his biography, the latter had difficulty finding material for it.

From his time onward, tradition became even more vague. This can be seen in the inability to produce the least chronological marker.[24] Saint Marcellus built up his reputation by punctuating it with ever more extraordinary miracles.[25] The last, and by that alone the most triumphant, was the one he performed on a dragon who had endeavored to devour the corpse of an unfaithful woman and had devastated the region. After battling him and striking him three times on the head with his cross, he succeeded in making him disappear. After the holy bishop's death, his body was buried in the church which was to take the name of Saint Marcellus. Very early on, the legend developed there of the "village of Christians" and the original site of the cathedral.[26] Over the course of the tenth century or perhaps earlier, the clergy took care to transfer his body to the cathedral. His cult does not seem to have been unusual. Be that as it may, it was to him that the religious community turned when it was decided to make a portal consecrated to the Virgin. The choice may have appeared odd, but one finds a number of explanations within a context which sought to exalt the Merovingian age. Saint Denis, first Bishop of Paris, had just been "revived" by Abbot Suger, who did not hesitate to put his statue on the pier of the west façade's portal that he had just finished (1140). For the cathedral's clergy, it was a matter of asserting its superiority over the other churches in the diocese: Saint Marcellus, already praised in the sixth century, would suit the purpose. He was depicted piercing the dragon's jaws with his cross, and the unfaithful woman was portrayed in her coffin at this feet. On either side of the pier, eight statue-columns were placed, representing the kings and queens of the Old Testament. Until the eighteenth century, if we are to believe Dom Montfaucon in the *Monumens de la monarchie françoise* (1724, vol. 1), people identified them as Merovingian sovereigns, whose names they provided. We do not know when this erroneous tradition began. It is likely that it is very old: by an easily understandable phenomenon of osmosis, the Merovingian significance was extended to the entire Gothic portal.

GOTHIC ARCHITECTURE AND THE TASTE FOR *SPOLIA*

Attention must be drawn to some characteristics of the cathedral's construction, which began in 1160 under Maurice de Sully. The bishop, who was truly extraordinary in both his work and his will, threw himself into a boldly "modern" project that sharply contrasted with the tentative beginnings of Gothic architecture.[27] The security of the design, the choice of elevation with its four levels, and the quality of the exceptional implementation underscore the care he put into formulating and executing the plan. His undertaking is even more remarkable in that the new edifice had just been profoundly "modernized." A portal dedicated to the Virgin had been sculpted for the west façade. A stained-glass window representing the triumph of the Virgin had been given by Abbot Suger. The archdeacon Étienne de Garlande had allocated large sums of money for the renovation, which was so good that it was called "new."[28] Carried away by the vast movement unleashed by Abbot Suger at Saint-Denis, Maurice followed the examples of other equally impetuous bishops: the cathedral of Sens (whose reconstruction was undertaken by Henri Sanglier [1122–42] at the end of his life); Noyon, begun around 1150; Senlis, about 1153; Laon, about 1160. Concurrent to this activity, the Bishop of Paris insisted that the new edifice conserve the monument that was being destroyed as fast as the new construction progressed. It is with this in mind that one must note the choice of plan, with its double aisles coming together at the sanctuary. It is the design of the ancient cathedral, as recent excavations have shown. Moreover, the reference to early Christian architecture is not unique: Abbot Suger considered it for the nave of Saint-Denis, eventually constructed with simple aisles. The decision to forego the transept—which did not show up in the plan but only in construction—held to the same conception. And what about the absence of chapels radiating from the ambulatory?

To this desire for conservation must be added the *spolia* (booty) of the destroyed building. Certainly, the age supplied other examples of this—Bourges, among others—but they were not so obvious. Thus this window dedicated to the triumph of the Virgin, given by Abbot Suger, was carefully dismantled in order to be placed in the Gothic cathedral.[29] It stayed there until the middle of the eighteenth century, when it was replaced by a large, white stained-glass window. As for the portal with statue-columns, it found a place on the right side of the west façade. Like the window, it was dedicated to the Virgin. To install it, sometime between 1210 and 1220, a certain number of adjustments were necessary in the arching. Most important, a lower lintel dedicated to scenes of the life of the Virgin and the childhood of Christ was added.[30] While this reassembly was being done, the portal exchanged its original appellation as portal of the Virgin for the Saint Anne portal. It must be said that the cult of the mother of the Virgin had definitely grown after the Count of Blois had sent from Constantinople to Chartres in 1204 for a relic of the saint: her head.

Figure 10.2
The most venerable saints of the diocese; portal of the Crowning of the Virgin, nineteenth century.

This historicizing taste persisted until the beginning of the thirteenth century when the west façade was constructed, while the portal consecrated to the Virgin was being built on its left. For the first time in medieval iconography, the statue-columns, which until then had depicted figures from the Old Testament and the Apostles, portray the most venerable saints of the diocese, whose relics were kept in the cathedral. Their choice reveals the important evolution that had been occurring since the middle of the twelfth century. One finds there Saint Stephen and Saint

Denis, who would have been placed on twelfth-century piers, but had been deliberately set aside. We know the fate which was in store for them thirty years after with the erection of the southern arm's portal which was consecrated to him. Saint Geneviève's presence clearly shows a desire to "reclaim" Saint Denis: she had constructed, around 475, according to the chronicler who wrote her biography around 520, a church above the tomb of the martyred bishop. As for Saint John the Baptist, his presence is explained by the fortuitous discovery in 1186 of relics: three precursory teeth, along with hair of the Virgin, an arm of Saint Andrew, stones from the stoning of Saint Stephen, and the brain pan of Saint Denis.[31] Two other figures were added: one religious, crosiered and mitered; the other civil, crowned, whose identity is uncertain, the traditional being unlikely.[32]

The Gallery of Kings makes use of another strategy which the popular mentality did not grasp. In the beginning of the thirteenth century, the architect laid out an arcature above the three portals in which were placed the statues of twenty-eight kings of Judah, as listed by Saint Matthew in his genealogy from Jesse to Joseph, including David riding a lion. It consists of the family tree of Jesse, depicted not in a vertical way, as had been the norm since Saint Denis, but horizontally. The subtleties of Isaiah's prophecy could hardly have been perceptible to a Parisian man of the street who, since the thirteenth century, had identified them as kings of France: Pepin, Charlemagne. . . . This interpretation, as obviously incorrect as it was for the Saint Anne portal, would endure until recent years. It is, in part, responsible for their destruction during the Revolution. It still encumbers a number of serious works. It has to be very old.[33] Thus, in the imagination of the man of the Middle Ages, poorly versed in religious iconography, the cathedral's façade became familiar to him through its glorification of the kings of France. This confusion, based on ignorance, played a not insignificant role in the perception of the cathedral.

NOTRE DAME OF PARIS AND PRESENT-DAY MEMORY

The cathedral could not be content merely to commemorate the past; it wanted to commemorate current events. Although we lack firm evidence, there is no doubt that the clergy was anxious to give a political dimension to the edifice. This wish threatened to allow political power to take precedence over religious power, as was customary in France. The king did not intervene in the construction: his gifts, when there at all, represented no more than a very small, which is not to say insignificant, part.[34] The reasons for this dearth could include the will of the king, who did not see his intervention as indispensable and was unaware of the clergy, who wished to guard its full independence. The answer is obvious for Philip Augustus, whom no source shows as taking the least interest in the building under construction. Nonetheless, he could follow the different stages from his palace situated a few hundred meters away. His financial resources were, then, entirely committed to the defense of the realm through the construction of fortresses and surrounding walls,[35] one of the most remarkable of which encircled the right bank of the capital with its fortress to the west: the Louvre. However, he could not have been unaware of it, and even took part for some years in an attempt to integrate the edifice into royal ceremony. In fact, it was in the building still under construction that the archbishop of Sens, Guy, proceeded in 1179 to crown Philip and Isabelle de Hainaut, whom he had just married. It is, moreover, in the sanctuary that the king laid to rest the body of the queen, who died on May 12, 1190, while giving birth to twins. Her tomb, discovered during the last century by Viollet-le-Duc, contained the silver matrix of his seal. The two events are unusual: burial of a royal family member in a cathedral, and the presence of the matrix, usually broken to prevent fraudulent use. They were rarely to occur again. However, Isabelle was not the first and only person to find a resting place in Notre Dame: Geoffroy, Duke of Brittany, third son of King Henry II, who died in an accident in Paris in 1186, was already there.[36] It is noteworthy that Philip Augustus had arranged funeral ceremonies worthy of Geoffroy's rank and, following Angevin custom, had not hesitated to choose the most attractive monument of the age. The last royal personage to be buried there was Philip, Count of Boulogne, son of Louis VIII (d. 1218). Later, Louis IX took the utmost care to prevent such actions: Saint-Denis was substituted then for good for the kings and queens, Royaumont for the children of France.[37] Everything happened as if Saint Louis had put an end to the clergy's desire—more or less expressed—to rival Reims and Saint-Denis. This defiance was expressed even more forcefully in 1239 at the moment of the triumphant arrival of the Crown of Thorns. One might have thought that it was being kept at Notre Dame while awaiting a permanent home: it was only very briefly exhibited there before being displayed in the palace's chapel and, finally, in the Saint-Chapelle, constructed for this purpose. The king had thus very forcefully marked out his domain.

This state of affairs was to last until the reign of Philip the Fair. In the battle which pitted the king against Pope Boniface VIII, the former relied on the clergy to defend the crown's authority. He did not hesitate on February 11, 1302, to burn the bull *Ausculta fili*, which marked an additional assertion of caesaro-papal claims. The pope had convened a council, which put Philip the Fair in a difficult position. To get out of this difficulty, the king and his councilors decided to convoke an extraordinary assembly during Holy Week—people later believed this to have been the origin of the States-General—to examine the bull (*Scire te volumus*), previously reduced to three propositions. The king made a second clever tactical move: he decided that the meeting would be held in the cathedral (April 10, 1302). A thousand people representing chapters and towns—prelates, doctors, barons—met with the king, who proposed "the reform of the realm and the Gallican church." The assembly ended with a letter drafted by the clergy to the pope, enjoining him to abandon the council.[38] Two years later, to celebrate his victory at Mons-en-Pévèle (August 18, 1304), the king had erected by the first eastern pillar in the southern part of the cathedral a wooden armed equestrian statue of himself. He had, incidentally, made an identical gift to the cathedral of Chartres.[39] For the first time, a representation of a living king was brought into a religious edifice. Legend was to seize quickly on this novel deed. Since the fifteenth century, it was claimed that the statue represented not Philip IV, but Philip VI, who, on his return from the East in 1328, had entered the edifice fully armed and had immortalized this act by having himself portrayed thus. The statue, an ex voto of gratitude, became a political statement. The inscription added during the reign of Henry II, glorifying the Salic law, contributed to the confusion. It led to a long and obscure polemic on the identification of the royal rider during the seventeenth century.

Thus, during the reign of Philip the Fair, the links between the two ends of the Île de la Cité were curiously brought together again, however strained they had been in the previous century. One must, though, take into account the fact that, in the meantime, the Palais de la Cité had been considerably altered following Philip the Fair's massive renovations, radically transforming the city's appearance. He added to it a no less important feature: the installation of sculpted representations of all the kings of France in the Great Hall for the glorification of the monarchy.[40] Thus, across a few meters, a long dialogue was established between the kings of Judah, the ancestors of Christ, and the ancestors of the living king. It thus explains how, later, the territories being well marked, the kings had revived the policy of the separation of powers articulated by Saint Louis.

Problems in the realm would challenge this policy. Once again, as under Philip Augustus, the cathedral was to be associated with death. Indeed, when Saint Louis's body was returned in 1271, it was deemed unthinkable not to make a stop there, but it was for a short time.[41] It nevertheless established a tradition which developed somewhat during the fourteenth century.[42] It also explains why Notre Dame was considered for the coronation of the young Henry VI. The ceremony took place on December 16, 1430.

The connection, lasting through these dramatic periods, between the cathedral and political authority was to endure. Upon entering the capital, Charles VII immediately went to the cathedral for a formal Te Deum (November 12, 1467). For the first time, Notre Dame was a part of current events (*l'histoire vivante*). This Te Deum, prelude to so many others, would be celebrated each year. Until 1793, every first Friday after Easter, the municipal body went to the edifice to thank Heaven for Paris's deliverance from English occupation.[43]

The celebration of the Te Deum was in no way to modify relations between the cathedral and the government. As in the past, the former remained a privileged site of worship, but it was hardly ever integrated into monarchical ceremony. The important places continued to be Reims and Saint-Denis. Joan of Arc was not wrong to persuade Charles VII to be crowned at Reims in order to be fully recognized as Charles VI's successor. The notion that the ceremony was legitimated by the location where it took place was still strong. The sixteenth century scarcely escaped this rule. Even if, as has been noted, the ceremonies became more numerous, they were of a religious nature. This was the case with the funeral rites of Queen Claude (November 5, 1526), the marriage of Francis II and Mary Stuart (1558), and many other ceremonies as well.[44] It was the same for the formal entry of Henry II into his good city of Paris. For the sovereign, it was a matter of boldly demonstrating the link between the king and his people: the varied Parisian population adequately represented the diversity of the nation, and Paris was the locus of the organs of government. In addition, the king attached a great deal of importance to this ceremony: it had to assure his power in a visual way; it was the tangible sign that Paris had become his place of residence. He had thought about this move since April 1547, but it did not come to pass until two years later (June 16, 1549). The formal retinue, which had been organized with the utmost care by the king, was content to make a quick stop at Notre Dame: the king prayed there, welcomed by the dean of the chapter in the absence of the bishop. Real life was beyond the king's contemplation, beyond the decor which wanted to be the very definition of artistic politics. Two days later, at the time of Catherine de Medici's entry, the stop was no longer important.[45] The most noteworthy deed, which aimed at exorcism, was the alliance renewed in 1582 by Henry III with the Swiss. This accord with the Protestants, signed by the most Christian King, took place, as it would once more in 1663, in the choir of the cathedral.

Like their predecessors, the Capetians, the Valois showed a certain prudence in preventing the cathedral from taking an overly important role in monarchical life. They had understood the danger which an overly interventionist episcopate could represent.

THE TRIUMPHANT CATHEDRAL

Everything was to change drastically with the accession of the Bourbons to the throne. They would develop privileged links to the cathedral, which would only strengthen over time. Religious conditions are alone enough to explain them. Paris, fiercely opposed to the Reformation, became one of the important centers in the struggle against the so-called reformed religion. The cathedral took a special role in this defense of the faith against the heir of the king (who had no heir-at-law), whose religion was not that of the Crown. On May 31, 1590, it was on the high altar that the Duke of Nemours and the leaders and magistrates of the city took an oath to die before surrendering the city to the King of Navarre. It was within its walls that the Bishop of Asti, Monsignor Panigarola, preached in 1590; it was there that the bulls of Pope Gregory XIV were posted on June 3, 1591. The health of the realm depended on the Catholic faith. Henry IV understood the full power of the message. His public conversion at Saint-Denis (July 23, 1593), and his coronation at Chartres (February 27, 1594) opened the doors of the capital to him, but peace was not yet concluded between the people and the man who claimed to be their king. On March 22, 1594, he made a meticulously arranged entry into Notre Dame, which ended his long march. He headed directly for the choir, where he was welcomed by the canons. A Te Deum that immediately burst forth from beneath the vaults ended the years of drama. The people thus recovered their king. The Bourbon married Notre Dame of Paris in that moment of reconciliation; his descendents would follow the path thus laid out. Notre Dame immediately took an essential part—as Reims remained in the hands of Leaguers—in the aura which enveloped the "new convert" who had humbly genuflected in the sanctuary.[46] His gesture had created a new legitimacy. Paris and Notre Dame were reunited. All the great deeds of the new reign were sealed there: the peace with the Spaniards (June 21) and, on June 29, 1610, the funeral ceremony of the king, with a gigantic crowd in attendance. It ended with an immense procession.

It was no longer conceivable that Paris would remain an ordinary bishopric. Gregory XV ended up giving in to the requests that were already piling up in the fourteenth century: on November 14, 1622, he proclaimed the bull that named Jean-François de Gondi first Archbishop of Paris. In February of the following year, Louis XIII published the bull,

giving it the desired solemnity by sealing the act with the great green wax
seal on green and red silk.

THE VOW OF LOUIS XIII

The close bond between the cathedral and the Bourbon monarchy took
on a special importance with the Vow of Louis XIII. The idea, as has
been recently shown, had been with the king a long time, since at least
the autumn of 1630.[47] Upon recovery from a terrible illness which failed
to defeat him in Lyons, he took care to write a first draft of the text of
1638: he "delivers himself and his realm, to God first, to the Empire of
the Most Powerful Lady, consecrate them to Her Majesty, entrust them
to their assistance, attest to the eternal nature of this votive offering by
erecting a monument for the world and the future." The day chosen for
the celebration was that of the Assumption. The chief difference between
this first document and the final resolution concerned the Parisian cathedral, which was not mentioned. It appeared soon after, in a letter from
Richelieu to the king dated May 9, 1636, in which he committed himself to making a gift of a silver lamp to the cathedral. It was installed on
October 9, 1636, before the altar of the Virgin. This gift could not have
seemed sufficient to the king, who had been committed to this celebration since 1630. On February 10, 1638, the king published the definitive
work in the form of a declaration which laid out his motivations and intentions: "To these causes, we have declared and do declare that taking
the most holy and most glorious Virgin as special protector of our Realm,
We especially dedicate our Person, our State, our Crown, and our subjects to her. . . . We will rebuild the great altar of the Cathedral Church
of Paris, with a picture of the Virgin holding in her arms her precious
son descended from the Cross; we will be depicted at the feet of the Son
and the Mother, offering them our crown and our Scepter." He established the first ceremony on August 15 of that same year, but took care
to indicate that it was to be revived each year on the same date and to be
followed by a procession in which various groups would participate. He
also ordered that a similar ceremony be celebrated in the cathedrals, and
the parish and monastic churches of the kingdom. But the essence of the
Declaration of 1638 was addressed to Paris.

   This fact is important because the cathedral showed a clear inferiority
with respect to Chartres. From earliest times, the cathedral of the Beauce
region had been associated with a very famous pilgrimage, thanks to the
Tunic of the Virgin, to the water miraculously drawn from the well of the
Saints-Forts, and, finally, to a statue of the Virgin and Child, so grimy that
it was thought to predate Christianity. At the beginning of the eleventh

century, Bishop Fulbert, in reconstructing the cathedral gutted by fire, restored a smaller church intended to welcome the crowds of pilgrims. There
existed nothing of its kind in Paris.[48] Certainly, Paris possessed a statue
of the Virgin and Child, also in wood, which could have rivaled the one
at Chartres. This statue, *Notre-Dame de Liesse*, calls to mind a work held
by Notre-Dame-de-Liesse near Laon. Anne of Austria early on showed
a special interest in her worship, undertaking the restoration of the altar
decoration, of which she was to become part; on either side were kneeling representations of the king and queen.[49] Miracles had already happened there and others were anticipated. It was in front of this statue that
Richelieu got the king to place the famous silver lamp. It was in fact a true
chandelier, with its six candelabra, six angels, and scenes from the life of
the Virgin. The Declaration of 1638 was to contribute to the spectacular
growth of the cult of the Virgin. Initially, people were satisfied with the
painting by Philippe de Champagne, today in the museum of Caen.

Louis XIV hoped to realize his father's wish. The decision was made
in 1698 and work began the following year. After many delays, a project
of Robert de Cotte was stopped and construction was finished in 1726.
In fact the entire sanctuary was redesigned to highlight better the very
beautiful sculpted group, the *Compassion de la Vierge devant le cadavre de
son fils descendu de la Croix*, by Nicolas Coustou. It was surrounded by
kneeling statues: Guillaume Coustou's Louis XIII offering his crown
and scepter, and Coysevox's Louis XIV, which the king had added to the
group because he wanted to be associated with his father's Declaration.[50]
The original meaning of the vow took on a deeper meaning after the
eagerly awaited birth of the Dauphin, deemed miraculous, on September 5, 1638. A link was immediately established between the two events:
God-given Louis (Louis Dieudonné) was considered to be the embodiment of the consecration of France to the Virgin. Louis XIV adopted his
father's Declaration on March 25, 1650, by associating himself with it:
"We desire to attest to the same gratitude and likewise submit Our self
[and] our crown to the sainted Virgin." In light of this it made sense that
God-given Louis be depicted facing his father, the regalia placed near his
knees. From that date on, parents began consecrating their children to
the Virgin in the manner of the queen, who, accompanied by the queen
mother, offered the Dauphin to Notre Dame on April 29, 1662, a custom
which still continues today.

Notre Dame of Paris thus became one of the major centers of the
French monarchy, besides Reims and Saint-Denis. Notre Dame even had
a tendency to supplant them, so much was the royal presence upheld there,
whereas it had become weakened in the other two sanctuaries. It became
the standard monument for the Bourbons' great ceremonies, the political

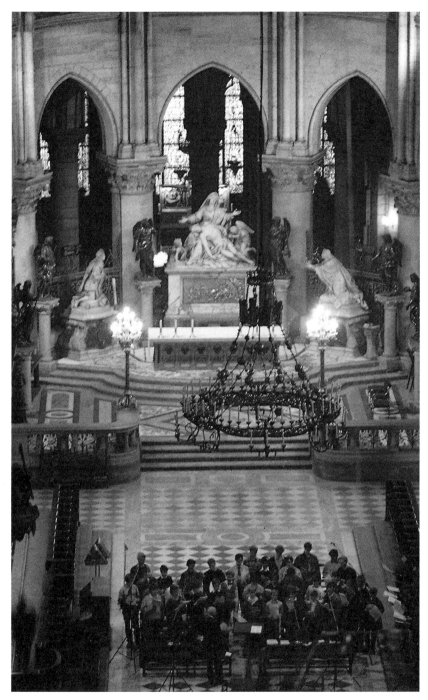

Figure 10.3
Interior view of the cathedral with the decoration of the choir redone by Louis XIV in fulfillment of the Vow of
Louis XIII: the *Vierge de Compassion* by Nicolas Coustou (1723) between the statues of Louis XIII, right, by
Guillaume Coustou (1715), and Louis XIV, left, by Coysevox (1715).

aspect of which could sometimes prevail over the religious significance. Certainly, as always, ceremonies remained ambiguous, and the government was satisfied with this ambiguity, which could only serve it.

The opening of the ceremony was the Te Deum, which obeyed very strict ceremonial rules according to whether or not the king and queen would be participating.[51] When present, they were seated in the middle of the canon choir, with the princes sitting in the high and low stalls. For both the coronation (1654) and the marriage of Louis XIV (1660), it was the people of Paris who were associated with the royal family, up to the highest dignitaries of the court and the clergy, in the presence of the Virgin. So too were the Te Deums intended to celebrate royal victories. Their number was reduced during the reign of Louis XV, even though eleven of them were presented in the year 1765 alone, to honor the birth of the Dauphin.

The army was not on the periphery. The blessing of the standards, which was done in the cathedral, took place in principle once every three years, presided over by the archbishop, who blessed flags and standards of the French guard, Swiss guard, and the musketeers.[52] The edifice became, consequently, the repository of flags taken from the enemy. The first such example seems to have been those taken from the Spanish at Avoin (1655), then Rheinfeld (1638), Rocroi (1643), Fleurus (1690), and Holland (1692). They were hung in narrow rows in the galleries, as shown in a precious drawing of 1779 by Gabriel de Saint-Aubin.[53] The cathedral thus participated in the glory of the king: paying homage to God for the weapons. In 1793, most of these flags were transferred to the church of the Invalides, which thus assumed the military heritage of Notre Dame.

NOTRE DAME AND DEATH

This association between the government and the church took on a spectacular dimension over the course of the seventeenth century when the cathedral was the theater for funeral services. If the monarchy had succeeded in developing a complex theory around the sovereign's death, which resulted in the assertion that kings never die, if it had found in Saint-Denis the edifice destined to house their mortal remains, it had not been able to express its gratitude toward the defunct great servants of the state. It lacked a Westminster. Certainly, on various occasions, the king had not hesitated to give exceptional funerals and tombs in Saint-Denis, but the examples of Du Guesclin in the fourteenth century, Louis de Sancerre and Guillaume de Chastel in the fifteenth century, and Turenne in the seventeenth century seem too out of the ordinary and were revoked later by Louis XIV, who finally adopted the recommendation of Saint Louis on his deathbed. Saint-Denis was to be reserved for kings and queens who had received unction. In the absence of a long-awaited pantheon, the monarchy took charge of not only the tomb but also the funeral observance. Notre Dame became the site for the glorification of great public servants, a postmortem triumph. Certainly, the cathedral had already been associated with death, as we have seen for the end of the Middle Ages, but not consistently so. In the sixteenth century, some funeral ceremonies took place there (Louise of Savoy, mother of Francis I, October 21, 1533), but usually there were formal services in the absence of the corpse. Examples include Henry VIII (March 19, 1546), Eleanor of Austria (April 24, 1558), the dowager queen of Scotland (August 9, 1560), the Duke of Guise (March 3, 1562), the Duke of Montpensier (March 21, 1608), the Emperor Matthias (April 27, 1619), the Duke of Savoy (March 28, 1638), and the wife of Charles-Emmanuel of Savoy and daughter of Henry IV (March 28, 1666). One observes an increase in the number of these ceremonies, obviously linked to the accession of the Bourbons to the throne, but there was no change in kind until then.

This shift occurred during the reign of Louis XIII and confirmed the role that the edifice then played in the monarchy. The Marshal of Guébriant, who died on November 11, 1643, of an arm wound during the siege of Rothweil, seems to have been the first to benefit from such an honor. Queen Anne of Austria took the utmost care in arranging the ceremony, demanding the presence of the body in the edifice and the attendance of court and city officials. At stake was the rewarding of a faithful and proud servant, but also the strengthening of certain loyalties which were in danger of weakening. The custom immediately took hold: funeral services followed one after another: the Duke of Brézé (November 13, 1646), Henry II of Condé (January 6, 1647), Mazarin (April, 1661). It would be tedious to cite the numerous personages thus honored: funeral services were supposed to draw attention to the merits of the deceased. Nevertheless, these ceremonies seemed quite pitiful compared with what was then being done in Italy. In 1666, Vigarini reproached the French for their ignorance in all matters that were properly called the *castrum doloris*. Indeed, these funeral services were not merely decorative; they participated fully in the work of the post-Tridentine Counter-Reformation. The council insisted on the opportunity to offer prayers for the dead, a practice challenged by the Protestants. It added to this that the funeral liturgy was to serve as consolation to the living. People in high places, who had benefited from so many favors when they were alive, were to serve as an example at the moment of their death by drawing attention to their virtues. The Jesuits underscored the lofty religious meaning of these funeral services. For various monarchs of Europe, it was a matter of exalting—even while dying—the monarchy while affirming the Catholic faith.[54] The grand dukes of Florence took immense advantage of this, which ended up reflecting back on their own family. France proved to be, in this respect, far behind. The Jesuit father Ménestrier,[55] familiar with Italian festivals, remarked on Italy's lead at the formal service for Anne of Austria, which was entrusted to him in Grenoble in 1666. He chose the theme of the "Crying Graces."

The first *castrum doloris* was the funeral service for the Duc de Beaufort, grandson of Henry IV, who died at the siege of Candie in 1669 in the war against the Turks. To celebrate his memory Pope Clement IX asked Bernini to design the catafalque for the ceremony on September 28, 1669. In Paris, it was Henri Gissey, designer of the king's chamber, who was given the task of decorating the cathedral for the ceremony on August 16, 1670. Gissey endeavored to Gallicize the obvious Italian influence (explained by the engraving that Bernini had sent): the catafalque was surrounded by skeletons carrying a tray of allegorical figures and candle stands. The monument was topped by a large statue. This short-term decoration was intended to exalt the monarchy through the Duke of Beaufort. The observance of death, from that date on, became inseparable from these "camps of sorrow," some of which were especially noteworthy.

Upon the death of Turenne in 1675, the king decided that a formal service would be observed at Notre Dame and entrusted the task to Bérain, who had just succeeded Gissey. He sent for Father Ménestrier, who conceived of a complex symbolic design consisting of an immense tower pierced with two openings which enabled one to see the catafalque. To clarify what might have remained mysterious for the faithful, the priest published a booklet in which he revealed all the clues to the production. The tower, evoking at first sight the Tower of Auvergne, was also a representation of the Virgin (*turris eburnean*). Her presence was all the more justifiable in that Turenne had abjured Protestantism several years earlier in this cathedral dedicated to Our Lady and, in this same place, had become one of the devotees of the Mother of Christ. But the tower would be linked to the Tower of David, high on the mountain of Zion, and thus to the king, who had ordered the funeral service. Even the best minds were repeatedly confused by this symbolism, though they were seduced by the quality of Bérain's implementation.[56] So, upon the death of the queen, the king no longer appealed to the Jesuit father and was content to erect a large urn supported by draped figures sheltering under an immense black dais attached to the arch.[57] This was a far cry from the project of the Jesuit, who had envisioned an immense pyre piled with the silver of Versailles, which the queen had just been deprived of by death. The break between the two men was credited to the publication of the

Figure 10.4
Castrum doloris: the structure erected for Turenne's funeral service, September 9, 1675, engraving by Bérain, for *Les Vertus chrétiennes et les Vertus militaires en deuil.*

work of Father Ménestrier, who explained in it the reasons motivating his ambition: he wanted funeral decorations to be placed on the same level as the other arts.

The Jesuit was not summoned for the Great Condé's "camp of sorrow" (March 10, 1687). Bérain adopted a new course of action: he completely hid the architecture of the canons' choir behind the central draperies, placed a canopy atop straight columns which supported an urn, and protected a catafalque topped by a pyramid surrounded by symbolic statues. It was in front of this decoration that Bossuet gave his funeral oration, which resonated fully there at the same time as it gave the *castrum doloris* its true meaning. Bérain and Bossuet succeeded where Father Ménestrier had failed.

The formula had been discovered and would recur a number of times over the course of the eighteenth century, without regaining the magnitude of the decor for the Great Condé. For the members of the royal family, the ceremony took place twice: first, at Notre Dame, so that the Parisian people could attend; next, at Saint-Denis, where the burial took place. At the end of the eighteenth century, one notes a rather clear evolution. For the death of Maria-Theresa (November 29, 1780), mother of Queen Marie-Antoinette, the ceremony took place after the six months of mourning (May 31, 1781) decreed by the king. Its great organizer had been Paris.

In the eyes of the public, the cathedral asserted itself, at the end of the old regime, as the major center of monarchical celebration. The Te Deum, the anniversary of the Vow of Louis XIII on August 15, funeral services, and the blessing of the standards recurred there at regular intervals, marking the life of the monarchy. Notre Dame of Paris became the echo chamber of a reality dulled by distance. The arrival of the king prompted an impressive cortege which left from Versailles. In the choir, the Swiss guards formed the personal guard of the king. After the ceremony, he returned to Versailles, leaving the palace and the Louvre empty. The cathedral had thus become the only place inhabited on rare occasions by the king. To its religious significance was added that of monarchical celebration in the Parisian's mind. Notre Dame would be at the heart of the debate unleashed by the Revolution.

NOTRE DAME IN TURMOIL

The strong bond established between monarchical authority and the cathedral would continue well beyond the autumn of 1789 and go on to benefit various regimes. Certainly, the relationship had not always been the same and depended above all on the nature of the government and its religious choice. Throughout the revolutionary era, one feels all the weight and fascination that the edifice could have on people's minds. All had been done to recover its aura in such a way that it would reflect back on the governments. Strange as it might seem, the monument was never closed.[58] It was defaced, emptied of its treasures, not to mention clergy, but the traditions continued, attracting a population whose support was by no means guaranteed. Great official acts found legitimation there, so much had its political significance prevailed over its religious role. Already born was the still vague idea that such gigantic and impressive edifices were exempt from common law and that the people were there for some reason. It is not inconceivable that ceremonies continued to be celebrated because they had been judged indispensable for calming Europe, disturbed by events taking place in France. The country could give a reassuring impression. Even on the day after the storming of the Bastille, Bailly, president of the National Assembly, went to Notre Dame with a deputation of the assembly to celebrate this triumph of the people with a Te Deum that suspiciously resembled those of the previous era. On August 13, a new Te Deum, intended to thank the Lord for the abolition of feudal rights, was sung.

Notre Dame took part in the great moments of the history of the nation. After the return of the king to Paris, the National Assembly held its first Parisian meeting (October 19, 1789) in the great hall of the archbishopric, constructed in the southern part of the cathedral, and it was precisely in this room that the property of the clergy was nationalized on November 1. A new Te Deum was sung under the vaults of the Gothic edifice on February 16, 1790, to celebrate the February 6 accord between the king and the nation, but in the following year there were hesitations over celebrating its anniversary with another Te Deum. It became clear that the memory of the past, so marked by memories of the monarchy, had to be replaced with a new one. It is from this point of view that one must note the celebrations of anniversaries. Not everything was done in the cathedral—one has only to think of July 14, 1790—but much took place there. The Te Deum of March 20, 1791, took on a particular importance: a deputation of the National Assembly, the Paris municipality, and the courts of the district of Paris were brought together to celebrate the restoration of the king's health. Yet another Te Deum was sung for the storming of the Bastille the day before the holiday (July 13, 1792), and on September 25, 1792, to celebrate the completion of the draft of the constitution and its acceptance by the king. In attendance was a delegation of the National Assembly, the electors of Paris, the municipality, and judges of the courts of Paris. The cathedral was not a symbol of Paris, but, as it claimed, of France. The black flag raised on March 8, 1793, to mark France's mourning following setbacks for the French armies attested to this.

This reclaiming of the cathedral in order to forge the vision (*l'imaginaire*) of the Revolution clashed with the highly visible reminders of the monarchy and the ostentatious signs of religion. Although the latter was still acceptable, the former was becoming unacceptable. Monarchical symbols would consequently disappear in as categorical a fashion as the king and queen had been made to disappear. In January 1793, the minister of the interior prescribed the destruction of the signs of superstition and feudalism.[59] Immediately, everything in the cathedral's decor that could evoke memories of the monarchy was destroyed. It was at this point that crowns and scepters were mutilated with scrupulous care. On October 23 of the same year, the council general of the commune, dissatisfied with the results, ordered the overthrow and destruction of "Gothic semblances of the kings of France." The entrepreneur entrusted with this operation removed more than a hundred statues from the west façade, making sure not to damage the architecture, and, in a symbolic gesture, had the heads separated from the bodies with a blow from a sledgehammer. Thus the punishment inflicted on Louis XVI was revisited on what were thought to be his ancestors. The condemnation became retroactive. No one doubted that the sculpted kings were the kings of France. Great scholars like Montfaucon lent their authority to an already deeply rooted thesis.

Figure 10.5
The standards in the cathedral's transept, gouache by Gabriel de Saint-Aubin, 1779.

Figure 10.6
Blessing of the flags in Notre-Dame de Paris, September 27, 1789, engraving after Prieur.

The cathedral, thus cleared out, was closed to worship on November 7, 1793. It could therefore accept a new assignment. On November 10, the Convention abolished the Catholic faith, advantageously replaced with that of Reason. Notre Dame immediately became the "Temple of Reason."[60] A festival was decreed for the establishment of the religion, which sought both continuity and discontinuity: "The musicians of the National Guard and others will sing patriotic hymns before the statue of Liberty erected in place of the former holy Virgin." In the nave, a mound was raised upon which stood a temple surrounded by busts of philosophers and bearing an inscription to the glory of philosophy. A torch symbolizing Liberty burned on the altar. A cortege of young girls, clothed in white and crowned, sang while waiting for the goddess Reason, who finally came to sit on the turf to listen to the hymns before going up to the temple to receive her worshippers' homage. That same evening, the Convention accompanied the people to sing the *Hymne à la Raison*, assigned to replace the traditional Te Deum. For the occasion, Marie-Joseph Chénier composed a *hymne à la Liberté*, which Gossec set to music.

The laicization of Notre Dame encountered real resistance, so much had the force of religion endured. Thus, two statues partially escaped the anticipated massacre. One was Saint Marcellus, whose face was mutilated. The other, most important, was that of the Virgin and Child situated on the pier of the northern arm of the transept. The flowers on the crown were discarded without anyone daring to touch the face. In the attempt to substitute one religion for another, the statue of the Virgin was replaced with that of the goddess of reason. As for the group entitled the *Voeu de Louis XIII*, Lenoir, out of a desire for preservation, undertook to safeguard it (the royal statues in 1792, and the pietà in 1793).

The festivals could continue and the celebrations of great events take place there: for example, on December 1, 1793, care was taken to read the Declaration of the Rights of Man to the assembled people; on February 18, 1794, the abolition of slavery was celebrated there. Nevertheless, the cult of reason was to reach its limits quickly. On May 12, 1794, the Temple of Reason was suppressed, the Supreme Being recognized, and the immortality of the soul proclaimed. A new inscription replaced the old (May 20, 1794).

The directory was to give back to religion the edifice served by the constitutional clergy (August 15, 1795). The ceremonies there took on a new significance. On January 21, 1797, the people observed the anniversary of Louis XVI's death by commemorating the oath of hatred to royalty and anarchy. But little by little religious activity regained the upper hand and, when there was a political ceremony, it also assumed a religious significance. In fact, Notre Dame became the locus of a *simultaneum* of religious and civil celebrations. An example of this was the funeral ceremony held on May 10, 1799, in memory of French plenipotentiaries murdered in Rastadt. A consular decree (January 12, 1800) made the decision to regulate use of the edifice more strictly: "The administrative authorities will determine the hours to be given over to the exercise of religion and to civil ceremonies in such a way as to prevent competition."[61]

A Te Deum was sung for the victory of Marengo (June 26, 1800). On July 14, 1800, instead of celebrating the storming of the Bastille, a solemn mass was sung for the victories won by the French army and to ask God for the reestablishment of the church and state. On July 15, there was a service for General Desaix, the Tower of Auvergne, and all those who had sacrificed their lives in defense of the Republic. In fact, in an almost surreptitious manner, civil ceremonies disappeared, or, rather, were absorbed into religious ceremony. A new state was reached on July 14, 1801: the solemn mass and the Te Deum were intended to thank the Lord for the blessings bestowed on the French people during the Revolution, for the Continental peace, and for the anniversary of the storming of the Bastille. Notre Dame was to inaugurate the policy of national reconciliation. It was celebrated in the presence of the *Voeu de Louis XIII*, replaced without the royal statues, on Easter Day 1802 (April 18), when the Concordat was signed. Consuls, senators, the legislative body, magistrates, and generals attended mass. Archbishops and bishops came next to take the oath at the hands of the First Consul. A stirring Te Deum ended the ceremony to celebrate the reestablishment of the Catholic religion. Bonaparte had taken the utmost care with the details of this ceremony, which was to revive a recent monarchical past that many participants still had in mind. The fate of the cathedral was closely associated with that of the First Consul. On the evening of August 14, he had a star nine meters in diameter mounted atop one of the towers of the edifice to announce his birthday. The next day was a national holiday.

The close connection between Napoleon and Notre Dame also explains the former's insistence in choosing Notre Dame of Paris as his coronation site. A reminder of the vanished monarchy, a reminder of the Revolution, it was more than any other edifice destined to become the symbol of the new legitimacy. It had to innovate without breaking with old and new traditions. Notre Dame became, rather, the place where the worlds of religion and civil authority were synthesized. The course of the ceremony had to follow these two axes. In the sanctuary, the most sacred part of the edifice, where the miracle of transubstantiation takes place each day, was the anointment and coronation, the essence of the sacred; in the first bay of the nave, to the west, was the constitutional oath, the essence of the secular. For the first part for the ceremony, the emperor had gotten back the regalia, restored for the occasion. For the second, the emperor, seated on a dais with twenty-four steps, was oriented toward the place of his coronation.

The regalia were not returned to the treasury of the abbey of Saint-Denis, where they had been kept during the old regime. Napoleon decided that they would henceforth belong to Notre Dame's treasury. The decision was two-fold. Napoleon, who was already thinking about having himself buried in the abbey, chose Paris over Saint-Denis, a good indicator of the cathedral's significance. The fact that the regalia were kept in a holy place and not in a museum gave them their symbolic significance. To this extra glorification was added even more the following year: on December 7, 1805, Millin returned to the canons the relics of the Passion bought by Saint Louis and housed until the Revolution in the Sainte-Chapelle, constructed for this purpose.[62] The sanctuaries of the former monarchy, Reims, Saint-Denis, and the Sainte-Chapelle, were reunited as one. The emperor's pact with the people of Paris had filtered through Notre Dame, bruised, certainly, but successfully defying time. It participated, as under the old regime, in the Te Deum of victories, the depositing of enemy flags (Austerlitz), funeral services, and baptisms (king of Rome).

NOTRE DAME DURING THE RESTORATION

The Restoration represented both continuity and change. It could not be a question of making a fresh start after all that had happened since the Revolution and ignoring some of the experiences of the empire. There was, on the other hand, a fierce desire to revive the past prior to 1789. For that reason alone, the major centers of monarchical ceremonies were to regain the significance that the Parisian cathedral had unlawfully co-opted. The rich archival evidence allows one to recover, if not the spirit of the ceremonies, at least the aspect which made them effective and gave them meaning.[63] When one comprehends the role of festivals in any paralyzed society, one easily understands the care that was taken in developing them. The splendor, greatness, mystery that enveloped the sacred was meant to assert the authority of the restored monarchy. The efficacy of each of these celebrations relied on a speech which clarified it. Each aspired to be a political assertion: the aggressiveness of certain declarations, of certain texts, was in keeping with this point of view. The most important—not only in terms of their significance but also because of their spectacular display and setting—took place in the cathedral. The alliance between the throne and the church, brutally interrupted by the Revolution, was once again powerfully affirmed, so much so that the clergy were invited to take an essential role in its accomplishment. Even more than in the eighteenth century, it was necessary to affirm that one could not advance without the other and that the monarchical principle drew its strength from the Catholic faith. The latter was experiencing a new momentum. Chateaubriand's *Genius of Christianity* was extended into politics. The coronation of Charles X, in this context, can be understood as the cleansing of a shameful past. Louis XVIII, aware of its importance, had thought about it. It was consistent with the Restoration, enabling the constitutional charter to be integrated in perpetuity. The affirmation of the religious origin of royal power was a major element in an overall plan. The second element, in terms of the significance given to it by virtue of its size, was the army, closely associated with all monarchical ceremony. It was a clever move, on the occasion of the marriage celebration of the Duke of Berry at Notre Dame (June 17, 1816), to renew the alliance with the Swiss. They were thus honored for their faithfulness to Louis XVI. This act underscored the reconciliation between the armies of the old regime and the new, the product of the Revolution and empire.

Once the general framework was set, the loci for celebrations had to be chosen. On this score as on so many others, it was necessary to remain faithful to the important monarchical centers. Saint-Denis consequently regained its position as cemetery of kings. The great funeral ceremonies

Figure 10.7

Vue du grand Vestibule, en forme de Tente, érigé à l'entrée du Palais Archiépiscopal derrière l'Église de Notre-Dame, on the occasion of the coronation of Napoleon I, December 2, 1804, by Fontaine and Percier.

Figure 10.8

The constitutional oath taken by Napoleon I in the cathedral, December 2, 1804, engraving by Le Coeur.

took place there: the Prince of Condé (May 26, 1818), the Duke of Berry (May 16, 1820), and Louis XVIII (October 26, 1824). Louis XVIII ordered that the leader of the émigré armies be honored as had been Du Guesclin, Sancerre, and Turenne, in coming to rest next to kings. It was also in the abbey that he had placed the gathered remains of Louis XVI and Marie Antoinette (January 18, 1821). However, when it came to the atonement ceremony in memory of Louis XVI, Louis XVII, Marie Antoinette, and Madame Elisabeth, Louis XVIII set the date and the place, in order to give it its real meaning. May 14, 1814 was reserved, as it was the birthday of Louis XVII as well as that of Henry IV. The place was Notre Dame of Paris, to give it its full expiatory significance. The entire Parisian people seemed to be participating and asking pardon there. The ceremony was supposed to erase the shameful memory of past eras with its austere grandeur and its solely religious aspect. The catafalque, surrounded by four statues, *Religion, Prudence, Charity,* and *Immortality,* had been placed in the choir; the mortuary chapel in the nave.[64]

When he had entered Paris several days before on May 3, Louis XVIII had made a stop at Notre Dame. Belanger, who had been put in charge of organizing this arrival, had sought to recreate the unanimity that had marked Louis XV's return from Metz. He evoked the return of the father to the bosom of his family. At Notre Dame, the king was welcomed by the whole clergy. He went to his seat at the entrance of the choir. Above the throne had been placed a picture of his hallowed ancestor, Louis IX. He heard the Te Deum there. He reestablished the celebration of the Vow of Louis XIII by ordering that the Declaration be read. France was once again consecrated to the Virgin. As for the army, it was closely associated with the Te Deum sung in the edifice.

At the same time that Notre Dame was regaining its religious meaning, it was becoming the locus of festivals of hope. The marriage of the Duke of Berry to Marie-Caroline of the Two Sicilies (June 17, 1816) held the hope of the monarchy's future, Louis XVIII and Angoulême having no heirs. Its importance accounts for the choice of this edifice. The decor sought to recall the pomp and circumstance of yesteryear even as it endeavored to be a political manifesto. It was in fact less the sacramental meaning which was exalted than the return of the monarchy. Medallions placed above the large arcades of the choir, decorated with allegorical scenes, were explained by inscriptions. At the back of the choir, the oriflamme was hung. The same importance was given to the baptism of the Duke of Bordeaux (May 1, 1821), which found an ideal setting in this same cathedral. Lecointe and Hittorff had at their disposal extraordinary financial resources which enabled them to give the ceremony the desired pomp. In a neo-Gothic decor, the four lines of Kings were brought together by their most popular representatives: Clovis, Charlemagne, Saint Louis, and Henry IV. They seemed to watch over this infant who was the future of the monarchy.

THE NEGLECTED CATHEDRAL

The break with the July Monarchy was abrupt. There was no doubt that the king of the French followed the policies of Charles X: Notre Dame had been the focal point of fifteen years of hatred. The anticlerical movement raged with an especial violence. On two occasions, the archbishop was assaulted by the crowd, excited by the ultra-Legitimist feelings of Monseigneur de Quélen. On July 29, 1830, protecting the endangered cathedral necessitated the intervention of the twelfth legion of the National Guard and, above all, that of Dupuytren, chief surgeon at the Hôtel-Dieu. February 14, 1831, was even more dramatic. Gunpowder was ignited during the anniversary service for the death of the Duke of Berry, still celebrated at Saint-Germain-l'Auxerrois. The torched buildings of the palace were not rebuilt, but razed. The isolation of the cathedral began with its southern flank, which then looked out on water. That same year, the statues of Louis XIII and Louis XIV were taken out of the sanctuary as a result of an ambiguous order, the instigator of which was not clearly identified. Their elimination was supposed to mark a break with the immediate past, but also with the more distant past which they evoked. Certainly, by virtue of this act the clergy recovered its peace of mind, but the cathedral lost a part of its meaning.

It was not until Fieschi's attempted assassination (July 28, 1835), which left eighteen dead and twenty-two wounded—Louis-Philippe miraculously escaped—that the king agreed to go to the cathedral for a Te Deum of gratitude. The ceremony was extended by the September Laws, which dealt with justice and regulation of the press. The Republic became illegal at the same time that power found its way back to Notre Dame. The deep change which affected the Catholic movement could only encourage this reconciliation, favored by Queen Marie-Amélie, around whom Guizot rallied. The nomination of Monseigneur Affre (1840) to the archiepiscopal seat, succeeding the overly Carlist Monseigneur de Quélen, was in keeping with these politics, which were clashing once more over the eternal academic debate. Lamennais and Montalembert had scarcely been heeded in their call for freedom of instruction. To dispel any lingering suspicions, Louis-Philippe paid a courtesy visit to the new archbishop on January 1, 1841. The cathedral immediately regained its privileged place in the symbolism of the new monarchy. The king had celebrated there his grandson's baptism with all the pomp worthy of the heir to the throne.

This ceremony was supposed to "legitimate," in the eyes of the Legitimists, this promise for the future. It was also at Notre Dame that the funeral service for the Duke of Orléans, the heir to the throne, killed in a
stupid carriage accident, took place (July 30, 1842). This death, in fact, put
an end to many hopes. Nonetheless, no one had dared to associate Notre
Dame with the most striking act of reconciliation of the reign: the chariot
returning Napoleon's ashes (December 15, 1840) passed under the Arc de
Triomphe and went directly to the Invalides. The monarch had managed
a policy of equilibrium which we know pleased no one, neither Orleanists, disturbed by the reconciliation, nor Legitimists, little convinced, nor
the clergy, which proved to be more and more indifferent.

1848: THE SECOND EMPIRE

The Revolution of 1848, in a departure from that of 1830, had scarcely
touched the church, whose solidarity with the July Monarchy was not at
all evident. Monseigneur Affre immediately showed his independence:
while going to deliver his words of peace on the barricades, he was mor-
tally wounded (July 25, 1848). The Parisian crowd thronged his funeral
in the presence of General Cavaignac. Monseigneur Sibour appeared to be
more flexible and was easily reconciled to the coup d'état of the prince-
president, Louis Napoleon.

Notre Dame recouped under the empire the privileged place it had
held under preceding monarchical regimes: it was to serve as a echo chamber for the regime, out of a desire to revive the prerevolutionary past as
well as the more recent empire and Restoration. Napoleon III's solicitude
was unfailing and was demonstrated more specifically in the interest he
took in the monument's repair and in the meaning he sought to give it.

Certainly, the decision to do a monumental restoration and the initial
work belonged to the preceding era.[65] The architect Godde had submitted, as far back as 1819, an important plan which was approved and even
financed, but was not executed. The Revolution of 1830 put an end to
this first attempt, which did not win all the votes anyway. The publication of Notre-Dame de Paris by Victor Hugo (1831) and the cabal started by
Didron against Godde attracted popular attention to the monument and its
unacceptable condition. The outburst of passionate public opinion led to
the decision to hold a competition in which Arveuf, Danjoy, Lassus, and
Viollet-le-Duc—all closely associated—participated. The plan submitted
by the last two was finally accepted (March 11, 1844). On July 19, 1845, a
law was passed for the restoration of the cathedral and the construction of
a sacristy. Although the plan was by and large accepted, it was nonetheless

Figure 10.9
The baptism of the Count of Paris, grandson of Louis-Philippe, May 2, 1841, gouache by Viollet-le-Duc.

subject to some reservations, a few of which deserve to be highlighted. They were not related to technique as much as to principles. In the report they had addressed to the minister of justice and religion (January 30, 1843), the architects had not hesitated to propose the restitution of "all the statues which decorated the portals, the Gallery of Kings, and the buttresses." The Chamber proved to be resistant to this absolutist dimension, fearing the reappearance of representations of the kings of France. Work nevertheless began and the rapidly exhausted funds were extended on March 29, 1851. After Lassus's death (1857), Viollet-le-Duc carried on alone, finishing the undertaking in time for the dedication on May 31, 1864. In the meantime, the monument under perpetual construction had seen state ceremonies follow one upon the other. The first, inaugurating the new regime, was the Te Deum of January 1, 1852, which celebrated the November 21–22 plebiscite. The prince-president "reestablished" imperial dignity there, taking the title of emperor of the French under the name Napoleon III, thus seeking to create a new legitimacy between the ephemeral reign of Napoleon II and his own. The vast majority of Catholics and the clergy favorably welcomed the new regime; the archbishop was the representative of this harmony. Louis Veuillot, in *L'Univers*, rallied to him enthusiastically, and a goodly number of prelates saw in him "the man on the right hand of God." The clergy's favor enabled him to attract the Legitimists. In addition, the clergy was associated with all solemn public celebrations. However, it was a political agreement of a tactical nature, which had, by virtue of that alone, its limits. The emperor's refusal to make religious marriage obligatory led Pope Pius IX to refuse to crown and anoint him.

Napoleon III obviously agreed to be married in church and sought to recall through pomp and circumstance the most beautiful ceremonies that had ever taken place in Notre Dame (January 30, 1853) while visibly affirming that his reign was in keeping with monarchical tradition.[66] On the lower bays of the two west towers, four statues symbolized this reconciliation between lines: *Charlemagne, Saint Louis, Louis XIV,* and *Napoleon*. The choice reveals the change in perspective from that of Louis XVIII: Clovis was abandoned, Louis XIV preferred over Henry IV, Napoleon made his appearance. In order to include Paris and pay homage to it, he had desired the depiction of the saints of the diocese. The province had not been forgotten: eighty-six flags of the *départements* hung in the gallery with openwork design. In this alone, the west façade was a manifesto. The baptism of the imperial prince (June 14, 1856) took on an even more solemn aspect: it was a pledge to the future. It took place in the presence of eighty-five prelates. To immortalize this brief moment, Napoleon III placed an order with Thomas Couture for a painting.[67] The painter never finished the work: "This ceremony received the child into the heart of the Church. . . . He is a prince who must maintain a dynasty, it is a national hope. . . . Napoleon I descends from heaven to earth to bless his descendent and touch his eagles with his formidable sword." The army was also associated with Notre Dame's imperial pomp at the time of the Te Deum for the victory of Sebastopol (September 17, 1855).

The commune was not unaware of all this: on April 2, 1871, it decreed as article 1 that the church is separate from the state, while article 2 eliminated the budget for worship. On May 26, it even tried to burn the edifice to reduce to nothing the old memories and especially the recent ones evoked by it; Monseigneur Darboy, finally, was shot in Montmartre, while a hostage of the commune.

THE CONTEMPORARY ERA

The fall of the empire and the new regime was to raise the problem of the relationship between church and state in a very new way. They were usually in conflict. Notre Dame of Paris particularly suffered the after-effects of this abrupt disengagement from political life. It had to rediscover the reason for its conception and construction: to be a house of God, intended to welcome the faithful. Like other cathedrals, it tried to return to a parish role. Claudel returned to the faith on Christmas Day 1886, while Péguy organized the great national pilgrimage to Chartres. It suffered, furthermore, from the environment which had just been created for it, which completely isolated it in the middle of the Île de la Cité, itself emptied of its population. The creation of this immense *parvis* was only, in truth, the public manifestation of an even deeper surgical operation. Haussmann's work was particularly drastic with respect to its treatment of the Île de la Cité. Three routes crossed from north to south along the axis of each of the bridges: the first touched the west façade of the edifice, the second the rue de la Cité and, the last, the boulevard du Palais. New buildings, heavy and disproportionate relative to the dimensions of the island, replaced the innumerable private dwellings: the immense Hôtel-Dieu, built to the north, which replaced the old one situated along the Seine; the Tribunal de Commerce; the barracks of the Cité, which have since become police headquarters. The soldiers drilled in the square along-side it on the *parvis*, which was 150 meters wide by 200 meters long, and soon at the palace itself. All this had an immediate effect on the island's population: it went from fifteen thousand inhabitants to five thousand by the end of the century. The cathedral of Paris was no longer at the center of urban life. It was isolated amid soulless administrative activity. The clergy painfully witnessed this isolation.[68]

NOTRE DAME'S LAST RESORT

The Republic ignores this great body which it simultaneously admires and dreads. It has recourse to it in each of its moments of despair, trying to move a God whom it otherwise pretends to be unaware of but whom it implores. In 1876, it was the reopening of the Chamber of Deputies; on January 16, 1881, public prayers. But it is death which seems to call this immense ship. The national funeral of Sadi Carnot, the president of the Republic, on June 26, 1894, presided over by Casimir Périer, gave rise to an immense cortege (July 1), which left from the Champs Élysées, passed the place de la Concorde, and the Hôtel de Ville, but stopped at Notre Dame before heading to the Pantheon. The same chariot was to be used for Félix Faure, another president, whose funeral was also held at Notre Dame (February 23, 1899). The decor devised for the occasion was inspired by the Restoration: the walls were hung with black draperies set off by white bands, trophy flags alternating with the president's initials. An immense catafalque surrounded by statues was placed in the sanctuary.[69]

Notre Dame will live, over the course of the twentieth century, by the rhythm of the joys and despairs of the nation; the archbishop welcomes both unhappy and happy believers, who suddenly discover that God, and especially Notre Dame, is the last resort. On September 13, 1916, forty thousand people thronged around Cardinal Amette to beg for divine mercy. But it was principally the vibrant Te Deum of Victory Day (November 17, 1918) which brought together the clergy, the army, the Republic, and Alsace. An Alsatian priest conducted the mass. The funeral of Marshal Foch (March 26, 1929) gathered together the Republic, the army, and the Allies. In 1934, it was Raymond Poincaré's funeral. In 1936, it was those of Charcot and his companions. In 1937, Cardinal Pacelli, the future Pope Pius XII, was to say in Notre Dame what is known as the *Vocation de la France*, which is embodied in Notre Dame, the soul of France. On May 21, 1944, public prayers were said for France. On this occasion, Cardinal Suhard dedicated the city and the diocese to the Virgin: "Our Lady of Paris, you who are both Queen of France and Queen of Peace, deign to listen to us." On August 26, 1944, a Te Deum of Victory was sung in the presence of General de Gaulle. On December 8, 1947, the funeral of General Leclerc. Finally, on November 12, 1970, the national funeral of General de Gaulle. Indeed, the entire people of France was at Colombey-les-Deux-Églises, lost in the middle of a crowd both moved

Figure 10.10
Le Te Deum de la Victoire, 17 novembre 1918,
drawing by Simont.

Figure 10.11
Generals de Gaulle and Leclerc at Notre Dame
for the Te Deum for the liberation of Paris,
August 26, 1944.

Figure 10.12
The funeral service for General de Gaulle at Notre-Dame de Paris, November 12, 1970.

and profoundly upset by this great loss. The universe belongs to Notre Dame, Notre Dame to the universe.

NOTES

1. Théodore Vacquer's layouts were published by Albert Lenoir, in *Statistique monumentale de Paris* (Paris, 1867).

2. According to Michel Fleury's *La Cathédrale mérovingienne Saint-Étienne de Paris: Plan et datation*, in *Mélanges Pétri* (Bonn, 1970), 211–20.

3. Charpentier, *Description historique et chronologique de l'église métropolitaine de Paris* (Paris, 1767), 19.

4. The subject's bibliography is particularly important. A synthetic account and recent bibliography can be found in *Histoire de la France religieuse*, ed. Jacques Le Goff and René Rémond (Paris: Éditions du Seuil, 1988), 1:39–167, by Paul-Albert Février.

5. Henri-Irénée Marrou, *Décadence romaine ou antiquité tardive, IIe-IVe siècles* (Paris: Édition du Seuil, "Points" coll., 1977).

6. See Paul-Albert Février, in *Histoire de la France urbaine*, ed. Georges Duby (Paris: Éditions du Seuil, 1980), vol. 1, pt. 4, pp. 399–493.

7. Alain Erlande-Brandenburg, *La Cathédrale* (Paris: Fayard, 1989), 55–75 (incl. bibliography).

8. The fascicles—seven at present—of the *Topographie chrétienne de la Gaule des origins au milieu de VIIIe siècle* (Paris: de Boccard, 1986–) are a precious source. They round off the various studies by Jean Hubert, brought together in two collections, *Art et vie sociale de la fin du monde antique au Moyen Âge* (Geneva: Droz, 1977); and *Nouveau Recueil d'études d'archéologie et d'histoire: De la fin du monde antique au Moyen Âge* (Geneva: Droz, 1985). The best example is the Geneva edition, available thanks to a series of search campaigns which took more than twenty years, undertaken by Louis Blondel and continued by Charles Bonnet. For the bibliography, see *Topographie religiouse . . .* (Vienna, 1986), 3:44–47.

9. Gregory of Tours, *Histoire des Francs*, bk. 2, chap. 28.

10. For these discoveries and their interpretation, the role played by the Historical Commission on Old Paris was exemplary. Following the move by Théodore Vacquer, whose notes were preserved in the Bibliothèque historique de la Ville de Paris, it preserved the search files made since then. Michel Fleury oversaw the publication of the *Carte archéologique de Paris* (Paris, 1971).

11. May Vieillard-Troiekouroff, "Les Anciennes Églises suburbaines de Paris (IVe-Xe siècles), Paris et Île-de-France," *Mémoires* 11 (1960): 165–66.

12. Alain Erlande-Brandenburg, *Les Roi est mort* (Geneva: Droz, 1975), 49–50.

13. Karl Richard Bruhl, *Palatium und civitas*, vol. 1, *Gallien* (Vienna, 1975), 6–33.

14. I have put forth the hypothesis that the edifice discovered in the middle of the nineteenth century, newly excavated by Michel Fleury, went back to the fourth century. With its five naves, its façade of thirty-six meters and length between eighty

and one hundred meters, it could not be dated any later. The different fragments discovered, for that matter, favor such a time sequence: columns of great age, marble capitals, mosaics; see *Notre-Dame de Paris* (Paris: Nathan, 1991), 13. Dom Dubois's studies have clearly showed the establishment of the cathedral in the Île de la Cité as far back as the fourth century: "L'Emplacement des premiers sanctuaires de Paris," *Journal des savants* (1968): 5–44; and "L'Organisation primitive de l'église de Paris du Ve au VIIIe siècle," *Cahiers de la Rotonde* 11 (1988).

15. The analysis of titles over the course of this period is especially tricky. The texts do not take judicial and everyday change into account until much later. In our time, it was not until 1990 that the Parisian subway station Chambre des députés took the name Assemblée nationale (adopted in 1959).

16. The analysis of texts brought together by Robert de Lasteyrie is hardly conclusive: *Cartulaire general de Paris*, vol. 1, *(528–1180)* (Paris, 1887).

17. De Lasteyrie, no. 28.

18. For the revival of Paris as capital, see Robert-Henri Bautier, "Quand et comment Paris devint capitale," *Bulletin de la Société de l'histoire de Paris et de l'Île-de-France* (1978): 17–46.

19. Jean Guerout, "Le Palais de la Cité à Paris, des origins à 1417," in *Paris et Île-de-France: Mémoires* 2 (1950): 112–24.

20. Jacques Thirion considerably revived the study of this portal by clearly showing that it antedated 1160: "Les plus anciennes sculptures de Notre-Dame de Paris," *Comptes rendus de l'Académie des inscriptions et belles-lettres* (1970): 85–112.

21. Jean Dérens and Michel Fleury, "La Construction de la cathédrale de Paris par Childebert 1er, d'après le *De ecclesia Parisiaca* de Fortunat," *Journal des savants* (1977): 247–56.

22. Alain Erlande-Brandenburg, "Un gisant royal du milieu du XIIe siècle provenant de Saint-Germain-des-Prés, à Paris," *Bulletin archéologique* 15 (1979): 33–50.

23. Dom Dubois, "Les Évêques de Paris: Des origins à l'avènement d'Hugues Capet," *Bulletin de la Société de l'histoire de Paris et de l'Île-de-France* (1969): 18–19.

24. Jacques Le Goff, "Culture écclesiastique et culture folklorique au Moyen Âge: Saint Marcel de Paris et le dragon," in *Pour un autre Moyen Âge* (Paris: Gallimard, 1977), 236–39.

25. Jean-Charles Picard, "Il était une fois un évêque de Paris appelé Marcel," in *Mélanges Pierre Riché* (La Garenne-Colombes, 1990), 79–91.

26. Dubois, "Les Évêques de Paris."

27. For Maurice de Sully, see Victor Mortet, "Maurice de Sully, évêque de Paris (1160–1196)," *Mémoires de la Société de l'histoire de Paris* 16 (1889): 105f. Pierre Michaud-Quantin, "Les évêques de Paris dans la seconde moitié du XIIe siècle," in *Huitième Centenaire de Notre-Dame de Paris* (Paris: Vrin, 1967), 23–33.

28. Erlande-Brandenburg, *Notre-Dame de Paris*, 23.

29. Victor Mortet and Paul Deschamps, *Recueil de texts relatifs à l'histoire de l'architecture . . .* (Paris: Picard, 1929), 86.

30. W. W. Clark and François J. Ladden, "Notes of the Archivoltes of the Sainte-Anne Portal of Notre-Dame de Paris," *Gesta* 25, no. 1 (1986): 109–18.

31. Alain Erlande-Brandenburg, "Une tête de prelate provenant du portail du

Couronnement de la Vierge à Notre-Dame de Paris," *Revue du Louvre et des musées de France* (1986): 186–91.

32. Dom Dubois, "Communication," *Bulletin de la Société nationale des antiquaires de France* (1987): 84–89.

33. *Les XXII manières du vilain,* fabliau dating back to 1284, published by Émile Mâle, in *L'Art religieux du XIIIe siècle en France* (Paris: Le livre de poche, 1990), 2:89.

34. Louis VII gave two hundred Parisian pounds. Queen Adèle, mother of Philip Augustus, gave twenty marks of silver in 1206, according to the *Cartulaire général de Notre-Dame de Paris,* published by B. Guérard, vol. 4, 79 and 153.

35. The sums spent are partially known. See Alain Erlande-Brandenburg, "L'Architecture militaire au temps de Philippe Auguste: Une nouvelle conception de la défense," in *La France de Philippe Auguste: Le temps des mutations* (Paris: CNRS, 1982), 597–607.

36. Erlande-Brandenburg, *Le Roi est mort,* 42–43, 77, 90.

37. Ibid., 78.

38. Jean Favier, *Philippe le Bel* (Paris: Fayard, 1978), 250–88.

39. Françoise Baron, "Le Cavalier royal de Notre-Dame de Paris," *Bulletin monumental* (1968): 141–54.

40. Guerout, 23–44, 128–43.

41. Erlande-Brandenburg, *Le Roi est mort,* 20.

42. Ralph E. Giesey, *Le Roi ne meurt jamais,* Fr. trans. (Paris: Flammarion, 1987), 64–67.

43. Pierre-Marie Auzas, *Les Grandes Heures de Notre-Dame de Paris* (Paris, 1951), 21, 24, 27.

44. For these ceremonies, see Auzas.

45. Jean-Pierre Babelon, *Paris au XVIe siècle* (Paris: Hachette, 1986), 61–64.

46. René Pillorget, *Paris sous les premiers Bourbons, 1594–1661* (Paris: Hachette, coll. "Nouvelle histoire de Paris," 1988), 13–14.

47. René Laurentin, *Le Voeu de Louis XIII: Passé ou avenir de la France* (Paris: OEIL, 1988), has especially insisted on the premises, publishing a number of texts never before brought together in the different appendixes.

48. Alain Erlande-Brandenburg, *Chartres* (Paris: Robert Laffont, 1986), 11–12.

49. Engraving by Balthazar Montcornet, *Le vray pourtraict de l'autel de la Vierge de l'église de Nostre-Dame de Paris,* published among others in the irreplaceable work by Maurice Vloberg, *Notre-Dame de Paris et le Voeu de Louis XIII* (Paris, 1926), pl. 11.

50. The Cabinet des estampes, in the Bibliothèque nationale, has a very important collection on the subject, the papers of Robert de Cotte, which has not been entirely explored.

51. For the alternative Te Deum, see Auzas. For the ceremonial, read Guillot de Montjoie, canon of the cathedral, who signed with the initials M.C.P.G. his *Description historique des curiosités de l'église de Paris* (Paris, 1763), 410–12.

52. De Montjoie, 412–13.

53. Published by Pierre du Colombier, *Notre-Dame de Paris: Mémorial de la France* (Paris: Plon, 1966), 160; Auzas, fig. 119.

54. François Souchal, *Les Slodtz: Sculpteurs et décorateurs du roi (1685–1764)* (Paris: de Boccard, 1967), 369.

55. Père Ménestrier, *Des décorations funèbres* . . . (Paris, 1683). See Roger-A. Weigert, *Jean Ier Bérain* . . . (Paris, 1937), 1:27.

56. Weigert, 42–43. Souchal, 376. Alain-Charles Gruber, *Les Grandes Fêtes et leurs décors à l'époque de Louis XVI* (Geneva: Droz, 1972), 103.

57. Gruber, 110.

58. Dubu, in *Description et annals de la basilique de Notre-Dame de Paris* (Paris, 1854), 279f., drew up the list of ceremonies which took place during the Revolution.

59. Alain Erlande-Brandenburg and Dierter Kimpel, "Le Statuaire de Notre-Dame de Paris avant les destruction révolutionnaires," *Bulletin monumental* (1978), 214. Fleury, in *Les Rois retrouvés*, 14–23.

60. Dubu, 279f.

61. Ibid., 29.

62. Ibid., 297.

63. Françoise Waquet, *Les Fêtes royales sous la Restauration ou l'ancien régime retrouvé* (Geneva: Droz and Flammarion, 1981), 69f.

64. Waquet, 78.

65. Jean-Michel Leniaud, *J.-B. Lassus (1807–1857) ou le temps retrouvé des cathédrales* (Geneva: Droz and Flammarion, 1980), 93.

66. Jean-Michel Leniaud, "Le marriage de Napoléon III à Paris," in *Congrès national des sociétés savants* (Paris, 1976), *Archéologie*, 309–21.

67. See the exhibition catalogue, *L'Art en France sous le second Empire* (Paris, 1979), 332.

68. Pierre Lavedan, *Histoire de l'urbanisme à Paris* (Paris: Hachette, coll. "Nouvelle histoire de Paris," 1975), 427–28.

69. Auzas, 36.

CHAPTER 11

SACRÉ COEUR OF MONTMARTRE

FRANÇOIS LOYER

A CONTESTED LANDMARK

Totally scorned by art historians, the Parisian basilica called the Sacré Coeur of Montmartre has long been the object of an ostracism of culture and ideological origin. The "discovery" of the nineteenth century, nearly fifteen years before its close, did not benefit art of the second half of the nineteenth century; it is still quite badly understood and unappreciated by the general public (whose judgment radically contrasts with the *passéisme* of Montmartre and the supposed modernity of the Eiffel Tower!). It is true that the continuation of the basilica's construction until the eve of World War I, after the heyday of the Art Nouveau movement, was disastrous, to say the least, to its public image. Curiously enough, Victor Laloux and the pompier style (*pompiérisme*) of the École des beaux-arts at the turn of the century were released from cultural purgatory earlier than the church, even though they were older by a quarter of a century and otherwise more interesting than what had been envisioned by Paul Abadie, one of Viollet-le-Duc's disciples.* A museum of the nineteenth century was created in the Orsay train station, but, for the basilica of Montmartre, the sole public reverberation was that of the

---

* Eugène Emmanuel Viollet-le-Duc (1814–79) was one of the most influential architect-theoreticians of the nineteenth century. His many restoration projects of medieval buildings, as well as his writing and teaching, made him a central figure in the Gothic revival. Paul Abadie (1812–84) drew the plans for Sacré Coeur, though he did not live to see it completed.—Ed.

419

Figure 11.1
Sacré Coeur, decorated by Ernest Pignon, in homage to the victims of the Commune on the centennial of that uprising.

terrorist bombers who celebrated the edifice's centennial in their own way
by blowing up one of its domes in 1974.

Can one consider Montmartre to be one of France's important centers? Ideologically, its past is laden.[1] Desired by the Catholic and royalist
majority just after the bloody events of the Paris Commune (1871), the
basilica is more an edifice of reconquest than of reconciliation (a situation
shared with Gaudi's Sagrada Familia). Imposing in form and position, the
building was a permanent insult, a defiance of republican political power
throughout the Third Republic. When the quarrels between religious and
civil power diminished, it would remain marked by the seal of the political
will which gave rise to it—a heavy and slightly shameful burden for the
clergy after Vatican II. A refuge of conservative intransigents, it has assumed *a contrario* perpetuation of Versailles' repression of the Commune—
another wall of the Fédérés,★ which only prayers will perhaps succeed one
day in cleansing of the civil war's blood and crimes.

It is thus with a very precise moment in the history of France in the
last quarter of the nineteenth century and with the views of the most
reactionary party (clerical and royalist) that the building is immediately
identified. The Sacré Coeur, from this perspective, is far from being the
true *heart* of France. It represents a France politically and socially fragmented. Had tourism not taken over, the basilica would perhaps be abandoned today, an immense, empty, and closed building like so many others
in existence in France, as a result of the decline of the Catholic faith.
Two steps away are the pimps and prostitutes of Pigalle, dominating the
Moulin-Rouge and the Folies-Bergère, which are spread across the lower
slopes of Montmartre. The neighborhood was saved by pictures of ur-
chins (*poulbots*), Parisian kids immortalized in the eye-catching drawings
of Francisque Poulbot (1879–1946); one would be at pains to find them
nowadays in this *quartier* so entirely devoted to the tourist industry. It is
interesting to note that painters of mediocre interest but who have had
a wise popular following, like Utrillo or Poulbot, did more for the fame
of the *quartier* than the greatest of the Postimpressionists or Cubists who
lived there. A similar mediocrity continues, thanks to the work of the
Japanese painters, in the art made on the place du Tertre, where tourists
push and shove between the easels of so-called landscape painters. What
would Adolf Loos have thought of this when he built for Tristan Tzara

★ The *Mur des Fédérés*, in Père Lachaise cemetery, is so named because the Communards
fled there and made their last stand against the Versailles troops. Those who surrendered
were executed at this wall, which immediately became sacred ground to the Left, from
Republicans to Communists—Ed.

his austere house on avenue Junot—a neighbor, as if in mockery, to that of Francisque Poulbot?★

All the same, the capital of "Paris by night," Montmartre, lives on as proud as ever above Paris, which it contemplates. And this is perhaps the secret of its timelessness: the basilica has withstood the test of time due to its location as well as its exceptional architecture (even if the latter is misunderstood). No tourist can remain unmoved by either the monument's power or the vastness of the landscape which unfolds beneath his feet. On the steps of the *parvis*, hundreds of people come to sit every day to watch night fall over Paris. On summer evenings, the show continues until quite late, with the jumbled and somewhat obnoxious sound of guitars (played by European tourists) mixed with that of the drums of African immigrants, coming from the neighboring quarter of the Goutte d'Or. There is only one other place in Paris that is equally favored, the *parvis* of the Notre Dame cathedral on the banks of the Seine. A handsome tribute to the architecture of the nineteenth century!

IN THE PARISIAN LANDSCAPE

If Montmartre has become one of the most important places in our country today, it is due neither to the circumstances of its construction nor to the political or religious views held about it over the course of a half century nor to the difficulties encountered in its erection, but rather to qualities that have to do with architecture and urban planning. The emptiness of its ideological meaning in a context entirely different from that of the past century has facilitated its dominance by the tourist industry. Nothing remains of the ideological debate between Montmartre and the Eiffel Tower—between the clerical monument and the lay monument which rise, facing each other, in the Parisian sky. But the two monuments feel none the worse for it.

At one hundred and four meters above the level of the river, Montmartre's summit is the highest point in Paris and the surrounding region. From here, the view extends over a more than fifty-kilometer radius, that is, even beyond the limits of the suburbs. In building on this site a monument, the domes of which are eighty-four meters high, the whole Parisian region has been marked with its imprint. The basilica is over half again as tall as the Eiffel Tower (188 meters versus 320 meters) and is nearly equal to that of the Maine-Montparnasse Tower, but with an entirely different

★ Tzara (1896–1963) was a French writer of Romanian origins who was hostile to all pretension in art. He is one of the principle founders of the Dada movement in the early twentieth century.

visual impact because of its extraordinary silhouette and materials. The immaculate whiteness of the edifice, marked by the design covering the main dome, and the sculptural dialogue between dome and campanile at the heart of the same powerful mass, violently contrasts with the grey and ochre tones of the Parisian landscape. It is at once a symbolic and plastic display of a tremendous intensity of expression. In fact, Montmartre is not made of Paris limestone (the color of which is beige, tending toward yellow), but of a white stone with an extremely fine grain, a sort of travertine which comes from the quarries of Souppes-sur-Loing, near Melun, eighty kilometers south of Paris. Only one other Parisian monument was built with the same material, the Arc de Triomphe de l'Étoile, an edifice also of colossal proportions, at least with respect to many triumphal arches, and of great importance in the urban setting.

Because of its position as well as its contrasting dialogue with its environment, Montmartre reorganizes Paris around it. This pool of glaring white, silhouetted by the sky, is as noticeable from the slopes of Trocadero atop which sits the Palais de Chaillot, as from the place de la Concorde (where it crowns the Palais de Gabriel), from the Tuileries or the Pont d'Austerlitz, along the quays of the Seine. It is along the axis of the rue Laffitte, on the Right Bank, that its appearance is most disconcerting, because it seems to fit into the façade of the neoclassical church Notre-Dame-de-Lorette: this beautiful illusion, like a picture postcard, is popular with tourists.

Less visible from the east (where the heights of Romainville conceal its nearness) and from the south (because of the distance) the basilica is most impressive looking from the west and especially from the north. One sees it behind the curve of the Seine, toward Saint-Germain-en-Laye and Maisons-Laffitte, and one does not lose sight of it, coming toward Paris from Montmagny or La Courneuve. Should one see this as symbolic? Unquestionably. Beyond the circumstantial aspect of Montmartre's position, the edifice was built at the junction of the German and Flemish roads, as if to ward off a new Prussian invasion. In the patriotic iconography of the Third Republic, Montmartre came to play a large role, lending its setting to the account of the life of Saint Denis (who, legend says, was decapitated there) as well as to that of Saint Geneviève, whose statue on the Pont de la Tournelle (Paul Landowski, 1928) creates a formal visible reminder with the basilica situated in the background.

While this plan—we will have occasion to come back to this—stems from a long history, Montmartre's silhouette departs from exemplars. In the French tradition, there is no model for an *architecture de site* (apart from military fortifications, which was one of France's innovations). A monument's architecture is always designed with respect to the site, in a relationship of unity and continuity involving materials and scale as well as rhythm and silhouette. In general, the effect of mass is more powerful, absorbing the facts of the landscape (whether it be a natural or constructed landscape). Montmartre totally rejects this osmosis of architecture and environment. It is an artificial foreign body, a heterogeneous megastructure, and asserts itself as such, appropriating for its benefit a new architectural effect that industrial buildings had just discovered. In this respect, it is sister to the gas distribution towers of La Villette—now destroyed, but which were for many years its companions in the cityscape of the Paris East. It is not, if you will, an architecture of integration, but rather of imposition.

Relationships

The basilica's real model is the East, in the mosques of the Golden Crescent which so powerfully reshaped the landscape of the Bosphorus, and in Istanbul (such as Suleymaniye or Yeni-Cami). Abadie's vision was not Byzantine, as one might have thought, but rather, in many ways, Ottoman. On this picture, with its formidable influence, another, no less strong, is superimposed: that of the astonishing Palais de Justice in Brussels, designed by Joseph Poelaert in 1861–62 and under construction as of 1866. When Abadie was at work the Palais de Justice was already built to the height of the cornice, and one could have discerned its final form, as it would appear some ten years later, in 1883. It is from Poelaert, in fact, that Abadie borrows the idea (which was later taken up by Sacconi for the Victor-Emmanuel monument in Rome) of a total restructuring of the landscape by a large-scale monument.

The theme was muted in the reconstruction of the Houses of Parliament in London and in the imperial additions to the Louvre, but with less imposing sites, less striking effects, more delicate scales. Here, as with Poelaert, all was to be sacrificed to the monumentality of the proportions, to the long-distance visibility of forms. The edifice was to be without detail, without any more visual information as one got closer, without any surprises, or incidental discourse, like the counterpoint of the main theme, as one approached. A totally unified symphonic composition, the form is held together entirely by the magnitude—as in Berlioz or Wagner—of the orchestral mass, like some gigantic choir in unison.

It is enough, to be convinced, to compare Montmartre with two generic models: the Major cathedral (begun in 1854) by Vaudoyer, and the Notre-Dame-de-la-Garde basilica (1853–72) by his student, Espérandieu, in Marseille. On an isolated, fortified prominence which serves to set it off, the small basilica has a significant silhouette, although it lacks the necessary mass. The cathedral, in spite of the unity imposed on it by Vaudoyer's

Figure 11.2
Major cathedral in Marseilles, taken by the photographer Mievemens around 1890.

installation of alternating strata and in spite of the powerful articulation of volume (to the point of disintegration), does not succeed in relating to its site except through the long, low line of the quay that serves as its base, on the harbor's edge. A monumental object on the scale of the landscape, but an object seemingly set down on its site, like a teapot on its tray. It is a problem that Poelaert and, after him, Abadie, succeeded in overcoming. The cityscape of Brussels without its Palais de Justice can no more be envisioned than that of Paris without Montmartre. Something essential would be missing.

The success of these monuments at the end of the Second Empire, around the 1870s, is comparable to that of the Garnier's Opéra (1861–75), nearly their contemporary. Julien Guadet, in the seminal article he dedicated to the Sacré Coeur, did not fail to point this out: "Nothing is more instructive in this regard than the comparison of these two works, both of which appeared almost at the same time as the competition, both aimed at realizing the modern type of a secular program: Garnier's Opéra, Abadie's Sacré Coeur church."[2] Even if we do not entirely share his conclusions it is our duty to point out the influence of Abadie's monument. Citing only examples not far from Paris, let me mention the names of Arthur Regnault and the Mellet brothers in Rennes, the Le Diberder brothers in Nantes, and Auguste Beignet in Angers.[3] These regional successors in western France felt the influence of Paul Abadie's personality. He was, for thirty-six years, the diocesan architect of the three bishoprics of La Rochelle, Angoulême, and Périgueux, at the junction between lower Poitou and Aquitaine, in a region with a medieval heritage as rich as it is original in comparison with thirteenth-century Île-de-France. Added to this was the profound impact that the basilica model would later have on the construction of pilgrimage churches. It had an international resonance and was a standard model for close to a century. One cannot ignore the significance of the Montmartre model on the Saint-Thérèse de Lisieux basilica (1929–68), designed by the Lille architect Louis-Marie Cordonnier.

THE REJECTED MONUMENT

The historical weight of the basilica of Montmartre in sacred art of the nineteenth and twentieth centuries has far surpassed the purely circum-stantial ambitions of its promoters. In emphasizing the circumstantial, it has transgressed its limits even beyond the level of the Fourvière basil-ica, despite the properties unique to this building. (Fourvière, despite its prominent position in Lyons above the confluence of the Rhône and the Saône rivers, does not have Montmartre's monumental scale, and appears a giant chapel from a distance.)

In the first pages of *La Cathédrale*, published in 1898, Joris-Karl Huys-mans demonstrates that all of Catholic opinion had been waiting for a long time for this revival of religious art that had been prefigured in the middle of the century by Louis-Auguste Boileau's idea of a "synthetic cathedral."[4] Taking Chartres as an exemplar, he describes the model of mystical space, monumental and imagined, which his generation seeks; he describes its stages of evolution from La Salette to Lourdes.

With the brilliant disrespect which is unique to him, Huysmans ana-lyzes the relationship between God and the public character of churches in salacious terms. La Salette, inaccessible by railroad, is a failure; Lourdes, much better situated, is a success aided by the publicity campaign of which Henri Lasserre and Émile Zola,* by virtue of their opposition, were the more or less voluntary promoters.[5] Speaking of Lourdes, Huysmans has this cruel sentence: "In order for this work [the Lourdes cathedral] to up-lift the masses, the writer assigned to this task must be a clever organizer as well as a man who has no personal style, no new idea. In a word, it re-quires a man without talent; and that is possible, since from the point of

* Emile Zola's (1840–1902) novel *Lourdes* was published in 1894.—Ed.

Figure 11.3
Model of Louis-Auguste Boileau's "synthetic cathedral," 1853.

view of art appreciation, the Catholic public is still a hundred feet below the secular public." Huysmans did not offer any opinions on architecture. He confined himself to tersely ridiculing the group around the Angevin sculptor, Barrème, in La Salette. Even so, his judgments meshed admirably with the conventional neo-Gothic work of H. D. Durand, realized between 1862 and 1872 (which L. Hardy's beautiful underground basilica of the Rosary, 1883–85, did not succeed in saving from mediocrity).

Abadie was to be the Zola of religious architecture: "It mattered little from then on, we can write [to extend the metaphor borrowed from Huysmans's book], that he denied the supernatural and endeavored to explain, with the weakest suppositions, the inexplicable cures. . . . [T]he confusion of his arguments, the poverty of his 'curative breath of the crowds' . . . , were they not excellent for persuading unbiased people . . . ?" Actually, the rationalist school, in which Abadie took part, hardly shared the religious convictions of its sponsors; it belonged, rather, to the world of freethinkers, in which Viollet-le-Duc was, in his time, one of the major figures. Religious architects were not required to share a belief; their talent was required to spread it to the crowds. At this time, Abadie would have been remarkable.

From this point of view, it is very striking that the founder of the plan for Montmartre was, if not an architect, at least related to one. This was Hubert Rohault de Fleury, a former navy officer turned *rentier*, who was the son of one of the most high-profile architects in Paris, Charles Rohault de Fleury, the designer of the Jardin des Plantes' greenhouses and the unfortunate rival of Charles Garnier (who had ousted him from the Opéra competition). Highly esteemed by Haussmann, Charles Rohault de Fleury was himself the offspring of the illustrious Hittorff (to whom he owed his career). These family connections played a decisive role in launching the Montmartre plan. The initial idea of a pilgrimage church goes back to Alexander Legentil, who was none other than Hubert Rohault de Fleury's brother-in-law. A rich fabric merchant and backer of the Petit Saint-Thomas (one of the first department stores), Legentil was to be, with Albert de Mun and Augustin Cochin, one of the promoters of social Catholicism—through the Société de Saint-Vincent-de-Paul, of which he was one of the prominent members. Taking refuge in Poitiers in 1870 during the siege of Paris, he edited the text of Voeu national au Sacré-Coeur,★ which Saint-Vincent-de-Paul's parish conferences then promoted.

The devotion to the Sacred Heart, dating from the seventeenth century, had witnessed an unusual growth, adapting an already ancient devotion linked to apparitions of Saint Marguerite-Marie Alacoque in Paray-le-Monial in 1675—evidence, in those times, of a struggle against theories, at first Protestant and later Jansenist, which posited a God indifferent to man, an imperturbable judge of his mistakes. In 1856, Pope Pius IX had revived this devotion by extending the purely French celebration of the Sacred Heart of Jesus (at the time of the octave of Corpus Christi) to the Universal Church.[6] During the bitter ultramontanist phase which marked the first part of the French Second Empire, from 1849 to 1860, this devotion appeared to be an attempt by papal authorities to take over Gallicanism. Things became more intense after 1860, when the pope became the victim of Italian unification. The year 1870 marks the annexation of the Papal States as well as the defeat of France by Prussia.

Catholic circles of the French Right then combined patriotic and religious feelings to demonstrate their disapproval of recent times:

> In the presence of troubles which desolate France and the perhaps greater troubles which threaten it, in the presence of sacrilegious attacks made in Rome against the Rights of the Church and the Holy

★ A group formed to promote the "National Wish"—the construction of the Sacré Coeur basilica to expiate the sins of the nation.—Trans.

Figure 11.4
Legentil, Baudon, Rohault de Fleury, and Beluze, founders of the Voeu national, lithograph by P. Gusman, 1891.

See and against the holy person of the Vicar of Jesus Christ, we
humble ourselves before God and uniting our love of the Church and
our Homeland, we recognize that we have been guilty and rightly
punished. And in order to make amends for our sins and obtain from
the infinite mercy of Sacred Heart of Our Lord Jesus Christ pardon
for our transgressions as well as the special assistance which only the
Supreme Pontiff can deliver from his captivity and end the troubles
of France, we promise to contribute to the construction, in Paris, of a
sanctuary dedicated to the Sacred Heart of Jesus.

The strange amalgamation which this text shows, in the emotion of the
moment, is full of undercurrents that events would clarify. They clearly
foreshadow the drama of the Commune of the following year. It was
understood by Catholic opinion in this way: an immense movement of
popular piety, in the years 1872–79, which would provide some seven
million gold francs expected for the competition. In 1873, the National
Assembly, the majority of which was royalist, even declared the construction to be of public utility and in adherence with the Voeu national du
Sacré-Coeur. It was within this context of making up for the transgressions of the Commune and the national upheaval after the defeat that the
1874 competition took place.

Things changed quickly: when work began, two years later, the Count
of Chambord had already abandoned the monarchical restoration urged
by his followers. The following year, Marshal MacMahon resigned and
was replaced by the Republican Jules Grévy. The isolation of the church,
in spite of the policy of Rallying [*Ralliement*] advocated by Léon XIII,
ended in a complete reversal of the trend in 1902, when the Radicals took
power. Montmartre, like Fourvière, became the target of antireligious attacks. More than forty-five million francs in all were spent between 1876
and 1910 for the basilica's construction, but without the participation of
the state (construction was entirely financed by collection money and individual gifts). Although the state was powerless to confiscate an edifice
that was entirely financed with private funds, it did not lessen attacks on
the symbol for which it stood. Georges Clemenceau, notably, tried to
get the namesake changed (following the example of Sainte-Geneviève
Church, which had become the Pantheon of the Republic). The history
of Montmartre is a little like that of the other France, rural and Catholic,
in the conflict which pitted it against the new society, urban and atheist,
the result of industrialization. Montmartre's history represents an extraordinary rejection of the change in cultures and mentalities at the dawn of
the twentieth century.

THE UPS AND DOWNS OF CONSTRUCTION

The year 1874 is of great importance in French architectural history because it is the year of the Montmartre competition and also that of the reconstruction of the Hôtel de Ville in Paris—the same architects answered both calls. For Montmartre, seventy-eight plans were submitted by architects who, for the most part, were rationally oriented (among whom were a large number of diocesans).[7] The shadow of Viollet-le-Duc hung over this jury as it had hung over the competition for Saint-Aubin de Rambouillet and Saint-Anne-d'Auray some years earlier. Sitting on the jury panel were the architects Duc, Guillaume, Labrouste, and Albert Lenoir, in addition to two city representatives (Alphand, Haussmann's former associate, as well as Ballu, from the city's architecture division), two politicians (de Cardaillac, director of civic buildings, and Chesnelong, a deputy), and, of course, the members of the Oeuvre de Voeu national. The results of the competition would demonstrate the rationalists' dominance. After Abadie, the first named, of course, were protégés of the Paris administration Davioud and Lameire (the architect of parks and gardens, and the painter-decorator—for the first time associates—who would become winners of the competition for the Palais du Trocadéro in the 1878 World's Fair), with Cazaux (inspector of public works in Paris) next. But prizes were given to the Douillard brothers, to Bernard and Tournade, Coisel, Moyaux, Roux, Raulin and Dillon, and Pascal, with honorable mention to Letz, Crépinet Leclerc, Magne *père et fils*, and Mayeux. Lastly, the jury offered distinction to de Baudot, Chipiez, Dabernat, the Douillard brothers (for their second plan), Gion, Métivier, Noguet, Phipps and Phene Spiers, Rouyer, Suisse, and Duclos. On this imposing list of names, the predominance of rationalists is obvious. The 1874 competition was an official sanction of this trend, in the face of the academic tradition it challenged.[8]

On the subject of the competition's circumstances, Julien Guadet's comments are harsh: "It goes without saying that after five minutes, in spite of the childish precaution of having the plans unsigned, everyone knew the designer of each plan. The success of Abadie's was prognosticated; it was actually chosen. One must speak frankly: it was a prudent choice; or rather, it was perhaps less a matter of choosing the plan than the man. He was then at the height of his powers, known for his beautiful works of religious architecture, tried and true." Abadie, in fact, had been for more than a quarter century a diocesan architect in southwestern France after beginning his career in 1845 as an inspector for the Notre Dame of Paris restoration under the direction of Jean-Baptiste Lassus and Viollet-le-Duc. An architect of historical monuments and restorer of the

Figure 11.5
Concours pour la souscription de l'église du Sacré-Coeur à Montmartre, plan by Magne, 1874.

Figure 11.6
Paul Abadie's plan for Sacré Coeur.

Figure 11.7
Sacré Coeur in Montmartre. Under construction, life drawing by the Count of Gourcy, 1880.

cathedral in Puy and one in Bordeaux and a large number of religious edifices in Angoumois, he was definitely not that uncultivated bungler caricatured by Louis Réau in a text that, to say the least, lacked restraint.[9] Architect of the city halls of Angoulême and Jarnac, the churches of Saint-Martial-Saint-Ausone in Angoulême, Notre Dame in Bergerac, and the Bastide in Bordeaux, he left a solid body of work in public architecture. The same year as the competition he succeeded Viollet-le-Duc, who was forced to resign from all his posts, as general inspector of diocesan edifices. In 1875, Abadie made a brilliant entry into the Académie des beaux-arts, after Charles Garnier but before Émile Vaudremer, although the latter was initially in a better position for election than Abadie. This official career, for the most part provincial, was marked by membership in the body of diocesan architects, who were rivals of the architects of civic buildings (winners of the Prix de Rome, which assured them the commissions from the public). The Montmartre competition, followed by entry into the Académie, was proof of the stunning triumph of the school of

Viollet-le-Duc, ten years after the failure of his lectures at the École des beaux-arts.[10]

Montmartre's construction, begun in 1876, was a major event: people quickly realized that the gypsum hill, eroded by the former plaster quarries (which they had tried to destroy at the end of the eighteenth century by blowing up the piers which supported them), was not fit for construction. Eighty-three masonry piers, each thirty-eight meters deep, had to be built to get a solid foundation. It is on these pilings, bonded by arches, that the foundations of the church rest. The work was long and costly. In 1900, the cupola was just being finished; from 1905 to 1910, the bell tower was completed, based on the designs of Lucien Magne, but the church was not consecrated until 1919.[11] The interior decor, done under Magne's direction, also dates to the beginning of the century: heavily criticized by art historians, it is nonetheless one of the most beautiful ensembles of religious art of the era, wonderfully rounding off Abadie's work.[12]

THE REFERENCE AND THE SCALE

From the start we have emphasized the qualities of Montmartre's *architecture de site*. Let us now, before going further, describe the overall plan in terms of its blueprint, and the qualities of its interior space. The play of volumes is conventional, packed with historical allusions, some of which are contradictory; there are even inadequacies or paradoxes in the conception of ornamentation and in the articulation of scales, which is deceptive. But all these elements contribute to the creation of an interior space whose evocative power is an outstanding example in French art, to which the furnishings and mural decoration greatly contribute. My hypothesis goes against current judgments, which is why it seems important to me to elaborate.

The basilica is not the traditional type with the long nave, but rather is based on a central plan, which a great many contemporaries have criticized. Its model is derived from a classical and, more precisely, French tradition, dating to the Renaissance. To the basic model of Saint Peter's in Rome, from which it is indisputably derived, it adds those of the Invalides' chapel of Saint Louis (where Napoleon is buried) and Sainte-Geneviève. With regard to the latter, it is like a reverse image: the same site of the church, the same ideological significance, same form, but with a somber, closed, cryptic interior space which is different. As for the Invalides, it harks back to the total domination of the central space by the transept and side chapels as well as the double tambour, the pendentives, and the elongated silhouette (inspired, of course, by Michelangelo's dome for Saint

Peter's, but silhouetted *à la française* in the manner of Hardouin-Mansart). These antecedents, which all arose out of royal architecture, had been, for the generation of the Second Empire, revived by Louis-Auguste Boileau, whose "synthetic cathedral" fascinated Anatole de Baudot as much as it did Paul Abadie.

Finally, it is appropriate to add to this collage of cultural references the Romano-Byzantine models of the time: Saint Mark in Venice and Saint-Front in Périgueux (which Abadie had restored), the domed churches of Aquitaine, and the choir of Germigny-des-Prés. French archaeological discoveries in the nineteenth century prevailed over the great Byzantine examples. Saint Sophia in Istanbul faded into the background, while discoveries in Syria (and, notably, the type of church found in Fusafah, which had just been unveiled in Melchior de Vogüé's big publication, *Syrie centrale: Archéologie civile et religieuse*, which appeared in two volumes in 1865 and later in 1877) exercised an influence. It is important, nevertheless, to emphasize that the plan, contrary to its neo-Roman stylistic appearance, remained deeply rooted in the classical tradition.

This is completely different from the form, marked by an excessive unity, the absence of articulation with the context, and the lack of scale, traits which strongly differ from the classical tradition (and owe much to the Gothic style of the Île-de-France, even if purely stylistic references are more or less nonexistent in the art of the thirteenth century). The excessive unity initially sets up a contrast between the relative scale of the big dome to the small domes: the former is double in size, a feature which Abadie borrows from Bramante's plan for Saint Peter's in Rome. Generally speaking, all the proportions are calculated to the ratio of 1:2, which gives the domes a silhouette set in a double square (about 21 by 42 meters for the main dome, 11.5 by 21 for the minor domes; the summit of the latter are over 42 meters high, to the starting point of the main dome, which culminates at 84 meters). This double proportion sharply contrasts with the classical rule of the golden ratio; it gives a nearly unruly vertical vigor to the silhouette. To this system other features of medieval origin are added, like the small side chapels which repeat the form on a different scale. The principle of repetition is applied with such rigor that the effect is dulled. Finally, the rigorous triangulation of volumes on the rigid outline of the plan suggests a form without variety. The concern for unity is such that even a dialogue between materials is forbidden. The edifice has neither framework nor roofing; the same stone serves for the walls' masonry, vaults, and roofs like some gigantic monolith (deliberately destroying the effect, even though heavy, of a simulated assemblage of imbrication covering the domes). Nowhere does one encounter lead revetment, still less tile or slate. Likewise, nowhere does one find bitonality, capable of delimiting design elements or levels. This edifice is just a block: one form, one material, one proportion.

For this reason, it is totally "other" in its immediate surroundings, like the Gothic cathedrals, whose enormous mass dwarfed their environment. There is no preparation for the cathedral in the approach: neither perspectives (except the almost absurd view of the carpet of green that stripes Montmartre to the south—even though the steep incline renders any effect of perspective impossible), nor framing, nor courtyard or forecourt, nor gates, nor columns, nor furniture, nor balustrade. It is a mess, placed there without concession to its surroundings. It dwarfs everything when viewed from behind. It is just as imposing when one ascends to its base via the rue du Chevalier-de-la-Barre, alongside the place du Tertre. Its very size insults the charming parish church Saint-Pierre de Montmartre on the other side of the street.

The sole elements of scale that are slightly smaller are the choir and the porch, underscoring the function of this stone mastodon. But it is noteworthy that, even on the level of ornamentation, this starkness of size is maintained. The façades are schematic, not very geometric, with very few moldings (*modénatures*), as if someone had feared to spend too much on sculpture. The middle range of perception is totally absent, which ensures that the approach to the edifice does not modify its impact, which reinforces the impression of the gigantic size of this object. Without any

Figure 11.8
The colossal statue
of Christ.

Figure 11.9
Religious procession during construction, after Jean Béraud, 1887.

preparation one suddenly goes from a colossal scale (from a distance) to the immediate, nearly tactile scale of the interior decoration. There, all of a sudden, the molding is born, the decor becomes abundant with quite beautiful details, like Magne's ornaments for the bronze doors, executed by Pierre Séguin. The artists of the nineteenth century had long studied medieval Italian art.

Here, Abadie proved to be far more modern than Charles Garnier. In fact, the Opéra's proportions are regular, the articulation of decors and treatment of the vicinity reinforce and clarify, in the purest of classical traditions. Abadie is seeking neither to direct the gaze nor to soften transitions but rather, through the sharp clash of elements, to startle, which is the essence of his architectural message. His art lies not in balance, but in *flash*: intense, unified, instantaneous—striking, in a word.

HIDDEN BEAUTIES

Montmartre's interior space pushes the dramatic intensity of contrast to its limits. To truly understand it, one must contrast it with Saint Sophia in

Figure 11.10
Inauguration du Sacré-Coeur. Monseigneur Rotelli gives the solemn blessing from the upper porch of the church, 1891.

Constantinople. Here, the central space is dominated by the cupola, which enriches the two large *culs-de-four*★ at the entrance and the choir, which in turn are articulated in the small semicircular chapels in the apse. The smaller vaulted spaces form a background which seems to push back the surrounding wall, using it to enhance the infinite perspective created by the rows of columns. The main source of lighting confirms the domination of the central volume, powerfully illuminated by the bays of the two large arches of the transept and by the many superimposed windows in the choir. On the walls this light is reflected onto the brilliant surfaces of the gold mosaic. The background is much darker, breaking up the shadows of the columns and vaults on distant luminous depths. Finally, the cupola is a gigantic crown of light with forty windows which allow calibrated shafts of light to penetrate, like powerful spotlights, the hazy half-light of interiors filled with the smoke of incense and candles. With each hour, the shafts of light shift from one wall to another, making the floor into a sort of gigantic sundial. Directional light, diffuse light, and contrasting lights come together to make this immense volume an ethereal play of forms, an architecture of intangible walls and changing effects, amid the soothing contemplation of one's thoughts.

It is completely different in Montmartre. This church is the largest and darkest Parisian monument (the opposite of Sainte-Geneviève, en-

---

★ This is a vault, supporting the dome, which is formed by a half-dome.—Ed.

tirely devoted to the rediscovery of Gothic transparence, which Soufflot made his ideal). Crossing a deep narthex preceded by tambour doors, one suddenly finds oneself in the colossal space of a transept with a vault fifty-five meters high; there are no prepared backgrounds, but rather empty walls which surround you on all sides, behind the four enormous piers of the dome. At the level of the vaults, some circular windows let in a rare, dazzling, raw light, while lighting also comes from the top of the cupola, reflected onto bare walls, free of any decoration. The disproportionate height lends a feeling of cramped space, lacking in magnitude, and, it must be confessed, without charm.

But the layout hides a surprise. Behind the transept is placed a deep choir, the length of which equals that of the transept. Below an enormous *cul-de-four*, richly decorated narrow arcading surrounds the main altar. No direct light penetrates there; after the services, the effect is lugubrious. Yet it is here that the most precious decorative details have been brought together—the marquetry stalls, the marble lecterns, a gilded ciborium—as well as the richest decorations. Everything is set off by colored-glass mosaics, while the vault is covered in an immense composition (475 meters square) executed for Henri-Marcel Magne after designs by Luc-Olivier Merson. In the same manner, in the choir, there is a beautiful mosaic by Magne that covers the cupola (lacking any lighting) of the chapel of the Virgin.

Was this an absurd choice? In fact, it is comprehensible only during ceremonies, when the light from altar candles all of a sudden illuminates the depths of the vault in a riot of colors and lights, in the sumptuous reflection of whites and golds. At the time of the service, the cryptic half-light of the choir is awakened, revealing the rich barrier that separates the

Figure 11.11
The choir mosaic commemorating the vote on the law of July 29, 1873, declaring the construction of the Sacré Coeur to be of public utility, as atonement for the crimes of the Paris Commune in 1871, detail.

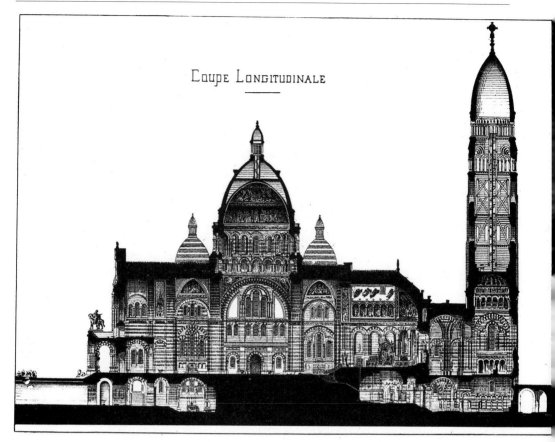

COUPE LONGITUDINALE

Figure 11.12
Cross-section of the Sacré Coeur.

liturgical choir from the nave. There, the two half-churches come together at this mystical frontier, where the altar for communion is placed. The contrast between spaces can now be better explained. This bare nave, dark and out of proportion, is the representation of the suffering church, in the darkness of sin and the misfortunes of the century; but the celebration of the Eucharist suddenly exalts the believer beyond the limits of his human condition and enables him to receive communion with the mystic happiness which awaits him in heavenly Jerusalem. This rather Manichean conception of the *religion of sin* was admirably expressed in Montmartre and given its complete architectural value, even if the religious vision of the nineteenth century is no longer ours.

It is not clear whether one should credit Abadie with the entire dramatic effect of this interior. Although the general idea was his, Julien Guadet—and after him, Hautecoeur—asserted that he had not wanted this decorative abundance. We owe the choir's mosaic decorations, desired by the clergy, to Lucien Magne, who designed the bell tower and was responsible for the interior fittings. It seems as though Magne perfectly understood the duality of Abadie's plan and that he synthesized it extremely forcefully in the choir's great mosaic—an exceptionally interesting work:

> One has the impression, when entering this sanctuary, that one is guided by the hierarchical succession of mosaic decorations: simple at the entrance, then everywhere in the choir furnishings, ending in a *hieratic flight* (if we are permitted this paradox) on the *cul-de-four* of the choir . . . drawing the eye toward the central point of convergence: a monumental Christ. . . . In his arms, he protects personages and public, with an attitude at once serene and stiff. One sees only him and the drapery of his white garment, which stands out against a deep blue sky, as do all the other elements of the decoration through which it passes, piercing them here and there with its colored intensity.[13]

The choir mosaic in Montmartre is the resolution of many formal conflicts that have marked the duality of the plan which divorces architecture from its environment. It at long last brings that comfort which is the ultimate goal of a dense and difficult architectural path. It sums up the edifice, it is the key to it, in an area where so many contradictory feelings and clashing views have been expressed until now. It conclusively proves that Montmartre is neither a political statement nor a backward-looking monument, but an intense moment—and how misunderstood—of architectural emotion.

NOTES

1. On this point, refer to a remarkable doctoral dissertation in the history of religions by the Abbé Jacques Benoist, *Le Sacré-Coeur de Montmartre: Spiritualité, art et politique (1870–1923); Contestation (1870–1990)* (Paris: Université de Paris-Sorbonne, 1991) (published by Éditions Ouvrières in 1992). Jacques Benoist was not satisfied with a mere history of the monument or its designers. He sought to situate the construction of the basilica in perspectives as much historical as theological to express its significance and analyze the debates of which this highly contested construction was the object for nearly a century.

2. Julien Guadet, "L'Église du Sacré-Coeur," in *La Revue de l'art ancien et moderne* (Paris, 1900): 103–20. Since the writing of this article, two important works have appeared à propos of Montmartre: Claude Laroche's exhibition devoted to *Paul Abadie architecte, 1812–1884*, and Abbé Jacques Benoist's dissertation.

3. Hélène Guéné and François Loyer, *L'Église, l'état et les architectes: Rennes 1870–1940* (Paris: Éditions Norma/Institut français d'architecture, 1995).

4. Bruno Foucart, "La 'cathédrale synthétique' de Louis Auguste Boileau," *Revue de l'art* 3 (1969): 49–66.

5. Joris-Karl Huysmans, *La Cathédrale* (Paris, 1898) (pp. 16–21 in the Livre de poche edition (Paris, 1964).

6. See hereinafter the text of René Rémond, "La Fille aînée de l'église," which relates, better than we can, the political significance of the devotion to the Sacred Heart in nineteenth-century France.

7. The plans are at present missing, having either been returned to the participants, destroyed by arson, which ravaged the basilica's archives several years ago, or, finally, having been filed elsewhere. As the edifice did not resort to state funds, no public archives exist; on the other hand, it is possible that some of the documentation got lost in the Archbishopric of Paris.

8. The announcement for the competition was made in the *Revue générale de l'architecture et des travaux publics* (Paris, 1874), cols. 47–48, and the results of it were commented on by L. Cernesson: "Concours pour la construction d'une église du Sacré-Coeur à Montmartre," cols. 181–85. See also *Le Moniteur des architectes* (1874), col. 38; and *La Gazette des architectes* (1874), 115. For the artists cited, see L.-Th. David de Penanrun, L. Roux, and E. Delaire, *Les Architectes élèves de l'École des beaux-arts* (Paris: Chaix, 1895).

9. For Paul Abadie, cf. E. Guillaume, "Discours prononcé par M. Guillaume, membre de l'Institut, sur la tombe de Paul Abadie," in *Encyclopédie d'architecture* (1884): 65–66. The biography of this high-caliber artist has still to be written. Louis Réau's violent polemic was published in *Les Monuments détruits de l'art français* (Paris: Hachette, 1959), 2:172–74: Abadie is described in it as being evil.

10. I speak here, obviously, of the famous lectures of 1863 at the École des beaux-arts. Unable to deliver them because of a hostile audience, Viollet-le-Duc published them under the title of *Entretiens sur l'architecture* (Paris: A. Morel, 1863–72).

11. The history of Montmartre was published by Paul Lesourd, *La Butte sacrée: Montmartre des origines au XXe siècle* (Paris: Spes, 1937), which is still the standard reference work. More recently, two catalogues were devoted to the exhibition Paul Abadie: Architecte, 1812–1884, curated by Claude Laroche: one by the Musée d'Angoulême, in 1984, the other by the Musée des Monuments français (published by the Réunion des Musées nationaux) in Paris in 1988. The revival of studies of Montmartre was also evidenced by the publication of David Harvey's *The Urban Experience* (Oxford: Blackwell, 1989), which devoted an entire chapter to Montmartre, "monument and myth."

12. Louis Hautecoeur, *Histoire de l'architecture classique en France*, vol. 7, *La Fin de l'architecture classique* (Paris: A. et J. Picard, 1957), 211–17.

13. Hélène Guéné, *Odorico: Mosaiste Art Déco* (Brussels: Archives de l'architecture moderne, 1991), 44, 46. In her dissertation in art history on an atelier of Italian mosaicists in Brittany, Hélène Guéné recounted the history of the revival of a technique neglected for more than three centuries before undergoing a spectacular development toward the end of the nineteenth century. This study owes much to the highly personal attention she gave to Montmartre and its decor.

CHAPTER 12

THE COLLÈGE DE FRANCE

CHRISTOPHE CHARLE

Ampère, Langevin, Berthelot, Cuvier, Laënnec, Claude Bernard, and Frédéric Joliot in the sciences; Bergson, Michelet, Marcel Mauss, Renan, Burnouf, Champollion, Edgar Quinet, Lucien Febvre in the humanities and social sciences. These are the names of nineteenth- and twentieth-century scholars whose fame went beyond the confines of their specialties. They constitute a list of laureates of past and present culture. Their common link is they were all professors at the Collège de France, across the rue Saint-Jacques.[*]

It is not simply the number of creative minds housed within the Collège de France that allows for its characterization as a *lieu de mémoire*. Not all the professors at the Collège have invented a science or inaugurated a new way to understand physics, chemistry, the natural sciences, medicine, philosophy, history, languages, ethnology, or literature. However, election to the Collège is the ultimate reward for the members of all universities, all pantheons, all bodies. Its history and functions dictate that the Collège de France participate in these various institutions, yet it cannot be reduced to any of these. Like the Sorbonne, it is committed to education founded on principles which were in opposition to those of the medieval Université. In breaking away from the corporatism of the clerics and the cult of tradition, the founders committed themselves to cultural change and in-

---

[*] The Sorbonne is located on one side of the rue Saint-Jacques in the Latin Quarter of Paris and the Collège de France is across the street.—Ed.

ternal diversity. The price: a certain dependence on institutional power. The seventeenth-century *académies* were established in order to control culture and to enlist writers and intellectuals to the service of royal glory. However, the link forged between the Collège and these institutions did not oblige the former to submit to glorify the sovereign ruler. Even during periods of decline the Collège de France never became a necropolis of knowledge.

In the words of Ernest Renan, one of the Collège's most famous professors, its success lies in "science being created." For this reason the Collège is the best example of one particular aspect of French power: cultural patronage. At several historical moments the king and later the state wanted to create a space of intellectual liberty, including freedom from the authority of the state. As a *lieu de mémoire*, the Collège de France is the first stone in the construction of an intellectual antiestablishment, a place where the scholar and the politician were able to begin their long chess match: the debate concerning French cultural history.

A free space was created thus by the central power. This was a site of innovation based on four centuries of tradition which provides a shelter for erudites cut off from the world and a haven for prophets who attract the masses. It also offers higher education without official students and almost without professors in the classic sense: all of these possible designations account for the fascination, touched by scandal, which this intellectual *lieu de mémoire* evokes. It is difficult to reconstruct and explain the genesis of these representations, which, like the historic past of France, are illustrated by a series of heroes or dramatic episodes, golden legends which obscure the true sources of the evolution of this institution.

I. THE HISTORY OF A REPRESENTATION

An Uninterrupted Creation

In the beginning, Guillaume Budé was able to secure a "dowry" in the name of philology and mathematics from the good king François I, who was clearly influenced by humanism. This money was in the form of six positions for royal readers.[1] In 1551 Henri II expanded the field of education to encompass philosophy by giving a chair to Ramus, which accentuated the opposition between the college of royal readers and the old Sorbonne. The new field was encroaching upon the domain of the Université and challenged its monopoly on education. This was compounded by the fact that Ramus was known for his attacks on Aristotle, so revered by the academics of the Sorbonne. The biography of Ramus exemplifies some of the paradoxes cited above. Owing to his sympathies with the

Reformation he attracted a huge audience to his first lecture (around two thousand people), but he was not satisfied with this success, since his philosophy classes were an opportunity to study all the scholarly disciplines. He even established a new chair of mathematics on his own, the first in a long series of these positions, which, unlike royal chairs, were awarded through competitive examinations. Forced out due to his heterodox beliefs, Ramus became the Collège's first martyr after his death following the massacre of Saint Bartholomew's Eve.[2]

Thus, from the outset, all the themes which characterize the Collège de France are in place: the princely or private patronage, the marginalization from official culture, and the freedom which always runs the risk of repression. There is also the innovation which is alternately encouraged by the institutional power or restrained at the mercy of political whims, encyclopedism allied with specialization which shatters the conventional scholarly divisions, and a call to individuals who defy or challenge traditional models. For example, among the first professors there were four Italians, one scholar each from Luxembourg and Flanders, and one man who had converted from Judaism.[3]

But if the principal elements which constitute the Collège de France's image were present as early as the sixteenth century, they were missing in the following years. Since the Collège was the prince's creation and thus suspect at the Sorbonne, it met with a backlash in the wake of the weakening royal power during the second half of the century. This reaction can also be attributed to the royal family's adoption of the new Catholic orthodoxy; as announced by the Council of Trent, this religious conservatism discouraged cultural innovation born of the humanism which was ascribed to the emergence of modern science during the seventeenth century. During this time royal patronage proceeded through other channels, primarily through the *académies* and other paid positions. The ways in which the Collège recruited professors, in the words of Abel Lefranc, its most sympathetic historian, tended toward the doubtful methods used by the old Université; the exploitation of substitutes, the corruption of the professors, and episodic teaching. In his inaugural lecture, Gabriel Monod refers to the miserably paid professors of the second half of the eighteenth century who "for lack of salary, did their best to discourage students in order to have some spare time."[4] With 800 to 900 *livres* per year, their salaries paled next to that of university professors who earned between 1500 and 1800 *livres*, allocated regularly thanks to the moneyed courts of the Université. The royal readers themselves fell victim to the risks of the always fragile prosperity of royal finances. As for the buildings, their story alone summarizes the shifting fortunes of François I's institution. The first stone was placed by the young Louis XIII and the final one was set during the reign of Louis XV after many incidents and conflicts with the Université, which owned part of the land. This antiinstitution was for many years a "noninstitution." Even more serious, it was in competition with establishments like the Jardin des Plantes.★ The members even devised a plan to relinquish the scientific chairs at the Collège de France to the Jardin des Plantes in the same way that twenty years earlier they had attempted to resolve the Collège's financial and space problems by partially consolidating with the Université.[5]

However, despite the internal and external menaces, this minimal institution succeeded in maintaining its autonomy and originality while the old Université's buildings and assets were destroyed in the chaos of the Revolution. Furthermore, the Collège de France was turned from an antiinstitution into a model institution by revolutionaries charged with creating a new system of secondary and higher education. While all French institutions felt the splintering of the 1790s, the Collège de France—along with the Jardin des Plantes, which at the very least changed its name to the Muséum d'histoire naturelle—was the only place where the events of these years did not change a thing.[6] This paradox can be explained once more by the skill with which the professors were able to develop and emphasize the secular image of their establishment, enriching and adapting it as different threats arose. The original pact between the rulers and the "men of letters" seems to have been reenacted. In the following excerpt from a 1770 essay, 241 years after Guillaume Budé, the professors denounce the abuses of which they were the victims and evoke the reasoning behind the "marriage proposal" presented in the name of philology by the humanist to the king of France: "The royal Collège still attracts the attention of all of learned Europe, and the man who has the noble ambition to restore the Collège will be assured that his name will go down in history."[7] This text repeats almost verbatim the wording in Louis XV's judgment given at the Conseil d'État the previous year and takes the royal protector at his word by demonstrating the concept which both parties had accepted.

> The King has accounted for the goals to which his Royal Collège was established and the present state of the chairs which were founded therein and His Majesty has recognized that by desiring to cultivate the emulation and love of letters in the hearts of his subjects, King François I established, under the name of the Royal Collège of France, a society of men of letters who he attached to his own service under the name of ordinary readers and who he intended would at the same time be devoted to public education in the position of

★ The Jardin des Plantes focused on natural history and the earth sciences.—Ed.

professor; that the principal goal of the founder was to find support in the aforesaid Royal Collège within all branches of human knowledge which are not taught or are taught imperfectly in the Université; that the two chairs of Hebrew established in the aforesaid Royal Collège are little frequented today; that one chair would suffice for this language and that it would be appropriate to apply the funds from the other chair to an object of public use; being that History is one of the most useful branches of human knowledge for all orders of citizens, it would be desirable that this profession not be completely ceded to some hirelings, and that in changing one of the aforementioned two chairs of Hebrew, that this would be in conformity with François I's original desire.[8]

This long citation shows the degree to which the social image of the Collège de France was established as early as the 1770s, not just by the professors defending their institution, but by the rulers charged with protecting it. Above all, in transforming two traditional chairs into two new chairs which are linked to the intellectual evolution, this proclamation institutes the mechanism of the Collège's auto-adaptation which accounts for the continual ascent of its prestige during the subsequent century. Between 1768 and 1781, no fewer than eleven chairs were created or changed titles. All of these modifications obeyed the new cultural configuration of the Enlightenment: penetrated by the sciences (physics, chemistry, astronomy), the ascension of literary disciplines (history, French literature, Oriental languages, natural law), and the retreat of humanist philology and subjects which are related to the clerical tradition (Hebrew, canon law). This reform, which predates the Revolution, explains the Collège de France's aversion to revolution and can be inscribed within the larger conditions of reform during the late eighteenth century; the founding of the technical schools (Ponts et Chaussées, Mines, etc.),★ and the school reforms following the expulsion of the Jesuits are other examples from the same period.[9] But the most important development was the success of this gentle evolution, where—the technical schools aside—the other creative impulses of the enlightened monarchy in decline were lost in the shuffle or in collision with corporate interests. This final period of the ancien régime enriched the image of the Collège de France. The Collège became an emblem of a possible enlightened despotism: what could have existed if only the thinkers and rulers had taken an interest in the intellectual domain. The history of French culture offers many examples of this concern,

★ The Écoles des mines is a school for mining engineers while the École des ponts et chaussées trains civil engineers.—Ed.

LE COLLÈGE ROYAL

DE FRANCE,

Après les Vacances de Pâques, reprendra ſes Exercices, le Lundi 2 Mai M. DCC. XCI.

JÉROME DE LA LANDE, Inſpecteur, veillera ſur l'exécution des Regles du Collége Royal.

LANGUES HÉBRAIQUE ET SYRIAQUE.

* * * * * * * *

LANGUE ARABE.

JEAN-JACQUES-ANTOINE CAUSSIN DE PERCEVAL, après avoir donné *les élémens de la Langue Arabe*, expliquera l'*Alcoran de Mahomet*, Lundi, Mercredi & Vendredi, à trois heures & demie.

LANGUES PERSANE ET TURQUE.

PIERRE-JEAN-MARIE RUFFIN, Chevalier de l'Ordre du Roi, Secrétaire du Roi, Interprete du Roi pour les Langues Orientales, ou en ſon abſence MICHEL VENTURD DE PARADIS, après avoir donné *les élémens de ces deux Langues*, expliquera l'*Histoire Turque de Timourlenk ou Tamerlan*, Lundi, Mardi & Mercredi, à onze heures.

LITTÉRATURE GRECQUE.

EDOUARD-FRANÇOIS-MARIE BOSQUILLON, Docteur-Régent de la Faculté de Médecine de Paris, ancien Profeſſeur de Chirurgie & de Botanique, de la Société de Médecine d'Edimbourg, expliquera *les Prognoſtics & les Aphoriſmes d'Hyppocrate*, Mardi, Jeudi & Samedi, à midi & demi.

JEAN-BAPTISTE GAIL, Aggrégé en l'Univerſité de Paris, de l'Académie d'Arras, expliquera l'*Electre de Sophocle*, Lundi, Mardi & Vendredi, à deux heures.

ÉLOQUENCE LATINE.

CHARLES-FRANÇOIS DUPUIS, de l'Académie Royale des Inſcriptions & Belles-Lettres, expliquera l'*Oraiſon de Cicéron contre Verrès, ſur les ſupplices*, Lundi, Mardi & Vendredi, à onze heures.

POESIE LATINE.

JACQUES DE LILLE, l'un des Quarante de l'Académie Françoiſe, & en ſon abſence, NICOLAS-JOSEPH SELIS, Profeſſeur de Rhétorique, des Académies de Berlin, de Lyon, d'Amiens, de la Rochelle, d'Orléans, de Rouen, explique,a *les Epitres d'Horace & le ſecond Livre de l'Eneïde*, Mercredi, Jeudi & Samedi, à onze heures.

LITTÉRATURE FRANÇAISE.

ANTOINE DE COURNAND, traitera de l'*Art Dramatique en France*, & donnera l'analyse des principaux chefs-d'œuvre en ce genre, Mardi, Jeudi & Samedi à dix heures.

MATHÉMATIQUES.

ANTOINE-REMI MAUDUIT, Profeſſeur de Mathématiques à l'Académie Royale d'Architecture, de l'Académie Electorale de Manheim, de l'Académie des Sciences & Arts de Metz, expliquera *les Elémens des Courbes*, Mardi, Jeudi & Samedi, à trois heures & demie.

ASTRONOMIE.

JÉROME DE LA LANDE, de l'Académie Royale des Sciences de Paris, de l'Académie Royale de Marine, de la Société Royale de Londres, de l'Académie Impériale de Pétersbourg, des Académies de Berlin, de Stockholm, d'Upſal, Bologne, Florence, Cortone, Mantoue, Rome, Naples, Padoue, Gottingen, Harlem, Roterdam, &c. Inſpecteur du Collége Royal, Directeur de l'Obſervatoire de l'Ecole Royale Militaire, continuera d'expliquer l'*Aſtronomie en général*, Mardi, Jeudi & Vendredi, à quatre heures.

PHYSIQUE GÉNÉRALE ET MATHÉMATIQUES.

JACQUES-ANTOINE JOSEPH COUSIN, de l'Académie Royale des Sciences, expliquera *la Théorie des Plantes* par le moyen de l'analyſe, Lundi, Mardi & Vendredi, à neuf heures.

PHYSIQUE EXPERIMENTALE.

LOUIS LE FEVRE DE GINEAU, traitera *de la Lumiere & des Fluides üëriformes*; Mardi, Jeudi & Samedi, à midi.

MEDECINE.

JOSEPH RAULIN, Docteur de la Faculté de Médecine de Montpellier, Médecin des Hôpitaux Royaux, Conſeiller & Médecin ordinaire du Roi, traitera *de la Rougeole, de la Petite-Vérole, & des différentes Méthodes d'Inoculation*, Lundi, Mercredi & Vendredi, à onze heures.

ANATOMIE.

ANTOINE PORTAL, Docteur de la Faculté de Montpellier, Conſeiller-Médecin de Monsieur, Frere du Roi, Profeſſeur-Adjoint d'Anatomie & de Chirurgie au Jardin des Plantes; de l'Académie Royale des Sciences, de l'Inſtitut de Bologne, des Académies de Turin, d'Edimbourg, de Harlem, de Padoue & de Montpellier, traitera *des Cauſes des Maladies & de leurs Siéges*, Lundi, Mardi, Jeudi, à cinq heures.

CHYMIE.

JEAN D'ARCET, Docteur Regent de la Faculté de Médecine de Paris, de l'Académie Royale des Sciences, de celle de Madrid, & de l'Académie Baſquaiſe, continuera *ces leçons de Chymie ſur le Règne Minéral*, Mardi, Jeudi & Samedi, à onze heures.

HISTOIRE NATURELLE.

LOUIS-JEAN-MARIE DAUBENTON, Garde & Démonſtrateur du Cabinet du Roi, de l'Académie Royale de Sciences, de la Société Royale de Médecine, des Académies de Londres, de Berlin, de Pétersbourg, de Dijon & de Nancy, & de l'Académie Baſquaiſe, traitera *du Règne Minéral*, Mardi, Jeudi & Samedi, à dix heures.

DROIT DE LA NATURE ET DES GENS.

MATTHIEU-ANTOINE BOUCHAUD, Conſeiller d'Etat, de l'Académie Royale des Inſcriptions & Belles-Lettres, Membre honoraire de l'Académie de Dijon & d'Arras, Profeſſeur de la Faculté de Droit, continuera d'expliquer *les différens devoirs de l'Homme & du Citoyen*, Lundi, Mardi & Samedi, à neuf heures & demie.

HISTOIRE ET PHILOSOPHIE MORALE.

PIERRE-CHARLES LEVESQUE, de l'Académie Royale des Inſcriptions & Belles-Lettres, traitera *de la Morale*, Lundi, Mercredi & Samedi, à quatreheures.

CHAIRE DE MATHÉMATIQUES FONDÉE PAR RAMUS.

ANTOINE-REMI MAUDUIT, Profeſſeur de Mathématiques à l'Académie Royale d'Architecture, de l'Académie Electorale de Manheim, de l'Académie des Sciences & Arts de Metz, expliquera les *Séries qui appartiennent au cercle*, Mardi, Jeudi & Samedi, à quatre heures & demie.

PHILIPPE-DENYS PIERRES, Premier Imprimeur du Roi, du Collége Royal de France, &c. 1791.

Figure 12.1

Flyer for the courses at the Collège de France.

from Napoleon's Egypt expedition to the creation of the Centre national de la recherche scientifique and Victor Duruy's École pratique des hautes études. During the nineteenth and twentieth centuries most of the promoters of the new disciplines excluded from the traditional university setting tried to use this gap in the French higher educational system by forging an alliance with their already established colleagues or even directly with the dominant powers.

Between the Rulers and the Sorbonne Nouvelle

The Collège de France thus continued to meet expectations at this time. The novel elements introduced during the nineteenth century were still united with the permanent fight for autonomy which set intellectual power against pure power. Higher education in general and the Collège de France in particular were among the principal stakes of this struggle. The historical stage is a matter of course for us because, like the founding period itself, there is a legendary quality about it. Under each regime the Collège had its martyrs, voluntary or not, prudent or provocative, courageous or ready to disavow everything. Tissot and Lefèvre-Gineau were too liberal during the 1823 Restoration; Mickiewicz, Quinet, and Michelet were too revolutionary and too anticlerical during the July Monarchy; Tissot, Michel Chevalier, Xavier des Portets, Alix Desgranges, and Lerminier were conditionally victimized after the establishment of the École d'administration by the provisional government of 1848; once again Mickiewicz, Quinet, Michelet, and Barthélemy-Saint-Hilaire were rebels with respect to Louis Napoleon's empire. Finally, after being sacrificed to clerical pressure during the liberal empire, Renan completed this list and inaugurated a new era. During the course of the Republic, Vichy aside, spiritual power invariably conquered temporal power, as exemplified by one of the first acts of the Government of National Defense in 1870: the restoration of his chair to Renan, the author of the *Vie de Jésus*.[10]

The time of prophets was followed by the period of mentors, from the confident and dominant power of the monarchies and the empire to the protective power of Gambetta's Athenian Republic. But if the Collège de France's small classrooms were simply one of the many nineteenth-century battle sites of liberty, limiting ourselves to this simplistic vision would effectively reduce the memory of the Collège de France to a poem from *La Légende des siècles** or to several chapters from Michelet's *History of France*. These episodes are indicative of a climate resulting from the sym-

---

* An epic collection of poems by Victor Hugo (1859, 1877, 1883).—Ed.

bolic resonance of arbitrary acts and the prestige of those who were thus victimized; for this reason they should be brought down to their proper size. A half dozen examples out of nearly two hundred professors between 1800 and 1900 is very little compared to the victims of purges in the other sectors of civil service, even under the Republic, for, like judges, they were under the supposed protection of theoretical tenure. The majority of professors remained outside the political arena or conformed to it, and their solidarity did not go beyond declarations of principle.[11] It was simple enough to find candidates to replace suspended or censured professors. Compared to the relationship between the Sorbonne and the rulers, that of the Collège de France was not particularly original.[12] Like Cousin, Villemain, and Guizot, the trio of July Monarchy martyrs from the Faculty of Letters at the Sorbonne, there was the trio of Collège professors suspended during the Restoration; the refusal of Barthélemy-Saint-Hilaire's oath is similar to that of Jules Simon, professor at the Faculty of Letters; corresponding to the liberal uproar in Saint-Beuve's classes at the Collège de France there were the attempts to sabotage Nisard's at the Sorbonne; the marginalization of Renan during the empire repeats that of Cousin after the 1851 coup d'état of Louis Napoleon.

All of these analogies concerning the same disciplines (philosophy, religion, history) prove that on the level of political fights, the literary Sorbonne and the Collège de France fulfilled the same function when confronted with threatening despotism. This memory has left more traces on the representation of the older of the two establishments undoubtedly because the heroes of these have remained on the same side of the barricade: that of the mind. However, this may be the very reason why Barthélemy-Saint-Hilaire has been forgotten. "The soul has triumphed," exclaimed Michelet upon his return to the Collège de France on March 6, 1848.[13] The heroes of the legendary Sorbonne politics, however, ultimately exercised some power, while the prophets of the Collège de France never left their chairs to take on governmental responsibilities, in part because this move implied the renouncing of ideals.

Nevertheless, political confrontation did not exhaust the interactions between the Collège de France, the institutional powers, and the traditional Université. On a purely intellectual level, the relative prestige of the two types of professorships and their autonomy with respect to external social demands went through contrasting phases; this progressive sedimentation helped to establish the final game of intentions between the two sides of the rue Saint-Jacques.

Until 1800 the division of labor was clear; the Collège de France mainly advanced the margins of classical studies dominant at the Sorbonne by devoting a series of chairs to rare languages: Hebrew, Arabic, Turkish,

Persian, Sanskrit, and Chinese. On the other hand, in the more traditional or scientific disciplines, the confusion between the two institutions was profound. The clearest proof is the relatively frequent accumulation of chairs by the same scholars, indeed the passage from one rostrum to the other in the course of one career. There were not yet many specialists nor even high-level classes in these disciplines; Boissonade taught Greek at the Collège de France and at the Faculty of Letters; Abbot Delille was presumably professor of Latin poetry at both institutions, as was Guéroult of Latin oratory, Guigniaut of ancient history, and Jouffroy of Greek and Latin philosophy. Within the sciences Claude Bernard, Balard, Binet, Biot, Libri, Liouville, Serret, and Thénard were named as professors at both institutions.

As for the relative prestige, the picture is no more precise. Except during the 1840s, superior individuals generally did not occupy the chairs at the Collège de France. In philosophy there were disciples but no masters, that is until the arrival of Bergson: Jouffroy and Barthélemy-Saint-Hilaire were there, but not Victor Cousin. Caro invited more people to the Sorbonne than did his contemporary, the unknown Charles Lévêque. The chair in French literature was no better off; the Collège recruited outmoded professors while at the Sorbonne it was the era of brilliant conversationalists: Villemain, Saint-Marc-Girardin, Saint-René Taillandier, and Faguet.[14] The Collège de France's brilliance was thus a result of its specialists—not one of the Sorbonne's strengths, except for those working in the exact sciences. Given the widespread resistance to the German style of erudition—the value of a professor was measured by the size of the audience attending his lectures—in the popular opinion of the period the Collège was viewed with ridicule or simply incomprehension. The 1860s were in this respect a pivotal moment symbolized by three names: Claude Bernard, Renan, and Berthelot. They were elected or named to the Collège de France by reason of their scientific titles and not, as in the case of certain of their colleagues, because of their social or political influence. Carried by the surge of interest in science and the combination of intellectual and moral reform following France's defeat in 1871, they were able to transcend the division of roles between, on the one side, intellectuals and scholars, and on the other, men of letters and thinkers. Impeccable on a purely scientific level, they developed a universal ideology based on the conclusions of their meticulous research. This message was even more powerful in that it attacked the dogmatic Catholic tradition and breathlessly filled the void with humanist culture.

This period, stretching from the 1860s to the 1880s, was one of the apogees in the history of the Collège de France, during which "it housed the leaders of the intellectual movement."[15] Meanwhile, the Sorbonne, obligated to its imitators and substitutes, was entombed in the routine of its twelve sacred chairs. However, as is often the case with intellectual history, this period set the scene for a reversal at the Sorbonne, or, more exactly, the Sorbonne Nouvelle, as it was called then. The new academic ideal which the most illustrious professors at the Collège de France embodied was slowly circulated throughout the higher education system. As George Weisz has shown, the reform of the traditional Université, initiated during the 1880s and 1890s, resulted in the Sorbonne Nouvelle of the Belle Époque; its champions and organizers formed the Société pour l'étude des questions d'enseignement supérieur, in which the best of the Collège de France and the young generation were assembled.[16] This association was primarily interested in increasing the number of chairs under the new model. Obtaining a chair involved a teaching focus and the implementation of an original research project which was designed to compete with the German system. The trendsetters of the Collège de France embodied this patriotic reasoning and they shared the same scientific ideology as the republican leaders; Berthelot embodied the two roles, given that he was deputy, senator, and then minister. Patriotic reasoning served to justify the new education system in the eyes of the public while furthering the interests and beliefs of the academic corporation. But the success of this attempt at renovation contributed to a reversal in the roles of the two sides of the rue Saint-Jacques. The Collège de France gradually lost its eminence through the deaths of many of its stars (Renan died in 1892, Claude Bernard in 1878) and through its members' departures into other academic or political activities (Berthelot became a permanent senator and secretary of the Academy of Sciences, etc.), while the Sorbonne, rejuvenated by the establishment of new chairs, acquired an academic body which was both innovative and attended by a large audience. In letters there were Fustel de Coulanges, Lavisse, Aulard, Ferdinand Brunot, Vidal de La Blache, Lanson, Durkheim, Seignobos, Boutroux, and Charles Andler; in the sciences Pasteur, Poincaré, Paul Appell, Émile Picard, Saint-Claire Deville, Pierre and Marie Curie were appointed. The new chairs at the Collège de France were geared toward increasingly more erudite specializations which served to distance the professors from the public. The establishment of the new positions also heeded social and political considerations which did not always dictate the choice of the best candidate. An example of the evolution of the first type is the transformation of the chair of Latin rhetoric into Latin philology in 1885, the creation of a chair of Celtic language and literature in 1882, and the replacement of the chair of history and morals, once held by Michelet, by a chair of French historical geography destined for Longnon.

There are many examples of the links between the Collège de France and diverse social or political concerns: the creation of a chair in history for the liberal pastor Albert Réville in 1880, another in 1892 in the history of science for the elderly Pierre Laffitte, the executor of Auguste Comte's will, and the 1897 chair of social philosophy accorded to the unknown scholar Izoulet at the expense of Durkheim. Izoulet was highly regarded in the political realm. These examples demonstrate the Collège de France's dependence on its protector, the republican state, which used the Collège to institutionalize anticlerical and antisocialist education. These cases were symptomatic of new, unfavorable circumstances for the Collège de France during this time of academic renewal. However, they should not eclipse the merit of the rest of the professors as a whole, especially in the sciences or rare languages. Nonetheless most of them were unknown to the public and did little to enhance the outward social image of their institution. Furthermore, thanks to academic reforms, the Sorbonne secured one further advantage over its rival; it supervised a steady audience of students who, contrary to the past, no longer attended classes as dilettantes; this was still the status, by definition, of the students at the Collège de France. While the professors at the Sorbonne aspired to combine novelty, prestige outside the university, and professional dignity, no professor at the Collège de France enjoyed these advantages until Bergson's election in 1900, or, even later, that of Gabriel Monod in 1905. Furthermore, the situation of these two scholars within the Collège was ambiguous; Bergson's subsequent fame should not obscure the fact that his admission into the Collège was quite complicated. Before his election to the chair of ancient philosophy he had lost that of modern philosophy to Gabriel de Tarde whose work was not even philosophical. Bergson's social success was in part due to a misunderstanding and a movement against positivism which dominated the Sorbonne. As for Gabriel Monod, one of the leaders of the academic reform and new history movement of the 1880s, his election to the Collège was ultimately facilitated through money provided by a private donor, the Marquise Arconati-Visconti. Although well within the tradition of the institution, his election was not thanks to a spontaneous effort on the part of the entire corps of professors.

The Collège de France and the Academic Hierarchy

Despite the short time during which Monod, the founder of the *Revue historique*, taught at the Collège de France, this episode can be seen as the symbol of its new position within the academic system of the twentieth century. Just like the Collège de France twenty years earlier, the Sorbonne

Figure 12.2
Michelet and Quinet
retaking possession
of their classes at the
Collège de France in
1848, by A. Brouilhet.

was a victim of its own success. The proliferation of chairs, the continual growth of the student population, the rise of pedagogic concerns to the detriment of research, all of these tendencies created by the reforms ran counter to the interests of the students. The scholars were monopolized more and more by scholarly tasks, and compared to that of their colleagues "across the street" their situation was deteriorating. The generation which benefited from the establishment of the new chairs at the Sorbonne toward the end of the nineteenth century lingered on, and length of service, a factor in intellectual fossilization, became one of the principal criteria within the established disciplines when there was a decision to be made between two candidates. On the other hand, liberated from this slavery, the Collège de France played the role of a haven, an enviable finale to

one's career despite the price of a smaller social court in one's youth. The 1926 nomination of Charles Andler, professor of Germanic studies at the Sorbonne for twenty-two years, just a few years before his retirement can be seen as a feature of the Collège de France's new, paradoxical role: the ultimate compensation for a distinguished career. The struggle between the teaching load and the difficulties in doing research at a university for the "masses" underlies Paul Hazard's remarks following his election to the Collège:

> We are encumbered by all kinds of burdens, the least of which is administering the *baccalauréat*. Can you believe that professors at the Sorbonne not only correct the examinations but also proctor them?

The Sorbonne had an enrollment of 4,100 students this year in letters; in July alone we awarded 2,000 *licences*★ and 7,000 *baccalau-
réats*. . . . When we are able to wearily steal some time for our own
work, we publish books which are condemned to oblivion with regard to the greater public. . . . My own work? Several months ago I
began to despair that I would never be able to complete it, crushed as
I was by academic burdens. But here a great event has occurred in my
life; the Collège de France is opening up its great doors to me and I
will joyously return to the work I was previously forced to abandon.[17]

The Collège de France's new function as ultimate compensation at
the end of various possible academic paths, less and less on a par with the
Sorbonne and more and more superior to it, had some important consequences, which only expanded as the university system grew larger throughout the twentieth century. While during the previous century a relative
equilibrium had existed between the chairs at the Sorbonne and those at
the Collège de France, the disparity grew during the years between the
two World Wars. The Faculty of Letters alone had more chairs than did
the Collège de France, which was composed of both literary and scientific
disciplines; the relative difficulty of securing a chair at the Collège was
growing. If we also consider the expanding number of possible candidates
from the professional schools and other academic institutions (Langues
orientales, École de pharmacie, École des chartes,† the École pratique des
hautes études, the schools of engineering, research laboratories, the Bibliothèque nationale, etc.), the competition for acceptance—the only possible
route of entry for many professors from peripheral institutions—became
even more fierce. The intensity was even greater, given that this less traditional course was becoming more tempting to academics. Finally, one
last element, absent from the Sorbonne, reinforced the Collège's preemi-
nent position (it can be said that earning a chair at the Collège de France
was as prestigious as being elected to the Institute of France,‡ or better yet
to the Académie française during the nineteenth century). This important element was the possibility of nominating individuals who were not
within academia but whose prestige, deriving from the intellectual field,
elevated the image of the Collège de France to that of the sixth academy

★ The *licence* is akin to a Master of Arts.—Ed.
† The École des chartes trains state archivists.—Ed.
‡ The Institute was composed of five academies: the Académie française, the Academy of
Sciences, the Academy of Fine Arts, the Académie of Moral and Political Sciences, and
the Academy for Inscriptions and Fine Letters.—Ed.

COLLÉGE ROYAL

DE FRANCE.

PREMIER SEMESTRE, 1847-1848.

MM. les Lecteurs et Professeurs Royaux ouvriront leurs Cours le Lundi 29 novembre 1847.

Astronomie.

M. BINET, membre de l'Institut, Académie Royale des Sciences, traitera de la Théorie des Orbites planétaires, les Mardis et Samedis, à trois heures et demie.

Mathématiques.

M. LIBRI, membre de l'Institut, Académie Royale des Sciences, et, en cas d'absence, M. AMIOT, agrégé de l'Université, traitera de la Géométrie analytique, et plus particulièrement de la Théorie des surfaces, les Lundis et Jeudis, à deux heures et demie.

Physique générale et mathématique.

M. BIOT, membre de l'Institut, Académie Royale des Sciences, et en son absence M. BERTRAND, docteur ès sciences, agrégé de l'Université, exposera comparativement les théories auxquelles les géomètres ont tenté à ramener les phénomènes de la capillarité, les Mardis et Samedis, à midi et demi.

Physique générale et expérimentale.

M. REGNAULT, membre de l'Institut, Académie Royale des Sciences, traitera de l'Optique météorologique et des phénomènes de la lumière polarisée, les Mercredis et Vendredis à midi et demi.

Chimie.

M. PELOUZE, membre de l'Institut, Académie Royale des Sciences, traitera de l'Analyse chimique, les Mardis et Samedis, à une heure moins un quart.

Médecine.

M. MAGENDIE, membre de l'Institut, Académie Royale des Sciences, et de l'Académie Royale de Médecine, et en son absence M. BERNARD, exposera les plus récentes découvertes sur la Physiologie et la Médecine, les Mercredis et Vendredis, à midi.

Histoire naturelle des corps inorganiques.

M. ÉLIE DE BEAUMONT, membre de l'Institut, [...] traitera des Climats terrestres aux différentes époques géologiques, les Mardis et Samedis, à [...]

Histoire naturelle des corps organisés.

M. DUVERNOY, membre de l'Institut, Académie Royale des Sciences, et correspondant de l'Académie Royale de Médecine, traitera de l'organisation des animaux en général, et plus particulièrement de ses rapports avec leurs instincts, les Mercredis et Vendredis, à une heure et demie.

Embryogénie comparée.

M. COSTE traitera du développement de l'espèce humaine, les Mardis et Samedis, à une heure.

Droit de la nature et des gens.

M. DE PORTETS traitera du Droit naturel, les Mardis et Samedis, à neuf heures.

Histoire des Législations comparées.

M. E. LERMINIER, et, en cas d'absence, M. RAPETTI, docteur en droit, exposera les Développements historiques de la coutume dans les législations modernes, les Mercredis et Samedis, à trois heures.

Économie politique.

M. MICHEL CHEVALIER traitera des Notions fondamentales de l'Économie politique, les Mercredis et Samedis, à midi.

Histoire et Morale.

M. MICHELET, membre de l'Institut, Académie Royale des Sciences morales et politiques, appliquera les Principes de la philosophie de l'histoire dans les deux années précédentes, à l'histoire des trois derniers siècles, les Lundis et Jeudis, à une heure.

Archéologie.

M. LETRONNE, membre de l'Institut, Académie Royale des Inscriptions et Belles-Lettres, est autorisé par M. le ministre à ne point faire son cours pendant le premier semestre de l'année scolaire 1847-1848.

Langues hébraïque, chaldaïque et syriaque.

M. QUATREMÈRE, membre de l'Institut, Académie Royale des Inscriptions et Belles-Lettres, expliquera le Pentateuque et les prophètes Isaïe et Jérémie, les Lundis et Mercredis, à une heure et demie.

Langue arabe.

M. CAUSSIN DE PERCEVAL expliquera le Coran, divers morceaux de la Circonstanche de M. de Sacy, et les Moallacat, les Mercredis et Vendredis, à huit heures et demie du matin.

Langue persane.

M. JULES MOHL, membre de l'Institut, Académie Royale des Inscriptions et Belles-Lettres, continuera l'explication du Schanh, épisode tiré de Ferdousi, les Mercredis et Vendredis, à dix heures et demie.

Langue turque.

M. ALIX DESGRANGES expliquera, 1° Abouli-Djenguiz ou aqeng Témur en turc oriental dialecte atheis-qepptchaq, s'le Chelfsre-Gueuz d'Aboul-Ghazi-Bahdan-Khan dialecte Djagataï, les Mercredis et Vendredis, à onze heures et demie.

Langue et Littérature chinoise et tartare-mandchou.

M. STANISLAS JULIEN, membre de l'Institut, Académie Royale des Inscriptions et Belles-Lettres, expliquera : 1° Le livre 90s de l'Encyclopédie littéraire de Matouantin, qui traite des ouvrages géographiques; 2° le texte tartare-mandchou du deuxième livre du philosophe Meng-tzeu, les Lundis et Jeudis, à cinq heures du soir.

Langue et Littérature sanskrite.

M. E. BURNOUF, membre de l'Institut, Académie Royale des Inscriptions et Belles-Lettres, expliquera le premier livre du Râmâyana, et le second livre de Manou, les Mercredis et Vendredis, à neuf heures et demie.

Langue et Littérature grecque.

M. BOISSONADE, membre de l'Institut, Académie Royale des Inscriptions et Belles-Lettres, professeur. Il sera suppléé par M. ROSSIGNOL, docteur ès lettres, qui expliquera le Philoctète de Sophocle, et le comparera avec les analyses et les fragments que l'antiquité nous a laissés du Philoctète d'Eschyle et de celui d'Euripide, les [...]

Éloquence latine.

M. NISARD traitera de Tacite, les Lundis et Vendredis à midi.

Poésie latine.

M. TISSOT, membre de l'Institut, Académie française, et, en cas d'absence, M. MAURICE MEYER, docteur ès lettres, exposera l'histoire, et commentera les principaux Fragments de la tragédie latine, les Mardis et Samedis, à midi.

Philosophie grecque et latine.

M. BARTHÉLEMY SAINT-HILAIRE, membre de l'Institut, Académie Royale des Sciences morales et politiques, traitera de la Philosophie dans l'antiquité, les Lundis et Vendredis, à une heure et demie.

Littérature française.

M. J.-J. AMPÈRE, membre de l'Institut, Académie française, et Académie Royale des Inscriptions et Belles-Lettres, exposera l'Histoire de la Littérature française au XVIII siècle, les Mercredis et Samedis, à une heure et demie.

Langue et Littérature slave.

M. ADAM MICKIEWICZ, chargé de la chaire à titre provisoire, ayant obtenu un congé, sera remplacé par M. CYPRIEN ROBERT, qui exposera, les Mardis, à midi et demi, l'Histoire littéraire des Slaves depuis les croisades jusqu'à Jean Huss. Les Samedis, à midi heures, il expliquera l'Epopée nationale de Cosindelich, l'Ozriconide et le dernier de Zalagorane.

Langues et Littératures d'origine germanique.

M. PHILARÈTE CHASLES traitera des auteurs, philosophes et publicistes allemands entre 1680 et 1850, les Mardis, à deux heures. Il expliquera le Merchant of Venice de Shakspeare, et la traduction allemande de M. Tieck, les Samedis à du heures et demie.

Langues et Littératures de l'Europe méridionale.

M. E. QUINET fera se cours les Lundis et Mercredis, à midi et demi.

Nota. Il y a pour chaque Cours un Registre où les auditeurs, qui voudront obtenir les certificats, devront s'inscrire

L'Administrateur du Collège royal de France,
LETRONNE.

TABLEAU DES JOURS ET HEURES DES COURS.

LUNDIS		MARDIS		MERCREDIS		JEUDIS		VENDREDIS		SAMEDIS	
MM.		MM.		MM.		MM.		MM.		MM.	
LIBRI	2 h. 1/2	DE PORTETS	9 heures	CAUSSIN DE PERCEVAL	8 h. 1/2	LIBRI	2 h. 1/2	CAUSSIN DE PERCEVAL	8 h. 1/2	DE PORTETS	9 heures
NISARD	Midi	BINET	3 h. 1/2	BURNOUF	9 h. 1/2	MICHELET	1 heure	BURNOUF	9 h. 1/2	ADAM MICKIEWICZ	12 heures
E. QUINET	Midi 1/2	TISSOT	Midi	MOHL	10 h. 1/2	STANISLAS JULIEN	5 heures	MOHL	Midi	PHILARÈTE CHASLES	10 h. 1/2
MICHELET	1 heure	ADAM MICKIEWICZ	Midi 1/2	ALIX DESGRANGES	11 h. 1/2			ALIX DESGRANGES	11 h. 1/2	BINET	3 h. 1/2
QUATREMÈRE	1 h. 1/2	BIOT	Midi 1/2	MICHEL CHEVALIER	Midi			NISARD	Midi	MICHEL CHEVALIER	Midi
BARTHÉLEMY S'-HILAIRE	1 h. 1/2	PELOUZE	1 heure	MAGENDIE	Midi			MAGENDIE	Midi	TISSOT	Midi
STANISLAS JULIEN	5 heures	COSTE	1 heure	RÉGNAULT	Midi 1/2			RÉGNAULT	Midi 1/2	PELOUZE	3/4
		ÉLIE DE BEAUMONT		E. QUINET	Midi 1/2			BARTHÉLEMY S'-HILAIRE	1 h. 1/2	ÉLIE DE BEAUMONT	1 heure
		PHILARÈTE CHASLES	2 heures	QUATREMÈRE	1 h. 1/2			DUVERNOY	1 h. 1/2	COSTE	1 heure
		AMPÈRE		AMPÈRE	1 h. 1/2					AMPÈRE	1 h. 1/2
				DUVERNOY	1 h. 1/2					LERMINIER	
				LERMINIER	3 heures						

Paris. — Typographie de Firmin Didot Frères, rue Jacob, 56.

Figure 12.3
Flyer for the courses for the first semester, 1847–48.

or to an intellectual club. Some examples, few in number but symbolically important, are globe-trotting political scientist André Siegfried, poet-thinker Paul Valéry, demographer-essayist Alfred Sauvy, theoretician and musician Pierre Boulez, and polymath Raymond Aron.

This survey of the evolution of the representation and intellectual function of the Collège de France clearly shows that through a historical ruse the Collège fulfills the function which its first promoters had originally imagined in their ambitious projects. Instead of reforming the Université, the Collège was established in its shadow and during the nineteenth century became both its counterpart and its complement; during the modern period of academic massification it was the innovator which the Université no longer was even within the traditional disciplines. But the twentieth-century lack of balance between the increasing number of candidates and the fixed number of chairs, which remains at the nineteenth-century level, serves to create a belated hope at the end of one's career.

II. "Formed of Men"

This study of the Collège's luminaries and exceptional periods has up until now only touched the tip of the iceberg. These facts, which involve the largely symbolic surface order, do not reveal the internal, everyday social functions of the Collège de France. In an ordinary university these operations can be measured through the traits of the students, while at the Collège de France, for lack of a formal audience, it is the professor's characteristics which are important. In the words of Étienne Pasquier as recorded by Abel Lefranc, the Collège de France is "formed of men."[18] Additionally, the instruction, the intellectual functions, and the students are dependent on the professor's renown (background, future, professional activities, intellectual perspectives, academic ideals).

But it is impossible to understand this essential key through historical analysis alone. Aside from several celebrities, we know very little about the professors of the ancien régime; systematic information can be found only about the nineteenth and twentieth centuries and the key elements of this analysis are based on these centuries.[19] The second difficulty within this sociological study is found in the diversity of the population in question: the Collège de France *omnia docet*, according to its motto. Thus scientists, doctors, lawyers, intellectuals, traditional professors, and unclassifiable people from all domains teach side by side in variable proportions. Tabulating their characteristics is tantamount to attempting to paint a picture of universities as a whole. However, from the details unique to the disciplines in question, we can assume that this picture would be slanted toward the margins of higher education. Even more useful for our purposes is to describe and if possible explain the originality of the Collège professors as regards their contributions to the originality of the institution where they teach. In order to assess this singularity we must evaluate the gap between the average professor at the Collège as compared to the corresponding categories in the rest of the Université or in the intellectual milieu. This gap is a function of two variables: the relative infrequency of the discipline being taught on the one hand, and the position of the Collège de France within the academic field on the other. This final element also depends on the period in question.

Sociological Analysis

A series of paradoxes comprise the sociology of the professors in the same way that contradictions characterize the institution as a whole: social extremes meet at the Collège de France. The Collège is the only academic establishment where the progeny of noble or bourgeois classes and the descendants of common people can be found conjunctively and even simultaneously. In the beginning of the nineteenth century, for example, there was the Marquis de Pastoret, scion of an old parliamentarian family of Provence, and Nicolas Vauquelin, the son of Normand farmhands. Similarly, around 1900, Henri d'Arbois de Jubainville, descendant of a noble family from Lorraine, and Paul Langevin, the child of Parisian workers, appeared in the same portrait: during the 1930s, André Siegfried, the son of a businessman MP and minister of trade, and Émile Coornaert, the son of a farmhand. These are not simply chance examples; it is statistically proven that custom and social tradition suited the literary and legal disciplines (international law, Celtic literature, political science) while social access was granted via the physical or social sciences. This is the standard mind/body opposition transported to the social realm.

The same diversity can be found in the geographical origins of the Collège professors. There were far more foreigners than in the rest of the university system (8.5 percent during the nineteenth century as compared to 1–2 percent at the Faculty of Letters in Paris), and Parisians remained overrepresented until the twentieth century, while during this same time their percentages were declining in the rest of the university. This is a consequence of the particular selectivity of the Collège. In order to teach certain unusual disciplines, especially in the beginning, it was often necessary to seek foreign specialists or French nationals raised abroad: for example, professor of Hebrew Salomon Munck, professor of Persian Jules Mohl, and professor of Assyrian archaeology Jules Oppert. All three of these men were German Jews prohibited from teaching in their country. In the same way, the overrepresentation of Parisians was a result of

Figure 12.4
Renan's funeral at the Collège de France, October 1892.

the underdevelopment of the sciences outside Paris. In order to conduct the research which a career at the Collège demanded, it was essential to enter into contact as soon as possible with the Parisian intellectual and scientific world; professors at the Collège de France were often former students of the Collège.

Another peculiarity of the professors as a whole was the relatively strong presence (more than 10 percent) of descendants of higher officials, mainly military officers and engineers. Their mostly scientific, intellectual vocations were undoubtedly a function of their privileged upbringings, but their backgrounds also could have diverted them from research. These sons of civil servants chose to challenge themselves instead of following in the footsteps of their fathers; examples can be found in Henry Le Chatelier and Camille Jordan, sons of public-sector engineers, or Paul Leroy-Beaulieu, the son of a préfet and deputy magistrate. But the choices by which these men subverted the expectations of their social environment in general characterized professors of more modest origins. Contrary to popular opinion, the proportion of the latter scarcely changed during the nineteenth and twentieth centuries, while the growth of university class sizes would seem to have favored social advancement. The share of professors of more modest backgrounds elected to the Collège before 1815, 1860, 1914, or 1939 remained between 20 and 30 percent. If higher education was more accessible in the twentieth century than in the nineteenth, the selection was also more severe, because a chair at the Collège de France became a prestigious claim. The details of the represented disciplines indicate an overselection of candidates: more so than within the traditional academic program. Certain intellectual directions within specialized fields at the Collège took on the hue of a series of coincidences, conversions, or reconversions such that individuals of modest means who benefited seemed like they had experienced authentic miraculous cures, whether it was Vauquelin, whose studies were sponsored by the nobles of his native village but who went to work at the age of fourteen before he was able to enjoy the protection of his mentor Fourcroy, or Jean-Louis Burnouf, the son of a weaver who won a fellowship to attend a Parisian high school, or Ernest Babelon, the son of a farmer and a student in Langres's seminar, or Salomon Munck, the son of a beadle in a synagogue who had originally planned on becoming a rabbi and ended his career as Renan's successor. As for Renan, the fatherless son of a grocery clerk was himself an example, as is well known, of an individual whose religious vocation turned scholarly.

Although these unusual social paths were more common at the Collège de France because the careers which led there did not have the same demanding character as elsewhere, we should not forget that—in accordance with the evolution outlined above—the majority of professors were descendents of the middle class which was already linked to the scholarly and academic institutions. This was the case with other academics as well. More and more frequently the children of cultivated clans found themselves beside others without such advantages. Thus, the ratio of doctors' or professors' children grew from a sixth of the Collège de France before 1860 to about a fourth during the Third Republic. Even the links between the Collège and higher education were at times very tight. During the nineteenth century seven of the professors at the Collège de France were the sons of former professors of the Collège: the Burnoufs, the Ampères, the Paris, the Havets, the Révilles, the Maspéros, and the Brillouins. To this list we can add the names of Sorbonne professors' sons: Pierre Boutroux, Jacques Duclaux, Guillaume Guizot, and others.[20] These internal connections were certainly rare, but less so than at the Sorbonne, and moreover they were temporally more consistent, as though the milieu of the Collège sui generis condoned it. In the first half of the nineteenth century these relations were undoubtedly the expression of a certain nepotism, but subsequently they became the mark of intellectual innovation born in a milieu which was "blessed by the muses." For example, É. Fauré-Frémiet was the son of Gabriel Fauré the music composer, grandson of the sculptor Frémiet, and son-in-law of the Collège professor Henneguy, himself the son-in-law of Proudhon and the son of a journalist.[21] Science was more frequently the product of a slow accumulation come to life within an advantageous milieu and less likely the romantic flash of genius as in the case of Champollion, the son of a bookseller from Figeac, or the miraculous intuition of twenty-two-year-old Balard, a provincial laboratory assistant who discovered bromine: his key to the doors of the Parisian scientific world.[22]

The Paths to Success

Beyond the diversity of their backgrounds, all the professors shared a compelling passion for the objects of their research. At the Sorbonne, intellectual distinction, most notably in letters, often led to more socially oriented pursuits. However, the majority of the Collège professors—except for those nominated with tainted criteria—practiced progressively more demanding intellectual asceticism: to be impassioned by a language which four or five people, or nobody, in France spoke; to spend years in laboratories which, until the beginning of the twentieth century, were unhealthily cobbled together; to search for hard-to-find inscriptions of documents; to wrestle with obscure or damaged texts. In a country like France where literature and brilliance were revered above all else, these were activities which were not a matter of course. Certainly, especially during the first half of the nineteenth century, these unusual interests allowed for careers to take off rapidly. Nearly 20 percent of the professors elected between 1789 and 1830 were younger than thirty-five, and this percentage falls below 10 percent only after 1860. Until this time the majority of professors were under forty years old at the time of their election to the Collège. But as the twentieth century neared and the prestige of the Collège de France grew, so did the average age at the time of nomination: from 43.7 years before 1830 to 48.1 for the period 1871–1914.[23]

The Sorbonne also manifested this delay of careers combined with the lengthening of training periods and the scarcity of chairs, but it does not have the same implication. Because of the details of the academic corps' renewal, the possibility of irregular programs was rare. Among the young professors of the twentieth century, for example, are Frédéric Joliot and Paul Langevin, who were both nominated at the age of thirty-seven, and

Paul Pelliot, nominated at thirty-three after returning from a productive mission to Asia. At the other end of the spectrum, the teaching profession on the rue des Écoles* takes on the hue of a second career. Charles Gide became a professor at the age of seventy-four, elected to a joint chair which was created for him after he retired as professor of political economy from the Faculty of Law, while Charles Nicolle earned the chair of medicine when he was sixty-six after a long career at the Pasteur Institute.[24] Identical examples can be found as early as the nineteenth century and prove the invariability of the Collège de France's double function: gambling on young and brilliant thinkers or honoring prophets late in life who remained in the shadows too long. The most extreme examples are Gaston Maspéro and Michel Bréal, elected at the ages of twenty-eight and thirty-two respectively, and Émile Deschanel and Charles Brown-Séquard, nominated at the ages of sixty-three and sixty-one.[25]

These early or late "miracles," just like the growing selectivity tempered by the creation of new chairs, somewhat blurred the career strategies in place at other institutions. The choices were in some way always paradoxical—both more and less exclusive than at the faculties. They were less exclusive because unlike the Sorbonne, nominees were not obliged to go through a series of ranks or extended apprenticeships at a lower level; more exclusive as well because, excluding the new chairs, the professors controlled the process of admissions; they could change the title of the chair and thus influence the profile of the possible candidates. Since each case was different, it is difficult to sketch a general picture of the elections. The written records are often insufficient and do not allow an understanding of the details of the process. The elections can be divided *grosso modo* into two general types: made-to-order polls without surprise, and difficult votes.

The election of Auguste Longnon to the chair of French historical geography (changed in 1892 from the chair of history and ethics) exemplifies the first case. While speaking with a journalist, Renan, the administrator of the Collège at the time and the influence behind the change, revealed with skeptical geniality the "secret of the game":

We wanted to substitute a precise title for the vague "history and ethics." So, why did we choose "French historical geography"? My God, it's just that we wanted Longnon to have this chair. This is the secret of the game. According to the rules, the professors will meet in a month to choose two candidates. We will consult with the Academy

* The rue des Écoles is in front of the Collège de France.—Ed.

On écoute aux fenêtres le cours de M. Bergson

Excelsior. Samedi 14 février 1914

ON ECOUTE AUX FENETRES LE COURS DE M.BERGSON

A L'ENTRÉE DE L'AMPHITHÉÂTRE

Mr BERGSON ARRIVANT AU COLLÈGE DE FRANCE

La foule qui s'est rendue hier au cours de M. Bergson était plus dense encore que de coutume. Il s'agissait, pour ses disciples et admirateurs, de lui témoigner leur joie à l'occasion de son élection. On écouta aux fenêtres la leçon du maître (Central-Excelsior-Photos.)

Figure 12.5
Bergson's success.

of Inscriptions and the Minister of Education will then name the person. Of course our choice is always approved; moreover, in this case it is already done. We only requested a chair of French historical geography because we wanted Longnon. My colleague from the Academy of Inscriptions, Mr. Longnon. . . .[26]

This custom-made election was thus nothing but the recognition of an already revered scholar. In the same way there were certain disciples who were elected to succeed their teachers even before they retired, after which the student naturally replaced them. Thus, Théodule Ribot, professor of experimental and applied psychology, was succeeded by his disciple Pierre Janet and, according to the testimony of Janet, voluntarily removed himself. "I would like to remember Ribot's sensitive scruples as he feared imposing too long upon me the role of his substitute teacher; he thus withdrew in order to leave the entire space to a younger person."[27] Others also went on their first unofficial campaigns before the corps of professors could ratify their colleague's choice: Bergson substituted for Lévêque, Langevin for Mascart, and so forth.

The second type of election is more interesting for historians because it better demonstrates the tensions and hidden motives in the teaching community than does the seeming unanimity of the first sort. In close votes two candidates of almost identical merit faced off, and secondary considerations or a keen campaign beforehand were often the basis of the final decision. In general these elections concerned strategic chairs—important either because of the prestige, the seniority, or the controversial discipline the professor would oversee. This type of election then became a pretext for symbolic and political overinvestments that also involved the events of the period in question. They generally involved literary chairs, but the scientific chairs were not exempt. According to Joseph Bédier, on July 1, 1900, a tight race set Marcel Brillouin, Mascart's substitute, against Marcel Deprez, a member of the Academy of Sciences and the substitute for Joseph Bertrand, the deceased holder of the chair in general and mathematical physics. The situation was made even more complex by the fact that out of twenty-eight professors present, only eight were scientists, as opposed to twenty men of letters. These professors thus held the key to the vote and yet could judge the candidates less on the content of their research than on the kind of intellect or scholar they epitomized. One (Brillouin), was a theoretician and more eclectic in his scientific interests, while the other (Deprez) was older and had more honors but had led a less academic career.[28] Brillouin won by a narrow margin (fifteen to thirteen), thanks to the addition of some literary votes. Bédier concludes his account by citing Renan:

What a strange establishment where a law reigns which is as constant as the laws of nature. As Renan said: "When the professors of the Collège must choose between two scientific candidates, the men of letters vote the most intelligently. Conversely, when the competition is between two men of letters, the scientists vote the most intelligently."[29]

Apart from the flattery which is so often present in commemorative texts such as this, what played in the minds of voters was most likely the social image of the two scholars. Maurice Lévy was appointed to defend Brillouin's case and skillfully focused his reasoning on the following point: "He has great erudition and clearly possesses that quality which the Collège de France should demand above all of its nominees: the orientation of one's work toward the most novel, most demanding of subjects."[30] This reasoning consisted partly in linking the candidate's profile with that of the institutional ideal; the professors who were the most committed to that ideal thus preferred Brillouin to the other scholar. Deprez was oriented more toward applied research, which was less valued at the Collège and thus less in accord with the spirit of the establishment.

For the chairs in letters, contested elections were more frequent and often involved extrascientific considerations, however little they might apply. The best example and the one for which there is a great deal of documentation is that of the election of Alfred Loisy to the chair of religious history, March 2, 1909. Several circumstances served to complicate the vote. First, Jean Réville, the previous holder of the post, died suddenly after only a year in the position. He had "naturally" succeeded his father, Albert, for whom the chair had been created by Jules Ferry in 1880 during an especially extreme anticlerical moment. Jean Réville thus did not have a chance to make his mark nor to train disciples or natural successors. Seven academics whose numerous qualifications were quite comparable found themselves competing for the position, which further broke up the votes and rendered difficult any attempt to establish a majority. Four of the seven taught at the École pratique des hautes études (in the fourth and fifth divisions): Maurice Vernes, Marcel Mauss, Jules Toutain, and Émile Amelineau. Two taught in universities outside Paris: Georges Foucart (Aix-en-Provence), the son of Paul Foucart, who was a professor at the Collège at the time, and Albert Dufourcq (Bordeaux). Finally, Louis Havet promoted the seventh candidate, Alfred Loisy, the former priest whose theories were at the center of the modernist controversy and hence condemned by the church. This injected an echo of the earlier religious and political battles which had culminated in the separation of church and state in 1905. This sudden rush of candidates from the École pratique des hautes études can be explained by the fact that this chair was the only one available for professors specializing in exotic subjects not taught at the university. Moreover, the candidates were all of the same generation, except for Vernes and Loisy, who were older. The winner would thus hold the chair for a period of time such that upon his retirement his competitors would be too old to campaign again. For almost all of them this was their last chance, and this made the election particularly bitter. They were all similar with respect to their qualifications (except for Loisy, but he had a group of influential friends at the Collège led by Louis Havet, whose seniority and role in the Dreyfus affair were great assets in the eyes of his colleagues), but each one advocated a different conception of religious history, based on ideological suppositions. In order to build a majority it was necessary to consolidate the different sympathies and aversions. The Catholics at the Collège hated Loisy because he fomented scandal in the church; furthermore, he was a victim of a negative public campaign. Vernes was Protestant, while Mauss was Jewish and also tainted by his socialist sympathies and sociological tendencies, which were influenced by his uncle, Durkheim. Foucart could thus count on the support of the Catholics and the friends of his professor father, especially Maspéro, his Egyptology professor. In much the same way Loisy was the candidate of choice for the anticlerical scholars, but he was restrained by the presence of the lesser candidates. The rumor even went that he had not really left the church and that it was possible that he was truly a Trojan horse proffered by the Catholics. This rumor could have diverted the Collège's far left from supporting him.

Five rounds of voting were needed to establish a majority. In the first Foucart led (twelve votes; with nine for Loisy, seven for Mauss, five for Toutain, two for Vernes, and one for Amelineau). As the voting progressed the majority was overturned; Loisy rallied the lesser candidates to block the right-wing nominee. Mauss and Vernes, the most distinctive candidates, lost their support to the former priest. Thus a new anticlerical block, reminiscent of the Combes's majority, was created.★ In the second, third, and fourth rounds Loisy won two more votes, then six, and then two more. In the fourth round Loisy and Foucart were almost tied (seventeen versus sixteen). In the fifth round Loisy won with three votes to spare. The more conservative Institute de France adopted an inverse order in the presentation of the candidate. However, in deference to tradition the minister Gaston Doumergue yielded to the Collège and was not unhappy to appoint an adversary of the church—the enemy of the regime.[31]

★ Émile Combes was anticlerical and prime minister from 1902 to 1905.—Ed.

Courses: Hermits and Messiahs

The diverse individuals, the heterogeneous careers, and the many elections generated great differences in the courses taught. Throughout the nineteenth century, the Université witnessed the establishment of an antithetical system: public courses, which were often attended by socialites or were directed at the constantly growing body of general students, and the German-style seminar. The latter were small, specialized groups whose purpose was training in research or methodology. This opposition was even institutionalized with the small seminars at the École pratique des hautes études on one side and the lecture classes at the Sorbonne on the other. But with the development of assistant professorships, the university faculty gradually began to teach using both types of pedagogy.

Without an a priori delineated public, the Collège de France offered classes spanning the entire range of styles encompassed by these two extremes, depending on the discipline and especially the personality of the professor in question. Certain professors used both styles concurrently, depending on the day of the week: lectures and seminars. In attempting to establish a systematic classification for these courses we decided that religious metaphors were the most convenient because pedagogical vocabulary is inadequate when describing the relations between the students, the professors, the eras, and the subjects. From the available accounts we can distinguish between several types of teaching styles; there was the hermit, who often talked only for his own benefit; the sect leader, who was frequently present in science laboratories; the high priests, who were the objects of cults in which the disciples were their students; and finally the messiahs, who sent their message out to the entire world with the help of their enthusiastic audience.

The hermit. Although he lends himself to an easy parody and fits into the stereotypes of the aged scholar ensconced in his ivory tower and cut off from the world, the hermit-professor lecturing to one or two people, indeed to an empty classroom, is not uncommon or even simply a historical curiosity. The majority of classes given in specialized fields, which made up the bulk of the courses at the Collège, were probably taught in these conditions up until the potential student population exploded even in the rare languages. What would have been a stigma at the Sorbonne was akin to an honor for certain professors—the sign of a high theoretical level: "It was fashionable to have no students in your classes at the Collège de France. We would joke among ourselves, 'I am teaching a serious course and I don't have any students.'"[32] In physics for example, Joseph Bertrand only had five students, and if there were twenty students in a class of Berthelot's, only ten were truly committed.[33] The situation

Figure 12.6
Marcellin Berthelot in his laboratory in the Collège de France, in 1927.

Figure 12.7
Paul Valéry teaching at the Collège de France, around 1937.

was even more serious for the obscure literary disciplines which had no professional prospects and held little interest for the general public. Thus after several months in 1846 Renan was the only student in Quatremère's Hebrew class: "He is troubled that he speaks into a void, but is it not a bit his own fault? Ah! if I were in his place, I swear . . . , I would know how to lecture and even better."[34] Renan kept his word. What best characterized his courses was less the size of his audience than their structure. According to Renan, "The true professor at the Collège de France does not prepare his lecture."[35] If we are to believe his disciple Loisy, Renan himself practiced this principle.

He did not prepare his lectures, or barely. At that time he was studying *Psalms*. He would take a verse, read it, translate it, read Septante's
Greek version as a comparison, cite the corrections of the work by
the oratorian Houbigant or a modern critic. He would weigh each
word and never prevented himself from digressing or repeating
things. In his opinion a professor at the Collège de France should
work in front of his students and hence he worked before us, I suspect a bit slower than in his office.[36]

The leader of the sect. We now leave the domain of solitary exercise for
the collective labor of the laboratory, the world of the experimental scientific disciplines which was becoming the true stage for the courses at the
Collège de France. The professor would suggest directions of research,
but the connection was not unilateral. Each discovery enriched the prob-
lematic for everyone as a function of the method elaborated in common.
The fashioning of the disciplines was much more complete, and a true
human community was created through the rituals, customs, options,
division of labor, and even the tensions. The professor was a supervisor,
the team leader to whom the students owed not only their knowledge
but their future as well. The description of Ranvier's laboratory (he was
a former assistant to Claude Bernard and, as such, a loyal advocate of the
experimental method) by one of his disciples and successors recreates this
atmosphere which is so unique to a pedagogy of collective research.

> Since the beginning of his career Ranvier created an atmosphere.
> He understood what the others did not; we gathered around him
> and very quickly a studio was formed. His collaborators and students
> were seduced by his imagination, the rigor of his methods, his pas-
> sion for research, and his constant discoveries, which they impatiently
> and inquisitively anticipated. Ranvier was "the boss." The appren-
> tices participated in his work and were interested in it as though it
> were their own; these beginners were also useful. He tested his way
> of thinking on them and in their flawed work he found elements for
> comparison and control. . . . Ranvier's teaching took place mainly in
> the laboratory. Few people attended his courses, generally his closest
> students, his collaborators, and some friends. In his lectures he gave
> neither an overview nor a synthesis.[37]

We can measure the originality of this sociability by comparing it to what
was done at the faculties, particularly at the Faculty of Medicine, where
dogmatic methods, large lecture courses, and clinical practice prevailed.
The nineteenth-century medical revolution did not evolve out of this

established religion, but rather it grew out of the laboratories of Claude Bernard and Ranvier at the Collège de France or of Pasteur at the École normale: these minor sects of snipers. Here we have moved from the suffering marginalization of the scientific hermit to the vindicated marginalization of the leader of a movement who awaits the recognition which his ideas merit.

The prophets. The successful prophets at the Collège de France fall into two categories: the high priests and the messiahs. In contrast to the preceding group, these professors had huge audiences, but they were the objects of differing overinvestments. The high priests attracted an intellectual overinvestment, while the messiahs attracted a political one. The former were thus more common than the latter, but the division between the two was sometimes difficult to detect. The best examples of high priests are Bergson and Valéry. Their classes created a sense of uneasiness in the participants that came from a misunderstanding at the heart of the pedagogical relationship. Valéry explained it to one of his correspondents in the following terms: classes are nothing but "hours filled with words":

> I lose myself from atop my chair!—Oh! if only I had five students like Renan, everything would work out! But a lecture hall filled with whomever they are is very tiring. I ask myself to whom should I direct my comments, to what level of knowledge, of desire, of tension; they must be satisfied.[38]

The poet who had to give courses on poetics was reduced to addressing himself in order to forget the lecture hall. The intellectually rigorous theoretician, the enemy of verbal improvisation, the writer of the idée fixe thus taught in a way that was the opposite of his own work.

> In these classes, where the genesis of different creations of the mind were harshly analyzed, where so many flattering illusions crumbled, where the importance of formal structures created a sort of generalized rhetoric, the freedom, the intransigence of judgments—like the tone, the hesitations, the reversals, the stammerings in a man who is capable of dazzling improvisations,—eloquently demonstrate the advantages of a form which would be flexible during difficult moments, independent of public acceptance, and resistant to verbal temptation as well as the desire for continuity and symmetry. A form which would be ultimately as supportive as possible of intellectual honesty: a lecture addressed to oneself.[39]

If Valéry's audience attended less for the lectures than to witness the genesis of poetry—in the valerian sense of the act of creation—Bergson's

audience came to pay homage to the cult of philosophy. According to
Étienne Gilson,

> In order to help better understand philosophers dead for many cen-
> turies, I evoke Bergson's example of living his philosophy before us.
> Ah! it is a great misfortune that he no longer teaches! It was amazing
> to hear him develop his ideas in public. The presence of this philoso-
> pher among the young students helped us to better understand what
> the lives of Socrates or Plato, surrounded by their disciples, must have
> been like.[40]

The paradox is that Bergson, like Valéry, never wanted to join in his disciples' fervor at all and often accepted it badly on account of the incidences
which the excess of press coverage never failed to create.[41] Contrary to legend, the crowds were not made up immediately of the elite public. They
were first composed of students who were disappointed by the courses
at the Sorbonne, in other words, as with the preceding case, heretics of
the official religion. Then Bergson's renown grew (he became a member
of the Institute and then of the Académie française), and the publicity
which certain writers generated by using him in their fight against academic positivism broadened his public to include a somewhat pretentious
element. Bergson, a rather traditional academic type, did not tolerate this
direction very well. He was the high priest of a misunderstood religion
despite himself; he sought an early retirement in order to recover the calm
necessary to finish his work.[42]

The truly prophetic courses, of which the best examples are those of
the romantic trilogy, Michelet, Quinet, and Mickiewicz, can be ascribed
not to a style linked to that time period, but to a deliberate, political enterprise which tried to translate the social and intellectual aspirations of
youth worried by the widespread opposition to progress. The justly celebrated 1847–48 lectures of Michelet, or the earlier ones given by Quinet and Mickiewicz, voluntarily left the domain of knowledge and were
transformed into improvised meetings during which the professor described the problem and delineated the action to be taken in the future.
The response of the ruling powers to this indictment is not at all surprising. An excerpt from Michelet's eighth lesson summarizes the romantic
philosophy underlying this impromptu speech, which was followed by a
written version; in some ways it came to life several weeks later through
the events of the revolution of 1848.

> What can scholars do without the people, or the people without
> scholars? Nothing. Everyone must cooperate on social action; more-

over we must alternate and exchange roles. The common man must climb aboard science and the scientist must fashion himself into the common man, he must refashion and restrengthen himself at the fountain of instinct and life.[43]

This is the opposite pole from the first type of class where the scholar renounced the world. Has the phenomenon reappeared? The recent past has seen these inspired prophecies reborn, at the Collège de France and elsewhere. The Collège de France is a *lieu de mémoire*, but the future springs from it as well.

The Collège de France ultimately offers a final paradox. In opposition to all the other French cultural institutions, the Collège does not have any true enemies. In May 1968 the students "seized" the Sorbonne and l'Odéon but not the Collège. It has also survived many other revolutions without damage. Let us push this reasoning further. It is possible that in imitation of the men in the year III (1794), the initiators of Edgar Faure's landmark law (1968) were inspired by the model of the Collège de France. What is the model for the university at Vincennes if it is not an extension of the pedagogical model established by François I in the age of universities for the masses: the admission of students without their *baccalauréat*, the recruitment of marginalized professors, the restructuring of the traditional disciplines, the rejection of short-term professional profits. Moreover, the esteemed institution recognizes this and over the years has elected several heretics whom the rebels have chosen as their heroes: Michel Foucault, Roland Barthes, and others.

But the ruling power has not forgotten its former protégé. It has renewed François I's solemn pact twice in recent years. The former president Giscard d'Estaing paid a visit to the professors in honor of the institution's four hundred fiftieth anniversary. His successor, François Mitterrand, requested of them a meditation on the "basic principles of teaching for the future" in a letter dated February 13, 1984.[44]

Four hundred and fifty years after its establishment the Collège de France is still inspirational; indeed it maintains a certain practice of cultural rebellion and at the same time secures the honor of our republican monarchs; it thus embodies orthodox heresy, essentially an academy without academicians. The Collège enjoys the privilege of extraterritoriality—only the professors of the Collège are exempt from the new mandatory retirement age. These qualities prove the degree to which the Collège de France has been able to link its founding myth with its real history. Although the Collège has refused entry to several highly regarded academics and welcomed some mediocre scholars, it has not been subjected to a litany of its errors, as has the Académie française and its forty-first member. As we

Figure 12.8

The Collège de France, 1976–77. 1. F. Lecoy. 2. G. Blin. 3. J. de Romilly. 4. G. Posener. 5. A. Horeau.
6. A. Chastel. 7. A. Leroi-Gourhan. 8. R. Aron. 9. A. Fessard. 10. E. Laroche. 11. J. Leray. 12. A. Bareau.
13. J.-P. Vernant. 14. J. Berque. 15. G. Duby. 16. J. de Ajuriaguerra. 17. J.-Cl. Pecker. 18. A. Lichnerowicz.
19. Cl. Lévi-Strauss. 20. Fr. Gros. 21. J.-L. Lions. 22. J. Vuillemin. 23. A. Miquel. 24. A. Caquot.
25. A. Abragam. 26. J. Delumeau. 27. J. Prentki. 28. G. Dagron. 29. Cl. Cohen-Tannoudji. 30. A. Jost.
31. R. Pfau. 32. R. Stein. 33. A. Sauvy. 34. J. Ruffié. 35. P.-M. Duval. 36. Fr. Jacob. 37. F. Morel.
38. L. Hambis. 39. P. Courcelle. 40. J. Benoit. 41. M. Froissart. 42. J.-P. Serre. 43. J.-P. de Morant.
44. J. Tits. 45. Y. Laporte. 46. J. Gernet. 47. E. Le Roy Ladurie. 48. P. Veyne.

have seen, much like the Sorbonne, it has had its moments of glory and periods of misfortune. If we are reminded of these highs and lows while at the Sorbonne, in crossing the rue Saint Jacques we remember only the heights. Perhaps Valéry found the answer to the enigma. When a German officer stopped him at the door to the Collège to ask, "What is taught at this school?," he answered: "This is a place where speech is free."[45]

NOTES

1. "Philology is like a poor girl who needs a husband, and we implore you to furnish a dowry." Letter from Guillaume Budé to François I (1529), quoted in Abel Lefranc, *Histoire du Collège de France depuis ses origines jusqu'à la fin du Premier Empire* (Paris: Hachette, 1893), 105.

2. "This great man died a martyr for the cause of the Collège de France"; Lefranc, 221. For more information on Ramus, see Charles Waddington, *Ramus: Sa vie, ses écrits et ses opinions* (Paris: Mayrueis, 1885).

3. Lefranc, 132.

4. Gabriel Monod, "La Chaire d'histoire du Collège de France," *La Revue bleue*, 1905 (excerpt): 10.

5. See Lefranc, 261.

6. See Lefranc, 288: classes continued even during the Reign of Terror.

7. Quoted in Lefranc, 255.

8. Quoted in Monod, 8–9.

9. See Dominique Julia, "Une réforme impossible: Le changement de cursus dans la France du XVIIIe siècle," *Actes de la recherche en sciences sociales* 47–48 (1983): 53–76; Roger Chartier, Marie-Madeleine Compère, and Dominique Julia, *L'Education en France du XVIe au XVIIIe siècle* (Paris: SEDES, 1976) chap. 7.

10. The Government of National Defense ruled France between September 4, 1870, and February 12, 1871. Paul Hazard, "Michelet, Quinet, Mickiewicz et la vie intérieure du Collège de 1838 à 1852," *Le Collège de France (1850–1930): Livre jubilaire composé à l'occasion de son quatrième centenaire* (Paris: PUF, 1932), 263–76; Jean Pommier, *Renan d'après des documents inédits* (Paris: Perrin, 1923), 228.

11. Hazard, 273.

12. See our paper: "La faculté des lettres de Paris et le pouvoir au XIXe siècle," Proceedings of *Le Personnel de l'enseignement supérieur en France aux XIXe et XXe siècles* (Paris: Éditions du CNRS, 1985), 151–66.

13. Jules Michelet, "Une année du Collège de France," in *Oeuvres complètes* (Paris: Flammarion, 1877), 592.

14. See Ferdinand Brunetière's very critical article, "Revue littéraire," *Revue des Deux Mondes*, April 1, 1885, 694–95. At this moment Paul Albert was named professor of Latin literature and then Émile Deschanel, former professor of rhetoric, was elected to the Collège as recompense for the political persecutions of which he was victim during the Second Empire rather than due to his academic merits.

15. Ernest Renan, *Questions contemporaines*, 142, cited in Lefranc, vii–viii.

16. George Weisz, *The Emergence of Modern Universities in France (1863–1914)* (Princeton: Princeton University Press, 1983).

17. Frédéric Lefèvre, *Une heure avec* (Paris: NRF, 1925), 3:271, 276.

18. "Basty en hommes"; Lefranc, 236.

19. See C. Delangle's thesis in progress on the professors of the Collège de France during the eighteenth and nineteenth centuries, and Agnès Lechat's master's thesis, "Les Professeurs du Collège de France de 1800 à 1914" (Thesis, University of Paris IV, 1984). We are currently collaborating on research concerning the professors of the twentieth century (up through 1939) and have published a comparative study of the professors of the Collège and other Parisian universities: "Le Champ universitaire parisien à la fin du XIXe siècle," *Actes de la recherche en sciences sociales* 47–48 (1983): 77–89. On the present era, see Pierre Bourdieu, *Homo academicus* (Paris: Éditions de Minuit, 1984), especially 140–44.

20. Lechat, 14.

21. From the archives of the Collège de France, CXII, file É. Fauré-Frémiet; National Archives, F17 26756, file Henneguy; *Qui êtes-vous?* (Paris: Delgrave, 1908).

22. Camille Matignon, "La Chimie générale au Collège de France," *Le Collège de France*, 95.

23. Lechat, 97.

24. Louis Renou, "Notice sur la vie et les travaux de Paul Pelliot," *Recueil de l'Institut*, 1950. André Langevin, *Paul Langevin, mon père* (Paris: EFR, 1971), 66. On Charles Gide, see National Archives, F17 21967. Paul Giroud, "Charles Nicolle," *Bulletin de l'Académie de médecine* (December 5, 1961): 714–22.

25. National Archives, F17 25852 (Maspéro), 21967 (Bréal), 25756 (Deschanel), 20293 (Brown-Séquard).

26. National Archives, F17 13556. Interview with *Temps*, 23 April 1892.

27. Pierre Janet, "Nécrologie de Théodule Ribot," *Annuaire de l'Association amicale des anciens élèves de l'École normale supérieure* (Paris: Hachette, 1919), 22.

28. Brillouin, born in 1854, had attended the École normale supérieure and was a professor there. Deprez, born in 1843, had attended the École des mines and was a professor at the Conservatoire national des arts et métiers, where he specialized in the transportation of electrical energy.

29. *Jubilé scientifique de Marcel Brillouin* (Paris: Gauthier-Villars, 1936), 4–5.

30. *Jubilé*, 4.

31. National Archives, F17 13556; Albert Houtin and Félix Sartiaux, *Alfred Loisy: Sa vie, son oeuvre*, (Paris: Émile Poulat, CNRS, 1960), 162–69.

32. The comments of Henry Le Chatelier as reported in François Le Chatelier, *Henry Le Chatelier* (Paris: François Le Chatelier, 1968), 189.

33. Le Chatelier, 188.

34. Pommier, 60.

35. Pommier, 322–23.

36. Lefèvre, 3:65

37. Justin Jolly, "Ranvier et la méthode expérimentale," *Le Collège de France*, 216–17.

38. Excerpts from a letter to Mme Roth-Mascagni, *Entretiens sur Paul Valéry* (Paris: PUF, 1972), 75.

39. Berne-Joffroy, "Souvenirs et digressions," *Paul Valéry vivant*, special issue of *Cahiers du Sud* (1946):185.

40. Lefèvre, 3:65.

41. Rose Mossé-Bastide, *Bergson éducateur* (Paris: PUF, 1955). The author reminds us of the principal events (69–71), especially the petition by the students who complained about the invasion of the lecture hall by idle spectators and the virtual riot after Bergson's election to the Académie française in January 1914. The windows had to be left open (in February!), which is confirmed by a photo in the newspaper *L'Excelsior*, 14 February.

42. See Mossé-Bastide, 73; and the National Archives, F17 22552. Bergson began soliciting substitutes in 1914 and requested his retirement in 1921, although he could have continued to teach until at least 1929. He was to become a sort of high priest of international knowledge through his role as president of the Commission of Intellectual Cooperation within the Society of Nations.

43. Michelet 535 (lecture of February 3, 1848).

44. *450e anniversaire de la fondation du Collège de France, 1530–1980* (Paris: Collège de France, 1981). The president spoke about the "home of French intelligence" in his speech (50). On the purpose of the meditation see, *Annuaire du Collège de France, 1983–1984*; and *Propositions pour l'enseignement de l'avenir élaborées à la demande de M. le Président de la République par les professeurs du Collège de France* (Paris: Collège de France, 1985).

45. Paul Valéry vivant, 19.

Figure 2.6   Inventories in Haute-Loire: the parish priest of Champels, sur-
              rounded by his parishioners, defends his steeple, March 1906. Biblio-
              thèque nationale, Paris. Photo © Bibliothèque nationale.

Figure 2.7   The sanctification of Sunday in a catechism, in pictures published
              by *La Croix* at the end of the nineteenth century. Coll. part. Photo
              © Jean-Loup Charmet.

Figure 2.8   The fortified churches of Thiérache: Plomion. Photo © Serge Chirol.

Figure 2.9   The church of Oradour-sur-Glane, in November 1944. Photo ©
              Lapi-Viollet.

Figure 2.10   Salvador Dalí, *Les Atavismes du crépuscule (phénomène obsessif)*, 1933–34.
              Kunstmuseum, Berne. Photo © Robert Descharnes/Dewart Pro Arte
              © ADAGP, 1992.

Figure 2.11   Jean-François Millet, *L'Angélus*, 1859. Musée du Louvre, Paris. Photo
              © Bulloz.

Figure 2.12   1789 : *L'Angélus* of Millet, taken by Yves Yacoël, 1981. Photo ©Yves
              Yacoël.

Figure 2.13   The steeple of Lavaur (Tarn) and its *jacquemart*. Photo © Cap/Roger-
              Viollet.

                          CHAPTER THREE

Figure 3.1   The painter of the Eiffel Tower. Photo © Marc Riboud/Magnum.

Figure 3.2   Cards and vignettes of different professional associations, 1848.
              Bibliothèque nationale, Paris. Photo © Bibliothèque nationale.

Figure 3.3   J. Raffaëlli, *Les Forgerons*. Musée de Douai. Photo © Bulloz.

Figure 3.4   *La Coulée*, stained glass window produced by the Majorelle work-
              shops in Nancy for the Aciéries de Longwy (Usinor) hotel in Mont-
              Saint-Martin. Photo © Service regional de l'Inventaire general en
              Lorraine. © SPADEM, 1992.

Figure 3.5   Caillebotte, *Les Raboteurs de parquets*, 1875. Musée d'Orsay, Paris.
              Photo © Réunion des Musées nationaux.

Figure 3.6   A locksmith at his forge, 1950s. Photo © Henri de Châtillon/Rapho.

Figure 3.7   A sculptor, Yves Loyer, in his shop, rue Chapon, 1980s. Photo D.R.

Figure 3.8   Cobbler. Revolutionary stamp. Musée Carnavalet, Paris. Photo
              © Bulloz.

Figure 3.9   A workshop of blind cobblers in Dijon at the beginning of the cen-
              tury. Coll. part. Photo © Kharbine/Tapabor.

Figure 3.10   A boot maker from Ménilmontant. Photo © Kharbine/Tapabor.

Figure 3.11   "The only woman in France practicing the profession of carpentry."
              Photo © Kharbine/Tapabor.

Figure 3.12   At the glass factory in Maubeuge. Photo © Kharbine/Tapabor.

Figure 3.13   Raymond Isidore, Chartres. Photo © Jacques Verroust.

Figure 3.14   Jean Gabin in Jean Renoir's *La Bête humaine*, 1938. Photo
              © Edimedia.

Figure 3.15   The locomotive, symbol of France, in Jean-Paul Goude's parade
              on the Champs-Élysées on the occasion of the bicentennial of the
              French Revolution, in 1989. Photo © Valérie Winckler/Rapho.

Figure 3.16   Catalogue from the arms and bicycle factory in Saint-Étienne.
              Photo © Kharbine/Tapabor.

CHAPTER FOUR

Figure 4.1   Industrial landscape between Lille and Roubaix (Nord). Photo
              © Henri Cartier-Bresson/Magnum.

Figure 4.2   The old Boeufs de La Villette market, in Paris. Photo © Richard
              Kalvar/Magnum.

Figure 4.3   A factory in Fourmies (Nord) has been transformed into the prin-
              cipal seat of the ecomuseum in the region of Fourmies-Trélon.
              Photo © Christophe Manquillet/Écomusée de la région Fourmies-
              Trélon.

Figure 4.4   The ironworks of Buffon (Côte-d'Or): the casting hall and the blast
              furnace, seen from the stairway of honor. Photo © Jacques Hiver/
              Association pour la sauve-garde et l'animation des Forges de Buffon.

Figure 4.5   The Dijonval factory, in Sedan (Ardennes). Photo D.R.

Figure 4.6   The castle of the Congo or Vaissier castle, near Tourcoing (Nord).
              Photo © Cap-Viollet.

Figure 4.7   The ruins of the factory of Fontaine-Guérard (Seine-Maritime).
              Photo Étienne Revault © CNMHS/SPADEM, 1992.

Figure 4.8   View of the entrance pavilion of the saltworks of Arc-et-Senans
              (Doubs). Photo © Marc Paygnard/Rapho.

Figure 4.9   Aerial view of the saltworks of Arc-et-Senans (Doubs). Photo
              © Marc Paygnard/Rapho.

Figure 4.10   The Sabatier shafts in the Raismes commune (Nord). Photo
              © P.-Ch. Guiollard.

Figure 4.11   The pithead frame for the Sainte-Fontaine shafts in Freyming-
              Merlebach (Moselle). Photo © P.-Ch. Guiollard.

Figure 4.12   The Hottinguer shafts in Épinac (Saône-et-Loire). Photo
              © P.-Ch. Guiollard.

Figure 4.13   The industrial wasteland of Cornillon in the Saint-Denis plain:
              the disused gas factory. Photo © Bruno Dicianni.

Figure 4.14   Between Port-sur-l'Escaut and Saint-Amand (Nord) in 1976. Photo
              © Henri Cartier-Bresson/Magnum.

Figure 4.15   The Vernes power plant built in 1918 on the Romanche, in Isère.
              Photo © Laurent Ménégoz.

CHAPTER FIVE

Figure 5.1   Jean Baudin with, in the background, Susana Azquinzer, storyteller.
              Coll. part. Photo D.R.

CHAPTER SIX

Figure 6.1   Durival, *De la vigne* (Paris, 1777). Bibliothèque nationale, Paris. Photo © Bibliothèque nationale.

Figure 6.2   *La Taille de la vigne*, miniature of *Livre des propriétés des choses*, by Barthélemy l'Anglais, fourteenth century. Photo © Roger-Viollet.

Figure 6.3   The pruning of vines in our era. Photo © R. Truchot/Explorer.

Figure 6.4   Vineyard at Saint-Émilion, in Bordelais. Photo © Nadeau/Explorer.

Figure 6.5   Vineyard at Andlau, in Alsace. Photo © S. Cordier/Explorer.

Figure 6.6   Vineyard near Saumur, on the banks of the Loire River. Photo © S. Jalain/Explorer.

Figure 6.7   Vineyards of Vosne-Romanée and Nuits-Saint-Georges, in Bourgogne. Photo © J.-P. Nacivet/Explorer.

Figure 6.8   *La Sainte Messe*, miniature of *La Journée du chrétien*, by the father of J.-K. Huysmans, 1852. Bibliothèque nationale, Paris. Photo © Bibliothèque nationale.

Figure 6.9   Flyer for Paul Court wine, 1900–1910. Musée de la publicité, Paris. Photo du Musée.

Figure 6.10   Party for the nomination of the mayor; engraving by Remhild, around 1850. Bibliothèque des arts décoratifs, Paris. Photo © J.-P. Vieil/Rapho.

Figure 6.11   *Nous l'avons eu votre Rhin allemand!* Engraving of the illustrated supplement of the *Petit Journal*, 1895. Bibliothèque nationale, Paris. Photo © Bibliothèque nationale.

Figure 6.12   *Réservez le vin pour nos poilus*; poster by Suzanne Ferrand, a student of the Paris public schools, sixteen years old, during World War I. Musée de la publicité, Paris. Photo du Musée.

Figures 6.13–6.14   Labels from Château Mouton Rothschild decorated with contemporary works of art, 1964, 1966, 1969, 1975. Photos coll. from the baron Philippe de Rothschild, with his kind authorization © ADAGP, 1992.

CHAPTER SEVEN

Figure 7.1   Watteau, *Assemblée dans un parc*, around 1715, detail. Musée du Louvre, Paris. Photo © Bulloz.

Figure 7.2   A tournament, miniature of *Roman du chevalier Tristan et de la reine Yseult*, fifteenth century. Musée Condé, Chantilly. Photo © Bulloz.

Figure 7.3   Miniature of *l'Histoire du grand Alexandre*, fifteenth century. Musée du Petit Palais, Paris. Photo © Bulloz.

Figure 7.4   Frontispiece of *La Guirlande de Julie*, by Nicolas Robert, book presented by Charles de Salles, future Duke of Montpensier, to Julie d'Angennes, eldest daughter of the Marquise de Rambouillet, January 1, 1642. Coll. part., Paris. Photo © Giraudon.

Figure 7.5   Watteau, *L'Indifférent*, 1716. Musée du Louvre, Paris. Photo © Bulloz.

Figure 7.6   Watteau, *L'Embarquement pour Cythère*, detail. Musée du Louvre, Paris. Photo © Bulloz.

Figure 7.7   *Madame Récamier l'Abbaye-aux-bois*, by François-Louis Dejuine, 1826.
              Coll. part. Photo © Bulloz.

Figure 7.8   Riesener, *Talma* (detail). Musée Carnavalet, Paris. Photo © Bulloz.

CHAPTER EIGHT

Figure 8.1   Watteau, *Étude de deux hommes conversant*. École des beaux-arts, Paris.
              Photo © Bulloz.

Figure 8.2   Angelo Decembrio, *De politia literaria*, around 1450, printed in 1540.
              Bibliothèque nationale, Paris. Photo © Bibliothèque nationale.

Figure 8.3   Abraham Bosse, *L'Ouïe*. Bibliothèque nationale, Paris. Photo
              © Bulloz.

Figure 8.4   Frontispiece of *Conversations* by Mademoiselle de Scudéry, new edi-
              tion, 1710, engraved by Sébastien Leclerc. Bibliothèque nationale,
              Paris. Photo © Bibliothèque nationale.

Figure 8.5   Rubens, *Le Jardin d'amour*, around 1630–40, detail. Musée du Prado,
              Madrid. Photo from museum.

Figure 8.6   Watteau, *La conversation*, 1712–1713. The Toledo Museum of Art.
              Don Edward Drummond Libbey. Photo from museum.

Figure 8.7   *Parceval de Grandmaison lisant des vers de son poème de Philippe Auguste*,
              in *Madame Ancelot: Un salon de Paris, 1824–1864* (Paris, 1866). Biblio-
              thèque nationale, Paris. Photo © Bibliothèque nationale.

Figure 8.8   *Rachel récitant des vers du rôle d'Hermione dans la tragédie d'Andromaque*,
              in *Madame Ancelot: Un salon de Paris, 1824–1864* (Paris, 1866). Biblio-
              thèque nationale, Paris. Photo © Bibliothèque nationale.

CHAPTER NINE

Figure 9.1   The café de Foy on July 12, 1789. Engraving by Berthault, after
              Prieur. Bibliothèque nationale, Paris. Photo © Bibliothèque
              nationale.

Figure 9.2   The café Procope in the eighteenth century. Engraving by Badou-
              reau, nineteenth century. Bibliothèque nationale, Paris. Photo
              © Bibliothèque nationale.

Figure 9.3   The interior of the café Lemblin in the galleries of the Palais-Royal
              in 1817. Engraving by Motte, after Boilly. Bibliothèque nationale,
              Paris. Photo © Bibliothèque nationale.

Figure 9.4   The café Frascati, drawn and engraved by Debucourt. Musée
              Carnavalet, Paris. Photo Ladet © Musées de la Ville de Paris,
              © SPADEM, 1992.

Figure 9.5   Guérard, *Boulevard des Italiens, le café Tortoni, 4 heures du soir*. Musée
              Carnavalet, Paris. Photo Toumazet © Musées de la Ville de Paris
              © SPADEM, 1992.

Figure 9.6   Merwart, *Le Cabaret du Chat-Noir: La première des projections d'ombres
              de "L'Épopée" dessinée par Caran d'Ache (1886)*. Musée Carnavalet,
              Paris. Photo Habouzi © Musées de la Ville de Paris, © SPADEM,
              1992.

Figure 9.7   Montmartre, *Le Lapin A. Gill*, around 1872. Bibliothèque nationale, Paris. Photo © Bibliothèque nationale.

Figure 9.8   Paul Fort (right) on the terrace of *La Closerie des Lilas*, around 1920. Photo © coll. Viollet.

Figure 9.9   Simone de Beauvoir in the café des Deux-Magots. Photo © Doisneau/Rapho.

CHAPTER TEN

Figure 10.1   Notre Dame of Paris. Photo © Marc Gantier/Rapho.

Figure 10.2   The most venerable saints in the diocese; gate of the Coronation of the Virgin, nineteenth century. Photo © Bulloz.

Figure 10.3   Interior view of the cathedral with the decoration of the choir redone by Louis XIV in execution of the Vow of Louis XIII: the *Vierge de Compassion* by Nicolas Coustou, 1723, between the statues of Louis XIII on the right by Guillaume Coustou (1715), and of Louis XIV, left, by Coysevox (1715). Photo © Jacqueline Guillot/Connaissance des Arts/Edimedia.

Figure 10.4   *Castrum doloris*: the apparatus dressed for the funeral of Turenne, September 9, 1675, in *Les Vertus chrétiennes et les Vertus militaires en deuil*, engraving by Berain. Bibliothèque nationale, Paris. Photo © Bibliothèque nationale.

Figure 10.5   The battle flags in the transept of the cathedral, gouache by Gabriel de Saint-Aubin, 1779. Musée des Beaux-Arts, Stockholm. Photo © Bulloz.

Figure 10.6   Benediction of the flags in Notre Dame of Paris, September 27, 1989, engraving after Prieur. Musée Carnavalet, Paris. Photo © Bulloz.

Figure 10.7   Fontaine and Percier, *Vue du grand Vestibule en forme de Tente, érigé à l'entrée du Palais Archiépiscopal derrière l'Église de Notre-Dame*, on the occasion of the coronation of Napoleon I, December 2, 1804. Bibliothèque nationale, Paris. Photo © Lauros—Giraudon.

Figure 10.8   The constitutional oath said by Napoleon, December 2, 1804, engraving by Le Coeur. Collection Pierre Joly, Paris. Photo © A. M. Joly.

Figure 10.9   The baptism of the Count of Paris, grandson of Louis-Philippe, May 2, 1841, gouache by Viollet-le-Duc. Musée du Louvre, on deposit at the Musée Notre-Dame. Photo © A.M. Joly.

Figure 10.10   *Le Te Deum de la Victoire, 17 novembre 1918*, drawing by Simont. Musée Notre-Dame, Paris. Photo © A. M. Joly.

Figure 10.11   The Generals de Gaulle and Leclerc at Notre Dame, at the time of the Te Deum of the liberation of Paris, August 26, 1944. Coll. Musée Notre-Dame. Photo © Lapi.

Figure 10.12   The funeral of General de Gaulle at Notre Dame of Paris, November 12, 1970. Photo © Gamma.

CHAPTER ELEVEN

Figure 11.1   Sacré Coeur, fixture by Ernest Pignon in homage to those who died in the commune, 1971. Photo coll. of the artist.

Figure 11.2   The cathedral of the Major de Marseille around 1890. Photo Mievemens. Bibliothèque du Patrimoine, Paris. Photo © Jean-Loup Charmet.

Figure 11.3   The "synthetic cathedral," by Louis-Auguste Boileau, perspective view, 1853. École nationale des beaux-arts, Paris. Photo © ENSBA.

Figure 11.4   MM. Legentil, Baudon, Rohault de Fleury, and Beluze, founders of the Voeu national, lithography by P. Gusman, 1891. Bibliothèque nationale, Paris. Photo © Bibliothèque nationale.

Figure 11.5   *Concours pour la souscription de l'église du Sacré-Coeur à Montmartre, projet de M. Magne*, 1874. Bibliothèque nationale, Paris. Photo © Bibliothèque nationale.

Figure 11.6   Plan by Paul Abadie for Sacré Coeur. Coll. René Hulot, Paris. Photo © Archives Jean-Loup Charmet.

Figure 11.7   *État actuel des travaux, église du Sacré-Coeur à Montmartre*, drawing from life by the Count de Gourcy, 1880. Bibliothèque nationale, Paris. Photo © Bibliothèque nationale.

Figure 11.8   *La Statue colossale du Christ*, 1891. Bibliothèque nationale, Paris. Photo © Bibliothèque nationale.

Figure 11.9   From Jean Béraud, *Le Cantique*, 1887. Bibliothèque nationale, Paris. Photo © Bibliothèque nationale.

Figure 11.10   *Inauguration de la basilique du Sacré-Coeur. Bénédiction solennelle donnée du haut du porche de l'église par Mgr Rotelli*, 1891. Bibliothèque nationale, Paris. Photo © Bibliothèque nationale.

Figure 11.11   Mosaic of the choir celebrating the vote on the law of July 29, 1873, declaring the construction of Sacré Coeur to be a public utility, in expiation of the crimes of the Paris Commune of 1871, detail. Photo © Roger-Viollet.

Figure 11.12   Cross-section of Sacré Coeur. Bibliothèque nationale, Paris. Photo © Bibliothèque nationale.

CHAPTER TWELVE

Figure 12.1   Poster of the courses at the Collège de France for the third trimester 1791. Archives du Collège de France, photo Jean-Loup Charmet © Gallimard.

Figure 12.2   A. Brouilhet, *Michelet et Quinet reprenant possession de leur cours au Collège de France en 1848*. Sorbonne, Paris, photo © Giraudon.

Figure 12.3   Poster for first-semester courses, 1847–48. Archives du Collège de France, photo Jean-Loup Charmet © Gallimard.

Figure 12.4   *Obsèques de Renan au Collège de France*, engraving by Méaulle from Meyer and Fichet, October 1892. Bibliothèque nationale, photo © Bibliothèque nationale, Paris.

Figure 12.5   "People listen at the windows to M. Bergson's courses," photo-graphic montage, *L'Excelsior*, February 14, 1914. Archives du Collège de France, photo Jean-Loup Charmet © Gallimard.

Figure 12.6   *Marcellin Berthelot dans son laboratoire du Collège de France*, 1927. Photo © Boyer-Viollet.

Figure 12.7   *Paul Valéry enseignant au Collège de France*, around 1937. Photo © Harlingue-Viollet.

Figure 12.8   The Collège de France, 1976–77. Coll. part., photo Tourte et Petion.

Chapters translated in published or projected volumes of *Rethinking France* can be found in *Les Lieux de mémoire* as follows.

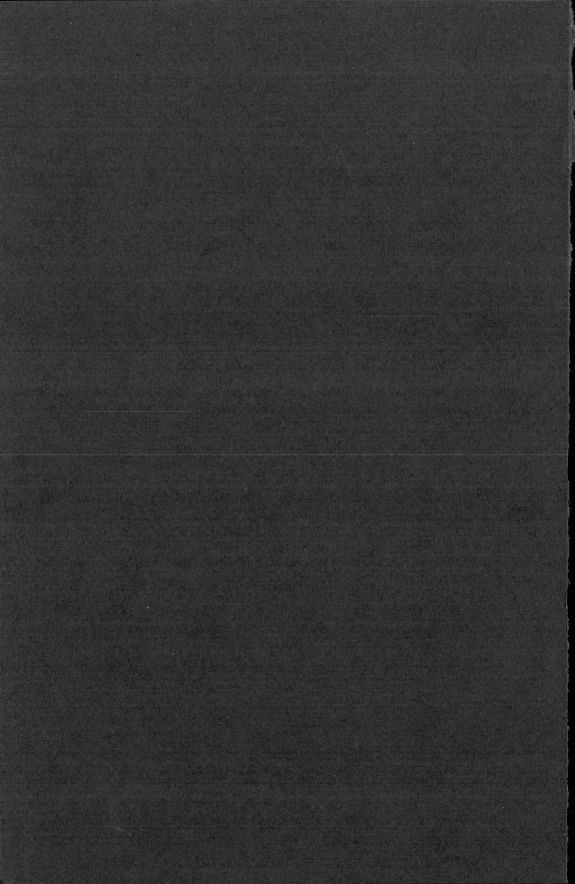